Houghton
Mifflin
Harcourt.

¡Avancemos!

AUTHORS

Estella Gahala | Patricia Hamilton Carlin

Audrey L. Heining-Boynton | Ricardo Otheguy | Barbara Rupert Mondloch

SPANISH 1

Cover Photography

Front cover: Illuminated National Palace in Plaza de la Constitución of Mexico City at sunset.
©Borna Mirahmadian/Shutterstock.
Inset: Charro mexicano, ©H. Sitton/zefa/Corbis

1
uno

¡Avancemos!

Celebraciones

CULTURA Interactiva Explora las celebraciones del mundo hispano

El Día de los Muertos,
Santiago Sacatepéquez, Guatemala

New Year's Eve, Madrid, Spain

DIGITAL SPANISH my.hrw.com

CULTURA Interactiva *pp. C2–C3, C4–C5, C6–C7, C8–C9, C10–C11, C12–C13, C14–C15, C16–C17, C18–C19, C20–C21, C22–C23, C24–C25*

LECCIÓN PRELIMINAR Nueva York

¡Hola!

Cultura
- **Un mural en Nueva York,** *p. 9*

Did you get it?
Student Self-Check
pp. 5, 9, 11, 15, 17, 19, 21, 24

¡AvanzaRap!
DVD
Sing and Learn

A performer wearing the colors of the Puerto Rican Flag

Dominican dancers in colorful costumes

UNIDAD 1 Estados Unidos
Un rato con los amigos

Cultura

 **¿Recuerdas?**
- weather expressions
  p. 36

 Did you get it?
Student Self-Check
pp. 34, 36, 39, 41, 44, 47

Una playa de Miami Beach,
Miami Beach, Florida

Paseo del Río, San Antonio, Texas

¡*AvanzaRap!*
DVD
Sing and Learn

Cultura
- **Explora México** *p. 82*
- **Uniformes escolares** *p. 92*
- **Los murales en México** *p. 97*
- **Una escuela internacional** *p. 102*

 ¿Recuerdas?
- after-school activities *p. 93*
- days of the week *p. 95*

PARA Y PIENSA **Did you get it?**
Student Self-Check
pp. 88, 90, 93, 95, 98, 101

La fuente de San Miguel en el Zócalo,
Puebla, México

El patio de una escuela secundaria,
México

Cultura
- El Museo de Antropología *p. 116*
- El autorretrato *p. 122*
- Mi clase favorita *p. 126*
- Arte de México y la República Dominicana *p. 128*
- Horarios y clases *p. 132*

 ¿Recuerdas?
- class subjects *p. 114*
- adjective agreement *p. 115*
- telling time *p. 124*

 PARA Y PIENSA **Did you get it?**
Student Self-Check
pp. 112, 114, 117, 119, 122, 125

¡*AvanzaRap!*
DVD
Sing and Learn

 DIGITAL SPANISH my.hrw.com

CULTURA Interactiva
pp. 136–137 186–187

ANIMATED GRAMMAR
pp. 145, 150, 159 169, 174, 183

@HOMETUTOR VideoPlus
pp. 143, 148, 153 167, 172, 177

 **Video/DVD**

Vocabulario
pp. 140–141, 164–165
Telehistoria
pp. 143, 148, 153 167, 172, 177

La Plaza de Colón en el Viejo San Juan,
San Juan, Puerto Rico

Una familia come en casa,
San Juan, Puerto Rico

¡AvanzaRap!
DVD
Sing and Learn

UNIDAD 4

España
En el centro

Cultura
- **Explora España** *p. 190*
- **El arte surrealista de España** *p. 203*
- **Climas diferentes** *p. 206*
- **Las memorias del invierno** *p. 210*

¿Recuerdas?
- numbers from 11 to 100 *p. 196*
- the verb **tener** *p. 198*
- after-school activities *p. 198*

PARA Y PIENSA **Did you get it?**
Student Self-Check
pp. 196, 198, 201, 203, 206, 209

 DIGITAL SPANISH my.hrw.com

CULTURA Interactiva pp. 190–191 240–241	**ANIMATED GRAMMAR** pp. 199, 204, 213 223, 228, 237	**@HOMETUTOR VideoPlus** pp. 197, 202, 207 221, 226, 231

 **Video/DVD**

Vocabulario *pp. 194–195, 218–219*
Telehistoria *pp. 197, 202, 207 221, 226, 231*

Una tienda de ropa, Madrid, España

El Teatro de la Comedia en la calle Príncipe, Madrid, España

Cultura

- **Los mercados** *p. 225*
- *Las meninas* *p. 230*
- **El fin de semana en España y Chile** *p. 234*
- **Pinturas de España y Chile** *p. 236*
- **¿Adónde vamos el sábado?** *p. 240*

 ¿Recuerdas?

- present tense of **-er** verbs *p. 220*
- the verb **ir** *p. 222*
- direct object pronouns *p. 229*
- **tener** expressions *p. 230*

PARA Y PIENSA **Did you get it?**

Student Self-Check
pp. 220, 222, 225, 227, 230, 233

¡AvanzaRap!
DVD
Sing and Learn

UNIDAD 5
Ecuador
¡Bienvenido a nuestra casa!

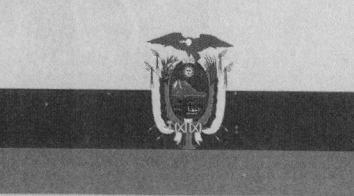

Cultura

- **Explora Ecuador** *p. 244*
- **Casas ecuatorianas** *p. 255*
- **Sitios geográficos** *p. 260*
- **Vivir en Ecuador** *p. 264*

 ¿Recuerdas?

- stem-changing verbs: **o → ue** *p. 250*
- location words *p. 254*
- colors *p. 255*
- clothing *p. 259*

PARA Y PIENSA **Did you get it?**

Student Self-Check
pp. 250, 252, 255, 257, 260, 263

Una casa tradicional con jardín, Quito, Ecuador

Una fiesta de cumpleaños, Quito, Ecuador

Cultura

¿Recuerdas?

Did you get it?

¡AvanzaRap!
DVD
Sing and Learn

Cultura

- **Explora la República Dominicana** *p. 298*
- **La Serie del Caribe** *p. 308*
- **El arte representativo** *p. 314*
- **Un club de deportes** *p. 318*

 ¿Recuerdas?

- numbers from 200 to 1,000,000 *p. 304*
- **gustar** with nouns *p. 306*
- comparatives *p. 309*

PARA Y PIENSA **Did you get it?**
Student Self-Check
pp. 304, 306, 309, 311, 314, 317

 DIGITAL SPANISH my.hrw.com

CULTURA Interactiva
pp. 298–299 348–349

ANIMATED GRAMMAR
pp. 307, 312, 321 331, 336, 345

@HOMETUTOR
VideoPlus
pp. 305, 310, 315 329, 334, 339

 **Video/DVD**
Vocabulario
pp. 302–303, 326–327
Telehistoria
pp. 305, 310, 315 329, 334, 339

Un partido en la escuela, Santo Domingo,
República Dominicana

Un día en la Playa Caribe, Juan Dolio,
República Dominicana

Cultura

- **La artista y su estilo** *p. 332*
- **El Festival del Merengue** *p. 338*
- **Dos atletas de alta velocidad** *p. 342*
- **Gestos y refranes** *p. 344*
- **Deportes favoritos** *p. 348*

 *¿Recuerdas?*

- **gustar** with nouns *p. 330*
- stem-changing verbs **o → ue** *p. 330*
- telling time *p. 332*

 PARA Y PIENSA **Did you get it?**

Student Self-Check
pp. 328, 330, 333, 335, 338, 341

¡AvanzaRap!
DVD
Sing and Learn

UNIDAD 7 Argentina
¡Una semana fenomenal!

DIGITAL SPANISH my.hrw.com

CULTURA Interactiva	**ANIMATED GRAMMAR**	**@HOMETUTOR VideoPlus**
pp. 352–353 402–403	*pp. 361, 366, 375 385, 390, 399*	*pp. 359, 364, 369 383, 388, 393*

Video/DVD

Vocabulario
pp. 356–357, 380–381
Telehistoria
*pp. 359, 364, 369
383, 388, 393*

La Casa Rosada, Buenos Aires, Argentina

El Parque de la Costa, El Tigre, Argentina

Lección
2

Tema: *Un día en el parque de diversiones* 378

¡AvanzaRap!
DVD
Sing and Learn

UNIDAD 8 Costa Rica
Una rutina diferente

Cultura
- **Explora Costa Rica** *p. 406*
- **El paisaje de Costa Rica** *p. 416*
- **El uso de *usted, tú* y *vos*** *p. 422*
- **Mi viaje a Costa Rica** *p. 426*
- **¡Vamos al museo!** *p. 428*

 ¿Recuerdas?
- preterite of **hacer** *p. 412*
- direct object pronouns *p. 414*
- parts of the body *p. 416*
- chores *p. 421*
- houses *p. 422*
- telling time *p. 424*

PARA Y PIENSA **Did you get it?**
Student Self-Check
pp. 412, 414, 417, 419, 422, 425

🌐 **DIGITAL SPANISH** my.hrw.com

CULTURA Interactiva
pp. 406–407
456–457

ANIMATED GRAMMAR
pp. 415, 420, 429
439, 444, 453

@HOMETUTOR
VideoPlus
pp. 413, 418, 423
437, 442, 447

💻 **Video/DVD**
Vocabulario
pp. 410–411, 434–435
Telehistoria
pp. 413, 418, 423
437, 442, 447

Una familia habla de las vacaciones,
San José, Costa Rica

Una tienda de artesanías y recuerdos,
San José, Costa Rica

Lección 2

Tema: ¡*Vamos de vacaciones!* **432**

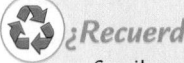

¡AvanzaRap!
DVD
Sing and Learn

Recursos

¡Avancemos!

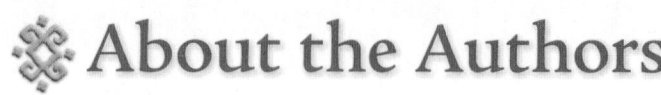

About the Authors

Estella Gahala

Estella Gahala received degrees in Spanish from Wichita State University, French from Middlebury College, and a Ph.D. in Educational Administration and Curriculum from Northwestern University. A career teacher of Spanish and French, she has worked with a wide variety of students at the secondary level. She has also served as foreign language department chair and district director of curriculum and instruction. Her workshops and publications focus on research and practice in a wide range of topics, including culture and language learning, learning strategies, assessment, and the impact of current brain research on curriculum and instruction. She has coauthored twelve basal textbooks. Honors include the Chevalier dans l'Ordre des Palmes Académiques and listings in *Who's Who of American Women, Who's Who in America,* and *Who's Who in the World.*

Patricia Hamilton Carlin

Patricia Hamilton Carlin completed her M.A. in Spanish at the University of California, Davis, where she also taught as a lecturer. Previously she earned a Master of Secondary Education with specialization in foreign languages from the University of Arkansas and taught Spanish and French at the K–12 level. Patricia currently teaches Spanish and foreign language/ESL methodology at the University of Central Arkansas, where she coordinates the second language teacher education program. In addition, Patricia is a frequent presenter at local, regional, and national foreign language conferences. In 2005, she was awarded the Southern Conference on Language Teaching's Outstanding Teaching Award: Post-Secondary. Her professional service has included the presidency of the Arkansas Foreign Language Teachers Association and the presidency of Arkansas's DeSoto Chapter of the AATSP.

Audrey L. Heining-Boynton

Audrey L. Heining-Boynton received her Ph.D. in Curriculum and Instruction from Michigan State University. She is a professor of Education and Romance Languages at The University of North Carolina at Chapel Hill, where she teaches educational methodology classes and Spanish. She has also taught Spanish, French, and ESL at the K–12 level. Dr. Heining-Boynton served as the president of ACTFL and the National Network for Early Language Learning. She has been involved with AATSP, Phi Delta Kappa, and state foreign language associations. In addition, she has presented both nationally and internationally and has published over forty books, articles, and curricula.

Ricardo Otheguy

Ricardo Otheguy received his Ph.D. in Linguistics from the City University of New York, where he is currently professor of Linguistics at the Graduate Center. He is also director of the Research Institute for the Study of Language in Urban Society (RISLUS) and coeditor of the research journal *Spanish in Context.* He has extensive experience with school-based research and has written on topics related to Spanish grammar, bilingual education, and Spanish in the United States. His work has been supported by private and government foundations, including the Rockefeller Brothers Fund and the National Science Foundation. He is coauthor of *Tu mundo: Curso para hispanohablantes,* and *Prueba de ubicación para hispanohablantes.*

Barbara Rupert Mondloch

Barbara Rupert Mondloch completed her M.A. at Pacific Lutheran University. She has taught Level 1 through A.P. Spanish and has implemented a FLES program in her district. Barbara is the author of CD-ROM activities for the *¡Bravo!* series. She has presented at many local, regional, and national foreign language conferences. She has served as president of both the Pacific Northwest Council for Languages (PNCFL) and the Washington Association for Language Teaching, and was the PNCFL representative to ACTFL. In 1996, Barbara received the Christa McAuliffe Award for Excellence in Education, and in 1999, she was selected Washington's "Spanish Teacher of the Year" by the Juan de Fuca Chapter of the AATSP.

John DeMado, Creative Consultant

John DeMado has been a vocal advocate for second-language acquisition in the United States for many years. He started his career as a middle/high school French and Spanish teacher, before entering the educational publishing profession. Since 1993, Mr. DeMado has directed his own business, John DeMado Language Seminars. Inc., a company devoted exclusively to language acquisition issues. He has authored numerous books in both French and Spanish that span the K–12 curriculum. Mr. DeMado wrote and performed the *¡AvanzaRap!* songs for Levels 1 and 2.

Carl Johnson, Senior Program Advisor

Carl Johnson received degrees from Marietta College (OH), the University of Illinois, Université Laval, and a Ph.D. in Foreign Language Education from The Ohio State University, during which time he studied French, German, Spanish, and Russian. He has been a lifelong foreign language educator, retiring in 2003 after 27 years as a language teacher (secondary and university level), consultant, and Director of Languages Other Than English for the Texas Department of Education. He has completed many publications relating to student and teacher language proficiency development, language textbooks, and nationwide textbook adoption practices. He also served as president of the Texas Foreign Language Association, Chair of the Board of the Southwest Conference on Language Teaching, and president of the National Council of State Supervisors of Foreign Languages. In addition, he was named Chevalier dans l'Ordre des Palmes Académiques by the French government.

Rebecca L. Oxford, Learning Strategy Specialist

Rebecca L. Oxford received her Ph.D. in educational psychology from The University of North Carolina. She also holds two degrees in foreign language from Vanderbilt University and Yale University, and a degree in educational psychology from Boston University. She leads the Second Language Education and Culture Program and is a professor at the University of Maryland. She has directed programs at Teachers College, Columbia University; the University of Alabama; and the Pennsylvania State University. In addition, she initiated and edited *Tapestry*, a series of student textbooks used around the world. Dr. Oxford specializes in language learning strategies and styles.

Contributing Writers

Louis G. Baskinger
New Hartford High School
New Hartford, NY

Jacquelyn Cinotti-Dirmann
Duval County Public Schools
Jacksonville, FL

Teacher Reviewers

Sue Arandjelovic
Dobson High School
Mesa, AZ

Susan K. Arbuckle
Mahomet-Seymour High School
Mahomet, IL

Kristi Ashe
Amador Valley High School
Pleasanton, CA

Shaun A. Bauer
Olympia High School, *retired*
Orlando, FL

Sheila Bayles
Rogers High School
Rogers, AR

Robert L. Bowbeer
Detroit Country Day Upper School
Beverly Hills, MI

Hercilia Bretón
Highlands High School
San Antonio, TX

Adrienne Chamberlain-Parris
Mariner High School
Everett, WA

Mike Cooperider
Truman High School
Independence, MO

Susan B. Cress
Sheridan High School
Sheridan, IN

Michèle S. de Cruz-Sáenz, Ph.D.
Strath Haven High School
Wallingford, PA

Lizveth Dague
Park Vista Community High School
Lake Worth, FL

Parthena Draggett
Jackson High School
Massillon, OH

Rubén D. Elías
Roosevelt High School
Fresno, CA

Phillip Elkins
Lane Tech College Prep High School
Chicago, IL

Maria Fleming Alvarez
The Park School
Brookline, MA

Michael Garber
Boston Latin Academy
Boston, MA

Marco García
Derry University Advantage Academy
Chicago, IL

David Gonzalez
Hollywood Hills High School
Hollywood, FL

Raquel R. González
Odessa Senior High School
Odessa, TX

Neyda Gonzalez-Droz
Ridge Community High School
Davenport, FL

Becky Hay de García
James Madison Memorial
  High School
Madison, WI

Fatima Hicks
Suncoast High School, *retired*
Riviera Beach, FL

Gladys V. Horford
William T. Dwyer High School
Palm Beach Gardens, FL

Pam Johnson
Stevensville High School
Stevensville, MT

Richard Ladd
Ipswich High School
Ipswich, MA

Patsy Lanigan
Hume Fogg Academic Magnet
  High School
Nashville, TN

Kris Laws
Palm Bay High School
Melbourne, FL

Kristen M. Lombardi
Shenendehowa High School
Clifton Park, NY

Elizabeth Lupafya
North High School
Worcester, MA

David Malatesta
Niles West High School
Skokie, IL

Patrick Malloy
James B. Conant High School
Hoffman Estates, IL

Brandi Meeks
Starr's Mill High School
Fayetteville, GA

Kathleen L. Michaels
Palm Harbor University High School
Palm Harbor, FL

Linda Nanos
Brook Farm Business Academy
West Roxbury, MA

Nadine F. Olson
School of Teaching and Curriculum
  Leadership
Stillwater, OK

Pam Osthoff
Lakeland Senior High School
Lakeland, FL

Nicholas Patterson
Davenport Central High School
Davenport, IA

Carolyn A. Peck
Genesee Community College
Lakeville, NY

Daniel N. Richardson
Concord High School, *retired*
Concord, NH

Rita E. Risco
Palm Harbor University High School
Palm Harbor, FL

Miguel Roma
Boston Latin Academy
West Roxbury, MA

Nona M. Seaver
New Berlin West Middle/High School
New Berlin, WI

Susan Seraphine-Kimel
Astronaut High School
Titusville, FL

Lauren Schultz
Dover High School
Dover, NH

Mary Severo
Thomas Hart Middle School
Pleasanton, CA

Clarette Shelton
WT Woodson High School, *retired*
Fairfax, VA

Maureen Shiland
Saratoga Springs High School
Saratoga Springs, NY

Irma Sprague
Countryside High School
Clearwater, FL

Mary A. Stimmel
Lincoln High School
Des Moines, IA

Karen Tharrington
Wakefield High School
Raleigh, NC

Alicia Turnier
Countryside High School
Clearwater, FL

Roberto E. del Valle
The Overlake School
Redmond, WA

Todd Wagner
Upper Darby High School, *retired*
Drexel Hill, PA

Ronie R. Webster
Monson Junior/Senior High School
Monson, MA

Cheryl Wellman
Bloomingdale High School
Valrico, FL

Thomasina White
School District of Philadelphia
Philadelphia, PA

Jena Williams
Jonesboro High School
Jonesboro, AR

Program Advisory Council

Louis G. Baskinger
New Hartford High School
New Hartford, NY

Linda M. Bigler
James Madison University
Harrisonburg, VA

Flora Maria Ciccone-Quintanilla
Holly Senior High School
Holly, MI

Jacquelyn Cinotti-Dirmann
Duval County Public Schools
Jacksonville, FL

Desa Dawson
Del City High School
Del City, OK

Robin C. Hill
Warrensville Heights High School
Warrensville Heights, OH

Barbara M. Johnson
Gordon Tech High School, *retired*
Chicago, IL

Ray Maldonado
Houston Independent School
  District
Houston, TX

Karen S. Miller
Friends School of Baltimore
Baltimore, MD

Dr. Robert A. Miller
Woodcreek High School
  Roseville Joint Union High School
  District
Roseville, CA

Debra M. Morris
Wellington Landings Middle School
Wellington, FL

Maria Nieto Zezas
West Morris Central High School
Chester, NJ

Rita Oleksak
Glastonbury Public Schools
Glastonbury, CT

Sandra Rosenstiel
University of Dallas, *retired*
Grapevine, TX

Emily Serafa Manschot
Northville High School
Northville, MI

La Telehistoria

Hi! My name is Alicia. My family and I live in Miami, Florida. My favorite thing to do is play soccer. At the Pan-American Youth Games, my team took second place. I made a lot of great friends from all over the world. I also met Trini Salgado, the best soccer player ever!

I got a T-shirt like hers, but I never got her to autograph it. She is always traveling to different countries, so maybe I can send my shirt to some of my soccer friends to try to get it signed.

Follow along in the ¡Avancemos! Telehistoria
to find out what happens to Alicia's T-shirt
as it travels from country to country.

SALGADO
10

Trini Salgado

En Parque de l

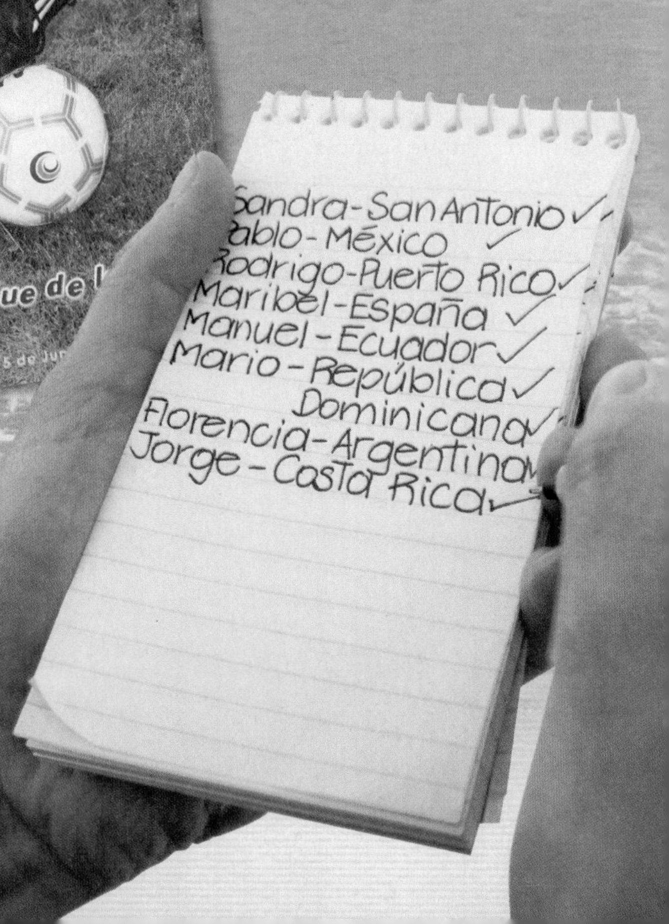

Próximo Sábado 15 de Jun

Sandra-San Antonio ✓
Pablo-MÉXICO ✓
Rodrigo-Puerto Rico ✓
Maribel-España ✓
Manuel-Ecuador ✓
Mario-República ✓
      Dominicana ✓
Florencia-Argentina ✓
Jorge-Costa Rica ✓

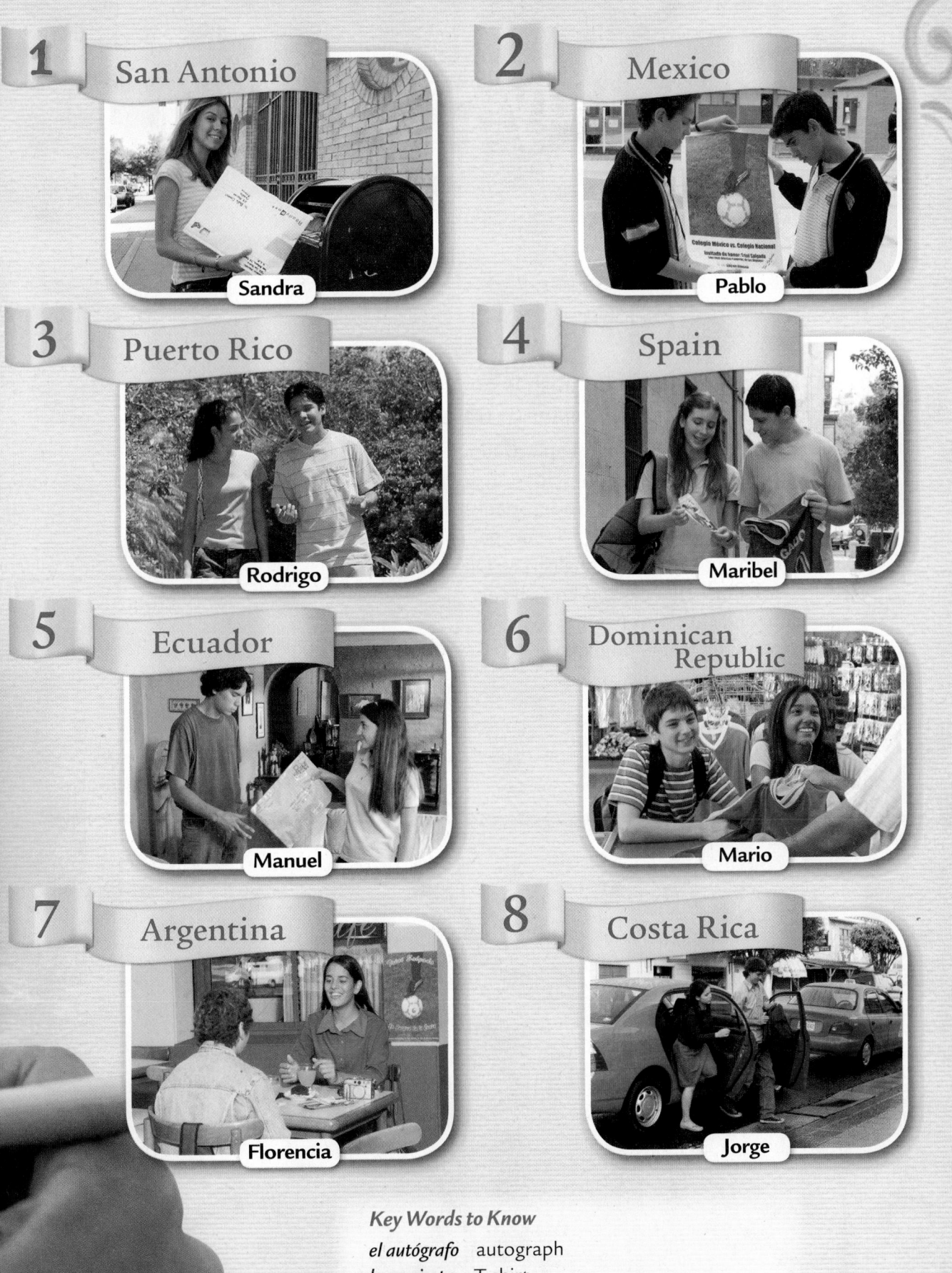

1 San Antonio — Sandra

2 Mexico — Pablo

3 Puerto Rico — Rodrigo

4 Spain — Maribel

5 Ecuador — Manuel

6 Dominican Republic — Mario

7 Argentina — Florencia

8 Costa Rica — Jorge

Key Words to Know
el autógrafo   autograph
la camiseta   T-shirt
el jugador (la jugadora) de fútbol   soccer player

Why Study Spanish?

Discover the world

Deciding to learn Spanish is one of the best decisions you can make if you want to travel and see the world.

More than 400 million people around the globe speak Spanish. After Chinese, English and Spanish are tied as the two most frequently spoken languages worldwide. Spanish is now the third most-used language on the Internet. In Europe, Spanish is the most popular foreign language after English. People who speak both Spanish and English can communicate with people from all around the globe, no matter where they find themselves.

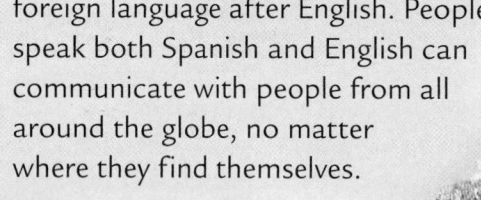

Explore your community

Inside the United States, Spanish is by far the most widely spoken language after English.

There are currently over 30 million Spanish speakers in the U.S. When you start to look and listen for it, you will quickly realize that Spanish is all around you—on the television, on the radio, and in magazines and newspapers. You may even hear your neighbors speaking it. Learning Spanish will help you communicate and interact with the rapidly growing communities of Spanish speakers around you.

Experience a new perspective

Learning a language is more than just memorizing words and structures.

When you study Spanish, you learn how the people who speak it think, feel, work, and live. Learning a language can open your eyes to a whole new world of ideas and insights. And as you learn about other cultures, you gain a better perspective on your own.

Create career possibilities

Knowing Spanish opens many doors.

If you speak Spanish fluently, you can work for international and multinational companies anywhere in the Spanish-speaking world. You can create a career working as a translator, an interpreter, or a teacher of Spanish. And because the number of Spanish speakers in the U.S. is growing so rapidly, being able to communicate in Spanish is becoming important in almost every career.

To the Student

Estimados estudiantes,

Perhaps you have already discussed 'why' it is important to speak other languages. But the real question for you, the student, is 'how' ... How do you acquire a second language? Overall, it is very important to be positive and to have a 'can do' attitude. If you speak a language, you are already a candidate to speak another one at some level. Above all, don't buy into the idea that you are either not smart enough or too old. These are myths. Ignore them!

Stay calm! It is natural to feel uncomfortable when you are trying to make yourself understood in another language or when listening to another language. However, if you are overly nervous, it will seriously block your ability both to speak and/or to understand that language. That is why it is important simply to stay calm. Use hand gestures, body language and facial expressions to make yourself understood, too. The idea is to stay in the second language and stay out of English as much as possible. If you stay calm, you can piece a message together. Really!

The same applies to listening to a native speaker. Stay calm! Don't worry about the words you may have missed. If you focus on them, the entire message will pass you by! Try to listen for the overall message instead of listening to each separate word.

Take risks in the second language. This is just what little children do when they are acquiring their first language. Everyone around them has more of that language than they do, yet they take risks to participate. Understand that native speakers are generally very appreciative when you try to use their language. Just use the best second language that you can on any given day and don't worry when you make mistakes. Errors in language are common and natural occurrences. It is only by making errors that you eventually come to improve your second language. Just as with athletics, drama, art and vocal/instrumental music, the only way you gain skill in your second language is through performance; by just doing it! Ability is acquired through trial and error. Communicating less than accurately in a second language is better than not communicating in that language at all! Please ... Don't let the rules of a language stop you from performing.

Make educated guesses. Look for clues to help you understand. Where is the conversation taking place? What words are similar in English? Go beyond just the words to find meaning by considering the speaker's facial expressions, hand gestures and general body language. Learn in advance how to say certain phrases like "Please. More slowly." in the second language. Above all, don't be afraid to guess! Even when people read, listen to someone or view a movie in their own native tongue, they still guess at the message being delivered. It is also that way in another language. Exploring the Internet for target language music, movies, blogs and social media can help you develop this skill.

¡Buena suerte!

John De Mado

Modes of Communication

What is communication?

When you attempt to understand someone or something, or make yourself understood, you are communicating. In any language, you rely on various skills to communicate: listening, reading, speaking, writing, and deciphering body language and other non-verbal cues. In English, you've been building these skills all your life, and are probably unaware how hard you worked as a child to make meaning. The good news is that these skills are already in place—you just have to be aware that you're developing them in new ways to learn Spanish.

What are the modes of communication?

Depending on the purpose of your communication, you are engaging in one of three modes: interpretive, interpersonal, or presentational. Say you click on an online ad for a clothing store in Buenos Aires. When you read the ad (or listen to it), you have to decipher the language to understand the ad. This is the interpretive mode. If you go into the store and talk to a sales clerk, you'll have to ask some questions and then understand the answers you get back. You might also exchange a text with your friend about where you're shopping. These direct exchanges with others are in the interpersonal mode. If you write a blog about shopping and post it online, this is presentational, since your audience isn't expected to immediately react and interact with you. In class, you may simulate experiences like shopping in a store. This situational practice will cover all three modes of communication and build your communication skills. It's also challenging! You'll find that you won't be equally strong across the modes, but that's okay. The key is to practice, practice, practice.

In *¡Avancemos!* you'll have lots of opportunity to practice. At the beginning of each lesson, you'll see examples of the types of interpretive, interpersonal, and presentational activities that you should be able to do at the end. In the **Todo junto** and **Repaso inclusivo** sections, you'll have the chance to put your interpretive, interpersonal and presentational skills to the test in fun, real-world ways.

How do I communicate better?

- **First, listen.** Listen to the vocabulary presentations as you read along. Listen to how individual words are pronounced and used in sentences. Use the Internet to find music, ads, and interviews that let you hear the language in a variety of contexts and accents. Pick out words you know. Can you understand well enough to get the gist?

- **Read.** Identify words that look like English words. Do known words let you guess the meaning of others? Pay attention to word order and patterns. Find Spanish-language magazines, interviews, or blogs. Ask why passages are worded the way they are. Use what you read as a model to express yourself.

- **Speak.** Don't read silently. Say words out loud and visualize them as you say them. Repeat words several times and use them in sentences. Imagine situations where those words would be useful and create a conversation. Speaking words in context helps you better remember them.

- **Write.** You remember language better if you write it down. Write sentences and arrange them to make conversations. Keep a class journal and write short entries daily. Write down expressions you come across and use them in conversations. Find a key-pal and exchange e-mails or instant messages.

- **Make it personal.** Use Spanish to talk about your experiences. In class, if you learn what people do, volunteer to say what you or a friend do. Ask the person next to you how he or she spends time and then retell what he or she said. You remember language better if you relate it to your experience.

- **Create contexts.** How will you use the language? Will you travel to a foreign country? Do you need it for a future career? Put yourself in the situations you'd encounter and talk your way through them. Identify difficulties and see if you can come up with creative ways to say something. This is why you study a foreign language.

- **Embrace the culture.** Language study opens up all kinds of travel and work opportunities, and gives you insights into ideas and perspectives you wouldn't otherwise have. You don't have to wait for your teacher to introduce foreign cultures to you. If you hear people in your town speaking Spanish, talk with them. Use your computer or smart phone to listen to radio broadcasts or stream movies. Better yet, look for travel and exchange opportunities!

What is language proficiency?

Proficiency is *how well* you understand and make yourself understood. Remember the clothing store? Say you ask the sales staff if they have a shirt in your size. If they do, you may ask how much the shirt costs, and if you can pay with a credit card. Your ability to keep the conversation going determines your proficiency. If you're a beginner, you won't be able to say much. That's okay—just do what you can!

 # How do I become proficient?

- **Determine what you are doing with the language.** Are you giving or getting information? Are you describing someone? Do you need to state a preference or make a recommendation? These are called language "functions" and they often require certain words and phrases. Learn new vocabulary and grammar with the idea that you'll use it to do specific things.

- **Remember that language has context.** If you recommend that your brother clean his room, or that a visitor go to the Fine Arts Museum, the function is the same—making a recommendation. However, the context suggests you'd use less formal language for the first than the second, and different vocabulary for chores and local landmarks. The trick is to take what you learn for one context and apply it to different situations.

- **Understand the social customs that go with the language.** If you want help from a sales clerk, how do you ask politely? Do you do something differently than you'd do in a mall in the United States? When learning, you may not be familiar with these customs, and Spanish-speakers will forgive your mistakes. However, your proficiency increases when you recognize and follow the social norms of other countries. So pay attention to cultural information that you see in the ***Nota cultural*** and ***Comparación cultural*** features and relate it to the language you're learning.

- **Build language control.** Learn vocabulary and follow grammar rules so you can express yourself accurately. When you first learn a language, saying something—*anything*—is critical, even if it sounds funny. Once you're farther along, being more accurate helps avoid confusion. To do so, practice grammar and memorize vocabulary daily, in multiple short sessions. The ***Presentación*** and ***Práctica*** sections give you the rules and plenty of practice. Then, go to the ***En contexto*** sections of your book and use the language in real-life conversations.

There just aren't enough hours in a school year for students to become proficient by going to class. Just as musicians won't play well if they don't practice outside of lessons, you'll have to follow these recommendations on your own to get beyond minimal proficiency. Remember, practice makes proficient!

El mundo

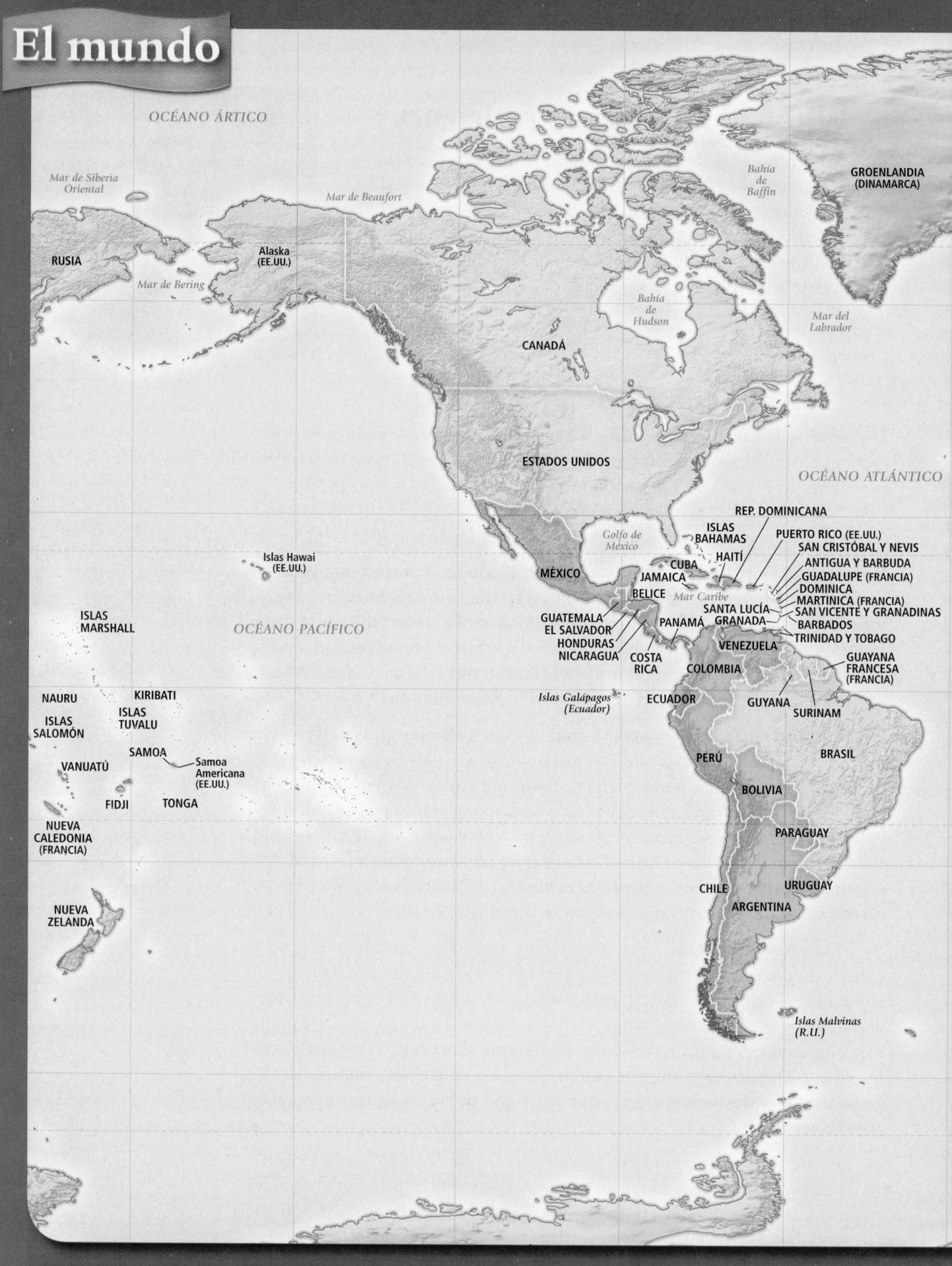

OCÉANO ÁRTICO

Mar de Siberia Oriental

Mar de Beaufort

GROENLANDIA (DINAMARCA)

Bahía de Baffin

RUSIA

Alaska (EE.UU.)

Mar de Bering

Mar del Labrador

Bahía de Hudson

CANADÁ

ESTADOS UNIDOS

OCÉANO ATLÁNTICO

Islas Hawai (EE.UU.)

Golfo de México

REP. DOMINICANA

ISLAS BAHAMAS

PUERTO RICO (EE.UU.)

SAN CRISTÓBAL Y NEVIS

MÉXICO

CUBA

HAITÍ

ANTIGUA Y BARBUDA

JAMAICA

GUADALUPE (FRANCIA)

BELICE

Mar Caribe

DOMINICA

ISLAS MARSHALL

OCÉANO PACÍFICO

GUATEMALA

SANTA LUCÍA

MARTINICA (FRANCIA)

EL SALVADOR

PANAMÁ

GRANADA

SAN VICENTE Y GRANADINAS

HONDURAS

BARBADOS

NICARAGUA

COSTA RICA

VENEZUELA

TRINIDAD Y TOBAGO

COLOMBIA

GUAYANA FRANCESA (FRANCIA)

Islas Galápagos (Ecuador)

ECUADOR

GUYANA

SURINAM

NAURU

KIRIBATI

ISLAS SALOMÓN

ISLAS TUVALU

PERÚ

BRASIL

VANUATÚ

SAMOA

Samoa Americana (EE.UU.)

BOLIVIA

FIDJI

TONGA

PARAGUAY

NUEVA CALEDONIA (FRANCIA)

URUGUAY

CHILE

ARGENTINA

NUEVA ZELANDA

Islas Malvinas (R.U.)

OCÉANO ÁRTICO

Mar de Kara

Mar de Barents

Mar de Laptev

Mar de Noruega

1	DINAMARCA	9	ESLOVENIA
2	HOLANDA	10	CROACIA
3	BÉLGICA	11	BOSNIA Y HERZEGOVINA
4	LUXEMBURGO	12	SERBIA Y MONTENEGRO
5	SUIZA	13	ALBANIA
6	REPÚBLICA CHECA	14	MACEDONIA
7	ESLOVAQUIA	15	BULGARIA
8	HUNGRÍA		

RUSIA

60°N

Mar de Ojotsk

Lago Baikal

LANDIA

SUECIA FINLANDIA

NORUEGA

REINO UNIDO

IRLANDA

Mar del Norte

ESTONIA
LETONIA
LITUANIA
BIELORRUSIA

POLONIA

ALEMANIA

UCRANIA
MOLDAVIA

KAZAKSTÁN

MONGOLIA

COREA DEL NORTE

Mar de Japón

FRANCIA

AUSTRIA

RUMANIA

Mar de Aral

GEORGIA

UZBEKISTÁN

KIRGUISTÁN

COREA DEL SUR

JAPÓN

ANDORRA

ESPAÑA

ITALIA

Mar Negro

TURQUÍA

Mar Caspio

TURKMENISTÁN

TAYIKISTÁN

CHINA

PORTUGAL

GRECIA

ARMENIA

AZERBAIYÁN

RALTAR (R.U.)

MARRUECOS

s Canarias (Esp.)

TÚNEZ

Mar Mediterráneo

MALTA

CHIPRE
LÍBANO

SIRIA

IRAQ

IRÁN

AFGANISTÁN

BUTÁN

NEPAL

TAIWÁN

OCÉANO PACÍFICO

Trópico de Cáncer

30°N

ISRAEL

JORDANIA

KUWAIT
QATAR

PAQUISTÁN

BANGLADESH

SAHARA CIDENTAL

ARGELIA

LIBIA

EGIPTO

BAHREIN

E.Á.U

OMÁN

INDIA

MYANMAR

LAOS

DE MAURITANIA

MALÍ

NÍGER

CHAD

SUDÁN

ARABIA SAUDITA

ERITREA

YEMEN

Mar Rojo

Mar Arábigo

TAILANDIA

VIETNAM

FILIPINAS

GUAM (EE.UU.)

SENEGAL

BURKINA FASO

BENIN

NIGERIA

REP. CENTRO-AFRICANA

ETIOPÍA

JIBUTI

Golfo de Bengala

CAMBOYA

Mar de China

MICRONESIA

BIA GUINEA

NEA SSAU

COSTA DE MARFIL

TOGO

GHANA

CAMERÚN

UGANDA

SOMALIA

SRI LANKA

BRUNEI

PALAÚ

LIBERIA

SIERRA LEONA

GUINEA ECUATORIAL

CONGO

GABÓN

KENIA

ISLAS MALDIVAS

MALASIA

Ecuador 0°

SANTO TOMÉ Y PRÍNCIPE

CABINDA (ANGOLA)

REP. DEM. DEL CONGO

BURUNDI

RUANDA

TANZANÍA

SEYCHELLES

SINGAPUR

INDONESIA

PAPÚA NUEVA GUINEA

ANGOLA

ZAMBIA

MALAWI

COMORES

TIMOR ORIENTAL

NAMIBIA

BOTSUANA

ZIMBABUE

MOZAMBIQUE

MADAGASCAR

MAURICIO

OCÉANO ÍNDICO

Trópico de Capricornio

AUSTRALIA

30°S

SUAZILANDIA

SUDÁFRICA

LESOTHO

0   1,000   2,000 millas

0   1,000   2,000 kilómetros

N
O   E
S

60°S

ANTÁRTIDA

Mapas **xxxix**

México y Centroamérica

ESTADOS UNIDOS

Washington, D.C.

OCÉANO ATLÁNTICO

Tijuana
Mexicali
Ciudad Juárez
Hermosillo
Chihuahua
Nuevo Laredo
SIERRA MADRE OCCIDENTAL
Baja California
MÉXICO
SIERRA MADRE ORIENTAL
Monterrey
Durango
San Luis Potosí
Tampico
Guadalajara
México, D.F.
Puebla
Veracruz
Acapulco
Oaxaca

Golfo de México

Mérida

ISLAS BAHAMAS
Nassau
Trópico de Cáncer
La Habana
CUBA
JAMAICA
Kingston

Belice
BELICE
Belmopan
HONDURAS
Tegucigalpa
Guatemala
GUATEMALA
San Salvador
EL SALVADOR
NICARAGUA
Managua
San José
COSTA RICA
Colón
Panamá
PANAMÁ

Mar Caribe

COLOMBIA

OCÉANO PACÍFICO

Ecuador

Quito
ECUADOR

PERÚ

N
O   E
S

0   250   500 millas
0   250   500 kilómetros

40°N

30°N

20°N

10°N

0°

10°S

110°O   100°O   90°O   80°O

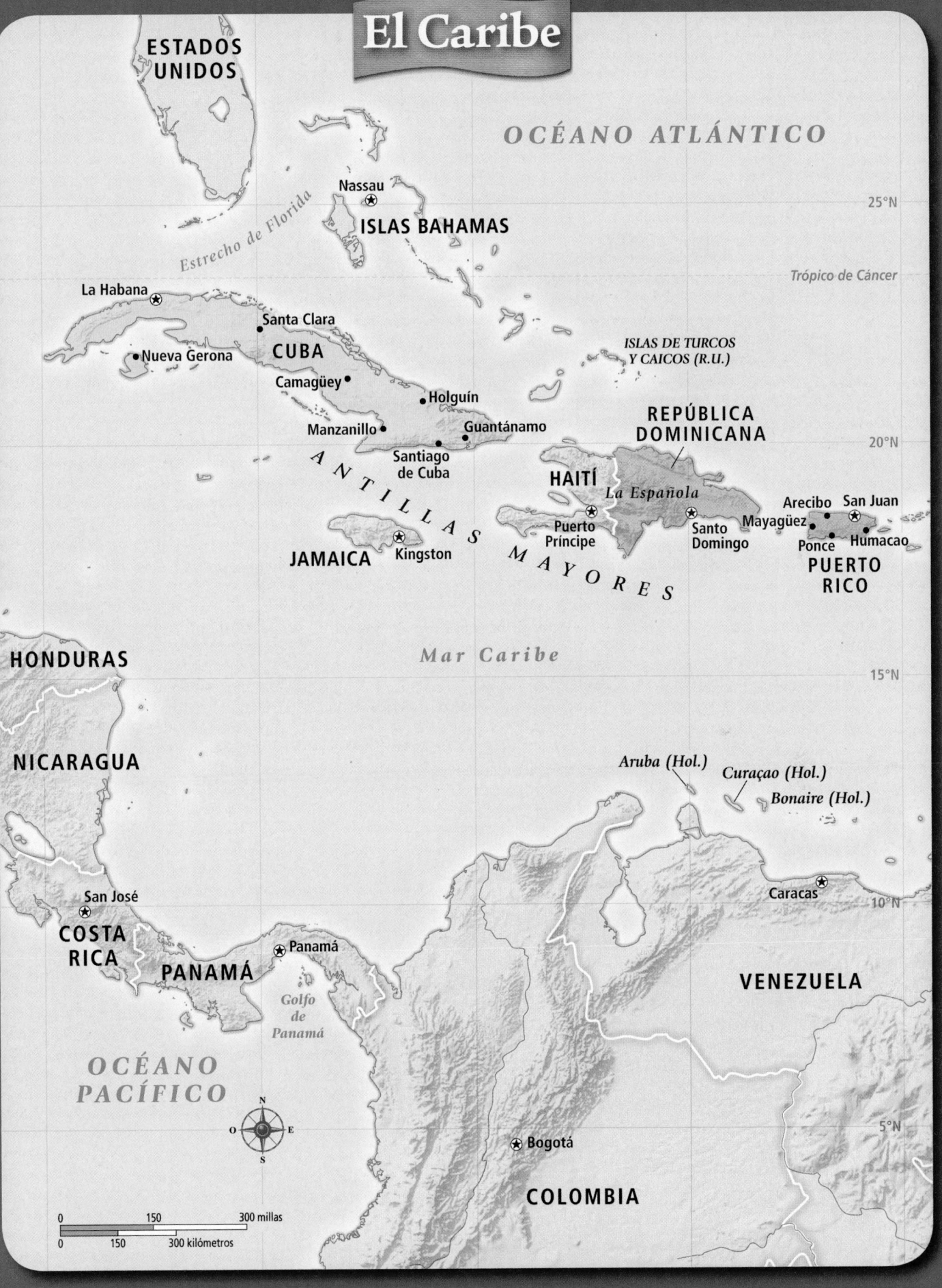

El Caribe

ESTADOS UNIDOS

OCÉANO ATLÁNTICO

Estrecho de Florida

Nassau

ISLAS BAHAMAS

Trópico de Cáncer

25°N

La Habana

Santa Clara

Nueva Gerona

CUBA

Camagüey

Holguín

Manzanillo

Guantánamo

Santiago de Cuba

ISLAS DE TURCOS Y CAICOS (R.U.)

REPÚBLICA DOMINICANA

20°N

HAITÍ

La Española

Arecibo

San Juan

Mayagüez

Puerto Príncipe

Santo Domingo

Ponce

Humacao

JAMAICA

Kingston

ANTILLAS MAYORES

PUERTO RICO

Mar Caribe

15°N

HONDURAS

NICARAGUA

Aruba (Hol.)

Curaçao (Hol.)

Bonaire (Hol.)

San José

Caracas

10°N

COSTA RICA

PANAMÁ

Panamá

Golfo de Panamá

VENEZUELA

OCÉANO PACÍFICO

N O E S

Bogotá

5°N

COLOMBIA

| 0 | 150 | 300 millas |
| 0 | 150 | 300 kilómetros |

Sudamérica

Mar Caribe

Barranquilla
Cartagena
Maracaibo
TRINIDAD Y TOBAGO
Puerto España

10°N

Lago
Maracaibo
Caracas
Río Orinoco

VENEZUELA
Georgetown
Paramaribo

OCÉANO
ATLÁNTICO

Medellín
GUYANA
Manizales
Bogotá
SURINAM
Cayena

COLOMBIA
GUAYANA
FRANCESA
(FRANCIA)

Cali

Otavalo
Río Negro
Ecuador 0°

Quito
Río Amazonas

ECUADOR
Guayaquil
Cuenca

Río Tapajós
Río Xingú
Río Madeira
Río Tocantins

PERÚ
Río São Francisco

Trujillo
BRASIL
10°S

C O R D I L L E R A

Callao
Lima

Lago
Titicaca
BOLIVIA
Brasilia

La Paz
Cochabamba

OCÉANO PACÍFICO
Bogotá
Santa Cruz

COLOMBIA
Sucre

Islas Galápagos
(Ecuador)
Quito
ECUADOR
PERÚ

GRAN CHACO
PARAGUAY
20°S

0   200   400 millas
0   200 400 kilómetros

Trópico de Capricornio

Asunción

CHILE
Salta

D E

San Miguel
de Tucumán

L O S

Resistencia

Córdoba
30°S

Valparaíso
Mendoza
Rosario
URUGUAY

A N D E S

Santiago
Buenos Aires
Montevideo

OCÉANO
PACÍFICO

ARGENTINA
La Plata

OCÉANO
ATLÁNTICO

Concepción

P A M P A S

Mar del Plata

Temuco
Bahía Blanca

40°S

P A T A G O N I A

N
O   E
S

0   250   500 millas
0   250 500 kilómetros

Estrecho de
Magallanes
Islas Malvinas (R.U.)
50°S

Tierra del Fuego

100°O   90°O   80°O   70°O   Cabo de Hornos   50°O   40°O   30°O   20°O

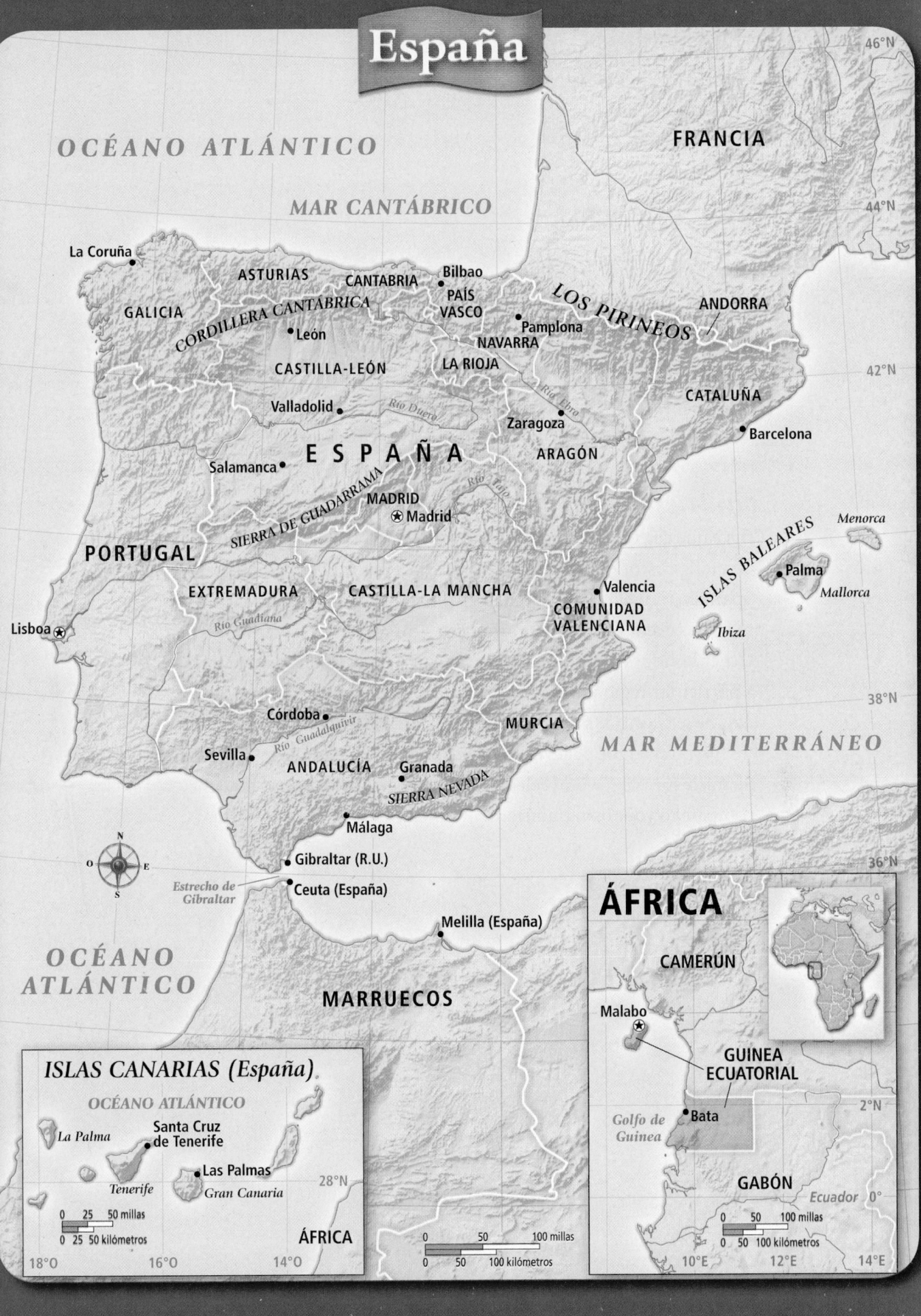

España

OCÉANO ATLÁNTICO

FRANCIA

MAR CANTÁBRICO

La Coruña

ASTURIAS
CANTABRIA
Bilbao
PAÍS VASCO
LOS PIRINEOS
ANDORRA

GALICIA
CORDILLERA CANTÁBRICA
León
Pamplona
NAVARRA
LA RIOJA

CASTILLA-LEÓN
Río Ebro
CATALUÑA

Valladolid
Río Duero
Zaragoza
ARAGÓN
Barcelona

ESPAÑA

Salamanca

Río Tajo

SIERRA DE GUADARRAMA
MADRID
Madrid

ISLAS BALEARES
Menorca
Palma
Mallorca

PORTUGAL

EXTREMADURA
CASTILLA-LA MANCHA

Río Guadiana
Valencia
COMUNIDAD VALENCIANA
Ibiza

Lisboa

38°N

Córdoba
Río Guadalquivir
MURCIA

MAR MEDITERRÁNEO

Sevilla
ANDALUCÍA
Granada
SIERRA NEVADA

Málaga
36°N

Gibraltar (R.U.)

N
O   E
S

Estrecho de Gibraltar
Ceuta (España)

Melilla (España)

OCÉANO ATLÁNTICO

MARRUECOS

ÁFRICA

CAMERÚN

Malabo

GUINEA ECUATORIAL

Golfo de Guinea
Bata
2°N

GABÓN
Ecuador   0°

ISLAS CANARIAS (España)

OCÉANO ATLÁNTICO

La Palma
Santa Cruz de Tenerife
Las Palmas
Tenerife
Gran Canaria
28°N

0   25   50 millas
0   25   50 kilómetros

ÁFRICA

0   50   100 millas
0   50   100 kilómetros

0   50   100 millas
0   50   100 kilómetros

18°O   16°O   14°O
10°E   12°E   14°E

46°N
44°N
42°N

Las celebraciones

The following lessons about holidays are provided for your personal enjoyment. You may choose to read them on your own, or your teacher may present them throughout the year.

Countries in the Spanish-speaking world often share the same celebrations and holidays. The celebrations are a result of a long history of traditions that reflect the mix of primarily Spanish, indigenous, and African cultures. Holidays celebrating religious events and beliefs are often similar between countries. Other holidays commemorate events or people that are important to a particular region. Many holidays, though celebrated on the same day, have traditions and customs that differ between countries.

As you read the pages of Celebraciones, you will discover how the Spanish-speaking world celebrates important holidays and how they compare to your own traditions.

Contenido

agosto

FERIA DE MÁLAGA

La Feria de Málaga celebrates King Ferdinand and Queen Isabella's triumphant entrance into the coastal city of Málaga on August 19, 1487. The pair claimed the city for the crown of Castile, an event this Spanish city has been celebrating for over 500 years. The *Feria de Málaga* now lasts for nine days and takes place in two parts of the city. Each day at noon the downtown fills with fairgoers. In the *Real,* a separate fairground, participants in *flamenco* dress or riding clothes ride on horseback or in horse-drawn carriages, or stroll, in a tradition known as *el paseo.* This daytime *feria* unfolds against a backdrop of music, singing, and dancing and ends at 6:00 p.m., when everyone goes home to rest. The celebration starts again at night in the *Real* and continues into the early morning hours. For this nightly *feria,* people gather in public and private *casetas,* to enjoy concerts, theatrical presentations, music, dance, and food. The last night of the *feria* ends with a city-sponsored concert followed by a spectacular fireworks display.

Feria de caballos More than a thousand riders and over a hundred horse-drawn carriages and carts participate in *el paseo.*

Música callejera Musicians play in the streets during the *feria.* Here a *panda,* or group, plays *verdiales,* traditional music that features guitars, tambourines, and tiny cymbals.

C2   Celebraciones

Una caseta offers free samples of *paella*, a rice and seafood dish that is a regional specialty from the coastal cities of Spain.

Una entrada a la feria Riders pass in front of one of the decorative entrances to a street in the historic downtown of Málaga.

Bailando flamenco Fairgoers perform folkloric dances such as *flamenco* and *sevillanas* in the streets, plazas, and *casetas,* wherever there is music.

Vocabulario para celebrar

los caballos	horses
las carretas	horse-drawn carriages
las casetas	small houses or tents
la feria	fair
el paseo	a walk, stroll, or ride

Comparación cultural

1. Does your town or city celebrate its beginnings or inauguration as a community, or is there a special "town day"? What events take place during the celebration?

2. What events in your community or region are similar to those of the *Feria de Málaga?* Describe them and then compare them to the *Feria de Málaga.*

Celebraciones **C3**

DÍA DE LA INDEPENDENCIA

El Día de la Independencia falls in September for many of the Spanish-speaking countries in the Americas. Mexico celebrates on September 15 and 16, with the *Grito de la Independencia,* music, fireworks, and parades. The first *Grito* occurred at dawn on September 16, 1810, when Padre Miguel Hidalgo y Costilla called to the people of Dolores to rise up against the Spanish crown. That rebellion led to the Mexican War of Independence.

Just two days later, on September 18, 1810, Chile declared its independence from Spain. Today Chile celebrates the date during a week of *fiestas patrias* that include parades, rodeos, dance competitions, and special foods.

Eleven years later, on September 15, 1821, a large part of Central America also proclaimed its independence from Spain, becoming El Salvador, Nicaragua, Guatemala, Costa Rica, and Honduras. These countries celebrate their independence on the 14 and 15 with a focus on students: parades, assemblies, and sports competitions.

México

El Grito de la Independencia On the night of September 15, the president of Mexico commemorates *el Grito* by ringing a bell, proclaiming *¡Que viva México!*, and waving the Mexican flag from a balcony above the Zócalo. Crowds gather below to participate in the *Grito*.

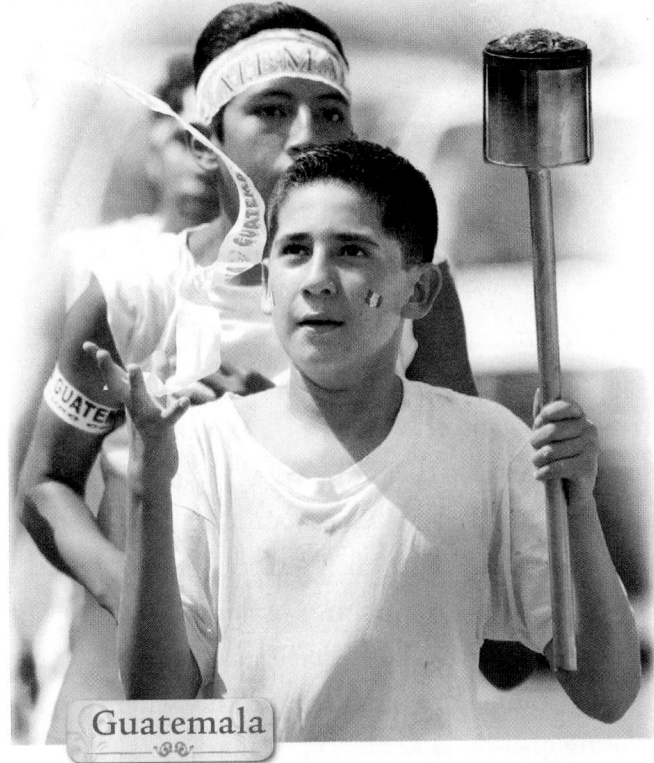

Fiestas patrias Costa Rican schoolchildren, dressed in colors of their country, dance in a parade.

Costa Rica

Guatemala

El recorrido de la antorcha Runners carrying a flaming torch start in Guatemala and end in Costa Rica. All along the route, uniformed schoolchildren wait expectantly for the torch to pass.

Vocabulario para celebrar

la antorcha	torch
la banda	band
las fiestas patrias	patriotic holidays
el grito	shout
el recorrido	run, journey
proclamar	to declare

Comparación cultural

1. Compare the way your town or city celebrates Independence Day with the celebrations in Mexico and Central America. How are they similar? Are there any differences?

2. How do you celebrate Independence Day? Do you participate in community events or have a special tradition?

Celebraciones **C5**

El 12 de Octubre

El 12 de Octubre has many different meanings in the Spanish-speaking world. For some people it is *el Día de Colón,* the day Christopher Columbus arrived in the Americas. For some, it is *el Día de la Hispanidad,* a day to celebrate one's connection with all other Spanish-speaking people, regardless of their country. And for others, it is *el Día de la Raza,* a day when indigenous people come together as a community and celebrate their heritage. Other Spanish speakers celebrate their mixed heritage of indigenous, African, and European cultures. How you celebrate depends very much on you and your family's origin and on the community where you live. For all Spanish-speaking groups, *el 12 de Octubre* marks a key turning point in the lives and cultures of the people in Spain and those living in the Americas.

Vocabulario para celebrar

Cristóbal Colón	Christopher Columbus
el Día Nacional	National Day
la hispanidad	the cultural community of Spanish speakers
la raza	race

México

Día de la Raza Indigenous groups gather in Mexico City dressed in their community's traditional outfits, some wearing pre-Columbian clothing and headdresses.

Chile

Día de la Raza A woman from the Pehuenche indigenous community gathers with other indigenous groups in downtown Santiago.

Nueva York

Día de la Hispanidad High school students carry flags representing all the American countries as they march in a parade down Fifth Avenue.

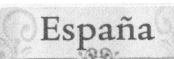

España

Día Nacional de España The Spanish government celebrates with a parade in Madrid.

Comparación cultural

1. How do you celebrate October 12 in your community or school? Is it similar to or different from the celebrations in Spanish-speaking countries? How so?

2. What does October 12 mean to you? Which of the Spanish names for the holiday has the most meaning for you? How would you rename the holiday to celebrate your heritage?

¡Día de los Muertos!

Estados Unidos

Las mojigangas People parade through the Pilsen-Little Village neighborhood of Chicago. Some carry *mojigangas*, giant papier-mâché puppets typically carried in Mexican processions.

On Día de los Muertos families visit the cemeteries and gravesites of their loved ones. They clean the sites and leave flowers and candles and, in many countries, they bring entire meals with special drinks and traditional breads to share with the deceased. Displays are set up next to the gravesite that include flowers, hand-crafted skeletons, colorful paper cutouts, candy skulls, personal items, and photos. Family members pass the night sharing food and conversation as they keep vigil for their ancestors.

The celebration of *Día de los Muertos* spans two days, November 1 and 2. Also known as *Día de los Difuntos*, the traditions originate in the centuries-old religious holiday *Día de Todos los Santos*. In the Americas, this holiday coincided with pre-Columbian festivals that celebrated the harvest, the new year, and honored the dead. The mix of cultures and traditions resulted in the celebration *Día de los Muertos*.

México

Las calaveras A display of dressed-up skulls and skeletons on a street in Mexico City

Ecuador

El pan de muertos This bread is made only for *Día de los Muertos*. In Ecuador, these breads are called *guaguas de pan*. *Guagua* is the Quechua word for "baby" and refers to the bread's shape. The *guaguas* are served with *colada morada*, a warm, purple-colored drink made from blueberries and raspberries.

México

El papel picado These tissue paper cutouts are a common holiday decoration. To celebrate *Día de los Muertos*, the cutouts form images of skeletons.

Guatemala

Vocabulario para celebrar

las calaveras	skulls
el cementerio	cemetery
los difuntos	deceased
el esqueleto	skeleton
el pan de muertos	special bread made for *Día de los Muertos*
el papel picado	paper cutouts
los santos	saints

Los barriletes Guatemalans celebrate by flying *barriletes*, or colorful kites, to which they attach messages for the deceased. The town of Santiago Sacatepéquez celebrates with a *barrilete* contest.

Comparación cultural

1. Does your family or community have a special day or specific traditions to remember the deceased? How are they similar to or different from the traditions of *Día de los Muertos*?

2. Centuries ago in Europe, the night of October 31, before All Saint's Day, was known as "All Hallows Eve." According to ancient beliefs, on this night the dead join the world of the living. Today we call this night Halloween. How would you compare the celebrations of Halloween and *Día de los Muertos*?

diciembre

Las Navidades

Las Navidades are celebrated throughout the Spanish-speaking world with family gatherings and special meals. Celebrations start in mid-December and, in some countries, extend to January 6.

Many families gather the night of December 24, or *la Nochebuena,* to share a special meal of traditional foods and drinks that vary depending on the country. *Tamales, empanadas,* and *buñuelos* are served in many countries. In Spain, there is turkey, or *pavo,* and *turrón.* In Argentina and Chile, where it is summer, people eat cold foods and salads.

The tradition of giving and receiving gifts also forms a part of *las Navidades.* In some countries, families exchange gifts at midnight on *la Nochebuena,* while in others children receive gifts the morning of December 25, and in other countries the gifts appear the morning of January 6. Often gifts are given primarily to children.

Panamá

Un desfile navideño The holiday parade in Panama City takes place in mid-December.

México

La noche de rábanos On the night of December 23, elaborate carvings made from radishes, or *rábanos,* are on display in Oaxaca's central plaza. The figures include people, animals, and even entire scenes. This unique tradition has been celebrated for over 100 years.

Argentina

Las empanadas Dancers dress as *empanadas* in Buenos Aires. These meat-filled pies are especially enjoyed during *las Navidades.*

Perú

El Día de los Reyes Magos In Peru and in many other Spanish-speaking countries, Argentina, the Dominican Republic, Paraguay, and Spain, children receive presents on January 6 from *los Reyes Magos*. In anticipation, children leave out a snack for the Three Kings, carrots or grass for the camels, and a pair of empty shoes for the gifts.

España

Un desfile navideño Circus elephants take part in Madrid's holiday parade on January 5. In Spain, parades on January 5 or 6 celebrate the arrival of *los Reyes Magos*.

Vocabulario para celebrar

la Nochebuena	Christmas Eve
los Reyes Magos	Three Kings
la rosca de reyes	sweet bread eaten on January 6
el turrón	almond nougat candy
los villancicos	seasonal Christmas songs

Comparación cultural

1. Do you and your family celebrate a holiday in December? If so, compare the traditions of your family to the traditions of *las Navidades*.

2. What special meals and foods do you associate with certain holidays? Describe the foods you traditionally enjoy on a holiday you celebrate.

3. What time of the year do you give or receive gifts and for what reason?

¡Año Nuevo!

Perú

La buena suerte In Lima, people believe touching a Chinese Lion brings happiness, good luck, and prosperity in the New Year. Ten percent of Peru's population is of Chinese descent.

España

La medianoche In Madrid, people gather in the Puerta del Sol, holding bags of 12 grapes as they wait for the 12 strokes of midnight from the Puerta del Sol clock, the city's official timekeeper.

El Año Nuevo celebrates the arrival of the New Year and *la Nochevieja* says goodbye to the old. In much of the Spanish-speaking world, traditions include making a toast, exchanging a kiss or hug, or eating twelve grapes—one for each stroke of midnight—to ensure your wishes come true for the New Year. Other good luck traditions include wearing yellow or red, eating a tablespoon of lentils, or carrying a suitcase around the block if you hope to take a trip. To wish someone a happy New Year, say *¡Feliz año nuevo!* or *¡Próspero año nuevo!*

On *Nochevieja,* there are also traditions for saying goodbye to the old year. Some people dress in masks representing *el año viejo.* Others build satirical figures called *los años viejos* that represent famous people or politicians. Adorned with poems or messages that poke fun at *el año viejo,* and filled with shavings and firecrackers, these figures are lit on fire at midnight, to burn and explode on street corners, as a final *despedida,* or farewell, to the old year.

Colombia

Paseo de los años viejos In Popayán, families and neighbors take their *año viejo* figures out for a final ride before the *Nochevieja* celebration. Later on, at midnight, they will burn the figures.

Guatemala

Baile de los Gigantes In Antigua, people celebrate the New Year with the folkloric "Dance of the Giants." These giant heads, or *cabezudos*, are similar to costumes used since the medieval period in Spain.

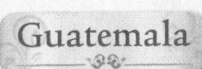

Vocabulario para celebrar

el Año Nuevo	New Year
el brindis	toast
las doce uvas	twelve grapes
las lentejas	lentils
la medianoche	midnight
la Nochevieja	New Year's Eve

Comparación cultural

1. How do you celebrate the New Year? Does your family or community have any special traditions? Are any of the traditions similar to the ones in Spanish-speaking countries? How are they similar or different?

2. If you were to build an *año viejo* representing the past year, what figure or event would you portray? Explain your choice.

febrero

¡Carnaval!

Carnaval marks a period of festivity prior to the beginning of Lent. Lent was, and for some still is, a 40-day period of solemnity and fasting with the removal of meat from the diet being a key feature. You can see the word *carne* (meat) in *Carnaval*; traditionally, this was the last chance to eat meat before the Lenten fast. Today, *Carnaval* often resembles a lively, multi-day party.

Falling in either February or March, *Carnaval* is typically celebrated during the five days that precede Ash Wednesday, the first day of Lent. In some countries, *Carnaval* lasts longer, overlapping other local celebrations. In many regions, traditions such as throwing water and eggs can start over a month before the actual holiday. The planning for the next year's parades, parties, and dance groups often starts as soon as the current *Carnaval* ends!

España

Disfraces Elaborate costumes are central to the *Carnaval* celebration. This costume, entitled "África soy yo," appeared in Las Palmas, in the Canary Islands.

Carnaval Revelers dance in Encarnación, site of the largest celebration in Paraguay.

Paraguay

México

Cascarones Breaking *cascarones* on the heads of friends and other party-goers is a *Carnaval* tradition. The sprinkling of confetti from these hollowed-out eggs is said to bring good luck, as seen here in Mazatlán.

Bolivia

Máscaras are a *Carnaval* tradition dating back to medieval Spain. This masked dancer is from the parade in Oruro, where some 40,000 folkloric dancers and musicians participate.

Bailarines folklóricos Dancers from the Mestizaje dance group perform in Barranquilla. The Colombian government proclaimed this city's *Carnaval* celebration, which combines indigenous, African, and European traditions, a National Cultural Heritage. UNESCO declared it a "Masterpiece" for its cultural uniqueness.

Colombia

Vocabulario para celebrar

los bailarines	dancers
la banda	musical band
Carnaval	Carnival
los cascarones	confetti-filled eggs
el disfraz	costume
las máscaras	masks

Comparación cultural

1. The ways in which *Carnaval* is celebrated in the Spanish-speaking world differ depending on the region. Why do you think the celebrations have evolved differently?

2. Compare the traditions of *Carnaval* to any holiday that you celebrate. Which one(s) are similar? How are they similar?

Las Fallas

Las Fallas is a weeklong festival in March that engulfs the city of Valencia, Spain. Tens of thousands of visitors from all over the world come to the city to experience *Las Fallas,* a week of pageants, music, flowers, and creative displays. Each day, the deafening explosions of thousands of firecrackers, *la mascletà,* fills the city at 2:00 p.m. and each night's celebration ends in fireworks.

The main characters of the celebration are the *ninots,* gigantic figures built of wood, plaster, and cardboard. The largest are up to several stories tall. Neighborhood organizations build these enormous figures during the preceding year. Then, during the week of *Las Fallas,* they display them in intersections, parks, and plazas throughout the city. The public visits the more than 400 *fallas* and votes for their favorite one. On the last night at midnight, all but the favorite are burned in enormous bonfires. Then one final, brilliant display of fireworks explodes over the city.

Los ninots These gigantic figures poke fun at well-known people or current events from the preceding year.

Las falleras During the festival, women dress in traditional outfits that include lace dresses, veils, jewelry, and colorful sashes.

CULTURA Interactiva
my.hrw.com
See these pages come alive!

Una falla iluminada Thousands of visitors come at night to see the illuminated *fallas*. This display was entered into a special contest, *la Sección Especial,* where a committee judges the *fallas* for creativity, gracefulness and charm, originality, and lighting.

La Cremà At midnight on the last night, the *fallas* are burned throughout the city. At the same time there are huge displays of colorful fireworks, which include explosions of roman candles and thousands of firecrackers.

Vocabulario para celebrar

La Cremà	burning of the *fallas*
las fallas	displays of figures
los falleros	celebrants of *Las Fallas*
los fuegos artificiales	fireworks
la mascletà	rhythmic explosion of large and small firecrackers
los ninots	large papier-mâché figures
quemar	to burn

Comparación cultural

1. Fireworks are a major part of *Las Fallas*. Does your community or region have fireworks displays? When and for what reasons?

2. Are there any other traditions in the festival of *Las Fallas* that are similar to traditions you follow in your community? What are they? Are they part of a specific celebration or season?

Semana Santa

La Semana Santa is one holiday during the year where in most Spanish-speaking countries entire towns, businesses, schools, and government close for at least four days, Thursday through Sunday. People that have relocated to other places often go back to their hometowns. Others take advantage of the long break to go to the countryside or beach. Entire communities come together for *Semana Santa* celebrations. In some places, religious processions fill the streets each day of the week from Palm Sunday to Easter; in others, Thursday and Friday are the most important days. Most *Semana Santa* traditions are hundreds of years old and originated in Spain, but many now have a unique twist due to the mix of cultures in each country.

México

Vestidos blancos Girls from San Miguel de Allende dress in white for the procession on *Viernes Santo*. In this town, the celebrations extend for two weeks, ending on *el Domingo de Pascua* with an explosion of papier-mâché figures in the center of town.

El Salvador

Alfombras de aserrín Rugs traditionally made of colored sawdust or sand, flowers, and fruits cover the streets where processions will pass in San Salvador. Artisans also now use modern industrial paints and sprays.

Ecuador

La fanesca Ecuadorians eat *fanesca,* a bean and grain soup with a fish base, only during *Semana Santa.* The soup is traditionally served with *bolitas de harina* (fritters), *plátano verde* (fried green plantain), fresh cheese, and *ají,* a spicy sauce.

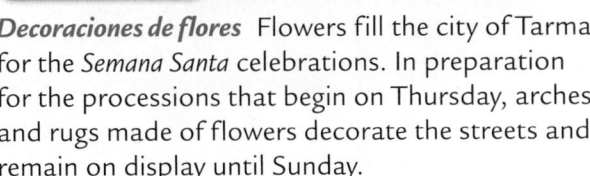

Perú

Decoraciones de flores Flowers fill the city of Tarma for the *Semana Santa* celebrations. In preparation for the processions that begin on Thursday, arches and rugs made of flowers decorate the streets and remain on display until Sunday.

Vocabulario para celebrar

las alfombras	rugs
las flores	flowers
las procesiones	processions
Semana Santa	Holy Week

México

Una procesión Mexicans celebrate Palm Sunday at the Metropolitan Cathedral in Mexico City.

Comparación cultural

1. What holidays do you celebrate with special parades or processions? What kinds of decorations do people use?

2. In what kind of event would most of the people in your community participate? Compare the event to *Semana Santa.*

¡Cinco de Mayo!

Cinco de Mayo has become a popular celebration thoughout the United States. However, not everyone who celebrates this uniquely Mexican holiday knows its origin. To find the reason, you must travel back to the year 1862 in Mexico. On May 5, in the town of Puebla de los Ángeles, the Mexican army, joined by farmers and townspeople, fought against the French and forced them to retreat. The Mexicans were led by General Ignacio Zaragoza and the town was later renamed Puebla de Zaragoza in his honor. Although the French went on to occupy Mexico City and assume a short-lived role in Mexico's government, *Cinco de Mayo* became a national holiday symbolizing Mexican unity.

A *Cinco de Mayo* celebration in Mexico includes dancing, music, and reenactments of the battle. In many parts of the U.S. where there is a large Mexican or Mexican-American community, you will often find *Cinco de Mayo* celebrations.

Los Ángeles

Mariachis y bailarines Folkloric dancers and musicians perform throughout the day in the Plaza Olvera during the *Cinco de Mayo* celebrations.

México

Reconstrucción de la batalla
A reenactment of the historic battle in Puebla commemorates Mexico's victory over the French.

Vocabulario para celebrar

los bailarines	dancers
la batalla	battle
el ejército	army
los franceses	French
los músicos	musicians
la reconstrucción	reenactment

Washington, D.C.

Bailarín folklórico A dancer performs in a traditional Mexican costume at the White House.

Comparación cultural

1. Do you know of a *Cinco de Mayo* celebration in your community or region? If so, how or where is it celebrated?

2. What important battles or historic events are celebrated in your community or state? How are they celebrated? Are they local or national holidays? Compare one of these holiday celebrations with the *Cinco de Mayo* celebrations.

junio

Inti Raymi

Inti Raymi, or the "Festival of the Sun," falls on June 21 or 22, the date of the southern hemisphere's winter solstice, the shortest day of the year. Indigenous communities throughout the Andean highland countries of South America celebrate the winter solstice with ceremonies designed to bring the Sun back and shorten the longest night. Incan in origin, *Inti Raymi* honored the sun as the source of light, heat, and life, and celebrated the start of a new planting season. The name *Inti Raymi* comes from the Quechua language: *inti* means "sun" and *raymi* means "festival." The largest festival takes place in Cuzco, Peru, the ancient capital of the Incan civilization and empire. In Cuzco, *Inti Raymi* has grown into a major tourist attraction. Thousands of people visit the city to enjoy the performances by folkloric groups and to watch the theatrical presentation of the Incan ceremony, the focal point of the celebration.

Perú

Presentación cultural de Inti Raymi
In Cuzco, professional actors and actresses interpret the roles of the Incan emperor and others.
Above: A woman carries offerings.
Right: The Incan emperor passes through the streets of Cuzco to the ruins of the Incan fortress, Sacsayhuaman.

Ecuador

Indígenas ecuatorianas A dance group from the Paktarinmi cultural organization forms a "sacred circle" with grains of corn, a pre-Incan rite. In Ecuador, which lies on the equator, this date is considered the summer solstice, rather than the winter.

Vocabulario para celebrar

el aymara	language of indigenous group from Bolivia and Peru
los incas	Incas, an ancient South American people
el quechua	language common to many South American indigenous groups and adopted and spread by Incas
el sol	sun

Bolivia

Los aymaras In the pre-Columbian ruins of Tihuanaku, an Aymara priest blows on a shell to celebrate the winter solstice, which marks the new year. The Aymara are one of two dominant indigenous groups in Bolivia, comprising 25 percent of the population. The other group, Quechua, makes up 30 percent.

Comparación cultural

1. In North America, June 21 is the summer solstice, or the longest day of the year, and December 21 is the winter solstice, or the shortest day of the year. What important holidays or events occur during this time of year?

2. In ancient civilizations, the appearance of the sun and moon were important events that helped mark the passing of time and the seasons. If you were to celebrate the winter or summer solstice, what would you include in your celebration?

Día de Simón Bolívar

Simón Bolívar, known as *El Libertador,* envisioned a united South America, a union for which he fought, but never attained. Despite this, he was instrumental in bringing about much of South America's independence from Spain and became one of its most revered leaders. His birthday is a national holiday in Venezuela, Ecuador, and Bolivia, and many cities and towns have plazas or monuments in his honor.

Born on July 24, 1783, in Caracas, Venezuela, Simón Bolívar strongly believed in freedom from Spanish rule and worked toward that goal as a political leader, writer, and military commander. With his troops, he liberated present-day Venezuela, then Colombia. He was then named president of Gran Colombia, a federation comprised of what is now Venezuela, Colombia, Panama, and Ecuador. He went on to lead his troops into Peru, aiding in the final defeat of Spain. For two more years, Bolívar maintained his leadership, writing the constitution of Bolivia, a country named in his honor. By 1827, his dream of unification dissolved amidst growing rivalries between the South American military leaders. Three years later Bolívar died, on December 17, 1830.

Colombia

Monumento a Simón Bolívar This monument marks the location of the Battle of Boyacá, where Bolívar's forces defeated the Spanish resulting in the liberation of Gran Colombia. To celebrate the anniversary of the battle, students form the colors of the Colombian flag.

Bolívares Venezuela's currency carries both Bolívar's name and image.

Venezuela

Ecuador

Líder de la Batalla de Pichincha Each year, the city of Quito commemorates the Battle of Pichincha, where Simón Bolívar sent troops under the command of Antonio José de Sucre to defeat the Spanish in one of the crucial battles in the fight for independence.

Simón Bolívar (1830), José Gil de Castro
José Gil de Castro, renowned painter of Chilean society and of the independence leaders, painted this portrait of Bolívar in the early 1800s.

Venezuela

Vocabulario para celebrar

la batalla battle
la independencia
   independence
El Libertador
   the liberator

Plaza de Bolívar This statue of Bolívar is located in the Plaza Bolívar, the historic, political, and commercial center of Caracas.

Comparación cultural

1. What famous leader in U.S. history would you compare with Simón Bolívar? Why? What do both leaders have in common?

2. What U.S. holidays are in honor of famous leaders? How are they celebrated? What other ways do we honor our important leaders?

Nueva York

Tema:

¡Hola!

¡AVANZA! **Let's get started**

- greet people and say goodbye
- introduce yourself and others
- ask and say how to spell names
- say where you are from
- exchange phone numbers
- say what day of the week it is
- describe the weather
- respond to classroom instructions

A performer wearing the colors of the Puerto Rican flag

Dominican dancers in colorful costumes

Nueva York   New York City has the largest Hispanic population of any city in the nation. During its annual Hispanic Day Parade, colorful floats, bands, costumed dancers, and flags from Spanish-speaking countries fill Fifth Avenue. *What cultural celebrations are there in your area?*

MODES OF COMMUNICATION

INTERPRETIVE	INTERPERSONAL	PRESENTATIONAL
Listen to weather reports and identify regional conditions. Read a phone directory and identify individual phone numbers.	With your classmates, introduce yourself and others, and say where you are from. Write an e-mail to a new pen-pal.	Give your personal information to someone. Write a comic-strip conversation.

A view of Lower Manhattan from the East River

New York, New York

✥ Hola, ¿qué tal?

¡AVANZA! **Goal:** Learn that friends and family in Spanish-speaking countries often greet each other with a kiss on the cheek, a hug, or a handshake. In formal settings, like a job, or when meeting for the first time, people shake hands. Practice expressions and gestures to greet and say goodbye to people. *Actividades 1–3*

A

Hola. ¿Cómo estás?

Bien. ¿Y tú?

Mal.

AUDIO

B **Juan:** ¡Hola, Miguel! ¿Qué tal?
 Miguel: Hola, ¿qué pasa?

C **Juan:** ¡Hasta luego, Ana!
 Ana: Hasta luego.

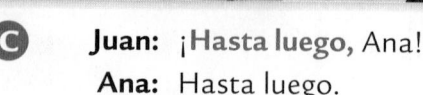

D **Srta. Daza:** Adiós.
 Sr. Ortega: Adiós, señorita.

Lección preliminar
2 dos

E **Sr. Martínez:** Buenos días, señora Ramos. ¿Cómo está usted?

Sra. Ramos: Regular. ¿Y usted?

Sr. Martínez: Más o menos.

F **Juan:** Buenas tardes. ¿Cómo estás?

Esteban: Muy bien.

G **Sra. Acevedo:** Hola, **buenas noches.**

Diana: Buenas noches, señora.

H **Sr. García:** Buenas noches, Diana.

Diana: **Hasta mañana, señor** García.

¡A responder! Escuchar

Listen to these people greeting and saying goodbye. Wave toward the front of the room if you hear a greeting or toward the back of the room if you hear a goodbye.

1 Muy bien

Leer Complete each expression.

1. ¿Cómo está...
2. Buenas...
3. ¿Qué...
4. Muy bien...
5. Hasta...

  a. tal?
  b. mañana.
  c. usted?
  d. tardes.
  e. ¿Y usted?

2 ¿Cómo estás?

Escribir Create a conversation to complete the speech bubbles of this cartoon strip.

Expansión
Write a conversation in which a teacher and student greet each other, ask how each other is doing, and say goodbye.

NOMBRES DE CHICOS

Alejandro	Juan
Andrés	Luis
Carlos	Manuel
Cristóbal	Mateo
Daniel	Miguel
David	Nicolás
Eduardo	Pablo
Esteban	Pedro
Felipe	Ramón
Guillermo	Ricardo
Jaime	Roberto
Jorge	Tomás
José	Vicente

NOMBRES DE CHICAS

Alejandra	Juana
Alicia	Luisa
Ana	María
Bárbara	Marta
Carmen	Natalia
Carolina	Patricia
Cristina	Raquel
Diana	Rosa
Elena	Sofía
Emilia	Susana
Florencia	Teresa
Gabriela	Verónica
Isabel	Yolanda

Manuel

Isabel

Nota

¿Cómo estás? and **¿Cómo está usted?** both mean *How are you?*

¿Cómo estás? and **¿Y tú?** are familiar phrases used with:

- a person your own age
- a relative
- a person you call by his or her first name

Other familiar greetings:
¿Qué tal? and **¿Qué pasa?**

¿Cómo está usted? and **¿Y usted?** are formal phrases used with:

- a person you don't know
- someone older
- a person to whom you want to show respect

3 | Buenos días

Hablar

According to the time of day, greet your partner as if he or she were the following people. Use a formal greeting or a familiar greeting, and appropriate gestures, depending on whom you address.

modelo: Sr. (Sra.) Vargas / 7 a.m.

A Buenos días, señor (señora) Vargas. ¿Cómo está usted?

B Muy bien.

1. your best friend / 10 p.m.
2. the school principal / 2 p.m.
3. Sr. (Srta.) López / 7 p.m.
4. your mother/father / 9 a.m.
5. Sr. (Sra.) Santos / 4 p.m.
6. your brother/sister / 9 p.m.
7. your coach / 11 a.m.
8. your Spanish teacher / 10 a.m.

AUDIO

Pronunciación   La letra h

In Spanish, the letter **h** is always silent.

Listen and repeat.

ha	he	hi	ho	hu
hace	helado	hispano	hola	humano

¡Hola, Hugo!

Hasta mañana, Héctor.

Get Help Online
my.hrw.com

PARA Y PIENSA

Did you get it?
1. Tell a friend good morning.
2. Ask a friend how he or she is.
3. Say goodbye to your teacher.

✾ ¡Mucho gusto!

AUDIO

A **Esteban:** Hola. **Me llamo** Esteban. ¿Y tú? **¿Cómo te llamas?**
  Diana: Me llamo Diana.
  Esteban: **Encantado,** Diana.
  Diana: **Igualmente.**

B **Diana:** **Te presento a** Esteban.
  Ana: **Encantada.**
  Esteban: Igualmente.

C **Srta. Machado:** **Perdón.** **¿Cómo se llama?**
  Srta. Daza: Me llamo Raquel Daza.

D **Srta. Machado:** **Le presento a** Ana Vega.
  Sr. Ortega: **Mucho gusto.**
  Ana: **El gusto es mío.**

E ¿Quién es? ¿Es Raúl?

No. Es Juan.

F ¿Cómo se llama?

Se llama Diana.

G **Rosa:** ¿Se llama Miguel?
Esteban: **Sí.** Se llama Miguel Luque.

¡A responder! Escuchar

Listen to four people make introductions. Point to yourself if you hear someone introducing themselves. Point to the person next to you if you hear someone introducing someone else.

4 ¿Cómo te llamas?

Leer Choose the correct response to each question or statement.

1. ¿Quién es?
   a. Es Hugo.
   b. Encantado.
   c. Me llamo Carlos.

2. Encantada.
   a. Le presento a Sergio.
   b. ¿Y tú?
   c. Igualmente.

3. Te presento a Joaquín.
   a. ¿Cómo se llama?
   b. Mucho gusto.
   c. Igualmente.

4. ¿Cómo te llamas?
   a. Perdón.
   b. Me llamo Isabel.
   c. Bien.

5. Me llamo Gabriel.
   a. Igualmente.
   b. Encantado.
   c. El gusto es mío.

6. Mucho gusto.
   a. Buenas tardes.
   b. ¿Quién es?
   c. El gusto es mío.

5 Conversación

Leer
Escribir

Complete the conversation with the correct words.

Carlos: Hola. Me __1.__ Carlos. ¿ __2.__ te llamas?

Beatriz: Me __3.__ Beatriz.

Carlos: __4.__ , Beatriz.

Beatriz: __5.__ .

6 Mucho gusto

Hablar Work in a group of four. Introduce yourself to each member of the group.

A Hola, me llamo...

B Encantado. Me llamo...

Expansión
Introduce yourself to your teacher.

7 | Te presento a...

Hablar Work in a group of three. Take turns introducing each other.

A Te presento a Tomás.

B Encantado(a), Tomás.

C Igualmente.

Comparación cultural

Un mural en Nueva York

How can artists give back to their neighborhood through their work? Artist Manuel Vega moved with his family from Puerto Rico to **New York** at a young age. He grew up in East Harlem and his works often depict neighborhood scenes inspired by his childhood. Vega was commissioned to restore this image, originally created by Hank Prussing in 1973, on a multi-story building in East Harlem.

The Spirit of East Harlem,
Manuel Vega

Compara con tu mundo *What childhood memory would you paint if you were creating a neighborhood mural? Compare it with the scene in Vega's mural.*

Get Help Online
my.hrw.com

PARA Y PIENSA

Did you get it? Complete each statement.

1. Me llamo...   **a.** a Maricela.
2. Te presento...   **b.** gusto, señor.
3. Mucho...   **c.** Walter.

❖El abecedario

Goal: Learn to say the Spanish alphabet. Then practice how to say the letters to spell different things. *Actividades 8–10*

AUDIO

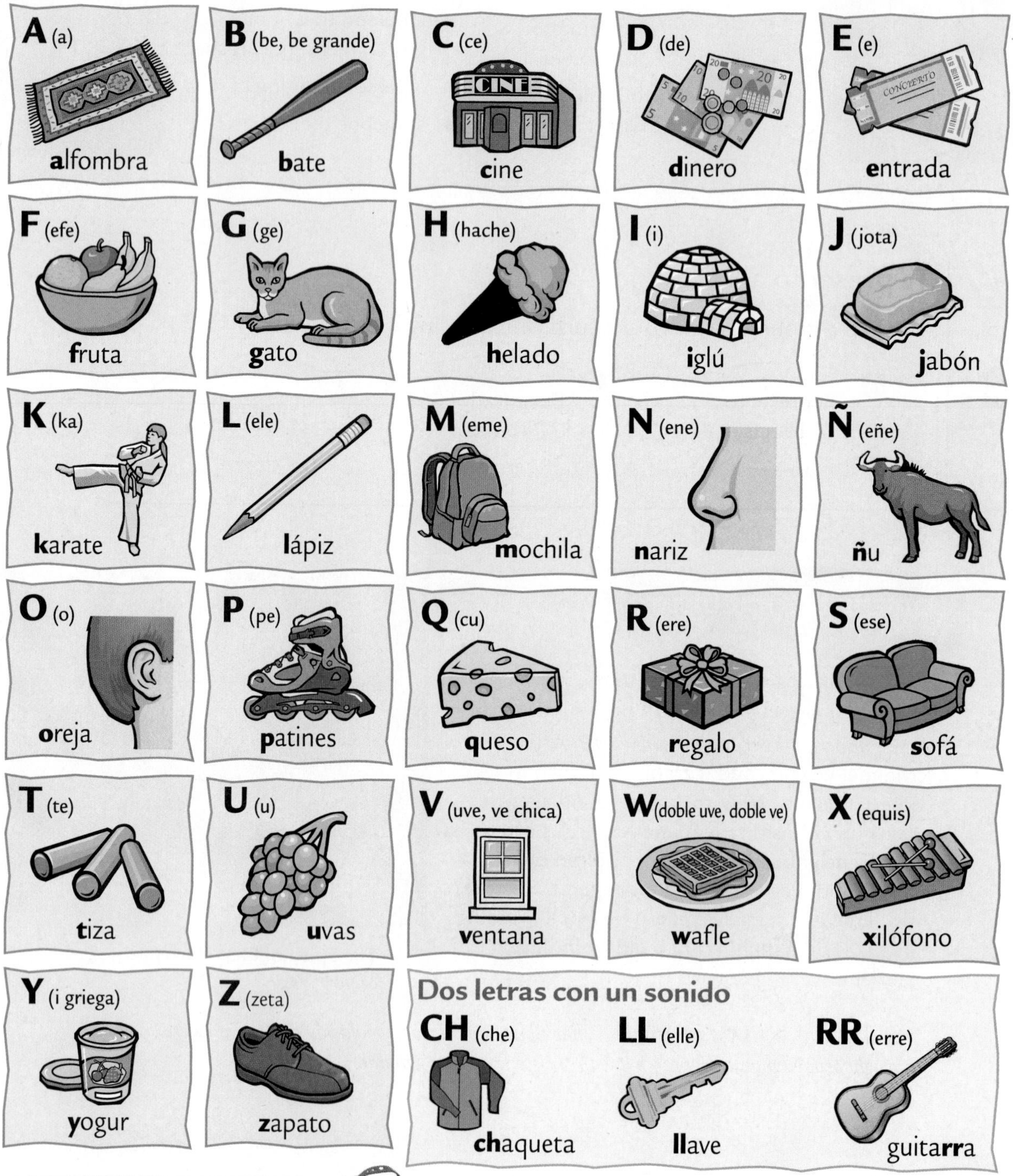

A (a) — **a**lfombra

B (be, be grande) — **b**ate

C (ce) — **c**ine

D (de) — **d**inero

E (e) — **e**ntrada

F (efe) — **f**ruta

G (ge) — **g**ato

H (hache) — **h**elado

I (i) — **i**glú

J (jota) — **j**abón

K (ka) — **k**arate

L (ele) — **l**ápiz

M (eme) — **m**ochila

N (ene) — **n**ariz

Ñ (eñe) — **ñ**u

O (o) — **o**reja

P (pe) — **p**atines

Q (cu) — **q**ueso

R (ere) — **r**egalo

S (ese) — **s**ofá

T (te) — **t**iza

U (u) — **u**vas

V (uve, ve chica) — **v**entana

W (doble uve, doble ve) — **w**afle

X (equis) — **x**ilófono

Y (i griega) — **y**ogur

Z (zeta) — **z**apato

Dos letras con un sonido

CH (che) — **ch**aqueta

LL (elle) — **ll**ave

RR (erre) — guita**rr**a

¡A responder! Escuchar

Listen to letters of the Spanish alphabet. Write each letter that you hear on a piece of paper and hold it up.

8 | Lista

Escuchar Escribir

Listen to someone dictate an invitation list for a party. Write down each name as it is spelled.

> **modelo:** You hear: de, a, ene, i, e, ele
> You write: Daniel

9 | Me llamo...

Hablar

Work in a group of three. Ask each person his or her name and write down the name as he or she spells it.

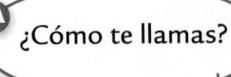

A ¿Cómo te llamas?

B Me llamo Shawna, S - H - A - W - N - A. (ese, hache, a, doble uve, ene, a)

Expansión
Continue the activity with your last name.

10 | ABC

Hablar

Spell aloud the following things for a partner. He or she will write the word. Then verify that your partner spelled the word correctly.

your middle name	your favorite singer	the name of
the name of your	your favorite sports	your town
school	team	¿ ?

AUDIO

Pronunciación   Las vocales

In Spanish, the vowels are **a, e, i, o,** and **u.** Each vowel is always pronounced the same way. Spanish vowels are always short and crisp.

Listen to and repeat these words.

a → as in *father*	enc**a**nt**a**d**a**	m**a**l	m**a**ñ**a**na
e → as in *hey*	m**e**nos	s**e**ñor	pr**e**s**e**nto
i → sounds like *meet*	**i**gualmente	ad**i**ós	b**i**en
o → as in *woke*	h**o**la	n**o**ches	cóm**o**
u → sounds like *boot*	**u**sted	m**u**cho	tú

Get Help Online
my.hrw.com

PARA Y PIENSA

Did you get it?   Recite the Spanish alphabet.

¿De dónde eres?

¡AVANZA! **Goal:** Look at the Spanish-speaking world and how Spanish speakers say where someone is from. Then practice what you have learned to ask where people are from. *Actividades 11–13*

AUDIO

Alicia, ¿de dónde eres?

Soy de **Estados Unidos.** Soy de la Florida.

Soy de **Estados Unidos.** ¿De dónde es usted?

Sr. Costas

Alicia

Isabel **es de la República Dominicana.**

Pablo es de **México.**

Susana es de **Costa Rica.**

Fernando es de **Ecuador.**

Marisol es de **Puerto Rico.**

Mariano es de **Argentina.**

Lección preliminar
doce

12

Los países hispanohablantes

Enrique es de **España**.

1. Estados Unidos
2. México
3. Cuba
4. República Dominicana
5. Puerto Rico
6. Guatemala
7. Honduras
8. El Salvador
9. Nicaragua
10. Costa Rica
11. Panamá
12. Venezuela
13. Colombia
14. Ecuador
15. Perú
16. Bolivia
17. Paraguay
18. Chile
19. Argentina
20. Uruguay
21. España
22. Guinea Ecuatorial
23. Filipinas
24. Guam

Color Key

Spanish is the official language.   Spanish is spoken.

¡A responder!   Escuchar

For each statement you hear, point to the person in the photo to whom it refers.

11 | Es de...

Escribir Hablar

Indicate where each person is from, according to the number on the map.

modelo: Guillermo / ⑦

Guillermo es de **Uruguay.**

1. Andrea / ⑤
2. Tomás / ⑧
3. Nicolás / ④
4. Sofía / ②
5. Verónica / ③
6. Mateo / ⑨
7. Consuelo / ①
8. Pablo / ⑥

12 | ¿De dónde eres?

Hablar

Ask a partner where he or she is from. Your partner will answer with the country listed.

modelo: Colombia

1. Venezuela
2. Panamá
3. México
4. Uruguay
5. España
6. Estados Unidos
7. El Salvador
8. Nicaragua

Ⓐ ¿De dónde eres?

Ⓑ Soy de Colombia.

Expansión
Ask a partner the same questions, using formal address.

Lección preliminar
14 catorce

13 | ¿Eres de Honduras?

Hablar

Ask a partner if he or she is from the country indicated. He or she will answer according to the number.

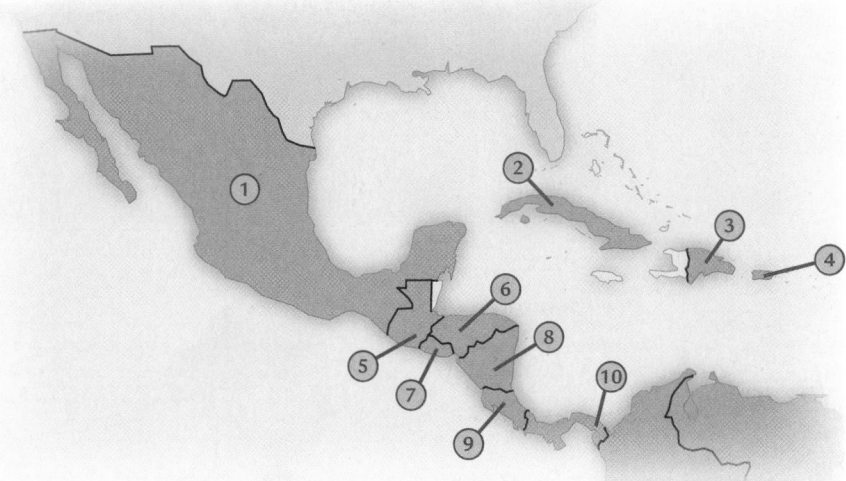

modelo: ① / ⑩

A ¿Eres de **México**?

B No. Soy de **Panamá.**

Estudiante A

1. ⑨   4. ⑩
2. ④   5. ⑤
3. ⑥   6. ⑧

Estudiante B

1. ③   4. ⑩
2. ④   5. ⑤
3. ②   6. ⑦

🌐 **Get Help Online**
my.hrw.com

PARA Y PIENSA

Did you get it? Match each question with the correct response.

1. ¿De dónde eres?   **a.** Es de Puerto Rico.
2. ¿De dónde es Hugo?   **b.** Soy de Colombia.
3. ¿Eres de México?   **c.** Sí, soy de México.

Mi número de teléfono

Goal: Learn how to say the numbers from zero to ten and how to exchange phone numbers. Then use what you have learned to say your home (or cellular) phone number. *Actividades 14–16*

AUDIO

¿Cuál es tu número de teléfono?

Es 7–6–4–9–0–8–1.

Perdón. ¿Cuál es su número de teléfono?

Mi número de teléfono es 2–5–3–7–1–0–9.

¡A responder! Escuchar

Listen to these numbers. If you hear an even number, raise your right hand. If you hear an odd number, raise your left hand.

14 | Matemáticas

Hablar Escribir

Give the answers to the following math problems using words.

modelo: 2 + 4

     seis

1. 8 − 3   **3.** 3 + 6   **5.** 1 + 9   **7.** 6 − 5   **9.** 10 − 8

2. 4 + 4   **4.** 7 − 7   **6.** 5 − 2   **8.** 7 + 0   **10.** 1 + 3

> **Expansión**
> Say each completed problem, using **más** (*plus*) and **menos** (*minus*).

15 | Teléfono

Hablar

Work in a group of five. Whisper a phone number to the person at your right. He or she will repeat it to the person at his or her right, and so on. Verify that the phone number you gave was repeated accurately.

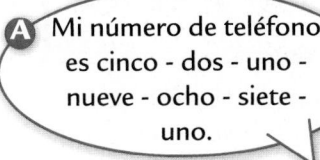

A Mi número de teléfono es cinco - dos - uno - nueve - ocho - siete - uno.

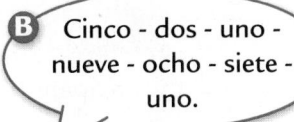

B Cinco - dos - uno - nueve - ocho - siete - uno.

C Cinco - dos - uno...

16 | ¿Quién es?

Hablar

Work with a partner. Look at this Buenos Aires phone directory and read a phone number at random. Your partner will say whose phone number it is.

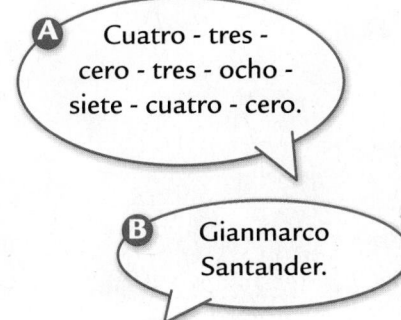

A Cuatro - tres - cero - tres - ocho - siete - cuatro - cero.

B Gianmarco Santander.

Santander Gemma
Lauerbach 3472 Pb 11- Capital Federal
Ciudad de Buenos Aires 4301-9203

Santander Genoveva
Löschner 244- Capital Federal
Ciudad de Buenos Aires 4921-4808

Santander Geraldo
López de Padilla 12 Pb 4- Capital Federal
Ciudad de Buenos Aires 4704-5960

Santander Giancarlo
Filippozzi 9903 Pb Casa- Capital Federal
Ciudad de Buenos Aires 4638-3123

Santander Gianmarco
Filippozzi 1099- Capital Federal
Ciudad de Buenos Aires 4303-8740

Santander Gregorio
Sta Marta 374 Pb 7- Capital Federal
Ciudad de Buenos Aires 4941-7819

Get Help Online
my.hrw.com

PARA Y PIENSA

Did you get it? Say these phone numbers.
   1. 6251-4209   **2.** 3708-9263   **3.** 4185-2760

Los días de la semana

AUDIO

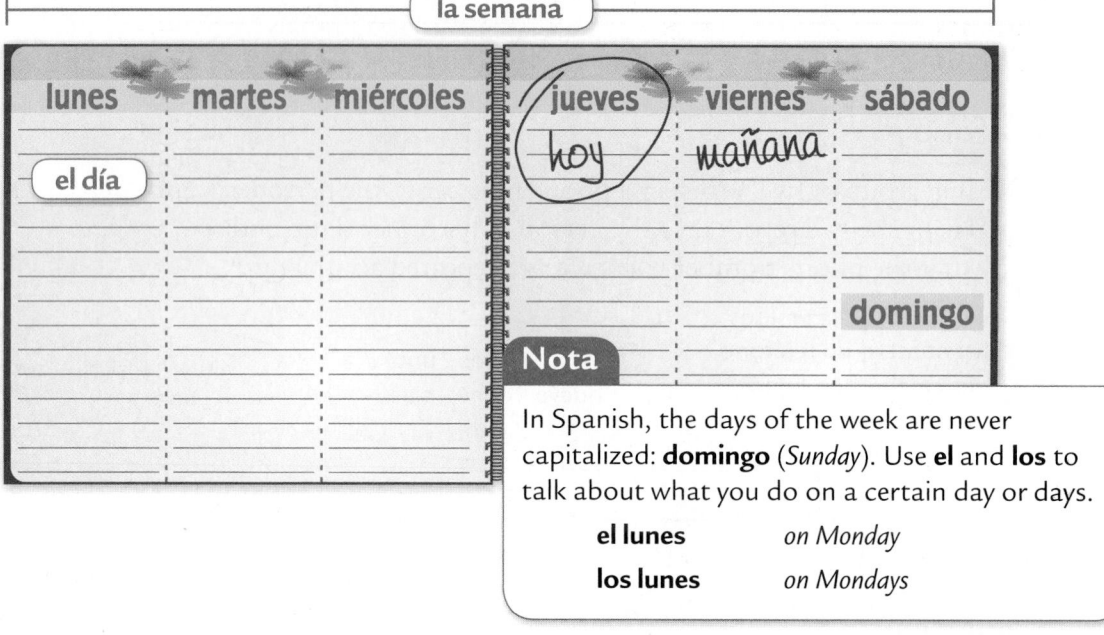

Nota

In Spanish, the days of the week are never capitalized: **domingo** (*Sunday*). Use **el** and **los** to talk about what you do on a certain day or days.

el lunes	*on Monday*
los lunes	*on Mondays*

A **Ana:** ¿Qué día es hoy?
Rosa: Hoy es jueves.

B **Juan:** ¿Hoy es viernes?
Esteban: No. Mañana es viernes.

¡A responder! Escuchar

Listen to the days of the week. If you hear a day that you have Spanish class, stand up. If you hear a day that you don't have Spanish class, remain seated.

17 Los días

Hablar
Escribir

Complete each list with the missing day of the week.

1. lunes, _____, miércoles, jueves
2. viernes, _____, domingo, lunes
3. _____, martes, miércoles, jueves
4. lunes, martes, miércoles, _____

5. _____, jueves, viernes, sábado
6. domingo, _____, martes, miércoles
7. sábado, _____, lunes, martes
8. martes, miércoles, jueves, _____

18 ¿Lógico o ilógico?

Escuchar

Listen to these statements about the days of the week. Write **L** if the statement you hear is **lógico** (*logical*) or **I** if it is **ilógico** (*not logical*).

modelo: You hear: Hoy es viernes. Mañana es domingo.
You write: I

19 ¿Qué día es?

Hablar

Ask a partner what day of the week it is. He or she will tell you what day of the week today is and what tomorrow is.

modelo: 6

A ¿Qué día es hoy?

B Hoy es **martes.** Mañana es **miércoles.**

1. 2
2. 12
3. 28
4. 15

5. 18
6. 3
7. 20
8. 16

SEPTIEMBRE

L	M	M	J	V	S	D
			1	2	3	4
5	6	7	8	9	10	11
12	13	14	15	16	17	18
19	20	21	22	23	24	25
26	27	28	29	30		

Get Help Online
my.hrw.com

PARA Y PIENSA

Did you get it?
1. Tell someone that today is Monday.   Hoy es _____.
2. Ask what day tomorrow is.   ¿Qué día es _____?

✤ ¿Qué tiempo hace?

¡AVANZA! **Goal:** Learn how to describe the weather. Then practice what you have learned to describe a sunny day, a rainy day, and a windy day. *Actividades 20–22*

¿Qué tiempo hace?

A Luis: Hace calor.

B Natalia: Hace sol.

C Jorge: Llueve.

D Andrea: Hace frío.

E Diego: Hace viento.

F Mariana: Nieva.

¡A responder! Escuchar

Listen to weather descriptions. Point to the photo of the person that corresponds to the description you hear.

20 | El tiempo

Escuchar

Listen to four meteorologists describe the weather in their region. Write the letter of the photo that corresponds to the weather description you hear.

a.    **b.**    **c.**    **d.**

21 | ¿Hace calor o hace frío?

Hablar

Work with a partner. Say whether it is cold or hot, according to the temperature given.

> **modelo:** 32°F / 0°C
> Hace frío.

1. 15°F / –9°C   **3.** 20°F / –6°C   **5.** 88°F / 32°C

2. 94°F / 35°C   **4.** 4°F / –16°C   **6.** 104°F / 40°C

Expansión
Say whether you think it is raining or snowing at these temperatures.

22 | ¿Qué tiempo hace?

Hablar

Tell what city you are from, and ask a partner what the weather is like. He or she will give you the weather conditions for that city.

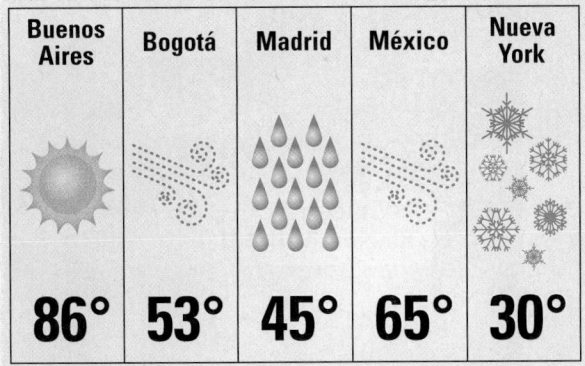

Buenos Aires	Bogotá	Madrid	México	Nueva York
86°	53°	45°	65°	30°

A Soy de la Ciudad de México. ¿Qué tiempo hace?

B Hace viento.

Get Help Online
my.hrw.com

PARA Y PIENSA

Did you get it? Match each question with the correct response.

1. ¿Qué tiempo hace?   **a.** No. Hace frío.

2. ¿Hace calor?   **b.** Hace viento.

3. ¿Llueve?   **c.** No. Hace sol.

En la clase

¡AVANZA! **Goal:** Learn some useful phrases used by teachers and students. Then practice what you have learned to use classroom phrases with others. ***Actividades 23–25***

AUDIO

En la clase

Abran los libros (en la página...)	*Open your books (to page . . .)*
Cierren los libros.	*Close your books.*
¿Cómo se dice...?	*How do you say . . .?*
Se dice...	*You say . . .*
¿Cómo se escribe (tu nombre)?	*How do you spell (your name)?*
Se escribe...	*It is spelled . . .*
¿Comprendes?	*Do you understand?*
Levanten la mano.	*Raise your hand.*
Más despacio, por favor.	*More slowly, please.*
No sé.	*I don't know.*
¿Qué quiere decir...?	*What does . . . mean?*
Quiere decir...	*It means . . .*
Repitan, por favor.	*Please repeat.*
Saquen una hoja de papel.	*Take out a piece of paper.*
Siéntense.	*Sit down.*
¿Tienen preguntas?	*Do you have questions?*
¿Verdad?	*Right?*

En el libro

Completa la conversación.	*Complete the conversation.*
Contesta las preguntas.	*Answer the questions.*
Escoge la palabra / la respuesta...	*Choose the word / answer . . .*
Escribe...	*Write . . .*
Escucha...	*Listen . . .*
Explica...	*Explain . . .*
Indica si es cierto o falso.	*Indicate whether it is true or false.*
Lee...	*Read . . .*
Pregúntale a otro(a) estudiante.	*Ask another student.*
Trabaja con otro(a) estudiante.	*Work with another student.*
Trabaja en un grupo de...	*Work in a group of . . .*

¡A responder! Escuchar

Listen to each classroom instruction and respond appropriately.

23 | Instrucciones

Leer | Match each picture with the correct instruction.

1.

2.

   a. Abran los libros en la página 7.
   b. Levanten la mano.
   c. Repitan, por favor.
   d. Siéntense.

3.

4.

24 | ¿Qué dices?

Escribir
Hablar

Indicate what you would say in each situation. Refer to the expressions on pages 22–23.

1. You want to thank your Spanish teacher.
2. Your teacher is speaking too fast.
3. You want to know how to say *book* in Spanish.
4. You want to know what **página** means.
5. You must admit that you don't have the answer to a question.
6. You wonder if your friend understands the lesson.

25 | ¿Cómo se dice?

Hablar

Ask a partner to say the following words in Spanish and how to spell them.

   modelo: Tuesday

1. Spanish
2. week
3. Thank you very much.
4. male teacher
5. See you later.
6. Friday
7. It's raining.

A ¿Cómo se dice *Tuesday*?

¿Cómo se escribe *martes*?

B Se dice *martes*.

Se escribe eme, a, ere, te, e, ese.

Expansión
Continue this activity with four more words of your choosing.

Get Help Online
my.hrw.com

PARA Y PIENSA

Did you get it?
1. Ask how to say the word *please*.
2. Ask a friend if he or she understands.

En resumen
Vocabulario

¡AvanzaRap!
DVD
Sing and Learn

Vocabulario

Greet People and Say Goodbye

Greetings

Buenos días.	Good morning.
Buenas tardes.	Good afternoon.
Buenas noches.	Good evening.
Hola.	Hello./Hi.

Say Goodbye

Adiós.	Goodbye.
Buenas noches.	Good night.
Hasta luego.	See you later.
Hasta mañana.	See you tomorrow.

Say How You Are

¿Cómo estás?	How are you? (familiar)
¿Cómo está usted?	How are you? (formal)
¿Qué tal?	How is it going?
Bien.	Fine.
Mal.	Bad.
Más o menos.	So-so.
Muy bien.	Very well.
Regular.	Okay.
¿Y tú?	And you? (familiar)
¿Y usted?	And you? (formal)
¿Qué pasa?	What's up?

Make Introductions

¿Cómo se llama?	What's his/her/ your (formal) name?
Se llama...	His/Her name is . . .
¿Cómo te llamas?	What's your (familiar) name?
Me llamo...	My name is . . .
Te/Le presento a...	Let me introduce you (familiar/ formal) to . . .
El gusto es mío.	The pleasure is mine.
Encantado(a).	Delighted./Pleased to meet you.
Igualmente.	Same here./ Likewise.
Mucho gusto.	Nice to meet you.
¿Quién es?	Who is he/she/it?
Es...	He/She/It is . . .

Say Which Day It Is

¿Qué día es hoy?	What day is today?
Hoy es...	Today is . . .
Mañana es...	Tomorrow is . . .
el día	day
hoy	today
mañana	tomorrow
la semana	week

Days of the week *p. 18*

Exchange Phone Numbers

¿Cuál es tu/su número de teléfono?	What's your (familiar/ formal) phone number?
Mi número de teléfono es...	My phone number is . . .

Numbers from zero to ten *p. 16*

Other Words and Phrases

la clase	class
el (la) maestro(a) de español	Spanish teacher (male/female)
el país	country
Perdón.	Excuse me.
por favor	please
(Muchas) Gracias.	Thank you (very much).
De nada.	You're welcome.
el señor (Sr.)	Mr.
la señora (Sra.)	Mrs.
la señorita (Srta.)	Miss
sí	yes
no	no

Describe the Weather

¿Qué tiempo hace?	What is the weather like?
Hace calor.	It is hot.
Hace frío.	It is cold.
Hace sol.	It is sunny.
Hace viento.	It is windy.
Llueve.	It is raining.
Nieva.	It is snowing.

Say Where You Are From

¿De dónde eres?	Where are you (familiar) from?
¿De dónde es?	Where is he/she from?
¿De dónde es usted?	Where are you (formal) from?
Soy de...	I am from . . .
Es de...	He/She is from . . .

Spanish-speaking countries *p. 13*

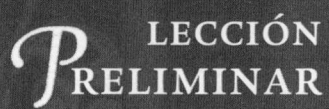
Repaso de la lección

¡LLEGADA!

@HOMETUTOR
my.hrw.com

¡AvanzaRap!
DVD
Sing and Learn

Now you can

- greet people and say goodbye
- introduce yourself and others
- ask and say how to spell names
- say where you are from

- exchange phone numbers
- say what day of the week it is
- describe the weather
- respond to classroom instructions

To review
- introductions pp. 6–7
- classroom instructions pp. 22–23

1 Listen and understand

You will hear four separate conversations. Put the drawings in order according to what you hear.

a.    **b.**    **c.**    **d.**

To review
- greet people pp. 2–3
- introductions pp. 6–7
- weather p. 20

2 Introduce yourself and others

Complete Enrique's e-mail message to his new e-pal.

Adiós	Hace	Hoy
calor	Hola	Soy
Cómo	tiempo	llamo

1. ,

¿ **2.** estás? Me **3.** Enrique. **4.** de Panamá. **5.** es sábado y hace **6.** . ¿Qué **7.** hace en Estados Unidos? ¿ _ **8.** frío?

9. ,

Enrique

To review
- origin pp. 12–13
- numbers p. 16

3 | Say where you are from

Look at these students' ID cards from the International Club.

Then complete the sentences that follow.

Club Internacional

NOMBRE:
Cristina Villaveces
PAÍS DE ORIGEN:
Venezuela
DOMICILIO:
332 Avenida de
las Américas
TELÉFONO:
241-0976

Club Internacional

NOMBRE:
Yolanda Hoyos
PAÍS DE ORIGEN:
Chile
DOMICILIO:
1902 Rúa Mayor
TELÉFONO:
397-2261

Club Internacional

NOMBRE:
Alejandro Cruz
PAÍS DE ORIGEN:
México
DOMICILIO:
214 Paseo Suárez
TELÉFONO:
898-1035

Club Internacional

NOMBRE:
Guillermo Morales
PAÍS DE ORIGEN:
España
DOMICILIO:
38 Calle Toro, 3ºD
TELÉFONO:
460-1853

1. ____ es de España.
2. El número de teléfono es ocho - nueve - ocho - uno - cero - tres - cinco. Se llama ____ .
3. Se llama Cristina. El número de teléfono es ____ .
4. La señorita de Chile se llama ____ .
5. Se llama Guillermo. El número de teléfono es ____ .
6. ____ es de México.

To review
- alphabet p. 10
- numbers p. 16
- days of the week p. 18

4 | Answer personal questions

Answer these questions using complete sentences.

1. ¿Cómo te llamas?
2. ¿Cómo se escribe tu nombre?
3. ¿De dónde eres?
4. ¿Cuál es tu número de teléfono?
5. ¿Quién es el (la) maestro(a) de español? ¿De dónde es?
6. ¿Cómo se llama el libro de español?
7. ¿Qué día es mañana?
8. ¿Qué tiempo hace hoy?
9. ¿Cómo se dice *country* en español?

Get Help Online
my.hrw.com

Estados Unidos

Un rato con los amigos

Lección 1

Tema: *¿Qué te gusta hacer?*

Lección 2

Tema: **Mis amigos y yo**

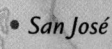

Alaska

Islas Hawai

«¡Hola!

**Nosotras somos Alicia y Sandra.
Somos de Estados Unidos.»**

Chicago •   Filadelfia •   *Nueva York*

Denver •   Estados Unidos

• San José

Los Ángeles
    Phoenix •   • *Albuquerque*

San Diego •   • Tucson

• El Paso   • Dallas
     • Houston

San Antonio •

      Miami •

Océano Atlántico

Golfo de México

Cuba

México

Mar Caribe

Océano Pacífico

Honduras
   / **Nicaragua**

**Costa
/ Rica**

Guatemala

El Salvador

Panamá

Población: 321.368.864

Población de ascendencia hispana: 50.477.594

Ciudad con más latinos: Nueva York
2.336.076

**Ciudad con mayor porcentaje de
latinos:** el este de Los Ángeles (97%)

Comida latina: el sándwich cubano,
burritos, fajitas

El sándwich cubano

Gente famosa: Sandra Cisneros (escritora),
Gloria Estefan (cantante), Eva Mendes (actriz),
Eloy Rodríguez (bioquímico)

Hispanic friends gather for a celebration in New York City

◀ **La ascendencia hispana** The over 40 million Hispanics living in the United States trace their roots to more than 20 nations. From September 15 to October 15, Hispanic Heritage Month celebrates the diverse backgrounds and cultures of these Americans. *Do you know anyone from a Spanish-speaking country?*

La comunidad cubana de Miami The Cuban American community thrives in Miami's Little Havana. **Calle Ocho** is known for its Cuban restaurants, cafés, and shops, and the nearby Freedom Tower houses the Cuban American Museum. *How have people from other countries shaped your community?* ▶

Miami's Freedom Tower, home to the Cuban American Museum

Dancers in traditional dress during the Fiesta San Antonio

◀ **Las celebraciones** San Antonio is proud of its unique multicultural history. The **Fiesta San Antonio,** a ten-day celebration with food, music, and parades, honors the heroes of the Alamo and the Battle of San Jacinto. La Villita, the city's oldest neighborhood, hosts many of the festival events. *How do people celebrate history and culture where you live?*

Estados Unidos

Tema:

¿Qué te gusta hacer?

¡AVANZA! **In this lesson you will learn to**
- talk about activities
- tell where you are from
- say what you like and don't like to do

using
- subject pronouns and **ser**
- **de** to describe where you are from
- **gustar** with an infinitive

♻ *¿Recuerdas?*
- weather expressions

Comparación cultural

In this lesson you will learn about
- *Los Premios Juventud,* an awards show in Miami
- Cuban-American artist Xavier Cortada
- free-time activities of students at a Florida school

Compara con tu mundo
This group of teenagers is spending the day at a beach. In southern Florida, beaches are open year-round and are popular places to do many different activities. *Where do you like to go with your friends in your free time? What do you like to do?*

¿Qué ves?

Mira la foto
What is the weather like?

Do you think that these teenagers are friends?

What activities do they like to do?

MODES OF COMMUNICATION

INTERPRETIVE	INTERPERSONAL	PRESENTATIONAL
Read a survey about what students in a dual-language school in Florida like to do. Listen to a conversation between friends and identify their likes and dislikes.	With other students, compare your after-school activities. Ask others where they're from.	Present a friend's likes and dislikes to the class. Write an email describing your likes and dislikes.

Una playa de Miami Beach
Miami Beach, Florida

Estados Unidos

treinta y uno **31**

✦ Presentación de VOCABULARIO

VIDEO DVD

AUDIO

A ¡Hola! Me llamo Teresa. **Después de** las clases, **me gusta pasar un rato con los amigos.** Me gusta **escuchar música o tocar la guitarra.**

tocar la guitarra

escuchar música

hablar por teléfono

leer un libro

dibujar

Miguel   Teresa   Alicia

B ¡Hola! Me llamo Miguel. A mí me gusta **hablar por teléfono, dibujar** y **estudiar.** Me gusta **pasear, pero** me gusta **más correr.** A ti, ¿qué te gusta hacer?

estudiar

pasear

correr

C ¡Hola! Me llamo Alicia. A mí me gusta **montar en bicicleta** y **jugar al fútbol. También** me gusta **andar en patineta.**

montar en bicicleta

jugar al fútbol

andar en patineta

D Hoy hace calor en Miami. **Antes de practicar deportes** me gusta **comprar agua.**

comprar

el refresco

las papas fritas

la fruta

el agua

la pizza

las galletas

el helado

E Me gusta **beber** agua o **jugo** pero no me gusta beber **refrescos.**

preparar la comida
comer
beber
el jugo

Más vocabulario

la actividad *activity*
alquilar un DVD *to rent a DVD*
aprender el español *to learn Spanish*
la escuela *school*
hacer la tarea *to do homework*
Expansión de vocabulario p. R2

F No me gusta **trabajar** los sábados y domingos. Me gusta **escribir correos electrónicos** y **descansar.** También me gusta **mirar la televisión.** ¿Te gusta pasar un rato con los amigos?

escribir correos electrónicos

descansar
mirar la televisión

@HOMETUTOR Interactive Flashcards
my.hrw.com

¡A responder!   Escuchar

Escucha la lista de actividades. Mientras escuchas, representa las actividades. *(Act out the activities as you hear them.)*

Práctica de VOCABULARIO

1 | El sábado

**Leer
Escribir**

Miguel, Teresa y Alicia hablan de las actividades que les gusta hacer. Completa la conversación con las palabras apropiadas. *(Complete the conversation about what they like to do.)*

> un libro
> un DVD
> bicicleta
> deportes
> la comida
> música
> la tarea

Alicia: Miguel, ¿te gusta escuchar **1.** los sábados?

Miguel: Sí, pero me gusta más practicar **2.** .
Teresa, ¿te gusta montar en **3.** ?

Teresa: No, no me gusta. Me gusta más leer **4.** .

Alicia: Teresa, ¿te gusta hacer **5.** los sábados?

Teresa: ¿Los sábados? No, sólo me gusta preparar **6.** , alquilar **7.** y descansar.

2 | ¿Te gusta?

**Escribir
Hablar**

Explica si te gusta o no te gusta comer o beber estas comidas y bebidas.
(Tell whether you like or don't like to eat or drink these foods and beverages.)

modelo: beber
(No) Me gusta beber refrescos.

1. comer

2. beber

3. comer

4. comer

5. beber

6. comer

> **Expansión**
> Compare your answers with a classmate's.

Más práctica   Cuaderno *pp. 1–3*   Cuaderno para hispanohablantes *pp. 1–4*

Get Help Online
my.hrw.com

PARA Y PIENSA

Did you get it?

1. Tell someone that you like to listen to music.   Me gusta _____ .
2. Ask a friend if he or she likes to do homework.   ¿Te gusta _____ ?

❖ VOCABULARIO en contexto

¡AVANZA! **Goal:** Listen to the words Alicia and Sandra use to talk about activities. Then practice what you have heard to talk about the activities you and others like to do. *Actividades 3–5*

♻ *¿Recuerdas?* Weather expressions p. 20

Telehistoria escena 1

 @HOMETUTOR View, Read and Record
my.hrw.com

STRATEGIES

 Cuando lees
Search for clues Look for clues in the picture before starting to read. Who's in the photos? What are they doing?

Cuando escuchas
Listen for intonation The way people speak, not just what they say, often reflects how they feel. Listen for Alicia's intonation. How does she feel about the activities mentioned?

VIDEO DVD

AUDIO

Sandra

Alicia

Papá

Alicia: *(on phone, to Sandra, a friend in San Antonio, Texas)* En Miami, hace calor. ¿Te gusta andar en patineta?

Sandra: No, me gusta más pasear o montar en bicicleta. Los sábados me gusta hacer la tarea.

Alicia: ¿Sí? Los sábados me gusta pasar un rato con amigos... ¡y dibujar! Y los domingos, ¡jugar al fútbol! Los viernes me gusta alquilar un DVD y comer pizza.

Sandra: Sí, sí. Mmm. Me gusta comer pizza y hablar por teléfono.

Alicia: ¿Hablar por teléfono? No me gusta hablar por teléfono. *(Father gives a look of disbelief.)*

Continuará... p. 40

También se dice

Miami To talk about riding bicycles, Sandra uses the phrase **montar en bicicleta.** In other Spanish-speaking countries you might hear:
• **muchos países** **andar en bicicleta**

3 | *Comprensión del episodio* A Alicia y a Sandra les gusta...

Escuchar Leer

Indica si lo que dicen Alicia y Sandra es cierto o falso. Si es falso, corrige la oración. *(Tell if what Alicia and Sandra say is true or false. Correct the false statements.)*

modelo: **Alicia:** Los viernes no me gusta comer pizza.
Falso. Los viernes me gusta comer pizza.

1. **Alicia:** Llueve en Miami.
2. **Sandra:** Me gusta correr los sábados.
3. **Alicia:** Me gusta pasar un rato con los amigos.
4. **Sandra:** Me gusta hacer la tarea los domingos.
5. **Alicia:** Los sábados me gusta alquilar un DVD.
6. **Sandra:** Me gusta hablar por teléfono.

4 | ¡Hace frío! ♻ *¿Recuerdas?* Weather expressions p. 20

Hablar

Habla con otro(a) estudiante de qué te gusta hacer en cada situación. *(Tell a partner what you like to do in each situation.)*

beber agua	leer un libro	pasear
correr	jugar al fútbol	mirar la televisión
descansar	montar en bicicleta	¿ ?

modelo: Hace viento.

A Hace viento. ¿Qué te gusta hacer?

B Me gusta mirar la televisión o descansar.

1. Hace frío y llueve.
2. Hace sol.
3. Hace viento y hace frío.
4. Hace calor.
5. Nieva y hace sol.
6. Llueve y hace calor.

Expansión
Write what you don't like to do for each weather expression.

5 | ¡Me gusta!

Escribir Hablar

Escribe una lista de tus actividades después de las clases. Luego compara las actividades con las de otros(as) estudiantes. *(Write a list of your after-school activities and compare them with other students'.)*

– escribir correos electrónicos
– practicar deportes
– dibujar
– andar en patineta

A ¿Te gusta pasear después de las clases?

B Sí, me gusta pasear.

C No, me gusta pasear antes de las clases.

 **Get Help Online**
my.hrw.com

PARA Y PIENSA

Did you get it? Fill in Alicia's sentences with the appropriate vocabulary word.

1. Me gusta _____ al fútbol.
2. ¿Te gusta escuchar _____ ?
3. También me gusta _____ pizza.

Presentación de GRAMÁTICA

Goal: Learn how to use subject pronouns and the verb **ser.** Then practice the forms of **ser** with **de** to talk about where you and others are from. *Actividades 6–9*

English Grammar Connection: Pronouns are words that take the place of nouns. **Subject pronouns** indicate who is being described or who does the action in a sentence.

We are friends.   **Nosotros** somos amigos.

Subject Pronouns and ser

ANIMATED GRAMMAR my.hrw.com

Ser means *to be*. Use **ser** to identify a person or say where he or she is from. How do you use this verb with **subject pronouns**?

Here's how:

	Singular			Plural	
yo	soy	*I am*	nosotros(as)	somos	*we are*
familiar → tú	eres	*you are*	vosotros(as)	sois	*you are* ← *familiar*
formal → usted	es	*you are*	ustedes	son	*you are*
él, ella	es	*he, she is*	ellos(as)	son	*they are*

Yo soy de Buenos Aires.   **Ellas son** de Venezuela.
I am from Buenos Aires.   *They are from Venezuela.*

Singular

Use **tú** with
- a friend
- a family member
- someone younger

Use **usted** with
- a person you don't know
- someone older
- someone to whom you want to show respect

Plural

- Use **vosotros(as)** with friends, family, and younger people only in Spain.

- Use **ustedes** with people you don't know, older people, and people for whom you want to show respect in Spain; use it in Latin America with any group of people.

- Use **nosotras, vosotras,** and **ellas** when all the people you are talking about are female.

Más práctica
Cuaderno *pp. 4–6*
Cuaderno para hispanohablantes *pp. 5–7*

@HOMETUTOR my.hrw.com
Leveled Practice
Conjuguemos.com

Práctica de GRAMÁTICA

6 | ¿Quién?

Escribe el pronombre que corresponde. *(Write the corresponding pronoun.)*

modelo: ella

1.

2.

3.

4.

5.

6.

Nota gramatical

Use **de** with the verb **ser** (p. 37) to talk about where someone is from.

Daniela y Sonia **son de** Miami.   Martín **es de** Honduras.

*Daniela and Sonia **are from** Miami.*   *Martín **is from** Honduras.*

7 | ¿De dónde son?

Leer
Escribir

Los amigos y maestros de Lucía son de diferentes lugares. Escribe la forma correcta de **ser** para saber de dónde son. *(Write the correct form of **ser**.)*

> Hola, me llamo Lucía. Mi amigo Andrés y yo **1.** de la República Dominicana. Yo **2.** de Santo Domingo y él **3.** de San Pedro de Macorís. La señora Muñoz y el señor Vázquez **4.** de Puerto Rico. Son mis maestros favoritos. Mis amigas Laura y Ana **5.** de Colombia. Laura **6.** de Bogotá y Ana **7.** de Cartagena. Y tú, ¿de dónde **8.** ?

Expansión
Write an e-mail message telling where at least five of your teachers and friends are from.

8 Los amigos de Alicia

Escribir

Alicia tiene muchos amigos y vas a conocerlos en los próximos capítulos. Escribe de dónde son. *(Alicia has many friends that you will meet. Write where they are from.)*

modelo: Maribel y Enrique / España
Maribel y Enrique son de España.

1. yo / Miami

2. Claudia y Pablo / México

3. Marisol / Puerto Rico

4. papá y yo / Miami

5. Fernando / Ecuador

6. Mario / la República Dominicana

9 De muchos países

Hablar

Pregúntale a otro(a) estudiante de dónde son los amigos de Miguel. Usa los pronombres. *(Ask another student where Miguel's friends are from. Use pronouns.)*

modelo: Luis: Bolivia

A ¿De dónde es Luis?

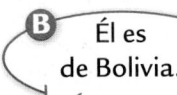

B Él es de Bolivia.

1. Leticia: Perú

2. Álvaro y Linda: Nicaragua

3. Isabel y Ángela: California

4. Andrés y Jorge: Uruguay

5. Ana Sofía y Elena: Panamá

6. Y tú, ¿ ?

Más práctica   Cuaderno *pp. 4–6*   Cuaderno para hispanohablantes *pp. 5–7*

🌐 **Get Help Online**
my.hrw.com

PARA Y PIENSA

Did you get it? Match the phrases to make a complete sentence.

1. Cristóbal y yo   **a.** soy de México.

2. Tomás   **b.** somos de Honduras.

3. Yo   **c.** es de la República Dominicana.

GRAMÁTICA en contexto

Goal: Notice how Alicia and her friends introduce people and say where they are from. Then use **ser** with **de** to tell where people are from. *Actividades 10–12*

Telehistoria escena 2

@**HOMETUTOR** View, Read
my.hrw.com and Record

STRATEGIES

VIDEO
DVD

AUDIO

Use appropriate expressions Pay attention to the expressions used by the characters to introduce someone. Is the register formal or informal? How do you know?

Listen for guesses How can you tell that Mr. Costas is guessing where Teresa and Miguel are from? What happens to his voice? Does he use non-verbal cues? What does he guess? What does Miguel guess about Mr. Costas?

Miguel

Sr. Costas

Teresa

Alicia

Alicia: ¡Hola! Señor Costas, le presento a dos amigos... Teresa y Miguel. Ellos son de...

Mr. Costas stops her because he wants to guess.

Sr. Costas: Tú eres de... ¿Puerto Rico? ¿Panamá? ¿Costa Rica?

Teresa: No, yo soy de...

Mr. Costas interrupts and gestures toward Miguel.

Sr. Costas: ¿Él es de México? ¿El Salvador? ¿Colombia?

Miguel: No, nosotros somos de *(pointing to himself)* Cuba y *(pointing to Teresa)* de Honduras. Y usted, ¿de dónde es?

Sr. Costas: Soy de...

Miguel: ¿Argentina? ¿Chile? ¿Cuba?

Sr. Costas: Soy de la Florida.

Continuará... p. 45

10 | *Comprensión del episodio* Los orígenes

Escuchar
Leer

Contesta las preguntas. *(Answer the questions.)*

1. Teresa y Miguel son los amigos de
   a. Alicia.
   b. el señor Costas.
   c. el señor Díaz.

2. ¿De dónde es Miguel?
   a. Es de Puerto Rico.
   b. Es de Cuba.
   c. Es de la República Dominicana.

3. ¿De dónde es Teresa?
   a. Es de Puerto Rico.
   b. Es de Costa Rica.
   c. Es de Honduras.

4. ¿Quién es de la Florida?
   a. Miguel
   b. el señor Costas
   c. Teresa

11 | Los famosos en Miami

Leer
Hablar

Comparación cultural

Juanes

Paulina Rubio

Los Premios Juventud

How have Latino performers and athletes affected popular culture in the United States? Los Premios Juventud is an awards show held in **Miami** and broadcast on Spanish-language television. Teens vote for their favorite stars in music, film, and sports. Past nominees include: Shakira and Juanes (Colombia), Paulina Rubio and Gael García Bernal (Mexico), Miguel Cabrera (Venezuela), and Jennifer Lopez (New York).

Compara con tu mundo *Who are your favorite figures in music, film, and sports, and why?*

Pregúntale a otro(a) estudiante sobre el origen de los famosos nominados para un Premio Juventud. *(Talk with a partner about where the nominees are from.)*

A ¿De dónde es Juanes?

B Juanes es de Colombia.

12 | ¿De dónde somos?

Hablar

Pregúntales a otros(as) estudiantes de dónde son. *(Ask other students where they are from.)*

A Nora, ¿de dónde eres?

B Soy de Miami. ¿Y tú?

También soy de Miami.

Expansión
As a class, compile the results into a chart to show where everyone is from.

🌐 **Get Help Online**
my.hrw.com

PARA Y PIENSA

Did you get it? Create sentences to tell where the people are from.

1. el Sr. Costas / la Florida
2. Alicia / Miami
3. Teresa y Miguel / Honduras y Cuba

Presentación de GRAMÁTICA

English Grammar Connection: An **infinitive** is the basic form of a **verb,** a word that expresses action or a state of being. In English, most infinitives include the word *to.* In Spanish, infinitives are always one word that ends in **-ar, -er,** or **-ir.**

I like to run.   Me gusta correr.

infinitive   infinitive

Gustar with an Infinitive

ANIMATED GRAMMAR
my.hrw.com

Use **gustar** to talk about what people like to do.

Here's how: Use phrases like **me gusta** + **infinitive.**

Me gusta **dibujar.**	*I like to draw.*
Te gusta **dibujar.**	*You (familiar singular) like to draw.*
Le gusta **dibujar.**	*You (formal singular) like to draw.* *He/She likes to draw.*
Nos gusta **dibujar.**	*We like to draw.*
Os gusta **dibujar.**	*You (familiar plural) like to draw.*
Les gusta **dibujar.**	*You (plural) like to draw.* *They like to draw.*

When you want to really emphasize or identify the person that you are talking about, add **a** + **noun/pronoun.**

A Sonia le gusta leer.   **A ella le gusta leer.**
Sonia likes to read.   *She likes to read.*

These are the **pronouns** that follow **a.**

A mí me gusta dibujar.	**A nosotros(as) nos gusta** dibujar.
A ti te gusta dibujar.	**A vosotros(as) os gusta** dibujar.
A usted le gusta dibujar.	**A ustedes les gusta** dibujar.
A él, ella le gusta dibujar.	**A ellos(as) les gusta** dibujar.

Más práctica
Cuaderno *pp. 7–9*
Cuaderno para hispanohablantes *pp. 8–11*

@HOMETUTOR my.hrw.com
Leveled Practice

✿ Práctica de GRAMÁTICA

13 | ¿Les gusta o no?

Escribir

Escribe lo que a estas personas les gusta o no les gusta hacer. *(Write what these people like and don't like to do.)*

modelo: a Luisa / preparar la comida
No le gusta preparar la comida.

1. a nosotras / comer pizza

2. a ustedes / estudiar

3. a ti / montar en bicicleta

4. a Alicia y a Miguel / aprender el español

5. a mí / escuchar música

6. a usted / trabajar

14 | ¿Qué les gusta hacer?

Hablar

Con otro(a) estudiante, di lo que a Alicia y a otros les gusta hacer, según las fotos. *(Tell what Alicia and others like to do.)*

Teresa

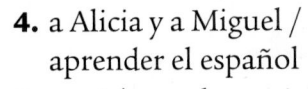
A ¿Qué le gusta hacer a Teresa?

B Le gusta leer un libro.

1. Alicia

2. ella

3. él

4. Alicia y Miguel

5. Teresa

6. ustedes

> **Expansión**
> For each person pictured, write a sentence stating what they don't like to do.

AUDIO

⬡ Pronunciación   Las letras p y t

When you pronounce the **p** and **t** in English, a puff of air comes out of your mouth. In Spanish, there is no puff of air. Listen and repeat.

pasar	**p**or favor	**P**uerto Rico
pizza	**p**ero	**p**a**p**as

Pe**p**e **p**re**p**ara las **p**a**p**as fritas.

fru**t**a	**t**elevisión	prac**t**icar
tocar	es**t**udiar	**t**area

¿**T**e gus**t**a mon**t**ar en bicicle**t**a?

15 | Las actividades

Escuchar
Escribir

Copia esta tabla en una hoja de papel. Escucha la descripción de lo que a Mariana y a sus amigos les gusta hacer los sábados y completa la tabla con **sí** o **no**. Luego contesta las preguntas. *(Copy this chart on a piece of paper. Listen to Mariana's description and complete your chart with **sí** or **no**. Then answer the questions.)*

¿Le gusta...?	descansar	pasear	mirar la televisión	tocar la guitarra
A Mariana	sí			
A Jorge		no		
A Federico				

1. ¿Qué le gusta hacer a Jorge?
2. ¿Qué le gusta hacer a Mariana?
3. ¿Qué le gusta hacer a Federico?
4. ¿Qué no le gusta hacer a Mariana?
5. ¿Qué no les gusta hacer a Jorge y a Federico?
6. ¿Qué les gusta hacer a los tres amigos?

Expansión
Write a list of the "top five" activities you like to do and the "bottom five" that you don't like to do. Compare with a classmate's.

16 | A mi amigo(a) le gusta

Hablar

Habla con otro(a) estudiante para saber qué le gusta y qué no le gusta hacer los sábados y domingos. Luego dile a la clase. *(Ask a classmate what he or she likes to do on weekends. Tell the class.)*

Comparación cultural

El arte de Miami

How would being Cuban American influence an artist's work? Growing up in **Miami,** artist Xavier Cortada learned about his Cuban heritage through his family and community around him. Many of his paintings reflect his identity as a Cuban American. His colorful painting *Music* presents a variety of instruments found in traditional Cuban music *(son, rumba, mambo, Afro-Latin jazz)* as well as American music. How many instruments can you identify?

Music (2005), Xavier Cortada

Compara con tu mundo *What would you paint to represent your community?*

Más práctica Cuaderno *pp. 7–9* Cuaderno para hispanohablantes *pp. 8–11*

🌐 **Get Help Online**
my.hrw.com

PARA Y PIENSA

Did you get it? Complete each sentence with the correct **gustar** phrase.

1. _____ correr. (a ella)
2. ¿_____ andar en patineta? (a ti)
3. _____ tocar la guitarra. (a nosotros)

Unidad 1 Estados Unidos
44 cuarenta y cuatro

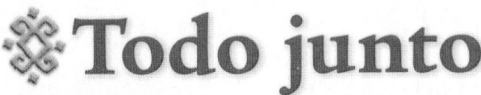

Todo junto

Goal: *Show what you know* Pay attention to Alicia and her friends as they describe the activities they like to do. Then use **ser** and **gustar** to say where you are from and what you like to do. *Actividades 17–21*

Telehistoria completa

@HOMETUTOR View, Read
my.hrw.com and Record

STRATEGIES

Cuando lees
Unlock the main idea Find repeated phrases that can unlock the overall meaning. Find all the phrases that contain the verb **gustar.** What is this scene about?

Cuando escuchas
Listen for cognates A cognate is a Spanish word that sounds like an English word and means the same thing. For example, *telephone* and **teléfono.** In the video, listen for at least three cognates.

Escena 1 *Resumen*
A Alicia y a Sandra les gusta hacer muchas actividades. Les gusta dibujar, comer pizza y más.

Escena 2 *Resumen*
Miguel es de Cuba y Teresa es de Honduras. El señor Costas es de la Florida.

VIDEO
DVD

AUDIO

Escena 3

Alicia: ¿Qué les gusta hacer?

Miguel: Me gusta mirar la televisión.

Teresa: No me gusta mirar la televisió Me gusta más tocar la guitarra o escuchar música.

Miguel: Me gusta comer.

Teresa: Sí, me gusta comer.

Alicia: ¡Nos gusta comer!

They stand to go eat.

Alicia: ¿Qué les gusta comer? ¿Pizza? ¿Les gusta comer helado? ¿Fruta? ¿Beber jugos?

Both say no, and they all sit. Teresa shows them the paper.

Alicia: ¿Trini Salgado? ¿En San Antonio? (*She quickly takes out her cell phone.*) ¡Sandra!

17 | Comprensión de los episodios   ¿Quiénes son?

Escuchar
Leer

Escribe el nombre de cada persona, según las descripciones.
(Write names according to the descriptions.)

1. No le gusta andar en patineta.
2. Es de Honduras.
3. Les gusta comer.
4. Es de la Florida.

5. Le gusta tocar la guitarra.
6. Es de San Antonio, Texas.
7. Le gusta hablar por teléfono.
8. Le gusta escuchar música.

> **Expansión**
> Write clues for another character from the Telehistoria and have a partner guess who it is.

---

18 | Comprensión de los episodios   Los amigos

Escuchar
Leer

Contesta las preguntas según los episodios. *(Answer the questions according to the episodes.)*

1.
a. ¿Cómo se llama?
b. ¿Qué le gusta hacer?
c. ¿Qué no le gusta hacer?

2.
a. ¿Cómo se llama?
b. ¿De dónde es?
c. ¿Qué le gusta hacer?

---

19 | Nuevos amigos

Digital
performance space

Hablar

STRATEGY Hablar

Boost your "speaking self-confidence" with positive statements To increase your speaking self-confidence, say something positive to yourself like: *I learn from my mistakes. I can say things now that I couldn't say last week.* Create your own positive statement. Say it to yourself before the speaking activity below.

Eres un(a) estudiante nuevo(a) en la escuela. Di a otros(as) estudiantes de dónde eres y lo que te gusta y no te gusta hacer. Haz una lista de las cosas que tienen en común. *(Talk with a group of students about where you are from and what you like and don't like to do. Make a list of things you have in common.)*

A Hola, me llamo Víctor. Soy de Chicago. Me gusta escuchar música y correr.

B Hola, me llamo Carolina y soy de Chicago también. No me gusta escuchar música pero me gusta practicar deportes.

C Hola. Me llamo Alex...

---

20 | Integración

**Leer
Escuchar
Hablar**

Lee el correo electrónico de Vanessa. Después escucha a Carmen y toma apuntes. ¿Qué les gusta hacer a las dos chicas? *(Read the e-mail from Vanessa, then listen to Carmen. Say what both of them like and don't like.)*

Fuente 1 Correo electrónico

¡Hola, Carmen! Soy Vanessa. Soy de Morelos, México. Me gusta mucho practicar deportes. También me gusta andar en patineta. No me gusta escuchar música. Después de las clases me gusta pasar un rato con los amigos y comer pizza. Los sábados y domingos no me gusta hacer la tarea. Me gusta más alquilar un DVD o descansar. ¿Y a ti? ¿Qué te gusta hacer?

Fuente 2 Escucha a Carmen

Listen and take notes
- ¿Qué le gusta hacer a Carmen?
- ¿Qué no le gusta hacer?

modelo: A las chicas les gusta...

21 | Un correo electrónico

Escribir

Vas a escribirle un correo electrónico a un(a) nuevo(a) amigo(a) en Puebla, México. Preséntate y explica de dónde eres y qué te gusta y no te gusta hacer. También escribe tres preguntas. *(Write your new e-pal, introducing yourself and telling him or her where you're from and what you like and don't like to do. Ask three questions.)*

modelo: Hola, Eva. Me llamo Ana, y soy de la Florida. Me gusta leer un libro, pero no me gusta mirar la televisión. ¿Te gusta hablar por teléfono?

Writing Criteria	Excellent	Good	Needs Work
Content	Your e-mail includes a lot of information and questions.	Your e-mail includes some information and questions.	Your e-mail includes little information and not enough questions.
Communication	Most of your e-mail is organized and easy to follow.	Parts of your e-mail are organized and easy to follow.	Your e-mail is disorganized and hard to follow.
Accuracy	Your e-mail has few mistakes in grammar and vocabulary.	Your e-mail has some mistakes in grammar and vocabulary.	Your e-mail has many mistakes in grammar and vocabulary.

Más práctica   Cuaderno *pp. 10–11*   Cuaderno para hispanohablantes *pp. 12–13*

Get Help Online
my.hrw.com

PARA Y PIENSA

Did you get it? Tell where these people are from and what they like to do, based on the Telehistoria.

1. Teresa / Honduras / tocar la guitarra
2. Alicia / Miami / comer
3. Miguel / Cuba / mirar la televisión

Lectura

Additional readings at **my.hrw.com**
SPANISH
InterActive Reader

¡AVANZA! **Goal:** Read about what students in a dual-language school in Florida like to do in their free time. Then compare the activities they like to do with what you like to do.

AUDIO

¿Qué te gusta hacer?

This is a survey about what students like to do in their free time. It was conducted among students at a dual-language school in Florida.

STRATEGY Leer
Use a judgment line Draw a line like this one with *least popular* on the left and *most popular* on the right. On the line, list all the activities in the survey according to their popularity.

leer estudiar	dibujar
least popular	most popular

¿Qué te gusta hacer?

Me gusta...

mirar la televisión ☐
pasar un rato con los amigos ✓
jugar videojuegos[1] ☐
trabajar ✓
jugar con los amigos ☐
dibujar ✓
practicar deportes ☐
escribir ☐
leer ✓
estudiar ☐
otras[2] actividades _tocar la guitarra_

_____

[1] videogames   [2] other

Una encuesta en la escuela

Resultados de la encuesta [3]

25 estudiantes respondieron [4] a las 11 categorías o actividades.

Actividades

mirar la tele	
pasar un rato	
videojuegos	
trabajar	
jugar	
dibujar	
deportes	
escribir	
leer	
estudiar	
otras	

5 10 15 20 25

Número de estudiantes

---

[3] survey   [4] replied

¡Interpreta!

Based on the chart and survey, answer the following questions.

1. How many students took the survey?
2. What are the three most popular activities and the three least popular activities?
3. Would you get the same results if you used the survey with your classmates? Give specific reasons why or why not.

¿Y tú?

Record your answers to the survey on the previous page and compare them to the results of these students.

La expedición de Hernando de Soto

Hernando de Soto

The map below shows one account of the expedition of Hernando de Soto, a sixteenth-century Spanish explorer. It is believed that de Soto's team traveled through ten present-day U.S. states, and through many Native American villages. The following table gives the latitude and longitude of four U.S. cities, as well as the villages that were close to these locations. Use the coordinates to find the city that corresponds to each Native American village.

NATIVE AMERICAN VILLAGE	LOCATION OF CITY	NAME OF CITY
Ucita	27° 56' N 82° 27' O	
Casqui	35° 15' N 90° 34' O	
Mabila	30° 41' N 88° 02' O	
Anhayca	30° 26' N 84° 16' O	

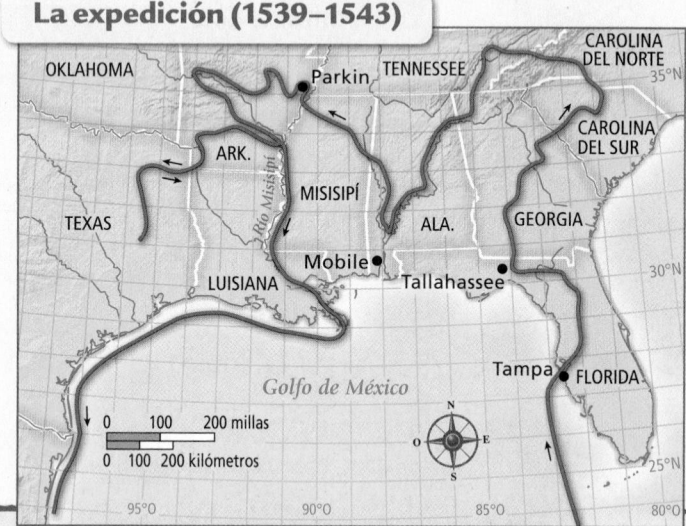

La expedición (1539–1543)

❖ Proyecto ① *Las matemáticas*

A common form of measurement during the time of de Soto was the league (**legua**). A league was based on the distance an average person could walk in an hour: 3.5 miles. Calculate what these distances would be in leagues.

Ucita to Anhayca:	204 miles
Anhayca to Mabila:	224 miles
Mabila to Casqui:	347 miles

❖ Proyecto ② *El lenguaje*

Many places in the United States have Spanish names. **Florida,** for instance, means *full of flowers.* Use an atlas or the Internet to find three places in the United States with Spanish names. Then write the meaning of each place.

❖ Proyecto ③ *La música*

The term "Tex–Mex" also describes music that blends elements of Mexico and the southwestern U.S. Most Tex–Mex music features the accordion, brought to Texas in the 1890s by German immigrants. Find an example of Tex–Mex music—such as Selena or Los Tigres del Norte—and listen to it. Then write a paragraph describing the instruments and the music and list the Spanish names of the instruments.

Los Tigres del Norte

En resumen
Vocabulario y gramática

ANIMATEDGRAMMAR
Interactive Flashcards
my.hrw.com

Vocabulario

Talk About Activities

alquilar un DVD	to rent a DVD	hacer la tarea	to do homework
andar en patineta	to skateboard	jugar al fútbol	to play soccer
aprender el español	to learn Spanish	leer un libro	to read a book
		mirar la televisión	to watch television
beber	to drink	montar en bicicleta	to ride a bike
comer	to eat		
comprar	to buy	pasar un rato con los amigos	to spend time with friends
correr	to run		
descansar	to rest	pasear	to go for a walk
dibujar	to draw	practicar deportes	to practice / play sports
escribir correos electrónicos	to write e-mails		
		preparar la comida	to prepare food / a meal
escuchar música	to listen to music		
estudiar	to study	tocar la guitarra	to play the guitar
hablar por teléfono	to talk on the phone	trabajar	to work

Snack Foods and Beverages

el agua (fem.)	water
la fruta	fruit
la galleta	cookie
el helado	ice cream
el jugo	juice
las papas fritas	French fries
la pizza	pizza
el refresco	soft drink

Other Words and Phrases

la actividad	activity
antes de	before
después (de)	afterward, after
la escuela	school
más	more
o	or
pero	but
también	also

Say What You Like and Don't Like to Do

¿Qué te gusta hacer?	What do you like to do?	Me gusta...	I like . . .
¿Te gusta...?	Do you like . . . ?	No me gusta...	I don't like . . .

Gramática

Nota gramatical: de to describe where you are from *p. 38*

Pronouns and ser

Ser means *to be*. Use **ser** to identify a person or say where he or she is from.

Singular		Plural	
yo	soy	nosotros(as)	somos
tú	eres	vosotros(as)	sois
usted	es	ustedes	son
él, ella	es	ellos(as)	son

Gustar with an Infinitive

Use **gustar** to talk about what people like to do.

A mí **me gusta** dibujar.
A ti **te gusta** dibujar.
A usted **le gusta** dibujar.
A él, ella **le gusta** dibujar.
A nosotros(as) **nos gusta** dibujar.
A vosotros(as) **os gusta** dibujar.
A ustedes **les gusta** dibujar.
A ellos(as) **les gusta** dibujar.

Practice Spanish with Holt McDougal Apps!

Lección 1
cincuenta y uno **51**

@**HOME**TUTOR
my.hrw.com

¡LLEGADA!

Now you can
- talk about activities
- tell where you are from
- say what you like and don't like to do

Using
- subject pronouns and **ser**
- **de** to describe where you are from
- **gustar** with an infinitive

To review
- **gustar** with an infinitive p. 42
- **de** to describe where you are from p. 38

1 | ## Listen and understand

AUDIO

Escucha a Pablo y a Sara hablar de sus actividades. Empareja las descripciones con el (los) nombre(s). *(Match according to what Pablo and Sara say about their activities.)*

1. Es de Puerto Rico.
2. Es de Miami.
3. Le gusta escuchar música.
4. No le gusta andar en patineta.
5. No le gusta comer frutas.
6. Le gusta comer helado.

a. Pablo
b. Sara
c. Pablo y Sara

To review
- **gustar** with an infinitive p. 42

2 | ## Say what you like and don't like to do

Escribe oraciones para describir las actividades que te gusta y no te gusta hacer. *(Write sentences describing the activities you like to do and don't like to do.)*

modelo: alquilar un DVD
(No) Me gusta alquilar un DVD.

1. beber refrescos
2. preparar la comida
3. hacer la tarea
4. descansar
5. escribir correos electrónicos
6. pasar un rato con los amigos
7. practicar deportes
8. trabajar
9. comprar libros
10. comer pizza

To review
- subject pronouns and **ser** p. 37
- **de** to describe where you are from p. 38

3 | Tell where you are from

Completa el mensaje con **ser.** *(Complete the e-mail with the appropriate form of **ser**.)*

> Hola, me llamo Eduardo. Yo **1.** de Miami. Y tú, ¿de dónde **2.**? Mis amigos y yo **3.** de diferentes países. Roberto **4.** de Chile y Yolanda **5.** de Perú. Nosotros **6.** estudiantes. El señor Santana y la señora Zabala **7.** maestros. Ellos **8.** de Cuba.

To review
- **gustar** with an infinitive p. 42

4 | Talk about activities

Indica qué actividades les gusta hacer a estas personas según las fotos.
(Tell what activities these people like to do, according to the photos.)

modelo: a José
A José le gusta tocar la guitarra.

1. a Sonia

2. a ellos

3. a usted

4. a nosotras

5. a ustedes

6. a ti

To review
- Miami's Freedom Tower p. 29
- Fiesta San Antonio p. 29
- Comparación cultural pp. 41, 44

5 | United States

Comparación cultural

Answer these culture questions.

1. What is inside Miami's Freedom Tower?

2. What occurs during Fiesta San Antonio?

3. Who votes for the winners of **Los Premios Juventud**?

4. What is Xavier Cortada's heritage?

Más práctica Cuaderno *pp. 12–23* Cuaderno para hispanohablantes *pp. 14–23*

Get Help Online
my.hrw.com

UNIDAD 1

Estados Unidos

Lección 2

Tema:
Mis amigos y yo

¡AVANZA! **In this lesson you will learn to**
- describe yourself and others
- identify people and things

using
- **ser** to describe what someone is like
- definite and indefinite articles
- noun-adjective agreement

♻ *¿Recuerdas?*
- snack foods, after-school activities
- **ser, gustar** with an infinitive

Comparación cultural

In this lesson you will learn about
- Latin-American and Tex-Mex food
- the tradition of making **cascarones**
- after-school activities in Miami and San Antonio
- students from Miami, Colombia, and Mexico

Compara con tu mundo
These Texas teens are exploring the Paseo del Río, one of San Antonio's main attractions. In this refreshing city retreat, people eat in restaurants, ride riverboats, or stroll along the river. *Does your city or town have a park or place of interest? What do people do there?*

¿Qué ves?
Mira la foto
¿Son amigos?
¿Qué les gusta hacer?
¿Llueve o hace sol?

MODES OF COMMUNICATION

INTERPRETIVE	INTERPERSONAL	PRESENTATIONAL
Read about other teens' favorite activities and compare your favorite activities to theirs.	Introduce yourself to someone.	Write a description of yourself for a yearbook.
Listen to descriptions of people and identify their physical and personality traits.	Take turns asking and saying what you are like and what you like to do.	Make a video presentation about yourself and what you like to do.

Paseo del Río
San Antonio, Texas

Presentación de VOCABULARIO

¡AVANZA! **Goal:** Learn how Sandra describes herself and her friends. Then practice what you have learned to describe yourself and others. *Actividades 1–2*

♻ *¿Recuerdas?* **ser** p. 37

VIDEO
DVD

AUDIO

A ¡Hola! Soy Sandra. Soy **artística** y **tengo pelo castaño.** A mi **amigo** Ricardo le gusta practicar deportes **porque** es **atlético.**

artística

atlético

B Alberto es **trabajador** y **estudioso.** Le gusta estudiar. David es **un poco perezoso.** No es **un estudiante muy bueno.** No le gusta trabajar.

trabajador

perezoso

Más vocabulario

bonito(a) *pretty*
guapo(a) *good-looking*
malo(a) *bad*

Expansión de vocabulario p. R2

C Soy **una persona** muy **organizada.** Mi **amiga** Ana es **inteligente** pero un poco **desorganizada.**

organizada

desorganizada

D Rafael es muy **alto,** pero Laura es **baja.** Manuel es **grande,** pero Francisco es **pequeño.** La señora Santa Cruz es un poco **vieja,** pero Rosita es **joven.**

E La señora Guardado es **pelirroja** y el señor Guardado **tiene** pelo castaño. Marco y Laura son **chicos** muy buenos. Marco tiene **pelo rubio** y Laura tiene pelo castaño.

F Yo soy un poco **seria,** pero mi amigo Alberto es muy **cómico. Todos** mis amigos son muy **simpáticos.** ¿Y tú? ¿Cómo eres?

@**HOMETUTOR**
my.hrw.com **Interactive Flashcards**

¡A responder!   Escuchar

Escucha estas descripciones de Sandra y sus amigos. Indica la persona en la foto que corresponde a cada descripción. *(Point to the person on these pages who matches each description you hear.)*

✤ Práctica de VOCABULARIO

1 | Los opuestos

Leer

Sandra describe a sus amigos pero Ricardo dice lo opuesto. Empareja la descripción de Sandra con la respuesta de Ricardo. *(Sandra describes her friends but Ricardo says the opposite. Match Sandra's description with Ricardo's response.)*

Sandra	Ricardo
1. Marco es pequeño.	**a.** No, es bueno.
2. Luisa es trabajadora.	**b.** No, es grande.
3. Pablo es organizado.	**c.** No, es desorganizado.
4. Joaquín es malo.	**d.** No, es perezosa.
5. Anabel es joven.	**e.** No, es serio.
6. Francisco es cómico.	**f.** No, es vieja.

Nota gramatical ♻ *¿Recuerdas?* **ser** p. 37

Use **ser** to describe what people are like.

La mujer **es** alta.   Los chicos **son** organizados.
*The woman **is** tall.*   *The boys **are** organized.*

---

2 | Porque...

Escribir
Hablar

Explica por qué a Ricardo y a Alberto les gusta o no les gusta hacer estas actividades. *(Explain why Ricardo and Alberto like or don't like the following activities.)*

serio	desorganizado
atlético	estudioso
artístico	trabajador

· **modelo:** A Ricardo le gusta practicar deportes porque es atlético.

1. A Ricardo le gusta hacer la tarea.

2. A Ricardo le gusta dibujar.

3. A Alberto no le gusta ser cómico.

4. A Alberto le gusta correr.

5. A Alberto no le gusta ser perezoso.

6. A Alberto no le gusta ser organizado.

Expansión
Draw, cut out pictures, or use clip art to illustrate all of the adjectives in the word bank.

Más práctica   Cuaderno *pp. 24–26*   Cuaderno para hispanohablantes *pp. 24–27*

🌐 **Get Help Online**
my.hrw.com

PARA Y PIENSA

Did you get it?
1. Say that Juan is short.
2. Say that David is artistic.
3. Say that Carlos is serious.

✤VOCABULARIO en contexto

¡AVANZA! **Goal:** Notice how Sandra and her friends describe themselves and each other. Then practice these words to describe others. *Actividades 3–4*

Telehistoria escena 1

@HOMETUTOR View, Read
my.hrw.com and Record

STRATEGIES

Cuando lees
Skim Find the main idea by skimming (rapidly glancing over) the text before reading it carefully. What is the main idea of the scene below?

Cuando escuchas
Find the humor Humor makes a scene fun and memorable. Listen for exaggeration, teasing, and jokes. What are some examples of humor in the following scene?

VIDEO
DVD

AUDIO

Sandra, speaking to Alicia via webcam, holds up Alicia's T-shirt.

Sandra: Es bonita. Pero te gusta más con el autógrafo de Trini Salgado, ¿no?

Alberto and Ricardo join Sandra.

Sandra: Alicia, te presento a mis amigos: Alberto y Ricardo.

Alberto: Hola, Alicia. Me llamo Alberto. Soy alto... no soy muy alto. Tengo pelo castaño, y soy muy trabajador. Pero me gusta mirar la televisión y escuchar música. *(He pulls CDs from his backpack.)*

Sandra: No, él no es perezoso pero es un poco desorganizado.

Ricardo: Hola, Alicia. ¿Qué tal? Me llamo Ricardo. Soy inteligente, simpático y estudioso. Me gusta practicar deportes porque soy atlético. Y me gusta dibujar porque soy muy artístico.

Sandra shows one of Ricardo's drawings that is not very good.

Sandra: Sí. Él es muy artístico.

Ricardo: Ella es cómica, ¿no?

Alberto: Ella no es muy seria.

Sandra: OK, OK. Adiós, Alicia. Hasta luego.

Continuará... p. 64

3 | Comprensión del episodio Las características

Escuchar
Leer

Copia el diagrama Venn en una hoja de papel para comparar a Ricardo y Alberto. Escribe sus diferencias debajo de sus nombres. En el centro escribe lo que tienen en común. *(Copy the Venn diagram and use it to compare Ricardo and Alberto. Write their differences below their names. In the center, write what they have in common.)*

Ricardo **Alberto**

Le gusta dibujar.

4 | Una entrevista

Leer
Hablar

Lee la entrevista con Raúl López, un joven futbolista famoso. Después, habla con otro(a) estudiante sobre el artículo. Usa por lo menos tres adjetivos para hacerle preguntas. *(Work with another student to talk about the article. Ask him or her questions using at least three adjectives.)*

A ¿Es Raúl perezoso?

B No, es trabajador porque le gusta estudiar.

ENTREVISTA

¡ESTRELLA DEL FUTURO!

Revista Estrella: Raúl, ¿cómo eres?

Raúl: Soy muy atlético. Me gusta mucho jugar al fútbol y practicar deportes. Pero también me gusta descansar.

Revista Estrella: Y eres un estudiante serio, ¿no?

Raúl: Sí, me gusta leer libros y estudiar.

Revista Estrella: ¿Te gusta escuchar música?

Raúl: Sí, me gusta escuchar música, pero me gusta más tocar la guitarra. También me gusta dibujar.

Expansión
Write an interview between you and your favorite actor or actress. Ask them what they are like and what they like to do.

Comparación cultural

Unas fajitas

La comida mexicana y Tex-Mex

How does local environment affect the food that people eat? Tex-Mex is a regional cuisine that combines styles of cooking from **Mexico** and **Texas.** Did you know that *nachos,* crispy tacos, tortilla chips with salsa, *fajitas,* and *chili con carne* are all Tex-Mex dishes? Common Tex-Mex ingredients include flour tortillas, yellow cheese, refried beans, and beef. In the interior of Mexico, traditional ingredients are corn tortillas, white cheese, black beans, chicken, seafood, and pork.

Compara con tu mundo *What are some restaurants in your community that serve foods from other countries?*

Get Help Online
my.hrw.com

PARA Y PIENSA

Did you get it? Fill in the appropriate adjective.

1. Alberto es trabajador. No es _____ .
2. A Ricardo le gusta practicar deportes. Es _____ .
3. A Ricardo le gusta hacer la tarea. Es _____ .

Unidad 1 Estados Unidos

Presentación de GRAMÁTICA

¡AVANZA! **Goal:** Learn about definite and indefinite articles. Then practice using these articles to identify people and things. *Actividades 5–9*

♻ *¿Recuerdas?* Snack foods p. 33, **gustar** with an infinitive p. 42

English Grammar Connection: Definite articles (in English, *the*) are used with nouns to indicate *specific* persons, places, or things. **Indefinite articles** (*a, an*) are used with nouns to indicate *nonspecific* persons, places, or things.

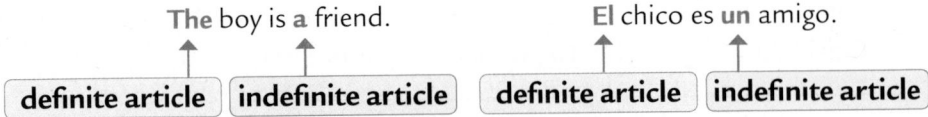

The boy is a friend.   El chico es un amigo.

| definite article | indefinite article | | definite article | indefinite article |

Definite and Indefinite Articles

ANIMATEDGRAMMAR
my.hrw.com

In Spanish, articles match nouns in gender and number.

Here's how: All Spanish nouns, even if they refer to objects, are either **masculine** or **feminine**.

- Nouns ending in **-o** are usually **masculine**.
- Nouns ending in **-a** are usually **feminine**.

		Definite Article	Noun	Indefinite Article	Noun
Masculine	Singular	el *the*	chico *boy*	un *a*	chico *boy*
	Plural	los *the*	chicos *boys*	unos *some*	chicos *boys*
Feminine	Singular	la *the*	chica *girl*	una *a*	chica *girl*
	Plural	las *the*	chicas *girls*	unas *some*	chicas *girls*

matches   *matches*

Los libros son para **la maestra**.   ***The** books are for **the** teacher.*

To form the **plural** of a noun, add **-s** if the noun ends in a vowel. Add **-es** if the noun ends in a consonant.

vowel ↴
estudiante → estudiant**es**

consonant ↴
mujer → muj**eres**

Más práctica
Cuaderno *pp. 27–29*
Cuaderno para hispanohablantes *pp. 28–30*

@**HOMETUTOR** my.hrw.com
Leveled Practice

Práctica de GRAMÁTICA

5 | ¿Cómo son las personas en la oficina?

Leer | Miguel describe a varias personas en la oficina de la escuela. Completa sus oraciones con **el, la, los, las.** *(Complete the sentences with the correct definite article.)*

1. ___ chicas son atléticas.
2. ___ maestra es inteligente.
3. ___ amigos son simpáticos.
4. ___ chico es pelirrojo.
5. ___ mujeres son artísticas.

6. ___ hombre es guapo.
7. ___ personas son organizadas.
8. ___ amigas son jóvenes.
9. ___ estudiantes son bajos.
10. ___ mujer es cómica.

Expansión
Choose three of the sentences and illustrate them.

6 | La lista de Sandra

Escuchar
Escribir

A Sandra le gusta comprar muchas cosas. Escucha y escribe una lista de lo que le gusta comprar, usando **el, la, los, las.** *(Listen and write a list of what Sandra likes to buy, using definite articles.)*

7 | ¿Qué es?   ♻ ¿**Recuerdas?** Snack foods p. 33

Hablar
Escribir

Identifica las comidas, usando **un, una, unos, unas.** *(Identify these foods using indefinite articles.)*

modelo: Son unas galletas.

1.
2.
3.
4.

5.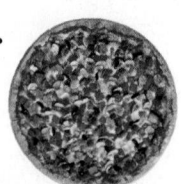
6.
7.
8.

8 | ¿Son estudiosos?

Hablar
Escribir

Describe a estas personas usando el verbo **ser** y **un, una, unos, unas.** *(Describe these people using **ser** and the correct indefinite article.)*

> **modelo:** chico cómico
> Daniel es un chico cómico.

1. chicas estudiosas
2. chicos serios
3. amigas trabajadoras
4. chico desorganizado

5. chica alta
6. chico alto
7. estudiante pelirroja
8. chico grande

Expansión
Choose one of the students from the picture and invent a complete description of him or her.

9 | ¿Qué te gusta más?

♻ ¿Recuerdas? gustar with an infinitive p. 42

Hablar

Pregúntale a otro(a) estudiante qué le gusta hacer más. *(Ask a partner what he or she likes to do more.)*

> **modelo:** comprar / fruta / papas fritas

1. leer / libro / correos electrónicos
2. hablar con / chicos / chicas
3. pasar un rato con / amigos / maestro
4. comer / galletas / pizza
5. beber / jugo / refresco
6. comprar / DVDs / libro

A ¿Te gusta más comprar una fruta o unas papas fritas?

B Me gusta más comprar una fruta.

Más práctica   Cuaderno *pp. 27–29*   Cuaderno para hispanohablantes *pp. 28–30*

🌐 **Get Help Online**
my.hrw.com

PARA Y PIENSA

Did you get it?
Match the article to its corresponding noun.

1. la
2. unas
3. el
4. unos

a. libro
b. hombres
c. televisión
d. frutas

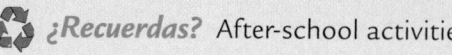 GRAMÁTICA en contexto

¡AVANZA! **Goal:** Listen to the conversation between Sandra and her friends. Then use definite and indefinite articles to talk about people. *Actividades 10–11*

♻ *¿Recuerdas?* After-school activities p. 32

Telehistoria escena 2

 @HOMETUTOR my.hrw.com View, Read and Record

STRATEGIES

Cuando lees
Answer questions related to context Knowing the context helps you understand the meaning. Ask yourself: Where is the action taking place?

Cuando escuchas
Listen for unstated wishes People often reveal their wishes without saying them out loud. How do Alberto and Ricardo make it obvious that they want to meet Ana?

VIDEO
DVD

AUDIO

Ricardo: Un helado.

Alberto: Unas papas fritas y un refresco.

Sandra: Un jugo y una pizza. *(Alberto looks over at another table.)*

Alberto: ¿Son las chicas de la clase de la señora García?

Ricardo: Sí, son Marta, Carla y...

Sandra: Ana.

Both boys look interested.

Alberto: ¿Quién es ella?

Sandra: Ella es la amiga de Carla. Es muy inteligente. Le gusta leer y tocar la guitarra.

Alberto: Me gusta escuchar música. Ana, ¿no?

Sandra: Sí. Y le gusta practicar deportes.

Ricardo: Yo soy atlético. Soy muy bueno.

Sandra: ¡Ay, los chicos! *(Leaving, Alberto trips and lands in the seat next to Ana and her friends.)*

Alberto: Uh... hola. Perdón.   **Continuará...** p. 69

También se dice

San Antonio Alberto says **unas papas fritas** to talk about French fries. In other Spanish-speaking countries you might hear:
• **España** **las patatas fritas**
• **Colombia, México**
  las papitas
To talk about juice, Sandra says **un jugo.** In other Spanish-speaking countries you might hear:
• **España** **el zumo**

10 Comprensión del episodio A corregir

Todas estas oraciones son falsas. Corrige los errores. *(Correct the errors.)*

1. Las chicas se llaman Marta, Beatriz y Ana.

2. Ana es la amiga de Sandra.

3. A Ricardo le gusta escuchar música.

4. Ana no es inteligente.

5. A Alberto le gusta tocar la guitarra.

6. Ricardo no es atlético.

Expansión
Write three false statements about the Telehistoria and ask a partner to correct them.

11 En el parque   ¿*Recuerdas?* After-school activities p. 32

Hablar

Escoge una persona o un grupo de personas de los dibujos. Según el modelo, dale pistas a otro(a) estudiante. Él o ella va a adivinar quién es o quiénes son. Túrnense para describir a todas las personas.

(Choose a person or a group of people from the drawings. Follow the model to give clues to another student, who will guess the people you describe. Change roles and describe everyone.)

A Es una chica. Le gusta tocar la guitarra.

B Es la chica de San Antonio.

San Antonio

Bogotá

AUDIO

Pronunciación   **La letra ñ**

The **ñ** sounds like the /ny/ of the word *canyon*. The letter **ñ** does not exist in English, but the sound does. Listen and repeat.

señor   España   mañana   pequeño   castaño

La señora es española.   **El señor es de España y tiene pelo castaño.**

🌐 **Get Help Online**
my.hrw.com

PARA Y PIENSA

Did you get it? Change the article to be more or less specific.

1. Ricardo es el amigo de Alberto.

2. Marta y Carla son las chicas de la clase de español.

3. Ana es la chica muy inteligente.

Presentación de GRAMÁTICA

¡AVANZA! **Goal:** Learn how to use adjectives with nouns. Then practice using adjectives to describe people. *Actividades 12–15*

English Grammar Connection: Adjectives are words that describe **nouns**. In English, the adjective almost always comes before the noun. In Spanish, the adjective usually comes after the noun.

before the noun
the **serious students**

after the noun
los **estudiantes serios**

Noun-Adjective Agreement

ANIMATED GRAMMAR
my.hrw.com

In Spanish, adjectives match the gender and number of the nouns they describe.

Here's how:

	Singular	Plural
Masculine	el chico alto *the tall boy*	los chicos altos *the tall boys*
Feminine	la chica alta *the tall girl*	las chicas altas *the tall girls*

- Adjectives that end in **-e** match both genders.

  el maestro inteligente
  la maestra inteligente

- Many adjectives that end in a **consonant** match both genders.

  el amigo joven
  la amiga joven

- Some adjectives that end in a **consonant** add **-a** to form the feminine singular. These exceptions have to be memorized.

  el chico trabajador
  la chica trabajadora

- To make an adjective plural, add **-s** if it ends in a **vowel**; add **-es** if it ends in a **consonant**.

  las chicas trabajadoras
  los chicos trabajadores

Más práctica
Cuaderno *pp. 30–32*
Cuaderno para hispanohablantes *pp. 31–34*

@HOMETUTOR my.hrw.com
Leveled Practice

Práctica de GRAMÁTICA

12 | Un correo electrónico

Leer

Alicia le escribe un correo electrónico a Sandra con una adivinanza. Escoge las palabras apropiadas entre paréntesis. *(Help Sandra solve the puzzle in Alicia's e-mail by choosing the correct words in parentheses.)*

A: Sandra

Asunto: ¡Una persona famosa en Miami!

Hola, amiga. Te gusta jugar al fútbol y eres **1.** (inteligente / inteligentes), ¿no? ¿Quién es la persona famosa en Miami? No es un chico **2.** (grande / grandes). No es una chica **3.** (pequeño / pequeña). Tiene pelo **4.** (castaño / castaña) y es una persona **5.** (simpático / simpática). Es una mujer **6.** (serio / seria) pero le gusta pasar un rato con los amigos. Los amigos de ella son **7.** (atléticos / atlético) también y les gusta practicar deportes. Ella se llama Trini...

Alicia

---

13 | Descripciones

Escribir

Escribe descripciones de las personas en el dibujo. *(Write descriptions of the people in the drawing.)*

alto(a)	desorganizado(a)
guapo(a)	serio(a)
atlético(a)	cómico(a)
estudioso(a)	¿ ?

Expansión
Choose a photo of people from a magazine. Describe the people in the photo.

14 | ¿Cómo son los amigos de clase?

**Escribir
Hablar**

Escribe descripciones de tres personas en la clase. Lee la descripción a otro(a) estudiante. Él o ella debe adivinar quién es. *(Write descriptions of three people in the class. Read the descriptions to a partner, who will guess the people being described.)*

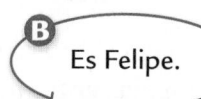

A Es un chico. Es alto, inteligente y atlético. Es un poco serio también. Tiene pelo castaño.

B Es Felipe.

Expansión
Describe someone you know to a partner. Your partner will try to draw that person.

15 | El arte tejano

Hablar

Comparación cultural

El arte en Texas

How do cultural traditions influence an artist's work? Cascarones are painted eggs filled with confetti. They are popular at Easter and events such as parties or graduations. They are also a common sight during Fiesta San Antonio, an annual city-wide celebration that honors the history and culture of San Antonio, **Texas**. But *cascarones* are not meant for decoration. Children sneak up on their friends and try to crack the eggs over their heads. If a *cascarón* is broken over your head, it is supposed to bring you good luck! Artists are often influenced by traditions like these. Carmen Lomas Garza is a Mexican-American artist who depicts scenes of traditional celebration. In her 1989 painting *Cascarones*, Lomas Garza presents a family making the colorful eggs.

Fiesta San Antonio

Compara con tu mundo *What are some traditions in your family and why are they important to you?*

Indica a una persona en la foto y pregúntale a otro(a) estudiante cómo es. Tu compañero(a) va a responder. Túrnense para describir a todas las personas. *(Point to a person in the photo and ask your partner what he or she is like. Change roles. Describe all the people in the photo.)*

A ¿Cómo es la chica?

B La chica es bonita.

Más práctica   Cuaderno *pp. 30–32*   Cuaderno para hispanohablantes *pp. 31–34*

Get Help Online
my.hrw.com

**PARA
Y
PIENSA**

Did you get it? Give the correct ending for each adjective.
1. una estudiante desorganizad _____
2. unos chicos simpátic _____
3. unas mujeres trabajador _____
4. un hombre grand _____

✤Todo junto

Goal: *Show what you know* Pay attention to how Sandra and her friends describe specific people. Then use definite and indefinite articles and adjectives to tell what someone is like. *Actividades 16–20*

Telehistoria completa

@**HOMETUTOR** View, Read
my.hrw.com and Record

STRATEGIES

Cuando lees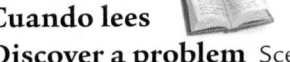
Discover a problem Scenes often reveal problems that the characters must solve. While reading the text below, search for a problem. What is it? Can it be solved?

Cuando escuchas
Listen for the parts Even a short scene can have parts, each with a somewhat different topic or action. These can be keys to meaning. How would you divide this scene?

Escena 1 *Resumen*

Alberto y Ricardo son amigos de Sandra. Alberto es un poco desorganizado. Ricardo es artístico.

Escena 2 *Resumen*

Ana es la amiga de Carla. A Ricardo y a Ana les gusta practicar deportes, y a Alberto y a Ana les gusta escuchar música.

VIDEO
DVD

AUDIO

Escena 3

The group enters a store where Trini Salgado will be signing autographs.

Alberto: Ana es bonita, inteligente, simpática... y nosotros somos inteligentes y simpáticos, ¿no?

Sandra: Sí, sí, ustedes son inteligentes, atléticos, cómicos. Ricardo, tú eres estudioso y Alberto, tú eres cómico.

Ricardo notices a woman in the store.

Ricardo: ¿Es Trini Salgado?

Alberto: ¿Quién?

Ricardo: La mujer seria. Tiene pelo castaño.

Sandra: No es ella. Es un poco baja. Trini es alta y más joven.

Ricardo finds the sign announcing Trini Salgado and points to the date.

Sandra: Pero... es el sábado. Hoy es domingo.

Ricardo: Sí, el sábado en San Antonio y el lunes en México.

Sandra: ¿México? ¿Puebla, México? Pablo, un amigo muy simpático de Alicia, es de México.

Sandra thinks of a plan to send the T-shirt to Pablo.

16 | *Comprensión de los episodios* ¿Cómo son?

Escuchar
Leer

Combina frases de las dos columnas para hacer oraciones sobre las personas en la Telehistoria. *(Combine phrases from the two columns to make sentences about the people in the Telehistoria.)*

1. Alberto y Ricardo son
2. Sandra es
3. Ana es
4. Ricardo es
5. Alberto es
6. Todos los chicos son
7. La mujer seria es
8. Pablo es

a. un poco baja.
b. una amiga de Ricardo y Alberto.
c. un amigo de Alicia.
d. jóvenes.
e. alto y trabajador.
f. cómicos.
g. inteligente y le gusta leer.
h. artístico y atlético.

17 | *Comprensión de los episodios* Los amigos

Escuchar
Leer

Escribe una descripción de los personajes de la Telehistoria según los tres episodios.
(Write descriptions of the Telehistoria characters.)

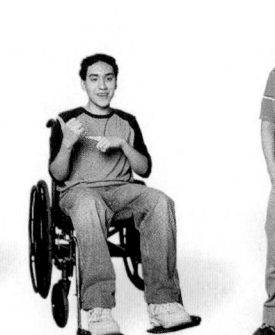

18 | Las personas famosas

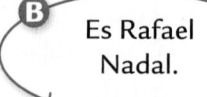
Digital
performance space

Escribir
Hablar

> **STRATEGY Hablar**
> **Practice pronunciation** To speak more fluently and accurately, practice the sounds of words you need to use in your descriptions. Paying attention to pronunciation will help you with cognates.

Escribe descripciones de tres personas famosas. Menciona lo que les gusta y no les gusta hacer. Lee tus descripciones a otro(a) estudiante.
(Write descriptions of three famous people, including what they like and don't like to do. Read the descriptions to a partner, who will guess the people being described.)

A Es un hombre. Tiene pelo castaño. Es muy atlético. Le gusta jugar al tenis. No es muy joven y no es muy viejo. Es de España. ¿Quién es?

B Es Rafael Nadal.

Expansión
Pick another celebrity and have a partner ask five yes/no questions to find out who it is.

19 | Integración

Leer
Escuchar
Hablar

Lee la página Web y escucha los mensajes de los chicos. Describe a los dos chicos. *(Read the Web page and listen to the boys' messages. Describe the two boys.)*

Fuente 1 **Página Web**

Amigos por correspondencia

Buscar en la Web [ ] Buscar Busca Imágenes

Alejandro
¡Hola! Soy de San José, Costa Rica. Soy un estudiante muy bueno. Soy inteligente y me gusta estudiar. Soy un poco serio pero también soy simpático.
¡Escucha!

Édgar
Soy de Colombia. Soy alto y tengo pelo castaño. Soy cómico y simpático. Soy inteligente pero no soy muy trabajador. No me gusta estudiar. ;-)
¡Escucha!

Fuente 2 **Audio en Internet**

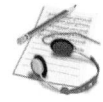

Listen and take notes
- ¿Cómo es Alejandro? ¿Qué le gusta hacer?
- ¿Cómo es Édgar? ¿Qué le gusta hacer?

modelo: Alejandro es un poco serio, pero Édgar es cómico...

20 | Un(a) amigo(a) perfecto(a)

Escribir

Describe el (la) amigo(a) perfecto(a) para una página especial en el anuario. ¿Cómo es? ¿Qué le gusta hacer? ¿Por qué? *(Describe the perfect friend for the yearbook. What is this person like? What does he or she like to do? Why?)*

modelo: Ella se llama Megan. Es bonita, inteligente y artística. Es una chica muy simpática. Le gusta escuchar música y...

Writing Criteria	Excellent	Good	Needs Work
Content	Your description includes a lot of information.	Your description includes some information.	Your description includes little information.
Communication	Most of your description is organized and easy to follow.	Parts of your description are organized and easy to follow.	Your description is disorganized and hard to follow.
Accuracy	Your description has few mistakes in grammar and vocabulary.	Your description has some mistakes in grammar and vocabulary.	Your description has many mistakes in grammar and vocabulary.

Más práctica Cuaderno *pp. 33–34* Cuaderno para hispanohablantes *pp. 35–36*

Get Help Online
my.hrw.com

PARA Y PIENSA

Did you get it? Create sentences with the following information.

1. Alberto / chico(a) / simpático(a)
2. Ricardo / estudiante / trabajador(a)
3. Sandra / persona / organizado(a)

Lectura cultural

Additional readings at my.hrw.com
SPANISH
InterActive Reader

¡AVANZA! **Goal:** Read about things to do in San Antonio and Miami. Then compare what teens do in those cities with what you like to do where you live.

Comparación cultural

AUDIO

Saludos desde [1]
San Antonio y Miami

STRATEGY Leer

Make a comparison chart
Create a chart like the one below to compare San Antonio and Miami.

	San Antonio	Miami
sitios de interés		
actividades		
comida		

En San Antonio, Texas, hay[2] parques de diversiones[3], museos[4], el Paseo del Río y el Álamo. Después de las clases, a los chicos y a las chicas les gusta pasar un rato con los amigos en El Mercado, donde es posible escuchar música de los mariachis y comer comida típica mexicana.

---

[1] **Saludos...** Greetings from   [2] there are
[3] amusement parks   [4] museums

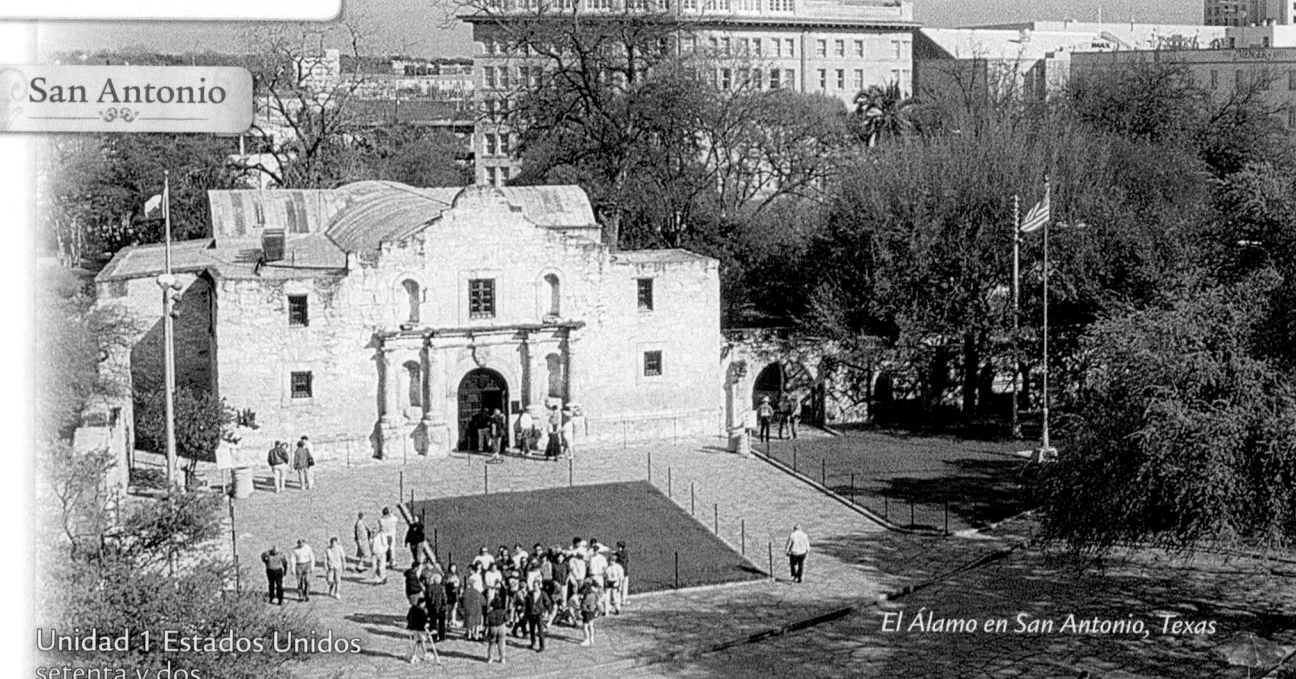

San Antonio

El Álamo en San Antonio, Texas

En Miami, Florida, si⁵ hace buen tiempo, a los chicos y a las chicas les gusta andar en patineta o montar en bicicleta. Después de las clases, a muchos chicos les gusta pasear con los amigos por la Calle Ocho, en la Pequeña Habana de Miami. ¡Es una pequeña Cuba en la Florida! Allí⁶ es posible comer sándwiches cubanos y beber jugo de mango.

_____

⁵ if   ⁶ There

Miami

Andar en patineta en Miami, Florida

PARA Y PIENSA

¿Comprendiste?
1. ¿Qué hay en San Antonio?
2. ¿Qué les gusta hacer a muchos chicos en Miami?
3. ¿Qué hay en la Pequeña Habana de Miami?

¿Y tú?
¿De dónde eres? ¿Qué te gusta hacer después de las clases?

Proyectos culturales

Comparación cultural

Platos tradicionales de México y Cuba

Why do traditional dishes change when they are brought from one country to another? In the U.S. we enjoy foods from many different Spanish-speaking countries. In many parts of the U.S. you can easily find dishes from Mexico, the Caribbean, Central America, and South America. Yet you might be surprised that those dishes aren't exactly the same as they are in their countries of origin. Here are two traditional recipes. The original list of ingredients for both has been modified to include foods more readily available in the U.S. They also reflect the widespread cooking practices and tastes that were already in place when the recipes were brought to this country.

Proyecto 1 *Salsa fresca*

México This is a common sauce in Mexico and all Central America. It is made from scratch and can be eaten as a dip with tortilla chips.

Ingredients for salsa fresca

4–5 fresh tomatoes, diced
1 onion, diced
1 green chile, diced
1 clove of garlic, crushed
Juice of 1 fresh lime

Instructions

Combine the ingredients in a bowl. Cover and let stand for an hour in the refrigerator so that the flavors mix. Serve with tortilla chips.

Proyecto 2 *Sándwich cubano*

Cuba This is a traditional Cuban lunch dish found throughout Florida. The sandwich is pressed in a special grill or on a skillet.

Ingredients for sándwich cubano

1 long sandwich roll
Slices of roast pork, ham, turkey, or bacon
Slice of Swiss or monterey jack cheese
Mustard or mayonnaise
Olive oil

Instructions

First brush the outside of the roll with olive oil. Then split it open and lay meat, cheese, and mustard or mayonnaise as desired. Put the sandwich in a hot skillet, placing a small, heavy skillet on top and pressing lightly. Cook three minutes or until cheese melts and bread is toasted.

En tu comunidad

Search the Internet for restaurants in your area that serve foods from Mexico, Cuba, or other Spanish-speaking countries. Which restaurants serve **salsa fresca** or **sándwiches cubanos**?

ANIMATEDGRAMMAR
Interactive Flashcards
my.hrw.com

Vocabulario

Describe Yourself and Others

¿Cómo eres? — *What are you like?*

Personality

artístico(a)	*artistic*
atlético(a)	*athletic*
bueno(a)	*good*
cómico(a)	*funny*
desorganizado(a)	*disorganized*
estudioso(a)	*studious*
inteligente	*intelligent*
malo(a)	*bad*
organizado(a)	*organized*
perezoso(a)	*lazy*
serio(a)	*serious*
simpático(a)	*nice*
trabajador(a)	*hard-working*

Appearance

alto(a)	*tall*
bajo(a)	*short (height)*
bonito(a)	*pretty*
grande	*big, large; great*
guapo(a)	*good-looking*
joven (pl. jóvenes)	*young*
pelirrojo(a)	*red-haired*
pequeño(a)	*small*
viejo(a)	*old*
Tengo...	*I have . . .*
Tiene...	*He / She has . . .*
pelo rubio	*blond hair*
pelo castaño	*brown hair*

People

el (la) amigo(a)	*friend*
la chica	*girl*
el chico	*boy*
el (la) estudiante	*student*
el hombre	*man*
la mujer	*woman*
la persona	*person*

Other Words and Phrases

muy	*very*
un poco	*a little*
porque	*because*
todos(as)	*all*

Gramática

Nota gramatical: ser to describe what someone is like *p. 58*

Definite and Indefinite Articles

In Spanish, articles match nouns in gender and number.

		Definite Article	Noun	Indefinite Article	Noun
Masculine	Singular	el	chico	un	chico
	Plural	los	chicos	unos	chicos
Feminine	Singular	la	chica	una	chica
	Plural	las	chicas	unas	chicas

Noun-Adjective Agreement

In Spanish, adjectives match the gender and number of the nouns they describe.

	Singular	Plural
Masculine	el chico alto	los chicos altos
Feminine	la chica alta	las chicas altas

Practice Spanish with Holt McDougal Apps!

Repaso de la lección

¡AvanzaRap!
DVD
Sing and Learn

¡LLEGADA!

Now you can
- describe yourself and others
- identify people and things

Using
- **ser** to describe what someone is like
- definite and indefinite articles
- noun-adjective agreement

To review
- definite and indefinite articles p. 61
- **ser** to describe what someone is like p. 58
- noun-adjective agreement p. 66

1 Listen and understand

AUDIO

Escucha a Carlos hablar de él mismo y de su maestra. Escribe una descripción de Carlos y de la señora Pérez, según lo que dice Carlos.
(Listen to Carlos describe himself and his teacher. Write a description of Carlos and Mrs. Pérez, according to what Carlos says.)

To review
- definite and indefinite articles p. 61

2 Identify people and things

Identifica a las personas en el dibujo. *(Identify the people in the drawing.)*

modelo: señor viejo / hombre
El señor viejo es un hombre de Honduras.

México   Honduras   Uruguay   Panamá   Bolivia   Argentina   Estados Unidos

1. chica pelirroja / estudiante
2. hombre grande / maestro
3. chicos pelirrojos / amigos
4. mujer joven / maestra

5. señora alta / mujer
6. chico atlético / estudiante
7. chico desorganizado / persona
8. hombres simpáticos / amigos

To review
• noun-adjective agreement p. 66

3 | Describe yourself and others

Lee este párrafo del diario de Alejandra. Completa la información con la forma correcta de la palabra entre paréntesis. *(Complete Alejandra's diary entry with the correct form of the word in parentheses.)*

> lunes
>
> Todos mis amigos son muy __1.__ (simpático). Miguel es un chico __2.__ (inteligente) y muy __3.__ (guapo). Beatriz es __4.__ (bonito) y __5.__ (estudioso). A Miguel y a Beatriz les gusta practicar deportes porque son __6.__ (atlético). Carmen y yo no somos __7.__ (atlético). Nosotras somos __8.__ (artístico). Todos nosotros somos unos estudiantes __9.__ (serio) y muy __10.__ (bueno).

To review
• **ser** to describe what someone is like p. 58
• noun-adjective agreement p. 66

4 | Describe yourself and others

Ramón y Ramona tienen características opuestas. Escribe oraciones para describirlos, según las descripciones. *(Ramón and Ramona are complete opposites. Write sentences describing them, based on the descriptions.)*

modelo: Ramón es malo.
Ramona es buena.

1. Ramón es viejo.
2. Ramona es seria.
3. Ramón es organizado.
4. Ramona es pequeña.
5. Ramón es perezoso.
6. Ramona es baja.

To review
• Comparación cultural pp. 54, 60, 68
• Lectura cultural pp. 72–73

5 | United States

Comparación cultural

Answer these culture questions.

1. What can people do at San Antonio's Paseo del Río?
2. Give an example of a Tex-Mex dish and a Mexican dish.
3. When do people generally use **cascarones** and what do they do with them?
4. What can people do in San Antonio's El Mercado and Miami's Calle Ocho?

Más práctica Cuaderno *pp. 35–46* Cuaderno para hispanohablantes *pp. 37–46*

Get Help Online
my.hrw.com

Estados Unidos

México

Colombia

AUDIO

Me gusta...

Lectura y escritura

1 **Leer** Read how José Manuel, Martina, and Mónica describe themselves and state their favorite activities.

2 **Escribir** Using the three descriptions as models, write a short paragraph about yourself.

STRATEGY Escribir
Use a personal chart
Make a chart showing information about yourself. This will help you write your description.

Categoría	Detalles
país de origen	
descripción física	
personalidad	
actividades favoritas	
comidas favoritas	

Step 1 Complete the chart by adding details about where you are from, a physical description, personality, and favorite activities and foods.

Step 2 Write your paragraph, including the information above. Review your writing and make final corrections. Write and illustrate your paragraph on cardstock to display in the classroom.

Compara con tu mundo

Use the paragraph you wrote to compare your personal description to a description by *one* of the three students. What similarities do you find? What differences?

Cuaderno *pp. 47–49*   Cuaderno para hispanohablantes *pp. 47–49*

Colombia

José Manuel

Me llamo José Manuel. Soy de Bogotá. Soy cómico y un poco desorganizado pero también soy estudioso. Después de hacer la tarea me gusta jugar al fútbol con mis amigos en el parque El Tunal. También me gusta mirar el fútbol en la televisión.

Estados Unidos

Martina

¡Hola! Me llamo Martina y soy de Miami. Soy inteligente, alta y atlética. Los domingos, me gusta montar en bicicleta. También me gusta preparar jugo de mango o de melón con mi amiga, María. Nos gusta beber mucho jugo porque en Miami hace calor.

México

Mónica

¿Qué tal? Me llamo Mónica y soy de México, D.F. Tengo pelo castaño y soy seria. Mis amigas Maite y Alejandra también tienen pelo castaño y son muy simpáticas. Maite y yo somos artísticas. Nos gusta tocar la guitarra. También nos gusta dibujar.

Repaso inclusivo
♻ Options for Review

Digital
performance space

¡AvanzaRap!
DVD
Sing and Learn

1 | Listen, understand, and compare

Escuchar

Listen to two teen radio reporters talk about typical after-school activities in Miami and San Antonio. Then answer the questions.

1. ¿Cómo son los estudiantes de Miami?
2. ¿Qué les gusta hacer a los estudiantes de Miami?
3. ¿Cómo son los estudiantes de San Antonio?
4. ¿Qué tiempo hace en San Antonio?
5. ¿Qué les gusta hacer a los estudiantes de San Antonio?

Are you and your friends like the students in Miami and/or San Antonio? Do you like to do the same kinds of activities?

2 | Oral presentation

Hablar

Your principal is making a video about your school and you are going to be a featured student. In a segment that lasts at least 30 seconds, introduce yourself, say where you are from, describe yourself, and talk about what you like to do after school.

3 | Role-play conversation

Hablar

Role-play a conversation with a new student at your school. The new student, played by your partner, will introduce himself or herself and ask you what you are like and what you and your friends like to do. Answer the new student's questions and ask questions of your own to get to know him or her. Your conversation should be at least two minutes long.

4 | Create a social media profile

Escribir

Bring in a photo of yourself and create a profile that you could post on a keypal exchange site or social media page.

5 | Do an interview

Work in a group of four. Create a talk show program to get to know your classmates. One of the members of your group will be the host and the others will be the guests. The host should ask the guests questions about what they are like, where they are from, and what they like to do. The guests should greet the host, introduce themselves, answer questions, and ask the host at least one question each. Remember that in real life the host and guests would want to show respect to each other, so use the appropriate register. Each person on the program should talk for at least two minutes.

6 | Create a collage

Hablar

Work with a partner to create individual collages. Use magazine clippings, photos, or your own drawings. Use the collage to introduce yourself to your partner, say where you are from, and show some of the things you like to do. When you finish, exchange your collages and use them to introduce each other to the class.

7 | Write a profile

Leer
Escribir

You are collecting information for this school's Web site. Read the questionnaire and write a profile of this student. Include his name, where he is from, and what he likes and doesn't like to do.

Escuela Secundaria Cuauhtémoc
Cuestionario estudiantil

Nombre: _Esteban Leñeros_

País de origen: _México_

ACTIVIDADES

¿Qué te gusta hacer? _practicar deportes, estudiar, comer enchiladas, escuchar música_

¿Qué no te gusta hacer? _andar en patineta, comer helado, dibujar_

México

⚜ ⚜

¡Vamos a la escuela!

Lección 1

Tema: **Somos estudiantes**

Lección 2

Tema: **En la escuela**

Estados Unidos

• Ciudad Juárez

• Chihuahua

BAJA
CALIFORNIA

Golfo de California

• Monterrey

México

Golfo de
México

Bahía de
Campeche

• Chichén Itzá

Zempoala •

«*¡Hola!*

Somos Pablo y Claudia.
Somos de México.»

Océano
Pacífico

Guadalajara •

• San Miguel de Allende

PENÍNSULA
DE YUCATÁN

México, D.F. ★

• Puebla

Oaxaca •

Guatemala

El Salvador

Población: 121.736.809

Área: 761.606 millas cuadradas

Capital: México, D.F. (Ciudad de México)

Moneda: el peso mexicano

Idiomas: español, maya y otras lenguas
indígenas; el país con más hispanohablantes
del mundo

Chocolate

Comida típica: tortillas, tacos, enchiladas

Gente famosa: Carlos Fuentes (escritor), Salma Hayek
(actriz), Mario Molina (químico), Thalía (cantante)

CULTURA Interactiva
my.hrw.com
See these pages come alive!

*Jóvenes en el Jardín Principal de
San Miguel de Allende*

◀ **Un rato con familia y amigos** In San Miguel de Allende, people of all ages go to the **Jardín Principal,** a tree-lined park in the center of town, to stroll, listen to live music, and spend time with family and friends. *When you want to spend time outside, where do you go?*

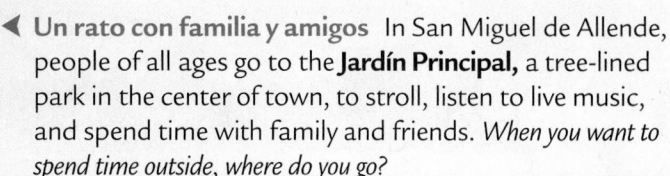

Las ruinas de Chichén Itzá The ruins of the ancient Mayan city of Chichén Itzá include structures built for worship, sports, and studying astronomy. The pyramid of **Kukulcán** was used as a temple. *What are some important buildings in your area used for?* ▶

La estatua de Chac-Mool y la pirámide de Kukulcán

*La biblioteca de la UNAM
con el mural mosaico*

◀ **Una universidad con mucha historia y arte** **La Universidad Nacional Autónoma de México (UNAM)** is one of the oldest universities in the Americas, and the largest public university in Mexico, with over 270,000 students. The library's mosaic mural depicts moments in the cultural history of Mexico. *What are some well-known universities in your area?*

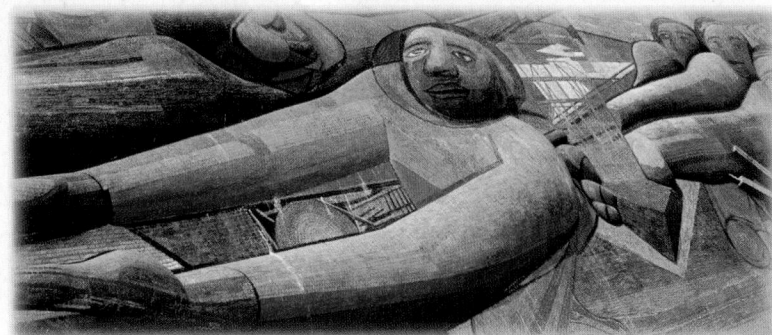

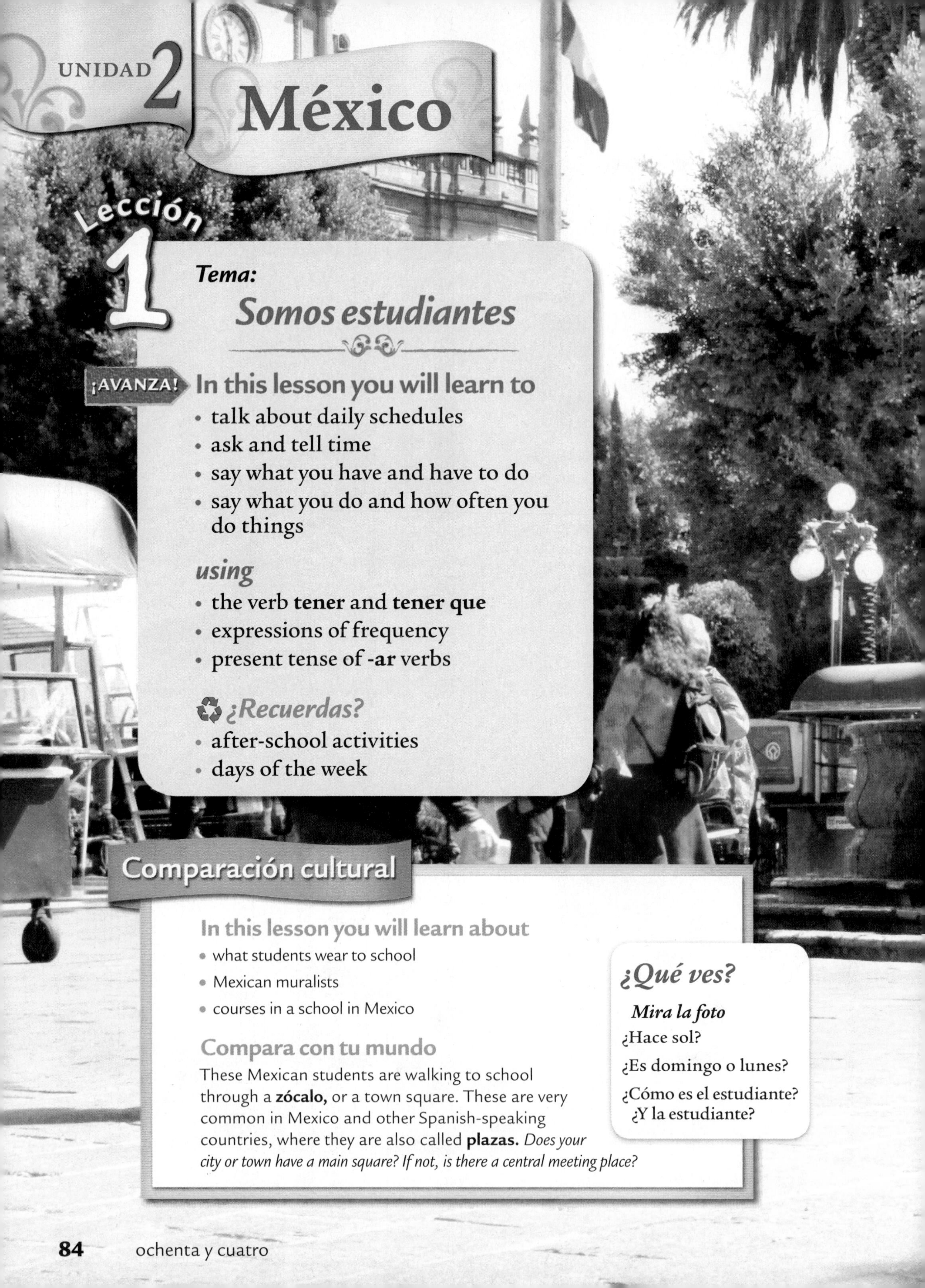

México

Lección 1

Tema:
Somos estudiantes

¡AVANZA! **In this lesson you will learn to**
- talk about daily schedules
- ask and tell time
- say what you have and have to do
- say what you do and how often you do things

using
- the verb **tener** and **tener que**
- expressions of frequency
- present tense of **-ar** verbs

♻ *¿Recuerdas?*
- after-school activities
- days of the week

Comparación cultural

In this lesson you will learn about
- what students wear to school
- Mexican muralists
- courses in a school in Mexico

Compara con tu mundo
These Mexican students are walking to school through a **zócalo,** or a town square. These are very common in Mexico and other Spanish-speaking countries, where they are also called **plazas.** *Does your city or town have a main square? If not, is there a central meeting place?*

¿Qué ves?
Mira la foto
¿Hace sol?
¿Es domingo o lunes?
¿Cómo es el estudiante? ¿Y la estudiante?

MODES OF COMMUNICATION

INTERPRETIVE	INTERPERSONAL	PRESENTATIONAL
Read about graduation requirements at an international school in Mexico. Listen to a conversation and identify details.	With other students, take turns asking about and describing what activities you have to do in school.	Say what you do and don't do in your classes. Write a description of your school schedule.

La fuente de San Miguel en el Zócalo
Puebla, México

Presentación de VOCABULARIO

¡AVANZA! **Goal:** Learn about Pablo's school and class schedule. Then practice what you have learned to talk about daily schedules. *Actividades 1–2*

VIDEO DVD

AUDIO

A ¡Hola! Me llamo Pablo. Mi amiga es Claudia. Somos estudiantes **en** Puebla, México. Me gusta **llegar** a clase **temprano.** Claudia, **¿qué hora es?**

CALENDARIO · FECHAS PARA RECORDAR

7:00 matemáticas
8:10 ciencias
9:15 usar la computadora
10:15 inglés
11:50 arte
12:30 historia
1:30 español
3:30 jugar al fútbol

el horario

B **¿A qué hora son** mis clases? Tengo **muchas** clases.

las matemáticas

La clase de **matemáticas** es **a las siete de la mañana.**

las ciencias

La clase de **ciencias** es **a las ocho y diez** de la mañana.

el inglés

La clase de **inglés** es **a las diez y cuarto** de la mañana.

el arte

La clase de **arte** es **a las doce menos diez** de la mañana.

la historia

La clase de **historia** es **a las doce y media de la tarde.**

el español

La clase de **español** es **a la una y media** de la tarde.

Unidad 2 México
86 ochenta y seis

C Son las ocho y diez y tengo la clase de ciencias. A Claudia **siempre** le gusta **contestar** las preguntas del maestro. Ella es muy inteligente. Yo **tengo que** estudiar **mucho** y **tomar apuntes** en clase.

enseñar

contestar

tomar apuntes

Más vocabulario

de vez en cuando *once in a while*
muchas veces *often, many times*
nunca *never*
todos los días *every day*
casi *almost*
difícil *difficult*
fácil *easy*
hay... *there is, there are. . .*
la hora *hour; time*
el minuto *minute*
¿Cuántos(as)...? *How many. . .?*

Expansión de vocabulario p. R3

D Tengo que **sacar una buena nota** en la clase de inglés. A Claudia y a mí nos gusta estudiar a las ocho **de la noche**. Es un poco **tarde** pero **necesito** estudiar. ¡No me gusta **sacar una mala nota**!

sacar una buena nota

el examen

usar la computadora

Numbers from 11 to 100

11	once	25	veinticinco
12	doce	26	veintiséis
13	trece	27	veintisiete
14	catorce	28	veintiocho
15	quince	29	veintinueve
16	dieciséis	30	treinta
17	diecisiete	31	treinta y uno
18	dieciocho	40	cuarenta
19	diecinueve	50	cincuenta
20	veinte	60	sesenta
21	veintiuno	70	setenta
22	veintidós	80	ochenta
23	veintitrés	90	noventa
24	veinticuatro	100	cien

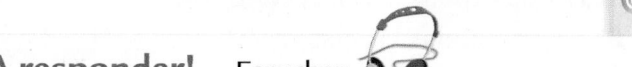

@**HOMETUTOR** my.hrw.com — **Interactive Flashcards**

¡A responder! Escuchar

Saca dos hojas de papel. En una escribe **la mañana,** y en la otra escribe **la tarde.** Escucha el horario de Pablo y levanta la hoja que indica cuándo tiene cada clase. *(On separate pieces of paper, write the words **la mañana** and **la tarde.** Listen to Pablo describe his schedule. Hold up the paper that indicates when he has each class.)*

Práctica de VOCABULARIO

1 | Las clases de Claudia

Escribir
Hablar

Identifica las clases de Claudia según la hora. *(Identify Claudia's classes according to the time.)*

modelo: a la una y diez
A la una y diez Claudia tiene la clase de español.

 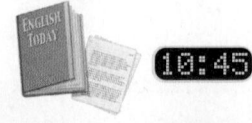

1. a las once menos cuarto
2. a las siete y media
3. a las doce

4. a las nueve menos veinte
5. a las nueve y cuarto
6. a las dos y media

Nota gramatical

For the numbers **21, 31,** and so on, use **veintiún, treinta y un,** and so on before a masculine noun and **veintiuna, treinta y una,** and so on before a feminine noun.

Hay **veintiún** maestros en la escuela.   Hay **treinta y una** personas en mi clase.

*There are **twenty-one** teachers in the school.*   *There are **thirty-one** people in my class.*

---

2 | ¿Cuántas personas?

Hablar

Habla con otro(a) estudiante sobre el número de personas en estas clases.

(Talk with a partner about the number of people in these classes.)

modelo: chicos / historia y arte (29)

A ¿Cuántos chicos hay en las clases de historia y arte?

B Hay veintinueve chicos en las clases de historia y arte.

1. chicas / matemáticas (16)
2. estudiantes / inglés y arte (58)
3. chicos / historia y ciencias (27)
4. estudiantes / historia y arte (62)
5. chicas / música y español (33)
6. estudiantes / arte (40)
7. chicas / todas las clases (71)
8. chicos / todas las clases (74)

Expansión
Tell how many people are in your other classes.

Más práctica   Cuaderno *pp. 50–52*   Cuaderno para hispanohablantes *pp. 50–53*

🌐 **Get Help Online**
my.hrw.com

PARA Y PIENSA   **Did you get it?**   **1.** Tell someone you like to draw in art class.
2. Say that there are 23 boys in math class.

VOCABULARIO en contexto

¡AVANZA! **Goal:** Listen to how Pablo and Claudia talk about at what time they will study. Then practice these words to ask and tell time. *Actividades 3–4*

Telehistoria escena 1

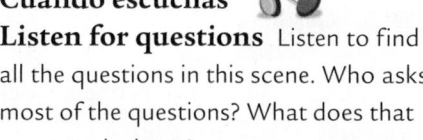

STRATEGIES

Cuando lees
Focus on time Read for expressions of time like **hoy** or **a las ocho.** How many can you find in this scene? What do they mean?

Cuando escuchas
Listen for questions Listen to find all the questions in this scene. Who asks most of the questions? What does that person ask about?

VIDEO
DVD

AUDIO

Claudia: Pablo, hay examen de ciencias mañana, ¿no?

Pablo: Sí... Me gusta la clase de ciencias, pero... sacar una buena nota, un 90 o un 100, ¡es difícil!

Claudia: Necesitas estudiar una o dos horas... ¿Te gusta estudiar con amigos?

Pablo: Sí... pero hoy no. ¡Hay fútbol! ¿Mañana?

Claudia: Sí. ¿En la escuela?

Pablo: Sí. ¿A las ocho de la mañana? ¿O más temprano?

Claudia: A las siete de la mañana. ¿Está bien?

Pablo: ¡Sí!

The bell rings, and they part ways for class.

Pablo: Hmmm... Hay chicas muy inteligentes en la escuela...

Continuará... p. 94

3 | *Comprensión del episodio*   Planes para estudiar

Escuchar
Leer

¿Es cierto o falso? Si es falso, di lo que es cierto. *(True or false? If it is false, say what is true.)*

1. Hay un examen en la clase de español mañana.
2. A Pablo le gusta estudiar con amigos, pero hoy no.
3. A Pablo le gusta la clase de ciencias.
4. Hay fútbol hoy.
5. La clase de ciencias es fácil.

Nota gramatical

- Use **Es la una** to say that it is one o'clock; use **Son las...** for any other time.

    Son las cinco.   *It is 5:00.*

- Use **y** + **minutes** for the number of minutes after the hour (up to 30).

    Son las dos **y diez.**   *It is 2:10.*

- Use **menos** + **minutes** for the number of minutes before the hour.

    Es la una **menos veinte.**   *It is 12:40.*

- Use **y** or **menos cuarto** for a quarter of an hour and **y media** for half an hour.

- To say at what time something happens, use **a la(s)...**

    La clase de arte es **a la** una y la clase de inglés es **a las** dos.

4 | El horario de clases

Escribir

Escribe a qué hora son las clases de Marisol. *(Write the times of Marisol's classes.)*

modelo: La clase de historia es a las siete de la mañana.

MARISOL AGUILAR

HORA	LUNES
7:00	HISTORIA
8:15	MATEMÁTICAS
9:30	INGLÉS
10:45	ARTE
1:05	CIENCIAS
2:10	ESPAÑOL

Expansión
Draw five clocks showing different times. Point to each one and ask a partner what time it is.

PARA
Y
PIENSA

🌐 **Get Help Online**
my.hrw.com

Did you get it?   Complete each sentence with the appropriate time.
1. El jueves Claudia tiene que llegar a la escuela _____ . (10:15)
2. Son _____ . (8:20)
3. A Pablo le gusta hacer la tarea _____ de la noche. (7:00)

Presentación de GRAMÁTICA

Goal: Learn how to form the verb **tener.** Then use this verb to say what people have and have to do and how often. *Actividades 5–7*

♻ *¿Recuerdas?* After-school activities p. 32

English Grammar Connection: Conjugating is changing the forms of a verb to indicate who is doing the action. For example, the English verb *to have* is conjugated as *I have, you have, he/she/it has, we have, they have.*

Claudia **has** a computer. | Claudia **tiene** una computadora.

⬆ | ⬆
conjugated verb | **conjugated verb**

The Verb tener

ANIMATED GRAMMAR
my.hrw.com

Use the verb **tener** to talk about what you have.
How do you conjugate this verb?

Here's how:

tener *to have*			
yo	**tengo**	nosotros(as)	**tenemos**
tú	**tienes**	vosotros(as)	**tenéis**
usted, él, ella	**tiene**	ustedes, ellos(as)	**tienen**

Tenemos clase el lunes. | ¿**Tienes** una bicicleta?
We have class on Monday. | *Do you have a bike?*

Tener + **que** + **infinitive** is used to talk about what someone has to do.

Tengo que estudiar. | Miguel **tiene que leer** un libro.
I have to study. | *Miguel has to read a book.*

Más práctica
Cuaderno *pp. 53–55*
Cuaderno para hispanohablantes *pp. 54–56*

@ **HOMETUTOR** my.hrw.com
Leveled Practice
🌐 Conjuguemos.com

❖ Práctica de GRAMÁTICA

5 | Las clases

Escribir

Escribe qué clases tienen estas personas, usando formas de **tener.**
*(Write what class these people have, using forms of **tener**.)*

1. yo

2. nosotros

3. Claudia y Pablo

4. tú

5. Claudia

6. ustedes

6 | ¿Qué tienen que hacer?

Escuchar
Escribir

Escucha la descripción de lo que Pablo y sus amigos tienen que hacer.
Luego escribe oraciones para indicar qué hora es y quién tiene que hacer
estas actividades. *(Listen and write sentences saying what time it is and who has to do the
following activities.)*

1. estudiar

2. usar la computadora

3. hacer la tarea

4. tocar la guitarra

5. trabajar

6. leer un libro

> **Expansión**
> Tell what you and your
> friends have
> to do today.

Comparación cultural

Uniformes escolares

*How does the way students dress reflect a
culture?* In **Mexico,** it is common for students
to wear uniforms in both public and private
schools. The type and color of the uniforms
can vary depending on the individual school.
Most students in the **Dominican Republic** also
wear uniforms. Public schools have the same
uniforms, while private school uniforms may vary.

Compara con tu mundo *Why do some schools
require uniforms? Are they common in your community?*

*Estudiantes en México y
la República Dominicana*

Nota gramatical

The expressions of frequency **siempre** and **nunca** are usually placed before the verb.

Antonio **siempre** toma apuntes.   *Antonio **always** takes notes.*

Rafael **nunca** llega a clase tarde.   *Rafael **never** arrives late to class.*

Mucho is usually placed after the verb.

Raquel estudia **mucho.**   *Raquel studies **a lot.***

De vez en cuando, muchas veces, and **todos los días** are usually placed at the beginning or the end of the sentence.

Todos los días Jaime trabaja.   *Jaime works **every day.***

Jaime trabaja **todos los días.**

---

7 Las obligaciones   **¿Recuerdas?** After-school activities p. 32

Hablar

Pregúntales a otros(as) estudiantes si tienen que hacer estas actividades. Ellos van a responder usando una expresión de frecuencia. *(Ask other students whether they have to do these activities. They will respond using an expression of frequency.)*

A ¿Tienen que tomar apuntes ustedes?

B Sí, tengo que tomar apuntes muchas veces.

C Sí, tengo que tomar apuntes de vez en cuando.

1.

2.

3.

4.

5.

6.

Expansión
Write three or four sentences about the activities you and your friends never have to do.

Más práctica   Cuaderno *pp. 53–55*   Cuaderno para hispanohablantes *pp. 54–56*

 **Get Help Online**
my.hrw.com

PARA Y PIENSA

Did you get it?   Answer each question with the word(s) in parentheses.
1. ¿Tiene que preparar la comida Juan? (nunca)
2. ¿Cuándo tenemos la clase de inglés? (todos los días)
3. ¿Tienes que usar la computadora? (siempre)

❖ GRAMÁTICA en contexto

¡AVANZA! **Goal:** Notice how Pablo and Claudia use the verb phrase **tener que** to talk about what they have to do at school. Then use **tener** and **tener que** to say what you and others have and have to do. *Actividades 8–10*

 ¿Recuerdas? Days of the week p. 18

Telehistoria escena 2

@ **HOMETUTOR** View, Read
my.hrw.com and Record

STRATEGIES

Cuando lees
Find the "tag questions" This scene contains the "tag question" **¿no?** Where are the tag questions in a sentence? How do they differ from questions like **¿Quién es?**

Cuando escuchas
Weigh the motive Listen for Pablo's reasons for not studying for the test. What are his reasons? Do they sound credible to you? Have you ever used them?

VIDEO
DVD

AUDIO

Pablo's cell phone rings.

Pablo: Hola... ¿Quién es? ¡Claudia! ¿Qué tal?... Sí, sí, a las siete. ¡Tenemos que estudiar mucho!

The next morning, Claudia and Pablo walk to class.

Claudia: Pablo, tienes que estudiar más, ¿no?

Pablo: Sí. Tenemos mucha tarea y los exámenes son muy difíciles.

Claudia: Pero te gusta sacar buenas notas, ¿no?

Pablo: Sí. Tenemos que estudiar más.

También se dice

México Pablo uses the word **tarea** to talk about homework. In other Spanish-speaking countries you might hear:
• **muchos países** los **deberes**

Continuará... p. 99

8 | *Comprensión del episodio* Un examen importante

Escuchar
Leer

Contesta las preguntas. *(Answer the questions.)*

1. ¿Qué tienen que hacer Pablo y Claudia?
  a. Tienen que descansar mucho.
  b. Tienen que estudiar.
  c. Tienen que enseñar.

2. ¿A qué hora tienen que estudiar?
  a. a las siete
  b. a las siete y media
  c. a las ocho

3. ¿Qué tienen Pablo y Claudia?
  a. muchos libros
  b. un poco de tarea
  c. mucha tarea

4. ¿Qué le gusta hacer a Pablo?
  a. Le gusta estudiar.
  b. Le gusta llegar tarde.
  c. Le gusta sacar buenas notas.

9 | Las responsabilidades   *¿Recuerdas?* Days of the week p. 18

Escribir

Escribe un e-mail a tu compañero(a). Pregúntale qué tarea tienes que hacer para todas tus clases. *(Write an e-mail to ask a classmate what you need to do for homework in each of your classes.)*

modelo:

```
Hola, Jeff.
¿Qué tarea hay? ¿Tengo que hacer tarea de
matemáticas?¿Qué tenemos que leer para la clase
de...?
```

Expansión
Work with a partner to write your classmate's response to your e-mail.

10 | ¿Y tú?

Hablar
Escribir

Contesta las preguntas. *(Answer the questions.)*

1. ¿Qué clases tienes? ¿Son fáciles o difíciles?

2. ¿A qué hora tienes la clase de español?

3. ¿Tienes que tomar apuntes? ¿En qué clases?

4. ¿Qué tienes que hacer todos los días?

5. ¿Qué tienes que hacer todos los sábados y domingos?

6. ¿Qué nunca tienes que hacer?

7. ¿Tienes que trabajar? ¿A qué hora?

8. ¿A qué hora necesitas llegar a la escuela?

Get Help Online
my.hrw.com

PARA Y PIENSA

Did you get it? **¿Tener** or **tener que?** Complete each sentence based on the Telehistoria with the correct form of the verb or expression.
  1. Pablo y Claudia _____ mucha tarea.
  2. Pablo _____ estudiar mucho.
  3. Ellos _____ un examen en la clase de ciencias.

❈ Presentación de GRAMÁTICA

¡AVANZA! **Goal:** Learn the forms of **-ar** verbs. Then practice using the verbs to say what people do. *Actividades 11–15*

English Grammar Connection: A **verb tense** is the form of the verb that shows *when* an action is happening. The **present tense** shows that an action is happening *now*. The Spanish present-tense verb form **estudiamos** can be expressed in English in three different ways: *we study, we are studying,* or *we do study*.

We **study** Spanish.

⬆

present-tense verb

Estudiamos español.

⬆

present-tense verb

Present Tense of -ar Verbs

ANIMATEDGRAMMAR
my.hrw.com

Many infinitives in Spanish end in **-ar.** How do you form the present tense of these verbs?

Here's how: In Spanish, the present tense is formed by changing the ending of the verb.

To form the present tense of a regular verb that ends in **-ar,** drop the **-ar** and add the appropriate **ending.**

habl~~ar~~ ◄ o, as, a, amos, áis, or an

hablar *to talk, to speak*			
yo	**habl**o	nosotros(as)	**habl**amos
tú	**habl**as	vosotros(as)	**habl**áis
usted, él, ella	**habl**a	ustedes, ellos(as)	**habl**an

Hablo inglés.

I speak English.
I am speaking English.
I do speak English.

¿**Habl**an español?

Do they speak Spanish?
Are they speaking Spanish?

Más práctica
Cuaderno *pp. 56–58*
Cuaderno para hispanohablantes *pp. 57–60*

@HOMETUTOR my.hrw.com
Leveled Practice
🌐 Conjuguemos.com

Práctica de GRAMÁTICA

11 | Somos buenos estudiantes

Hablar Escribir

Pablo, Claudia y sus amigos son buenos estudiantes. Explica si siempre o nunca hacen lo siguiente. *(Tell whether good students always or never do the following.)*

modelo: Claudia / llegar a clase temprano
Claudia **siempre** llega a clase temprano.

1. yo / escuchar en clase
2. Pablo / tomar apuntes
3. nosotros / sacar malas notas
4. Claudia y Pablo / estudiar
5. tú / contestar preguntas
6. Diego y yo / llegar a clase tarde
7. Lorena / mirar la televisión
8. ustedes / sacar buenas notas

Expansión
Say how often you do these things.

12 | El fin de semana

Leer Escribir

A Sandra le gusta pasar un rato con los amigos. Completa el párrafo con la forma correcta del verbo apropiado. *(Complete the paragraph with the correct form of the appropriate verb.)*

escuchar	pasar
tocar	montar
alquilar	dibujar
estudiar	practicar

Nosotros **1.** en bicicleta después de las clases. Amy y Rosa **2.** deportes y yo **3.** la guitarra. A mi amigo Eduardo no le gusta descansar. Él **4.** inglés o **5.** para la clase de arte. Es muy artístico. Si llueve, nosotros **6.** música en un café o **7.** un DVD. ¿Dónde **8.** tú un rato con los amigos?

13 | ¿Qué estudias?

Hablar

Con otro(a) estudiante, habla de tu horario y lo que estudias. *(Talk with a partner about your schedule and what you study.)*

A ¿Estudias ciencias?

B Sí, tengo la clase de ciencias a las once.

Comparación cultural

Los murales en México

How does society affect public artwork? From the 1920s to the 1950s, the Mexican government commissioned artists to paint the walls of public buildings. Diego Rivera, José Orozco and David Alfaro Siqueiros were the three most notable muralists. Their art promoted their political and social views on Mexican history and government, education, social security, class structure, and technology.

Compara con tu mundo What would you paint in a mural representing your community?

Detalle de Por una seguridad completa para todos los mexicanos (1952–1954)

14 | ¿En la escuela?

Hablar

Pregúntale a otro(a) estudiante si hace estas actividades en la escuela. Usa expresiones de frecuencia. *(Ask another student if he or she does these activities at school. Use expressions of frequency.)*

modelo: dibujar

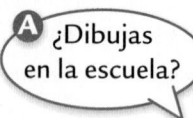

A ¿Dibujas en la escuela?

B No, nunca dibujo en la escuela.

1. estudiar
2. escuchar música
3. comprar refrescos
4. practicar deportes
5. tocar la guitarra
6. pasar un rato con los amigos

Expansión
Say how often you do these activites on Sundays.

15 | Un sábado típico

Escribir Hablar

Describe lo que haces los sábados y con qué frecuencia. Usa los verbos de la lista. Luego compara tus actividades con las de otros(as) estudiantes.

(Use verbs from the list to describe what you do on Saturdays and how often you do it. Then compare your activities with other students'.)

alquilar	estudiar	escuchar	trabajar
comprar	descansar	usar	¿ ?

modelo: Siempre hablo por teléfono los sábados. Muchas veces paso un rato con las amigas. Nosotras alquilamos un DVD...

AUDIO

Pronunciación   El sonido ch

In Spanish, the **ch** sounds like the *ch* of the English word *chip*.

Listen and repeat.

cha	che	chi	cho	chu
mucha	noche	chico	dieciocho	churro

Muchas chicas escuchan música de Pancho Sánchez.

Más práctica   Cuaderno *pp. 56–58*   Cuaderno para hispanohablantes *pp. 57–60*

Get Help Online
my.hrw.com

PARA Y PIENSA

Did you get it?   Complete each sentence with the correct form of the verb in parentheses.

1. Nosotros _____ la computadora mucho. (usar)
2. Yo _____ la comida de vez en cuando. (preparar)
3. Los chicos _____ en la clase de arte. (dibujar)
4. ¿ _____ tú sacar una buena nota? (necesitar)

Todo junto

¡AVANZA! **Goal:** ***Show what you know*** Pay attention to how Pablo and Claudia use **tener** and **-ar** verbs to talk about their test and what they do after school. Then use these verbs to say what you and others do during and after school. ***Actividades 16–20***

Telehistoria completa

@HOMETUTOR my.hrw.com **View, Read and Record**

STRATEGIES

Cuando lees
Look for the unexpected As you read, look for two surprises involving Pablo. What are they? Why are they unexpected? What did you expect to happen?

Cuando escuchas
Listen for cognates Listen for cognates like **examen** (exam, test). What cognates do you hear? What English word(s) do they sound like? What do they mean?

Escena 1 ***Resumen***
Pablo y Claudia necesitan estudiar porque tienen un examen de ciencias.

Escena 2 ***Resumen***
Pablo y Claudia hablan por teléfono. Tienen que estudiar más.

Escena 3

VIDEO DVD

AUDIO

Pablo: ¡Claudia! En el examen de ciencias, tengo… ¡un 90!

Claudia: ¡Y yo, un 100!

Pablo: ¿Estudiamos, tú y yo, todos los días?

Claudia: Sí… pero tú necesitas tomar buenos apuntes, ¿no? *(Pablo grins.)* ¿A qué hora practican fútbol?

Pablo: Muchas veces practicamos a las cinco. Mañana practicamos temprano, a las tres y media. ¿Y tú? ¿Qué necesitas hacer mañana?

Claudia: ¿Mañana? Estudiar y hacer la tarea de ciencias.

Claudia says goodbye and leaves. As his friend Roberto walks up, Pablo distractedly pulls Alicia's T-shirt out of his bag and puts it on.

Roberto: ¡Ay, Pablo, qué interesante!

Pablo, embarrassed, takes the shirt off quickly.

16 | Comprensión de los episodios ¿Quién es?

Escuchar Leer

¿A quién se refieren estas oraciones? ¿A Claudia, a Pablo o a los dos? Escribe el (los) nombre(s) y la forma correcta del verbo entre paréntesis. *(Do these sentences refer to Claudia, Pablo, or both? Write the name(s) and the correct form of the verb in parentheses.)*

Pablo

Claudia y Pablo

Claudia

1. _____ (tener) que practicar fútbol.
2. _____ (llegar) a la escuela a las siete de la mañana.
3. _____ (hablar) por teléfono.
4. _____ (necesitar) estudiar una o dos horas.

5. _____ (tener) un examen de ciencias.
6. _____ (sacar) una buena nota.
7. _____ (estudiar) para la clase de ciencias mañana.
8. _____ (practicar) a las tres y media mañana.

17 | Comprensión de los episodios ¿Qué hacen?

Escuchar Leer

Completa las oraciones con información de los episodios. *(Finish the sentences.)*

1. Pablo y Claudia tienen que...
2. A las siete Pablo y Claudia...
3. Mañana Claudia...
4. Pablo necesita tomar...
5. Claudia y Pablo sacan...

18 | ¿Qué tienes que hacer?

Digital **performance space**

Hablar

STRATEGY Hablar
Create a dialogue of your own Use the model question and substitute different school subjects. Use the model answer, but change verbs, or use multiple verbs in a single sentence. Bring in humor if you can.

Habla con otro(a) estudiante de lo que haces y qué tienes que hacer en tus clases. *(Talk with a partner about what you do and have to do in your classes.)*

A ¿Qué tienes que hacer en la clase de matemáticas?

B Tengo que tomar apuntes. Siempre escucho en clase...

19 | Integración

Leer
Escuchar
Hablar

Mañana los maestros tienen una reunión y el horario de clases es diferente. Lee el horario de Manuel y escucha el mensaje del director. Indica a qué hora necesita llegar Manuel a sus clases. *(Tell at what time Manuel needs to arrive at each of his classes.)*

Fuente 1 Horario de clases

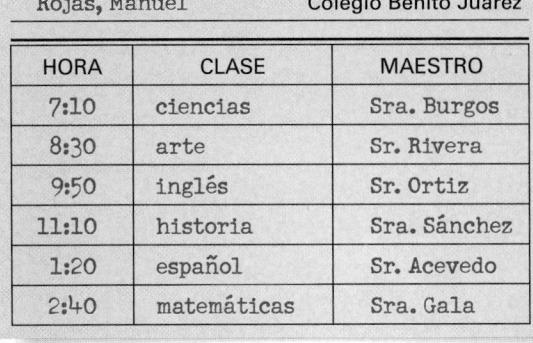

Rojas, Manuel		Colegio Benito Juárez
HORA	CLASE	MAESTRO
7:10	ciencias	Sra. Burgos
8:30	arte	Sr. Rivera
9:50	inglés	Sr. Ortiz
11:10	historia	Sra. Sánchez
1:20	español	Sr. Acevedo
2:40	matemáticas	Sra. Gala

Fuente 2 Mensaje del director

Listen and take notes
- ¿Cuántos minutos después de la hora normal son las clases de la mañana? ¿Las clases de la tarde?

modelo: Manuel necesita llegar a la clase de... a las...

20 | Tu horario

Digital performance space

Escribir

Escribe un e-mail a un(a) amigo(a) de Cuba para describir tu horario y preguntar sobre su horario. ¿Qué necesita hacer para la escuela y con qué frecuencia? ¿Qué tiene que hacer cuando no hay clases? *(Write an e-mail to your Cuban friend, describing your schedule. Ask about his/her schedule. What does s/he need to do for school or outside of school?)*

modelo: ¿Qué clases hay en tu horario? ¿Qué necesitas hacer para la clase de matemáticas?

Writing Criteria	Excellent	Good	Needs Work
Content	Your description includes a lot of information.	Your description includes some information.	Your description includes little information.
Communication	Most of your description is organized and easy to follow.	Parts of your description are organized and easy to follow.	Your description is disorganized and hard to follow.
Accuracy	Your description has few mistakes in grammar and vocabulary.	Your description has some mistakes in grammar and vocabulary.	Your description has many mistakes in grammar and vocabulary.

Expansión
Take turns with a partner writing responses to the questions.

Más práctica   Cuaderno *pp. 59–60*   Cuaderno para hispanohablantes *pp. 61–62*

Get Help Online
my.hrw.com

PARA Y PIENSA

Did you get it? Write the correct form of **tomar, estudiar,** or **practicar.**

1. Claudia siempre _____ buenos apuntes.
2. Pablo tiene que _____ fútbol a las cinco.
3. Pablo y Claudia _____ todos los días.

Lectura

¡AVANZA! **Goal:** Read about the requirements for graduating from an international school in Mexico. As you read these documents, compare them with the course requirements needed to graduate from your school.

AUDIO

Una escuela internacional en México

The following pages are from the student handbook for Colegio Internacional.

STRATEGY Leer
Use what you know As you read the graduation requirements of Colegio Internacional, use what you know. Find words that sound and look somewhat similar to those in English — cognates like **ciencias** or **matemáticas.** Then use the context and what you already know to guess what **desarrollo humano and optativas** mean.

MANUAL DEL ESTUDIANTE

Estudiantes en el Colegio Internacional

«A mí me gusta mucho el Colegio Internacional. Las clases son muy buenas. Los maestros son trabajadores y muy inteligentes. Y los estudiantes son súper simpáticos. Siempre tenemos que trabajar mucho, pero... ¡¿dónde no?! Y también en la escuela hay muchas actividades después de las clases. ¡Es una escuela excelente!»
–Marta Ramos, estudiante

COLEGIO INTERNACIONAL

Requisitos para graduarse de bachillerato

A continuación [1], los requisitos para graduarse con los dos certificados: el certificado mexicano y el certificado estadounidense.

Clase	Número de unidades
Inglés	4 unidades
Español	4 unidades
Matemáticas	4 unidades
Ciencias	4 unidades
Ciencias Sociales de México	1 unidad
Historia de México II	1 unidad
Geografía de México	1 unidad
Derecho [2]	1 unidad
Ciencias Sociales	3 unidades
Computación	0,5 unidades
Educación Física	0,5 unidades
Desarrollo Humano [3]	1 unidad
Optativas [4]	2 unidades
Total	**27 unidades**

COLEGIO INTERNACIONAL

---

[1] **A...** following are   [2] Law
[3] Human Development   [4] Electives

PARA Y PIENSA

¿Comprendiste?
1. ¿Cuántas clases necesitas para los dos programas?
2. ¿Cuántas unidades de matemáticas tienes que tomar?

¿Y tú?
¿Qué clases del Colegio Internacional hay en tu escuela? ¿Cómo son?

✤ Conexiones   *La historia*

El pueblo de Zempoala

In 1577, the Spanish crown sent a questionnaire to Mexico to get information about its territories in the New World. The responses that were sent back included local maps drawn by indigenous mapmakers.

The map below depicts the town (**pueblo**) of Zempoala, located in the modern Mexican state of Hidalgo. Research Zempoala to learn more about the town and this map. Then choose three specific map symbols not listed in the legend (**leyenda**) and explain what you think they mean.

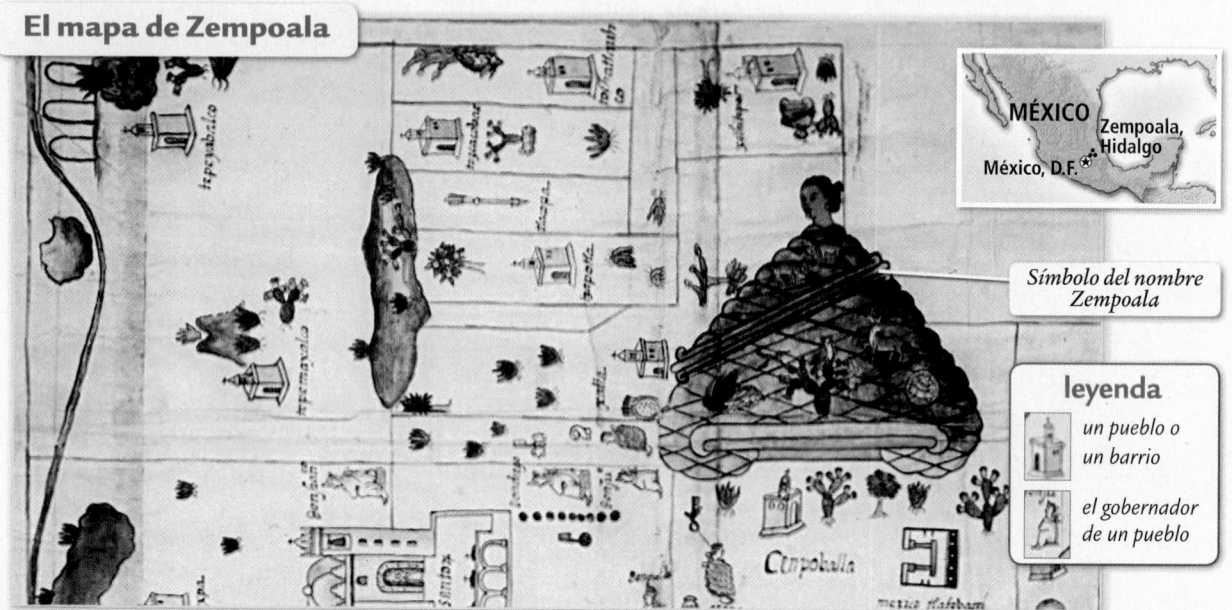

El mapa de Zempoala

MÉXICO
Zempoala, Hidalgo
México, D.F.

Símbolo del nombre Zempoala

leyenda
un pueblo o un barrio
el gobernador de un pueblo

✤ Proyecto ① *El arte*

Draw a map of your town or city similar to the one of Zempoala. Give information about people, buildings, roads, and vegetation. Use symbols like the ones in the map above and label them in Spanish.

✤ Proyecto ② *Las ciencias sociales*

In 1968, Mexico established a televised system of secondary schools called **Telesecundaria.** Today, educational video programs are broadcast via satellite to more than 15,000 schools. Write two paragraphs about the use of technology in education. How is it used in your school? Can you think of other ways it can be used in education?

✤ Proyecto ③ *La salud*

The map of Zempoala shows a number of cacti. The cactus has been an important source of food and medicine for people in Mexico for many years. Make a list of different types of cacti found in Mexico and create a chart showing how people have used them for health and beauty purposes.

Un nopal con flores

Vocabulario

Tell Time and Discuss Daily Schedules

¿A qué hora es...?	At what time is ...?	la hora	hour; time
¿Qué hora es?	What time is it?	el horario	schedule
A la(s)...	At . . . o'clock.	menos	to, before (telling time)
Es la... / Son las...	It is . . . o'clock.		
de la mañana	in the morning (with a time)	el minuto	minute
		...y cuarto	quarter past
de la tarde	in the afternoon (with a time)	...y (diez)	(ten) past
		...y media	half past
de la noche	at night (with a time)		

Describe Classes

School Subjects

el arte	art
las ciencias	science
el español	Spanish
la historia	history
el inglés	English
las matemáticas	math

Classroom Activities

contestar	to answer
enseñar	to teach
llegar	to arrive
necesitar	to need
sacar una buena / mala nota	to get a good / bad grade
tomar apuntes	to take notes
usar la computadora	to use the computer

Describe Frequency

de vez en cuando	once in a while
muchas veces	often, many times
mucho	a lot
nunca	never
siempre	always
todos los días	every day

Other Words and Phrases

casi	almost
¿Cuántos(as)...?	How many . . . ?
difícil	difficult
en	in
el examen (pl. los exámenes)	exam, test
fácil	easy
hay...	there is, there are . . .
muchos(as)	many
tarde	late
temprano	early
tener que	to have to

Numbers from 11 to 100 *p. 87*

Gramática

Notas gramaticales: Numbers *p. 88*, Telling time *p. 90*, Expressions of frequency *p. 93*

The Verb tener

Use the verb **tener** to talk about what you have.

tener *to have*			
yo	tengo	nosotros(as)	tenemos
tú	tienes	vosotros(as)	tenéis
usted, él, ella	tiene	ustedes, ellos(as)	tienen

Tener + que + infinitive is used to talk about what someone has to do.

Present Tense of -ar Verbs

To form the present tense of a regular verb that ends in **-ar,** drop the **-ar** and add the appropriate **ending.**

hablar *to talk, to speak*			
yo	**habl**o	nosotros(as)	**habl**amos
tú	**habl**as	vosotros(as)	**habl**áis
usted, él, ella	**habl**a	ustedes, ellos(as)	**habl**an

Repaso de la lección

@ HOMETUTOR
my.hrw.com

¡LLEGADA!

Now you can
- talk about daily schedules
- ask and tell time
- say what you have and have to do
- say what you do and how often you do things

Using
- the verb **tener** and **tener que**
- expressions of frequency
- present tense of **-ar** verbs

To review
- the verb **tener** and **tener que** p. 91
- expressions of frequency p. 93
- present tense of **-ar** verbs p. 96

1 | Listen and understand

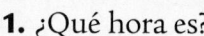
AUDIO

Escucha a Martín y a Lupe hablar de sus clases y empareja la información.
(Match according to what you hear Martín and Lupe say about their activities.)

1. ¿Qué hora es?
2. ¿A qué hora es la clase de historia?
3. ¿En qué clase tiene que sacar una buena nota Martín?
4. ¿En qué clases contestan muchas preguntas?
5. ¿Cómo es la maestra de ciencias?
6. ¿En qué clase usan la computadora?

a. joven
b. en la clase de ciencias
c. Son las diez y cuarto.
d. Es a las diez y media.
e. en las clases de inglés y ciencias
f. en la clase de historia

To review
- the verb **tener** and **tener que** p. 91

2 | Say what you have and have to do

Indica qué clases tienen Beto y sus amigos a estas horas y qué tienen que hacer. *(Tell what classes Beto and his friends have at these times and what they have to do.)*

 **8:00** modelo: Adela: arte / dibujar
Adela tiene la clase de arte a las ocho.
Tiene que dibujar.

1. **9:15** yo: historia / tomar muchos apuntes
2. **10:30** ustedes: matemáticas / estudiar los problemas
3. **11:45** tú: español / hablar español
4. **1:20** David y yo: inglés / contestar muchas preguntas
5. **2:15** Lilia: ciencias / usar la computadora
6. **3:30** Eva y Víctor: música / tocar la guitarra

To review
• present tense **-ar** verbs p. 96

3 | Talk about daily schedules

Lee la información sobre Pati León. Complétala con la forma correcta de los verbos entre paréntesis. *(Read the information about Pati León. Then complete the information with the correct form of the verbs in parentheses.)*

Mi horario es muy bueno. Yo __1.__ (trabajar) mucho los lunes, martes y miércoles. Los jueves Gustavo y yo __2.__ (andar) en patineta. Los viernes Gustavo __3.__ (descansar), pero yo __4.__ (montar) en bicicleta con Eloísa y Héctor. Ellos __5.__ (practicar) deportes casi todos los días. Los viernes nosotros __6.__ (comprar) una pizza y __7.__ (mirar) la televisión. ¿Y los sábados y domingos? Muchas veces mis amigos y yo __8.__ (pasear). ¿Y tú? ¿También __9.__ (pasar) un rato con los amigos los sábados y domingos?

To review
• expressions of frequency p. 93
• present tense of **-ar** verbs p. 96

4 | Say what you do and how often you do things

Escribe oraciones para decir con qué frecuencia estas personas hacen las siguientes actividades. *(Tell how often these people do the following activities.)*

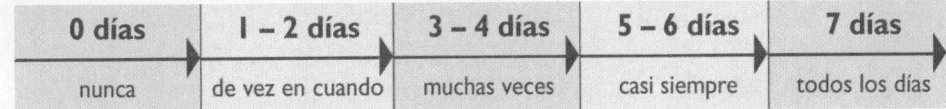

0 días	1 – 2 días	3 – 4 días	5 – 6 días	7 días
nunca	de vez en cuando	muchas veces	casi siempre	todos los días

modelo: nosotros / mirar un DVD (2 días)
Miramos un DVD de vez en cuando.

1. Roberta / contestar preguntas (0 días)
2. tú / hablar español (5 días)
3. Nicolás / practicar deportes (6 días)
4. yo / escuchar música (3 días)
5. Carlos y Pilar / estudiar historia (2 días)
6. nosotros / tocar la guitarra (4 días)
7. los maestros / usar la computadora (7 días)

To review
• Chichén Itzá p. 83
• Comparación cultural pp. 84, 92, 97

5 | Mexico and the Dominican Republic

Comparación cultural

Answer these culture questions.

1. What is Chichén Itzá and what can you find there?
2. What are **zócalos**?
3. What do many students in Mexico and the Dominican Republic wear to school?
4. Who are three famous Mexican muralists?

Get Help Online
my.hrw.com

Más práctica Cuaderno *pp. 61–72* Cuaderno para hispanohablantes *pp. 63–72*

México

LECCIÓN 2

Tema:

En la escuela

¡AVANZA! **In this lesson you will learn to**
- describe classes and classroom objects
- say where things are located
- say where you are going
- talk about how you feel

using
- the verb **estar**
- the conjugated verb before the subject to ask a question
- the verb **ir**

♻ **¿Recuerdas?**
- class subjects
- telling time

Comparación cultural

In this lesson you will learn about
- museums of anthropology and artist Frida Kahlo
- schools in Mexico, the Dominican Republic, and Paraguay
- Huichol yarn painting and Taino rock art

Compara con tu mundo
School years vary from country to country. Mexican students go to school from the end of August until June, with short breaks in December and April. *How is this different or similar to your school year?*

¿Qué ves?

Mira la foto

¿Hay una escuela en la foto?

¿Pablo dibuja o escucha música?

¿Qué practican las chicas?

MODES OF COMMUNICATION

INTERPRETIVE	INTERPERSONAL	PRESENTATIONAL
Listen to interviews with teachers.	Talk to a school counselor about your classes and after-school activities.	Give a guided tour of your school to new students.
Read students' descriptions of what they do during and after school in Spanish-speaking countries.	Answer a post card from a pen-pal by describing your classes.	Write an article about your typical school day.

El patio de una escuela secundaria
México

Presentación de VOCABULARIO

Goal: Learn about Pablo and Claudia's school and how they spend their day. Then practice what you have learned to talk about your school day. *Actividades 1–3*

VIDEO
DVD

AUDIO

A La clase de historia no es **aburrida** porque la maestra es **interesante.** La clase es **divertida** pero es difícil. **Cuando** una clase no es fácil, tengo que trabajar mucho. Necesito sacar buenas notas.

el pizarrón
la tiza
el borrador
la silla
la ventana
el reloj
el mapa
el escritorio

B En la escuela siempre tengo mi **mochila.**

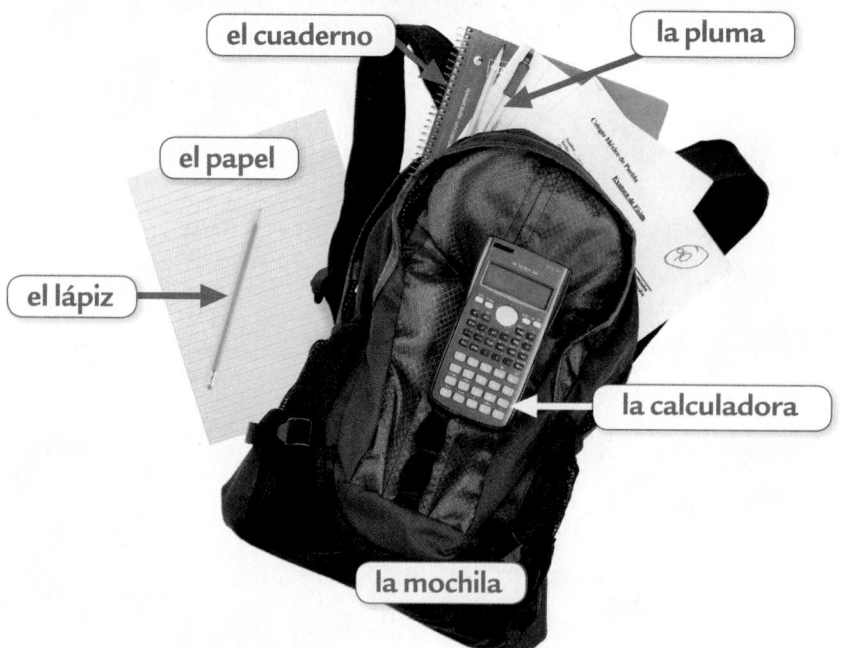

el cuaderno
el papel
el lápiz
la pluma
la calculadora
la mochila

En México se dice...

In Mexico the word for *chalk* is **el gis.**

Más vocabulario

¿(A)dónde? *(To) Where?*
¿Cuándo? *When?*
deprimido(a) *depressed*
emocionado(a) *excited*
ocupado(a) *busy*
el problema *problem*
la puerta *door*
Expansión de vocabulario p. R3

C Mi escuela es grande. Hay **una cafetería, un gimnasio** y **una biblioteca**.

la cafetería

el gimnasio

la biblioteca

el pasillo

los baños

la oficina del director

D Me gusta pasar un rato con Claudia en la biblioteca.
Claudia usa la computadora pero yo tengo que estudiar.

cansado(a)

nervioso(a)

contento(a)

tranquilo(a)

enojado(a)

triste

@HOMETUTOR   Interactive
my.hrw.com   Flashcards

¡A responder!   Escuchar

Escucha la lista de adjetivos. Dibuja una cara para cada uno. *(Listen to the list of adjectives and draw a face representing each one.)*

✤ Práctica de VOCABULARIO

1 | Para la escuela

Hablar
Escribir

¿Qué tienen en la Tienda Martínez? Nombra las cosas. *(Name the items at Tienda Martínez.)*

PARA LA ESCUELA...

5 por **30** pesos

25O pesos

3 pesos

2 por **80** pesos

300 pesos

5 por **IO** pesos

Tenemos todo para tus clases en **TIENDA MARTÍNEZ**
Avenida Hermanos Soriano 80, Puebla, México

2 | ¿Qué lugar es?

Leer
Escribir

Claudia habla de varios lugares en la escuela. Completa las oraciones con la palabra apropiada. *(Complete the sentences with the appropriate place word.)*

biblioteca	cafetería
gimnasio	baños
oficina del director	clase

En el gimnasio hay dos **1.** , uno para chicas y uno para chicos. Tenemos que correr y practicar deportes en el **2.** . Hay muchos libros en la **3.** . Nos gusta comer pizza y pasar un rato con los amigos en la **4.** . Hablamos con el director en la **5.** . Hay escritorios y pizarrones en la **6.** .

3 | ¿Cuántos hay en la clase?

Hablar

Habla con otro(a) estudiante sobre lo que hay en la clase. *(Talk with another student about objects in the classroom.)*

modelo: mapa

pizarrón	puerta	tiza
mapa	escritorio	¿ ?
ventana	reloj	

A ¿Cuántos mapas hay en la clase?

B Hay tres mapas en la clase.

Expansión
Tell what objects aren't in your room.

Más práctica   Cuaderno *pp. 73–75*   Cuaderno para hispanohablantes *pp. 73–76*

🌐 Get Help Online
my.hrw.com

PARA Y PIENSA

Did you get it?
1. Name three rooms in your school.
2. Name three objects you could find in your classroom.

VOCABULARIO en contexto

¡AVANZA! **Goal:** Identify the words Pablo and Claudia use to talk about what they do after school. Then use the words you have learned to describe classes and classroom objects. *Actividades 4–5*

♻ *¿Recuerdas?* Class subjects p. 86

Telehistoria escena 1

@HOMETUTOR my.hrw.com **View, Read and Record**

STRATEGIES

Cuando lees
Look for exclamations Many sentences below are exclamations. Exclamations reveal emphasis, warning, or emotions. How many exclamation-type sentences can you find? Why is each one used?

Cuando escuchas
Listen for emotions What different emotions do Claudia and Pablo show? How do they express them? How would you feel in their place?

VIDEO DVD

AUDIO

Maestro
Pablo
Claudia

A poster announces Trini Salgado's guest appearance in the school gym.

Maestro: Trini Salgado, ¿eh? ¿Y vas tú al gimnasio?

Pablo: ¡Sí!

Maestro: ¡Muy divertido! *(later on in science class...)* ¿Quién contesta la pregunta? ¿Pablo? Bueno, ¡al pizarrón!

Pablo tries, but gets the problem wrong. Claudia goes to the board and corrects it. The bell rings and they leave class together.

Claudia: Pablo, ¿vamos a la biblioteca? Estudiamos, hacemos la tarea y llegamos bien al gimnasio... ¡Trini Salgado, Pablo!

Pablo: ¡Sí! Necesito estudiar, ¡y tú enseñas muy bien! ¿Y tu mochila? *(He points to her backpack, which she has left in the classroom.)*

Claudia: ¡Gracias, Pablo!

Continuará... p. 118

También se dice

México The teacher uses the word **pizarrón** to call Pablo to the board. In other Spanish-speaking countries you might hear:
• **muchos países** la pizarra

Lección 2
ciento trece **113**

4 | Comprensión del episodio   En clase

Describe lo que pasa en el episodio. Empareja frases de cada columna.
(Describe what happens in the episode by matching phrases from each column.)

1. Pablo no contesta la pregunta
2. Después de Pablo, Claudia contesta
3. Pablo y Claudia necesitan ir
4. Pablo necesita
5. Claudia no tiene
6. Claudia enseña

a. la pregunta en el pizarrón.
b. la mochila.
c. estudiar con Claudia.
d. a la biblioteca y al gimnasio.
e. porque el problema es difícil.
f. muy bien.

5 | ¿Cómo son las clases?   ¿Recuerdas? Class subjects p. 86

Hablar

Describe las clases a otro(a) estudiante. *(Describe your classes to another student.)*

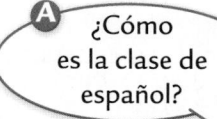 **A** ¿Cómo es la clase de español?

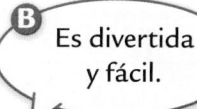 **B** Es divertida y fácil.

1.

2.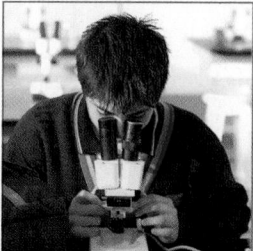

3.

4.

5.

6.

Expansión
Present your answers to the class and give reasons for your descriptions.

Get Help Online
my.hrw.com

 **PARA Y PIENSA**

Did you get it? Tell where Pablo and Claudia are going by writing **la biblioteca** or **el gimnasio.**
1. Pablo y Claudia tienen que estudiar.
2. Pablo necesita practicar fútbol.
3. Ellos necesitan un libro.

Presentación de GRAMÁTICA

Goal: Learn to use the verb **estar** to talk about location and condition. Then practice using **estar** to say and ask where things are located and how people feel. *Actividades 6–9*

English Grammar Connection: There are two ways to say the English verb *to be* in Spanish: **ser** and **estar.** You already learned **ser** (see p. 37).

The Verb estar

ANIMATEDGRAMMAR
my.hrw.com

Use **estar** to indicate location and say how people feel.

Here's how:

estar	*to be*		
yo	**estoy**	nosotros(as)	**estamos**
tú	**estás**	vosotros(as)	**estáis**
usted, él, ella	**está**	ustedes, ellos(as)	**están**

Pedro **está** en la cafetería.   *Pedro **is** in the cafeteria.*

Use **estar** with the following words of location.

al lado (de)	**debajo (de)**	**dentro (de)**	**encima (de)**
cerca (de)	**delante (de)**	**detrás (de)**	**lejos (de)**

Use the word **de** after the location word when a specific location is mentioned. When **de** is followed by the word **el,** they combine to form the contraction **del.**

La biblioteca **está al lado** de la cafetería.   La tiza **está encima del** borrador.
*The library **is next to the** cafeteria.*   *The chalk **is on top of the** eraser.*

Estar is also used with **adjectives** to say how someone feels at a given moment.

El maestro **está tranquilo.**   Las chicas **están cansadas.**
*The teacher **is** calm.*   *The girls **are** tired.*

♻ ***¿Recuerdas?*** Adjectives agree in gender and number with the nouns they describe (see p. 66).

Más práctica
Cuaderno *pp. 76–78*
Cuaderno para hispanohablantes *pp. 77–79*

@HOMETUTOR my.hrw.com
Leveled Practice
🌐 Conjuguemos.com

✥ Práctica de GRAMÁTICA

6 | ¿Dónde están?

Hablar
Escribir

Di dónde están las personas según Pablo. (*Tell where people are, according to Pablo.*)

modelo: el señor Díaz
El señor Díaz está en la oficina.

1. ustedes

2. yo

3. Miguel y Alejo

4. Sergio

5. Claudia y yo

6. Cristina y Sarita

Expansión
Choose two places and name something you would find in each.

7 | Las salas del museo

Hablar

Comparación cultural

El museo de antropología

What do ancient artifacts teach us about a culture? The National Museum of Anthropology in Mexico City contains artifacts from **Mexico's** many indigenous cultures. A main attraction is the *Piedra del Sol*, or Sun Stone, an Aztec calendar that weighs almost 25 tons. In **Paraguay,** the Andrés Barbero Museum of Ethnography in Asunción contains tools, musical instruments, and artwork from its indigenous cultures.

Compara con tu mundo *What items might people find 1,000 years from now that give clues about life in the 21st century?*

Piedra del Sol

1. Sala Mexica (Azteca)
2. el patio central
3. la oficina
4. Sala Norte de México
5. Sala Maya
6. Sala Oaxaca
7. Sala Tolteca
8. Sala Teotihuacán
9. Sala Preclásico
10. Sala de Introducción a la Antropología
11. el auditorio

El Museo Nacional de Antropología

Un plano de El Museo Nacional de Antropología en la Ciudad de México

Usa el plano para decirle a otro(a) estudiante dónde están las salas del museo. (*Tell your partner where the rooms are located in the museum.*)

A ¿Dónde está la Sala Tolteca?

B La Sala Tolteca está al lado de la Sala Teotihuacán.

You already know that you can use rising intonation to ask a yes/no question.
You can also switch the position of the **verb** and the **subject** to form a question.

María tiene una patineta.   ¿**Tiene María** una patineta?
María has a skateboard.   *Does María have a skateboard?*

8 | Las emociones

Hablar

Habla con otro(a) estudiante de cómo están estas personas. *(Talk with another student about how these people are feeling.)*

modelo: el maestro / nervioso
el maestro ☺

A ¿Está nervioso el maestro?

B No, está tranquilo.

Estudiante A

1. Pablo / tranquilo
2. Claudia / triste
3. los maestros / cansado
4. los amigos / enojado
5. las amigas / emocionado
6. tú / ocupado

Estudiante B

Pablo 😆
Claudia 🙁
los maestros 😴
los amigos 😠
las amigas 🙁
yo ¿ ?

9 | ¿Qué es?

Hablar

Dale pistas a otro(a) estudiante sobre un objeto del dibujo. Él o ella tiene que adivinar el objeto. *(Give clues to another student. He or she has to guess the object.)*

A Está encima del cuaderno. Está al lado del libro.

B Es la calculadora.

Expansión
Give clues to your partner about objects that are in your classroom.

Más práctica   Cuaderno *pp. 76–78*   Cuaderno para hispanohablantes *pp. 77–79*

🌐 **Get Help Online**
my.hrw.com

PARA Y PIENSA

Did you get it?   1. Tell someone that you are near the windows.
2. Ask Pablo if he is nervous.

✿GRAMÁTICA en contexto

¡AVANZA! **Goal:** Listen to how Pablo and Claudia use **estar** to talk about how Pablo feels. Then practice using **estar** to talk about emotions and locations.
Actividades 10–12

Telehistoria escena 2

@HOMETUTOR View, Read
my.hrw.com and Record

STRATEGIES

Cuando lees
Read for motives behind actions
This scene contains a physical action related to Pablo's complaints. What is the action, and what are his complaints? Are his complaints justified?

Cuando escuchas
Listen for feelings What feelings are mentioned in this scene? How does Pablo explain how he feels? Have you ever felt this way?

VIDEO
DVD

AUDIO

Claudia: Eh, Pablo, ¿qué pasa? ¿Estás deprimido? ¿Estás enojado?

Pablo: No, no estoy enojado... Estoy nervioso... Tengo que estar en el gimnasio a las cinco pero tengo que hacer la tarea.

Pablo leaves the library. Later Claudia joins him outside.

Pablo: Ay, Claudia, nunca descanso... Me gusta pasar un rato con los amigos... Y ¡esta mochila!

Claudia: ¿Qué pasa?

Pablo starts swinging his backpack back and forth.

Pablo: Aquí tengo libros, cuadernos, plumas, calculadoras... ¡estoy cansado!

Suddenly Pablo lets go of his backpack.

Pablo: ¡Ay! ¿Dónde está mi mochila?

Claudia: ¡Pablo, tu mochila!

She points to his backpack, which is caught in a basketball hoop.

Continuará... p. 123

También se dice

México To say he has pens in his backpack, Pablo uses the word **plumas.** In other Spanish-speaking countries you might hear:
• **muchos países**
 el bolígrafo, el boli

10 | Comprensión del episodio   El problema de Pablo

Lee las oraciones y decide si son ciertas o falsas. Si son falsas, corrígelas.
(Decide if these sentences are true or false. Correct the false statements.)

1. Claudia y Pablo están en la oficina.
2. Pablo está nervioso porque tiene que jugar al fútbol.
3. Claudia tiene que estar en el gimnasio a las cinco.
4. Pablo está enojado.
5. A Claudia y a Pablo les gusta pasar un rato con los amigos.
6. Pablo está deprimido porque tiene libros, cuadernos, plumas y calculadoras en la mochila.

11 | ¿Cuándo?

Hablar

Pregúntale a otro(a) estudiante cuándo tiene estas emociones. *(Ask another student when he or she feels these emotions.)*

A ¿Cuándo estás triste?

B Estoy triste cuando saco una mala nota.

Estudiante A
1.
2.
3.
4.
5.
6.

Estudiante B
sacar una buena / mala nota
escuchar música
practicar deportes
trabajar
estudiar
¿ ?

12 | ¡A jugar! ¿Dónde estoy?

Hablar

Estás en varios lugares de la escuela. Da pistas y los otros estudiantes van a adivinar dónde estás. *(You are in various parts of the school. Give clues for other students to guess where you are.)*

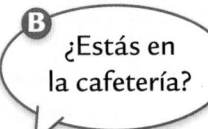

A Compro papas fritas y jugo. Paso un rato con los amigos. Estoy tranquilo.

B ¿Estás en la cafetería?

Expansión
Describe where these places are located.

Get Help Online
my.hrw.com

PARA Y PIENSA

Did you get it?   Give three sentences about Pablo and Claudia using the verb **estar.** Use one of the following words in each sentence:
la biblioteca, nervioso(a), el gimnasio.

✦ Presentación de GRAMÁTICA

> **¡AVANZA!** **Goal:** Learn how to form the verb **ir** in order to say where you and others are going. Then practice using **ir** to say where you go during and after school. *Actividades 13–16*

English Grammar Connection: Remember that **conjugating** is changing the forms of a verb to indicate who is doing the action (see p. 91). In English, *to go* is conjugated as *I go, you go, he/she/it goes, we go, they go.*

Pablo **goes** to the cafeteria at twelve.   Pablo **va** a la cafetería a las doce.

↑ **conjugated verb**   ↑ **conjugated verb**

The Verb ir

ANIMATED GRAMMAR
my.hrw.com

Use **ir** to talk about where someone is going.
How do you form the present tense of this verb?

Here's how:

ir *to go*			
yo	voy	nosotros(as)	vamos
tú	vas	vosotros(as)	vais
usted, él, ella	va	ustedes, ellos(as)	van

Use **ir** with the word **a** to say that someone is going to a specific place.
When **a** is followed by the word **el**, they combine to form the contraction **al**.

Voy a la biblioteca.   Los estudiantes **van al** gimnasio.
I'm going to the library.   *The students are going to the gym.*

To ask where someone is going, use **¿adónde**...?

¿Adónde vas?
Where are you going?

Más práctica
Cuaderno *pp. 79–81*
Cuaderno para hispanohablantes *pp. 80–83*

@HOMETUTOR my.hrw.com
Leveled Practice
Conjuguemos.com

✵ Práctica de GRAMÁTICA

13 | ¿Un estudiante serio?

Leer
Escribir

Claudia y Pablo hablan en la escuela. Completa la conversación con formas de **ir.** *(Complete the conversation, using forms of* **ir.***)*

Claudia: ¡Tengo mucha tarea en la clase de inglés! Yo __1.__ a la biblioteca… ¿ __2.__ tú y yo?

Pablo: No, yo no __3.__ a la biblioteca hoy.

Claudia: ¿No __4.__ tú a la biblioteca? ¡Tienes que hacer la tarea!

Pablo: Sí, pero necesito comprar pizza y un refresco. Mis amigos y yo __5.__ a la cafetería. Después yo __6.__ al gimnasio y ellos __7.__ a la clase de matemáticas.

Claudia: ¿ __8.__ Carlos al gimnasio?

Pablo: No, él __9.__ a la biblioteca.

Claudia: ¡Ay, Pablo! Tú también necesitas ir. ¿ __10.__ tú y Carlos mañana?

Pablo: Sí, todos nosotros __11.__ mañana.

14 | ¿Adónde van?

Escuchar
Escribir

¿Adónde van Pablo y las otras personas? Escucha la descripción y escribe oraciones para decir adónde van estas personas. *(Listen to the description and write sentences to tell where these people are going.)*

la cafetería	la clase de inglés
el gimnasio	la clase de matemáticas
la biblioteca	la oficina de la directora

1. Pablo   **3.** Martín y Sara   **5.** María y Claudia

2. Claudia   **4.** la maestra de inglés   **6.** el señor Treviño

---

✵ Pronunciación ✵   La letra d

AUDIO

In Spanish, the letter **d** has two sounds. At the beginning of a sentence, after a pause, or after the letters **l** or **n,** the **d** sounds like the English *d* in *door*. In all other cases, the **d** sounds like the *th* of the word *the*.

Listen and repeat, paying close attention to the two sounds of **d.**

comi**d**a	**d**iverti**d**o	¿**D**ónde está **D**avi**d**?
a**d**iós	fal**d**a	**D**aniel está al la**d**o **d**e la puerta.
la**d**o	gran**d**e	¿A**d**ónde vas con mi cua**d**erno?

15 | ¿Cuándo vas a...?

Hablar

Pregúntale a otro(a) estudiante cuándo va a estos lugares. *(Ask a partner when he or she goes to these places.)*

A ¿Cuándo vas a la oficina?

B Voy a la oficina cuando tengo problemas.

modelo: la oficina

Estudiante A

1. el gimnasio
2. la oficina
3. la escuela
4. la biblioteca
5. la cafetería
6. la clase de...

Estudiante B
tengo (que)
necesito
hay
¿ ?

Expansión
Tell the class when your partner goes to the places in the activity.

16 | ¿Y tú?

Hablar Escribir

Contesta las preguntas. *(Answer the questions.)*

1. ¿A qué hora vas a la escuela?
2. ¿Cuándo van tú y tus amigos(as) a la cafetería?
3. ¿Adónde vas después de la clase de español?
4. ¿Vas mucho a la oficina del (de la) director(a)?
5. ¿Adónde vas cuando tienes que estudiar?
6. ¿Qué hay dentro de tu mochila?

Comparación cultural

El autorretrato

What does a self-portrait reveal about an artist?
Mexican artist Frida Kahlo painted many self-portraits, including *Autorretrato con collar*. She was influenced by the indigenous cultures of **Mexico** in both her style of painting and style of clothing. She often wore traditional native clothing, as depicted in the photograph. How do you think she depicted herself in her self-portraits?

Compara con tu mundo *What would you include in a portrait of yourself and why?*

Una fotografía de Frida Kahlo

Más práctica Cuaderno *pp. 79–81* Cuaderno para hispanohablantes *pp. 80–83*

Get Help Online
my.hrw.com

PARA Y PIENSA

Did you get it? Tell where the following people are going.

1. Teresa / la cafetería
2. los estudiantes / la oficina del director
3. nosotros / el gimnasio
4. yo / la clase de matemáticas

✺ Todo junto

¡AVANZA!

Goal: *Show what you know* Notice how Pablo and Claudia use **ir** to talk about where they are going, and **estar** to say where things are. Then use **ir** and **estar** to talk about your own schedule. *Actividades 17–21*

♻ *¿Recuerdas?* Telling time p. 90

Telehistoria completa

@HOMETUTOR View, Read
my.hrw.com and Record

STRATEGIES

Cuando lees
Read for locations This scene mentions specific places people are going. What are those places? Alicia's T-shirt is now located in a specific place. Where is it?

Cuando escuchas
Notice the problems In this scene, Pablo's problems go from bad to worse. What are the problems? How does he react?

Escena 1 *Resumen*
Pablo no contesta la pregunta en la clase de ciencias porque el problema es difícil. Claudia contesta la pregunta.

Escena 2 *Resumen*
Pablo no está contento porque tiene mucho que hacer y no tiene la mochila con la camiseta de Alicia.

VIDEO
DVD

AUDIO

Escena 3

Roberto   Pablo   Claudia

Roberto approaches, holding a poster.

Roberto: ¿Qué pasa?

Claudia: Vamos al gimnasio. Bueno, Pablo va al gimnasio, yo voy a la cafetería...

Pablo: ¡Necesito ir al gimnasio a las cinco, y son las cinco menos cuarto!

Claudia: ¡Y necesita la mochila! Dentro está la camiseta de Alicia.

Pablo: A las cinco Trini Salgado va al gimnasio, y yo...

Roberto: No, no. ¡A las cuatro!

Pablo: No... ¡A las cinco!

Roberto: Mira... a las cuatro.

He shows his autographed poster to Pablo. It says four o'clock.

Pablo: *(dejectedly)* No...

17 | Comprensión de los episodios   ¡A organizar!

Escuchar
Leer

Pon las oraciones en orden para describir los episodios. *(Put the events in order to describe the episodes.)*

1. La camiseta está en la mochila y Pablo no tiene la mochila.

2. Pablo y Claudia hablan con Roberto.

3. Claudia y Pablo van a la biblioteca y estudian.

4. Pablo está nervioso; tiene que ir al gimnasio a las cinco.

5. Pablo va a la clase de ciencias y no contesta la pregunta.

18 | Comprensión de los episodios   ¡A describir!

Escuchar
Leer

Describe lo que pasa en estas fotos. Incluye dónde están y cómo están las personas en las fotos. *(Describe what is happening in the photos.)*

modelo: Pablo está en la clase de ciencias. Va al pizarrón porque tiene que contestar una pregunta. Está nervioso.

1. 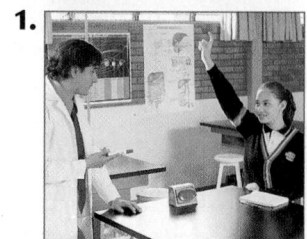   **2.**    **3.**

19 | ¿Adónde vamos?

♻ **¿Recuerdas?**
Telling time p. 90

Digital performance space

Hablar

> **STRATEGY Hablar**
>
> **Make it lively** Keep the discussion interesting! Add as many details about your classes as possible. Don't just talk about your classes; include other places in your school.

Habla con otros(as) estudiantes sobre adónde van y a qué hora. *(Talk with other students about schedules.)*

A ¿A qué hora van ustedes a la cafetería?

B Voy a la cafetería a las doce y media.

C Voy a la cafetería a la una.

Expansión
Write a summary of the classes that you have in common with other members of your group.

20 | Integración

Leer
Escuchar
Hablar

Raquel y Mario necesitan estudiar en la biblioteca. Lee la agenda de Raquel y escucha el mensaje de Mario. Luego indica cuándo van a la biblioteca y explica por qué no estudian a las otras horas mencionadas. *(Tell when Raquel and Mario will go to the library to study. Explain why they won't go at the other times mentioned.)*

Fuente 1 Agenda personal

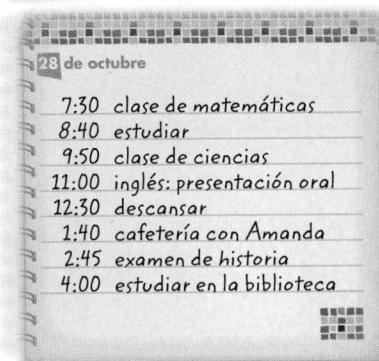

28 de octubre

7:30 clase de matemáticas
8:40 estudiar
9:50 clase de ciencias
11:00 inglés: presentación oral
12:30 descansar
1:40 cafetería con Amanda
2:45 examen de historia
4:00 estudiar en la biblioteca

Fuente 2 Un mensaje por teléfono

Listen and take notes
• Escribe qué hace Mario y a qué hora.

modelo: Ellos van a la biblioteca a las... No estudian a las siete y media porque...

21 | El periódico escolar

Escribir

Tú tienes que escribir un artículo para el periódico escolar sobre tu día típico en la escuela. Explica a qué clases vas, cómo son y qué usas en cada clase.
(Write an article for the school paper about your typical school day.)

modelo: Yo siempre estoy muy ocupado. A las siete y media voy a la clase de matemáticas. La clase es muy divertida. Usamos calculadoras, pero no es fácil. A las ocho y cuarto...

Writing Criteria	Excellent	Good	Needs Work
Content	Your article includes a lot of information.	Your article includes some information.	Your article includes little information.
Communication	Most of your article is organized and easy to follow.	Parts of your article are organized and easy to follow.	Your article is disorganized and hard to follow.
Accuracy	Your article has few mistakes in grammar and vocabulary.	Your article has some mistakes in grammar and vocabulary.	Your article has many mistakes in grammar and vocabulary.

Expansión
Interview your teacher and write about a typical day for him or her.

Más práctica   Cuaderno *pp. 82–83*   Cuaderno para hispanohablantes *pp. 84–85*

Get Help Online
my.hrw.com

PARA Y PIENSA

Did you get it?   Complete each sentence with the correct forms of **estar** and **ir + a.**

1. A la una Pablo ___ en la clase de arte, pero a las dos ___ la cafetería.
2. ¿Dónde ___ Roberto y Claudia? Ellos ___ la cafetería.
3. Claudia ___ nerviosa porque ___ la oficina de la directora.

✦ Lectura cultural

¡AVANZA! **Goal:** Read the excerpts from the essays of two students from Mexico and the Dominican Republic. Then compare the descriptions of their favorite classes and talk about your favorite class.

Comparación cultural

AUDIO

Mi clase favorita

STRATEGY Leer

Use the title The title *Mi clase favorita* helps you anticipate the contents of the reading. Write down the things that you would expect to find, then search for them.

Expected contents	Actual contents
El (La) maestro(a)...	
La clase...	
Más información:	

Below are compositions by two finalists who entered the essay contest called "Mi clase favorita."

Tomás Gutiérrez Moreno
Colegio de la Providencia
Guadalajara, México

 Mi nombre es Tomás Gutiérrez Moreno. Soy de Guadalajara, México. Estudio en el Colegio de la Providencia.

 La historia es muy interesante; es mi clase favorita. Me gusta mucho estudiar el pasado 1 de México. Soy estudioso y siempre saco buenas notas en la clase.

 En la universidad deseo 2 estudiar historia. Deseo ser maestro y enseñar historia mexicana en Guadalajara.

---
1 past   2 I wish to

Mural en la Biblioteca Central de la Universidad Nacional Autónoma de México en la Ciudad de México

México

María González
Colegio San Esteban
San Pedro de Macorís, República Dominicana

Me llamo María González. Soy de la República Dominicana. Estudio en el Colegio San Esteban.

Tengo dos clases favoritas: el inglés y el español. Deseo estudiar idiomas[3] en Santo Domingo, la capital, y después, trabajar en mi país.

El turismo es muy importante para[4] la economía de la República Dominicana. Deseo trabajar en un hotel, en las famosas playas[5] de Punta Cana o de Puerto Plata.

---

[3] languages   [4] for   [5] beaches

PARA Y PIENSA

¿Comprendiste?

1. ¿Dónde estudia Tomás?
2. ¿Cómo es Tomás?
3. ¿De dónde es María?
4. ¿Qué le gusta estudiar más a María?

¿Y tú?
¿Cuál es tu clase favorita? ¿Cómo es?

❖ Proyectos culturales

Arte de México y la República Dominicana

How does art reflect a culture's view of the natural world? Many cultures use art to capture the beauty and wonder of their natural surroundings. Two indigenous groups whose art can still be appreciated are the Huichol of **Mexico** and the Taino of the Greater Antilles (including what is now known as the **Dominican Republic**).

❖ Proyecto ① *Yarn Painting*

México Some Huichol still live in the isolated mountains of western Mexico. They make yarn paintings of birds, flowers, and other natural shapes. Make your own Huichol-style yarn painting.

Materials for yarn painting
Cardboard
2–3 colors yarn
Glue

Instructions
1. On a piece of cardboard, draw a pencil outline of the design you'd like to make.
2. Place one strand of yarn along the outline's length. Glue the yarn to the cardboard.
3. Fill in the design by laying yarn just inside the outline you made, coiling the yarn around until the figure is filled.
4. Section off the background and fill it in the same way.

❖ Proyecto ② *Rock Drawing*

República Dominicana The Taino lived in the islands of the Caribbean until the 16th century. Their rock art can still be seen in the caverns of the Dominican Republic. Try making your own rock art.

Materials for rock drawing
Rock
Pencil
Optional: Markers, pens, or chalk

Instructions
1. Begin by finding a smooth, oval rock about the size of your hand with an adequate surface for drawing.
2. Use a pencil to sketch the animal or design you'd like to make.
3. Then use a black felt tip pen to make it permanent. Add color by using colored felt tip pens or colored chalk.

❖ En tu comunidad

Visit an arts and crafts store or a museum in your community. Look for any items that have been influenced by Spanish-speaking cultures.

En resumen
Vocabulario y gramática

ANiMaTeDGRaMMaR
Interactive Flashcards
my.hrw.com

Vocabulario

Describe Classroom Objects

el borrador	eraser	el pizarrón (pl. los pizarrones)	board, chalkboard
la calculadora	calculator		
el cuaderno	notebook	la pluma	pen
el escritorio	desk	la puerta	door
el lápiz (pl. los lápices)	pencil	el reloj	clock; watch
		la silla	chair
el mapa	map	la tiza	chalk
la mochila	backpack	la ventana	window
el papel	paper		

Describe Classes

aburrido(a)	boring
divertido(a)	fun
interesante	interesting

Say Where Things Are Located

al lado (de)	next to	dentro (de)	inside (of)
cerca (de)	near (to)	detrás (de)	behind
debajo (de)	underneath, under	encima (de)	on top (of)
delante (de)	in front (of)	lejos (de)	far (from)

Places in School

el baño	bathroom
la biblioteca	library
la cafetería	cafeteria
el gimnasio	gymnasium
la oficina del (de la) director(a)	principal's office
el pasillo	hall

Talk About How You Feel

cansado(a)	tired	nervioso(a)	nervous
contento(a)	content, happy	ocupado(a)	busy
deprimido(a)	depressed	tranquilo(a)	calm
emocionado(a)	excited	triste	sad
enojado(a)	angry		

Other Words and Phrases

¿(A)dónde?	(To) Where?
¿Cuándo?	When?
cuando	when
el problema	problem

Gramática

Nota gramatical: Conjugated verb before the subject to ask a question *p. 117*

The Verb estar

Use **estar** to indicate location and say how people feel.

estar *to be*			
yo	estoy	nosotros(as)	estamos
tú	estás	vosotros(as)	estáis
usted, él, ella	está	ustedes, ellos(as)	están

The Verb ir

Use **ir** to talk about where someone is going.

ir *to go*			
yo	voy	nosotros(as)	vamos
tú	vas	vosotros(as)	vais
usted, él, ella	va	ustedes, ellos(as)	van

Practice Spanish with Holt McDougal Apps!

¡AvanzaRap!
DVD
Sing and Learn

Repaso de la lección

Lección 2

@HOMETUTOR
my.hrw.com

¡LLEGADA!

Now you can

- describe classes and classroom objects
- say where things are located
- say where you are going
- talk about how you feel

Using

- the verb **estar**
- the conjugated verb before the subject to ask a question
- the verb **ir**

To review

- the verb **estar** p. 115
- the conjugated verb before the subject to ask a question p. 117
- the verb **ir** p. 120

AUDIO

1 Listen and understand

Copia esta tabla en una hoja de papel. Escucha los mensajes de teléfono y completa la tabla. Usa la información para escribir oraciones. *(Copy the chart. Listen to the phone messages and complete the chart. Write sentences using the information.)*

La hora	¿Dónde está Ana?	¿Adónde va Ana?
modelo: 8:00	delante de la clase de arte	clase de español
10:15		
12:30		
2:45		
4:10		

modelo: A las ocho Ana está delante de la clase de arte.
Ella va de la clase de arte a la clase de español.

To review

- the verb **estar** p. 115
- the conjugated verb before the subject to ask a question p. 117

2 Talk about how you feel

Escribe preguntas para verificar cómo están todos. *(Write questions to find out how these people are feeling.)*

 modelo: Bárbara
¿Está emocionada Bárbara?

1. Jorge y Pilar

2. las maestras

3. la directora

4. usted

5. tú

6. ustedes

To review
• the verb **ir** p. 120

3 | Say where you are going

Lee el correo electrónico de Mario y complétalo con las formas correctas de **ir**. *(Read Mario's e-mail message and complete it with the correct forms of **ir**.)*

Hola, Luis. Yo __1.__ a la clase de ciencias en quince minutos. Es una clase interesante, pero es difícil. A las doce y media mis amigos y yo __2.__ a la cafetería. Después Inés __3.__ al gimnasio y Jerónimo __4.__ a la oficina del director. A las cinco ellos __5.__ a la biblioteca para estudiar. ¿Adónde __6.__ tú después de las clases?

To review
• the verb **estar** p. 115

4 | Say where things are located

Escribe oraciones para decir dónde están los borradores de la señora Romero. *(Write sentences telling where Mrs. Romero's students have put the erasers.)*

modelo: pizarrón (cerca / lejos)
Un borrador está cerca del pizarrón.

1. reloj (al lado / debajo)   **4.** ventana (delante / detrás)
2. silla (debajo / encima)   **5.** escritorio (encima / delante)
3. mochila (dentro / debajo)   **6.** maestra (lejos / detrás)

To review
• Comparación cultural pp. 108, 116, 122
• Lectura cultural pp. 126–127

5 | Mexico and the Dominican Republic

Comparación cultural

Answer these culture questions.

1. When do Mexican students attend school?
2. How did indigenous cultures influence Frida Kahlo?
3. What can you find in Mexico City's National Museum of Anthropology?
4. Why is tourism important in the Dominican Republic?

Más práctica   Cuaderno *pp. 84–95*   Cuaderno para hispanohablantes *pp. 86–95*

Get Help Online
my.hrw.com

México

Paraguay

República Dominicana

AUDIO

Horarios y clases

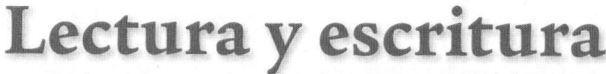

Lectura y escritura

1 **Leer** School subjects and daily schedules vary around the world. Read how Rafael, Andrea, and Juan Carlos spend a typical day at school.

2 **Escribir** Using the three descriptions as models, write a short paragraph about your daily schedule.

> **STRATEGY** **Escribir**
> **Create a schedule** Draw two large clocks, one for a.m. and the other for p.m. Write your school schedule on these clocks.

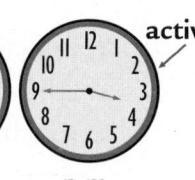

actividad

clase

a.m.   p.m.

Step 1 Complete the two clocks by listing your classes and after-school activities. Use arrows to point to the correct times.

Step 2 Write your paragraph. Make sure to include all the classes, activities, and times. Check your writing by yourself or with help from a friend. Make final corrections.

Compara con tu mundo

Use the paragraph you wrote to compare your school schedule to the schedule of *one* of the three students. What are the similarities in the schedules? What are the differences?

Cuaderno *pp. 96–98*   Cuaderno para hispanohablantes *pp. 96–98*

Paraguay — *Andrea*

¿Qué tal? Me llamo Andrea y estudio en Asunción, Paraguay. Mis clases son en la tarde, de la una a las cinco. En la escuela los estudiantes tienen muchas clases. Todos los días, tengo clases de español, ciencias, historia y matemáticas. También tengo clase de guaraní[1]. Después de las clases, voy al gimnasio y practico deportes. De vez en cuando uso la computadora en la biblioteca.

[1] an indigenous language spoken in Paraguay

República Dominicana — *Rafael*

¡Hola a todos! Me llamo Rafael y estudio en una escuela en Santo Domingo. Tengo clases todos los días de las ocho de la mañana a la una de la tarde. A las diez tenemos un descanso de quince minutos. Luego, voy a la clase de historia. Es interesante y yo tomo muchos apuntes. En la tarde muchas veces paso un rato con los amigos.

México — *Juan Carlos*

¡Hola! Soy Juan Carlos. Soy estudiante en México, D.F. En la escuela necesito trabajar mucho porque tengo nueve clases. Las clases son de las siete de la mañana a las dos de la tarde. ¡Tengo que llegar muy temprano! Mi clase favorita es la clase de matemáticas. Es interesante y divertida. Después de las clases mis amigos y yo estudiamos en la biblioteca.

Repaso inclusivo
♻ Options for Review

¡AvanzaRap!
DVD
Sing and Learn

Digital
performance space

1 | Listen, understand, and compare

Escuchar

Javier interviewed teachers and administrators at his school for Teacher Appreciation Day. Listen to his report and answer the questions.

1. ¿Qué enseña el señor Minondo?
2. ¿Qué deporte practica el señor Minondo?
3. ¿Quién es la señora Cruz?
4. ¿Qué le gusta hacer a la señora Cruz?
5. ¿Cómo son los maestros?

Are your teachers and administrators like those at Javier's school? What kind of activities do your teachers like to do after classes?

2 | Give a school orientation

Hablar

You are giving a talk at an orientation meeting for students who are new to your school. Greet the new students, introduce yourself, and give them some background information about yourself: what classes you have, what you like to do after school, etc. Then, describe your school, telling them where the gym, cafeteria, and other locations around the school are. Finish by describing some of the classes that are available and what they have to do in each class. Your talk should be at least two minutes long.

3 | Talk with a school counselor

Hablar

Role-play a conversation with a school counselor. The counselor wants to know what your classes are like and what you like to do after classes. Answer your partner's questions, tell him or her what you do in each class, and ask a few questions of your own about the school. Your conversation should be at least two minutes long.

4 | Write a brochure

Escribir

Create a brochure about your school that would be helpful to a new student from a Spanish-speaking country. Describe places in the school, classes offered, school supplies needed, teachers, and extracurricular activities. Your brochure should have illustrations and at least six sentences. Display your brochure in class or post it to a class website.

5 | Interview at a new school

Hablar

Role-play an interview in which you are seeking admission to a school in Mexico. Your partner is the interviewer at the school. The interviewer should ask you questions about your classes and activities. Answer his or her questions and ask a few of your own about the school. Remember to use appropriate register and expressions of courtesy. The interview should be at least two minutes long.

6 | Hold a press conference

Hablar
Escribir

Hold a mock press conference. You and your classmates are reporters and have to ask your teacher questions about his or her school schedule and favorite activities. Use the answers to write a short profile of your teacher that could appear in a Spanish edition of the school newspaper. The profile should have at least five sentences.

7 | Write a postcard

Leer
Escribir

You received the following postcard from your new pen pal in Mexico. Write back, answering all of your pen pal's questions and asking a few of your own. Your letter should have at least eight sentences.

PUEBLA

Hola. Me llamo Manuel Salazar. Soy de Puebla, México. Soy estudioso y atlético. Soy un estudiante organizado. Siempre saco buenas notas. ¿Cómo eres tú? ¿Cómo son tus clases? Tengo clases difíciles pero los maestros son muy simpáticos. Estudio mucho y también paso un rato con los amigos. Me gusta jugar al fútbol y andar en patineta. ¿Qué te gusta hacer con los amigos?

Tu amigo,

Manuel

Puerto Rico

❧❧

Comer en familia

Océano Atlántico

Lección 1
Tema: **Mi comida favorita**

Lección 2
Tema: **En mi familia**

Golfo de México

Cuba

Puerto Rico

México

Honduras

República Dominicana

Mar Caribe

Guatemala

Nicaragua

Costa Rica

El Salvador

Panamá

«**¡Hola!**

Somos Marisol y Rodrigo.
Somos de Puerto Rico.»

Venezuela

Colombia

Océano Atlántico

Arecibo   San Juan

Mayagüez   **Puerto Rico**   EL YUNQUE   Culebra

Humacao   Vieques

Ponce   Guayama

Mar Caribe

Población: 3.598.357

Área: 3.515 millas cuadradas

Capital: San Juan

Moneda: el dólar estadounidense

Idiomas: español, inglés (los dos son oficiales)

Comida típica: pasteles, arroz con gandules, pernil

Gente famosa: Julia de Burgos (poetisa), Roberto Clemente (beisbolista), Rosario Ferré (escritora), Luis Muñoz Marín (político)

Pasteles

CULTURA Interactiva
my.hrw.com *See these pages come alive!*

Una familia come en la playa

◄ Comidas al aire libre Many Puerto Ricans enjoy informal gatherings at a beach or park, where families can spend the day together, barbecue, and listen to music. **Pinchos** (skewers of chicken or pork) are popular at barbecues and snack stands. *Where do people like to eat outdoors where you live?*

Casas de colores vivos San Juan is famous for its well-preserved colonial quarter, called **Viejo San Juan.** Its narrow streets are lined with brightly-colored houses with balconies. *What are some historic areas close to where you live?* ▶

Casas coloniales en el Viejo San Juan

La Cascada de la Coca en El Yunque

◄ Un parque nacional El Yunque is the only tropical rain forest in the care of the U.S. Forest Service. The park has many waterfalls, such as the Cascada de la Coca, and is home to the **coquí,** a tiny tree frog named for its distinctive song. *What are some features of other parks in the United States?*

Puerto Rico

Tema:

Mi comida favorita

¡AVANZA! **In this lesson you will learn to**
- talk about foods and beverages
- ask questions
- say which foods you like and don't like

using
- interrogative words
- **gustar** with nouns
- present tense of **-er** and **-ir** verbs
- the verb **hacer**

♻ *¿Recuerdas?*
- **gustar** with an infinitive
- snack foods
- the verb **estar**
- telling time

Comparación cultural

In this lesson you will learn about
- traditional cooking
- historic landmarks in Puerto Rico
- grocery shopping in Puerto Rico

Compara con tu mundo

These teenagers are buying ice cream from a street vendor. Another popular cold treat in Puerto Rico is **la piragua,** a kind of shaved ice with fruit syrup. *What do you like to eat or drink during hot weather?*

¿Qué ves?

Mira la foto

¿Están contentos los chicos?

¿Están delante o detrás del señor?

¿Qué les gusta comer a los chicos?

MODES OF COMMUNICATION

INTERPRETIVE	INTERPERSONAL	PRESENTATIONAL
Understand what others say about food and beverages.	Talk about foods and beverages you prefer to eat.	Write a description of foods and beverages that you like or dislike.
Read a supermarket ad and shopping list and identify items.	Write a letter about what's good and bad at your school cafeteria.	Say what foods you like and where they sell them.

La Plaza de Colón
en el Viejo San Juan
San Juan, Puerto Rico

Presentación de VOCABULARIO

Goal: Learn about what Rodrigo and Marisol eat for breakfast, lunch, and dinner. Then practice what you have learned to talk about foods and beverages. *Actividades 1–2*

♻ *¿Recuerdas?* **gustar** with an infinitive p. 42

VIDEO
DVD

AUDIO

A ¡Hola! Me llamo Rodrigo y ella es Ana. Son las ocho de la mañana. **Es importante** comer **un desayuno nutritivo** todos los días.

el desayuno

los huevos

el pan

B Cuando **tengo hambre,** me gusta comer **huevos** y **pan.** Cuando **tengo sed,** bebo **jugo de naranja.** Me gusta mucho porque es **rico.** Nunca bebo **café** porque es **horrible.**

las bebidas

el jugo de naranja

la leche

el café

el cereal

el yogur

de fresa

En Puerto Rico se dice...

In Puerto Rico the word for *orange juice* is **el jugo de china.** The word for *banana* is **el guineo.**

Más vocabulario

¿Cómo? *How?*	¿Quién(es)? *Who?*
¿Cuál(es)? *Which?*	compartir *to share*
¿Por qué? *Why?*	otro(a) *other*
¿Qué? *What?*	*Expansión de vocabulario* p. R4

C Es la una y **ahora** Marisol y yo comemos **el almuerzo.** En la cafetería **venden** muchas **comidas:** sándwiches, hamburguesas y **sopa.** También venden **bebidas:** leche, jugos y refrescos.

el sándwich de jamón y queso

el almuerzo

la hamburguesa

la sopa

D Marisol y yo compramos fruta **para** mi papá: **manzanas, bananas** y **uvas. La cena** es a las siete y **tengo ganas de** comer. Siempre como mucho cuando mi mamá prepara la comida.

las uvas

la manzana

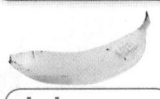

la banana

la cena

@**HOMETUTOR**
my.hrw.com
Interactive Flashcards

¡A responder! Escuchar

En un papel escribe **desayuno** y en otro escribe **almuerzo.** Escucha la lista de comida. Para cada comida, levanta el (los) papel(es) correcto(s) para indicar cuándo la comes. *(Write **desayuno** and **almuerzo** on separate pieces of paper. Then hold up the correct paper[s] based on the foods you hear.)*

Práctica de VOCABULARIO

1 | ¡A jugar! Busca, busca

Escribir

Busca y escribe las ocho comidas escondidas en este dibujo de una cafetería.

(Find and list the eight hidden foods.)

2 | ¿Qué te gusta más?

♻ **¿Recuerdas?** gustar with an infinitive p. 42

Hablar

Habla con otro(a) estudiante sobre qué te gusta comer o beber más.

(Tell what you like more.)

A ¿Te gusta más comer papas fritas o pizza?

B Me gusta más comer pizza.

1.

2.

3.

4.

5.

6.

Expansión
Tell what items you like to eat or drink at dinner.

Más práctica   Cuaderno *pp. 99–101*   Cuaderno para hispanohablantes *pp. 99–102*

🌐 **Get Help Online**
my.hrw.com

PARA Y PIENSA

Did you get it?
1. Name three breakfast foods.   2. Name three lunch foods.

Unidad 3 Puerto Rico
142 ciento cuarenta y dos

✾ VOCABULARIO en contexto

¡AVANZA! **Goal:** Identify the words Rodrigo and Marisol use to ask questions. Then practice these words to ask questions and give answers. *Actividades 3–4*

♻ *¿Recuerdas?* Snack foods p. 33

Telehistoria escena 1

@HOMETUTOR View, Read
my.hrw.com and Record

STRATEGIES

Cuando lees
List the question words As you read, list the words that indicate questions, such as **Qué** in **¿Qué amiga?** Save the list so that you can add more question words as you encounter them.

Cuando escuchas
Think about motives In this scene, Marisol asks questions repeatedly. Think of possible reasons why she does this. Which reason seems the most probable to you?

VIDEO
DVD

AUDIO

Marisol

Rodrigo

Rodrigo and Marisol walk to the grocery store. Rodrigo is counting his money.

Marisol: ¿A la escuela? ¿Por qué vas a la escuela hoy? Es sábado.

Rodrigo: Trini Salgado llega hoy y necesito un autógrafo en una camiseta. Es importante.

Marisol: ¿En una camiseta? ¿Qué camiseta?

Rodrigo: Tengo una amiga...

Marisol: *(teasing him)* ¿Una amiga? ¿Qué amiga? ¿Cómo se llama?

Rodrigo: Se llama Alicia.

Marisol: ¿De dónde es?

Rodrigo: Es de Miami. *(He loses count and starts over, sighing.)*

Marisol: ¿Cuándo tienes que estar en la escuela?

Rodrigo: A las cuatro de la tarde. *(Rodrigo loses count.)* ¡Y por favor! ¡No más preguntas! *(He starts to count again.)*

Marisol: Quince, veinte, cuarenta... **Continuará...** p. 148

También se dice

Puerto Rico Rodrigo uses the word **la camiseta** when he mentions Alicia's T-shirt. In other Spanish-speaking countries you might hear:
• **Argentina** la remera
• **Perú** el polo
• **Venezuela** la franela
• **México** la playera

3 | *Comprensión del episodio*   **Muchas preguntas**

Escuchar
Leer

Completa las preguntas con la palabra interrogativa apropiada y escoge la respuesta correcta según el episodio.
(Complete the questions with the appropriate question word and choose the correct answer.)

cómo   quién   qué
dónde   por qué

1. ¿ _____ necesita Rodrigo?

2. ¿ _____ se llama la amiga de Rodrigo?

3. ¿De _____ es Alicia?

4. ¿ _____ va a la escuela Rodrigo?

5. ¿ _____ es Trini Salgado?

a. Es de Miami.

b. porque Trini Salgado está allí

c. un autógrafo

d. Alicia

e. una atleta famosa

Expansión
Write two more questions and answers about the Telehistoria.

4 | **¿Cómo es?**   ♻ **¿Recuerdas?** Snack foods p. 33

Hablar

Habla con otro(a) estudiante para describir las siguientes comidas y bebidas en la cafetería. *(Describe the following foods and drinks in your school's cafeteria.)*

A ¿Cómo es la leche?

B La leche es buena.

Estudiante **A**

1.   2.   3.   4.

5.   6.   7.   8.

Estudiante **B**

nutritivo(a)
bueno(a)
malo(a)
horrible
rico(a)

🌐 **Get Help Online**
my.hrw.com

PARA Y PIENSA

Did you get it?   Choose the correct interrogative word.

1. ¿(Qué / Quiénes) son las amigas de Rodrigo?

2. ¿(Cuándo / Cuál) llega Trini Salgado?

3. ¿(Quién / Por qué) necesita Rodrigo el autógrafo?

Presentación de GRAMÁTICA

¡AVANZA! **Goal:** Learn how to use **gustar** with nouns. Then practice using this verb to express what foods you like and don't like. *Actividades 5–9*

English Grammar Connection: In English, the phrase *I like* doesn't change. In Spanish, there are two ways to say it, depending on whether what you like is singular or plural. This is because the Spanish phrase **me gusta** literally means that something *is pleasing to me*.

Gustar with Nouns

ANIMATEDGRAMMAR
my.hrw.com

 ¿Recuerdas? You have already learned to use gustar with infinitives to say what people like to do (see p. 42).

To talk about the things that people like, use **gustar** + **noun**.

Here's how:

If what is liked is singular, use the **singular** form gusta.

If what is liked is plural, use the **plural** form gustan.

Singular
me gusta **la sopa**
te gusta **la sopa**
le gusta **la sopa**
nos gusta **la sopa**
os gusta **la sopa**
les gusta **la sopa**

Plural
me gustan **los jugos**
te gustan **los jugos**
le gustan **los jugos**
nos gustan **los jugos**
os gustan **los jugos**
les gustan **los jugos**

matches singular noun

Me gusta **el cereal.**
I like cereal.

matches plural noun

Me gustan **las uvas.**
I like grapes.

Notice that the singular and plural forms of **gustar** match what is liked, not the person who likes it.

Más práctica
Cuaderno *pp. 102–104*
Cuaderno para hispanohablantes *pp. 103–105*

@HOMETUTOR my.hrw.com
Leveled Practice

Práctica de GRAMÁTICA

5 En el supermercado

Leer
Escribir

Indica lo que les gusta o no les gusta a estas personas en el supermercado, según la descripción. *(Indicate what these people like and don't like.)*

modelo: El yogur es horrible. (a Rodrigo)
A Rodrigo no le gusta el yogur.

1. Las uvas son ricas. (a ti)
2. La sopa es buena. (a Marisol)
3. El cereal es malo. (a nosotros)
4. Los huevos son horribles. (a mí)
5. El café es muy bueno. (a usted)
6. Los jugos son nutritivos. (a ellos)

Expansión
Say whether you like each of the items listed.

6 Las comidas favoritas

Hablar

Comparación cultural

Tostones

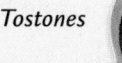

La cocina criolla

How do historical influences affect the food that people eat?
Traditional cooking in **Puerto Rico,** known as *la cocina criolla,* combines Spanish, African, and indigenous influences. *Tostones* (fried plantains) are a common side dish. Popular snack foods are *alcapurrias* (fried plantains stuffed with meat) and *bacalaítos* (codfish fritters). In **El Salvador,** traditional cuisine blends indigenous and Spanish influences. A typical food is the *pupusa,* a corn tortilla filled with beans, pork, and cheese. *Pupusas* are often served with *curtido,* a spicy coleslaw. *Semita,* a sweet bread layered with pineapple marmalade, is also popular.

Pupusas

Compara con tu mundo *Which of these dishes would you most like to try and why?*

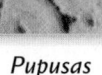

Usa la información para hablar sobre las comidas preferidas en Puerto Rico y El Salvador. *(Talk with a partner about food preferences in both countries.)*

A ¿A quiénes les gustan los tostones?

B A los chicos de Puerto Rico les gustan.

Pronunciación: Las letras r y rr

AUDIO

In Spanish, the letter **r** in the middle or the end of a word is pronounced by a single tap of the tongue against the gum above the upper front teeth. The letter **r** at the beginning of a word or **rr** within a word is pronounced by several rapid taps called a trill. Listen and repeat.

para	**cereal**	**beber**	**yogur**
rico	**rubio**	**horrible**	**pizarrón**

El cereal y el yogur son ricos; no son horribles.

7 | Opiniones

Hablar

Trabaja en un grupo de tres y hablen de las comidas y bebidas que les gustan y no les gustan. *(Talk in a group of three about what you like and don't like.)*

la pizza	el jugo de naranja
las manzanas	la leche
las uvas	¿ ?

A ¿A ustedes les gusta la pizza?

B A mí no me gusta la pizza. No me gusta el queso.

C Sí, a mí me gusta la pizza con jamón.

8 | El menú

Leer Hablar

Pregúntale a otro(a) estudiante qué comidas del menú le gustan más y por qué. *(Ask your partner questions about the foods he or she likes more and why.)*

A ¿Te gusta más el desayuno uno o el desayuno dos?

B Me gusta más el desayuno dos porque me gusta el cereal y no me gustan los huevos.

Restaurante Borinquen

Desayunos (de 8:00 a 11:00)
1. Huevos fritos o revoltillo con jamón $4.00
2. Cereal frío y fruta $4.00
3. Frutas frescas
   (uvas, guineos, manzanas), yogur $3.50

Bebidas incluidas: jugo de china, café o leche

Almuerzos (de 12:00 a 3:00)
1. Hamburguesa americana, papas fritas $5.50
2. Sándwich de jamón y queso, con fruta $6.50
3. Pizza con jamón y queso $5.50
4. Asopao de vegetales
   (sopa tradicional de Puerto Rico) $4.00

Bebidas incluidas: jugos, refrescos o café
Postres incluidos: helado, flan o pastel del día

9 | ¿Y tú?

Escribir Hablar

Contesta las preguntas. *(Answer the questions.)*

1. ¿Qué comida te gusta cuando tienes mucha hambre?
2. ¿Qué bebida te gusta cuando tienes mucha sed?
3. ¿Cuál es una comida nutritiva?
4. ¿Qué comidas nutritivas te gustan y no te gustan?
5. ¿Qué comidas en la cafetería de la escuela te gustan?
6. ¿Qué comidas en la cafetería de la escuela no te gustan?

Expansión
Talk with a partner. Compare your answers in a Venn diagram.

Más práctica   Cuaderno *pp. 102–104*   Cuaderno para hispanohablantes *pp. 103–105*

🌐 **Get Help Online**
my.hrw.com

PARA Y PIENSA

Did you get it?
1. Tell a friend you like eggs for breakfast.
2. Say that José likes pizza with ham.
3. Ask a friend why he or she doesn't like fruit.

❖GRAMÁTICA en contexto

Telehistoria escena 2

@HOMETUTOR View, Read
my.hrw.com and Record

STRATEGIES

Cuando lees
Organize with a chart To keep thoughts organized, make a chart listing Rodrigo's and Marisol's likes and dislikes about breakfast foods. Are your preferences more like Rodrigo's or more like Marisol's?

Cuando escuchas
Use mental pictures to remember words Listen for names of foods. For each name you hear, picture the food mentally. Remember these words by repeatedly linking them to the mental pictures.

VIDEO
DVD

AUDIO

Marisol: ¿Qué te gusta comer en el desayuno?

Rodrigo: Me gustan el cereal, el yogur, las frutas... Y a ti, Marisol, ¿qué te gusta comer en el desayuno?

Marisol: No me gusta el yogur y no me gustan los huevos.

Rodrigo: ¿Te gustan las frutas? ¿Las uvas, las manzanas?

Marisol: No me gusta comer mucho en el desayuno.

Rodrigo: ¡Tienes que comer bien en el desayuno! ¿Te gusta el pan? ¿O la leche?

Marisol: Me gustan las galletas. Tengo hambre.

Rodrigo: Sí. ¡Porque no te gusta comer mucho en el desayuno!

Continuará... p. 153

10 | Comprensión del episodio   ¿Un desayuno grande?

Escuchar
Leer

Contesta las preguntas sobre el episodio. *(Answer the questions.)*

1. ¿Qué le gusta comer a Rodrigo en el desayuno?
2. ¿A quién no le gustan los desayunos grandes?
3. ¿Qué le gusta comer a Marisol?
4. ¿Por qué tiene hambre Marisol?

11 | En el desayuno y el almuerzo

Escribir

Escribe una descripción de qué comidas y bebidas te gustan y no te gustan en el desayuno y el almuerzo. *(Write a description of what foods and drinks you like and don't like for breakfast and lunch.)*

> **modelo:** En el desayuno me gusta el pan. Para beber, me gusta el jugo de naranja. También me gustan las bananas. Es importante comer fruta. No me gustan los huevos. Son horribles. En el almuerzo...

12 | Una entrevista

Hablar
Escribir

Pregúntale a otro(a) estudiante qué le gusta y no le gusta en el almuerzo. Escribe sus respuestas. Luego compara lo que les gusta a los dos, usando un diagrama de Venn. *(Ask a classmate what he or she likes and doesn't like for lunch. Write the responses. Compare your likes and dislikes, using a Venn diagram.)*

> **modelo:** A Nicolás le gustan los sándwiches de queso en el almuerzo. También le gusta la fruta. No le gusta la pizza...

A mí   **A Nicolás**

Me gustan las hamburguesas. | Nos gusta la fruta. | No le gusta la pizza.

Expansión
Present your common likes and dislikes to the class.

Get Help Online
my.hrw.com

PARA Y PIENSA

Did you get it?   Complete each sentence based on the Telehistoria with the correct form of **gustar.**
1. A Marisol no le _____ la comida nutritiva.
2. A Rodrigo le _____ el cereal.
3. A Marisol le _____ las galletas.

Presentación de GRAMÁTICA

¡AVANZA! **Goal:** Learn how to form **-er** and **-ir** verbs. Then use these verbs and **hacer** to talk about school activities and what you and others eat and drink. *Actividades 13–16*

♻ *¿Recuerdas?* The verb **estar** p. 115

English Grammar Connection: Remember that the **present tense** shows an action happening now (see p. 96).

Present Tense of -er and -ir Verbs

ANIMATEDGRAMMAR
my.hrw.com

Regular verbs that end in **-er** or **-ir** work a little differently than regular **-ar** verbs. How do you form the present tense of regular **-er** and **-ir** verbs?

Here's how:

The endings for **-er** and **-ir** verbs are the same except in the **nosotros(as)** and **vosotros(as)** forms. The letter change in these two forms matches the ending of the infinitive.

vend**er** *to sell*			
yo	vend**o**	nosotros(as)	vend**emos**
tú	vend**es**	vosotros(as)	vend**éis**
usted, él, ella	vend**e**	ustedes, ellos(as)	vend**en**

-er verbs = -**emos**, -**éis**

Mario **vende** comida en la cafetería.
*Mario **sells** food in the cafeteria.*

compart**ir** *to share*			
yo	compart**o**	nosotros(as)	compart**imos**
tú	compart**es**	vosotros(as)	compart**ís**
usted, él, ella	compart**e**	ustedes, ellos(as)	compart**en**

-ir verbs = -**imos**, -**ís**

Compartimos** las uvas.
***We are sharing** the grapes.*

Más práctica

Cuaderno *pp. 105–107*
Cuaderno para hispanohablantes *pp. 106–109*

@HOMETUTOR my.hrw.com
Leveled Practice
🌐 Conjuguemos.com

Práctica de GRAMÁTICA

13 | ¿Comer o beber?

Escribir Hablar

Indica lo que estas personas comen o beben. *(Tell what these people eat or drink.)*

> **modelo:** Rodrigo (cereal)
> Rodrigo come cereal.

1. Rodrigo y Marisol (uvas)
2. tú (refrescos)
3. ustedes (pan)
4. Marisol y yo (sopa)
5. Ana (hamburguesas)
6. usted (sándwiches)
7. yo (jugo de naranja)
8. los maestros (café)

14 | ¿En la cafetería o en clase?   ♻ *¿Recuerdas?* The verb **estar** p. 115

Escribir Hablar

Di qué hacen estas personas e indica dónde están ahora: en la cafetería o en clase. *(Tell what these people are doing and where they are right now.)*

> **modelo:** Marisol / vender fruta
> Marisol vende fruta. Ahora está **en la cafetería.**

1. yo / beber leche
2. ellas / leer un libro
3. tú / comer yogur
4. Rodrigo / aprender el español
5. ustedes / escribir en el pizarrón
6. tú y yo / compartir una pizza

> **Expansión**
> Tell who does these things at your school.

15 | Actividades en el almuerzo

Escuchar Escribir

Escucha las descripciones de Marisol y sus amigos y toma apuntes. Luego escribe oraciones para describir qué hacen. Usa elementos de cada columna. *(Listen to Marisol and her friends and take notes. Then write sentences saying who does what, using elements from each column.)*

1. Marisol
2. la cafetería
3. Rodrigo y Mateo
4. Carmen
5. Raúl y David
6. Laura y Diana

Nota gramatical

The verb **hacer** is irregular in the present tense only in the **yo** form: **hago.**
In the other forms, it follows the pattern for **-er** verbs. (See p. R19 for the complete conjugation.)

Hago un sándwich.   Carmen **hace** la tarea.

I am making a sandwich.   *Carmen is doing her homework.*

16 | ¿Con quién?

Hablar

Pregúntale a otro(a) estudiante con quién hace las siguientes actividades.

(Ask a partner with whom he or she does the following activities.)

modelo: comer pizza

A ¿Con quién comes pizza?

B Como pizza con Alicia.

1. correr
2. compartir el almuerzo
3. hacer la tarea
4. comer ¿ ?

5. escribir correos electrónicos
6. beber ¿ ?

Expansión
Tell when and where you do each activity.

Comparación cultural

La Plaza de Colón

La Plaza de Colón

How do some cities reflect their historical colonial past? In Old San Juan you will find cobblestone streets, Spanish colonial buildings, and many plazas as part of Puerto Rico's Spanish heritage. The Plaza de Colón is popular with both tourists and locals. A statue of Christopher Columbus in the center of the square includes plaques commemorating the explorer's achievements.

Compara con tu mundo *What is a well-known landmark in your area? Why is it important?*

Más práctica   Cuaderno *pp. 105–107*   Cuaderno para hispanohablantes *pp. 106–109*

🌐 **Get Help Online**
my.hrw.com

PARA Y PIENSA

Did you get it?   Complete each sentence with the correct form of the verb in parentheses.

1. ¿Qué _____ ellas? (hacer) Ellas _____ el desayuno. (comer)
2. ¿Qué _____ tú? (hacer) Yo _____ un libro. (leer)
3. ¿Qué _____ Rafael? (hacer) Rafael _____ un refresco. (beber)

✸ Todo junto

¡AVANZA! **Goal:** *Show what you know* Pay attention to the **-er** and **-ir** verbs Rodrigo and Marisol use to talk about eating healthy food. Then practice these verbs and **gustar** to talk about lunchtime in the cafeteria. *Actividades 17–21*

♻ *¿Recuerdas?* Telling time p. 90

Telehistoria completa

@HOMETUTOR View, Read
my.hrw.com and Record

STRATEGIES

Cuando lees
Find the twist There is sometimes a "twist," or something unexpected, toward the end of a story or scene. Find the twist in this scene. What is it? Why is it unexpected?

Cuando escuchas
Listen for attitude changes To understand the scene fully, notice people's attitudes. At the beginning of the scene, what are Marisol's and Rodrigo's contrasting attitudes? Whose attitude changes during the scene? Why?

Escena 1 *Resumen*
Rodrigo necesita el autógrafo de Trini Salgado para Alicia. Tiene que estar en la escuela a las cuatro de la tarde.

Escena 2 *Resumen*
Rodrigo compra comida. Le gusta la comida nutritiva. Marisol tiene hambre porque no le gusta comer mucho en el desayuno.

Escena 3

VIDEO
DVD

AUDIO

Marisol stops to order an ice cream.

Rodrigo: ¿Helado? ¿En el almuerzo?

Marisol: Sí, tengo ganas de comer helado. ¿Compartimos?

Rodrigo: El helado no es nutritivo.

Marisol: ¡Pero es muy rico!

Rodrigo: ¿Qué comes en la cena? ¿Una hamburguesa con papas fritas?

Marisol: ¿Venden papas fritas?

Rodrigo: Tienes que comer comidas buenas.

Marisol: Sí, sí. Yo como comida nutritiva de vez en cuando.

Rodrigo: ¿Sí? ¿Qué comes?

Marisol: Me gusta la sopa.

Rodrigo: La sopa es muy buena.

Marisol: Necesito una bebida.

Marisol walks away. Rodrigo sneaks a taste of her ice cream.

Rodrigo: El helado es muy rico.

17 | *Comprensión de los episodios* ¡A completar!

Escuchar
Leer

Completa las siguientes oraciones, según los episodios. *(Complete the following sentences, based on the episodes.)*

1. Rodrigo necesita...

2. La amiga de Miami se llama...

3. En el desayuno Rodrigo come...

4. Marisol tiene hambre porque...

5. Marisol tiene ganas de...

6. Cuando Marisol compra una bebida, Rodrigo...

18 | *Comprensión de los episodios* Organiza la información

Escuchar
Leer

Escribe un artículo sobre Marisol o Rodrigo. Organiza la información usando este mapa. *(Write an article about Marisol or Rodrigo using a map like this one to organize information.)*

¿cuándo?

¿qué?

¿quién?
Marisol

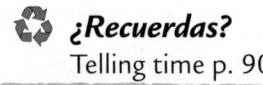

¿cómo?
simpática

19 | ¿Qué hacen en la cafetería?

♻ **¿Recuerdas?**
Telling time p. 90

Digital **performance space**

Hablar

STRATEGY Hablar

Think and practice in advance First write down words or phrases you want to say. Then practice pronouncing them aloud. Say them in sentences several times and you will be ready for your conversation!

Trabaja en un grupo de tres. Habla con los otros estudiantes de lo que haces en la cafetería. Incluye a qué hora vas y qué venden allí. También explica qué comes y bebes, y por qué. *(Work in a group of three to talk about what you do in the cafeteria.)*

A ¿A qué hora van ustedes a la cafetería? ¿Qué hacen?

B Como en la cafetería a la una. Venden fruta, sándwiches, leche y otras bebidas. Los lunes como pizza y bebo jugo porque no me gusta la leche.

C Yo compro una manzana y leo un libro...

20 | Integración

Leer
Escuchar
Hablar

Lee el anuncio del Supermercado Grande. Después escucha el anuncio de radio del Supermercardo Econo. ¿Qué comidas te gustan a ti y en cuál supermercado las venden? *(Read the newspaper ad and listen to the radio ad. Say what foods you like and where they sell them.)*

Fuente 1 Anuncio

Fuente 2 Anuncio de radio

Listen and take notes
- ¿Qué comidas venden en el Supermercado Econo?
- ¿Qué venden en la cafetería?

modelo: A mí me gustan las uvas. Venden uvas en el Supermercado Grande...

21 | La cafetería de la escuela

Escribir

Escríbele una carta al (a la) director(a) de la escuela para describir qué te gusta y no te gusta en la cafetería y por qué. Hazle las preguntas que tienes. *(Write a letter to your principal about what you like or dislike in the cafeteria and why. Ask any questions you have.)*

modelo: Sr. Hogan:
¿Cómo está usted? Me gusta la escuela pero no me gusta mucho la cafetería. No es muy grande y hay muchos estudiantes. ¿Por qué no venden...

Writing Criteria	Excellent	Good	Needs Work
Content	Your letter includes a lot of information.	Your letter includes some information.	Your letter includes little information.
Communication	Most of your letter is organized and easy to follow.	Parts of your letter are organized and easy to follow.	Your letter is disorganized and hard to follow.
Accuracy	Your letter has few mistakes in grammar and vocabulary.	Your letter has some mistakes in grammar and vocabulary.	Your letter has many mistakes in grammar and vocabulary.

Expansión
Write a reply letter from the principal to you that responds to your questions and comments.

Más práctica   Cuaderno *pp. 108–109*   Cuaderno para hispanohablantes *pp. 110–111*

Get Help Online
my.hrw.com

PARA Y PIENSA

Did you get it? Complete the first sentence with a form of **gustar,** and the second sentence with the correct form of **compartir** or **beber.**
1. A Rodrigo le _____ la fruta. Él _____ jugo de naranja.
2. A Rodrigo y a Ana les _____ los sándwiches. Siempre _____ un sándwich.

Lectura

¡AVANZA! **Goal:** Read a section from a supermarket ad and then a shopping list. Compare this information with the foods and beverages you eat and drink.

AUDIO

¡A comprar y a comer!

The following is a supermarket ad from Supermercados La Famosa and a shopping list.

STRATEGY Leer
Don't translate; use pictures!
Sketch and label pictures of the foods and beverages on the shopping list. Below each picture, write the brand or type of item you can buy at Supermercados La Famosa.

SUPERMERCADOS LA FAMOSA
TENEMOS BUENOS PRECIOS Y PRODUCTOS SUPERIORES

Hamburguesas El bohío, 1.5 lbs.
$4.29

$1.79
Queso americano de sándwich Vitarroz 12 oz. [1]

Jamón de sándwich Astor
$5.79/LB. [2]

Uvas de California
$1.59/LB.

Yogur de mango La Yogurt
$1.09

$1.29
Queso crema La Cremosa 8 oz.

Leche condensada La Fe 14 oz.
.99¢

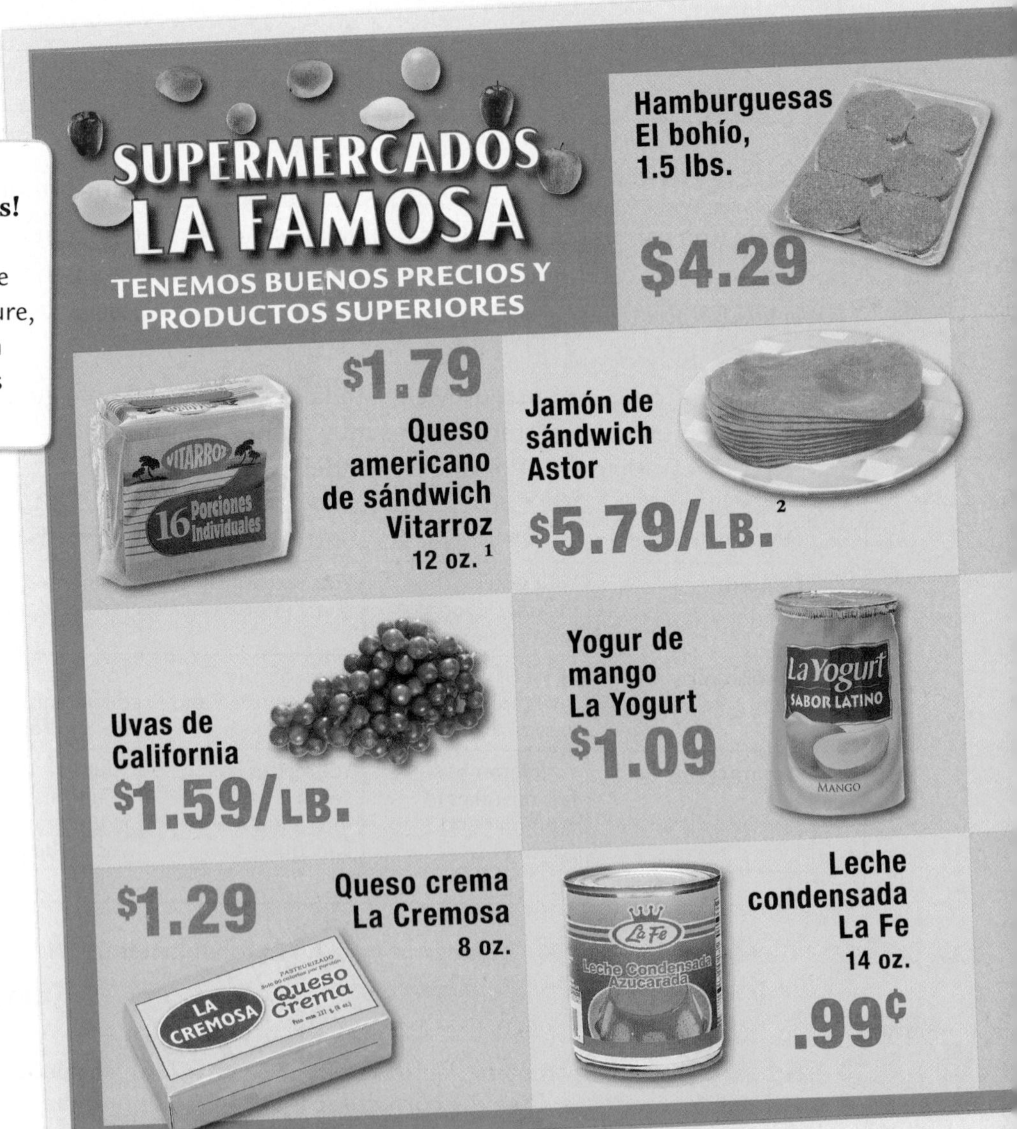

[1] onzas   [2] libra

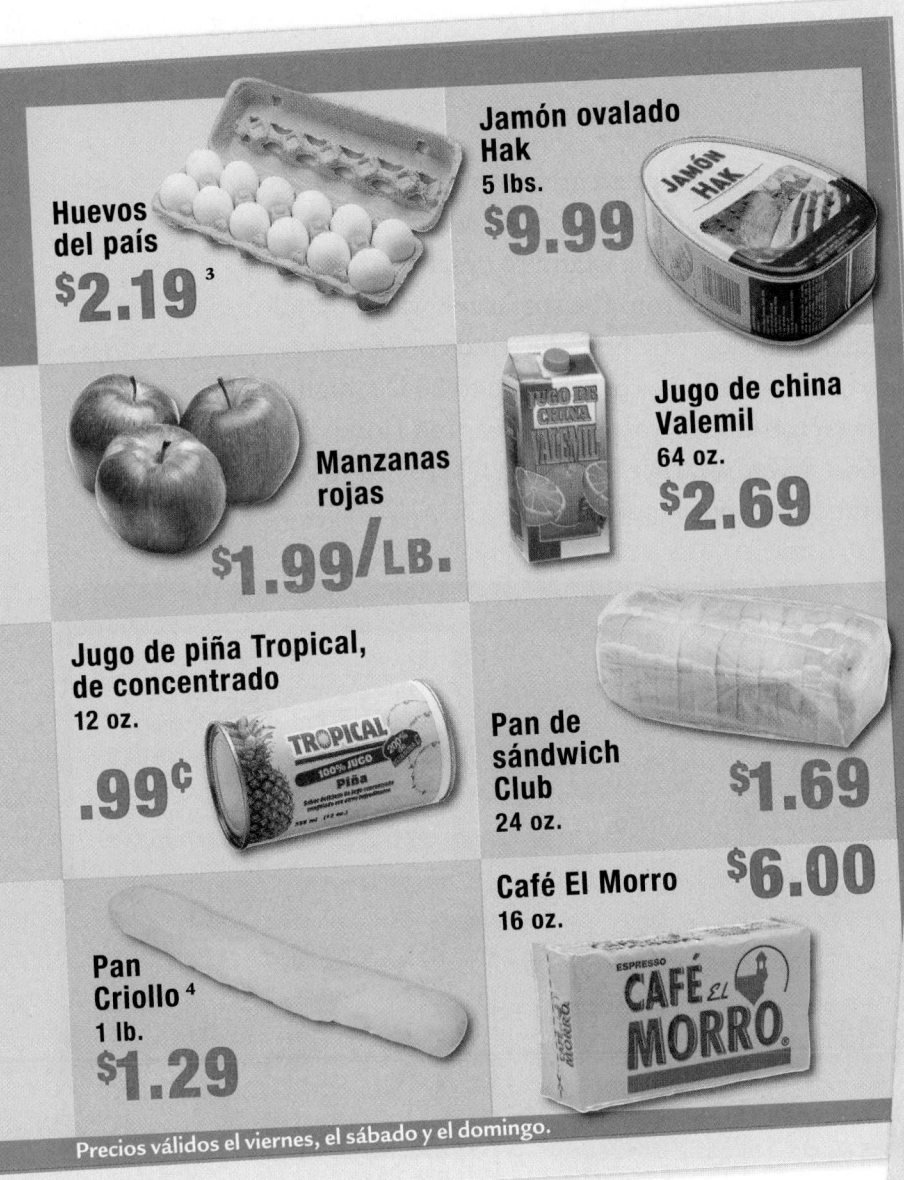

Huevos del país
$2.19 [3]

Jamón ovalado Hak
5 lbs.
$9.99

Manzanas rojas
$1.99/LB.

Jugo de china Valemil
64 oz.
$2.69

Jugo de piña Tropical, de concentrado
12 oz.
.99¢

Pan de sándwich Club
24 oz.
$1.69

Café El Morro
16 oz.
$6.00

Pan Criollo [4]
1 lb.
$1.29

Precios válidos el viernes, el sábado y el domingo.

Lista de compras

café

huevos

leche condensada

jugo de china

pan

yogur

cereal

jamón de sándwich

queso de sándwich

uvas

manzanas

---

[3] En Puerto Rico usan dólares estadounidenses

[4] bread similar to French bread

PARA Y PIENSA

¿Comprendiste?

1. ¿Qué hay en la lista que no está en la circular?

2. ¿Qué venden en Supermercados La Famosa que no está en la lista?

3. ¿Qué frutas hay en la lista?

¿Y tú?
¿Qué comida de Supermercados La Famosa comes tú? ¿Qué bebes?

Conexiones   *Las ciencias*

Los huracanes

The Caribbean island of Puerto Rico is located in an area prone to hurricanes (**huracanes**). The word *hurricane* comes from the Taino word *hurákan*, which was used by the pre-Columbian inhabitants of the island to describe these storms (**tormentas**). Hurricanes draw energy from the surface of warm tropical waters and from moisture in the air. The extreme winds of 74 miles per hour or more can create storm surges—domes of water up to 20 feet high and 100 miles wide—and can spawn tornadoes, torrential rain, and floods. Research and write about the most severe weather condition where you live. Create a diagram or drawing to illustrate your report.

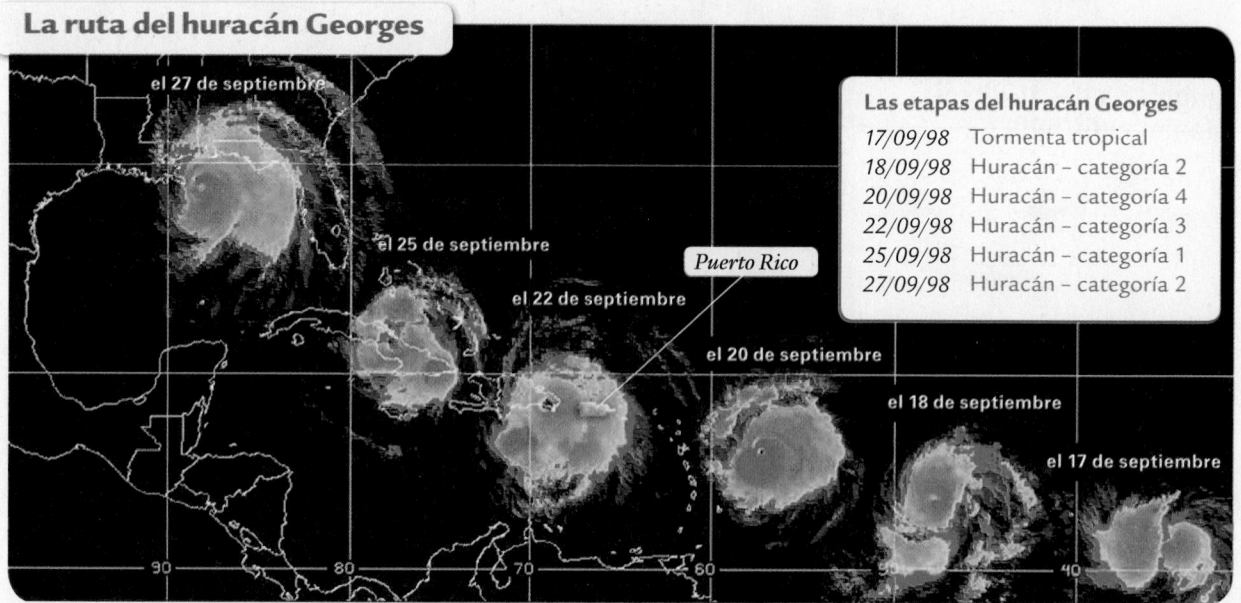

La ruta del huracán Georges

el 27 de septiembre
el 25 de septiembre
el 22 de septiembre
Puerto Rico
el 20 de septiembre
el 18 de septiembre
el 17 de septiembre

Las etapas del huracán Georges	
17/09/98	Tormenta tropical
18/09/98	Huracán – categoría 2
20/09/98	Huracán – categoría 4
22/09/98	Huracán – categoría 3
25/09/98	Huracán – categoría 1
27/09/98	Huracán – categoría 2

Proyecto 1 *Las matemáticas*

Hurricane Georges passed over Puerto Rico at a speed of about 24 kilometers per hour (**kilómetros por hora**). Find the distance from Humacao to Mayagüez in kilometers and calculate the time it took for the storm to move from one city to the other.

Proyecto 2 *La historia*

Research another major hurricane that has hit Puerto Rico in the past two decades. Draw a map showing the trajectory of the hurricane. Then write a paragraph describing the storm.

Proyecto 3 *La geografía*

Compare this map to the one on page xxxi to name three other countries that were hit by Hurricane Georges. Make a chart in Spanish showing the three countries, the dates of the storm, and the category of the hurricane at the time it hit.

La playa Ocean Park, Puerto Rico, durante el huracán Georges

En resumen
Vocabulario y gramática

Vocabulario

Talk About Foods and Beverages

Meals		For Breakfast		For Lunch	
el almuerzo	*lunch*	el café	*coffee*	la hamburguesa	*hamburger*
la bebida	*beverage, drink*	el cereal	*cereal*	el sándwich de	*ham and cheese*
la cena	*dinner*	el huevo	*egg*	jamón y queso	*sandwich*
compartir	*to share*	el jugo de naranja	*orange juice*	la sopa	*soup*
la comida	*food; meal*	la leche	*milk*		
el desayuno	*breakfast*	el pan	*bread*	**Fruit**	
vender	*to sell*	el yogur	*yogurt*	la banana	*banana*
				la manzana	*apple*
				las uvas	*grapes*

Describe Feelings		Ask Questions		Other Words and Phrases	
tener ganas de...	*to feel like . . .*	¿Cómo?	*How?*	ahora	*now*
tener hambre	*to be hungry*	¿Cuál(es)?	*Which?; What?*	Es importante.	*It's important.*
tener sed	*to be thirsty*	¿Por qué?	*Why?*	horrible	*horrible*
		¿Qué?	*What?*	nutritivo(a)	*nutritious*
		¿Quién(es)?	*Who?*	otro(a)	*other*
				para	*for; in order to*
				rico(a)	*tasty, delicious*

Gramática

Notas gramaticales: Interrogative words *p. 144,* The verb **hacer** *p. 152*

Gustar with Nouns

To talk about the things that people like, use
gustar + noun.

Singular
me gusta **la sopa**
te gusta **la sopa**
le gusta **la sopa**
nos gusta **la sopa**
os gusta **la sopa**
les gusta **la sopa**

Plural
me gustan **los jugos**
te gustan **los jugos**
le gustan **los jugos**
nos gustan **los jugos**
os gustan **los jugos**
les gustan **los jugos**

Present Tense of -er and -ir Verbs

vender *to sell*	
vendo	vendemos
vendes	vendéis
vende	venden

compartir *to share*	
comparto	compartimos
compartes	compartís
comparte	comparten

Repaso de la lección

@HOMETUTOR
my.hrw.com

¡LLEGADA!

Now you can
- talk about foods and beverages
- ask questions
- say which foods you like and don't like

Using
- interrogative words
- **gustar** with nouns
- present tense of **-er** and **-ir** verbs
- the verb **hacer**

To review
- **gustar** with nouns p. 145
- present tense of **-er** and **-ir** verbs p. 150

AUDIO

1 Listen and understand

Lola nunca come comidas tradicionales. Escucha la entrevista en la radio y escribe **el desayuno, el almuerzo o la cena,** según cuándo come o bebe cada cosa. *(Listen to the radio interview and write at what meal Lola eats and drinks each item.)*

1. huevos
2. café
3. leche
4. hamburguesas
5. banana
6. refresco
7. pan
8. cereal

To review
- present tense of **-er** and **-ir** verbs p. 150
- the verb **hacer** p. 152

2 Talk about foods and beverages

Escribe lo que hacen estas personas en la cafetería. *(Write what these people are doing in the cafeteria.)*

modelo: Daniel / comer
Daniel come pan.

1. Irene / beber

2. ustedes / compartir

3. yo / hacer

4. nosotros / vender

5. yo / comer

6. tú / hacer

7. los estudiantes / beber

8. Trinidad y yo / compartir

To review
· interrogative words p. 144

3 | Ask questions

Gilberto es un nuevo estudiante. Es la hora de almuerzo y está en la cafetería con Julia. Completa la conversación con palabras interrogativas.
(Complete the conversation with interrogative words.)

> **modelo:** ¿<u>Cuál</u> es el sándwich del día?
> Es el sándwich de jamón y queso.

Gilberto: ¿ __1.__ está el yogur?

Julia: Está al lado de las frutas.

Gilberto: ¿ __2.__ no venden pizza?

Julia: Porque hoy no es viernes.

Gilberto: ¿ __3.__ venden los martes?

Julia: Venden hamburguesas.

Gilberto: ¿ __4.__ es la sopa?

Julia: Es muy rica.

Gilberto: ¿ __5.__ prepara la comida?

Julia: La señora Aguirre.

Gilberto: ¿ __6.__ personas trabajan en la cafetería?

Julia: Nueve o diez.

Gilberto: ¿ __7.__ compramos la bebida?

Julia: Ahora, con la comida.

Gilberto: ¿ __8.__ vamos después del almuerzo?

Julia: A la clase de inglés.

To review
· **gustar** with nouns p. 145

4 | Say which foods you like and don't like

Estas personas están en el supermercado y hablan de comidas y bebidas. Escribe oraciones sobre lo que les gusta o no les gusta, según las opiniones.
(Write sentences about the foods these people like and dislike.)

> **modelo:** la señora Medina: «El yogur es bueno.»
> A la señora Medina le gusta el yogur.

1. ustedes: «No, el yogur es horrible.»

2. Adán y Susana: «Necesitamos manzanas. Son nutritivas.»

3. el señor Chávez: «El café es bueno.»

4. nosotros: «No, el café es malo.»

5. yo: «Tengo ganas de comer uvas.»

6. tú: «Las hamburguesas son ricas.»

To review
· El Yunque p. 137
· Comparación cultural pp. 138, 146, 152

5 | Puerto Rico and El Salvador

Comparación cultural

Answer these culture questions.

1. What is El Yunque and what can you find there?

2. What is a popular cold treat in Puerto Rico?

3. What can you find in Plaza de Colón?

4. Describe some popular foods from Puerto Rico and El Salvador.

Get Help Online
my.hrw.com

Más práctica Cuaderno *pp. 110–121*   Cuaderno para hispanohablantes *pp. 112–121*

Puerto Rico

Lección

2

Tema:
En mi familia

¡AVANZA! **In this lesson you will learn to**
- talk about family
- ask and tell ages
- express possession
- give dates
- make comparisons

using
- **de** to show possession
- possessive adjectives
- comparatives

♻ *¿Recuerdas?*
- the verb **tener,** describing others
- numbers from 11 to 100
- after-school activities

Comparación cultural

In this lesson you will learn about
- government elections
- portraits and instruments from Puerto Rico and Peru
- **quinceañeras** in Puerto Rico and Peru
- meals in Puerto Rico, El Salvador, and Peru

Compara con tu mundo

In many Spanish-speaking countries, families share time together at the table long after a meal is over. This custom is called **la sobremesa.** *Does your family have any traditions involving mealtimes? What are they?*

¿Qué ves?

Mira la foto
¿Tiene sed Rodrigo?

¿Qué beben los señores, café o refrescos?

¿Cómo es la chica?

MODES OF COMMUNICATION

INTERPRETIVE	INTERPERSONAL	PRESENTATIONAL
Read people's descriptions of their typical Sunday meals to compare them to meals with your family. Listen to a call-in radio show and identify the advice given.	Describe the ideal family and compare your opinion to others'. Ask and answer questions about your classes and your likes and dislikes.	Describe a friend to your classmates. Plan for a family reunion by making a seating chart.

Una familia come en casa
San Juan, Puerto Rico

※ Presentación de VOCABULARIO

VIDEO
DVD

AUDIO

A Soy Rodrigo. **Vivo** en Puerto Rico con **mis padres.** Ellos tienen dos **hijos.** Yo soy **su hijo** y **mi hermana** Ana es su **hija.** Te presento a las otras personas en **nuestra familia.**

los abuelos

la abuela   el abuelo

María y Cristóbal

los padres

la madre   el padre

Celia y José

los tíos

la tía   el tío

Camila y Pablo

los hermanos

el hermano   la hermana

Rodrigo y Ana

el perro

Capitán

el gato

Príncipe

los primos

el primo   la prima

Tito y Éster

B **¿Cuántos años tienes** tú? Yo **tengo** quince **años.** Ana, mi hermana **menor,** tiene nueve años. Soy su **hermano mayor.**

C ¿**Cuál es la fecha?** Hoy **es el primero de abril.** Es mi **cumpleaños.** ¿Cuándo es **tu** cumpleaños?

los meses

enero
febrero
marzo
abril
mayo
junio
julio
agosto
septiembre
octubre
noviembre
diciembre

abril

¡Feliz cumpleaños!

Numbers from 200 to 1,000,000

200	doscientos(as)	700	setecientos(as)
300	trescientos(as)	800	ochocientos(as)
400	cuatrocientos(as)	900	novecientos(as)
500	quinientos(as)	1,000	mil
600	seiscientos(as)	1,000,000	un millón (de)

Más vocabulario

la madrastra	*stepmother*	**la fecha de nacimiento**	*birth date*
el padrastro	*stepfather*	**ya**	*already*

Expansión de vocabulario p. R4

@**HOMETUTOR** **Interactive Flashcards**
my.hrw.com

¡A responder!   Escuchar

Escucha las oraciones sobre la familia de Rodrigo. Si la oración es cierta, levanta la mano izquierda; si es falsa, levanta la mano derecha.
(Listen to the sentences about Rodrigo's family. If the sentence is true, raise your left hand; if it is false, raise your right hand.)

Práctica de VOCABULARIO

1 | La familia de Rodrigo

Hablar
Escribir

Indica la relación de cada persona con Rodrigo. Usa el árbol genealógico de la página 164. *(Tell how each person is related to Rodrigo.)*

modelo: José es el padre.

1.
2.
3.
4.
5.
6.
7.

Expansión
Draw your own family tree or that of a famous family. Explain how the people are related.

Nota gramatical

In Spanish, **'s** is never used. To show possession, use **de** and the **noun** that refers to the owner/possessor.

el gato **de Marisa**   *Marisa's cat*   los primos **de Juan**   *Juan's cousins*

---

2 | La familia de Marisol

Leer

Combina las frases para describir las relaciones entre las personas de la familia de Marisol. *(Match the descriptions.)*

1. El padre de mi madre es...
2. Las hermanas de mi padre son...
3. La hija de mi padre es...
4. Los hijos de mis padres son...
5. Las hijas de mi tía son...
6. La hermana de mi tía es...

a. mi hermana.
b. mi madre.
c. mis tías.
d. mi abuelo.
e. mis primas.
f. mis hermanos.

Más práctica   Cuaderno *pp. 122–124*   Cuaderno para hispanohablantes *pp. 122–125*

🌐 **Get Help Online**
my.hrw.com

PARA
Y
PIENSA

Did you get it?   Fill in the blank with the correct vocabulary word.
1. El _____ de tus tíos es tu primo.
2. Los _____ de tus padres son tus abuelos.
3. Las _____ de tu madre son tus tías.

❈ VOCABULARIO en contexto

¡AVANZA! **Goal:** Identify the words Marisol and Rodrigo use to talk about birthdays and other family members. Then practice the words you have learned to ask and tell a person's age. *Actividades 3–4*

♻ *¿Recuerdas?* The verb **tener** p. 91, numbers from 11 to 100 p. 87

Telehistoria escena 1

@HOMETUTOR View, Read
my.hrw.com and Record

STRATEGIES

Cuando lees
Analyze the scene This scene starts out calmly and ends with a problem. What do the characters talk about at the beginning? What is the problem, and whose problem is it?

Cuando escuchas
Remember, listen, and predict
Before listening, remember why Rodrigo wanted Alicia's T-shirt. What happens to the T-shirt in this scene? After listening, predict what will happen next.

VIDEO
DVD

AUDIO

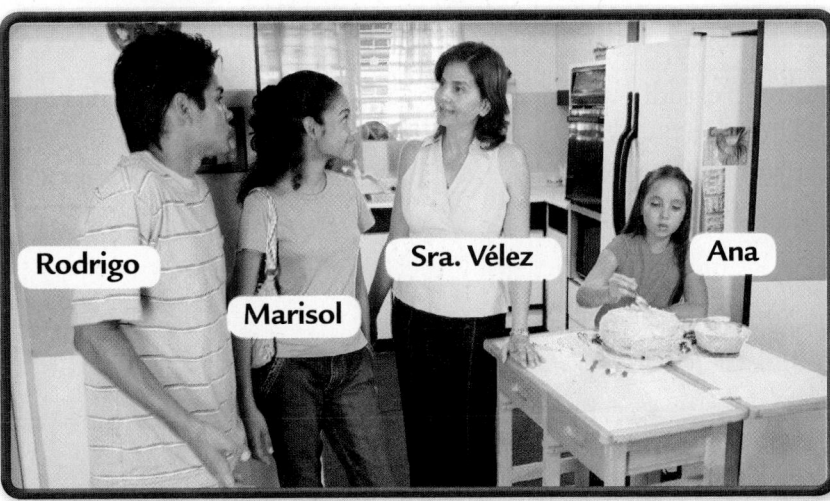

Rodrigo · Marisol · Sra. Vélez · Ana

Rodrigo and Marisol arrive in Rodrigo's kitchen.

Marisol: Señora Vélez, ¿es su cumpleaños?

Sra. Vélez: No, es el cumpleaños de Ana.

Marisol: ¡Feliz cumpleaños! ¿Cuántos años tienes?

Ana: Hoy tengo nueve años. Mañana, ¡diez!

Marisol: ¿Mañana? ¿El veintiocho de febrero?

Rodrigo: No. El primero de marzo.

Marisol: El cumpleaños de mi abuela es el primero de marzo.

Ana: Ah, ¿sí? ¿Cuántos años tiene?

Marisol: Tiene sesenta y ocho años.

Rodrigo: Mamá, ¿dónde está la camiseta?
Trini Salgado está en la escuela a las cuatro.

Continuará... p. 172

También se dice

Puerto Rico Marisol uses the word **abuela** to talk about her grandmother. In other Spanish-speaking countries you might hear:
• **Perú, Argentina** **la mamama**

3 | Comprensión del episodio   Un cumpleaños

**Escuchar
Leer**

Indica si las oraciones son ciertas o falsas. Si es falsa, escribe lo que es cierto.
(Tell if the statements are true or false. Correct the false statements to make them true.)

1. Es el cumpleaños de la señora Vélez.
2. Mañana es el veintiocho de febrero.
3. El cumpleaños de Ana es en el mes de febrero.
4. El cumpleaños de la abuela de Marisol es el primero de marzo.

Nota gramatical   ♻️ *¿Recuerdas?* The verb **tener** p. 91

Use the verb **tener** to talk about how old a person is.

¿Cuántos años **tiene** tu amiga?   ¿Violeta? **Tiene** quince años.
How old is your friend?   *Violeta? She's fifteen years old.*

---

4 | ¿Cuántos años tienen?   ♻️ *¿Recuerdas?* Numbers from 11 to 100 p. 87

Hablar

Habla con otro(a) estudiante sobre cuántos años tienen estas personas de
la familia de Rodrigo.
Si es necesario, usa
el árbol genealógico de
la página 164. *(Talk with
a partner about the ages of the
people in Rodrigo's family.)*

47 años

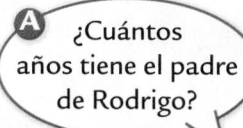

A ¿Cuántos años tiene el padre de Rodrigo?

B Tiene cuarenta y siete años.

1. 9 años

2. 10 años

3. 66 años

4. 14 años

5. 38 años

6. 45 años

7. 39 años

8. 64 años

Expansión
Say how old the
members of your
family are.

🌐 **Get Help Online**
my.hrw.com

**PARA
Y
PIENSA**

Did you get it? Give each
age, using **tener** and the
word for each number in
parentheses.

1. Marisol _____ _____ años. (14)
2. El gato de la familia Vélez _____ _____
   años. (8)
3. Los padres de Marisol _____ _____ años. (52)

Presentación de GRAMÁTICA

¡AVANZA! **Goal:** Learn to express possession. Then practice using possessive adjectives to talk about your family members and to give dates. *Actividades 5–8*

♻ *¿Recuerdas?* After-school activities p. 32, describing others p. 58

English Grammar Connection: Possessive adjectives tell you who owns something or describe a relationship between people or things. The forms of possessive adjectives do not change in English, but they do change in Spanish.

They are **my** cousins.   Ellos son **mis** primos.

Possessive Adjectives

ANIMATEDGRAMMAR
my.hrw.com

In Spanish, **possessive adjectives** agree in number with the nouns they describe.

Here's how:

Singular Possessive Adjectives	
mi *my*	**nuestro(a)** *our*
tu *your (familiar)*	**vuestro(a)** *your (familiar)*
su *your (formal)*	**su** *your*
su *his, her, its*	**su** *their*

Plural Possessive Adjectives	
mis *my*	**nuestros(as)** *our*
tus *your (familiar)*	**vuestros(as)** *your (familiar)*
sus *your (formal)*	**sus** *your*
sus *his, her, its*	**sus** *their*

Es **mi** tía.
*She is **my** aunt.*

Son **mis** tías.
*They are **my** aunts.*

Nuestro(a) and **vuestro(a)** must also agree in gender with the nouns they describe.

agrees
Nuestra abuela tiene 70 años.
***Our** grandmother is 70 years old.*

agrees
Nuestros abuelos viven en San Francisco.
***Our** grandparents live in San Francisco.*

Más práctica
Cuaderno *pp. 125–127*
Cuaderno para hispanohablantes *pp. 126–128*

@HOMETUTOR my.hrw.com
Leveled Practice

Práctica de GRAMÁTICA

5 | Las familias

Leer

Marisol habla de las familias y sus animales. Escoge el adjetivo posesivo correcto para expresar lo que dice. *(Choose the correct possessive adjectives.)*

1. Nosotros tenemos tres primas. (Nuestros / Nuestras) primas son altas.
2. Ustedes tienen un abuelo. (Su / Nuestro) cumpleaños es el dos de abril.
3. Mi familia y yo tenemos una gata vieja. (Nuestra / Su) gata es Rubí.
4. Yo tengo dos hermanos mayores. (Mi / Mis) hermanos son estudiosos.
5. Mis abuelos tienen un perro. (Su / Mi) perro es perezoso.
6. ¡Feliz cumpleaños! Hoy tienes quince años. Es (tu / su) cumpleaños.

6 | ¿Qué hacen?   *¿Recuerdas?* After-school activities p. 32

Leer
Escribir

Usa un adjetivo posesivo y escribe qué actividades hacen estas personas.
(Restate the relationship with a possessive adjective and tell what activities these people do.)

> **modelo:** La hermana de Alicia es inteligente. (sacar buenas notas)
> Su hermana saca buenas notas.

1. Los abuelos de nosotros no son muy serios. (escuchar música rock)
2. Los tíos de ustedes son trabajadores. (trabajar mucho)
3. La prima de Marisol no es perezosa. (hacer la tarea)
4. La madre de Rodrigo es atlética. (practicar deportes)
5. La hermana de nosotros es muy estudiosa. (leer muchos libros)
6. El padrastro de Luz es simpático. (pasar un rato con la familia)

> **Expansión**
> Write what these people don't do, based on the descriptions.

Comparación cultural

Las elecciones en Puerto Rico

What do elections reveal about a culture? **Puerto Rico** is a commonwealth of the United States. Puerto Ricans have U.S. citizenship and those living on the mainland can vote in presidential elections. On the island, Puerto Ricans vote for their governor and local legislature. Voter turnout is high, often over 80 percent. Puerto Rico has three main political parties: the *Partido Popular Democrático* favors the current political status, the *Partido Nuevo Progresista* wants Puerto Rico to become the 51st state, and the *Partido Independentista Puertorriqueño* supports independence from the U.S.

Compara con tu mundo *What issues would motivate you to vote when you are 18?*

Residencia y oficina del gobernador, Viejo San Juan

Nota gramatical

To give the date, use the following phrase: **Es el** + **number** + **de** + **month.**

> Hoy **es el diez de diciembre.**   *Today is the tenth of December.*

Only the first of the month does not follow this pattern.

> **Es el primero de diciembre.**   *It is December first.*

The year is expressed in **thousands** and **hundreds.**

> **mil cuatrocientos** noventa y dos   *1492*

---

7 | Unos puertorriqueños famosos

Hablar

Trabaja con otro(a) estudiante.
Usa la línea cronológica para
decir las fechas de nacimiento
de estos puertorriqueños famosos.
(Use the timeline to give the birth dates.)

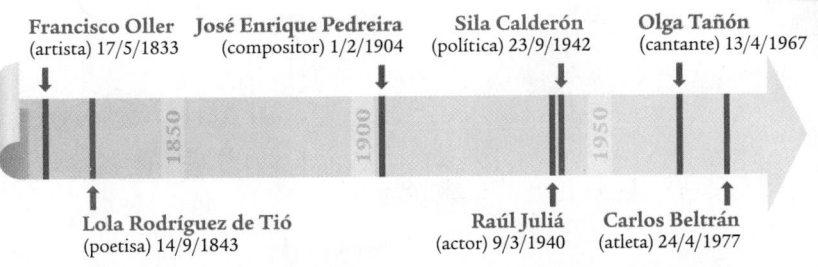

A ¿Cuál es la fecha de nacimiento de Carlos Beltrán?

B Su fecha de nacimiento es el veinticuatro de abril de mil novecientos setenta y siete.

Francisco Oller (artista) 17/5/1833
José Enrique Pedreira (compositor) 1/2/1904
Sila Calderón (política) 23/9/1942
Olga Tañón (cantante) 13/4/1967

1850   1900   1950

Lola Rodríguez de Tió (poetisa) 14/9/1843
Raúl Juliá (actor) 9/3/1940
Carlos Beltrán (atleta) 24/4/1977

Expansión
Write six sentences about the birth dates of your family members and friends.

---

8 | ¿Cómo son?   ♻ ***¿Recuerdas?*** Describing others p. 58

Hablar

Habla con otro(a) estudiante sobre las personas y animales domésticos en tu familia. *(Talk about your family and pets.)*

modelo: serio(a)

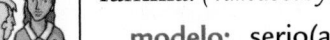

A ¿Hay una persona seria en tu familia?

B Sí, mi tío David es muy serio.

1. atlético(a)
2. cómico(a)
3. desorganizado(a)
4. inteligente
5. perezoso(a)
6. artístico(a)
7. simpático(a)
8. trabajador(a)
9. ¿ ?

Más práctica   Cuaderno *pp. 125–127*   Cuaderno para hispanohablantes *pp. 126–128*

🌐 **Get Help Online**
my.hrw.com

PARA Y PIENSA

Did you get it?   Fill in the correct possessive adjective and dates.

1. El cumpleaños de _____ *(my)* madrastra es _____ . (6/9)
2. El cumpleaños de _____ *(our)* hermano es _____ . (25/1)
3. El cumpleaños de _____ *(his)* amigo es _____ . (17/4)

GRAMÁTICA en contexto

Goal: Listen to the possesive adjectives Marisol and Rodrigo use to talk about the members of his family. Then use possessive adjectives to talk about your family and the birthdays of people you know. *Actividades 9–11*

Telehistoria escena 2

@HOMETUTOR View, Read
my.hrw.com and Record

STRATEGIES

Cuando lees
List and practice words While reading, list the words for family members, such as **madre.** Then practice! Say these words aloud several times. Say them in sentences and create questions with them.

Cuando escuchas
Track the people and actions While listening, identify the people involved and the actions. What does each one say? Who helps solve the key problem? What new problem arises?

VIDEO
DVD

AUDIO

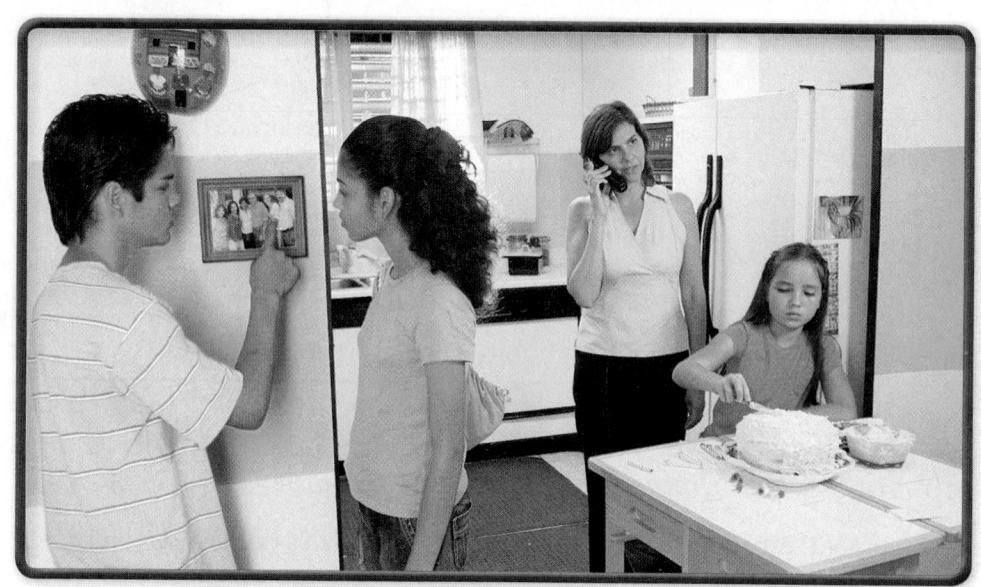

Rodrigo: ¿Dónde está la camiseta?

Sra. Vélez: ¡Ah, tus primos! *(She picks up the phone and dials.)*

Rodrigo: *(explaining to Marisol)* Ellos comen con nosotros todos los viernes. A nuestros primos les gusta jugar al fútbol.

Sra. Vélez: *(on the phone)* ¿Camila? Es Celia. Tengo una pregunta...

Rodrigo: Es mi tía Camila. La tía Camila es la madre de Éster y Tito. Mis primos tienen catorce y diez años.

Marisol: *(pointing to a family portrait)* ¿Es tu familia?

Rodrigo: Mi madre tiene dos hermanas: Inés y Mónica. Mi padre tiene un hermano, Sergio, y una hermana, Camila.

Sra. Vélez: Rodrigo, tu primo Tito tiene la camiseta de tu amiga Alicia.

Rodrigo: *(to Marisol)* Mi primo tiene perros muy grandes. ¡No me gustan los perros de Tito!

Continuará... p. 177

9 | Comprensión del episodio Una familia grande

Escuchar
Leer

Completa las oraciones para describir el episodio. *(Complete the sentences.)*

1. La madre de Rodrigo
  a. no tiene la camiseta.
  b. no tiene hermanas.

2. Los primos de Rodrigo
  a. comen en su casa todos los días.
  b. comen en su casa todos los viernes.

3. A los primos de Rodrigo
  a. les gusta jugar al fútbol.
  b. les gusta hablar por teléfono.

4. La tía Camila
  a. es la madre de Tito y Éster.
  b. es la hermana de Inés y Mónica.

5. El padre de Rodrigo
  a. tiene dos hermanas.
  b. tiene una hermana.

6. A Rodrigo
  a. no le gusta la camiseta.
  b. no le gustan los perros.

10 | ¿Cuál es tu fecha de nacimiento?

Hablar

Pregúntales a ocho estudiantes cuáles son sus fechas de nacimiento. Haz una tabla con la información. Comparte los resultados con la clase. *(Find out the birth dates of eight classmates and make a chart. Share the results with the class.)*

A ¿Cuál es tu fecha de nacimiento?

B Mi fecha de nacimiento es el quince de enero de...

enero	febrero	marzo
Sandy 15/1/...	Lillian 24/2/...	
Doug 21/1/...		

11 | Tu familia

Escribir

Escribe un párrafo sobre tu familia. Incluye las respuestas a las siguientes preguntas. *(Write a paragraph about your family. Include the answers to the following questions.)*

- ¿Es grande o pequeña tu familia?
- ¿Cuántos hermanos y hermanas tienes?
- ¿Cómo son las personas de tu familia?
- ¿Cuántos años tienen las personas de tu familia?

modelo: Mi familia es grande. Tengo tres hermanos y una hermana. Mi madre tiene treinta y siete años. Es...

Expansión
Say what each family member likes to do on his or her birthday.

Get Help Online
my.hrw.com

PARA Y PIENSA

Did you get it? Using complete sentences, tell the birthdays of the following people.
  1. Camila (12/6) **2.** Éster (1/10) **3.** Tito (28/3) **4.** Celia (17/1)

✵ Presentación de GRAMÁTICA

Goal: Learn to make comparisons. Then use them to describe your family, your friends, and yourself. *Actividades 12–15*

English Grammar Connection: Comparatives are expressions used to compare two people or things. In English, comparative adjectives are formed by adding *-er* to the end of a word or by using *more, less,* and *as.*

Rodrigo is **taller** than his sister.   Rodrigo es **más alto** que su hermana.

Comparatives

ANIMATEDGRAMMAR
my.hrw.com

There are several phrases in Spanish used to make comparisons.

Here's how: Use the following phrases with an **adjective** to compare two things. The adjectives agree with the first noun.

agrees

más... que *more . . . than*	Mi abue**la** es **más artística** que mi padre. *My grandmother is **more** artistic **than** my father.*
menos... que *less . . . than*	La clase de ciencias es **menos divertida** que la clase de inglés. *Science class is **less** fun **than** English class.*
tan... como *as . . . as*	Tus hermanas son **tan serias** como la maestra. *Your sisters are **as** serious **as** the teacher.*

When a comparison does not involve an adjective, use these phrases.

más que... *more than . . .*	Me gusta ir a la biblioteca **más que** al gimnasio. *I like to go to the library **more than** to the gym.*
menos que... *less than . . .*	Me gustan las hamburguesas **menos que** los tacos. *I like hamburgers **less than** tacos.*
tanto como... *as much as . . .*	¿Te gusta hablar **tanto como** escuchar? *Do you like to talk **as much as** listen?*

There are a few irregular comparative words. They agree in number with the first noun.

mayor	**menor**	**mejor**	**peor**
older	*younger*	*better*	*worse*

agrees

Mis tío**s** son **mayores** que mi tía.
*My uncles are **older** than my aunt.*

Más práctica
Cuaderno *pp. 128–130*
Cuaderno para hispanohablantes *pp. 129–132*

@**HOMETUTOR** my.hrw.com
Leveled Practice

✦ Práctica de GRAMÁTICA

12 | Sus familias

Escribir

Completa las oraciones con **que** o **como** para describir a las familias de Rodrigo y Marisol. *(Complete the sentences with **que** or **como**.)*

1. Marisol es tan simpática _____ su madrastra.
2. Ana es menor _____ Rodrigo.
3. Marisol corre tanto _____ sus padres.
4. Rodrigo tiene menos hermanos _____ José.
5. El tío Pablo toca la guitarra mejor _____ la tía Camila.
6. Ester es mayor _____ Tito.

> **Expansión**
> Rewrite the sentences with another comparative.

13 | Comparaciones

Escribir
Hablar

Mira los dibujos y haz comparaciones usando **más... que, menos... que, tan... como** o **tanto como.** *(Make a comparison for each drawing using the correct phrase.)*

modelo: Nicolás / grande / Sara
Nicolás es más grande que Sara.

1. Nora / alto(a) / Patricia

2. Marcos / serio(a) / José

3. Ana / perezoso(a) / Alí

4. Pablo / desorganizado(a) / Pedro

5. María / atlético(a) / David

6. A Elena / gustar / correr / escuchar música

AUDIO

Pronunciación **La letra** j

The **j** in Spanish sounds similar to the English *h* in the word *hello.*

Listen and repeat.

jamón   mujer   dibujar   joven   junio   hija

La mujer pelirroja es joven. El cumpleaños del hijo es en julio.

14 | Capitán y Príncipe

Escuchar
Escribir

Ana habla de sus animales, Capitán y Príncipe. Escucha su descripción y decide si las siguientes oraciones son ciertas o falsas. *(Listen to the description and indicate whether the following sentences are true or false.)*

1. La familia de Ana tiene más perros que gatos.
2. Príncipe es tan simpático como Capitán.
3. Capitán es más grande que Príncipe.
4. A Príncipe le gusta comer más que descansar.
5. Príncipe es menor que Capitán.
6. Capitán es más perezoso que Príncipe.

Expansión
Correct the false statements.

15 | Compara a las personas

Escribir

Comparación cultural

Los retratos

How do portraits represent the people in a country?
Rafael Tufiño was born in New York and moved to **Puerto Rico,** his parents' homeland, as a child. Much of his work reflects the people and culture of Puerto Rico. In addition to paintings like *Lavandera*, he painted many portraits of his mother, giving them the title *Goyita*. These portraits came to represent not just his mother, but Puerto Rican women overall. Fernando Sayán Polo, an artist from **Peru,** also reflects the people of his country through his artwork. His painting *Niña campesina sonriente* depicts a young girl wearing traditional Andean dress. Look for a copy of Fernando Sayán Polo's *Niña campesina sonriente* in the library or on the Internet and compare the girl with the woman in *Lavandera*.

Lavandera (1960),
Rafael Tufiño

Compara con tu mundo   *If you had to paint a portrait of someone famous, which person would you choose and why? How would you portray him or her?*

Escribe cinco oraciones para comparar a la mujer de *Lavandera* con la niña de *Niña campesina sonriente. (Write five sentences comparing the two people in the paintings.)*

> **modelo:** La mujer es mayor que la chica. La chica es más...

Más práctica   Cuaderno *pp. 128–130*   Cuaderno para hispanohablantes *pp. 129–132*

Get Help Online
my.hrw.com

PARA Y PIENSA

Did you get it?
1. Say that your brother is taller than your father.
2. Say that you like apples as much as bananas.
3. Say that math class is better than art class.

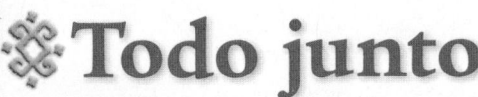 **Todo junto**

¡AVANZA! **Goal:** *Show what you know* Notice the comparative words Marisol and Rodrigo use to talk about why Rodrigo doesn't like Tito's dogs. Then use comparative words and possessive adjectives to describe your family and friends. *Actividades 16–20*

Telehistoria completa

STRATEGIES

Cuando lees
Work with comparisons This scene contains comparisons of animals and of people. How many comparisons do you see? Write down the "comparison words." Practice them in sentences.

Cuando escuchas
Remember, listen, and predict At the beginning of this scene, Marisol is calm. How does she change and why? Does this happen suddenly or slowly? How do you know?

Escena 1 *Resumen*
Mañana es el cumpleaños de Ana, la hermana de Rodrigo. Rodrigo está nervioso porque no tiene la camiseta de Alicia.

Escena 2 *Resumen*
Tito, el primo de Rodrigo, tiene la camiseta. A Rodrigo no le gustan los perros de Tito.

VIDEO DVD

AUDIO

Escena 3

Tito

Rodrigo and Marisol are walking to Tito's house.

Marisol: ¿No te gustan los perros? Son simpáticos.

Rodrigo: Me gustan más los gatos. Son más simpáticos que los perros.

Marisol: Los perros son menos perezosos que los gatos.

Rodrigo: Los perros de Tito son perezosos y muy grandes. ¡Son tan grandes como tú!

They stop outside the gate and look around. Tito appears, wearing Alicia's T-shirt, which is filthy.

Tito: ¡Hola, Rodrigo! Tu camiseta.

Suddenly the dogs begin growling. Rodrigo and Marisol run away frightened.

16 Comprensión de los episodios ¿Rodrigo, Marisol o Tito?

Escuchar
Leer

¿A quién de los tres se refiere cada oración? *(To whom does each sentence refer?)*

1. Pasa un rato con su tía Celia.
2. Tiene perros muy grandes.
3. El cumpleaños de su abuela es el primero de marzo.
4. Necesita la camiseta de su amiga Alicia.
5. Come con la familia de Rodrigo todos los viernes.
6. Es menor que Rodrigo.
7. No le gustan los perros.
8. Tiene la camiseta de Alicia.

Rodrigo

Tito

Marisol

17 Comprensión de los episodios ¿Comprendiste?

Escuchar
Leer

Contesta las preguntas según los episodios. *(Answer the questions.)*

1. ¿Cuándo es el cumpleaños de Ana?
2. ¿A qué hora está Trini Salgado en la escuela?
3. ¿A quién le gustan más los gatos, a Rodrigo o a Marisol?
4. ¿Cuántos años tienen los primos de Rodrigo?
5. ¿Cuántas hermanas tiene la madre de Rodrigo?
6. ¿Quién tiene la camiseta de Alicia?

18 La familia ideal

Hablar

Digital
performance space

STRATEGY Hablar
Consider your beliefs Before the conversation, consider your beliefs about families. What is an ideal family? Describe it on paper and then aloud. Do you know such a family?

Trabaja en un grupo de tres para expresar y apoyar opiniones sobre la familia ideal. Incluye tus respuestas a las siguientes preguntas. *(Offer and support opinions about the ideal family. Include your answers to these questions.)*

Para organizarte
- ¿Es grande o pequeña la familia? ¿Dónde vive?
- ¿Cuántas personas hay en la familia?
- ¿Cómo son las personas de la familia? ¿Qué hacen?
- ¿Cuántos años tienen las personas de la familia?

A Una familia pequeña es buena.

B Una familia grande es mejor que una familia pequeña porque es más interesante.

C No, una familia cómica es mejor porque...

Expansión
Give a summary of your group's opinions to the class.

19 | Integración

Digital **performance space**

Leer
Escuchar
Hablar

Lee el cartel de una familia que busca una casa para su perro. Después escucha el anuncio de radio de una organización para la protección de animales. Empareja cada perro con un miembro de tu familia y explica tu decisión. *(Read the flyer and listen to the radio announcement. Match each dog to someone in your family and explain your choices.)*

Fuente 1 Cartel

Es tan inteligente como su madre y... ¡más activo!

Le gusta correr, nadar y jugar al fútbol. ¡Es más atlético que yo! ☺

Vamos a Nueva York en enero y Rayo no va con nosotros. ☹

Si necesitas un amigo, Rayo necesita una familia.

Llámanos: 555-8231

Rayo
Labrador marrón.
Tiene un año.

Fuente 2 Anuncio de radio

Listen and take notes
• ¿Cómo es Dino?
• ¿Qué le gusta hacer a Dino?

modelo: Rayo es un buen perro para mi primo Alberto. Rayo es menos tranquilo que Dino y a mi primo le gusta correr...

20 | Un amigo nuevo

Digital **performance space**

Escribir

Tu familia va a recibir a un(a) estudiante de Puerto Rico. Escríbele una carta para describir a los miembros de tu familia. Usa comparativos. *(Write a letter to an exchange student comparing members of your family.)*

modelo: ¡Hola! Te presento a mi familia. Tengo dos hermanos. Yo soy mayor que mis hermanos. Mi hermano Lance es menor que...

Writing Criteria	Excellent	Good	Needs Work
Content	Your letter includes a lot of information.	Your letter includes some information.	Your letter includes little information.
Communication	Most of your letter is organized and easy to follow.	Parts of your letter are organized and easy to follow.	Your letter is disorganized and hard to follow.
Accuracy	Your letter has few mistakes in grammar and vocabulary.	Your letter has some mistakes in grammar and vocabulary.	Your letter has many mistakes in grammar and vocabulary.

Expansión
Write comparisons of your friends.

Más práctica Cuaderno *pp. 131–132* Cuaderno para hispanohablantes *pp. 133–134*

 **Get Help Online**
my.hrw.com

PARA Y PIENSA

Did you get it? Create sentences based on the Telehistoria using possessive adjectives and comparatives.
1. los perros (de Tito) / tan grande / Marisol
2. el primo (de Rodrigo) / menor / él
3. los perros (de Tito) / más perezoso(a) / los gatos

Lectura cultural

Additional readings at my.hrw.com
SPANISH
InterActive Reader

¡AVANZA! **Goal:** Read about the **quinceañera** celebrations in Peru and Puerto Rico. Then compare the parties and talk about the activities at the birthday parties you go to.

Comparación cultural

AUDIO

La quinceañera

STRATEGY Leer

Compare and contrast Draw a Venn diagram like this one. Use it to compare the **quinceañera** celebrations of Peru and Puerto Rico.

Perú   Puerto Rico

La fiesta[1] de quinceañera es muy popular en muchos países de Latinoamérica. Es similar al *Sweet Sixteen* de Estados Unidos. Muchas veces hay una ceremonia religiosa y una fiesta con banquete. En la fiesta hacen un brindis[2] en honor a la quinceañera y después todos bailan un vals[3].

La chica que celebra su cumpleaños también se llama la quinceañera. En Perú (y otros países) la quinceañera tiene catorce o quince damas de honor[4]: una por cada[5] año que tiene. No hay un menú especial de banquete, pero en Perú es común comer comida típica del país, bailar y escuchar música tradicional.

---

[1] party   [2] toast   [3] **bailan...** dance a waltz
[4] **damas...** maids of honor   [5] **por...** for each

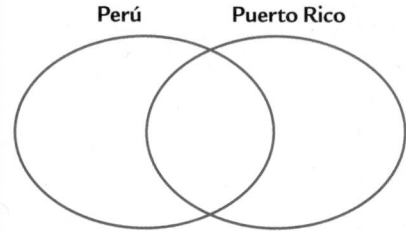

Comida tradicional

Perú

*Una quinceañera en Puerto Rico con
familia y amigos*

En Puerto Rico, la celebración se llama el quinceañero. Muchas veces las chicas tienen la gran fiesta en su cumpleaños número dieciséis (por influencia del *Sweet Sixteen*) y no en el cumpleaños de los quince años.

Puerto Rico

En el banquete de una quinceañera de Puerto Rico es normal comer comida típica del país, como arroz con pollo[6]. Todos bailan y escuchan música del Caribe: salsa, merengue, reggaetón y el hip-hop cubano.

---

[6] chicken and rice dish

PARA
Y
PIENSA

¿Comprendiste?
1. ¿Qué fiesta en Estados Unidos es similar a la fiesta de quinceañera?
2. ¿Cuántas damas de honor tiene una quinceañera en Perú?
3. ¿Cuándo tienen la fiesta las chicas de Puerto Rico?

¿Y tú?
¿Te gustan las fiestas de cumpleaños? ¿Qué haces en las fiestas?

❈ Proyectos culturales

Instrumentos de Puerto Rico y Perú

How do certain instruments and music become associated with a particular region? Percussion instruments that produce strong beats and rhythms are the base of much of the music of **Puerto Rico.** In **Peru,** the **zampoña** is a wind instrument that adds a deep and distinctive sound to traditional Andean music.

❈ Proyecto ❶ *Percussion*

Puerto Rico Make your own rhythm on a homemade percussion instrument.

Materials for your own percussion instrument

An object that can be used as a "found" percussion instrument, such as:
- coffee or juice can
- yogurt cup with pebbles, sand or seeds, secured inside with a lid on top
- wooden, plastic, or metal spoons
- pan lid and long-handled brush
- upside-down basket

Instructions

Practice making a rhythm pattern you can repeat on your "found" percussion instrument. Try creating different tones by striking the instrument in different places or with different objects.

❈ Proyecto ❷ *Zampoña*

Perú Use these simple materials to create your own **zampoña.**

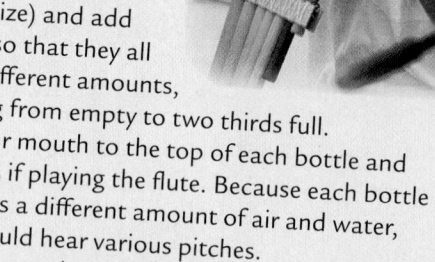

Materials for zampoña

4 or more plastic or glass bottles, all the same size
Water

Instructions

1. Bring to class four or more bottles (all the same size) and add water so that they all have different amounts, ranging from empty to two thirds full.
2. Put your mouth to the top of each bottle and blow as if playing the flute. Because each bottle contains a different amount of air and water, you should hear various pitches.
3. Add tape so that the bottles are connected in a row. Arrange the bottles according to their pitch, from low to high.

❈ En tu comunidad

Find out if any Andean music groups play in your community, perhaps at a cultural heritage fair or at a local university. Share your findings with the class.

En resumen
Vocabulario y gramática

Vocabulario

Talk About Family

la abuela	grandmother	la madrastra	stepmother
el abuelo	grandfather	la madre	mother
los abuelos	grandparents	el padrastro	stepfather
la familia	family	el padre	father
la hermana	sister	los padres	parents
el hermano	brother	el (la) primo(a)	cousin
los hermanos	brothers, brother(s) and sister(s)	los primos	cousins
		la tía	aunt
la hija	daughter	el tío	uncle
el hijo	son	los tíos	uncles, uncle(s) and aunt(s)
los hijos	son(s) and daughter(s), children		

Ask, Tell, and Compare Ages

¿Cuántos años tienes?	How old are you?	mayor	older
		menor	younger
Tengo... años.	I am . . . years old.		

Give Dates

¿Cuál es la fecha?	What is the date?
Es el... de...	It's the . . . of . . .
el primero de...	the first of . . .
el cumpleaños	birthday
¡Feliz cumpleaños!	Happy birthday!
la fecha de nacimiento	birth date

Pets

el (la) gato(a)	cat
el (la) perro(a)	dog

Other Words and Phrases

vivir	to live
ya	already

Numbers from 200 to 1,000,000 p. 165

Months p. 165

Gramática

Notas gramaticales: de to express possession p. 166, **tener... años** p. 168, Giving dates p. 171

Possessive Adjectives

In Spanish, **possessive adjectives** agree in number with the nouns they describe. **Nuestro(a)** and **vuestro(a)** must also agree in gender with the nouns they describe.

Singular Possessive Adjectives		Plural Possessive Adjectives	
mi *my*	**nuestro(a)** *our*	**mis** *my*	**nuestros(as)** *our*
tu *your (familiar)*	**vuestro(a)** *your (familiar)*	**tus** *your (familiar)*	**vuestros(as)** *your (familiar)*
su *your (formal)*	**su** *your*	**sus** *your (formal)*	**sus** *your*
su *his, her, its*	**su** *their*	**sus** *his, her, its*	**sus** *their*

Comparatives

Use the following phrases with an adjective to compare two things.
  más... que
  menos... que
  tan... como

When a comparison does not involve an adjective, use these phrases.
  más que...
  menos que...
  tanto como...

There are a few irregular comparative words.

mayor	menor	mejor	peor
older	younger	better	worse

Repaso de la lección

@HOMETUTOR
my.hrw.com

¡AvanzaRap!
DVD
Sing and Learn

¡LLEGADA!

Now you can
• talk about family
• ask and tell ages
• express possession
• give dates
• make comparisons

Using
• **de** to express possession
• possessive adjectives
• comparatives

To review
• **de** to express possession p. 166
• possessive adjectives p. 169

AUDIO

1 | Listen and understand

Marcos tiene una foto de su familia y explica quiénes son. Escucha a Marcos y luego indica su relación con las siguientes personas. *(Listen to Marcos describe a family photo and indicate each person's relationship to him.)*

modelo: Pedro
Pedro es el hermano de Marcos.

1. Elena y Rosa
2. Julio
3. Norma

4. Alberto
5. Diego y Felipe
6. Carmen

To review
• possessive adjectives p. 169

2 | Talk about family

Escribe oraciones para describir las relaciones de estas personas y sus edades. Usa adjetivos posesivos. *(Tell what family members these people have, and what their ages are. Use possessive adjectives.)*

modelo: yo / hermano menor (5 años)
Yo tengo un hermano menor. Mi hermano tiene cinco años.

1. Bárbara / hermana mayor (19 años)
2. tú / dos primos (7 y 11 años)
3. nosotros / abuelo (67 años)
4. Manuel y Óscar / padre (34 años)
5. yo / perro (5 años)
6. ustedes / madre (36 años)
7. tú y yo / dos tíos (48 y 44 años)
8. usted / abuela (81 años)
9. ellas / dos gatos (2 años)
10. yo / tía (30 años)

3 | Make comparisons

To review
• comparatives p. 174

Josefina describe a su gato, Memo, y a su perro, Sancho. Lee la descripción y escoge las palabras apropiadas. *(Read Josefina's description of her pets and choose the appropriate words.)*

> Memo, mi gato, y Sancho, mi perro, viven con mi familia. Memo tiene diez años y Sancho tiene cinco. Memo es **1.** (menor / mayor) que Sancho. Pero Sancho es **2.** (tan / más) grande que Memo y come más **3.** (como / que) él. Memo come **4.** (mejor / menor) comida que Sancho porque come buena comida para gatos. Sancho come comida **5.** (mayor / menos) nutritiva porque muchas veces come pizza y papas fritas. Memo y Sancho son muy perezosos. Memo es **6.** (tanto / tan) perezoso como Sancho. Descansan mucho. A Memo le gusta descansar **7.** (tanto / más) como a Sancho. Pero Memo y Sancho no son aburridos. También les gusta jugar un poco todos los días. Jugar con ellos es más divertido **8.** (como / que) mirar la televisión.

4 | Give dates

To review
• **de** to express possession p. 166

Escribe oraciones con las fechas de cumpleaños de estas personas. *(Write sentences giving these people's birthdays.)*

modelo: el señor Gómez: 13/4
El cumpleaños del señor Gómez es el trece de abril.

1. Berta: 23/12   **4.** Olga: 5/8   **7.** la maestra: 30/9

2. Emilio y Emilia: 1/2   **5.** Germán: 15/10   **8.** Luis: 27/3

3. la señora Serrano: 14/1   **6.** el director: 11/6   **9.** Víctor: 12/11

5 | Puerto Rico and Peru

To review
• Comparación cultural pp. 162, 170, 176
• Lectura cultural pp. 180–181

Comparación cultural

Answer these culture questions.

1. What do people do during **la sobremesa**?

2. Which political positions do people vote for in Puerto Rico?

3. Who does Rafael Tufiño portray in *Goyita*?

4. What are some **quinceañera** traditions? Describe at least three.

Más práctica Cuaderno *pp. 133–144* Cuaderno para hispanohablantes *pp. 135–144*

Get Help Online
my.hrw.com

Perú

El Salvador

Puerto Rico

AUDIO

¿Qué comemos?

Lectura y escritura

1 **Leer** Meals vary for people around the world. Read how María Luisa, Silvia, and José enjoy a meal on Sundays.

2 **Escribir** Using the three descriptions as models, write a short paragraph about a typical Sunday meal.

> **STRATEGY** **Escribir**
> **Make a mind map** To write about a real or imaginary Sunday meal, make a mind map like the one shown.

La comida del domingo

¿Dónde?   ¿Qué?   ¿Con quién?

Step 1 Complete the mind map of your Sunday meal by adding details to the categories of place (where you eat), foods (what you eat), and people (with whom you eat).

Step 2 Write your paragraph. Make sure to include all the information from your mind map. Check your writing by yourself or with help from a friend. Make final corrections.

Compara con tu mundo

Use the paragraph you wrote to compare your Sunday meal to a meal described by *one* of the three students. Share your paragraph with the class and mention something similar to or different from the meals described by the three students.

Cuaderno *pp. 145–147*   Cuaderno para hispanohablantes *pp. 145–147*

CULTURA Interactiva
my.hrw.com
See these pages come alive!

El Salvador

María Luisa

Hola, soy María Luisa. Yo soy de El Salvador. Los domingos, voy con mi hermana mayor y mi prima a Metrocentro[1]. Después de pasear unas horas, vamos a un café porque estamos cansadas y tenemos sed y hambre. En el café venden sándwiches, refrescos y jugos de papaya, mango, melón y otras frutas. A mí me gusta más la horchata[2]. Es una bebida muy rica.

[1] popular mall in San Salvador

[2] beverage made of rice, water, and milk

Perú

Silvia

Yo soy Silvia y vivo en Lima, Perú. Todos los domingos comemos la cena con mis tíos. Mi tío Ricardo siempre prepara su comida favorita, el ceviche[3]. A mí me gusta más el ají de gallina[4] que hace mi abuela. ¡Es mejor que el ceviche de mi tío! Después de la cena, mis padres y mis tíos beben café y hablan. Mis primos y yo comemos helado y escuchamos música.

[3] fish marinated in lime juice   [4] spicy chicken and potato dish

Puerto Rico

José

¿Qué tal? Me llamo José. Vivo en San Juan, Puerto Rico. Todos los domingos, mi familia y yo comemos el almuerzo en un restaurante. Nos gusta comer carne asada[5]. Es muy, muy buena. También me gustan los tostones[6]. ¡Pero los tostones de mi madre son más ricos que los tostones en un restaurante!

[5] barbecued   [6] fried plantains

Repaso inclusivo
♻ Options for Review

¡*AvanzaRap!*
DVD
Sing and Learn

1 | Listen, understand, and compare

Escuchar

Listen to this episode from a call-in radio show giving advice to teens. Then answer the questions.

1. ¿Cómo es Diana? ¿Qué problema tiene?
2. ¿Por qué tiene que estudiar Diana?
3. ¿Qué le gusta hacer a Diana? ¿Y a Óscar?
4. ¿Óscar es mayor o menor que Diana? ¿Cuántos años tienen?
5. ¿Qué va a hacer Diana?

Do you have siblings or cousins? Do you have a lot in common or are you very different? Explain.

2 | Present a friend

Hablar

Bring in a photo or drawing of your best friend or a person you admire. Introduce the person to the class and talk about what personality traits, favorite activities, and favorite foods you have in common. Then mention your differences. Prepare to talk for at least three minutes.

3 | Get to know a new student

Hablar

Role-play a conversation in which you are an exchange student from Puerto Rico, and your partner is your host brother or sister. Introduce yourself and ask about his or her classes, likes and dislikes, and what his or her family is like. Then answer his or her questions for you. Your conversation should be at least four minutes long.

4 | Plan a family reunion

Escribir

Your family is hosting a reunion with all of your extended family members. You are in charge of organizing a breakfast for everyone. Create a seating chart, and label each seat with the person's name, age, and relation to you. Write what breakfast foods and drinks each person likes and doesn't like.

5 | Talk with a nutritionist

Hablar

Work in a group of four. Three members of the group are siblings and the fourth is a nutritionist. The nutritionist should ask each family member's age, at what time they eat their meals, their food likes and dislikes, and what they do after school. The nutritionist should tell them what healthy foods they have to eat and the activities they have to do. Each person should talk for at least two minutes.

6 | Display your family tree

Hablar
Escribir

Work with a partner to create a poster of your family tree or that of a TV family. Use photos or make drawings of each family member. Label each person's name, age, birthday, favorite activity, and favorite food. Use the family tree to describe your family to your partner, making comparisons between family members. Then present your partner's family to the class.

7 | Compare twins

Leer
Escribir

Read this chart from a magazine article about Manolo and Martín Santos, twins that were recently reunited after being separated at birth. Then write a paragraph comparing the two men. Include at least six comparisons.

MUCHAS COINCIDENCIAS

Manolo
Nacimiento: 30/7, a las 2:20 de la tarde
Personalidad: serio, muy artístico
Profesión: Maestro de español. Enseña cuatro clases. Trabaja 45 horas en la semana.
Familia: dos hijos (Enrique y Arturo) y una hija (Rebeca)
Actividades: Le gusta practicar deportes: correr, montar en bicicleta, jugar al fútbol.

Martín
Nacimiento: 30/7, a las 2:22 de la tarde
Personalidad: cómico, muy artístico
Profesión: Maestro de español. Enseña seis clases. Trabaja 52 horas en la semana.
Familia: dos hijos (Eduardo y Ángel) y dos hijas (Rebeca y Rosa)
Actividades: Le gusta practicar deportes: andar en patineta, jugar al fútbol, jugar al golf.

La historia increíble de los hermanos Santos

Correr, montar en bicicleta, jugar al fútbol, andar en patineta, jugar al fútbol

UNIDAD 4

España

En el centro

Lección 1
Tema: **¡Vamos de compras!**

Lección 2
Tema: **¿Qué hacemos esta noche?**

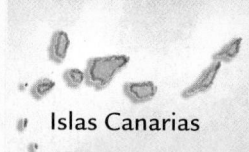
Islas Canarias

«¡Hola!
**Somos Maribel y Enrique.
Vivimos en Madrid, la capital.»**

Francia

España

León

Salamanca

Andorra

Barcelona

Portugal

Madrid ★

Valencia

Islas Baleares

Océano
Atlántico

Sevilla

Granada

Mar Mediterráneo

Ceuta

Melilla

Argelia

Marruecos

Población: 48.146.134

Área: 194.897 millas cuadradas

Capital: Madrid

Moneda: el euro (lo comparte con otros 25 países)

Idiomas: castellano (español), catalán, gallego, vasco

Comida típica: tortilla española, paella, gazpacho

Gente famosa: Carmen Amaya (bailaora), Francisco de Goya (artista), Ana María Matute (escritora), Severo Ochoa (bioquímico)

Paella

190 ciento noventa

CULTURA Interactiva
my.hrw.com
See these pages come alive!

◀ **Aficionados del fútbol** Official songs, or **himnos oficiales,** are an important part of the Spanish soccer experience. Fans of the Real Madrid team sing **¡Hala Madrid!** *(Let's go, Madrid!),* especially during games against rival team FC Barcelona, known as **El Barça.** *What teams have sports rivalries where you live?*

Un jugador de fútbol del Real Madrid

El arte y la literatura Pablo Picasso, one of the 20th century's greatest artists, portrayed traditional Spanish themes in his work. He made this print of fictional characters Don Quijote and Sancho Panza exactly 350 years after Cervantes wrote his famous novel, *El ingenioso hidalgo Don Quijote de la Mancha. What other works of Picasso are you familiar with?* ▶

Don Quijote (1955), Pablo Picasso

◀ **Las costumbres regionales** During the **Feria de Abril** celebration, girls wear Seville's traditional costume, **el traje de sevillana. Sevillanas** are similar to **flamenco,** which involves singing, dance, and guitar as well as rhythmic clapping or foot taps. *What type of music and dress would be considered typically American?*

Bailarinas de flamenco en Sevilla

UNIDAD **4**

España

Lección 1

Tema:

¡Vamos de compras!

¡AVANZA! **In this lesson you will learn to**
- talk about what clothes you want to buy
- say what you wear in different seasons

using
- **tener** expressions
- stem-changing verbs: **e → ie**
- direct object pronouns

♻ *¿Recuerdas?*
- numbers from 11 to 100
- the verb **tener**
- after-school activities

Comparación cultural

In this lesson you will learn about
- surrealism and Salvador Dalí
- climates around the world
- Spanish poet and novelist Antonio Colinas

Compara con tu mundo

These teenagers are shopping for clothes in Madrid, Spain. While there are department stores (**almacenes**) and some shopping centers (**centros comerciales**) in Madrid, many people also shop at small stores like the one pictured here. *Where do you like to shop for clothes?*

¿Qué ves?

Mira la foto

¿La chica está al lado del chico?

¿Quién es más alto, el chico o la chica?

¿Cómo están ellos?

MODES OF COMMUNICATION

INTERPRETIVE	INTERPERSONAL	PRESENTATIONAL
Read store coupons and listen to store ads to describe the clothing you want to buy and learn how much it costs.	Discuss shopping for clothes. With classmates, describe the clothing you wear for various activities and in different seasons.	Describe what others are wearing. Write a poem about what you wear and like to do during a particular season.

Una tienda de ropa
Madrid, España

✿ Presentación de VOCABULARIO

¡AVANZA! **Goal:** Learn about the clothes Enrique and Maribel like to wear. Then practice what you have learned to talk about clothes and how much they cost. *Actividades 1–2*

♻ *¿Recuerdas?* Numbers from 11 to 100 p. 87

VIDEO
DVD

AUDIO

A ¡Hola! Me llamo Enrique. **Voy de compras** al **centro comercial** con mi amiga, Maribel. **Queremos** comprar **ropa nueva.** A Maribel le gusta ir a todas **las tiendas.**

B Voy a comprar **una camisa** y **unos jeans. Cuestan** treinta euros. El **vestido** de Maribel **cuesta** veinte euros. Es un buen **precio.**

la tienda

ir de compras

el centro comercial

Enrique

la camisa

la chaqueta

los jeans

los calcetines

Maribel

la blusa

los pantalones

los zapatos

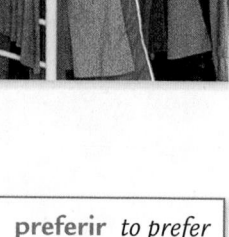
el vestido

el precio

22€

Más vocabulario

cerrar *to close*	**preferir** *to prefer*
¿Cuánto cuesta(n)?	**tener suerte**
How much does it (do they) cost?	*to be lucky*
el dólar *dollar*	
empezar *to begin*	
entender *to understand*	

Expansión de vocabulario p. R5

En España se dice...

In Spain the word for *jeans* is **los vaqueros.** They also use **los tejanos.**

C Me gusta **llevar** ropa **blanca, roja** y **marrón.** A Maribel le gusta llevar **una camiseta verde** y **unos pantalones cortos azules.**

roja | verde | amarilla | anaranjada | **la camiseta**

marrones | azules | blancos | negros | **los pantalones cortos**

D Maribel **piensa** que **el vestido** es un poco **feo.** Ella **tiene razón;** no es muy bonito. Ella compra otro vestido que le gusta más.

pensar

pagar

el dinero

los euros

E En España hay cuatro **estaciones.** Maribel siempre **tiene calor durante el verano.** Me gusta **el invierno,** pero siempre **tengo frío.**

las estaciones

la primavera | el verano

el otoño | el invierno

tener calor

el sombrero

tener frío

el gorro

@**HOMETUTOR** my.hrw.com | **Interactive Flashcards**

¡A responder! Escuchar

Escucha las siguientes descripciones de ropa. Levanta la mano si llevas la ropa que escuchas. *(Listen to the following descriptions of clothes. Raise your hand if you are wearing that item.)*

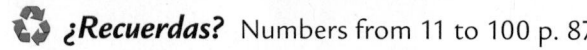

Práctica de VOCABULARIO

1 | Los precios de la ropa   ♻ ¿Recuerdas? Numbers from 11 to 100 p. 87

¿Recuerdas? Numbers from 11 to 100 p. 87

Escribir Hablar

Indica cuánto cuesta la ropa. *(Tell how much the clothing costs.)*

modelo: la camisa
La camisa cuesta veintiocho euros.

1. el vestido
2. los jeans
3. los zapatos
4. la chaqueta
5. la camiseta
6. los pantalones cortos
7. la blusa

2 | Ropa de muchos colores

Hablar

Pregúntale a otro(a) estudiante de qué color es cada artículo de ropa.
(Ask a partner the color of the clothing items.)

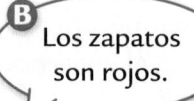

A ¿De qué color son los zapatos?

B Los zapatos son rojos.

1.    2.    3.    4.

5.    6.    7.    8.

Expansión
Make your own price list. A partner will ask you how much the items cost.

Más práctica   Cuaderno *pp. 148–150*   Cuaderno para hispanohablantes *pp. 148–151*

🌐 **Get Help Online**
my.hrw.com

PARA Y PIENSA

Did you get it? Ask how much the following items cost.
1. the white socks   3. the orange jacket
2. the blue dress   4. the red shorts

VOCABULARIO en contexto

¡AVANZA! **Goal:** Pay attention to the different articles of clothing Enrique and Maribel talk about. Then practice these words and **tener** expressions to say what you wear in different seasons. *Actividades 3–4*

♻ *¿Recuerdas?* The verb **tener** p. 91, after-school activities p. 32

Telehistoria escena 1

@HOMETUTOR **View, Read and Record**
my.hrw.com

STRATEGIES

Cuando lees
Scan for details Before reading, quickly scan the scene to discover basic details: Who's in the scene? What are they doing? Where are they? What time is it? What's the season?

Cuando escuchas
Listen for wishes Listen to Maribel and Enrique express where they want to go. Who gets his or her way in this scene? How does this happen?

VIDEO DVD

AUDIO

Enrique

Maribel

Maribel is opening a package from Alicia.

Enrique: ¿Es una camiseta?

Maribel: *(reading a flyer from the package)* Sí. Y Trini está en el centro comercial del Parque de las Avenidas de las doce a la una de la tarde.

Enrique: ¿Dónde está el Parque de las Avenidas?

Maribel: Necesito un mapa. ¿Vamos?

They start walking. Enrique stops and points at a store.

Enrique: ¡Una tienda de ropa! ¡Y yo necesito comprar una chaqueta! ¡Tengo frío!

Maribel: ¡Eres muy cómico! En el verano, cuando hace calor, ¿necesitas una chaqueta?

Enrique: ¿Hace calor? Yo no tengo calor.

Maribel: En el invierno, cuando hace frío, llevas pantalones cortos. Y durante la primavera, ¡nunca llevas calcetines!

Enrique: ¡Me gusta ser diferente! ¿No necesitas unos zapatos nuevos?

Maribel: *(reluctantly)* ¡Vale! Diez minutos. **Continuará...** p. 202

También se dice

España Maribel uses the word **vale** to say *OK*. In other Spanish-speaking countries you might hear:
• **México** órale, sale, ándale
• **Cuba** dale

3 | *Comprensión del episodio*   La ropa apropiada

Escuchar
Leer

Escoge la palabra o frase correcta para completar las oraciones, según el episodio. *(Complete the sentences by choosing the correct word or phrase, according to the episode.)*

1. Maribel tiene _____ .

2. Trini está en _____ .

3. Enrique necesita comprar _____ .

4. Enrique lleva _____ en el invierno.

5. Enrique nunca lleva _____ en la primavera.

6. A Enrique le gusta ser _____ .

a. pantalones cortos

b. diferente

c. calcetines

d. una camiseta

e. el centro comercial

f. una chaqueta

Nota gramatical   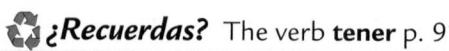 *¿Recuerdas?* The verb **tener** p. 91

Tener is used to form many expressions that in English would use the verb *to be.*

tener **calor**	*to be hot*	tener **razón**	*to be right*
tener **frío**	*to be cold*	tener **suerte**	*to be lucky*

En el invierno **tengo frío,** y en el verano **tengo calor.**
In winter, I'm cold, and in summer, I'm hot.

---

4 | ¿Qué ropa llevas?    *¿Recuerdas?* After-school activities p. 32

Hablar

Túrnense para contestar preguntas sobre qué ropa llevan en estas situaciones.
(Take turns answering questions about what you wear in these situations.)

A ¿Qué ropa llevas cuando paseas?

B Llevo pantalones, una camiseta y un sombrero.

Estudiante A

1. montar en bicicleta
2. tener calor
3. practicar deportes
4. tener frío
5. ir a la escuela
6. ¿ ?

Estudiante B

gorro
pantalones cortos
chaqueta
camiseta
vestido
¿ ?

Expansión
Take turns asking your partner what he or she wears in different weather conditions.

Get Help Online
my.hrw.com

PARA Y PIENSA

Did you get it?   Enrique likes to be different. Complete each sentence with the correct form of **tener calor** or **tener frío.**

1. En el verano, Enrique _____ y lleva una chaqueta.

2. En el invierno, él lleva pantalones cortos porque _____ .

3. Cuando Maribel tiene calor, Enrique _____ .

❖Presentación de GRAMÁTICA

¡AVANZA! **Goal:** Learn how to form **e → ie** stem-changing verbs. Then use these verbs to talk about clothes you and others want to buy. *Actividades 5–8*

English Grammar Connection: There are no stem-changing verbs in the present tense of English.

Stem-Changing Verbs: e → ie

ANIMATEDGRAMMAR
my.hrw.com

In Spanish, some verbs have a stem change in the present tense.
How do you form the present tense of **e → ie** stem-changing verbs?

Here's how:

Stem-changing verbs have regular **-ar, -er,** and **-ir** present-tense endings.
For **e → ie** stem-changing verbs, the **e** of the stem changes to **ie** in all forms except **nosotros(as)** and **vosotros(as).**

stem changes to

quer**er**   **qui**e**ro**

querer	*to want*
quiero	queremos
quieres	queréis
quiere	quieren

Other **e → ie** stem-changing verbs you have learned are **cerrar, empezar, entender, pensar,** and **preferir.** In stem-changing verbs, it is the next-to-last syllable that changes.

> Paula **prefiere** el vestido azul.
> *Paula **prefers** the blue dress.*

Notice that when one verb follows another, the **first verb** is conjugated and the second is in its **infinitive** form.

> ¿**Quieres** mirar la televisión o leer un libro?
> ***Do you want** to watch television or read a book?*

Más práctica
Cuaderno *pp. 151–153*
Cuaderno para hispanohablantes *pp. 152–154*

@HOMETUTOR my.hrw.com
Leveled Practice
Conjuguemos.com

❖ Práctica de GRAMÁTICA

5 | Todos quieren ropa

Escribir

Enrique y Maribel miran un catálogo de ropa y describen la ropa que quieren ellos y otros. Usa las fotos para decir qué ropa quieren.
(Write sentences describing the clothing items these people want.)

modelo: la madre de Enrique
La madre de Enrique quiere la blusa anaranjada.

1. Maribel
2. tú
3. vosotros
4. usted
5. yo
6. los amigos de Maribel
7. mis amigas y yo
8. ustedes

Terráqueo - Ropa para este planeta   ROPA DE TEMPORADA

1. 49 €
2. 13,05 €
3. 24 €
4. 13,95 €
5.
6.
7. 69 €
8. 6 €   44 €
12 €

LLAME AL 555 22 13 40 O VISÍTENOS EN WWW.TERRAQUEO.ES   23

Expansión
Write about what you prefer to buy when you go shopping.

6 | El regalo de cumpleaños

Leer
Escribir

Maribel quiere comprar un regalo para su hermana. Completa lo que dice. *(Complete the paragraph with the correct form of the appropriate verb.)*

querer	entender
cerrar	pensar
preferir	empezar

Mañana celebramos el cumpleaños de mi hermana mayor. Voy a la tienda de ropa porque ella **1.** una chaqueta nueva. Ya tiene dos chaquetas, pero ella **2.** que los otras chaquetas son feas. Mis padres no **3.** por qué necesita tres chaquetas. Pero ahora el otoño **4.** y a ella no le gusta tener frío. Mis hermanos y yo vamos a la tienda Moda 16. Yo **5.** otra tienda pero ellos tienen el dinero. Tenemos que llegar antes de las ocho porque la tienda **6.** a las ocho.

7 | ¿Tiene suerte en la tienda?

**Escuchar
Escribir**

Enrique está en el centro comercial. Escucha lo que dice y contesta las preguntas. *(Listen to Enrique's story and answer the questions.)*

1. ¿Qué estación empieza?
2. ¿Qué quiere comprar Enrique?
3. ¿Prefiere tener frío o calor él?
4. ¿Qué quiere comprar Micaela?
5. ¿Qué no entiende Enrique?
6. ¿Quién tiene suerte?

8 | ¿Qué piensas de la ropa?

Hablar

Habla con otro(a) estudiante sobre la ropa de varios colores. *(Talk with a classmate about your opinions on clothes.)*

A ¿Quieres comprar un sombrero marrón?

B No, pienso que los sombreros marrones son feos. Prefiero los sombreros negros. (Sí, quiero comprar un sombrero marrón.)

Expansión
List the clothes you and your partner want in order of preference. Share your preferences with the class.

Más práctica Cuaderno *pp. 151–153* Cuaderno para hispanohablantes *pp. 152–154*

🌐 **Get Help Online**
my.hrw.com

**PARA
Y
PIENSA**

Did you get it? Complete each sentence with the correct form of the appropriate verb: **empezar, cerrar,** or **pensar.**

1. Yo _____ que la blusa amarilla es bonita.
2. Ya hace frío cuando _____ el invierno.
3. El centro comercial _____ a las nueve de la noche.

✤ GRAMÁTICA en contexto

¡AVANZA! **Goal:** Listen to the **e → ie** stem-changing verbs that Enrique and Maribel use while they are shopping for clothes. Then use the stem-changing verbs to talk about your clothing preferences. *Actividades 9–10*

Telehistoria escena 2

@HOMETUTOR View, Read
my.hrw.com and Record

STRATEGIES

Cuando lees
Look for color words In this scene, Enrique and Maribel discuss colors and types of clothing. Which color words do you find?

Cuando escuchas
Disregard stereotypes Who wants to keep looking at clothes and who is worried about being late? Is this expected? Why or why not?

VIDEO
DVD

AUDIO

Maribel: Tenemos que estar en el centro comercial a las doce, ¿entiendes?

Enrique: Sí, entiendo. Dos minutos más. ¿Prefieres los vaqueros negros o los pantalones verdes?

Maribel: Prefiero ir al centro comercial, ¡ahora!

Enrique: Quiero la camisa blanca.

Vendedora: Tenemos camisas en color azul y en verde. ¿Queréis ver?

Maribel: *(to the clerk)* No, gracias. *(to Enrique, frustrated)* Pero Enrique, ¿una tienda de ropa? ¿No prefieres ir de compras al centro comercial?

Enrique: No. No quiero comprar la ropa en el centro comercial. Los precios no son buenos. *(still shopping)* ¿Te gustan los pantalones cortos azules?

Maribel: *(rushing him)* Sí, sí. Y me gustan los calcetines rojos, la camisa amarilla y los zapatos marrones...

Enrique: No, no, no. ¿Rojo, amarillo y marrón? No, no me gustan.

Continuará... p. 207

9 | *Comprensión del episodio* En la tienda de ropa

**Escuchar
Leer**

¿Quién prefiere las siguientes cosas, Maribel o Enrique?

(Who prefers the following things—Maribel or Enrique?)

1. ir de compras en una tienda de ropa
2. la camisa amarilla
3. la camisa blanca
4. los calcetines rojos
5. los zapatos marrones
6. ir al centro comercial temprano

Maribel

Enrique

10 | La ropa y las estaciones

Hablar

Habla con otro(a) estudiante de lo que prefieres llevar y no llevar durante cada estación. *(Talk about what you prefer to wear and not wear during each season.)*

A ¿Qué prefieres llevar durante el verano?

B Prefiero llevar pantalones cortos. Nunca llevo chaqueta durante el verano.

Expansión
Describe what your partner is wearing.

Comparación cultural

El arte surrealista de España

How might dreams influence an artist's work? Artist Salvador Dalí from **Spain** is well known for his surrealist paintings. In surrealist art, the imagery reflects an artist's imagination and is often inspired by dreams. *La persistencia de la memoria,* considered one of Dalí's masterpieces, shows pocket watches that appear to be melting. Many interpret this painting as a commentary about the nature of time. What do you think Dalí's message is?

Compara con tu mundo *Can you think of a dream you had that would make an interesting painting?*

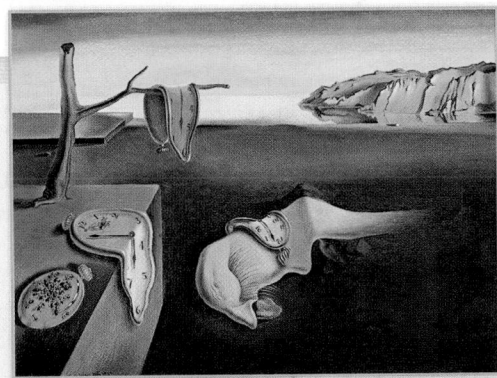

La persistencia de la memoria *(1931), Salvador Dalí*

Get Help Online
my.hrw.com

PARA Y PIENSA

Did you get it? Complete each sentence based on the Telehistoria with the correct form of the verb in parentheses.

1. Enrique _____ que van al centro comercial. (entender)
2. Maribel _____ ir al centro comercial. (preferir)
3. Enrique _____ comprar la camisa blanca. (querer)

 # Presentación de GRAMÁTICA

¡AVANZA! **Goal:** Learn how to use direct object pronouns. Then practice using them to talk about the clothes you wear and those you want to buy. *Actividades 11–14*

English Grammar Connection: Direct objects receive the action of the verb in a sentence. They answer the question *whom?* or *what?* about the verb. The direct object can be a **noun** or a **pronoun.**

Luisa is buying the **blouse.** Luisa is buying **it.**   Luisa compra la **blusa.** Luisa **la** compra.

noun   pronoun   noun   pronoun

Direct Object Pronouns

ANIMATEDGRAMMAR
my.hrw.com

Direct object **pronouns** can be used to replace **direct object nouns.**

Here's how:

	Singular		Plural	
	me	*me*	**nos**	*us*
	te	*you (familiar)*	**os**	*you (familiar)*
masculine	**lo**	*you (formal), him, it*	**los**	*you, them* — *masculine*
feminine	**la**	*you (formal), her, it*	**las**	*you, them* — *feminine*

The **direct object noun** is placed *after* the **conjugated verb.**

The **direct object pronoun** is placed directly *before* the **conjugated verb.**

replaced by

Quiero la **camisa** azul.   **La quiero.**

I want the blue **shirt.**   *I want* **it.**

When an **infinitive** follows the **conjugated verb**, the **direct object pronoun** can be placed *before* the **conjugated verb** or be *attached* to the **infinitive.**

replaced by

Quiero comprar **zapatos** negros.   Y **los** quiero comprar hoy.

I want to buy black **shoes.**   *or* Y **quiero** comprar**los** hoy.

And I want to buy **them** *today.*

Más práctica
Cuaderno *pp. 154–156*
Cuaderno para hispanohablantes *pp. 155–158*

HOMETUTOR my.hrw.com
Leveled Practice

❋Práctica de GRAMÁTICA

11 | Ropa para una fiesta

Leer

Maribel y su amiga hablan de la ropa que quieren comprar para la fiesta del sábado. Completa sus mensajes instantáneos con los pronombres correctos. *(Complete the instant messages by choosing the correct direct object pronouns.)*

---

mensajero instantáneo

pelirroja16: Quiero comprar un vestido azul pero no tengo mucho dinero. ¿ _1._ (Lo/La) compro?

busco_rebaja: Mmm... _2._ (me/te) entiendo. Bueno, ¿cuánto cuesta el vestido?

pelirroja16: Veintinueve euros. Y tú, ¿qué necesitas comprar? ¿Una blusa blanca?

busco_rebaja: Ya _3._ (la/los) tengo. Necesito unos zapatos. Los zapatos negros son más elegantes. ¿ _4._ (Me/Os) entiendes?

pelirroja16: Sí, tienes razón. Si quieres zapatos negros, _5._ (nos/los) venden en la Tienda Betún.

busco_rebaja: ¡Vale! También venden vestidos azules. _6._ (Nos/Los) tienen por veinte euros.

Expansión
Write what you and your friends prefer to wear to a party.

12 | Lo que Enrique quiere

Escribir

Identifica lo que Enrique quiere y no quiere comprar. Usa pronombres. *(Use direct object pronouns to tell what Enrique wants or doesn't want to buy.)*

modelo: No le gustan **los zapatos anaranjados.**
No **los** quiere comprar. (No quiere comprar**los.**)

1. Los pantalones son feos.

2. No le gusta la camiseta.

3. Le gustan mucho las camisas.

4. Prefiere los calcetines verdes.

5. El sombrero es horrible.

6. Prefiere los zapatos azules.

7. No necesita pantalones cortos.

8. Prefiere la chaqueta blanca.

🎧 **AUDIO**

Pronunciación **La letra c con a, o, u**

Before **a, o,** or **u,** the Spanish **c** is pronounced like the /k/ sound in the English word *call.* Listen and repeat.

ca →	**ca**misa	**ca**lor	to**ca**r	nun**ca**
co →	**co**mprar	**co**rto	po**co**	blan**co**
cu →	**cu**mpleaños	**cu**ando	**cu**aderno	es**cu**ela

Carmen compra pantalones cortos. Carlos tiene calor; quiere una camiseta.

Before a consonant other than **h,** it has the same sound: **clase, octubre.**

13 | Unos modelos cómicos

Hablar | Maribel y Enrique van a una tienda y combinan ropa de muchos colores. Pregúntale a otro(a) estudiante quién lleva la ropa que describes.
(Ask a partner about Maribel's and Enrique's clothing.)

modelo: gorro

A ¿Quién lleva **el gorro verde**?

B Enrique **lo** lleva.

1. zapatos
2. camisa
3. chaqueta
4. pantalones cortos
5. jeans
6. ¿ ?

14 | ¿Qué llevas en julio?

Hablar | **Comparación cultural**

Climas diferentes

How does geography affect a country's climate? Countries near the equator have rainy and dry seasons, but have warm temperatures year-round. Countries in the northern and southern hemispheres have opposite seasons. For example, in **Spain,** July is a summer month and the weather is often hot, but in **Chile** it is a winter month. Chile's varied terrain, from beaches to mountains, and length (over 2,600 miles) create many different climates.

Barcelona, España

Compara con tu mundo *How does the geography of your area affect the climate?*

Los Andes en Chile

En julio, tú y otro(a) estudiante van a **Chile, México, España, Puerto Rico, Argentina** y **Nueva York.** Pregúntale qué ropa lleva. *(Ask a partner what he or she wears in these places in July.)*

A ¿Llevas una camiseta en Chile en julio?

B No, no la llevo. Llevo una chaqueta y...

Más práctica Cuaderno *pp. 154–156* Cuaderno para hispanohablantes *pp. 155–158*

Get Help Online
my.hrw.com

PARA Y PIENSA

Did you get it? In each sentence, use the correct direct object pronoun.
1. Luisa quiere los pantalones blancos. Ella _____ compra.
2. No quiero la blusa nueva. ¿ _____ quieres tú?
3. Nosotros preferimos las camisas azules. _____ compramos.

❋ Todo junto

Goal: *Show what you know* Listen to Maribel and Enrique talk to the salesclerk about what Enrique wants to buy. Then use **e → ie** stem-changing verbs and direct object pronouns to talk about clothing preferences. *Actividades 15–19*

Telehistoria completa

@HOMETUTOR View, Read
my.hrw.com and Record

STRATEGIES

Cuando lees
Identify cultural practices Currency varies from country to country. Identify the currency that Enrique and Maribel use to pay for purchases.

Cuando escuchas
Take the "emotional temperature" Find out who has the greatest intensity of feeling by listening to voices. Who is the most upset and why?

Escena 1 *Resumen*
Maribel tiene que ir al centro comercial porque necesita el autógrafo de Trini. Pero Enrique quiere ir de compras en una tienda.

Escena 2 *Resumen*
Enrique y Maribel están en una tienda, y Enrique quiere comprar mucha ropa. Maribel prefiere ir al centro comercial.

VIDEO DVD

AUDIO

Escena 3

Maribel: Enrique, tienes que pagar. Son las once y media.

Enrique: Un gorro verde. ¡Lo quiero comprar! ¡Tengo que comprarlo!

Maribel: Enrique, ¡pero tú ya tienes un gorro verde!

Enrique: Sí, pero nunca lo llevo.

Maribel: Quieres una chaqueta, ¿no?

Enrique: Tienes razón. La chaqueta... la necesito. *(to the salesclerk)* ¿Vende chaquetas?

Vendedora: ¿En verano? No. Las vendo en el otoño.

Enrique: ¿Cuánto cuesta todo?

Vendedora: Los pantalones cuestan treinta euros, la camisa cuesta veinticinco, y el gorro, quince. Son setenta euros.

Enrique: ¡Mi dinero! ¡No lo tengo!

Maribel: ¡No te entiendo! ¿Quieres ir de compras y no tienes dinero?

Enrique: Está en mi mochila. ¿Dónde está mi mochila? ¿Tienes dinero? En el centro comercial yo compro la comida.

Maribel: ¿Con qué piensas pagar? No tienes dinero.

15 | Comprensión de los episodios   ¿Cierto o falso?

**Escuchar
Leer**

Lee las oraciones y di si son ciertas o falsas. Corrige las oraciones falsas.
(Read the sentences and say if they are true or false. Correct the false statements.)

1. Enrique piensa que los precios son buenos en el centro comercial.
2. Maribel prefiere llegar al centro comercial a las doce.
3. Maribel necesita comprar una chaqueta.
4. Enrique tiene setenta euros para comprar su ropa.
5. A Maribel le gusta ser diferente.
6. Enrique prefiere llevar una chaqueta en el invierno.
7. Enrique compra una chaqueta en la tienda de ropa.

16 | Comprensión de los episodios   Analizar la historia

**Escuchar
Leer**

Contesta las preguntas sobre los episodios. *(Answer the questions about the episodes.)*

1. ¿Qué estación es?
2. ¿Dónde quiere comprar ropa Enrique?
3. ¿De qué color es el gorro?

4. ¿Cuánto cuestan los pantalones? ¿La camisa? ¿El gorro?
5. ¿Qué problema tiene Enrique?

Expansión
Retell the episode, substituting the equivalent prices in dollars for the items mentioned.

17 | ¡A jugar! Un juego de quién

Digital **performance space**

Hablar

> **STRATEGY Hablar**
> **Prepare and don't stress out** Create a list of useful questions and possible answers. Include various types of clothes. Review your verb endings. Then just talk!

Da una pista sobre una persona de la clase. Las otras personas de tu grupo te van a hacer preguntas para adivinar quién es. Sigue el modelo. *(Give a clue about someone in your class. The other members of your group will ask you yes/no questions to identify who it is.)*

A Lleva jeans azules.

B ¿Tiene el sombrero verde?

Sí, lo tiene. (No, no lo tiene.)

C ¿Lleva zapatos blancos?

Sí, los lleva. (No, no los lleva.)

¿Es David?

Sí, ¡tienes razón! (No, no tienes razón.)

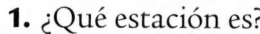

18 | Integración

Leer
Escuchar
Hablar

Digital
performance)space

Lee el cupón de descuentos (*discounts*) y escucha el anuncio de la tienda. Describe qué ropa quieres comprar para tus amigos(as) y cuánto cuesta.

(Describe four items you want to buy for your friends and how much each item costs.)

Fuente 1 Cupón

Fuente 2 Anuncio

Listen and take notes
• ¿Qué venden en la tienda?
• ¿Cuánto cuesta la ropa?

modelo: Quiero comprar un
vestido verde para Emily. Cuesta...

19 | Un poema de la estación

Digital
performance)space

Escribir

Escribe un poema sobre una de las estaciones. Incluye los siguientes elementos. *(Write a poem that talks about one of the seasons by including the following elements.)*

Para organizarte:
· *el nombre de la estación* ⟶ verano
· *dos colores que describen la estación* ⟶ verde, azul
· *tres cosas que quieres* ⟶ quiero zapatos, helado, camisetas
· *cuatro actividades que prefieres hacer* ⟶ prefiero jugar, pasear, leer, descansar
· *una descripción de cómo estás* ⟶ tengo calor

modelo:

Writing Criteria	Excellent	Good	Needs Work
Content	Your poem includes all of the elements.	Your poem includes some of the elements.	Your poem includes a few of the elements.
Communication	Most of your poem is easy to follow.	Parts of your poem are easy to follow.	Your poem is hard to follow.
Accuracy	Your poem has very few mistakes in grammar and vocabulary.	Your poem has some mistakes in grammar and vocabulary.	Your poem has many mistakes in grammar and vocabulary.

Expansión
Display your poem on a visual that reflects what you have expressed.

Más práctica Cuaderno *pp. 157–158* Cuaderno para hispanohablantes *pp. 159–160*

🌐 **Get Help Online**
my.hrw.com

PARA Y PIENSA

Did you get it? Answer each question based on the Telehistoria with **sí,** using direct object pronouns.
1. ¿Necesita Enrique la chaqueta?
2. ¿Prefiere Enrique el gorro verde?
3. ¿Quiere comprar Enrique la comida?

 **¡AVANZA!**   **Goal:** Read a poem by a Spanish poet. Then talk about what you have read and describe winter in your region.

AUDIO

Las memorias del invierno

Antonio Colinas is a poet and novelist from León, in northern Spain. He published the following poem in 1988.

STRATEGY Leer

Find the feelings Find phrases that show the poet's feelings and write them in a chart like the one below. Write the feeling after each phrase.

Emotions in *Invierno tardío* by Colinas

- Phrase: es como primavera temprana
  Feeling: está feliz
- Phrase:
  Feeling:
- Phrase:
  Feeling:

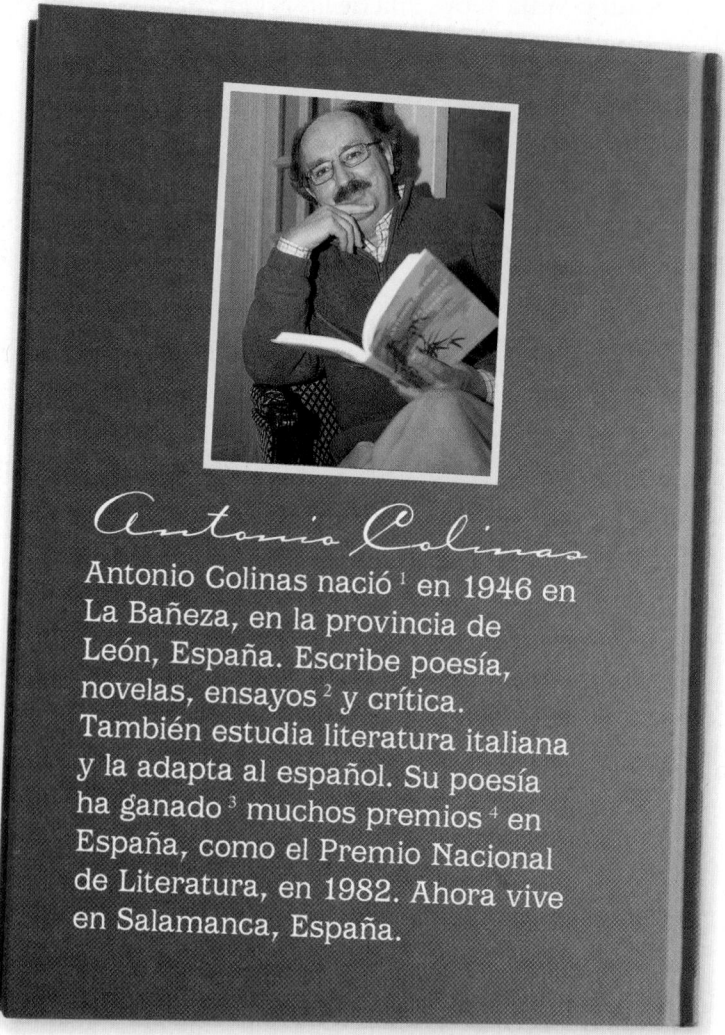

Antonio Golinas nació [1] en 1946 en La Bañeza, en la provincia de León, España. Escribe poesía, novelas, ensayos [2] y crítica. También estudia literatura italiana y la adapta al español. Su poesía ha ganado [3] muchos premios [4] en España, como el Premio Nacional de Literatura, en 1982. Ahora vive en Salamanca, España.

---

[1] was born   [2] essays   [3] has won   [4] awards

Invierno tardío

No es increíble cuanto ven mis ojos[5]:

nieva sobre el almendro florido[6],

nieva sobre la nieve.

Este invierno mi ánimo[7]

es como primavera temprana,

es como almendro florido

bajo la nieve.

Hay demasiado[8] frío

esta tarde en el mundo[9].

Pero abro la puerta a mi perro

y con él entra en casa[10] calor,

entra la humanidad.

---

[5] **ven...** my eyes see
[6] **sobre...** on the flowery almond tree
[7] spirit   [8] too much   [9] world   [10] house

<56>

PARA Y PIENSA

¿Comprendiste?

1. ¿De dónde es Antonio Colinas? ¿Qué escribe? ¿Dónde vive ahora?

2. ¿Dónde está la persona en el poema? ¿Qué mira? En tu opinión, ¿está triste o contenta la persona?

3. ¿Piensas que el perro es un buen amigo? ¿Por qué?

¿Y tú?

¿Cómo es el invierno en tu región? ¿Qué te gusta hacer?

Conexiones *El arte*

Los árabes en España

For almost 800 years, from 711 to 1492, the Moors, Arab Muslims from northern Africa, occupied an area in southern Spain called **Al-Andalus,** now known as **Andalucía.** This was a period of rich cultural exchange in the arts, sciences, mathematics, agriculture, and architecture.

The Alhambra palace in Granada is a notable example of Moorish architecture in Spain. The interior is exquisitely detailed, bright, and airy. Ornately carved pillars and arches open onto sunny courtyards. The walls and ceilings are decorated with intricate geometric designs.

Design a courtyard based on the architectural styles illustrated in these pictures of the Alhambra. Create a drawing or model to show your design.

El patio de los leones

La Alhambra

Un arco musulmán

Los jardines del Generalife

Proyecto 1 *La música*

Moorish civilization had a lasting influence on the music of Spain. The guitar may be derived from the oud, a type of lute and a classic Arab instrument. The word **guitarra** comes from the Arabic *qithara*. Some contemporary music is similar to the music played during the Moorish rule. Research and write about the musical group *Al-Andalus*. Include the members of the group, the places where they perform, and a description of their music.

Proyecto 2 *La salud*

Olives have always been a part of Spanish tradition. Olive seeds that date back 8,000 years have been found in Spain. The majority of olive trees grown in the country are found in **Andalucía.** Spain is also one of the world's foremost producers of olive oil. Research and write about the health and beauty benefits of olives and olive oil. Describe how they are used on a daily basis.

Proyecto 3 *El lenguaje*

The Moors brought many concepts and inventions to Spain. The Arabic words for many of these things still exist in Spanish. Often these words begin with **al-** or **a-.** Some examples are **almohada, álgebra, algodón,** and **ajedrez.** Using a Spanish-English dictionary, write the meanings of these words. Then find three more Spanish words that begin with **al-,** write their English definitions, and use the Internet or the library to find out if they have Arabic origin.

En resumen
Vocabulario y gramática

ANiMATEDGRAMMAR
Interactive Flashcards
my.hrw.com

Vocabulario

Talk About Shopping

el centro comercial	shopping center, mall	el dólar	dollar
¿Cuánto cuesta(n)?	How much does it (do they) cost?	el euro	euro
		ir de compras	to go shopping
Cuesta(n)...	It costs . . . (They cost . . .)	pagar	to pay
		el precio	price
el dinero	money	la tienda	store

Describe Clothing

la blusa	blouse	nuevo(a)	new
los calcetines	socks	los pantalones	pants
la camisa	shirt	los pantalones cortos	shorts
la camiseta	T-shirt		
la chaqueta	jacket	la ropa	clothing
feo(a)	ugly	el sombrero	hat
el gorro	winter hat	el vestido	dress
los jeans	jeans	los zapatos	shoes
llevar	to wear		

Colors

amarillo(a)	yellow	marrón (pl. marrones)	brown
anaranjado(a)	orange		
azul	blue	negro(a)	black
blanco(a)	white	rojo(a)	red
		verde	green

Expressions with tener

tener calor	to be hot
tener frío	to be cold
tener razón	to be right
tener suerte	to be lucky

Discuss Seasons

la estación (pl. las estaciones)	season
el invierno	winter
el otoño	autumn, fall
la primavera	spring
el verano	summer

Other Words and Phrases

durante	during
cerrar (ie)	to close
empezar (ie)	to begin
entender (ie)	to understand
pensar (ie)	to think, to plan
preferir (ie)	to prefer
querer (ie)	to want

Gramática

Nota gramatical: tener expressions *p. 198*

Stem-Changing Verbs: e → ie

For **e → ie** stem-changing verbs, the **e** of the stem changes to **ie** in all forms except **nosotros(as)** and **vosotros(as).**

querer	to want
quiero	queremos
quieres	queréis
quiere	quieren

Direct Object Pronouns

Direct object pronouns can be used to replace direct object nouns.

Singular		Plural	
me	me	nos	us
te	you (familiar)	os	you (familiar)
lo	you (formal), him, it	los	you, them
la	you (formal), her, it	las	you, them

Practice Spanish with Holt McDougal Apps!

Repaso de la lección

¡LLEGADA!

Now you can
- talk about what clothes you want to buy
- say what you wear in different seasons

Using
- **tener** expressions
- stem-changing verbs: **e → ie**
- direct object pronouns

To review
- stem-changing verbs: **e → ie** p. 199
- direct object pronouns p. 204

AUDIO

1 | Listen and understand

Escucha a Paula hablar de la ropa. Para cada artículo de ropa, indica si quiere comprarlo o no. Usa pronombres de objetos directos. *(Listen to Paula and indicate whether she wants to buy each article of clothing or not. Use direct object pronouns.)*

1.

2.

3.

4.

5.

6.

To review
- stem-changing verbs: **e → ie** p. 199

2 | Talk about what clothes you want to buy

Fernando va de compras con sus padres. ¿Qué dice? *(Tell what Fernando says about his shopping experience.)*

preferir	cerrar	entender
empezar	pensar	querer

Las clases __1.__ el lunes y necesito ropa. Yo __2.__ comprar unas camisetas y unos pantalones pero no tengo mucho dinero. Yo __3.__ las camisetas a las camisas. Yo no __4.__ por qué una camiseta cuesta más en el centro comercial que en otras tiendas. Mi amiga Carla __5.__ que hay ropa más bonita y menos cara en la tienda Moda Zaragoza. Necesito ir hoy porque la tienda __6.__ los domingos.

To review
- **tener** expressions p. 198
- stem-changing verbs: **e → ie** p. 199

3 | Talk about what clothes you want to buy

Indica si estas personas tienen calor o tienen frío basado en lo que piensan comprar. *(Indicate if these people are hot or cold based on what they are thinking about buying.)*

> **modelo:** Ana / blusa de verano
> Ana piensa comprar una blusa de verano porque tiene calor.

1. Juan y yo / gorros

2. yo / pantalones cortos

3. tú / chaqueta

4. Laura y Carlos / camisetas de verano

5. ustedes / calcetines de invierno

6. Pilar / vestido de primavera

To review
- direct object pronouns p. 204

4 | Say what you wear in different seasons

Escribe oraciones para decir quién prefiere llevar la ropa. *(Tell who prefers to wear these clothing items.)*

> **modelo:** los zapatos negros (Juan)
> Juan los prefiere llevar. (Juan prefiere llevarlos.)

1. los pantalones cortos (Rosa)

2. las camisas azules (ellas)

3. el sombrero rojo (yo)

4. la camiseta anaranjada (Carlos)

5. el gorro negro (ellos)

6. la blusa amarilla (nosotros)

7. los calcetines blancos (ustedes)

8. la chaqueta marrón (tú)

9. los zapatos marrones (usted)

10. el vestido verde (Amanda)

To review
- **Sevillanas** p. 191
- Comparación cultural pp. 203, 206
- Lectura pp. 210–211

5 | Spain and Chile

Comparación cultural

Answer these culture questions.

1. What are the characteristics of **sevillanas**?

2. How do the climates of Spain and Chile differ in July and why?

3. What are some characteristics of surrealist art?

4. What season is represented in Antonio Colinas' poem? How does the speaker of the poem feel and why?

Más práctica   Cuaderno *pp. 159–170*   Cuaderno para hispanohablantes *pp. 161–170*

Get Help Online
my.hrw.com

España

Lección

2

Tema:

¿Qué hacemos esta noche?

─────❧❧❧─────

¡AVANZA! **In this lesson you will learn to**

- describe places and events in town
- talk about types of transportation
- say what you are going to do
- order from a menu

using

- the verb **ver, ir a** + infinitive
- stem-changing verbs: **o → ue**
- stem-changing verbs: **e → i**

♻ ¿Recuerdas?

- present tense of **-er** verbs
- the verb **ir, tener** expressions
- direct object pronouns

Comparación cultural

In this lesson you will learn about

- local markets
- art from Spain and Chile
- weekend activities in Spain, Guatemala, and Chile

Compara con tu mundo

Maribel and Enrique are near the Teatro de la Comedia, where many traditional Spanish plays are performed. *What do you and your friends like to do on weekends?*

¿Qué ves?

Mira la foto

¿Es viejo el teatro?

¿Lleva pantalones o un vestido Maribel?

¿De qué color es la camisa de Enrique?

MODES OF COMMUNICATION

INTERPRETIVE	INTERPERSONAL	PRESENTATIONAL
Understand what a tourist guide says.	Discuss what you can buy in markets in Spanish-speaking countries.	Write a newspaper article about your favorite restaurant.
Read a tourist brochure and identify destinations.	Write an e-mail to your family to discuss plans for the weekend.	Describe a restaurant visit, including the food and the cost.

**El Teatro de la Comedia
en la calle Príncipe**
Madrid, España

Presentación de VOCABULARIO

¡AVANZA!

Goal: Learn about what Enrique and Maribel do when they go out. Then practice what you have learned to describe places and events in town. *Actividades 1–2*

♻ *¿Recuerdas?* Present tense of **-er** verbs p. 150

VIDEO DVD

AUDIO

A En **el centro** de Madrid hay muchos **lugares** para comer. Maribel y yo queremos ir a **la calle** de Alcalá para **encontrar** un buen **restaurante**. ¿Vamos **a pie, en coche** o **en autobús**?

a pie

en coche

en autobús

B En **el menú** hay muchos **platos principales**. Si te gusta **la carne,** hay **bistec.** Si no, también hay **pescado.**

el camarero

el menú

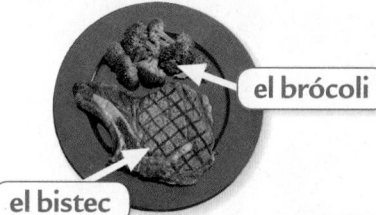

el brócoli

el bistec

las patatas

el pollo

la ensalada

las verduras

el tomate

el pescado

el arroz

el pastel

C **La cuenta** es veinticinco euros. ¿Cuánto dinero necesitamos para **la propina**?

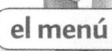

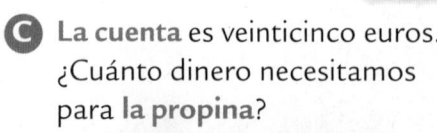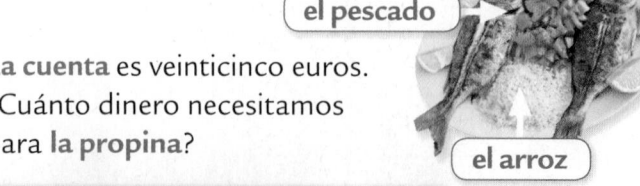

la cuenta

En España se dice...

In Spain the word for *cake* is **la tarta.** The word for *beans* is **las alubias.**

D **Tomamos** el autobús para ir al **cine.** Vamos al Cine Ideal para **ver una película.**

el cine

la ventanilla

las entradas

Más vocabulario

allí *there*
almorzar *to eat lunch*
costar *to cost*
los frijoles *beans*
la música rock *rock music*
poder *to be able, can*
servir *to serve*
tal vez *perhaps, maybe*
volver *to return, to come back*

Expansión de vocabulario p. R5

E **Aquí** en Madrid también hay **teatros** y **parques** pero yo prefiero ir a **un concierto** para escuchar música.

el teatro

el parque

el concierto

F Vamos a **un café.** **De postre** nos gusta **pedir un pastel.** Después, Maribel está muy cansada. Es la hora de **dormir.**

el café

la mesa

dormir

@**HOMETUTOR**
my.hrw.com
Interactive Flashcards

¡A responder!   Escuchar

Escucha a la camarera. Escribe la comida que menciona.
(Listen to the server. Write the food that she mentions.)

Práctica de VOCABULARIO

1 | Diversiones en el centro

Leer Empareja cada palabra con la descripción correspondiente. *(Match each word with its definition.)*

1. Es una persona que trabaja en un café.
2. Es el lugar adonde vas para comer.
3. Vas aquí para ver una película.
4. La necesitas para ir a un concierto.
5. Lo comes después del plato principal.
6. Compras entradas aquí.

a. la ventanilla
b. el restaurante
c. la camarera
d. la entrada
e. el cine
f. el postre

Nota gramatical ♻ *¿Recuerdas?* Present tense of **-er** verbs p. 150

Ver has an irregular **yo** form in the present tense: **veo.**

> **Veo** muchos autobuses en el centro.   *I **see** a lot of buses downtown.*

---

2 | ¿Qué ves en el restaurante?

Hablar Los señores Ortiz están en el restaurante Los Reyes. Pregúntale a otro(a) estudiante qué ve. *(Ask a partner what he or she sees in the restaurant.)*

A ¿Qué ves en el restaurante?

B Allí veo una silla.

Expansión
Create a menu for your own café. Include prices.

Más práctica   Cuaderno *pp. 171–173*   Cuaderno para hispanohablantes *pp. 171–174*

🌐 **Get Help Online**
my.hrw.com

PARA Y PIENSA

Did you get it?
1. Name three things you would find in a restaurant.
2. Name three places where you and your friends might go to have fun.

VOCABULARIO en contexto

¡AVANZA! **Goal:** Focus on how Maribel and Enrique talk about where they go and how they get there. Then practice these words and **ir a +** infinitive to talk about types of transportation and what you are going to do.
Actividades 3–4

 ¿Recuerdas? The verb **ir** p. 120

Telehistoria escena 1

@HOMETUTOR
my.hrw.com
View, Read
and Record

STRATEGIES

Cuando lees
Think about timing Consider timing while reading. How long will Enrique's plan take? Will they see Trini? Why or why not?

Cuando escuchas
Enter the scene As you listen to Enrique's travel plan, enter the scene. If you were Maribel, would you feel calm or nervous about Enrique's ideas? Why?

VIDEO
DVD

AUDIO

Enrique

Maribel

Enrique: ¿Trini Salgado está en el centro comercial del Parque de las Avenidas a las doce?

Maribel: Sí. Y ya es tarde. Enrique, ¡por favor!

Enrique: ¡Vale! ¿Y cómo vamos a llegar allí? ¿En autobús?

Enrique puts the T-shirt in his bag so that Maribel can open the map.

Maribel: Podemos empezar aquí en el parque. El centro comercial está allí. ¿Cuál es la calle?

Enrique: Calle Poveda. ¡Es fácil! Tomamos el autobús al centro. Vamos a pie a la biblioteca —aquí. Mi madre está allí. Ella tiene coche. ¡Llegamos al centro comercial en coche!

Maribel: ¡Pero, Enrique! Son las once y cuarenta y cinco. Vamos a llegar tarde. ¿Qué voy a hacer?

Enrique: ¡Ah! El autobús setenta y cuatro va al centro comercial. Llega aquí a las doce y llega al centro comercial a las doce y media.

Maribel: ¡Vale!

También se dice

España Enrique says **el autobús** to talk about taking the bus. In other Spanish-speaking countries you might hear:
- **Puerto Rico, República Dominicana, Cuba** **la guagua**
- **México** **el camión**
- **muchos países** **el colectivo, el micro**

Continuará... p. 226

3 | *Comprensión del episodio* ¿Cómo piensan llegar?

Escuchar
Leer

Lee las oraciones y decide si son ciertas o falsas. *(Read the sentences and tell whether they are true or false.)*

1. Maribel y Enrique no tienen mapa.

2. La madre de Enrique está en la biblioteca.

3. El centro comercial está en la calle Poveda.

4. Enrique quiere ir a pie al centro comercial.

5. El autobús llega al centro comercial a las doce.

Nota gramatical   *¿Recuerdas?* The verb **ir** p. 120

To talk about what you are going to do, use a form of **ir a** + **infinitive.**

¿Qué **van a hacer** ustedes?   Vamos **a mirar** una película.
*What **are you going to do?***   ***We're going to watch** a movie.*

Vamos **a** can also mean *Let's.*

---

4 | ¿Qué vas a comer?

Hablar

Pregúntale a otro(a) estudiante qué va a comer esta semana. *(Ask a partner what he or she is going to eat this week.)*

Ⓐ ¿Vas a comer carne?

Ⓑ Sí, voy a comer carne. Es rica. (No, no voy a comer carne. Es horrible.)

1.    **2.**    **3.**    **4.**

5.    **6.**    **7.**    **8.**

Expansión
Organize this list of foods from your favorite to your least favorite. Compare it with a classmate's.

Get Help Online
my.hrw.com

PARA Y PIENSA

Did you get it?   Complete each sentence with the correct phrase to tell what form of transportation is used.

1. Maribel va a la escuela _____ ; va a tomar el cuarenta y dos.

2. Enrique y su hermano van a ir _____ al parque; les gusta pasear.

3. Maribel y su mamá van al concierto _____ porque no quieren llegar tarde.

Presentación de GRAMÁTICA

Goal: Learn how to form **o → ue** stem-changing verbs. Then practice using these verbs to talk about going out with friends. *Actividades 5–8*

English Grammar Connection: Remember that there are no stem-changing verbs in the present tense of English (see p. 199). In Spanish, **o → ue** stem changes happen in all three classes of verbs: **-ar, -er,** and **-ir.**

Stem-Changing Verbs: o → ue

ANIMATED GRAMMAR
my.hrw.com

Some verbs have an **o → ue** stem change in the present tense. How do you form the present tense of these verbs?

Here's how:

Remember that stem-changing verbs have regular **-ar, -er,** and **-ir** endings. For **o → ue** stem-changing verbs, the last **o** of the stem changes to **ue** in all forms except **nosotros(as)** and **vosotros(as).**

poder *to be able, can*	
p**ue**do	p**o**demos
p**ue**des	p**o**déis
p**ue**de	p**ue**den

Carmen p**ue**de ir al concierto.
*Carmen **can** go to the concert.*

Other verbs you know that have this stem change are **alm**o**rzar, c**o**star, d**o**rmir, enc**o**ntrar,** and **v**o**lver.**

Almu**erzo** a la una.
***I eat lunch** at one o'clock.*

Antonio, ¿cuándo **v**u**elves**?
*Antonio, when **are you coming back**?*

Más práctica
Cuaderno *pp. 174–176*
Cuaderno para hispanohablantes *pp. 175–177*

@HOMETUTOR my.hrw.com
Leveled Practice
Conjuguemos.com

Práctica de GRAMÁTICA

5 | Un concierto de música rock

Leer
Escribir

Maribel habla con su amiga, Toni, sobre cuándo pueden ir a un concierto. Completa lo que dice con formas de **poder.** Usa el póster para contestar su pregunta. *(Complete what Maribel says with forms of **poder** and answer her question, based on the poster.)*

> Nosotros queremos ir a un concierto el viernes o el sábado, pero ¿cuándo? Yo no **1.** ir el viernes en la noche porque tengo que trabajar. Manolo no **2.** ir el sábado en la noche. Ana y Miguel no **3.** ir el viernes en la noche y el sábado en la tarde no van a estar aquí. Enrique y su hermano no **4.** ir el sábado en la tarde porque van a un restaurante con su primo. Y Toni, tú no **5.** ir el sábado en la noche. ¿Cuándo **6.** ir todos nosotros?

Presenta LOS Rebeldes

en el Centro Cívico, Madrid
Entrada: 18€ en la ventanilla
Fecha: 22–23 de abril
Hora: el viernes por la tarde (19:00) y por la noche (22:00)
el sábado por la tarde (14:00) y por la noche (21:00)

6 | Las actividades en el centro

Escribir

Combina frases de las dos columnas con la forma correcta del verbo para describir las actividades de estas personas en el centro. *(Write sentences by conjugating the verbs and combining the phrases.)*

modelo: el camarero / no poder trabajar / en el restaurante
El camarero no puede trabajar en el restaurante.

las entradas para
  el concierto / costar

yo / almorzar

vosotros / encontrar la calle

tú / poder jugar al fútbol

usted / dormir bien

nosotros / volver al centro

en el mapa

con amigos en el parque

después de comer mucho

quince euros

en el café con mi familia

en autobús

Expansión
Choose three verbs from this activity and write three sentences about yourself.

7 | Todos tienen excusas

Hablar

Habla con otro(a) estudiante sobre las actividades que ustedes no pueden hacer este fin de semana. Di que no puedes e inventa una excusa. *(Give excuses for what you cannot do.)*

modelo: ir a un concierto

A ¿Vas a ir a un concierto?

B No, no puedo ir a un concierto. Voy a ir al cine con mi hermano.

1. ir al teatro
2. dormir diez horas
3. practicar deportes
4. almorzar en un café
5. pasar un rato con los amigos
6. ver una película en el cine
7. ir al centro
8. comprar ropa

Expansión
Make plans with a classmate to do two of these activities this weekend.

8 | ¡Vamos a ir de compras!

Hablar

Comparación cultural

Chichicastenango, Guatemala

El Rastro en Madrid, España

Los mercados

How do local markets reflect the culture of an area? Every Sunday, tourists and locals head to El Rastro, one of the oldest flea markets in Madrid, **Spain,** to search for bargains amid the hundreds of stalls. Vendors offer a wide variety of items such as antiques, secondhand clothing, CDs, books, maps, and art. In **Guatemala,** the town of Chichicastenango hosts a popular market in which you can find handicrafts from the Maya-Quiché culture. Many vendors wear the traditional dress of their region and sell colorful textiles, including Mayan blouses called *huipiles.* Other common items include fruits and vegetables, masks, baskets, candles, and flowers.

Compara con tu mundo *What type of souvenir might a visitor to your community purchase?*

Pregúntale a otro(a) estudiante dónde puedes encontrar **libros, discos compactos, fruta, arte, verduras, mapas,** y **huipiles.** *(Ask your partner where you can find these items.)*

A ¿Dónde puedo encontrar libros?

B Encuentras libros en El Rastro.

Más práctica Cuaderno *pp. 174–176* Cuaderno para hispanohablantes *pp. 175–177*

 **Get Help Online**
my.hrw.com

PARA Y PIENSA

Did you get it? Complete each sentence with the correct form of the appropriate verb: **poder, costar, almorzar,** or **dormir.**

1. El pescado _____ diez dólares.
2. Nosotros _____ a la una en el café.
3. Yo _____ ocho horas.
4. Ellos no _____ contestar.

✿ GRAMÁTICA en contexto

¡AVANZA!

Goal: Identify the **o → ue** stem-changing verbs Enrique and Maribel use to talk about things to do in the city. Then practice using these verbs to talk about where you go. *Actividades 9–10*

Telehistoria escena 2

HOMETUTOR View, Read and Record
my.hrw.com

STRATEGIES

Cuando lees
Compare scenes As you read this scene, compare it to Scene 1. How are these scenes alike in terms of Enrique's promises and his behavior? What trends do you find?

Cuando escuchas
Identify causes A negative feeling can have more than one cause. Listen for the causes of Maribel's anxiety and concerns. How many causes are there? What are they?

VIDEO
DVD

AUDIO

Enrique: ¿Qué vas a hacer hoy por la tarde?

Maribel: Después de ir de compras, quiero volver al centro. Hay un concierto de música rock, o puedo ir al cine a ver una película... ¡o puedo ir al teatro!

Enrique: ¡Un concierto de rock! ¿Puedo ir?

Maribel: Mmm... ¡quiero ir al teatro! Vamos al teatro.

Enrique: ¿Al teatro? Pero las entradas cuestan mucho, y...

After the trouble he caused, Enrique decides to go along with Maribel's idea.

Enrique: ¡Vale! Vamos al teatro.

Maribel: *(amused)* No, vamos al concierto.

Enrique: ¡Muy bien! Voy a comprar las entradas.

Maribel: ¡Pero, Enrique! El autobús...

Enrique: La ventanilla está allí, cerca del café. Vuelvo en dos minutos.

As he runs to buy the tickets, Maribel sees the bus approaching. She decides to go alone, but realizes she no longer has the T-shirt.

Maribel: ¡La camiseta! ¡No encuentro la camiseta! ¡Enrique!

Continuará... p. 231

9 | *Comprensión del episodio* Planes para la tarde

Escuchar Leer

Completa las oraciones con la frase que corresponde. *(Complete the sentences with the corresponding phrase.)*

1. Después de ir de compras, Maribel quiere...
2. Enrique no quiere ir al teatro porque...
3. Maribel y Enrique van...
4. El autobús llega...
5. Enrique va a comprar las entradas...

a. cuando Enrique va a comprar las entradas.
b. volver al centro.
c. a un concierto de música rock en la tarde.
d. y tiene la camiseta.
e. las entradas cuestan mucho.

10 | ¿Qué encuentras?

Hablar

Habla con otro(a) estudiante sobre qué encuentras en estos lugares. *(Talk about what you find in these places.)*

A ¿Qué encuentras en una biblioteca?

B Encuentro libros y computadoras allí.

1.

2.

3.

4.

5.

6.

Expansión
Write a description of what people can do in each of these places.

Get Help Online
my.hrw.com

PARA Y PIENSA

Did you get it? Complete each sentence based on the Telehistoria with the correct form of the verb in parentheses.
1. Maribel _____ ir al cine o al teatro. (poder)
2. Maribel no _____ la camiseta. (encontrar)
3. Enrique _____ tarde y los dos no van al centro comercial. (volver)

Lección 2
doscientos veintisiete **227**

Presentación de GRAMÁTICA

Goal: Learn how to form **e → i** stem-changing verbs. Then practice using these verbs to order from a menu. *Actividades 11–14*

¿Recuerdas? Direct object pronouns p. 204, **tener** expressions p. 198

English Grammar Connection: Remember that there are no stem-changing verbs in the present tense of English (see p. 199). There are, however, a number of stem-changing verbs in Spanish.

Stem-Changing Verbs: e → i

ANIMATED GRAMMAR
my.hrw.com

Some **-ir** verbs have an **e → i** stem change in the present tense. How do you form the present tense of these verbs?

Here's how:

For **e → i** stem-changing verbs, the last **e** of the stem changes to **i** in all forms except **nosotros(as)** and **vosotros(as).**

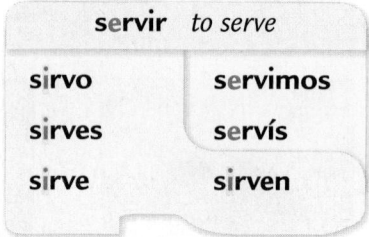

servir	*to serve*
sirvo	ser**vi**mos
sirves	ser**ví**s
sirve	**si**rven

El camarero **si**rve la comida.
*The waiter **serves** the food.*

Another verb you know with this stem change is **pedir.**

¿**Pi**des una ensalada?
***Are you ordering** a salad?*

Siempre **pe**dimos pollo.
***We** always **order** chicken.*

Más práctica
Cuaderno *pp. 177–179*
Cuaderno para hispanohablantes *pp. 178–181*

@HOMETUTOR my.hrw.com
Leveled Practice
Conjuguemos.com

Práctica de GRAMÁTICA

11 | ¿Qué piden?

Escribir Hablar

Describe qué piden las personas. *(Tell what these people are ordering.)*

modelo: yo
Yo pido carne.

1. tú

2. mis amigas

3. yo

4. vosotros

5. mi madre

6. Maribel

7. mis abuelos y yo

8. ustedes

 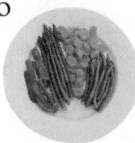 

12 | ¿Quién sirve la comida?

 ¿Recuerdas? Direct object pronouns p. 204

Escribir Hablar

Describe qué piden estas personas y quién sirve la comida. *(Tell what these people ask for and who serves it.)*

modelo: Maribel: bebida (la camarera)
Maribel pide una bebida y la camarera la sirve.

1. yo: ensalada (Enrique)
2. mi amigo: pollo (sus padres)
3. tú: pescado (yo)
4. mis amigas y yo: verduras (vosotros)
5. usted: patatas (nosotros)
6. vosotros: postre (el camarero)

> **Expansión**
> Talk about what you ask for and what your family serves for breakfast, lunch, and dinner.

AUDIO

Pronunciación | La letra c con e, i

Before **e** and **i**, the Spanish **c** is pronounced like the *c* in *city*.

Listen and repeat.

ce → cero   centro   cerrar   quince

ci → cien   cine   precio   estación

In many regions of Spain, the **c** before **e** and **i** is pronounced like the *th* of the English word *think*.

13 | ¿Qué sirven en el café?

Escuchar
Escribir

Enrique está en un café y habla con los camareros. Escribe oraciones para explicar qué sirven estas personas. *(Listen and write sentences to tell what these people are serving.)*

1. los camareros   **3.** el camarero   **5.** Luis y José
2. el señor Fuentes   **4.** la camarera   **6.** Ana

14 | ¿Qué pides del menú?   **¿Recuerdas?** tener expressions p. 198

Hablar

Pregúntale a otro(a) estudiante qué pide en un restaurante en las siguientes situaciones. *(Ask a partner what he or she orders in a restaurant in the following situations.)*

modelo: bebida / en el almuerzo

A ¿Qué bebida pides en el almuerzo?

B Pido leche o un refresco.

1. comida / en el almuerzo
2. bebida / cuando tienes frío
3. bebida / en el desayuno
4. comida / cuando tienes calor
5. comida / cuando tienes hambre
6. bebida / cuando tienes mucha sed

Expansión
Write about other things that you ask for at home and at school.

Comparación cultural

Las meninas

Why might an artist create a version of another artist's masterpiece? Diego Velázquez served as the official painter for King Philip IV of **Spain** and painted many portraits of the royal family. *Las meninas* shows the *Infanta* (princess) and her attendants. Velázquez included himself in the painting. Three centuries later, Pablo Picasso, also from Spain, completed 58 interpretations of this painting. What similarities and differences do you notice?

Las meninas (1656),
Diego Velázquez

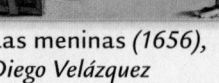

Las meninas (Infanta Margarita) (1957), Pablo Picasso

Compara con tu mundo *What famous artwork would you like to try to re-create and why?*

Más práctica   Cuaderno *pp. 177–179*   Cuaderno para hispanohablantes *pp. 178–181*

🌐 **Get Help Online**
my.hrw.com

PARA Y PIENSA

Did you get it? Complete each sentence with the correct form of **pedir** or **servir**.

1. En la cena los camareros _____ arroz con pollo.
2. Mi madre hace un pastel y lo _____ de postre.
3. Nosotros no _____ mucho porque no tenemos mucha hambre.

Todo junto

Telehistoria completa

@HOMETUTOR View, Read and Record
my.hrw.com

STRATEGIES

Cuando lees
Analyze the communication Analyze this scene's communication by answering these questions: Why does Maribel order so much food? What is the effect?

Cuando escuchar
Listen for contrasts Listen for contrasts during the scene. Examples: What do Maribel and Enrique order? Who promises to pay, and who actually pays?

Escena 1 *Resumen*
Enrique y Maribel pueden tomar el autobús setenta y cuatro al centro comercial. Piensan llegar a las doce y media.

Escena 2 *Resumen*
Enrique va a comprar las entradas para un concierto. El autobús llega pero Enrique no está. Maribel no tiene la camiseta.

VIDEO DVD

AUDIO

Escena 3

They arrive at an outdoor restaurant.

Enrique: Es un restaurante muy bonito.

Maribel: Pero no tengo el autógrafo de Trini.

Enrique: Vamos a pedir la comida. ¡Yo pago!

Maribel: Ah, ¿pagas tú? Ahora pido toda la comida del menú.

The waiter arrives.

Maribel: Señor, ¿sirven pescado hoy?

Camarero: No, hoy no tenemos pescado.

Maribel: Quiero empezar con una ensalada. De plato principal quiero el pollo con verduras y... Sí, y filete con patatas.

Camarero: ¿Dos platos principales? ¿Filete y pollo?

Enrique: Es mucho, ¿no?

Maribel: Sí. Y de postre quiero un arroz con leche.

Enrique: *(nervously)* Pan y agua, por favor.

Maribel: Él va a pagar la cuenta.

Enrique: *(nods, then remembers)* ¡Maribel! ¡Mi mochila! ¡No tengo dinero!

Maribel: *(smiling)* Ay, Enrique, yo sí tengo dinero.

15 | Comprensión de los episodios   ¿Quién lo hace?

Lee estas oraciones e indica a quién se refieren—a Enrique o a Maribel. *(Read these sentences and tell to whom they refer—Enrique or Maribel.)*

1. Quiere volver al centro después de ir de compras.

2. Piensa que las entradas cuestan mucho.

3. No encuentra la camiseta.

4. Piensa que el restaurante es muy bonito.

5. Pide mucha comida.

16 | Comprensión de los episodios   Problemas en el centro

Contesta las preguntas según los episodios. *(Answer the questions according to the episodes.)*

1. ¿Cómo quieren ir Maribel y Enrique al centro comercial?

2. ¿Adónde va el autobús setenta y cuatro?

3. ¿Por qué no quiere ir al teatro Enrique?

4. ¿Por qué está enojada Maribel?

5. ¿Qué pide Maribel en el restaurante?

17 | Clientes y camareros

> **STRATEGY Hablar**
> **Plan the whole scene** Plan the whole scene from start to finish. What would the waiter or waitress say before, during, and after the meal? What would the customers say at each stage?

Trabaja en un grupo de tres. Preparen una escena en un café con un(a) camarero(a) y clientes para representar en clase. *(Prepare a scene in a café.)*

Para organizarte:
- qué comidas y bebidas piden
- qué sirve el (la) camarero(a)
- cuánto cuesta la comida (la cuenta y la propina)

Camarero(a) Buenas tardes. ¿Quieren ver el menú?

Cliente 1 Buenas tardes. Sí, por favor. Tenemos mucha hambre.

Ustedes pueden pedir el pollo con patatas. Es mucha comida.

Cliente 2 Tal vez, pero hoy tengo ganas de comer...

18 Integración

Lee el folleto y escucha al guía turístico. Describe cinco actividades que vas a hacer, adónde vas a ir y cómo puedes llegar. *(Describe five activities you are going to do, where, and how you can get there.)*

Fuente 1 Folleto del hotel

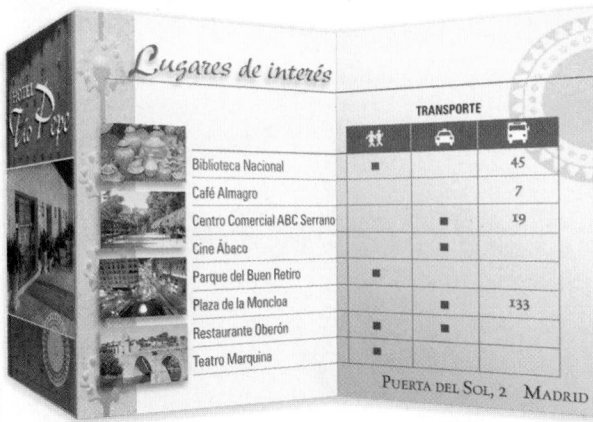

Fuente 2 Anuncio del guía turístico

Listen and take notes

- ¿Qué actividades menciona el guía?
- ¿En qué lugares puedes hacer las actividades?

modelo: Voy a comer pescado. Voy al Restaurante Oberón. Puedo ir a pie o en coche...

19 Una crítica culinaria

Escribes críticas para la sección de restaurantes del periódico. Escribe un párrafo sobre tu restaurante favorito. Explica qué sirven, qué pides, cómo es la comida, cómo son los camareros y cuánto cuesta la comida. *(Write a review of your favorite restaurant.)*

modelo: El restaurante Salazar es muy bueno. Los camareros son trabajadores. De plato principal sirven...

Writing Criteria	Excellent	Good	Needs Work
Content	Your review includes a lot of information.	Your review includes some information.	Your review includes little information.
Communication	Most of your review is organized and easy to follow.	Parts of your review are organized and easy to follow.	Your review is disorganized and hard to follow.
Accuracy	Your review has few mistakes in grammar and vocabulary.	Your review has some mistakes in grammar and vocabulary.	Your review has many mistakes in grammar and vocabulary.

Más práctica   Cuaderno *pp. 180–181*   Cuaderno para hispanohablantes *pp. 182–183*

Get Help Online
my.hrw.com

PARA Y PIENSA

Did you get it? Choose the correct verb to make each sentence logical according to the Telehistoria.

1. Maribel y Enrique (almuerzan / encuentran) en un restaurante bonito.
2. Maribel (sirve / pide) mucha comida.
3. Enrique no (puede / vuelve) pagar.

Lectura cultural

Additional readings at **my.hrw.com**
SPANISH
InterActive Reader

¡AVANZA! **Goal:** Read about weekend activities in Spain and Chile. Then talk about what each city offers and compare these activities with what you do on weekends.

Comparación cultural

AUDIO

El fin de semana en España y Chile

STRATEGY Leer

List attractions and places
Use a table like the one below to list attractions and the places where they can be found.

	conciertos	zoológico	botes
Madrid	Parque del Buen Retiro		
Santiago de Chile			

España

Los habitantes de Madrid, España, y Santiago de Chile hacen muchas actividades en el fin de semana. Van a parques, restaurantes, teatros, cines y otros lugares divertidos. También van de compras.

En Madrid hay muchos lugares interesantes para pasar los fines de semana. La Plaza Mayor tiene muchos cafés y restaurantes. Hay un mercado de sellos[1] los domingos. El Parque del Buen Retiro es un lugar perfecto para descansar y pasear. En este parque hay jardines[2], cafés y un lago[3] donde las personas pueden alquilar botes. Hay conciertos allí en el verano. Otro parque popular es la Casa de Campo. Hay un zoológico, una piscina[4], un parque de diversiones[5] y un lago para botes.

Hay muchas tiendas en el centro. El almacén[6] más grande es El Corte Inglés: allí los madrileños[7] pueden comprar ropa, comida y mucho más.

---

[1] **mercado...** stamp market   [2] gardens   [3] lake
[4] swimming pool   [5] **parque...** amusement park
[6] department store   [7] people of Madrid

El Parque del Buen Retiro en Madrid

En Santiago de Chile las personas pasan los fines de semana en muchos lugares. Siempre hay mucha actividad en la Plaza de Armas, la parte histórica de Santiago. Hay conciertos allí los domingos.

La Plaza de Armas

El parque del Cerro Santa Lucía es perfecto para pasear. Los santiaguinos[8] pueden ver jardines y el panorama de Santiago. El Cerro San Cristóbal en el Parque Metropolitano es un lugar favorito para comer, correr y montar en bicicleta. Hay jardines, piscinas, un zoológico, cafés y restaurantes en el parque.

Los santiaguinos van a tiendas en el centro y a centros comerciales como Alto Las Condes. En el Mercado Central pueden comprar pescado y frutas y comer en restaurantes con precios baratos[9].

---

[8] people of Santiago, Chile   [9] inexpensive

Chile

¿Comprendiste?
1. ¿Qué hay en la Plaza Mayor y la Plaza de Armas los domingos?
2. ¿A qué parques van los madrileños y los santiaguinos?
3. ¿Dónde pueden ir de compras los habitantes de Madrid y Santiago?

¿Y tú?
¿Cuál(es) de estos lugares en Madrid y Santiago quieres visitar? ¿Adónde vas los fines de semana donde vives? ¿Qué haces allí?

PARA Y PIENSA

Cerro San Cristóbal

✤ Proyectos culturales

Pinturas de España y Chile

What messages can an artist communicate through a painting? When you look at a painting, you might see something different than what the artist originally intended when he or she painted it. In fact, a single work of art can have a number of different interpretations.

España Landscape near El Escorial
(1932), Ignacio Zuloaga y Zabaleta

Chile La Siesta
(1872), Pedro Lira

☀ Proyecto ❶ *Interpret and investigate*

Interpreting the two paintings above from **Spain** and **Chile.**

Instructions
1. After looking at each painting, describe it to yourself. What message do you get from it? As you scan the painting, does any particular point draw your attention?
2. Use the Internet or your school's library to learn more about the two paintings. You might look up information about the artists and whether the paintings reflect personal events in their lives.

☀ Proyecto ❷ *Your own painting*

Now try your hand at being an artist.

Materials for your own painting
Construction paper
Charcoal pencil, colored pencils or pens, watercolor paint, paintbrushes

Instructions
Create a landscape scene on construction paper. Use the paintings above as an inspiration.

☀ En tu comunidad

Visit the website of a museum in your part of the country that contains works of art from a Spanish-speaking country. What can you learn about that country by examining the artwork? Record your impressions in a journal.

En resumen
Vocabulario y gramática

ANIMATEDGRAMMAR
Interactive Flashcards
my.hrw.com

Vocabulario

Describe Places in Town

el café	café
el centro	center, downtown
el cine	movie theater; the movies
el parque	park
el restaurante	restaurant
el teatro	theater

Describe Events in Town

el concierto	concert
las entradas	tickets
la música rock	rock music
la película	movie
la ventanilla	ticket window

Getting Around Town

a pie	by foot
la calle	street
en autobús	by bus
en coche	by car
encontrar (ue)	to find
tomar	to take

In a Restaurant

el (la) camarero(a)	(food) server
costar (ue)	to cost
la cuenta	bill
de postre	for dessert
el menú	menu
la mesa	table
el plato principal	main course
la propina	tip

Ordering from a Menu

pedir (i)	to order, to ask for
servir (i)	to serve

For Dinner

el arroz	rice
el bistec	beef
el brócoli	broccoli
la carne	meat
la ensalada	salad
los frijoles	beans
el pastel	cake
la patata	potato
el pescado	fish
el pollo	chicken
el tomate	tomato
las verduras	vegetables

Other Words and Phrases

allí	there
almorzar (ue)	to eat lunch
aquí	here
dormir (ue)	to sleep
el lugar	place
poder (ue)	to be able, can
tal vez	perhaps, maybe
ver	to see
volver (ue)	to return, to come back

Gramática

Notas gramaticales: The verb **ver** *p. 220*, **ir a** + infinitive *p. 222*

Stem-Changing Verbs: o → ue

For o → **ue** stem-changing verbs, the last **o** of the stem changes to **ue** in all forms except **nosotros(as)** and **vosotros(as).**

poder *to be able, can*	
p**ue**do	podemos
p**ue**des	podéis
p**ue**de	p**ue**den

Stem-Changing Verbs: e → i

For e → **i** stem-changing verbs, the last **e** of the stem changes to **i** in all forms except **nosotros(as)** and **vosotros(as).**

servir *to serve*	
s**i**rvo	servimos
s**i**rves	servís
s**i**rve	s**i**rven

Repaso de la lección

¡AvanzaRap!
DVD
Sing and Learn

¡LLEGADA!

Now you can
- describe places and events in town
- talk about types of transportation
- say what you are going to do
- order from a menu

Using
- **ir a** + infinitive
- stem-changing verbs: **o → ue**
- stem-changing verbs: **e → i**

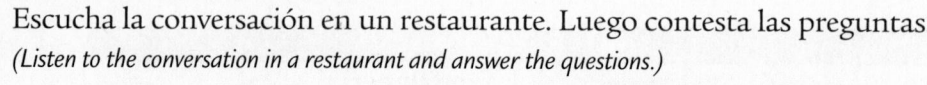

To review
- stem-changing verbs: **o → ue** p. 223
- **ir a** + infinitive p. 222
- stem-changing verbs: **e → i** p. 228

1 | Listen and understand

🎧 AUDIO

Escucha la conversación en un restaurante. Luego contesta las preguntas. *(Listen to the conversation in a restaurant and answer the questions.)*

1. ¿Cuántas personas van a comer?
2. ¿Cómo son los platos principales?
3. ¿Qué pide Raúl con el bistec?
4. ¿Qué pide Raúl para beber?
5. ¿Qué pide Tere de plato principal?
6. ¿Quién pide el pastel de postre?

To review
- **ir a** + infinitive p. 222

2 | Say what you are going to do

¿Qué van a hacer estas personas el sábado? ¿Cómo van a ir? *(Tell what people are going to do on Saturday and how they plan to go there.)*

modelo: Angélica / almorzar en un restaurante
Angélica va a almorzar en un restaurante.
Va a ir en autobús.

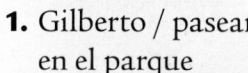

1. Gilberto / pasear en el parque

2. yo / volver al centro

3. las chicas / beber refrescos en un café

4. tú / ver una película en el cine

5. nosotros / escuchar música rock

6. vosotros / ir al teatro

To review
• stem-changing verbs: **o → ue** p. 223

3 | Describe places and events in town

Tomás describe sus actividades. Completa su mensaje con la forma correcta del verbo apropiado.
(Complete the e-mail message with the correct form of the appropriate verb.)

encontrar	almorzar
poder	volver
costar	dormir

Los domingos por la tarde, yo __1.__ en el restaurante Casa Serrano con mi familia. Nosotros __2.__ platos muy buenos en el menú y la comida no __3.__ mucho.
Yo nunca __4.__ comer todo porque sirven mucha comida.
Nosotros __5.__ a casa a las tres o a las cuatro. Muchas veces mis hermanos menores están cansados y __6.__ dos horas. Me gusta pasar los domingos con mi familia. Es un día muy tranquilo.

To review
• stem-changing verbs: **e → i** p. 228

4 | Order from a menu

Describe los problemas en el restaurante. *(Describe the problems in the restaurant.)*

modelo: Leonor: carne / el camarero: pescado
Leonor pide carne, pero el camarero sirve pescado.

1. tú: agua / la camarera: leche
2. yo: brócoli / el camarero: patatas
3. ustedes: bistec / los camareros: pollo
4. Nicolás: ensalada / el camarero: tomates
5. nosotros: arroz / los camareros: verduras
6. vosotros: pastel / la camarera: helado

To review
• Comparación cultural pp. 216, 225, 230
• Lectura cultural pp. 234–235

5 | Spain, Guatemala, and Chile

Comparación cultural

Answer these culture questions.

1. What is featured at Madrid's Teatro de la Comedia?
2. What can you find at Madrid's Rastro and Chichicastenango's market?
3. Who is depicted in *Las meninas*?
4. What can you see and do in Madrid's Parque del Buen Retiro and Santiago's Parque Metropolitano?

Get Help Online
my.hrw.com

Más práctica Cuaderno *pp. 182–193* Cuaderno para hispanohablantes *pp. 184–193*

Guatemala
España
Chile

AUDIO

¿Adónde vamos el sábado?

Lectura y escritura

1 **Leer** Activities that young people do vary around the world. Read what Anita, Rodrigo, and Armando do for fun on Saturdays.

2 **Escribir** Using the three descriptions as models, write a short paragraph about what you like to do on Saturdays.

STRATEGY Escribir
Create an activity chart
To write about what you do for fun on Saturdays, use an activity chart like the one shown.

Categoría	Detalles
lugares	
ropa	
actividades	

Step 1 Complete the chart with details about where you go, what you wear, and what you do for fun on Saturdays.

Step 2 Write your paragraph. Make sure to include all the information from your chart. Check your writing by yourself or with help from a friend. Make final corrections.

Compara con tu mundo

Use the paragraph you wrote to compare the activities you do for fun to the activities described by *one* of the three students. How are the activities similar? How are they different?

Cuaderno *pp. 194–196*   Cuaderno para hispanohablantes *pp. 194–196*

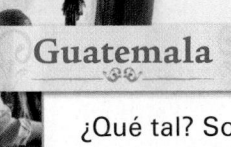

Guatemala

Anita

¿Qué tal? Soy Anita y me gusta escuchar música folklórica. El sábado mis amigos y yo pensamos ir a un concierto de marimba[1] en el centro. Las entradas no cuestan mucho y los conciertos son muy buenos. ¿Qué ropa voy a llevar? Quiero llevar un vestido porque es primavera y hace calor. Mis amigos prefieren llevar camisetas y jeans.

[1] musical instrument resembling a xylophone

España

Rodrigo

¡Hola! Me llamo Rodrigo y vivo en Madrid. El sábado quiero ir de compras con mi hermano. Siempre necesito comprar camisetas y calcetines. Muchas veces los encuentro en el centro comercial. Se llama Xanadú y tiene tiendas, restaurantes y ¡un parque de nieve! Allí puedes practicar deportes de invierno durante todo el año. A mi hermano le gusta la nieve en el verano, pero a mí no. En el verano ¡prefiero tener calor!

Chile

Armando

¡Hola! Me llamo Armando y soy de Santiago, Chile. En septiembre puedes ir a muchos rodeos porque hay muchas fiestas nacionales en Chile. El sábado voy a ir a un rodeo con mis amigos para ver a los huasos[2]. Pienso llevar unos jeans nuevos y una chaqueta porque no quiero tener frío. Quiero llevar un sombrero de vaquero[3], pero no puedo. ¡Cuestan mucho!

[2] Chilean cowboys   [3] cowboy

Repaso inclusivo
♻ Options for Review

¡AvanzaRap!
DVD
Sing and Learn

1 | Listen, understand, and compare

Escuchar

Listen to Mrs. Estrada and her son, Carlitos, order a meal at a restaurant. Then answer the questions.

1. ¿Qué tiene ganas de comer Carlitos?
2. ¿Qué pide para empezar? ¿Y de plato principal?
3. ¿Qué plato pide la señora Estrada para empezar?
4. ¿Qué no sirven hoy en el restaurante?
5. ¿Qué van a beber ellos?

Which order most resembles what you like to eat? What foods and drinks do you order when you go to restaurants?

2 | Present a family outing

Hablar

Prepare a presentation about a family outing to a restaurant. Bring in a photo of your own or one from a magazine. Talk about the clothes each person is wearing, what food the restaurant serves, what each person orders, and how much it costs. You should talk for at least three minutes.

3 | Compare school days

Hablar

Take turns interviewing a partner about his or her day at school. Ask about the classes your partner prefers, what he or she eats for lunch and what he or she thinks about the cafeteria food. Finish by asking what he or she prefers to do after school, and at what time he or she is going to do things today after school.

4 | Make a flier

Escribir

As president of the Spanish club, you have been put in charge of a booth at the upcoming international food fair. You have decided to serve breakfast dishes from Spain and Mexico. Use the Internet to learn about Spanish and Mexican cuisine. Create a flier to advertise what food and beverages you will serve, at what time you will be serving them, and how much the tickets cost. Your flier should have illustrations and describe in detail each dish.

5 | Help find a lost child

Hablar

Role-play a situation in which you are a mall employee in customer service. Your partner is shopping at the mall with a younger cousin, but can't find him or her. Interview your partner to find out as much descriptive information as possible, including age, physical characteristics, and clothing. Your conversation should be at least three minutes long.

6 | Create a fashion show

Hablar
Escribir

Work in a group of five. Individually, write a detailed description of the clothes you are wearing. Include color, where the clothes are from, where you can buy each item, how much they cost, and in what season(s) you can wear them. Your description should have at least eight sentences. Then perform the fashion show for the class, reading each other's descriptions as each "model" walks down the runway.

7 | Plan a weekend with family

Leer
Escribir

You are studying in Barcelona, Spain, for the summer and your parents are coming to visit. Read this newspaper supplement to find out about the weekend's events. Then write an e-mail to your parents, and suggest what you can do and where you can go together or separately during the weekend. Keep in mind everyone's likes and dislikes. Your e-mail should have at least six suggestions.

Suplemento especial – fin de semana

GUÍA DEL OCIO - BARCELONA

VIERNES

Cena especial
Comida española típica, con música de flamenco.
Restaurante Casals (de las 21.30 a las 23.30 h)

Concierto
Los hermanos Pujols tocan música rock.
Plaza Cataluña (a las 14.30 h)

SÁBADO

Películas
Terror en el centro
Hollywood. Película de terror. Dos chicos de Nueva York van en autobús cuando llegan unos extraterrestres horribles.
Cines Maremagnum (a las 16.00 y 18.30 h)

Mi tía loca
España. Película cómica. La historia de una chica y su tía favorita.
Cine Diagonal Mar (a las 13.30 y 21.00 h)

Comprar y pasear
La calle que lo tiene todo: libros, ropa, comida ¡y más!
Las Ramblas (todo el día)

DOMINGO

Eliminar el cáncer
Puedes pasear y donar dinero para combatir el cáncer.
Parque Güell (a las 10.00 h)

Compras
Los mejores precios del verano en las tiendas de ropa.
Centro Comercial Barcelona Glorias (de las 10.30 a las 20.30 h)

Concierto de Beethoven
La orquesta de Barcelona toca música clásica. Un concierto para toda la familia.
Teatro Liceu (a las 20.00 h)

UNIDAD 5

Ecuador

¡Bienvenido a nuestra casa!

Lección 1
Tema: **Vivimos aquí**

Lección 2
Tema: **Una fiesta en casa**

«¡Hola!
Somos Fernando y Elena.
Somos de Quito, Ecuador.»

Venezuela
Colombia
Ecuador
Islas Galápagos
Perú
Océano Pacífico
Bolivia
Chile
Paraguay
Argentina
Uruguay

Océano Pacífico
Otavalo
Quito
Coca
Saquisilí
Ecuador
Guayaquil
RUINAS DE INGAPIRCA
Cuenca
Machala

Población: 15.868.396

Área: 109.483 millas cuadradas

Capital: Quito

Moneda: el dólar estadounidense, desde *(since)* el año 2001

Idiomas: español, quechua y otras lenguas indígenas

Comida típica: locro, fritada, llapingachos

Gente famosa: Alexandra Ayala Marín (periodista), Gilda Holst (escritora), Julio Jaramillo (cantante), Jefferson Pérez (atleta)

Canguil, tostado, chifles

Jóvenes ecuatorianos aplauden al equipo nacional

◀ **Nuestra pasión: el fútbol** In Ecuador, major-league soccer games are played on weekends in the cities of Quito and Guayaquil, while informal games are played at any time, in every city, town, and village. These fans of the **Selección Nacional** team hope for an appearance at the World Cup (**Copa Mundial**). *Where and when is your favorite sport played?*

Las montañas de los Andes Not far from the capital city of Quito lies the 19,347-foot Cotopaxi, the world's highest active volcano. The Andes mountain range, which stretches 4,500 miles north to south along the western coast of South America, has many mountains that reach 20,000 feet or more. *What mountain ranges in the United States are you familiar with?* ▶

El volcán Cotopaxi y la ciudad de Quito

◀ **La ropa tradicional** In *Las floristas*, Camilo Egas shows indigenous women from the market town of Otavalo, north of Quito. They are wearing traditional clothing: white blouses and layered white and black skirts with red sashes, along with gold or red coral jewelry. *How do people in the United States express themselves through the clothing they wear?*

Las floristas (1916), Camilo Egas

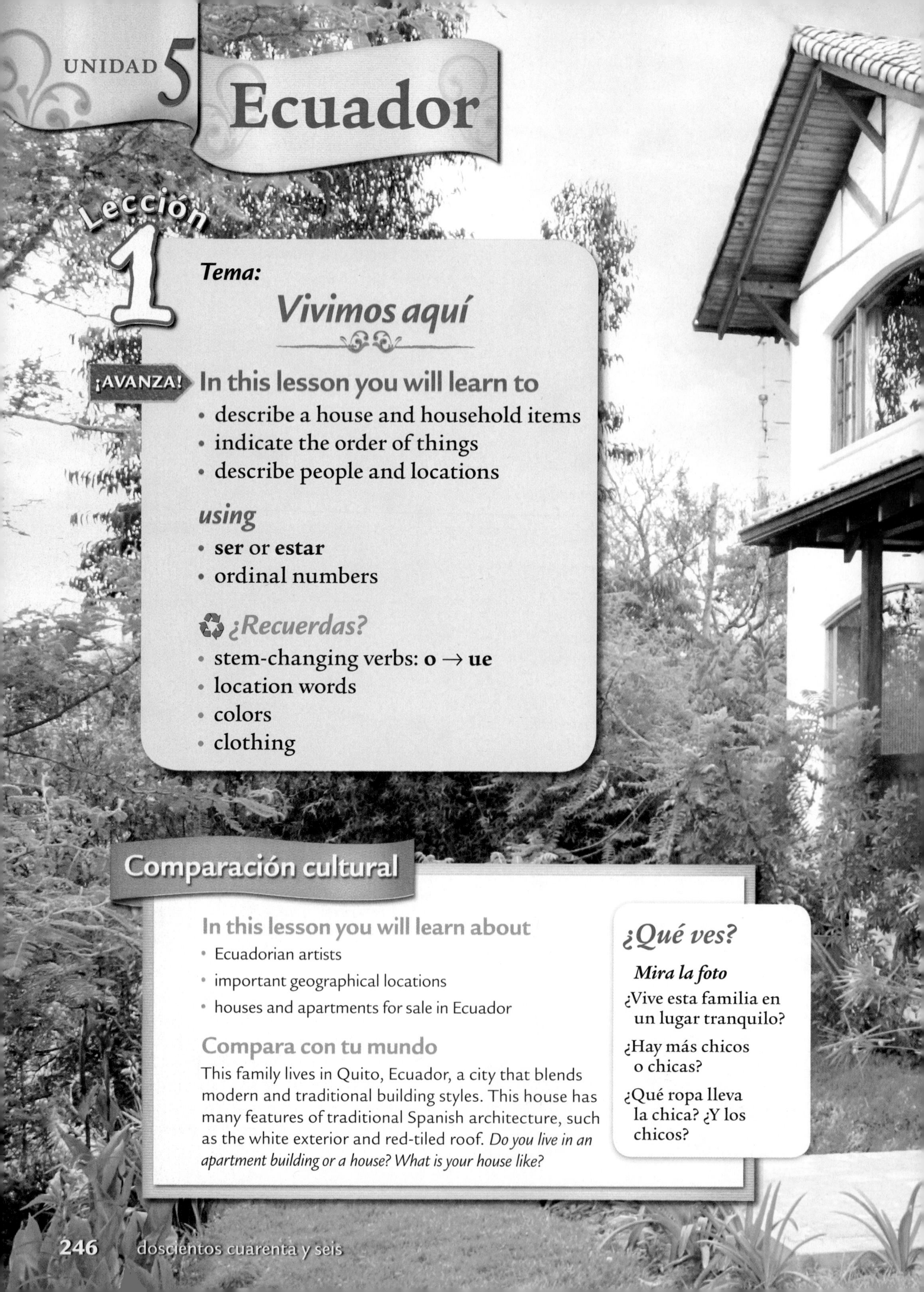

Ecuador

Lección 1

Tema:

Vivimos aquí

¡AVANZA! **In this lesson you will learn to**
- describe a house and household items
- indicate the order of things
- describe people and locations

using
- **ser** or **estar**
- ordinal numbers

♻ *¿Recuerdas?*
- stem-changing verbs: **o → ue**
- location words
- colors
- clothing

Comparación cultural

In this lesson you will learn about
- Ecuadorian artists
- important geographical locations
- houses and apartments for sale in Ecuador

Compara con tu mundo

This family lives in Quito, Ecuador, a city that blends modern and traditional building styles. This house has many features of traditional Spanish architecture, such as the white exterior and red-tiled roof. *Do you live in an apartment building or a house? What is your house like?*

¿Qué ves?

Mira la foto

¿Vive esta familia en un lugar tranquilo?

¿Hay más chicos o chicas?

¿Qué ropa lleva la chica? ¿Y los chicos?

MODES OF COMMUNICATION

INTERPRETIVE	INTERPERSONAL	PRESENTATIONAL
Listen to a voice mail asking you to help with party plans. Read real-estate ads from Ecuador and determine which properties better suit certain people.	Take turns describing your house or apartment to others.	Present a plan to furnish a dorm room. Write a real-estate ad to advertise a house for sale.

Una casa tradicional con jardín
Quito, Ecuador

Presentación de VOCABULARIO

¡AVANZA!   **Goal:** Learn about what Manuel's house is like. Then practice what you have learned to describe a house and household items. *Actividades 1–2*

♻ *¿Recuerdas?* Stem-changing verbs: **o → ue** p. 223

VIDEO
DVD

AUDIO

la casa

el jardín

el patio

A ¡Hola! Me llamo Manuel. Vivo en **una casa** grande. Tiene dos **pisos.** Hay **un patio** y **un jardín** detrás de la casa.

B A Elena y a mí nos gusta jugar **videojuegos** en **la sala.** En **la cocina** preparamos la comida y en **el comedor** comemos todos los días.

la sala

el sillón

el sofá

los videojuegos

el televisor

la alfombra

la cocina

el suelo

el comedor

C Cuando **subimos la escalera,** llegamos a mi **cuarto.** Allí me gusta estudiar, escuchar mis **discos compactos** y descansar.

subir

la escalera

el espejo

el radio

la cómoda

D En mi cuarto tengo **un tocadiscos compactos, un radio** y otras **cosas.**

el cuarto

las cortinas

la lámpara

la cama

E Mi amigo Fernando piensa que vivir en **un apartamento** es **ideal.** Prefiere vivir en un apartamento donde puede ver el centro de Quito.

el apartamento

la planta baja

el primer piso

Más vocabulario

el armario *closet*
bajar *to descend*
el lector DVD *DVD player*
los muebles *furniture*
Expansión de vocabulario p. R6

@**HOMETUTOR** Interactive
my.hrw.com Flashcards

¡A responder!   Escuchar

Escucha la lista de las cosas que hay en la casa. Indica la foto del cuarto donde se encuentra cada cosa. *(Listen to the list of items found in a house and point to the photo of the room in which each item is found.)*

❖ Práctica de VOCABULARIO

1 | ¿Dónde encuentras...? ♻ ¿Recuerdas? Stem-changing verbs: o → ue p. 223

Escribir
Hablar

Indica dónde encuentras estas cosas. *(Indicate where you would find these items.)*

modelo: ¿sala o jardín?
Encuentro un televisor en la sala.

1. ¿cuarto o cocina?

2. ¿comedor o baño?

3. ¿cocina o sala?

4. ¿baño o patio?

5. ¿jardín o cuarto?

6. ¿comedor o sala?

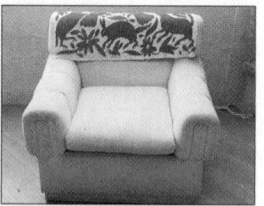

2 | ¿Qué es?

Escribir
Hablar

Lee las descripciones de cosas o lugares en la casa. Identifica la cosa o el lugar.
(Read the clues to identify things and places in a house.)

modelo: Hay una mesa y sillas, y la familia come aquí pero no prepara
la comida aquí.
Es el comedor.

1. Son para las ventanas y las cierras en la noche.
2. La necesitas para bajar al primer piso.
3. Está en el suelo de una sala.
4. Lo usas para ver un DVD.
5. La usas para leer en la noche.
6. Lo usas para escuchar discos compactos.

> **Expansión**
> Write your own clues
> for other parts of the
> house for a partner
> to guess.

Más práctica Cuaderno *pp. 197–199* Cuaderno para hispanohablantes *pp. 197–200*

🌐 **Get Help Online**
my.hrw.com

PARA Y PIENSA

Did you get it? Name three items that can be found in . . .
1. la sala **2.** el cuarto

⚜ VOCABULARIO en contexto

Telehistoria escena 1

@HOMETUTOR
my.hrw.com
View, Read and Record

STRATEGIES

Compare uses of the verb This scene contains expressions with **ir a...** Identify whether each expression states a fact, offers a suggestion, or makes plans.

Draw a map Draw a map showing the places Fernando goes in this scene. To whom is he talking in each place? What are they talking about?

VIDEO DVD

AUDIO

Sra. Cuevas   Fernando

Elena   Manuel

Mrs. Cuevas is working in the garden when Fernando arrives.

Fernando: ¿Cómo está, señora Cuevas? ¿Está Manuel?

Sra. Cuevas: ¿Qué tal, Fernando? Sí, escucha discos compactos en su cuarto...

Fernando: Ah, gracias. Voy a subir.

Sra. Cuevas: ...o está en la sala. Le gusta mucho jugar videojuegos con Elena. ¿Van a estudiar?

Fernando: Sí.

Sra. Cuevas: Bueno. ¡Ah! *(She hands him a package.)* Fernando, es para Manuel.

Fernando takes it and walks inside, where Elena and Manuel are playing videogames in the living room.

Fernando: Hola.

Manuel: *(distracted)* Hola, Fernando.

Elena: Hola, Fernando. ¿Van a estudiar aquí en la sala, en el comedor o en el cuarto de Manuel?

Fernando: *(shrugging his shoulders)* ¿Manuel?

Elena: ¡Manuel! *(She turns off the television to get his attention.)*

Manuel: ¡OK! ¿Qué tal si estudiamos en mi cuarto?

También se dice

Ecuador To say where Manuel is, Mrs. Cuevas uses the word **cuarto.** In other Spanish-speaking countries you might hear:
• **España** la habitación
• **Argentina, Chile** la pieza
• **México** la recámara
• **muchos países** la alcoba, el dormitorio

Continuará... p. 256

3 | *Comprensión del episodio* La casa de la familia Cuevas

Escuchar
Leer

Lee las oraciones y decide quién lo hace: ¿Fernando, la señora Cuevas, Manuel y/o Elena? *(Read the sentences and tell who is being described.)*

> **modelo:** Van a estudiar.
> Manuel y Fernando van a estudiar.

1. Va a subir la escalera para ver a Manuel.
2. Le gusta mucho jugar videojuegos con Elena.
3. Habla con Fernando cuando él llega a la casa.
4. Habla con Fernando porque Manuel no escucha.

4 | Las cosas que hay en la casa

Hablar

Describe las cosas en la casa. Otro(a) estudiante tiene que adivinarlas. *(Describe these household items for a partner to guess.)*

una mesa	un disco compacto
un televisor	una cama
una cómoda	un radio

A Puedes encontrarlo en muchos lugares: la sala, la cocina, tu cuarto. Lo usas para escuchar música o deportes.

B Es un radio.

5 | El apartamento ideal

Escribir

Escribe una descripción del apartamento ideal. *(Describe an ideal apartment.)*

> **modelo:** El apartamento ideal es grande.
> En la sala hay...

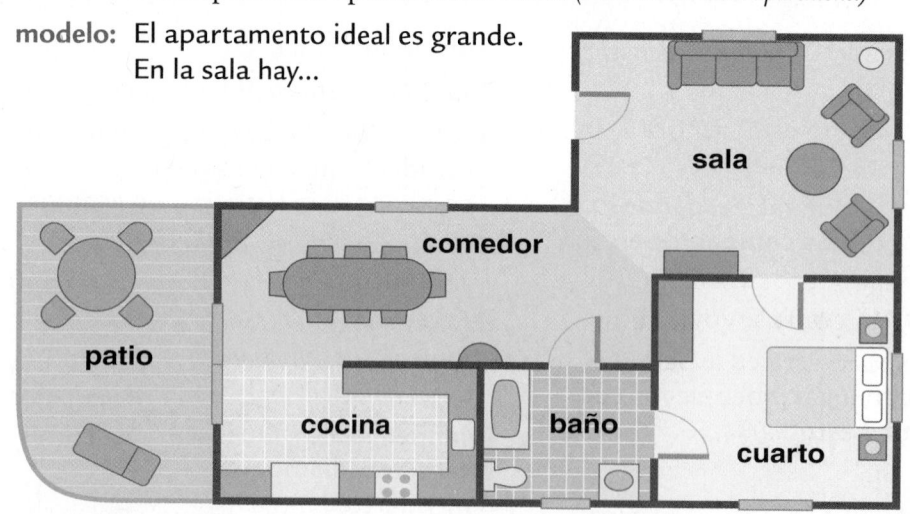

sala

comedor

patio

cocina

baño

cuarto

Expansión
Read your description to a partner, who will draw a floor plan of your ideal apartment.

🌐 **Get Help Online**
my.hrw.com

PARA Y PIENSA

Did you get it? Name items Manuel may use to do the following.
  1. escuchar música   **2.** estudiar   **3.** jugar videojuegos

Unidad 5 Ecuador
252 doscientos cincuenta y dos

Presentación de GRAMÁTICA

Goal: Learn the differences between **ser** and **estar.** Then practice using these two verbs to describe people and locations. **Actividades 6–10**

♻ *¿Recuerdas?* Location words p. 115, colors p. 195

English Grammar Connection: Remember that there are two ways to say the English verb *to be* in Spanish: **ser** and **estar** (see pp. 37 and 115).

Ser or estar

ANIMATEDGRAMMAR
my.hrw.com

Ser and **estar** both mean *to be.* How do you know which verb to use?

Here's how:

Use **ser** to indicate origin: where someone or something is from.

> **Soy** de Quito.
> *I'm from Quito.*

Use **ser** to describe personal traits and physical characteristics.

> Los estudiantes **son** inteligentes.
> *The students **are** intelligent.*

Ser is also used to indicate professions.

> La señora Ramírez **es** maestra.
> *Mrs. Ramírez **is** a teacher.*

Remember that you also use **ser** to identify people or things and to give the time and the date.

Use **estar** to indicate location: where someone or something is.

> Quito **está** en Ecuador.
> *Quito **is** in Ecuador.*

Estar is also used to describe conditions, such as how someone feels.

physical: ¿Cómo **estás**?   **Estoy** bien.
*How **are you**?*   *I'm fine.*

emotional: **Estamos** contentos.   **Están** enojados.
***We are** happy.*   ***They are** angry.*

Más práctica
Cuaderno *pp. 200–202*
Cuaderno para hispanohablantes *pp. 201–203*

@HOMETUTOR my.hrw.com
Leveled Practice
Conjuguemos.com

Práctica de GRAMÁTICA

6 | El apartamento de Fernando

 ¿Recuerdas? Location words p. 115

Escribir

Ayuda a Fernando a describir su apartamento. Escribe oraciones con esta información, utilizando **ser** y **estar.** *(Using the information given, write sentences with* **ser** *and* **estar.***)*

> **modelo:** el apartamento: grande / cerca de la escuela
> El apartamento es grande. Está cerca de la escuela.

1. la sala: marrón / lejos de la escalera

2. las cortinas: nuevo / delante de las ventanas

3. el cuarto: pequeño / en la planta baja

4. el sillón: blanco / cerca del sofá

5. las lámparas: feo / encima de las mesas

6. el jardín: bonito / en el patio

7. la cómoda: grande / en el cuarto

8. la alfombra: viejo / debajo del sofá

> **Expansión**
> Describe these items in your home.

7 | Un sábado con la familia

Leer
Escribir

Manuel describe un sábado por la mañana en su casa. Completa lo que dice con la forma correcta de **ser** o **estar.** *(Complete the description with the correct form of* **ser** *or* **estar.***)*

> Los sábados yo no __1.__ cansado porque duermo mucho. Bajo a la cocina a las diez; mis padres y Elena ya __2.__ allí. Elena __3.__ mi hermana. Ella __4.__ un poco perezosa. Mi padre y yo preparamos el desayuno. La cocina __5.__ grande y amarilla. La mesa y las sillas __6.__ cerca de la ventana. Las cortinas __7.__ blancas. La alfombra __8.__ de Otavalo, en Ecuador. Después del desayuno, mi familia y yo __9.__ contentos porque vamos a jugar al fútbol. Nosotros __10.__ muy atléticos.

8 | Los amigos de Manuel

Escuchar
Escribir

Manuel describe a varias personas. Escucha su descripción y toma apuntes. Contesta las preguntas. *(Listen to Manuel's description and take notes. Then answer the questions.)*

1. ¿Cómo está Manuel hoy?

2. ¿De dónde es Rosa?

3. ¿Cómo es ella?

4. ¿Dónde está su casa?

5. ¿De dónde son José y Carlos?

6. ¿Cómo son ellos?

7. ¿Dónde está su apartamento?

8. ¿Cómo es su apartamento?

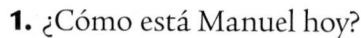

9 | Mi casa

Comparación cultural

Casas ecuatorianas

Nochebuena
(alrededor de 1990),
Targelia Toaquiza

How do landscapes reflect a community's way of life? The Tigua artists from the **Ecuadorian Andes** are known for their colorful paintings, created with chicken feather brushes on sheephide. Their artwork shows the world around them: mountains, valleys, farms, and livestock. Tigua paintings, such as *Nochebuena* by Targelia Toaquiza, are typically landscapes that show scenes of community life, such as festivals, indigenous traditions, harvests, and everyday rural activities.

Compara con tu mundo *What would a painting showing community life in your area include?*

Escribe una descripción del lugar donde tú vives. Explica dónde está y cómo es. *(Write a description of where you live.)*

> **modelo:** Mi casa está cerca de la escuela. Es blanca y está al lado de una casa amarilla. También está cerca del parque...

10 | ¡A jugar! ¿Cómo es?   ♻ *¿Recuerdas?* Colors p. 195

Hablar

Trabaja en un grupo de tres y túrnense para describir los dibujos. La última persona que tiene una descripción original gana. *(In a group of three, take turns describing each drawing. Try to be the last person who can add something new without repeating.)*

A Es una sala.

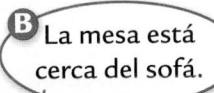
B La mesa está cerca del sofá.

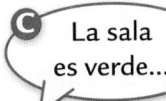
C La sala es verde...

1.
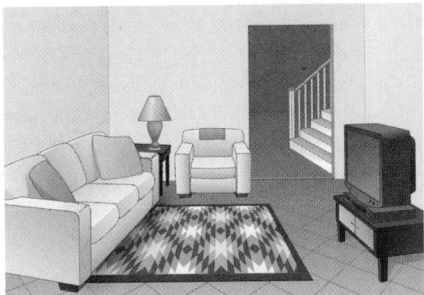

2.

Más práctica   Cuaderno *pp. 200–202*   Cuaderno para hispanohablantes *pp. 201–203*

Get Help Online
my.hrw.com

PARA Y PIENSA

Did you get it? Complete each sentence with the correct form of **ser** or **estar.**

1. Nosotros _____ en la cocina.
2. Voy a mi cuarto porque _____ cansado.
3. El espejo _____ de Bogotá.
4. Los jardines _____ bonitos.

❊ GRAMÁTICA en contexto

¡AVANZA! **Goal:** Identify the ways **ser** and **estar** are used in Manuel and Fernando's conversation about themselves and things in the house. Then use these verbs to talk about people and things in your life. *Actividades 11–13*

Telehistoria escena 2

@ **HOMETUTOR** View, Read
my.hrw.com and Record

STRATEGIES

Cuando lees
Consider the influence of the setting
Early in this scene, you find out whether Manuel's bedroom is neat or messy. This has a big influence on the action in the scene. How and why?

Cuando escuchas
Find the real feelings How does Elena describe Manuel? Is she sincere, or is she saying the opposite of what she feels? How can you tell?

VIDEO
DVD

AUDIO

Manuel: ¡Mi cuaderno no está aquí!

Fernando: *(distracted)* Y, ¿encima de la cama? ¿Y cerca de la lámpara? ¿Y en el armario? ¿En la cómoda?

Manuel looks around, but Fernando finds the notebook on the floor.

Fernando: Manuel, ¡eres muy desorganizado! ¡Todas tus cosas están en el suelo!

Meanwhile, Elena sees the package from Alicia in the living room and calls upstairs.

Elena: ¡Manuel! ¡Manueeeel!

Manuel: *(He goes downstairs.)* ¿Qué quieres? Estoy muy ocupado.

Elena: Sí, tú eres muy estudioso.

She gives him the package. Manuel opens it, dropping the T-shirt on the floor to read the letter. He goes back to his room.

Fernando: *(reading the letter)* ¿Tienes que ir al centro de Quito? ¿A ver a Trini Salgado?

Manuel: Sí. ¡Alicia quiere el autógrafo de Trini! Es importante. Tenemos que ir.

As they leave, Fernando realizes that Manuel forgot the T-shirt.

Fernando: Manuel... ¿y la camiseta?   **Continuará...** p. 261

También se dice

Ecuador When asking where Manuel's notebook is, Fernando uses the word **el armario.** In other Spanish-speaking countries you might hear:
• **España el armario empotrado**
• **muchos países el clóset**

11 *Comprensión del episodio* Los problemas de Manuel

Escuchar
Leer

Di si las siguientes oraciones son ciertas o falsas. Corrige las oraciones falsas.
(Tell whether the following sentences are true or false. Correct the false sentences.)

1. Manuel es muy organizado.

2. Manuel está tranquilo.

3. Manuel no puede encontrar su calculadora.

4. Todas las cosas de Manuel están en el suelo.

5. Fernando y Manuel tienen que ir al centro comercial.

6. Quieren ver a Trini.

7. Fernando quiere el autógrafo de Trini Salgado.

8. Fernando y Manuel tienen que ir, y Manuel tiene la camiseta.

12 Una persona importante

Escribir

Escribe una descripción de una persona importante en tu vida. Usa las siguientes preguntas. *(Write about someone special in your life. Use the following questions.)*

Para organizarte:

- ¿Quién es?
- ¿Cómo es?
- ¿De dónde es?
- ¿Dónde está ahora?
- ¿Cómo estás cuando pasas un rato con él o ella?

modelo: Mi madre es simpática y trabajadora. Es más alta que mi padre. Es de Seattle, Washington, pero está en Portland ahora...

13 Mi cuarto

Hablar

Descríbele tu cuarto a otro(a) estudiante. Él o ella va a dibujarlo.
(Describe your room to a partner. He or she will draw it.)

modelo: Mi cuarto es grande. La puerta está al lado de la cómoda. El televisor y los videojuegos están encima de la cómoda...

Expansión
Write a description of someone else's drawing.

Get Help Online
my.hrw.com

PARA Y PIENSA

Did you get it? Choose the correct verb in each sentence based on the Telehistoria.

1. Manuel (es / está) muy desorganizado.

2. Todas las cosas (son / están) en el suelo.

3. El cuaderno no (está / es) encima de la cama.

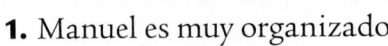

Presentación de GRAMÁTICA

Goal: Learn how to use ordinal numbers. Then practice them to indicate the order of things, and to talk about the floors of a house or building. **Actividades 14–16**

♻ **¿Recuerdas?** Clothing p. 194

English Grammar Connection: In both English and Spanish, **ordinal numbers** indicate position in a series or the order of items.

in **second** place   en **segundo** lugar

Ordinal Numbers

ANIMATED GRAMMAR
my.hrw.com

When used with a noun, an **ordinal number** must agree in number and gender with that noun.

Here's how:

Ordinal Numbers			
primero(a)	*first*	**sexto(a)**	*sixth*
segundo(a)	*second*	**séptimo(a)**	*seventh*
tercero(a)	*third*	**octavo(a)**	*eighth*
cuarto(a)	*fourth*	**noveno(a)**	*ninth*
quinto(a)	*fifth*	**décimo(a)**	*tenth*

Ordinals are placed before **nouns.**

before the noun ⌐   *agrees*

Es la **primera película** de María Conchita Alonso.
*It's the **first** movie of María Conchita Alonso.*

agrees

Nuestro apartamento está en el **octavo piso.**
*Our apartment is on the **eighth** floor.*

Primero and **tercero** drop the **o** before a **masculine singular noun.**

drops the o ⌐
Enero es el **primer mes** del año.
*January is the **first** month of the year.*

Más práctica
Cuaderno *pp. 203–205*
Cuaderno para hispanohablantes *pp. 204–207*

@HOMETUTOR my.hrw.com
Leveled Practice

❊ Práctica de GRAMÁTICA

14 | ¿En qué piso?

Escribir

Escribe en qué piso vive cada familia. *(Tell on which floor each family lives.)*

> **modelo:** Gutiérrez (2)
> La familia Gutiérrez vive en **el segundo piso.**

1. Díaz (7) **4.** Ponce (1) **7.** García (3)

2. Granados (5) **5.** Romero (9) **8.** Martínez (8)

3. Santiago (10) **6.** Sánchez (6) **9.** Cabral (4)

15 | La primera persona lleva...   ♻ *¿Recuerdas?* Clothing p. 194

Hablar

Estas personas hacen cola. Pregúntale a otro(a) estudiante qué llevan, usando números ordinales. *(Use ordinal numbers to ask what the people in line are wearing.)*

A ¿Qué lleva la **primera** persona?

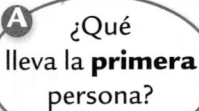

B La **primera** persona lleva **jeans, una camiseta marrón** y...

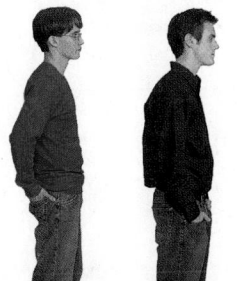

> **Expansión**
> Ask your partner about the physical appearance of the people in the line.

AUDIO

▶ Pronunciación ◀   La acentuación

In Spanish, just like in English, certain syllables are stressed more than others. If a word ends in a vowel, **n**, or **s,** and there is no written accent, the next-to-last syllable is stressed.

> **sa**la   **su**ben   cor**ti**nas   aparta**men**to

If a word ends in a consonant other than **n** or **s,** the natural stress falls on the last syllable of the word.

> mu**jer**   re**loj**   ba**jar**   i**deal**   televi**sor**

Words that have written accents are stressed on the syllable with the accent.

> jar**dín**   si**llón**   **lám**para   so**fá**   **dé**cimo

16 | Los pisos del almacén

Hablar

Pregúntale a otro(a) estudiante a qué piso del almacén vas para encontrar las siguientes cosas. *(Ask a partner to what floor you go to find the following items.)*

A ¿A qué piso voy para comprar sopa?

B Necesitas ir a la planta baja para comprar sopa.

1.

2.

3.

4.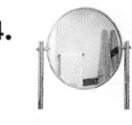

5.

6.

ALMACÉN

5	MUEBLES
4	DECORACIÓN
3	APARATOS ELECTRÓNICOS
2	ROPA DE MUJERES
1	ZAPATOS
Planta Baja	CAFETERÍA

Comparación cultural

Mitad del Mundo

Sitios geográficos

How does a country's location in the world make it unique?
Ecuador is located on the equator, which divides the northern and southern hemispheres. The Mitad del Mundo monument marks the location of the equator. There you can stand with one foot in each hemisphere. Ushuaia, in the province of Tierra del Fuego in **Argentina,** is the southernmost city in the world. It is known as *la ciudad del fin del mundo* (the city at the end of the earth). Located a little over 600 miles from Antarctica, it is a common starting point for arctic explorations.

Compara con tu mundo *What geographical locations are important in the United States and why?*

Ushuaia, Argentina

Más práctica Cuaderno *pp. 203–205* Cuaderno para hispanohablantes *pp. 204–207*

🌐 **Get Help Online**
my.hrw.com

PARA Y PIENSA

Did you get it? Say that you are on the following floors.
1. sixth **2.** ninth **3.** second **4.** third

❊ Todo junto

¡AVANZA!

Goal: *Show what you know* Identify how Manuel, his mother, and Fernando use **ser** and **estar** to talk about different places in the house. Then practice these verbs and ordinal numbers to describe houses and apartments. *Actividades 17–21*

Telehistoria completa

@HOMETUTOR   View, Read
my.hrw.com   and Record

STRATEGIES

Cuando lees
Read to know whether and where
You already know that Manuel has lost the T-shirt. Read to find out whether he finds it. If so, where?

Cuando escuchas
Notice reactions As you listen, consider the reactions of Manuel, his mother, and Fernando to the T-shirt dilemma. How does each one react? How can you tell?

Escena 1 *Resumen*
Fernando va a la casa de Manuel porque necesitan estudiar. Pero a Manuel le gusta más jugar videojuegos.

Escena 2 *Resumen*
Manuel no puede encontrar su cuaderno. Fernando piensa que Manuel es muy desorganizado.

Escena 3

VIDEO
DVD

AUDIO

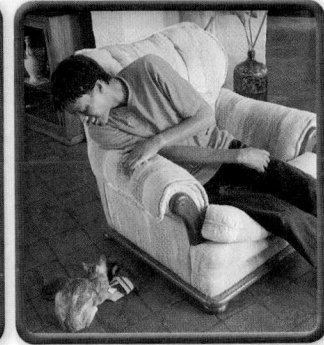

Manuel: ¡Mamá! ¡La camiseta! ¿Dónde está?

Sra. Cuevas: ¿Qué camiseta?

Manuel: La camiseta de Alicia, mi amiga de Miami.

Sra. Cuevas: Ay, hijo. Aquí en el jardín no está. Tiene que estar en la casa.

Manuel: ¡Mamá! ¡Por favor!

Sra. Cuevas: Manuel, estoy ocupada.

Manuel goes back inside, where Fernando is waiting in the living room.

Manuel: ¿Dónde está? Aquí en la mesa no está.

Fernando: No está encima de la mesa. No está en tu cuarto.

Manuel: ¡No, tiene que estar aquí!

Fernando: ¿En el comedor? ¿En la cocina?

Fernando notices something next to his chair.

Fernando: Manuel, aquí hay un gato al lado del sillón.

Manuel: Sí, es Fígaro, el gato de Elena. ¿Y qué?

Fernando: El gato está encima de ¡una camiseta!

17 | Comprensión de los episodios   ¿En qué orden?

Pon las oraciones en orden para describir los episodios. *(Put the sentences in order according to the episodes.)*

a. La camiseta está debajo del gato.

b. Manuel y Elena están en la sala.

c. Fernando llega a la casa de Manuel.

d. Manuel no encuentra su cuaderno.

e. La camiseta de Alicia no está en el jardín.

f. Fernando y Manuel van a estudiar en el cuarto de Manuel.

g. Fernando habla con la señora Cuevas.

h. Manuel habla con la señora Cuevas.

18 | Comprensión de los episodios   Descríbelos

Escuchar
Leer

Contesta las preguntas según las fotos. *(Answer the questions.)*

1.

a. ¿Quiénes son?

b. ¿Cómo son?

c. ¿Dónde están?

d. ¿Cómo están?

2.

a. ¿Quién es?

b. ¿Cómo es?

c. ¿Dónde está?

d. ¿Cómo está?

19 | Una visita a tu casa

Digital
performance space

Hablar

STRATEGY Hablar
Use graphics while you talk For your current or ideal house or apartment, take photos, find photos in magazines or on the Internet, or make detailed drawings with objects' colors shown in each room. Use the graphics while talking with your partner.

Descríbele tu apartamento, tu casa o la casa ideal a otro(a) estudiante. Dile cómo es cada cuarto y qué hay en los cuartos. *(Describe your home or your dream house to a partner.)*

modelo: Vivo en un apartamento. Está en el décimo piso. Hay una sala grande con muchos muebles. En la sala hay un sofá negro...

Expansión
Tell which rooms you like the most and why.

20 | Integración

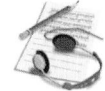

Leer
Escuchar
Hablar

Tú y tu familia van a vivir un año en Quito y necesitan un apartamento. Mira la lista de una agencia de alquiler y escucha el mensaje telefónico de un agente. Describe cuál es el mejor apartamento para ustedes. *(Describe which apartment is best for you and your family.)*

Fuente 1 Lista de apartamentos

Calle Olmedo, 38 Apartamento en el centro de Quito. Cuesta 1.300 dólares al mes. Está en el tercer piso. Tiene tres cuartos con muchos armarios y dos baños. La sala es un poco pequeña pero la cocina es muy grande. Hay un patio pequeño. Está cerca de tiendas y restaurantes.

Calle de los Olivos, 45 Apartamento lejos del centro. Cuesta 1.050 dólares al mes. Está en el primer piso. Tiene cinco cuartos y tres baños. La cocina es grande y la sala es bonita. El apartamento tiene muchas ventanas y armarios grandes. No tiene patio, pero hay un parque cerca.

Calle Simón Bolívar, 76 Apartamento cerca del centro. Cuesta 1.125 dólares al mes. Está en el décimo piso y puedes ver todo el centro. Tiene dos cuartos y un baño. La sala es grande y la cocina también. También hay un patio bonito. Está cerca de los cines y los teatros.

Fuente 2 Mensaje telefónico

Listen and take notes
- ¿Cómo es el apartamento y dónde está?
- ¿Cuánto cuesta?

modelo: Quiero vivir en el apartamento de la calle... porque...

21 | Una casa increíble

Escribir

Escribe un anuncio para vender una casa. Di dónde está, cómo es, y qué cuartos y muebles tiene. *(Write a detailed ad that you would use to sell a house.)*

modelo:

> **¡Casa bonita!** Está cerca del centro. Es grande y tiene cinco cuartos y cuatro baños. La escalera es muy bonita. Ya tiene muebles. En la sala hay un sofá y dos sillones.

Writing Criteria	Excellent	Good	Needs Work
Content	Your ad includes a lot of information.	Your ad includes some information.	Your ad includes little information.
Communication	Most of your ad is organized and easy to follow.	Parts of your ad are organized and easy to follow.	Your ad is disorganized and hard to follow.
Accuracy	Your ad has few mistakes in grammar and vocabulary.	Your ad has some mistakes in grammar and vocabulary.	Your ad has many mistakes in grammar and vocabulary.

Expansión
Post your description to your class website as if you were a real state agent trying to sell it.

Más práctica   Cuaderno *pp. 206–207*   Cuaderno para hispanohablantes *pp. 208–209*

Get Help Online
my.hrw.com

PARA Y PIENSA

Did you get it?   Use **ser, estar,** and an ordinal number to complete the sentences.
1. Fígaro _____ el gato de Elena. No _____ tranquilo.
2. Fígaro vive en el _____ piso. (7)

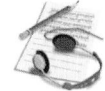

Lección 1
doscientos sesenta y tres   **263**

Lectura

¡AVANZA! **Goal:** Read advertisements for houses and apartments for sale in Ecuador. Then compare the two places and talk about where you prefer to live.

AUDIO

STRATEGY Leer

Use a checklist and explain Make a checklist showing which place—apartment or house—is more useful for a single person, a small family, and a large family. List reasons.

	el apartamento	la casa	¿Por qué?
una persona			
una familia pequeña			
una familia grande			

Vivir en Ecuador

The following are an apartment brochure from Quito and a real-estate ad from Guayaquil.

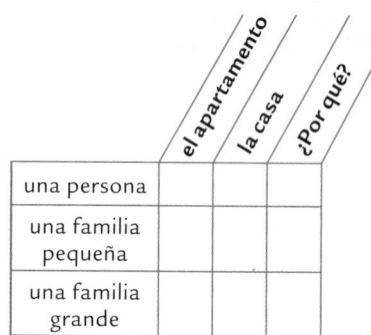

COMEDOR

CUARTO

COCINA

SALA

LAS CAMELIAS
COMUNIDAD RESIDENCIAL

EL QUITEÑO MODERNO

- Construcción antisísmica [1]
- Jardines comunales
- Sauna
- Gimnasio
- Portero [2] de 24 horas
- Áreas verdes y recreativas
- Cerca de tiendas, supermercados y restaurantes

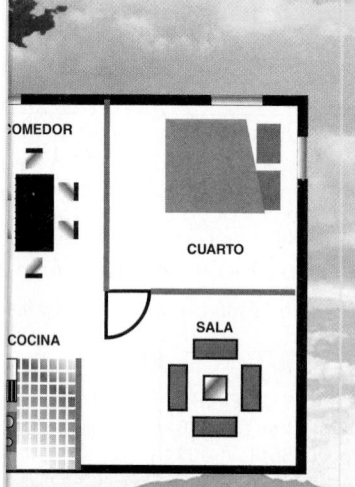

¿Quieres estar cerca de todo? El Quiteño Moderno está en un lugar muy conveniente.

Desde [3] el noveno piso puedes ver todo el centro.

Apartamento de 95 metros cuadrados [4] $65.000

RESIDENCIAS PICHINCHA
AV. EL INCA, 32
TELÉFONO 244-5502

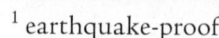

[1] earthquake-proof   [2] Doorman   [3] From   [4] square

Cerro Santa Ana
Comunidad privada de 18 residencias

Aquí puedes ir de compras o al cine y en unos minutos volver a tu casa cerca del río[5] Guayas. Cerro Santa Ana es para las personas a quienes les gusta el aire puro tanto como un lugar urbano.

$130.000

Casa ultramoderna de dos pisos con acceso fácil a Guayaquil

- 4 cuartos
- sala-comedor
- cocina

- oficina de lavar[6]
- 2 garajes

La casa está en un lugar tranquilo pero no está muy lejos de Guayaquil. Puedes preparar la comida en el patio y hay zonas para practicar deportes.

Cerro Santa Ana | Escalón 68 | Teléfono 231-6687

---

[5] river   [6] washing machines

PARA Y PIENSA

¿Comprendiste?
1. ¿Cómo es el apartamento y dónde está? ¿Y la casa?
2. ¿Qué puedes hacer en los dos lugares?
3. ¿Cuál es mejor para una familia, el apartamento o la casa? ¿Por qué?

¿Y tú?
Explícale a otro(a) estudiante dónde prefieres vivir y por qué.

Conexiones   *Las matemáticas*

Las ruinas de Ingapirca

At one time, the Incan empire stretched from modern-day Colombia to Chile. At Ingapirca, an important settlement in Ecuador, the Incas built a majestic temple called El Templo del Sol (Temple of the Sun). Carved into a steep rocky cliff, the temple served as a fortress and place of worship.

Many Incan buildings have withstood centuries of earthquakes. The Incas used large stone blocks of different shapes for building. Often the blocks, as well as the doors and windows, were wider at the base and narrower at the top.

Look at the images below. Write two paragraphs comparing the shapes you see in the buildings to other shapes such as circles, squares, and triangles. Give the names and a description of the shapes you discuss. Make an illustration for each shape.

El Templo del Sol

Las ruinas de Sacsayhuaman, Perú

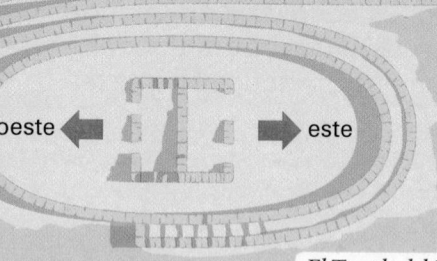

oeste ← → este

El Templo del Sol

Proyecto 1 *Las ciencias sociales*

The external walls of the buildings at Ingapirca were made of chiseled blocks that fit together so precisely that no mortar was needed to hold them. Research and report on how the Incas may have cut, transported, and fit these huge blocks without the use of iron tools or wheels.

Proyecto 2 *La historia*

Research the Incan empire and create a map showing its size. Then write a paragraph about its population, duration, and political structure.

Proyecto 3 *El lenguaje*

There are many different indigenous groups and languages in Ecuador. The most common indigenous language, Quechua, was also spoken by the Incas. Spanish and English have borrowed many words from Quechua. Use the Internet or a library to find four or five Quechua words that are used in Spanish. Write the words in Spanish, then explain what they mean in English.

Vocabulario

Describe a House			
el apartamento	apartment	el jardín	garden
el armario	closet; armoire	(pl. los jardines)	
bajar	to descend	el patio	patio
la casa	house	el piso	floor (of a building)
la cocina	kitchen	la planta baja	ground floor
el comedor	dining room	la sala	living room
el cuarto	room; bedroom	subir	to go up
la escalera	stairs	el suelo	floor (of a room)
ideal	ideal		

Describe Household Items	
la cosa	thing
el disco compacto	compact disc
el lector DVD	DVD player
el radio	radio
el televisor	television set
el tocadiscos compactos	CD player
los videojuegos	video games

Furniture			
la alfombra	rug	la lámpara	lamp
la cama	bed	los muebles	furniture
la cómoda	dresser	el sillón	armchair
las cortinas	curtains	(pl. los sillones)	
el espejo	mirror	el sofá	sofa, couch

Ordinal Numbers	
primero(a)	first
segundo(a)	second
tercero(a)	third
cuarto(a)	fourth
quinto(a)	fifth
sexto(a)	sixth
séptimo(a)	seventh
octavo(a)	eighth
noveno(a)	ninth
décimo(a)	tenth

Gramática

Ser or estar

Ser and **estar** both mean *to be*.

- Use **ser** to indicate origin.
- Use **ser** to describe personal traits and physical characteristics.
- **Ser** is also used to indicate professions.
- You also use **ser** to express possession and to give the time and the date.

- Use **estar** to indicate location.
- **Estar** is also used to describe conditions, both physical and emotional.

Ordinal Numbers

When used with a noun, an **ordinal number** must agree in number and gender with that noun.

- **Ordinals** are placed before nouns.
- **Primero** and **tercero** drop the **o** before a masculine singular noun.

Repaso de la lección

@HOMETUTOR
my.hrw.com

¡LLEGADA!

Now you can
• describe a house and household items
• indicate the order of things
• describe people and locations

Using
• **ser** or **estar**
• ordinal numbers

To review
• **ser** or **estar** p. 253

1 | Listen and understand

AUDIO

Escucha a Rebeca describir su casa. Indica si las oraciones son ciertas o falsas.
(Listen to Rebeca describe her house and tell whether the statements are true or false.)

1. La casa es muy bonita.

2. Hay un sillón en la sala.

3. En el comedor hay diez sillas.

4. El baño está detrás del comedor.

5. En el segundo piso hay tres cuartos y dos baños.

6. El cuarto de Rebeca es azul.

To review
• ordinal numbers p. 258

2 | Indicate the order of things

El señor Cabrera tiene que ayudar a los residentes de su edificio de apartamentos a mover unos muebles. Indica en qué piso están estas cosas.
(Tell on what floor of the apartment building these items are.)

modelo: PB
Las alfombras están en la planta baja.

1. 4°

2. 5°

3. 6°

4. 3°

5. 7°

6. 1°

7. 2°

8. 8°

To review
• **ser** or **estar**
  p. 253

3 | Describe a house and household items

Joaquín describe su casa en un correo electrónico. Completa su mensaje con la forma correcta de **ser** o **estar**. *(Complete the email message with the correct form of **ser** or **estar**.)*

Hola, amigo. Aquí __1.__ yo en mi casa. Nuestra casa __2.__ al lado del parque. La casa __3.__ blanca y muy bonita. Ahora mi hermano y yo __4.__ en nuestro cuarto. Muchos discos compactos __5.__ en el suelo porque nosotros no __6.__ muy organizados. ¿Y tú? ¿Tú __7.__ organizado o desorganizado? El cuarto de nuestros padres __8.__ al lado de nuestro cuarto. Su cuarto __9.__ más grande que nuestro cuarto. ¿Cómo __10.__ tu casa?

To review
• **ser** or **estar**
  p. 253

4 | Describe people and locations

Describe a estas personas y explica dónde y cómo están. *(Describe these people, their locations, and how they feel.)*

modelo: Ernesto (artístico / en el parque / tranquilo)
Ernesto es artístico. Está en el parque. Está tranquilo.

1. las maestras (simpáticas / en la escuela / contentas)
2. tú (estudioso / en la biblioteca / nervioso)
3. la señora Moreno (seria / deprimida / en el pasillo)
4. nosotros (cómicos / en el teatro / emocionados)
5. mi hermano menor (malo / en su cuarto / enojado)
6. yo (inteligente / en clase / ocupado)

To review
• Comparación
  cultural pp. 246,
  255, 260

5 | Ecuador and Argentina

Comparación cultural

Answer these culture questions.

1. What are some characteristics of traditional Spanish architecture?
2. What are some features found in Tigua paintings?
3. What does Ecuador's **Mitad del Mundo** monument mark?
4. Why is Ushuaia, Argentina, known as **la ciudad del fin del mundo**?

Más práctica   Cuaderno *pp. 208–219*   Cuaderno para hispanohablantes *pp. 210–219*

Get Help Online
my.hrw.com

Ecuador

Lección

2

Tema:

Una fiesta en casa

⚜️ ⚜️

¡AVANZA! **In this lesson you will learn to**

- plan a party
- talk about chores and responsibilities
- tell someone what to do
- say what you just did

using

- more irregular verbs
- affirmative **tú** commands
- **acabar de** + infinitive

♻️ *¿Recuerdas?*

- **tener que,** interrogative words
- expressions of frequency
- direct object pronouns

Comparación cultural

In this lesson you will learn about

- a festival honoring Quito, and textiles in Otavalo
- folk dances and traditional crafts, like **tapices** and **molas**
- throwing parties in Ecuador, Argentina, and Panama

Compara con tu mundo

This photo shows a teenager's birthday party in Quito, Ecuador. In Latin America it is common to celebrate with family and perhaps a few close friends. *Where and with whom do you like to celebrate your birthday?*

¿Qué ves?

Mira la foto

¿Están en un parque las personas?

¿Elena sirve pastel o una pizza?

¿Qué muebles hay?

MODES OF COMMUNICATION

INTERPRETIVE	INTERPERSONAL	PRESENTATIONAL
Read about celebrations across the Spanish-speaking world to identify cultural customs. Listen to a message to get directions for what you need to do.	Plan a party with others. Write a note to someone saying what preparations you've done and what that person needs to do.	Write a paragraph describing your favorite celebration and comparing it to others in Spanish-speaking countries. Describe plans for a surprise party to the class.

Una fiesta de cumpleaños
Quito, Ecuador

❖ Presentación de VOCABULARIO

VIDEO
DVD

AUDIO

A ¡Hola! Soy Elena. Vamos a **dar una fiesta** porque es el cumpleaños de Manuel, pero es **un secreto.** Antes de **celebrar, hay que limpiar** la cocina porque está **sucia.**

cortar el césped

limpiar la cocina

barrer el suelo

lavar los platos

sacar la basura

darle de comer al perro

B **Acabamos de** limpiar la cocina pero **todavía** tenemos que trabajar. Toda la casa **debe** estar **limpia.**

hacer la cama

planchar la ropa

Más vocabulario

abrir *to open*	**salir** *to leave, to go out*
buscar *to look for*	**si** *if*
invitar a *to invite (someone)*	**traer** *to bring*
recibir *to receive*	

Expansión de vocabulario p. R6

pasar la aspiradora

C Mi papá quiere **ayudar** con **los quehaceres** pero no **cocina** muy bien. Prefiere **poner la mesa.**

cocinar

poner la mesa

D Son las cuatro y **los invitados** van a **venir** a las cinco. Papá **pone las decoraciones** y Fernando **envuelve un regalo** para Manuel.

decorar

las decoraciones

el globo

envolver

el regalo

el papel de regalo

E Cuando Manuel llega, todos **dicen** «¡Sorpresa!» Yo **canto** «Feliz cumpleaños» y mis padres **bailan.**

la fiesta de sorpresa

los invitados

cantar

bailar

@HOMETUTOR
my.hrw.com

Interactive
Flashcards

¡A responder! Escuchar

Escucha la lista de actividades. Mientras escuchas, representa las actividades. *(Listen to the list of activities. Act out the activities as you hear them.)*

Práctica de VOCABULARIO

1 La fiesta de cumpleaños

Leer

Lee las pistas que describen una fiesta de cumpleaños. Identifica las palabras de la lista. *(Read the clues to identify the words.)*

papel de regalo	invitados	globos
regalo	decoraciones	secreto

1. Las usas para decorar la casa.

2. Son las personas en la fiesta.

3. Lo abres si celebras tu cumpleaños.

4. Son decoraciones de colores.

5. Hay una fiesta de sorpresa y no debes decirlo.

6. Lo usas para envolver un regalo.

2 ¿Qué hay que hacer?

Escribir Hablar

Mira las fotos e identifica qué hay que hacer para limpiar la casa. *(Identify what must be done.)*

modelo: Hay que limpiar la cocina.

1.

2.

3.

4.

5.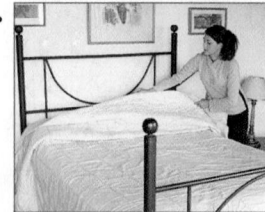

6.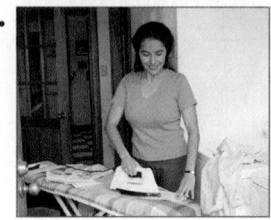

> **Expansión**
> Write about the two chores you like to do most and least.

Más práctica   Cuaderno *pp. 220–222*   Cuaderno para hispanohablantes *pp. 220–223*

Get Help Online
my.hrw.com

PARA Y PIENSA

Did you get it?   Name four things you do before having a party at your house.

VOCABULARIO en contexto

¡AVANZA! **Goal:** Identify the words Fernando and the Cuevas family use to talk about the preparations they have to do before Manuel's party. Then use what you have learned to talk about your chores and responsibilities. *Actividades 3–4*

 *¿Recuerdas?* **tener que** p. 91

Telehistoria escena 1

VIDEO
DVD

AUDIO

@HOMETUTOR View, Read
my.hrw.com and Record

STRATEGIES

Cuando lees
Consider cultural customs How do Manuel's family and friends prepare for his birthday party? How are teenagers' birthdays usually celebrated in the United States? What are some differences and similarities?

Cuando escuchas
Listen for cognates This scene has several cognates, including **sorpresa.** Listen for them. Which ones do you recognize? How do they help you with understanding?

The Cuevas family is preparing for a party. Fernando arrives with a gift.

Fernando: ¿Y los regalos? ¿Dónde...?

Sra. Cuevas: En la mesa.

Elena: Fernando, ¿qué regalo traes para Manuel?

Fernando: Un videojuego. Lo acabo de envolver.

Sr. Cuevas: Un videojuego. ¡Qué sorpresa!

Fernando: ¿Puedo ayudar?

Elena: Sí, puedes abrir la puerta a los invitados.

Fernando: Ay, prefiero preparar la comida. ¡Me gusta cocinar!

Sr. Cuevas: Bueno. Puedes ayudar en la cocina.

Guests begin to arrive, and everyone starts to wonder when Manuel is coming.

Sra. Cuevas: ¿Qué hora es? *(to Elena)* ¿Dónde está tu hermano?

Fernando: Acabo de hablar por teléfono con Manuel. Va a venir.

Continuará... p. 280

3 | *Comprensión del episodio* **Preparan una celebración**

Escuchar
Leer

Escoge la respuesta correcta. *(Choose the correct answer.)*

1. Los regalos están
   a. en la cocina.
   b. en el comedor.
   c. en la mesa.

2. Fernando acaba de
   a. envolver el regalo.
   b. ayudar en la cocina.
   c. abrir la puerta a los invitados.

3. Fernando trae
   a. un DVD para Manuel.
   b. un disco compacto para Manuel.
   c. un videojuego para Manuel.

4. Fernando prefiere
   a. abrir la puerta a los invitados.
   b. jugar videojuegos.
   c. preparar la comida.

4 | **Las obligaciones en casa** *¿Recuerdas?* **tener que** p. 91

Hablar

Pregúntale a otro(a) estudiante si tiene que hacer estos quehaceres en casa. Si no, ¿quién los tiene que hacer? *(Ask a classmate if he or she has to do these chores. If not, who has to do them?)*

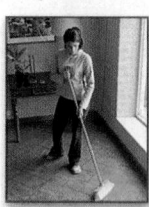

A ¿Tienes que barrer el suelo?

B Sí, tengo que barrer el suelo. (No, no tengo que barrer el suelo. Mi padre tiene que hacerlo.)

1.

2.

3.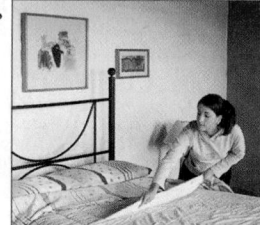

4.

5.

6.

Expansión
Compare your chores with a partner's. Which do you have in common?

 **Get Help Online**
my.hrw.com

PARA Y PIENSA

Did you get it? Complete each sentence with the appropriate vocabulary word.
  1. Manuel saca _____ antes de ir a la escuela.
  2. El señor Cuevas corta _____ los sábados.
  3. Fernando necesita pasar _____ porque sus abuelos van a venir.

Presentación de GRAMÁTICA

¡AVANZA! **Goal:** Learn the forms of six more irregular verbs. Then practice using these verbs to talk about parties. *Actividades 5–8*

♻ *¿Recuerdas?* Interrogative words p. 140

English Grammar Connection: Just as the English verb *to be* does not follow a pattern in the present tense (*I am, you are, he/she/it is,* etc.), **irregular verbs** in Spanish do not follow the pattern of regular or stem-changing verbs.

More Irregular Verbs

ANiMaTeDGRaMMaR
my.hrw.com

Dar, decir, poner, salir, traer, and **venir** are all irregular. How do you form the present tense of these verbs?

Here's how:

Decir has several irregular forms. Only the **nosotros(as)** and **vosotros(as)** forms are regular.

> **Dicen** que es una fiesta de sorpresa.
> *They say that it is a surprise party.*

decir	*to say, to tell*
d**i**go	decimos
d**i**ces	decís
d**i**ce	d**i**cen

Venir is similar to **tener,** except that the **nosotros(as)** and **vosotros(as)** forms have **-ir** endings, while **tener** uses **-er** endings.

> ¿De dónde **vienes**?
> *Where **are you coming** from?*

venir	*to come*
ven**g**o	venimos
v**i**enes	venís
v**i**ene	v**i**enen

Some verbs are irregular only in the **yo** form of the present tense.

> **Do**y una fiesta.
> *I am giving a party.*

dar	*to give*	**do**y
poner	*to put, to place*	**pon**go
salir	*to leave, to go out*	**sal**go
traer	*to bring*	**tra**igo

Más práctica
Cuaderno *pp. 223–225*
Cuaderno para hispanohablantes *pp. 224–226*

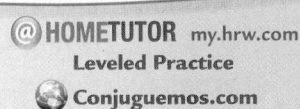
@ HOMETUTOR my.hrw.com
Leveled Practice
🌐 Conjuguemos.com

✤Práctica de GRAMÁTICA

5 | ¿Lo haces?

**Hablar
Escribir**

Di si haces estas cosas en una fiesta de sorpresa. *(Tell whether you do the following at a surprise party.)*

> **modelo:** salir con amigos antes de la fiesta
> (No) Salgo con amigos antes de la fiesta.

1. poner la mesa con platos bonitos
2. dar diez regalos
3. salir de la fiesta muy temprano
4. venir a la fiesta con amigos
5. traer libros de historia
6. decir «¡Feliz cumpleaños!»

> **Expansión**
> Describe in 3–4 sentences a typical birthday celebration in your family.

6 | ¡Vamos a celebrar!

**Leer
Escribir**

Comparación cultural

Preparan los carritos de madera (wooden cars) para las fiestas.

Fiestas de Quito

How do people show pride for their community? On December 6, *quiteños* celebrate Fiestas de Quito, a festival honoring the anniversary of the founding of Quito, **Ecuador,** in 1534. The week-long celebration includes many parades, concerts, and dances. Some residents perform *serenatas quiteñas,* musical tributes to their city. Other popular activities are fireworks displays and the Reina de Quito beauty pageant. Many young people build and decorate wooden cars to race in competitions for their age level.

Compara con tu mundo *Is there an event that celebrates your area or region?*

Manuel y Fernando hablan por teléfono. Completa su conversación con la forma correcta del verbo apropiado. *(Complete the conversation with the correct form of the appropriate verb.)*

dar	traer
decir	poner
salir	venir

Manuel: ¿Cuándo __1.__ a mi casa? Tenemos que decorar los carritos para las Fiestas de Quito.

Fernando: __2.__ de aquí en quince minutos y llego en media hora.

Manuel: Elena __3.__ que la carrera (*race*) empieza a las dos.

Fernando: Hay un desfile (*parade*) después. ¿Vas a traer tu guitarra?

Manuel: Sí, yo la __4.__ . Quiero tocar una serenata quiteña.

Fernando: ¡Y yo voy a cantar! ¿Qué hacemos después del desfile?

Manuel: Elena y yo __5.__ una fiesta en casa. Ahora ella prepara la ensalada y yo __6.__ la mesa.

Fernando: Bueno, llego en media hora. ¡Hasta luego!

7 | Una fiesta en la clase

Hablar

Hay una fiesta en la clase de español. Pregúntale a otro(a) estudiante si trae estas cosas a la fiesta y por qué. *(Ask a partner whether he or she is bringing these things to the class party, and why or why not.)*

A ¿Traes DVDs a la fiesta?

B Sí, traigo DVDs porque quiero ver películas. (No, no traigo DVDs porque no quiero ver películas.)

1.

2.

3.

4.

5.

6.

8 | Hay que preparar ♲ *¿Recuerdas?* Interrogative words p. 140

Hablar

Tu amigo(a) ayuda a organizar una fiesta de cumpleaños. Pregúntale a otro(a) estudiante sobre los preparativos. *(Ask a partner about a party he or she is helping organize.)*

modelo: ¿cuándo? / dar la fiesta

A ¿Cuándo das la fiesta?

B Doy la fiesta el sábado.

1. ¿cuántos(as)? / venir a la fiesta
2. ¿qué? / traer a la fiesta
3. ¿dónde? / poner las decoraciones
4. ¿qué? / servir para comer y beber
5. ¿por qué? / dar la fiesta

6. ¿qué? / cantar los invitados
7. ¿qué? / decir los invitados
8. ¿cuándo? / salir los invitados

Expansión
Write down the description of the party and present it to the class.

Más práctica Cuaderno *pp. 223–225* Cuaderno para hispanohablantes *pp. 224–226*

🌐 **Get Help Online**
my.hrw.com

PARA Y PIENSA

Did you get it? Complete each sentence with the correct form of one of the irregular verbs you just learned.

1. Yo _____ la mesa porque los invitados van a llegar.
2. Isabel _____ que el pastel es muy rico.
3. Yo _____ los regalos a la fiesta.

✤ GRAMÁTICA en contexto

¡AVANZA! **Goal:** Pay attention to the irregular verbs that Manuel, his family, and his friends use to talk about what to do at his party. Then use them to talk about what you and others do at parties. *Actividades 9–11*

♻ *¿Recuerdas?* Expressions of frequency p. 93

Telehistoria escena 2

@**HOMETUTOR** View, Read
my.hrw.com and Record

STRATEGIES

Cuando lees
Predict based on visuals Predict what might happen, based on the photos. Does Manuel get the T-shirt signed? Was Manuel surprised, or did he know about the party?

Cuando escuchas
Consider two kinds of language Notice feelings based on both spoken language and body language, such as facial expressions, posture, and gestures. How does Manuel feel about Fernando's present? How do you know?

VIDEO
DVD

AUDIO

Manuel

Manuel arrives home with Alicia's T-shirt, admiring the autograph.

Manuel: ¡El autógrafo de Trini Salgado!

Elena: *(in the backyard)* ¡Allí viene Manuel!

Manuel enters the yard.

Todos: ¡Sorpresa!

Sra. Cuevas: ¡Feliz cumpleaños, hijo!

Elena: ¡Aquí viene el pastel!

Manuel blows out the candles while people clap.

Manuel: Y, ¿qué hago ahora?

Fernando: ¡Abrir los regalos! Yo los traigo.

Manuel: *(opening a gift)* ¡Qué sorpresa! ¡Un videojuego! No lo tengo. Muchas gracias, Fernando.

Fernando: Hmmm... Y, ¿qué hacemos ahora?

Sr. Cuevas: ¡A bailar todos! **Continuará...** p. 285

También se dice

Ecuador When serving the cake, Elena uses the word **el pastel.** In other Spanish-speaking countries you might hear:
• **España** la tarta
• **Puerto Rico** el bizcocho
• **muchos países** el queque, la torta

9 | Comprensión del episodio   Muchas sorpresas

Escuchar
Leer

Contesta las preguntas. *(Answer the questions.)*

1. ¿Quiénes dan la fiesta?
2. ¿Quién viene?
3. ¿Quién trae los regalos?
4. ¿Quiénes dicen «¡Sorpresa!»?
5. ¿Qué recibe Manuel de Fernando?
6. ¿Qué quiere hacer el señor Cuevas?

10 | ¿Con qué frecuencia?   ♻ **¿Recuerdas?** Expressions of frequency p. 93

Hablar

Habla con otros(as) estudiantes sobre la frecuencia con que haces las siguientes actividades. *(Tell how often you do these activities.)*

A ¿Con qué frecuencia sales con amigos?

B Salgo con amigos de vez en cuando.

C Nunca salgo con amigos.

1.
2.
3.
4.
5.
6.

Expansión
Write a summary of your group's responses and present it.

11 | ¿Y tú?

Escribir

Contesta las preguntas. *(Answer the questions.)*

1. ¿Das muchas fiestas? ¿A quién(es) invitas?
2. ¿Quién pone la mesa en tu casa?
3. ¿Qué traes a tus clases?
4. ¿A qué hora sales de la casa en la mañana?
5. ¿A qué hora vienes a la escuela?
6. ¿Qué dices cuando recibes un regalo?

🌐 **Get Help Online**
my.hrw.com

PARA Y PIENSA

Did you get it?   Complete each sentence based on the Telehistoria with the correct form of **venir, traer,** or **decir.**
1. Elena _____ que Manuel _____ a la fiesta.   2. Fernando _____ un regalo.

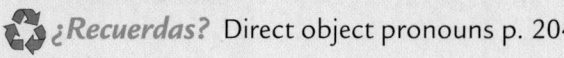 Presentación de GRAMÁTICA

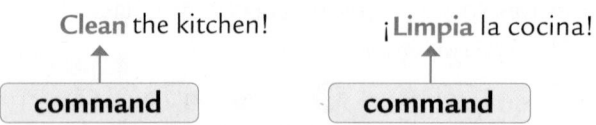

¡AVANZA!

Goal: Learn how to give affirmative **tú** commands and use **acabar de** + infinitive. Then tell someone what to do and say what you just did.
Actividades 12–15

♻ *¿Recuerdas?* Direct object pronouns p. 204

English Grammar Connection: In both English and Spanish, **affirmative commands** are used to tell someone to do something.

Clean the kitchen!	¡Limpia la cocina!
↑	↑
command	**command**

Affirmative tú Commands

ANIMATEDGRAMMAR
my.hrw.com

Use **affirmative tú commands** with a friend or a family member.

Here's how:

Regular **affirmative tú commands** are the same as the **él/ella** forms in the present tense.

Infinitive	Present Tense	Affirmative tú Command
lavar	(él, ella) **lava**	¡Lava los platos!
barrer	(él, ella) **barre**	¡Barre el suelo!
abrir	(él, ella) **abre**	¡Abre la puerta!

Some verbs you know have irregular **affirmative tú commands.**

Infinitive	decir	hacer	ir	poner	salir	ser	tener	venir
Affirmative tú Command	di	haz	ve	pon	sal	sé	ten	ven

If you use an **affirmative command** with a **direct object pronoun,** attach the pronoun to the end. Add an accent when you attach a pronoun to a command of two or more syllables to retain the original stress (see p. 259).

¡**Cierra** la ventana!	*becomes*	¡**Ciérrala**!
Close the window!		**Close** it!
¡**Pon** la mesa ahora!	*becomes*	¡**Ponla** ahora!
Set the table now!		**Set** it now!

Más práctica
Cuaderno *pp. 226–228*
Cuaderno para hispanohablantes *pp. 227–230*

@HOMETUTOR my.hrw.com
Leveled Practice
Conjuguemos.com

Práctica de GRAMÁTICA

12 ¿Quién tiene que hacerlo?

Escribir

Manuel siempre le dice a Elena lo que tiene que hacer. Usa los mandatos para escribir lo que le dice. *(Write Manuel's commands to Elena.)*

modelo: limpiar la cocina
Limpia la cocina, por favor.

1. lavar los platos
2. planchar la ropa
3. venir a casa
4. barrer el suelo
5. salir temprano
6. hacer la cama
7. cortar el césped
8. ser buena
9. sacar la basura
10. traer el pastel
11. ir a la tienda
12. poner la mesa

Expansión
Write five commands you would hear in the classroom.

13 ¿Debo hacerlo?

¿Recuerdas? Direct object pronouns p. 204

Hablar

Tú y otro(a) estudiante preparan una fiesta de cumpleaños. Pregúntale lo que debes hacer. Sigue el modelo. *(Ask a partner what you should do to prepare for a party. Follow the model.)*

modelo: comprar el papel de regalo

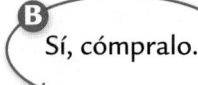

A: ¿Debo comprar el papel de regalo?

B: Sí, cómpralo.

1. traer las bebidas
2. preparar la comida
3. buscar los globos
4. poner las decoraciones
5. limpiar la cocina
6. envolver los regalos
7. abrir la puerta a los invitados
8. servir el pastel
9. pasar la aspiradora
10. sacar la basura

AUDIO

Pronunciación — Las letras b y v

In Spanish, the **b** and **v** are pronounced almost the same. As the first letter of a word, at the beginning of a sentence or after the letters **m** and **n, b** and **v** are pronounced like the hard *b* in the English word *boy.*

In the middle of a word, **b** and **v** have a softer sound, made by keeping the lips slightly apart.

Listen and repeat.

basura	**venir**	**alfombra**	**invitar**
deber	**todavía**	**globo**	**acabar**

Bárbara baila la cumbia en Colombia.
Debes subir al octavo piso.

14 | Una casa sucia

Escuchar La casa de Elena está sucia y su madre necesita ayuda. Escucha las situaciones y escribe un mandato para cada una. *(Write the mother's commands to Elena.)*

Nota gramatical

When you want to say that something has just happened, use the verb phrase **acabar de** + **infinitive.**

Acabamos de **comprar** el pastel para la fiesta.   ***We just bought*** *the cake for the party.*

Acaban de **cortar** el césped.   ***They just cut*** *the grass.*

15 | ¿Ayudas?

Hablar Tú y otro(a) estudiante tienen muchos quehaceres. Usa un mandato para decirle lo que tiene que hacer. Él o ella va a contestar que acaba de hacerlo.
(Tell a partner what chores to do. Your partner will answer that he or she just did them.)

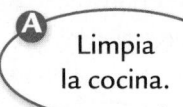

A Limpia la cocina.

B La acabo de limpiar. (Acabo de limpiarla.)

Comparación cultural

Los textiles de Otavalo

Why are traditional crafts important to a culture?
Many tourists visit the town of Otavalo for its Saturday market to find woven sweaters, rugs, and other items. The Otavalos, an indigenous group from **Ecuador,** have practiced weaving for centuries and are famous worldwide for their textiles. Common designs include landscapes, animals, and geometric patterns. The Otavalos take pride in their heritage and have achieved economic success selling their work both locally and internationally.

Textiles en el mercado de Otavalo

Compara con tu mundo *What are some traditional U.S. crafts?*

Más práctica Cuaderno *pp. 226–228*   Cuaderno para hispanohablantes *pp. 227–230*

🌐 **Get Help Online**
my.hrw.com

PARA Y PIENSA

Did you get it? Give the affirmative **tú** command of each verb. Then say you just did it.
1. decorar la sala   **2.** hacer los quehaceres   **3.** cortar el césped

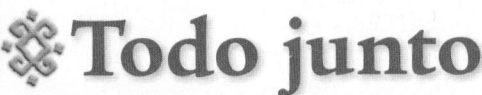

Todo junto

Telehistoria completa

@HOMETUTOR View, Read
my.hrw.com and Record

STRATEGIES

Cuando lees
Find the key event A key event at the end of this scene causes big trouble. What is this event? Why is it important? What hints do you find earlier in the scene?

Cuando escuchas
Listen for commands What are the family members doing? Why wasn't the catastrophe at the end prevented?

Escena 1 *Resumen*
Fernando trae un regalo a la fiesta de sorpresa para Manuel y quiere ayudar a la familia. Manuel todavía no está en casa.

Escena 2 *Resumen*
Manuel llega a la fiesta con el autógrafo de Trini Salgado. Hay pastel, y él abre los regalos de los invitados.

VIDEO DVD

AUDIO

Escena 3

After the party, the family begins to clean up.

Sra. Cuevas: *(to Elena)* Pon los platos sucios allí.

Sr. Cuevas: Elena, barre el suelo, saca la basura y yo lavo la ropa.

Elena: ¿Y Manuel? ¿Por qué no ayuda?

Sra. Cuevas: Acaba de celebrar su cumpleaños. Hoy no tiene que limpiar.

Elena: *(to Manuel)* ¿Vienes a ayudar? Toma. *(She tries to hand him the broom.)*

Manuel: ¡Elena! Ahora, ¡no! Tengo que buscar la camiseta de Alicia. ¿Dónde está? ¿Mamá...?

Manuel and Elena go into the laundry room and find their father.

Elena: La camiseta de Alicia... ¿Dónde está?

Sr. Cuevas: ¡Ahh! ¡Acabo de lavarla!

16 | Comprensión de los episodios   No es cierto

Escuchar
Leer

Todas estas oraciones son falsas. Corrígelas. *(Correct these false statements.)*

1. El padre de Manuel dice que quiere cantar en la fiesta.
2. Fernando abre la puerta a los invitados.
3. La madre de Elena lava la ropa.
4. Manuel tiene que ayudar.
5. Los padres de Manuel tienen la camiseta de Alicia.
6. El padre de Manuel acaba de planchar la camiseta.

> **Expansión**
> Once correct, put these sentences in the order in which they occur.

17 | Comprensión de los episodios   ¡A buscar!

Escuchar
Leer

Busca la información en los episodios y escríbela en una hoja de papel.
(Look for the following in the episodes and write down the information on a piece of paper.)

> **modelo:** un quehacer que Fernando hace
>   Fernando ayuda en la cocina.

1. un regalo que Manuel recibe
2. un quehacer que Fernando no quiere hacer
3. dos cosas que hacen con la camiseta
4. dos actividades que hacen en la fiesta
5. dos quehaceres que Elena tiene que hacer
6. un quehacer que el señor Cuevas hace

18 | ¡Qué organizados!

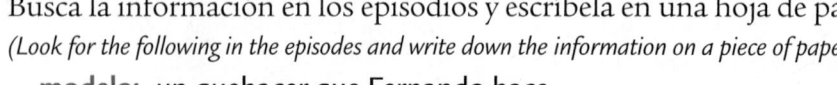

Hablar

> **STRATEGY Hablar**
> **Combine imagination with organization** Think creatively while organizing. To do this, consider questions like these: Is the party for a special occasion? Will it be inside or outside? When will it be? How many guests will there be? Is there a theme for party activities, decorations, and food?

Trabaja con un grupo para planear una fiesta. Habla sobre la comida, las decoraciones y los quehaceres. Todos son muy organizados. Dile a otro(a) estudiante lo que tiene que hacer. Él o ella va a decir que lo acaba de hacer.
(You are planning a party with a group. Tell another student to do something. He or she will say that he or she just did it.)

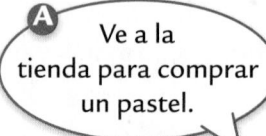

A Ve a la tienda para comprar un pastel.

B Acabo de ir a la tienda. Ya tengo el pastel. Pon la mesa.

C Acabo de poner la mesa. Barre el suelo.

19 | Integración

Leer
Escuchar
Hablar

Digital performance space

Tú y tu amigo(a) son participantes en un programa de televisión, ¡**Limpia ya!** Escucha el mensaje para aprender cuál es tu misión y mira los planos de la casa. Luego, explica lo que tú haces y dile a tu amigo(a) qué hacer. *(Explain which rooms you are cleaning and what chores you are doing and tell your friend what to do.)*

Fuente 1 Los planos de la casa

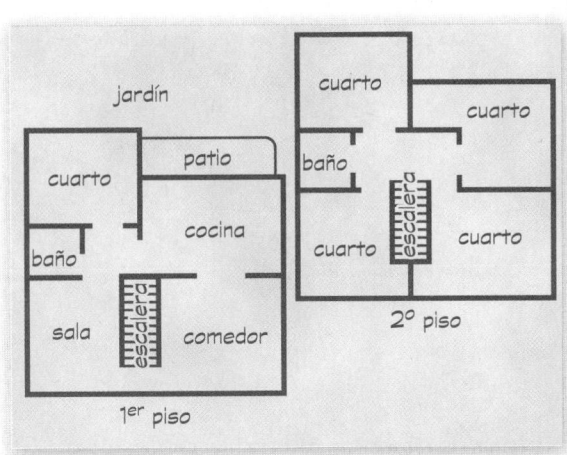

Fuente 2 Instrucciones para la misión

Listen and take notes
- ¿Qué quehaceres tienen que hacer?
- ¿Donde tienen que hacerlos?

modelo: Yo subo al segundo piso y... Roberto, sal al jardín y...

20 | Una casa bonita y limpia

Digital performance space

Escribir

Para darle una sorpresa a tu familia, quieres limpiar toda la casa. Necesitas la ayuda de tu hermano(a), pero no está en casa. Escríbele una nota para decirle qué acabas de hacer y qué debe hacer él o ella. *(Write a note to your sibling, telling him or her what to do and what you just did.)*

modelo: ¡Queremos una casa limpia! En el baño, acabo de sacar la basura. Barre el suelo, por favor. En la sala...

Writing Criteria	Excellent	Good	Needs Work
Content	Your note includes a lot of information.	Your note includes some information.	Your note includes little information.
Communication	Most of your note is organized and easy to follow.	Parts of your note are organized and easy to follow.	Your note is disorganized and hard to follow.
Accuracy	Your note has few mistakes in grammar and vocabulary.	Your note has some mistakes in grammar and vocabulary.	Your note has many mistakes in grammar and vocabulary.

Más práctica Cuaderno *pp. 229–230* Cuaderno para hispanohablantes *pp. 231–232*

Get Help Online
my.hrw.com

PARA Y PIENSA

Did you get it? Give Elena three more commands for chores to do around the house.

Lectura cultural

Additional readings at my.hrw.com
SPANISH
InterActive Reader

¡AVANZA!   **Goal:** Read about two traditional dances of Ecuador and Panama. Then compare the two dances and talk about when you go dancing.

Comparación cultural

AUDIO

Bailes folklóricos de Ecuador y Panamá

STRATEGY Leer

Draw key aspects Draw pictures of the **sanjuanito** and the **tamborito.** Label key aspects of your drawings. Then add more details by writing captions describing each dance.

Los bailes folklóricos de Latinoamérica representan una combinación de culturas. Ayudan a formar una identidad nacional y continuar las tradiciones de las personas que viven allí. A muchas personas de Ecuador y Panamá les gusta bailar cuando celebran fiestas.

Hay muchos bailes de influencia indígena[1] en Ecuador. Uno de los bailes más populares se llama el sanjuanito. El sanjuanito tiene un ritmo alegre[2] y es una buena representación de la fusión de culturas indígenas y españolas.

Para bailar, chicos y chicas forman un círculo y muchas veces bailan con pañuelos[3] en las manos[4]. Es posible ver el baile del sanjuanito todo el año en celebraciones en casa, pero es más común durante el festival de San Juan en junio.

---

[1] indigenous   [2] **ritmo...** upbeat rhythm
[3] scarves   [4] hands

Ecuador

Un baile tradicional en Mitad del Mundo, Ecuador

Un baile folklórico, Ciudad de Panamá

En Panamá, es muy popular bailar salsa en fiestas o discotecas[5], pero el baile nacional es el tamborito. El tamborito usa ritmos de influencia africana, pero también tiene orígenes indígenas y españoles.

Las personas bailan con el sonido[6] de palmadas[7] y tambores[8] africanos. El tamborito es popular durante fiestas grandes y celebraciones regionales, como Carnaval. Para bailar en los festivales, las chicas llevan polleras (los vestidos tradicionales de Panamá) y los chicos llevan el dominguero (pantalones negros con una camisa blanca).

---

[5] nightclubs   [6] sound   [7] handclaps   [8] drums

PARA Y PIENSA

¿Comprendiste?

1. ¿Qué influencias culturales forman el baile del sanjuanito? ¿Y el tamborito?
2. ¿Qué artículos de ropa usan para bailar en Ecuador? ¿Y en Panamá?
3. ¿En qué tipo de fiestas bailan el sanjuanito y el tamborito?

¿Y tú?

¿Te gusta bailar en fiestas? ¿Sales para bailar o bailas en casa? ¿Qué ropa llevas cuando bailas? Si no bailas, ¿quieres aprender?

❈ Proyectos culturales

Arte textil de Ecuador y Panamá

How do different cultures express themselves through crafts?
Indigenous Otavalans are famous for the beautiful woolen textiles sold in a weekly market in Otavalo, **Ecuador.** In the San Blas Islands of **Panama,** women from the Kuna culture design and produce **molas,** which are pieces of fabric art that are traditionally sewn onto women's blouses. The crafts from both the Otavalan and the Kuna cultures are colorful, unique creations that have become representative of the people that make them.

Proyecto ① Tapestry design

Ecuador Otavalan tapestries often use a design of geometric shapes and can depict people, objects of everyday life, and scenes of nature. Create a tapestry design in the Otavalan style.

Materials for making a tapestry design
Construction paper
Colored pens and pencils

Instructions
Think about the variety of objects the Otavalans weave. Then draw your own design using construction paper and colored pens or pencils.

Proyecto ② Las molas

Panamá The Kuna women make **molas** out of several layers of colorful fabric. Make a **mola** out of paper.

Materials for making a mola
Construction paper (3 colors)
Piece of plain paper
Scissors
Glue

Instructions
1. Cut out a shape on plain paper to use as the pattern for your **mola.**
2. Trace the pattern onto a sheet of construction paper. Cut out the shape and set aside the sheet of paper.
3. Use scissors to trim your original pattern to make it smaller. Repeat step two on a second piece of construction paper.
4. Layer the two pieces of construction paper into a third one so that all the colors are visible.

En tu comunidad

Where can local artists in your community sell their work? What advantages would an artist have who is able to communicate with potential customers in Spanish?

En resumen
Vocabulario y gramática

Vocabulario

Plan a Party

bailar	to dance	el globo	balloon
cantar	to sing	los invitados	guests
celebrar	to celebrate	invitar a	to invite (someone)
dar una fiesta	to give a party		
las decoraciones	decorations	salir	to leave, to go out
decorar	to decorate		
la fiesta de sorpresa	surprise party	el secreto	secret
		venir	to come

Talk About Gifts

abrir	to open
buscar	to look for
envolver (ue)	to wrap
el papel de regalo	wrapping paper
recibir	to receive
el regalo	gift
traer	to bring

Talk About Chores and Responsibilities

acabar de...	to have just . . .	limpiar (la cocina)	to clean the kitchen
ayudar	to help	limpio(a)	clean
barrer el suelo	to sweep the floor	pasar la aspiradora	to vacuum
cocinar	to cook		
cortar el césped	to cut the grass	planchar la ropa	to iron
darle de comer al perro	to feed the dog	poner la mesa	to set the table
		los quehaceres	chores
deber	should, ought to	sacar la basura	to take out the trash
hacer la cama	to make the bed	sucio(a)	dirty
lavar los platos	to wash the dishes		

Other Words and Phrases

decir	to say, to tell
hay que	one has to, one must
poner	to put, to place
si	if
todavía	still; yet

Gramática

Nota gramatical: acabar de + infinitive *p. 284*

More Irregular Verbs

Dar, decir, poner, salir, traer, and **venir** are all irregular.

decir	to say, to tell
digo	decimos
dices	decís
dice	dicen

venir	to come
vengo	venimos
vienes	venís
viene	vienen

Some verbs are irregular only in the **yo** form of the present tense.

dar	poner	salir	traer
doy	pongo	salgo	traigo

Affirmative tú Commands

Regular **affirmative tú commands** are the same as the **él/ella** forms in the present tense.

Infinitive	Present Tense	Affirmative tú Command
lavar	(él, ella) **lava**	¡Lava los platos!
barrer	(él, ella) **barre**	¡Barre el suelo!
abrir	(él, ella) **abre**	¡Abre la puerta!

There are irregular **affirmative tú commands.**

decir	hacer	ir	poner	salir	ser	tener	venir
di	haz	ve	pon	sal	sé	ten	ven

Repaso de la lección

¡LLEGADA!

¡AvanzaRap!
DVD
Sing and Learn

Now you can
- plan a party
- talk about chores and responsibilities
- tell someone what to do
- say what you just did

Using
- more irregular verbs
- affirmative **tú** commands
- **acabar de** + infinitive

To review
- more irregular verbs p. 277
- affirmative **tú** commands p. 282
- **acabar de** + infinitive p. 284

AUDIO

1 | Listen and understand

El señor Robles y sus estudiantes hablan de una fiesta. Escucha la conversación y empareja las personas con las oraciones correspondientes.
(Listen to Mr. Robles and his students. Then match each person with the appropriate sentence.)

1. La fiesta es para ella.
2. No deben hablar de la fiesta.
3. Va a traer los globos.
4. Va a ayudar a limpiar.
5. Va a poner las decoraciones.
6. Va a traer pizza.

a. Andrés
b. Carla
c. Samuel
d. el señor Robles
e. la directora
f. los estudiantes

To review
- more irregular verbs p. 277

2 | Plan a party

Natalia da una fiesta para su hermano y habla con Catalina, una amiga. Completa sus mensajes instantáneos con la forma correcta del verbo apropiado. *(Complete the instant messages with the correct form of the appropriate verb.)*

dar	salir
decir	traer
poner	ven

○○○

mensajero instantáneo

chica_cómica: Catalina, yo __1.__ una fiesta de sorpresa para Hugo el sábado. Hay mucho que hacer.

Cati268: El sábado llego a tu casa temprano para ayudar. También yo __2.__ los refrescos.

chica_cómica: Yo decoro la casa y mamá __3.__ la mesa.

Cati268: ¿Cuándo __4.__ Hugo?

chica_cómica: A las dos. Los invitados __5.__ «¡Feliz cumpleaños!», y él abre los regalos.

Cati268: Y después de comer el almuerzo, todos nosotros __6.__ de la casa para comer pastel en un café.

To review
• affirmative **tú** commands p. 282

3 | Tell someone what to do

Alfredo es muy perezoso. Usa mandatos para escribir lo que él le dice a su hermana. *(Write Alfredo's commands to his sister.)*

> **modelo:** venir a mi cuarto
> Ven a mi cuarto.

1. traer mi mochila
2. buscar mi libro de ciencias
3. envolver el regalo para mamá
4. ponerlo en el escritorio
5. ir a la tienda
6. hacer todos mis quehaceres

To review
• **acabar de** + infinitive p. 284

4 | Talk about chores and responsibilities

Escribe qué acaban de hacer Fernando y otros. *(Write what these people have just done.)*

> **modelo:** Elena
> Elena acaba de barrer el suelo.

1. mamá

2. yo

3. papá

4. ellos

5. Elena

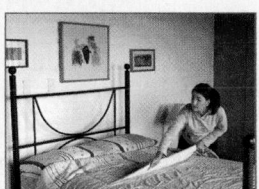

6. Elena y yo

To review
• **las montañas** p. 245
• Comparación cultural pp. 278, 284
• Lectura cultural pp. 288–289

5 | Ecuador and Panama

Comparación cultural

Answer these culture questions.

1. What is the world's highest active volcano? Where is it located?
2. What is celebrated during **Fiestas de Quito**? How?
3. Who are the Otavalos and what are they known for?
4. How do you dance **el sanjuanito**? What instruments are used in **el tamborito**? Where are these dances popular?

Más práctica   Cuaderno *pp. 231–242*   Cuaderno para hispanohablantes *pp. 233–242*

Get Help Online
my.hrw.com

Panamá
Argentina
Ecuador

AUDIO

¡Así celebramos!

Lectura y escritura

1 Leer Party celebrations vary around the world. Read how María Elena, Carla, and Daniel enjoy parties and celebrations.

2 Escribir Using the three descriptions as models, write a short paragraph about a celebration of your own.

STRATEGY Escribir

Use a chart Complete this chart to describe a celebration.

tipo de fiesta

lugar	invitados	comida	actividades

Step 1 Complete the chart with details about the type of celebration, location, guests, food, and activities.

Step 2 Write your paragraph. Make sure to include all the information from the chart. Check your writing by yourself or with help from a friend. Make final corrections. Read your paragraph aloud to the class.

Compara con tu mundo

Use the paragraph you wrote to compare your celebration to a celebration described by *one* of the three students. What is similar? What is different?

Cuaderno *pp. 243–245*   Cuaderno para hispanohablantes *pp. 243–245*

CULTURA Interactiva
my.hrw.com
See these pages come alive!

Panamá
María Elena

¡Saludos desde Panamá! Me llamo María Elena. Mi familia y yo acabamos de decorar la casa para celebrar la Navidad[1]. El 24 de diciembre es muy importante en Panamá. Las familias comen la cena tarde y a las doce de la noche abren los regalos. Mis hermanos y yo siempre decoramos el árbol de Navidad[2]. También me gusta envolver regalos con papel. Quiero dar y recibir muchos regalos este año.

[1] Christmas   [2] **árbol...** Christmas tree

Argentina
Carla

¡Hola! Me llamo Carla y vivo en el norte de Argentina. Todos los años celebramos un gran festival. En el festival podemos ver a los gauchos[3] con sus caballos[4], escuchar música típica y comer comida rica. Siempre llevo un vestido bonito para participar en los bailes típicos con otros chicos y chicas.

[3] Argentinean cowboys   [4] horses

Ecuador
Daniel

¡Hola! Me llamo Daniel y vivo en Cuenca, Ecuador. Para la fiesta del año nuevo, muchas personas hacen figuras grandes de papel maché. Las figuras son de muchos colores y muchas veces son muy cómicas. La noche del 31 de diciembre mis padres dan una fiesta. Invitan a muchas personas. Limpiamos toda la casa, ponemos la mesa y compartimos una cena rica con nuestra familia y los otros invitados.

Repaso inclusivo
♻ Options for Review

¡AvanzaRap!
DVD
Sing and Learn

1 | Listen, understand, and compare

Escuchar

Gabriela is giving a surprise party. Listen to her phone message. Then answer the following questions.

1. ¿Qué acaba de hacer Gabriela?
2. ¿Qué sirve Gabriela?
3. ¿Qué traes tú a la fiesta?
4. ¿Dónde vive la señora Domínguez? ¿Y Jorge y Marlene?
5. ¿Qué tiene la señora Domínguez? ¿Y Jorge y Marlene?
6. ¿Qué debes hacer si los invitados llegan temprano?

Have you ever given or gone to a surprise party? How did others help prepare for the party?

2 | Give orders

Hablar

You have designed a personal robot to perform your everyday tasks for you. Your friend asks if he or she can borrow your robot for a day, but your robot only listens to you. Your friend tells you what his or her schedule is and what has to be done, and you give the commands to your robot.

3 | Plan a surprise party

Hablar

Work in a group of four to plan a surprise party for a close friend or family member. Each member of your group should take on a role: food coordinator, invitation designer, guest list creator, and activities organizer. Describe your party plans to the class.

4 | Have a yard sale

Escribir

You want to earn some extra money by holding a yard sale. Make a flier to advertise what you are selling: books, personal items, clothing, and furniture. Include information such as the date, time, and location of the sale. Display your flyer in the classroom. As a follow-up activity, ask your classmates what they think they would buy.

5 | Furnish a dorm room

Hablar

Role-play a conversation between college roommates. You and your partner need to furnish your dorm room. Discuss with your partner the items that you want to have in your room, where those items will go, and what color your room should be. Once you come to an agreement on what your room will look like, draw a sketch and present it to the class.

6 | Design a family home

Hablar
Escribir

Your partner has contracted you to design a floor plan for a house that will fit his or her family's personalities and lifestyles. Interview your partner to find out what his or her family is like and what they like to do. Also find out what they like and dislike about where they live now. Take notes and use the information to write a proposal. Present it to your partner.

7 | Prepare a dinner

Leer
Escribir

Your family has invited your Spanish teacher home for dinner tonight. Your parents left you this note telling you to do some dinner preparations. Read the note and write another note saying that you have just done certain tasks and make excuses as to why you can't do the other items.

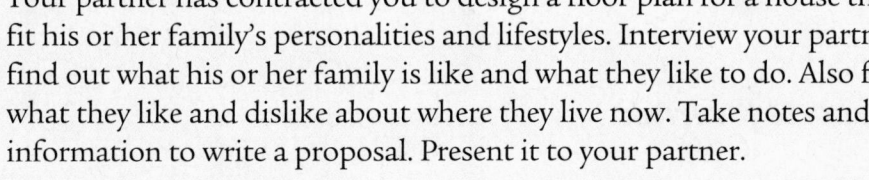

Necesitamos ir a trabajar y no podemos
preparar todo. Por favor:

haz la tarea temprano
ve a la tienda para comprar el postre
prepara la ensalada
cocina el pollo y las patatas
limpia la cocina
lava los platos
saca la basura
pon la mesa

Hablamos más tarde. ¡Gracias!

UNIDAD 6

República Dominicana

Mantener un cuerpo sano

Lección 1
Tema: **¿Cuál es tu deporte favorito?**

Lección 2
Tema: **La salud**

Océano
Atlántico

República Dominicana

Puerto Rico

Golfo de México

Cuba

México

Mar Caribe

Honduras

Nicaragua

Guatemala

Costa
Rica

El Salvador

Panamá

«¡Hola!

**Somos Mario e Isabel.
Somos de la República Dominicana.»**

Venezuela

Colombia

Océano Atlántico

Haití   República
          Dominicana   Punta
          Santo   Cana
          Domingo Juan
                    Dolio

Mar Caribe

Población: 10.478.756

Área: 18.815 millas cuadradas;
comparte la isla de La Española
con Haití

Capital: Santo Domingo

Moneda: el peso dominicano

Idioma: español

Frutas tropicales

Comida típica: mangú, cazabe, la bandera

Gente famosa: Julia Álvarez (escritora), Juan Luis
Guerra (cantante), Pedro Martínez (beisbolista),
Oscar de la Renta (diseñador)

CULTURA Interactiva
my.hrw.com
See these pages come alive!

Una familia de pescadores en una playa de Pedernales

◀ **La importancia del Mar Caribe** The white sand beaches of the Dominican Republic are popular with Dominican and international tourists. The clear blue waters and coral reefs are ideal for snorkeling and diving. *What can tourists enjoy in your area?*

El deporte nacional Baseball is considered the Dominican Republic's national sport. It can be played throughout the year because of the country's warm climate, and fans can see professional games from October through February. *What sports are popular where you live?* ▶

Juegan al deporte nacional en Santo Domingo

El Altar de la Patria en la capital

◀ **Un monumento de la Independencia** Santo Domingo's **Altar de la Patria** (Altar of the Nation) is a memorial dedicated to the heroes of the Dominican Republic's fight for freedom from Haiti in 1844. The monument's walkway contains a 32-point nautical star, considered kilometer one, from which all distances within the country are measured. *How are heroes honored in your country's capital?*

República Dominicana

1

Tema:

¿Cuál es tu deporte favorito?

¡AVANZA! **In this lesson you will learn to**
- talk about sports
- talk about whom you know
- talk about what you know

using
- the verb **jugar**
- the verbs **saber** and **conocer**
- the personal **a**

♻ *¿Recuerdas?*
- numbers from 200 to 1,000,000
- **gustar** with nouns
- comparatives

Comparación cultural

In this lesson you will learn about
- Caribbean baseball championships
- Dominican artist Juan Medina
- sports clubs in Santo Domingo

Compara con tu mundo

Baseball has been a popular pastime in the Dominican Republic since the late 1800s, especially in the southeast of the country. Most Dominican players in the U.S. major leagues come from this region. *Do you like to play or watch sports with your friends? Which is your favorite?*

¿Qué ves?

Mira la foto

¿Practican un deporte estas personas?

¿Son atléticas o perezosas?

¿Cuántas personas llevan camisetas rojas?

MODES OF COMMUNICATION

INTERPRETIVE	INTERPERSONAL	PRESENTATIONAL
Read a brochure for a sports club and identify features you like.	Discuss what you know about sports and sports personalities.	Create and present a radio ad for a sports store.
Listen to two broadcasters evaluate two sports teams to predict who will win a match.	Take turns talking about which sports you like.	Write whether or not boys and girls should play sports on the same team and why.

Un partido en la escuela
Santo Domingo, República Dominicana

✿ Presentación de VOCABULARIO

¡AVANZA! **Goal:** Learn what sports Mario and Isabel like to play. Then use what you have learned to talk about sports. *Actividades 1–2*

♻ *¿Recuerdas?* Numbers from 200 to 1,000,000 p. 165

VIDEO DVD

AUDIO

A ¡Hola! Me llamo Mario. Soy **atleta** y mi deporte **favorito** es **el béisbol.** Hoy tenemos **un partido** con **el equipo** rojo.

el jugador

el guante

el casco

la pelota

el béisbol

los aficionados

el bate

el equipo

la jugadora

el campo

B Acabamos de **perder** el partido, cuatro a cinco. Mi amiga Isabel y su equipo son **los ganadores.** Tal vez debo practicar otro deporte.

4 equipo azul

perder

ganar

5 equipo rojo

los campeones

Más vocabulario

el estadio *stadium*
patinar *to skate*

Expansión de vocabulario p. R7

En la República Dominicana se dice...

In the Dominican Republic the word for *baseball game* is **el juego de pelota.**

C Me gusta **nadar,** pero **la piscina** está lejos de mi casa. **El voleibol** es divertido, pero prefiero el béisbol.

la natación

la piscina

el voleibol

D De vez en cuando voy al **campo** para jugar al **fútbol americano,** pero es difícil **comprender las reglas.** Me gusta **el básquetbol,** pero nunca **gano.** También voy a **la cancha** de **tenis,** pero siempre hay muchas personas allí. Puedo **patinar en línea,** pero es **peligroso.** ¡Es mejor jugar al béisbol!

el fútbol americano

el básquetbol

la cancha

el tenis

la raqueta

patinar en línea

los patines en línea

@**HOMETUTOR** my.hrw.com **Interactive Flashcards**

¡A responder!   Escuchar

Escucha la lista de palabras asociadas con los deportes. Si es una palabra que asocias con el béisbol, levanta la mano. *(Raise your hand if the word you hear is associated with baseball.)*

Práctica de VOCABULARIO

1 | ¿Qué necesitan?

Leer | Isabel describe los artículos deportivos que sus amigos tienen y/o los deportes que quieren practicar. Identifica la cosa que necesita. *(For each situation, identify the sports-related item that Isabel's friend needs.)*

> bate
> casco
> patines en línea
> pelota
> piscina
> raqueta

1. Ya tiene una pelota y quiere jugar al tenis.
2. Ya tiene una pelota y un guante y quiere jugar al béisbol.
3. Tiene un casco y quiere patinar en línea.
4. Ya tiene una pelota y va a jugar al fútbol americano.
5. Quiere nadar.
6. Está en la cancha y quiere jugar al básquetbol.

2 | La tienda de deportes   **¿Recuerdas?** Numbers from 200 to 1,000,000 p. 165

Escribir Hablar | La tienda Mundo de Deportes, en Santo Domingo, vende muchos artículos deportivos. Di cuánto cuestan estas cosas. *(Tell how much these items cost.)*

modelo: Un bate cuesta tres mil setecientos treinta pesos.

RD$3,730

¡Atención, atletas!
En nuestra tienda, tenemos
los precios más bajos.

RD$1,800   3 por RD$180   RD$2,620   RD$2,300

RD$5,475   RD$435

MUNDO DE DEPORTES
Avenida 27 de febrero, 104
Santo Domingo, República Dominicana
809-555-5707

> **Expansión**
> Write four sentences comparing the cost of these items.

Más práctica   Cuaderno *pp. 246–248*   Cuaderno para hispanohablantes *pp. 246–249*

Get Help Online
my.hrw.com

 **PARA Y PIENSA**

Did you get it?   Say what you would need to play the following sports.
1. el básquetbol   2. el béisbol   3. el tenis

¡AVANZA! **Goal:** Identify the words Isabel and Mario use to talk about sports. Then practice what you have learned to talk about sports. *Actividades 3–4*

♻ *¿Recuerdas?* **gustar** with nouns p. 145

Telehistoria escena 1

 @**HOMETUTOR** View, Read
my.hrw.com and Record

STRATEGIES

Cuando lees
Brainstorm before reading
Brainstorm English words for equipment used in baseball, swimming, in-line skating, tennis, football, and other sports. Which items on your list are in the Telehistoria?

Cuando escuchas
Listen for non-responses Some statements or questions don't receive responses. Listen for Mario's last questions to Isabel. Does she respond? Does Mario expect a response? Why or why not?

VIDEO
DVD

AUDIO

Isabel is on first base, where Mario is playing.

Isabel: Hoy tu equipo va a perder el partido, Mario. Mi equipo siempre gana.

Mario: Sí, Isabel, eres muy buena jugadora de béisbol. Pero hoy nosotros vamos a ser los campeones.

Isabel: ¿Qué vas a hacer después de las clases? ¿Vamos al café?

Mario: Tengo que comprar un regalo. Es el cumpleaños de mi hermano.

Isabel: ¿Qué vas a comprar? Es un atleta. Le gusta el béisbol, ¿no?

Mario: Sí, pero tiene un bate y pelotas de béisbol.

Isabel: ¿Le gusta patinar en línea?

Mario: Sí, pero los patines en línea cuestan mucho dinero.

Isabel: ¿Le gusta el fútbol americano? ¿El tenis? La natación, ¿le gusta?

Mario: Sí, le gusta nadar pero, ¿qué puedo comprar? ¿Una piscina? ¿Agua?

Isabel's teammate hits a home run, and Mario's team loses.

Continuará... p. 310

También se dice

República Dominicana Mario uses the word **piscina** to joke about buying a swimming pool. In other Spanish-speaking countries you might hear:
• **México** **la alberca**
• **Argentina** **la pileta**

3 | Comprensión del episodio   ¿Quién gana?

Completa las oraciones con información del episodio. *(Complete the sentences.)*

| un bate | los campeones | ganar |
| jugadora de béisbol | patines en línea | un regalo |

1. Isabel piensa que su equipo va a _____ .

2. Mario piensa que él y su equipo van a ser _____ .

3. Isabel es una buena _____ .

4. Mario tiene que comprar _____ después de las clases.

5. El hermano de Mario no necesita _____ .

6. Mario no quiere comprar _____ porque cuestan mucho.

4 | ¿Te gustan los deportes?   ¿*Recuerdas?* **gustar** with nouns p. 145

Hablar

Pregúntale a otro(a) estudiante si le gustan estos deportes. *(Ask a partner whether he or she likes the following sports.)*

A ¿Te gusta el fútbol?

B Sí, me gusta el fútbol. (No, no me gusta el fútbol.)

1.

2.

3.

4.

5.

6.

Expansión
Use a Venn diagram to compare your sports preferences with a partner's.

Get Help Online
my.hrw.com

PARA Y PIENSA

Did you get it?   Complete each sentence with the appropriate vocabulary word.

1. Cuando Isabel gana un partido, ella es _____ .

2. Al hermano de Mario le gusta nadar; su deporte favorito es _____ .

3. Mario lleva _____ porque el béisbol puede ser peligroso.

Presentación de GRAMÁTICA

Goal: Learn how to form the verb **jugar**. Then practice using **jugar** to talk about playing sports. *Actividades 5–9*

♻ *¿Recuerdas?* Comparatives p. 174

English Grammar Connection: There is more than one way to say the English verb *to play* in Spanish. Use **jugar** when you mean playing a sport or a game; use **tocar** when you mean playing a musical instrument or a CD.

The Verb jugar

Use **jugar** to talk about playing a sport or a game. How do you form the present tense of this verb?

Here's how:

Jugar is a stem-changing verb in which the **u** changes to **ue** in all forms except **nosotros(as)** and **vosotros(as).**

jugar *to play*	
j**ue**go	j**u**gamos
j**ue**gas	j**u**gáis
j**ue**ga	j**ue**gan

When you use **jugar** with the name of a sport, use **jugar a + sport.**

Mi primo **juega al fútbol.**
My cousin plays soccer.

Jugamos al fútbol americano.
We play football.

Juegan al béisbol en la República Dominicana.
They play baseball in the Dominican Republic.

Más práctica
Cuaderno *pp. 249–251*
Cuaderno para hispanohablantes *pp. 250–252*

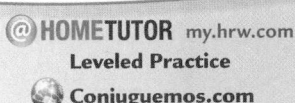
@HOMETUTOR my.hrw.com
Leveled Practice
🌐 Conjuguemos.com

❖ Práctica de GRAMÁTICA

5 | Una familia activa

Leer
Escribir

La familia de Mario es muy atlética. Completa su descripción con formas de **jugar** y luego contesta la pregunta. *(Complete Mario's description of his family with forms of **jugar**. Then answer his question.)*

Mi familia practica muchos deportes. Yo __1.__ al béisbol en un equipo. Mi hermano __2.__ también. Él y mi hermana __3.__ al voleibol los sábados. Mis padres __4.__ mucho al tenis. Ellos __5.__ casi todos los días. Nosotros no __6.__ al fútbol americano, pero lo miramos en la televisión. ¿Y tú? ¿A qué deportes __7.__ ?

Expansión
List your family members and tell what sports they play or like to watch.

6 | ¿A qué juegan?

Escuchar
Escribir

Estos atletas hablan de los lugares donde juegan. Escucha las descripciones y escribe a qué juegan estas personas. *(Listen to the descriptions and write what sports these people play.)*

1. Elena
2. Rogelio y José
3. el equipo
4. los maestros
5. Tomás
6. la atleta

7 | ¿Para qué equipo?

Hablar

Comparación cultural

La Serie del Caribe

How do professional athletes support their home countries? Every February, Winter League championship teams from four countries compete in baseball's *Serie del Caribe,* or Caribbean Series. Many major league ballplayers have taken part in the Winter Leagues. Miguel Tejada and David Ortiz have represented the **Dominican Republic.** Other players include Johan Santana and Miguel Cabrera for **Venezuela,** Oliver Pérez and Vinny Castilla for **Mexico,** and Carlos Beltrán and Iván Rodríguez for **Puerto Rico.**

David Ortiz juega para los Red Sox de Boston en un partido contra los Phillies de Filadelfia.

Compara con tu mundo *How does the Serie del Caribe compare to other sports championships you are familiar with?*

Pregúntale a otro(a) estudiante para qué equipo juegan los jugadores de las Ligas de Invierno. *(Ask what team each player plays for.)*

A ¿Para qué equipo juega Oliver Pérez?

B Pérez juega para el equipo de México.

8 | ¿Dónde juegas?

Hablar

Mira las fotos de estos deportes. Pregúntale a otro(a) estudiante dónde los juega. *(Ask a partner where he or she plays these sports.)*

1.
2.
3.

4.
5.
6.

Expansión
Quiz a partner on sports that famous athletes play.

9 | ¿A qué juegas mejor?

 ¿Recuerdas? Comparatives p. 174

Hablar

Habla con otro(a) estudiante sobre a qué juegas mejor. *(Tell what sports you play better than others.)*

A ¿Juegas mejor al fútbol americano o al béisbol?

B No juego al fútbol americano porque no comprendo las reglas. Juego mejor al béisbol.

1
2.
3.
4.

5.
6.
7.
8.

Más práctica   Cuaderno *pp. 249–251*   Cuaderno para hispanohablantes *pp. 250–252*

Get Help Online
my.hrw.com

PARA Y PIENSA

Did you get it?   Create sentences that tell the sports each of the following people play, using **jugar.**

1. Ana y yo / el béisbol
2. ustedes / el básquetbol
3. el hermano de Rosa / el voleibol
4. yo / el tenis

❈ GRAMÁTICA en contexto

Goal: Pay attention to the forms of **jugar** that Isabel and Mario use to talk about sports and sports equipment. Then use **jugar** to say what sports people play. *Actividades 10–11*

Telehistoria escena 2

@**HOMETUTOR** View, Read
my.hrw.com and Record

STRATEGIES

Cuando lees
Make a mindmap for related words
Write the name of a piece of sports equipment, such as **el casco,** in the center circle. In outside circles, write as many sports as possible that use that piece of equipment.

Cuando escuchas
Listen for stressed words When Mario and Isabel talk about possible gifts, listen for the way they stress or emphasize certain words to show their preferences.

VIDEO
DVD

AUDIO

Isabel and Mario are in a sporting goods store, looking for a gift.

Isabel: Un guante de béisbol. Me gusta para tu hermano.

Mario takes the glove and puts it back on the shelf.

Isabel: Me gusta la raqueta.

He also takes the racket and puts it back. Isabel picks up a basketball.

Mario: No, una bola de básquetbol, no. Es un regalo para mi hermano; no es tu cumpleaños.

Isabel: ¿Necesita un casco?

Mario: No, pero necesito un casco para jugar al tenis.

Isabel: ¡Un partido de tenis no es peligroso!

Mario: Tú no juegas al tenis con mi hermano.

Isabel: *(laughing)* No, no juego al tenis. Pero me gusta el voleibol. ¿Tu hermano juega al voleibol?

Continuará... p. 315

También se dice

República Dominicana
Mario uses the word **bola** to talk about the ball. In other Spanish-speaking countries you might hear:
• **muchos países** **el balón**

10 | Comprensión del episodio   Buscan un regalo

Escuchar
Leer

Di si la oración es cierta o falsa. Si es falsa, escribe lo que es cierto. *(Tell whether it is true or false. Correct the false statements.)*

1. Isabel piensa que un guante de béisbol es un buen regalo.
2. Mario quiere comprar una pelota de básquetbol.
3. Es el cumpleaños de Isabel.
4. Mario necesita un bate para jugar al tenis con su hermano.
5. Es peligroso cuando Mario juega al tenis con su hermano.
6. Isabel juega al tenis.

11 | Un atleta famoso

Hablar

Eres reportero(a) y tu amigo(a) es un(a) atleta famoso(a). Entrevista a otro(a) estudiante, usando estas preguntas. *(Interview a partner.)*

1. ¿A qué deporte juegas?
2. ¿Dónde juegas?
3. ¿Qué necesitas hacer para ser campeón (campeona) en tu deporte?
4. ¿Qué prefieres, ser jugador(a) o aficionado(a)? ¿Por qué?
5. ¿Quién es tu atleta favorito(a)? ¿A qué deporte juega?
6. ¿Qué te gusta hacer después de un partido? ¿Qué haces cuando pierdes?

> **Expansión**
> Use the answers to write an article.

AUDIO

Pronunciación   **La letra g con a, o, u**

Before **a, o, u,** and consonants, the Spanish **g** is pronounced like the *g* in the English word *game*.

Listen and repeat.

ga	**go**	**gu**	**g** + consonant
ganar	ten**go**	**gu**ante	re**g**las

A **G**re**g**orio le **g**usta ju**g**ar al béisbol en a**g**osto.

Get Help Online
my.hrw.com

PARA Y PIENSA

Did you get it?   Complete each sentence based on the Telehistoria with the appropriate form of the verb **jugar.**
1. Isabel no _____ al tenis.
2. Cuando Mario y su hermano _____ al tenis, Mario necesita un casco.
3. A Isabel le gusta _____ al básquetbol.

Presentación de GRAMÁTICA

Goal: Learn how to form **saber** and **conocer**, as well as use the personal **a.** Then use them to talk about whom and what you know. *Actividades 12–15*

English Grammar Connection: There are two ways to say the English verb *to know* in Spanish: **saber** and **conocer.**

The Verbs saber and conocer

ANiMaTeDGRaMMaR
my.hrw.com

In Spanish, there are two verbs that mean *to know.* How do you form the present tense of **saber** and **conocer** and use them correctly?

Here's how: Both **saber** and **conocer** have irregular **yo** forms in the present tense.

saber	*to know*
sé	sabemos
sabes	sabéis
sabe	saben

conocer	*to know*
conozco	conocemos
conoces	conocéis
conoce	conocen

Use **saber** to talk about factual information you know.

Sé cuánto cuesta el bate.
I know how much the bat costs.

¿**Sabes** a qué hora empieza el partido?
Do you know what time the game begins?

You can also use **saber** + **infinitive** to say that you know how to do something.

Nicolás **sabe** **patinar** muy bien.
Nicolás knows how to skate very well.

Use **conocer** when you want to say that you are familiar with a person or place.

Conozco a tu hermano David.
I know your brother David.

Mi prima **conoce** Santo Domingo.
My cousin knows (is familiar with) Santo Domingo.

You also use **conocer** to talk about meeting someone for the first time.

Queremos **conocer** a los jugadores.
We want to meet the players.

Más práctica
Cuaderno *pp. 252–254*
Cuaderno para hispanohablantes *pp. 253–256*

@HOMETUTOR my.hrw.com
Leveled Practice
Conjuguemos.com

Práctica de GRAMÁTICA

12 | Un correo electrónico de Alicia

Leer

Alicia le escribe un correo electrónico a Mario. Escoge el verbo correcto entre paréntesis. *(Complete Alicia's e-mail to Mario by choosing the correct verb in parentheses.)*

Hola, Mario:

¿Qué tal? ¿ **1.** (Sabes / Conoces) tú que Trini Salgado acaba de ganar otro partido de fútbol? Ella **2.** (sabe / conoce) jugar muy bien. Es campeona. Ella **3.** (sabe / conoce) a muchos campeones de deportes también. Yo **4.** (sé / conozco) que ella va a ir a la capital de tu país. ¿La **5.** (sabes / conoces) tú? Yo no la **6.** (sé / conozco) todavía, pero es mi jugadora favorita y tú y yo **7.** (sabemos / conocemos) que la quiero **8.** (saber / conocer). Mario, yo no **9.** (sé / conozco) dónde está la camiseta. **10.** ¿(Saben/ Conocen) Isabel y tú dónde está la camiseta?

Tu amiga, Alicia

Nota gramatical

When a specific person is the direct object of a sentence, use the personal **a** *after* the verb and *before* the person.

No conozco **a** Raúl.   Ayudo **a** la maestra.
I don't know Raúl.   *I am helping the teacher.*

13 | ¿Qué saben? ¿Qué conocen?

Escribir

¿Qué saben y conocen estas personas? Escribe oraciones con **saber** o **conocer**. *(Write about what and whom these people know, using **saber** or **conocer**.)*

modelo: mi madre (cuándo empieza el partido)
　　　　Mi madre sabe cuándo empieza el partido.

1. las campeonas (nadar muy bien)
2. yo (un jugador de béisbol)
3. el equipo (el estadio de fútbol)
4. tú (dónde está la cancha)
5. mis amigos y yo (la República Dominicana)
6. los jugadores (Trini Salgado)
7. yo (qué equipo va a ganar)
8. Ana (cuánto cuesta el casco)
9. tú (las ganadoras)
10. nosotros (patinar en línea)
11. ustedes (quién es el campeón)

Expansión
Write three things you know how to do well and three things you don't.

14 | ¡A charlar!

Hablar

Trabaja en un grupo de tres. Habla de lo que sabes y conoces en el mundo de los deportes. *(Talk with a group of three about what and whom you know in sports.)*

A ¿Saben jugar al voleibol ustedes?

B Sí, sé jugar al voleibol. Juego los sábados con mis hermanos.

C No, no sé jugar al voleibol. No comprendo las reglas...

Expansión
Ask your group three more questions about a topic other than sports. Use **saber** or **conocer.**

1. las reglas de...
2. un lugar donde juegan al...
3. unos aficionados de...
4. el (la) atleta...
5. un lugar donde... es muy popular
6. ¿ ?

15 | ¿Qué saben hacer tus amigos?

Escribir

Escribe un párrafo sobre tus amigos u otras personas y lo que ellos saben hacer. *(Write a paragraph about friends or other people you know and what they know how to do.)*

modelo: Mi amigo Sean sabe tocar la guitarra. Toca todos los días...

Comparación cultural

El arte representativo

How can artists represent the people of their country through their artwork? Juan Medina, an artist from the **Dominican Republic**, has experimented with different styles of art, combining traditional and modern techniques. Some of his paintings are inspired by his Dominican heritage, showing the history, people, and social and political issues of his country. *Vendedora de flores* shows a flower vendor. Vendors and their carts are found throughout Santo Domingo, selling everything from shaved ice to coffee to flowers to newspapers.

Compara con tu mundo How would you represent a typical sight or activity in your community through artwork?

Vendedora de flores (alrededor de 1990), Juan Medina

Más práctica Cuaderno *pp. 252–254* Cuaderno para hispanohablantes *pp. 253–256*

🌐 **Get Help Online**
my.hrw.com

PARA Y PIENSA

Did you get it? Complete each sentence with the correct form of **saber** or **conocer.** Use the personal **a** if necessary.
1. ¿ _____ ustedes jugar al voleibol?
2. Yo _____ María muy bien porque es mi amiga.
3. Nosotros _____ que el fútbol americano puede ser peligroso.

❖ Todo junto

Telehistoria completa

@HOMETUTOR View, Read
my.hrw.com and Record

STRATEGIES

Cuando lees
Scan for the details Before reading carefully, scan the scene for these details: Who is Trini Salgado? What is she doing today? Who is a bigger fan of Trini: Alicia or Mario's brother?

Cuando escuchas
Go for the goals While listening, consider Mario's two goals in this scene. What are they? Does he fulfill both goals during the scene?

Escena 1 *Resumen*
En un partido de béisbol, Mario habla con Isabel. Él tiene que comprar un regalo para el cumpleaños de su hermano.

Escena 2 *Resumen*
Isabel y Mario buscan un regalo en una tienda de deportes. Mario no sabe qué va a comprar.

Escena 3

VIDEO
DVD

AUDIO

Mario points to a soccer jersey.

Mario: ¡Es como la camiseta de Alicia! ¿Conoces a Trini Salgado? Ella está aquí, en Santo Domingo.

Isabel: Lo sé. ¿Alicia la conoce?

Mario: No, pero Trini es su jugadora de fútbol favorita. Alicia quiere un autógrafo en la camiseta. Y yo debo encontrar a Trini...

Vendedor: ¿Buscan a Trini Salgado? *(Mario and Isabel nod.)* ¿Saben dónde encontrar a Trini Salgado?

Mario and Isabel shake their heads, and the clerk turns up the radio.

«La jugadora de fútbol Trini Salgado va a estar en el estadio hoy a las seis de la tarde. Los primeros quinientos aficionados pueden conocer a Trini.»

Mario: ¡Vamos! *(He buys the jersey.)*

Isabel: ¿A tu hermano le gusta Trini Salgado?

Mario: No sé. ¡Pero sé que le gustan las camisetas con autógrafos de atletas importantes!

16 | *Comprensión de los episodios* ¿A quién(es) describen?

Escuchar
Leer

Identifica a quién(es) describen estas oraciones:
a Mario, a Isabel o a los dos. *(Tell whom these sentences describe: Mario, Isabel, or both.)*

1. Piensa que va a ganar el partido de béisbol.
2. Su equipo de béisbol siempre gana.
3. Dice que el tenis es peligroso.
4. Va a una tienda de deportes.
5. Compra una camiseta de fútbol.
6. Dice que debe encontrar a Trini.

Isabel

Isabel y Mario   **Mario**

17 | *Comprensión de los episodios* Regalo para un atleta

Escuchar
Leer

Contesta las preguntas, según los episodios. *(Answer the questions, based on the Telehistoria.)*

1. ¿A qué juegan Isabel y Mario?
2. ¿Qué tiene que hacer Mario después de las clases?
3. ¿Necesita un casco el hermano de Mario?

4. ¿Dónde va a estar Trini a las seis?
5. ¿Quiénes pueden conocer a Trini?
6. ¿Qué compra Mario para su hermano?

18 | Un anuncio de radio

Digital performance space

Escribir
Hablar

STRATEGY Hablar
Use logical steps to meet the goal Use logical steps to create a radio ad, such as: (a) make a chart containing types of key information, like **qué hay en la tienda,** in column 1 and specific examples for each type in column 2; (b) choose the best examples; (c) write an exciting ad; and (d) record and present it.

Trabaja en un grupo de tres. Escriban un anuncio de radio para una tienda de deportes. Preséntenlo a la clase. Deben incluir el nombre de un deporte y un(a) atleta famoso(a), lo que venden en la tienda y los precios. *(Work in a group of three. Create a radio ad and present it to the class.)*

A Si quieres conocer a Trini Salgado, ven a la tienda El Deportista el sábado.

B Tenemos pelotas de fútbol, ropa... ¡y mucho más!

C El sábado, las pelotas de fútbol cuestan setecientos pesos. Puedes recibir un autógrafo de la jugadora...

Expansión
Create a radio ad for a professional sports game.

19 | Integración

Digital **performance** space

Leer
Escuchar
Hablar

Lee el anuncio de un partido y escucha a los comentaristas. Luego di qué equipo va a ganar y por qué. *(Read the ad and listen to the sports broadcasters' commentary. Then tell which team you think will win and why.)*

Fuente 1 Anuncio

LA ASOCIACIÓN DOMINICANA DE BASQUETBOL PRESENTA...
¡Un partido entre dos equipos excelentes!

Los Cometas — El equipo con el mejor récord contra Los Pumas

José Luis Tejada, el centro más alto de la liga

Los Pumas — El equipo con el mejor récord de la liga: 15-1

El equipo con más puntos por partido

¿Quién va a ganar? Vas a saberlo hoy. El partido empieza a las 4:00 de la tarde en el Centro de Deportes Solimar.

Fuente 2 Comentarios

Listen and take notes
- ¿Cómo juegan los equipos?
- ¿Cómo practican antes de los partidos?

modelo: El equipo de Los... va a ganar el partido porque...

20 | Un foro deportivo

Digital **performance** space

Escribir

En un foro en línea, debates este tema: Hay chicas que quieren jugar en los equipos con los chicos, por ejemplo, en los equipos de fútbol americano. ¿Piensas que es buena o mala idea? ¿Por qué? *(Do you think it's a good or bad idea for boys and girls to play on the same sports teams? Explain your answer.)*

modelo: Es una buena idea. Si las chicas pueden jugar al fútbol americano, deben jugar en el equipo de los chicos. Conozco a unas chicas que juegan...

Writing Criteria	Excellent	Good	Needs Work
Content	Your argument is supported with many reasons.	Your argument is supported with some reasons.	Your argument is supported with few reasons.
Communication	Your argument is organized and easy to follow.	Your argument is somewhat organized and easy to follow.	Your argument is disorganized and hard to follow.
Accuracy	Your argument has few mistakes in grammar and vocabulary.	Your argument has some mistakes in grammar and vocabulary.	Your argument has many mistakes in grammar and vocabulary.

Expansión
Exchange what you wrote with a partner and write a response to what he/she wrote.

Más práctica   Cuaderno *pp. 255–256*   Cuaderno para hispanohablantes *pp. 257–258*

Get Help Online
my.hrw.com

PARA Y PIENSA

Did you get it? Fill in the paragraph with the correct form of **saber** or **conocer.**

Trini Salgado _____ jugar al fútbol muy bien. Alicia y sus amigos la _____ , y ellos _____ que ella va a estar en el estadio en Santo Domingo.

Lectura

¡AVANZA! **Goal:** Read a flier for a sports club in the Dominican Republic. Then describe the club and compare it with any sports facilities you know.

AUDIO

Un club de deportes

This is a brochure for a sports club in Santo Domingo.

STRATEGY Leer

Make a mind map Make a mind map of the sports club in Santo Domingo, showing everything the club offers. Add circles! Highlight the features you like most.

El club en Santo Domingo

béisbol

Palacio
de los Deportes

¿Eres atlético?
¿Te gusta practicar deportes?
Si la respuesta es sí, ven al Palacio de los Deportes.

¿Te gusta nadar?
Tenemos una piscina olímpica.

¿Te gusta jugar al tenis?
Tenemos cinco canchas de tenis.

¿Te gusta jugar al béisbol?
Tenemos un campo de béisbol.

¿Te gusta jugar al básquetbol?
Tenemos d os canchas de básquetb ol.

¿Quieres comer después de jugar?
Tenemos un café que sirve comidas y bebidas ricas y nutritivas.

Palacio de los Deportes

Para nuestros socios [1]...

Si no sabes practicar los siguientes deportes, tenemos clases de...

- natación
- tenis
- artes marciales
- ejercicios aeróbicos

Si quieres jugar con otras personas, hay equipos de...

- básquetbol
- béisbol
- voleibol

Horas

lunes a viernes	6:00 de la mañana a 9:00 de la noche
sábado	7:00 de la mañana a 6:00 de la tarde

Membresías [2]
Hay membresías personales y familiares [3]. Puedes pedir la lista de los precios.

Dirección [4]
Calle Mella, 100
Santo Domingo

Teléfono
(809) 583-1492

---

[1] members   [2] memberships   [3] family   [4] address

PARA Y PIENSA

¿Comprendiste?

1. ¿A qué puedes jugar en el Palacio de los Deportes?

2. ¿Qué puedes hacer si no sabes nadar?

3. Si quieres jugar con un equipo, ¿a qué puedes jugar?

¿Y tú?

Si eres socio(a) de un club de deportes, compara tu club con el Palacio de los Deportes. Si no, ¿quieres ser socio(a) del Palacio de los Deportes? Explica.

Conexiones · *Las ciencias sociales*

La bandera dominicana

The colors and symbols of the Dominican flag reflect the country's long struggle for independence from France, Spain, and Haiti. It was not until 1844 that the Dominican Republic finally gained its independence.

On the Dominican flag, blue stands for liberty (**libertad**), red for the fire and blood of the fight for independence (**independencia**), and white for faith and sacrifice (**sacrificio**).

Write a description of the coat of arms (**el escudo de armas**). Research and explain the symbolism of the laurel branch (**rama de laurel**) and the palm branch (**rama de palma**).

El simbolismo de la bandera dominicana

Libertad

Sacrificio

Independencia

El escudo de armas

Rama de palma

Rama de laurel

Proyecto 1 *La historia*

Research and write about the Dominican struggle for independence from 1800 to 1844. Include specific facts such as dates, countries that were involved, and important people.

Proyecto 2 *El arte*

Flags combine geometric shapes, colors, symbols, and mottos. Design a flag for your school and explain the meaning of each element you use. Include a motto and labels in Spanish.

Proyecto 3 *La educación física*

In many countries, people fly their flag and sing their national anthem at sporting events. Write a paragraph about the role of flags and anthems in sports. Why do you think this tradition started?

El equipo nacional de fútbol femenino

ANIMATEDGRAMMAR
Interactive Flashcards
my.hrw.com

Vocabulario

Sports

el básquetbol	basketball
el béisbol	baseball
el fútbol americano	football
nadar	to swim
la natación	swimming
patinar	to skate
patinar en línea	to in-line skate
el tenis	tennis
el voleibol	volleyball

Sports Equipment

el bate	bat
el casco	helmet
el guante	glove
los patines en línea	in-line skates
la pelota	ball
la raqueta	racket

Talk About Sports

comprender las reglas	to understand the rules
favorito(a)	favorite
ganar	to win
el partido	game
peligroso(a)	dangerous
perder (ie)	to lose

Locations and People

los aficionados	fans	el equipo	team
el (la) atleta	athlete	el estadio	stadium
el campeón (pl. los campeones), la campeona	champion	el (la) ganador(a)	winner
		el (la) jugador(a)	player
el campo	field	la piscina	swimming pool
la cancha	court		

Gramática

Nota gramatical: The personal **a** *p. 313*

The Verb jugar

Jugar is a stem-changing verb in which the **u** changes to **ue** in all forms except **nosotros(as)** and **vosotros(as).**

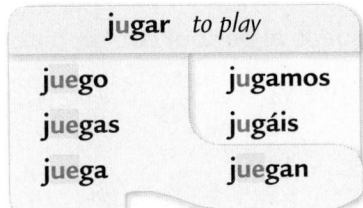

jugar	*to play*
juego	jugamos
juegas	jugáis
juega	juegan

When you use **jugar** with the name of a sport, use **jugar a + sport.**

The Verbs saber and conocer

Both **saber** and **conocer** mean to know and have irregular **yo** forms in the present tense.

saber	*to know*
sé	sabemos
sabes	sabéis
sabe	saben

conocer	*to know*
conozco	conocemos
conoces	conocéis
conoce	conocen

- Use **saber** to talk about factual information you know. You can also use **saber** + **infinitive** to say that you know how to do something.

- Use **conocer** when you want to say that you are familiar with a person or place. You also use **conocer** to talk about meeting someone for the first time.

Practice Spanish with Holt McDougal Apps!

Repaso de la lección

¡LLEGADA!

Now you can
- talk about sports
- talk about whom you know
- talk about what you know

Using
- the verb **jugar**
- the verbs **saber** and **conocer**
- the personal **a**

To review
- the verb **jugar** p. 307
- the verbs **saber** and **conocer** p. 312
- the personal **a** p. 313

AUDIO

1 | Listen and understand

Escucha una entrevista entre Tina y Sergio Martínez, un atleta famoso. Luego escoge la respuesta correcta. *(Listen as Tina interviews the famous athlete Sergio Martínez. Then choose the correct answer.)*

1. Sergio es jugador de...
   a. fútbol americano.
   b. béisbol.

2. También Sergio sabe jugar...
   a. al voleibol.
   b. al tenis.

3. Sergio dice que el fútbol americano es un poco...
   a. aburrido.
   b. peligroso.

4. Sergio no conoce a...
   a. muchos de sus aficionados.
   b. muchos jugadores.

5. Sergio...
   a. corre mucho.
   b. nada mucho.

6. Sergio sabe...
   a. patinar en línea.
   b. dibujar bien.

To review
- the verb **jugar** p. 307

2 | Talk about sports

Escribe a qué juegan estas personas y qué artículos usan. *(Write what sports these people play and what equipment they use.)*

modelo: Adriana
Adriana juega al béisbol con un bate.

1. tú

2. Horacio y Mercedes

3. Santiago

4. nosotros

5. yo

6. ustedes

To review
• the verbs **saber** and **conocer** p. 312

3 | Talk about whom and what you know

Completa el correo electrónico con la forma correcta de **saber** o **conocer**.
*(Complete the e-mail message with the correct form of **saber** or **conocer**.)*

```
Hola, Norma.
Yo no  1.  qué voy a hacer el sábado. Quiero jugar al
tenis. Yo  2.  a una chica que juega muy bien. Se
llama Ana. ¿Y tú? ¿  3.  jugar al tenis? ¿Por qué no
jugamos el sábado con Ana? Nosotras  4.  un parque
con muchas canchas. ¿Tú  5.  el Parque Miraflores?
Está cerca de mi casa. ¿Tú  6.  dónde está la calle
Olmeda? Allí está el parque. Hablamos esta noche.
Hasta luego,
Estela
```

To review
• the personal **a** p. 313

4 | Talk about sports

Escribe oraciones para describir la importancia de los deportes en tu vida diaria. Usa la **a** personal si es necesario. *(Write sentences describing the importance of sports in your daily life. Use the personal **a**, if needed.)*

modelo: ver / mis atletas favoritos en la televisión
(No) Veo a mis atletas favoritos en la televisión.

1. comprender / las reglas de muchos deportes
2. invitar / mis amigos a los partidos de fútbol americano
3. practicar / dos o tres deportes
4. mirar / muchos deportes en la televisión
5. ayudar / mis amigos a aprender las reglas de fútbol
6. conocer / muchos jugadores de mi equipo favorito

To review
• **El deporte nacional** p. 299
• **Altar de la Patria** p. 299
• Comparación cultural pp. 308, 314

5 | Dominican Republic and Venezuela

Comparación cultural

Answer these culture questions.

1. When is professional baseball played in the Dominican Republic?
2. What does the **Altar de la Patria** monument commemorate?
3. What is the **Serie del Caribe**? Which countries participate?
4. What is featured in Juan Medina's painting *Vendedora de flores*?

Más práctica   Cuaderno *pp. 257–268*   Cuaderno para hispanohablantes *pp. 259–268*

Get Help Online my.hrw.com

República Dominicana

Lección **2**

Tema:

La salud

**¡AVANZA!** **In this lesson you will learn to**
- talk about parts of the body
- make excuses
- say what you did
- talk about staying healthy

using
- the verb **doler**
- preterite of **-ar** verbs
- preterite of **-car, -gar, -zar** verbs

♻ *¿Recuerdas?*
- **gustar** with nouns
- stem-changing verbs: **o → ue**
- telling time

Comparación cultural

In this lesson you will learn about
- artist Amaya Salazar and a merengue festival
- gestures and sayings
- famous athletes and outdoor sports in the Dominican Republic, Honduras, and Venezuela

Compara con tu mundo

These teens are playing on a beach in the Dominican Republic. Beaches are popular places to do a variety of activities, from surfing to a simple game of catch. *What outdoor activities do you like to do to stay healthy?*

¿Qué ves?

Mira la foto
¿Hace frío?

¿Llevan camisas o camisetas los dos chicos?

¿Qué hacen Isabel y Mario?

Un día en la Playa Caribe
Juan Dolio, República Dominicana

�֍ Presentación de VOCABULARIO

¡AVANZA! **Goal:** Learn about what Mario and Isabel do to stay healthy. Then use what you have learned to talk about parts of the body. *Actividades 1–2*

VIDEO
DVD

AUDIO

A Soy Isabel. En **la playa** Mario y yo siempre usamos **bloqueador de sol**. Si no lo usamos, **tomar el sol** puede ser malo para **la piel**.

la playa

el mar

el bloqueador
de sol

tomar el sol

B En la República Dominicana hay muchas actividades que son buenas para **la salud**. Yo **camino**, pero también puedes **hacer esquí acuático** o **bucear**. A Mario le gusta **levantar pesas**.

caminar

hacer esquí
acuático

bucear

levantar pesas

Más vocabulario

anoche *last night*
ayer *yesterday*
comenzar *to begin*
terminar *to end*
Lo siento. *I'm sorry.*
¿Qué hiciste (tú)? *What did you do?*
¿Qué hicieron ustedes? *What did you do?*

Expansión de vocabulario p. R7

C Si hacemos actividades en la playa, usamos bloqueador de sol en todo **el cuerpo: la nariz, las orejas, los brazos, las piernas...**

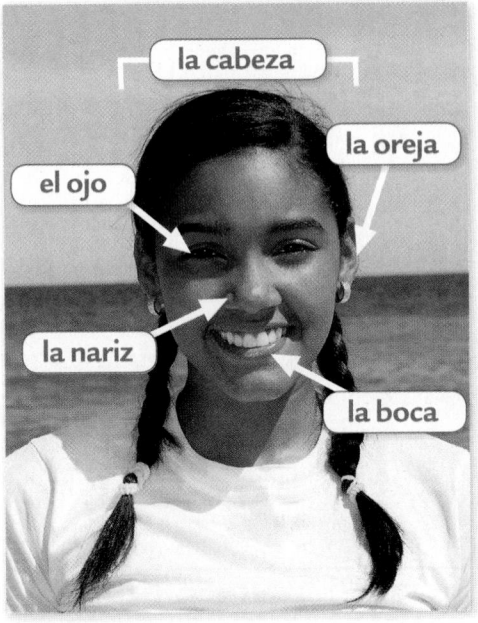

la cabeza
la oreja
el ojo
la nariz
la boca

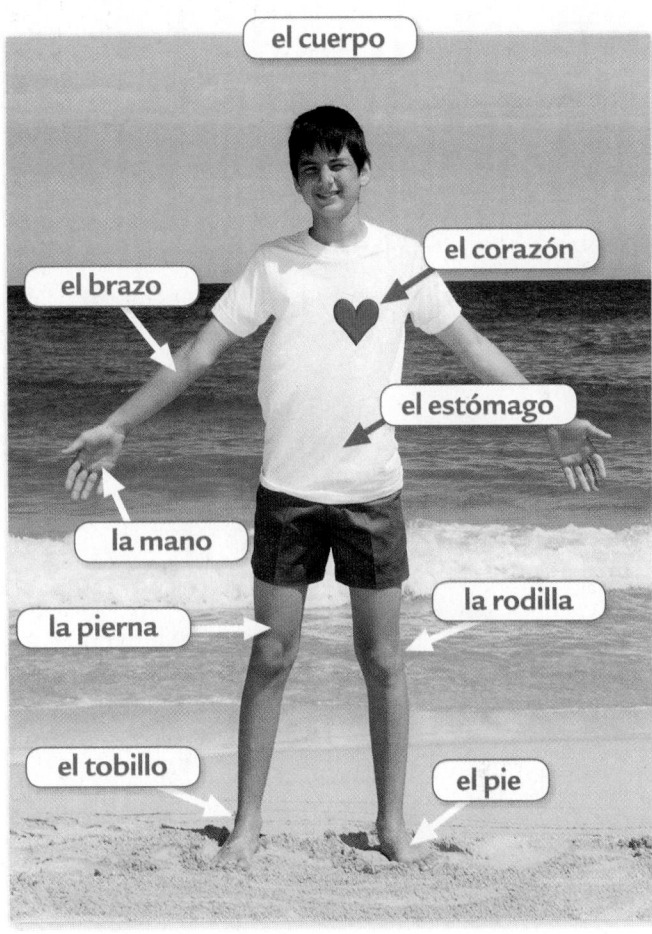

el cuerpo
el brazo
el corazón
el estómago
la mano
la rodilla
la pierna
el tobillo
el pie

D Mario es **fuerte** pero ahora está **herido. Le duele** mucho **el tobillo.**

fuerte

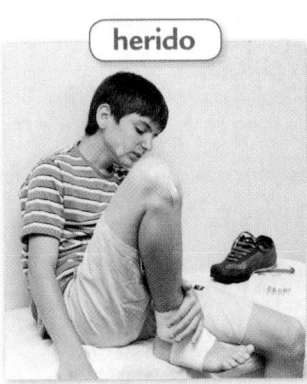

herido

E Yo soy muy **sana** pero de vez en cuando estoy **enferma.**

sana

enferma

@HOMETUTOR
my.hrw.com
Interactive
Flashcards

¡A responder!   Escuchar

Levántate. Escucha al atleta profesional hablar de lo que le duele. Señala las partes del cuerpo que menciona. *(Stand up. Point to each part of the body as it is mentioned.)*

❊ Práctica de VOCABULARIO

1 | Las partes del cuerpo

Escribir
Hablar

Identifica las partes del cuerpo. *(Identify the body parts.)*

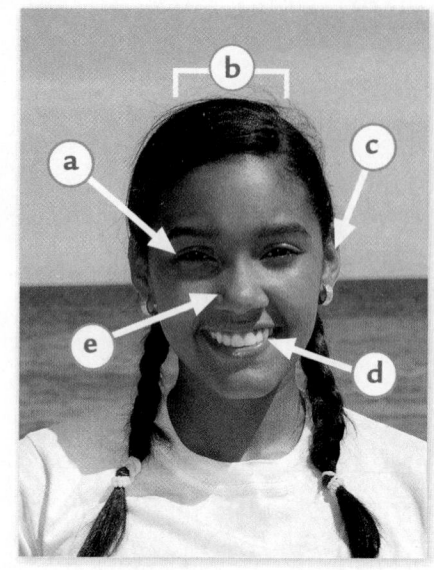

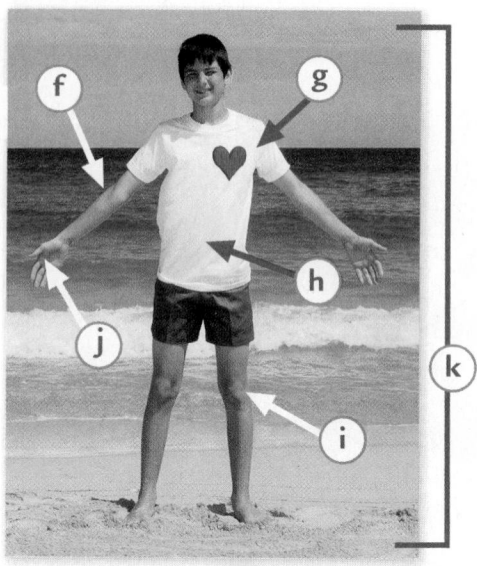

2 | ¿Qué usas?

Escribir
Hablar

Identifica qué partes del cuerpo usas cuando haces estas actividades.
(Tell what parts of the body you use to do these activities.)

la boca	las manos	los ojos	los pies
los brazos	la cabeza	las piernas	¿ ?

modelo: nadar
      Cuando nado, uso los brazos, las piernas, las manos y los pies.

1. caminar

2. comer

3. bucear

4. dibujar

5. levantar pesas

6. patinar

7. jugar al fútbol

8. bailar

9. mirar la televisión

10. hacer esquí acuático

Expansión
Write a description of an alien. Read your description to a partner, who will draw it.

Más práctica   Cuaderno *pp. 269–271*   Cuaderno para hispanohablantes *pp. 269–272*

Get Help Online
my.hrw.com

**PARA
Y
PIENSA**

Did you get it?
   1. Name three parts of your face.
   2. Name three parts of your leg.

✤VOCABULARIO en contexto

¡AVANZA! **Goal:** Notice the words Isabel and Mario use to talk about what happens to Mario. Then use **doler** to say what hurts and make excuses. *Actividades 3–4*

♻ *¿Recuerdas?* **gustar** with nouns p. 145, stem-changing verbs:
o → ue p. 223

Telehistoria escena 1

@HOMETUTOR **View, Read**
my.hrw.com **and Record**

STRATEGIES

Cuando lees
Draw and label Draw an outline of a body. Label the body parts that Mario and Isabel mention in this scene. Which others do you know?

Cuando escuchas
Listen for the action This scene has a lot of action. Listen to what happens to Mario. What does Isabel do and say in response? Will they go to their planned destination?

VIDEO
DVD

AUDIO

Mario

Isabel

Mario and Isabel get on their bicycles.

Mario: ¡Tenemos que ser los primeros aficionados en el estadio!

Isabel: Mario, ¿sabes montar en bicicleta?

Mario: Sí, sí, ¡es fácil!

Isabel: ¡Necesitas el casco!

Mario wobbles on his bicycle and crashes into a fruit cart.

Mario: ¡No estoy herido!

Isabel: Pero, ¿y el tobillo? ¿Y la pierna?

Mario: Soy fuerte y sano...

Isabel: Y la cabeza, ¿Mario? ¡Tienes la piel muy roja! ¡La nariz! Abre la boca. ¿Puedes caminar?

Mario: Sí. Me duele un poco el pie... pero puedo caminar.

Isabel: No, no debes caminar.

Mario: Pero... ¡Y Trini Salgado!

Isabel: ¿Trini Salgado? ¡Un autógrafo no es importante! Vamos... **Continuará...** p. 334

También se dice

República Dominicana
Mario uses the common phrase **es fácil** to describe riding a bike. In other Spanish-speaking countries you might hear:
• **Puerto Rico** **es un guame**
• **España** **está tirado**
• **muchos países** **es pan comido, es coser y cantar**

3 | Comprensión del episodio   Un accidente

Escuchar
Leer

Combina las frases para describir el episodio. *(Match phrases from the two columns to form sentences about the episode.)*

1. Van en bicicleta porque
2. Mario piensa que
3. Mario no debe caminar
4. Mario tiene
5. La salud de Mario es

  a. la piel muy roja.
  b. más importante que un autógrafo.
  c. montar en bicicleta es fácil.
  d. quieren ser los primeros en el estadio.
  e. porque está herido.

Nota gramatical   ♻ *¿Recuerdas?* **gustar** with nouns p. 145

When you want to say what hurts, use **doler (ue).** This verb functions like **gustar.**

agrees

Me duele la cabeza. *My head hurts.*

agrees

Le duelen los brazos. *His arms hurt.*

With **doler,** you use a definite article with parts of the body.

---

4 | ¿Quieres ir a la playa?   ♻ *¿Recuerdas?* Stem-changing verbs: **o → ue** p. 223

Hablar

Pregúntale a otro(a) estudiante si quiere hacer estas actividades en la playa. Él o ella va a decir que no puede porque le duele una parte del cuerpo. *(Ask a partner if he or she wants to do these activities. Your partner will decline, saying something hurts.)*

A ¿Quieres tomar el sol en la playa?

B Lo siento, pero no puedo. Me duele la piel.

1.
2.
3.
4.
5.
6.

Expansión
With a partner, exchange invitations to do something via e-mail or text. Decline the invitations politely and explain that something hurts.

🌐 **Get Help Online**
my.hrw.com

PARA Y PIENSA

Did you get it?   Complete each sentence based on the Telehistoria with the correct form of **doler.**

1. A Mario _____ la cabeza.
2. También a él _____ el pie y la pierna.

Presentación de GRAMÁTICA

Goal: Learn how to form the preterite of **-ar** verbs. Then practice using the verbs to say what you did and talk about staying healthy. *Actividades 5–8*

♻ *¿Recuerdas?* Telling time p. 90

English Grammar Connection: The **preterite** is a tense used to express an action completed at a definite time in the past. This tense is usually referred to as the past tense in English. In English, regular verbs in the past tense end in *-ed*.

You **lifted** weights yesterday.   Usted **levantó** pesas ayer.

↑   ↑

past tense   **preterite**

Preterite of Regular -ar Verbs

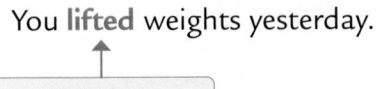

ANIMATED GRAMMAR
my.hrw.com

Use the preterite tense to talk about actions completed in the past. How do you form the **preterite** of regular **-ar** verbs?

Here's how: To form the **preterite** of a regular **-ar** verb, add the appropriate preterite ending to the verb's stem.

nadar	to swim
nadé	**nad**amos
nadaste	**nad**asteis
nadó	**nad**aron

Notice that the **yo** and **usted/él/ella** forms have an accent over the final vowel.

Nadé en el mar.   Mariana **patin**ó.
I swam in the sea.   *Mariana skated.*

The **nosotros(as)** form is the same in the preterite as in the present tense. Use the context to determine the tense of the verb

Caminamos en la playa anoche.
We walked on the beach last night.

Más práctica
Cuaderno *pp. 272–274*
Cuaderno para hispanohablantes *pp. 273–275*

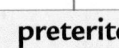 **@HOMETUTOR** my.hrw.com
Leveled Practice
🌐 Conjuguemos.com

Práctica de GRAMÁTICA

5 | ¿Cuándo terminaron? ♻ ¿Recuerdas? Telling time p. 90

Escribir
Hablar

Ayer Isabel y otros caminaron. ¿Qué dice Isabel sobre cuándo terminaron?
(Indicate when these people finished their walks.)

> **11:30** modelo: mi madre
> Mi madre terminó a las once y media.

1. yo **10:45**

2. Mario y un amigo **12:20**

3. tú **1:15**

4. Carlota **9:50**

5. ustedes **10:10**

6. nosotros **3:40**

7. mis hermanas **1:55**

8. mi padre **9:30**

6 | Una playa en la República Dominicana

Leer
Escribir

Fernando y su familia fueron a la playa ayer. Completa su descripción de lo que hicieron. Escribe la forma apropiada en el pretérito del verbo correcto entre paréntesis. *(Write the appropriate preterite form of the correct verb in parentheses.)*

Ayer mi familia y yo **1.** (decorar / pasar) un rato en la playa de Boca Chica. Mis padres **2.** (invitar / celebrar) a mis abuelos también. Mi madre **3.** (trabajar / preparar) sándwiches y yo **4.** (limpiar / ayudar) con las bebidas. Mis hermanos **5.** (usar / bucear) en el mar y yo **6.** (tomar / usar) el sol. Después, toda la familia **7.** (nadar / ganar). Y tú, ¿ **8.** (caminar / nadar) en el mar ayer?

> **Expansión**
> Write a paragraph about a trip you and someone you know took to the beach.

Comparación cultural

Bosque escondido (2005), Amaya Salazar

La artista y su estilo

How do artists reflect a distinctive style in their painting? Bright pastel colors, glowing light, and abstract images that reveal hidden figures are common elements in Amaya Salazar's work. This painter from the **Dominican Republic** is also a sculptor and muralist. Many consider her painting to have a magical or dreamlike quality. What images can you find hidden in this painting of a tropical forest?

Compara con tu mundo *How would you describe the style, colors, and images used by your favorite artist? How does his or her work compare to that of Amaya Salazar?*

7 | ¿Lo hiciste?

Hablar

Habla con otro(a) estudiante sobre lo que hiciste la semana pasada.
(Talk about what activities you did last week.)

A ¿Montaste en bicicleta?

B Sí, monté en bicicleta en el parque. (No, no monté en bicicleta.)

1.

2.

3.

4.

5.

6.

Expansión
Create a Venn diagram to compare your answers with your partner's.

8 | Durante el fin de semana

Hablar

Trabaja en un grupo de tres. Habla de lo que hicieron el fin de semana pasado. *(In a group of three, talk about what you did last weekend.)*

comprar un almuerzo sano   caminar en la playa
estudiar   mirar la televisión
levantar pesas   trabajar
nadar en una piscina   ¿ ?

A ¿Compraron ustedes un almuerzo sano?

B Sí, compré una ensalada.

C No, mis amigos y yo compramos papas fritas.

Más práctica Cuaderno *pp. 272–274*   Cuaderno para hispanohablantes *pp. 273–275*

Get Help Online
my.hrw.com

PARA Y PIENSA

Did you get it? Complete each sentence with the preterite form of the verb in parentheses.

1. Ayer mis amigos y yo _____ en el mar. (bucear)
2. Tú _____ el sol mucho y ahora tu piel está roja. (tomar)
3. José y Ricardo _____ pesas para ser más fuertes. (levantar)

❖GRAMÁTICA en contexto

¡AVANZA! **Goal:** Pay attention to how Mario and Isabel use the preterite to tell the doctor about Mario's accident. Then use the preterite of regular **-ar** verbs to talk about past actions. *Actividades 9–11*

Telehistoria escena 2

@**HOMETUTOR** View, Read
my.hrw.com and Record

STRATEGIES

Cuando lees
Pay attention to register Read the conversation. Does the doctor use "usted" or "tú" when addressing Mario? Why? Would it be different if the patient were older?

Cuando escuchas
Listen for incomplete sentences Listen for the sentence that Mario starts, but does not complete. Finish his sentence using previous knowledge gained in scene 1.

VIDEO
DVD

AUDIO

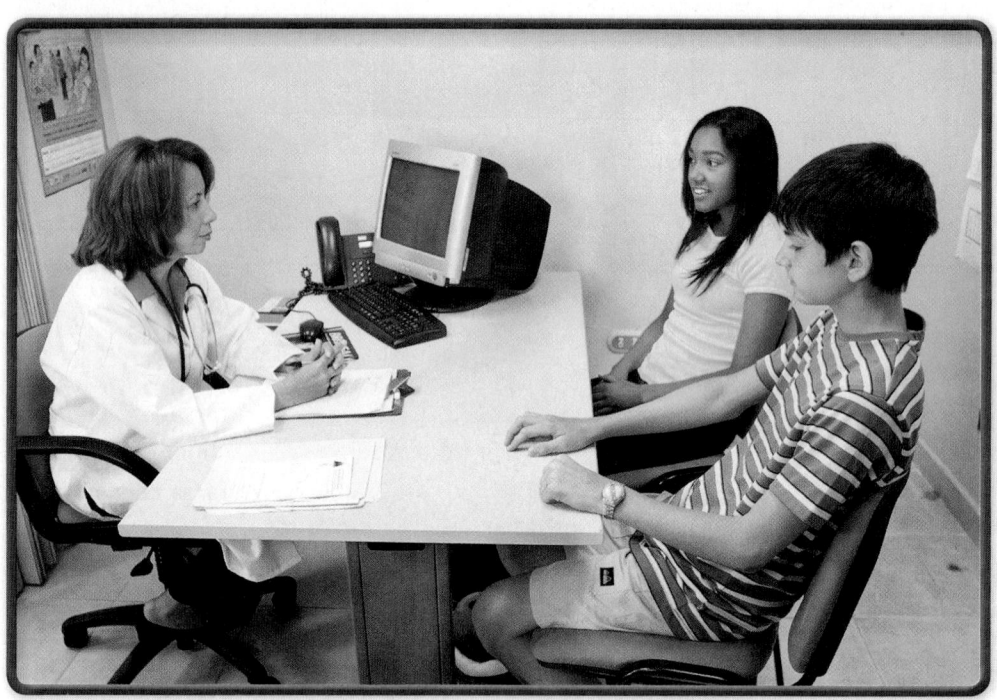

Isabel takes Mario to the doctor's office.

Doctora: ¿Mario Álvarez? ¿Está usted enfermo?

Isabel: Le duelen la pierna y la cabeza. Lo ayudé a caminar.

Doctora: *(to Mario)* ¿Qué hiciste?

Isabel: Pues, montó en su bicicleta... ¡cerca de unas frutas!

Mario: Monté en mi bicicleta...

Doctora: ¿Llevaste un casco?

Isabel: Sí, ¡pero Mario piensa que es Lance Armstrong!

Mario: Isabel, ¡el señor de las frutas caminó delante de mi bicicleta!

Isabel: Y allí... ¡Pum!

Doctora: Mario, ¿sabes montar en bicicleta?

Mario: Sí, es fácil.

Doctora: ¿Te gustó?

Mario: Ahora estoy herido, ¡pero me gustó!

Doctora: *(to Isabel)* Para la salud de tu amigo, no más bicicletas, ¡por favor! **Continuará...** p. 339

9 Comprensión del episodio Hablan con la doctora

Escuchar
Leer

Indica si estas oraciones son ciertas o falsas según el episodio. Corrige las oraciones falsas. *(Tell whether these sentences are true or false. Correct the false statements.)*

1. A Mario le duelen la cabeza y los brazos.

2. El señor de las frutas caminó detrás de Mario.

3. Mario llevó casco.

4. La doctora piensa que Mario es Lance Armstrong.

5. A Mario le gustó montar en bicicleta.

6. Ahora Isabel está herida.

10 De vacaciones con tu familia

Escribir

Estás de vacaciones en la playa con tu familia y le escribes una tarjeta postal a un(a) amigo(a). Describe lo que hicieron ayer. *(Write a postcard about what you and your family did yesterday on vacation at the beach.)*

modelo:

Playa Caribe

¡Hola! ¡Estamos en la República Dominicana!

Ayer yo buceé en el mar. Mi hermana tomó el sol ...

11 ¿Qué hicieron tú y tus amigos?

Escribir
Hablar

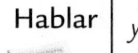

Describe lo que tú y tus amigos hicieron recientemente. *(Describe what you and your friends did recently.)*

1. ¿Alquilaron ustedes un DVD interesante?

2. ¿Con quién hablaste por teléfono ayer?

3. ¿Qué hiciste tú en la biblioteca ayer?

4. ¿Dónde escucharon ustedes buena música?

5. ¿Qué miraste en la televisión anoche?

6. ¿Qué hicieron ustedes en el centro comercial?

Expansión
Write three original questions and ask them to a partner.

Get Help Online
my.hrw.com

PARA Y PIENSA

Did you get it? Create sentences using each verb in the preterite tense.
1. Isabel y Mario / llevar cascos
2. Mario / no montar en bicicleta muy bien
3. El señor de las frutas / caminar delante de Mario

❧ Presentación de GRAMÁTICA

English Grammar Connection: The spelling of some verbs in English changes in the past tense when *-ed* is added: for example, *admit → admitted, stop → stopped, picnic → picnicked.* Spanish also has verbs that change their spelling in the preterite.

Preterite of -car, -gar, -zar Verbs

ANIMATED GRAMMAR
my.hrw.com

There is a spelling change in the preterite of regular verbs that end in **-car, -gar,** or **-zar.** How do you write the verb forms that have a change in spelling?

Here's how:

Regular verbs that end in **-car, -gar,** or **-zar** have a spelling change in the **yo** form of the preterite. This change allows these words to maintain their original sound.

bus**c**ar	c	becomes →	**qu**	(yo) bus**qu**é
ju**g**ar	g	becomes →	**gu**	(yo) ju**gu**é
almor**z**ar	z	becomes →	**c**	(yo) almor**c**é

Busqu**é** el bloqueador de sol. Él **bus**có las toallas.
*I **looked for** the sunscreen. He **looked for** the towels.*

Jugu**é** al béisbol. Ellas **ju**garon al fútbol.
*I **played** baseball. They **played** soccer.*

Almorcé a la una. ¿A qué hora **almor**zaste tú?
*I **ate lunch** at one o'clock. What time **did you eat lunch**?*

Más práctica
Cuaderno *pp. 275–277*
Cuaderno para hispanohablantes *pp. 276–279*

@HOMETUTOR my.hrw.com
Leveled Practice
Conjuguemos.com

Práctica de GRAMÁTICA

12 | La agenda de Isabel

Escribir

Mira la agenda de Isabel y completa lo que dice ella sobre las actividades de la semana pasada. Sigue el modelo. *(Complete what Isabel says she did last week. Follow the model.)*

> modelo: «_____ a las cuatro el martes.»
> «Practiqué el piano a las cuatro el martes.»

lunes	martes	miércoles	jueves	viernes	sábado
3:00 jugar al béisbol	3:30 pagar las entradas	3:00 tocar la guitarra con Roberto	5:00 practicar el piano	4:00 practicar el piano	10:00 nadar
5:00 practicar el piano	4:00 practicar el piano	5:00 buscar un vestido nuevo	7:00 estudiar	8:00 llegar a la fiesta	11:00 limpiar la casa
8:00 estudiar	7:00 comenzar un libro nuevo		9:00 sacar la basura		12:30 practicar el piano
					1:00 almorzar con Luz María
					7:30 alquilar un DVD

domingo
3:00 jugar al béisbol
5:00 practicar el piano
8:00 estudiar

1. «_____ a la una el sábado.»
2. «_____ a las ocho el viernes.»
3. «_____ a las siete el martes.»
4. «_____ a las tres y media el martes.»
5. «_____ a las tres el miércoles.»
6. «_____ a las cinco el miércoles.»
7. «_____ a las tres el domingo.»
8. «_____ a las nueve el jueves.»

13 | Muchas preguntas

**Escuchar
Escribir**

Mario quiere saber lo que hiciste ayer. Escucha sus preguntas y escribe tus respuestas. *(Listen to Mario's questions and then write your answers.)*

> modelo: ¿Pagaste el almuerzo?
> Sí, pagué el almuerzo. (No, no pagué el almuerzo.)

> **Expansión**
> Explain why, where, and/or with whom you did these activities.

AUDIO

Pronunciación   La letra g con e, i

Before **e** and **i**, the **g** in Spanish is pronounced like the Spanish **j,** or **jota.**

Listen and repeat.

ge	→	inteligente	Argentina	Jorge	general
gi	→	gimnasio	digital	página	Sergio

Jorge corre en el gimnasio.   **Regina tiene una cámara digital.**

14 | Me duele...

Hablar

Pregúntale a otro(a) estudiante por qué no hizo estas cosas hoy. Él o ella va a decir que le duele una parte del cuerpo. *(Ask a partner why he or she didn't do these things today. Your partner will answer by saying something hurts.)*

A ¿Por qué no sacaste una buena nota?

B No saqué una buena nota porque me duele la cabeza.

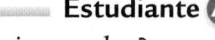

modelo: sacar una buena nota

Estudiante A
1. jugar al ¿?
2. practicar deportes
3. almorzar mucha comida
4. tocar la guitarra
5. llegar temprano a clase
6. ¿?

Estudiante B
los pies
el estómago
las piernas
la mano
la cabeza
¿?

Expansión
Tell about activities you can't do when something hurts.

15 | Un día en el festival

Escribir

Comparación cultural

El Festival del Merengue

How do music and dance reflect the culture of a country? Merengue is a lively style of music and dance that many consider a symbol of the **Dominican Republic.** Musicians use instruments such as the *güiro,* maracas, accordion, saxophone, and drums to play its characteristic rhythm. The Festival del Merengue takes place every summer in Santo Domingo. The ten-day event includes music, parades, arts and crafts fairs, cart races, and a wide variety of Dominican foods.

El Festival del Merengue

Compara con tu mundo *Do you know of any similar festivals in your area?*

Fuiste al Festival del Merengue. Describe el día. *(Describe your day at the festival.)*

pistas: llegar, tocar, almorzar, comenzar, escuchar, bailar

modelo: El festival comenzó a las diez...

Más práctica   Cuaderno *pp. 275–277*   Cuaderno para hispanohablantes *pp. 276–279*

Get Help Online
my.hrw.com

PARA Y PIENSA

Did you get it? Complete each sentence with the preterite form of the appropriate verb: **comenzar, jugar, llegar,** or **practicar.**
1. Yo _____ a casa temprano.
2. ¿Ustedes _____ al tenis ayer?
3. El partido _____ a las siete.
4. Yo _____ deportes anoche.

Todo junto

Telehistoria completa

@**HOMETUTOR** my.hrw.com View, Read and Record

STRATEGIES

Cuando lees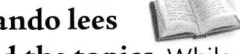
Find the topics While reading, find at least two or three topics in this scene. One is the doctor's suggestions for Mario's health. What other topics can you identify?

Cuando escuchas
Listen for the implied meaning Listen for the unstated meaning to answer these questions: Will Mario ever get Trini's autograph? Is Mario strong and healthy now?

Escena 1 *Resumen*
Mario está herido y no puede ir con Isabel al estadio para ver a Trini Salgado.

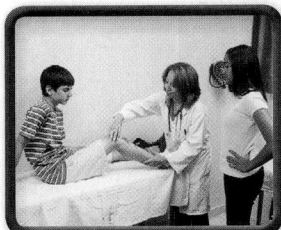

Escena 2 *Resumen*
Isabel ayuda a Mario a caminar. A él le duelen la pierna y la cabeza. Ellos hablan con una doctora.

Escena 3

VIDEO DVD

AUDIO

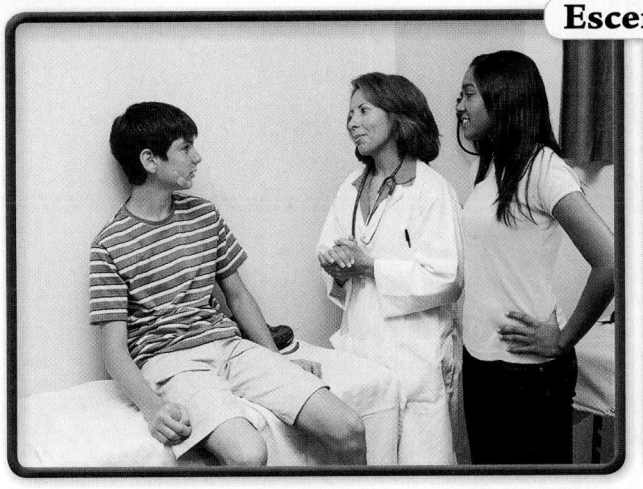

Doctora: El tobillo está bien. ¿Te duele la rodilla?

Mario: No. *(The doctor touches Mario's knee, and he yelps.)* Un poco.

Doctora: No puedes jugar al fútbol, y no puedes jugar al béisbol por cuatro semanas.

Mario: ¿Puedo levantar pesas?

Doctora: Levantar pesas, sí, con los brazos. Con las piernas, no...

Isabel: Muchas gracias, doctora. Adiós.
The doctor leaves. Mario turns to Isabel.

Mario: ¡Ay, el autógrafo para Alicia! Comencé a...

Isabel: Sí, Mario, lo siento. Comenzaste a buscar a Trini, pero ¿qué podemos hacer? *(They stand to leave.)*

Isabel: ¿Vamos a la playa mañana? El mar es bueno para los enfermos.

Mario: ¡No estoy enfermo!

16 | Comprensión de los episodios   ¡A completar!

Completa las oraciones para describir lo que pasó en los episodios.
(Complete the sentences.)

1. Isabel y Mario quieren ser los primeros...
2. Mario no está enfermo, pero...
3. Isabel y Mario buscaron a Trini Salgado porque...
4. El señor de las frutas...
5. A Mario le duele la rodilla y no puede...
6. Mario puede levantar pesas, pero...

17 | Comprensión de los episodios   ¿Qué pasó?

Contesta las preguntas sobre los episodios. *(Answer the questions.)*

1. ¿Qué buscaron Isabel y Mario?
2. ¿Qué llevó Mario?
3. ¿Le gustó a Mario montar en bicicleta?
4. ¿Qué le duele a Mario?

18 | ¿Qué hiciste para la salud?

Hablar

STRATEGY Hablar

Draw a Venn diagram for similarities and differences While talking,
make a Venn diagram. In one circle list healthy things *you* did that your partner did
not. In the other circle, list what *your partner* did that you did not. In the overlap,
list what *you both* did.

Habla con otro(a) estudiante sobre las actividades sanas que hiciste el mes
pasado. Explícale qué beneficios tienen, dónde las hiciste y con quién. *(Talk
with a partner about the healthy activities you did last month. Explain what benefits the activities have
for your health, where you did them, and with whom.)*

caminar	levantar pesas
jugar al ¿ ?	nadar
practicar deportes	almorzar bien

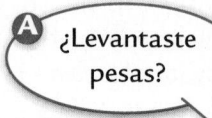 **A** ¿Levantaste pesas?

B Sí, levanté pesas porque es bueno para los brazos. Levanté pesas en el gimnasio con mi amigo Fernando...

19 | Integración

Leer
Escuchar
Hablar

Lee el artículo y escucha la entrevista. Compara lo que tú hiciste durante la semana para la salud con lo que estas personas hicieron. Decide si eres tan sano(a) como ellos. *(Compare what you did last week to stay healthy to what these people did.)*

Fuente 1 Artículo del periódico

Ricardo, ¿qué hiciste para ganar?

Ricardo Núñez es el campeón olímpico de natación. Él nos explicó cómo ganó el año pasado. Es un atleta muy trabajador. «Yo soy una persona muy seria. Practico todos los días. Este fin de semana nadé por dos horas el sábado y el domingo levanté pesas en el gimnasio por tres horas». Para él, la comida es muy importante. «Ayer preparé un desayuno muy sano... cereal, jugo de naranja y pan. Hoy almorcé una ensalada y sopa de pollo». Núñez también tiene que descansar. «También descanso. Ayer alquilé una película muy buena... una película de natación».

Fuente 2 Entrevista de radio

Listen and take notes
- ¿Qué deportes practicó la chica?
- ¿Qué almorzó?

modelo: Durante la semana yo...

20 | Un poema diamante

Escribir

Escribe un poema diamante sobre algo que te hace sentir sano(a). *(Write a diamond poem about something that makes you feel healthy.)*

Para organizarte: **modelo:**
- *el nombre del lugar o de la actividad* ——————→ la playa
- *una descripción* ————————————→ agua bonita
- *tres cosas que hiciste* ———————→ tomé el sol, caminé, miré el agua
- *otra descripción* ——————————→ agua tranquila
- *otro nombre* ————————————→ el mar Caribe

Writing Criteria	Excellent	Good	Needs Work
Content	Your poem includes most of the required elements.	Your poem includes some of the required elements.	Your poem includes few of the required elements.
Communication	Most of your poem is organized and easy to follow.	Parts of your poem are organized and easy to follow.	Your poem is disorganized and hard to follow.
Accuracy	Your poem has few mistakes in grammar and vocabulary.	Your poem has some mistakes in grammar and vocabulary.	Your poem has many mistakes in grammar and vocabulary.

Más práctica   Cuaderno *pp. 278–279*   Cuaderno para hispanohablantes *pp. 280–281*

Get Help Online
my.hrw.com

PARA Y PIENSA

Did you get it? Complete each sentence based on the Telehistoria with the preterite form of the verb in parentheses.
1. Mario _____ a buscar a Trini. (comenzar)
2. Isabel y Mario no la _____ . (encontrar)

Lectura cultural

¡AVANZA!

Goal: Read about two world-class athletes from the Dominican Republic and Venezuela. Then compare them and talk about the sports you play.

Comparación cultural

AUDIO

Dos atletas de alta velocidad

STRATEGY Leer
Chart the data In a chart, record the following data for Félix and for Daniela.

	país	deporte	medallas	año(s) que ganó
Félix				
Daniela				

Latinoamérica tiene una gran historia de deportes y de atletas ganadores. Algunos [1] practican su deporte día y noche, en las calles y pistas [2] que están muy lejos de los aficionados y cámaras de televisión.

Félix Sánchez es uno de los atletas más dominantes en los 400 metros de vallas [3]. Estadounidense de nacimiento, Sánchez decidió representar a la República Dominicana, el país de sus padres, en competiciones internacionales. En los Juegos Olímpicos del 2000 en Sydney, Australia, Félix Sánchez llegó en cuarto lugar. Para tener motivación, Sánchez prometió [4] llevar el brazalete que llevó en Sydney hasta [5] ganar una medalla de

---

[1] Some [2] tracks [3] hurdles [4] promised [5] until

República Dominicana

Félix Sánchez con la bandera dominicana

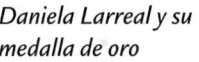

oro[6]. Lo llevó por cuatro años. En los Juegos Olímpicos del 2004, ganó la primera medalla de oro para la República Dominicana y se hizo[7] héroe nacional. Después de ganar, el triunfante Sánchez caminó delante de los aficionados con la bandera[8] dominicana en las manos.

Muchas personas montan en bicicleta pero pocos van tan rápido como la ciclista venezolana Daniela Larreal. Ella ganó tres medallas de oro en los Juegos Bolivarianos en el 2001. En el 2003, se hizo campeona de la Copa Mundial[9] de Ciclismo de Pista. En agosto del 2005, ella ganó otra medalla de oro en los Juegos Bolivarianos. Llegó a los 500 metros con un tiempo de 35,56 segundos. «Qué rico es volver a estar en unos Bolivarianos y ganar nuevamente otra medalla», comentó la campeona.

Daniela Larreal y su medalla de oro

---

[6] gold   [7] became   [8] flag   [9] **Copa...** World Cup

PARA Y PIENSA

¿Comprendiste?
1. ¿Qué deporte practica Félix Sánchez? ¿Y Daniela Larreal?
2. ¿Qué ganó Sánchez? ¿Y Larreal?
3. Haz una comparación de los dos atletas. ¿Qué hacen? ¿De dónde son?

¿Y tú?
¿Practicas un deporte? ¿Cuál? ¿Ganaste medallas?

❖ Proyectos culturales

Gestos y refranes

How can gestures and proverbs facilitate communication? When you speak, you communicate with more than just words. When you move your hands, face, or body while you speak, you are using gestures. You can also use gestures to communicate without words. Some gestures are universally understood, yet others are only understood within one language or cultural group. **Refranes,** or proverbs, are short, well-known sayings that express a basic truth or idea. Like gestures, some **refranes** are unique to one language, while others are similar in many languages.

❖ Proyecto ① Los gestos

With a partner, practice using gestures common in Spanish-speaking countries.

Instructions
1. Study the photos that illustrate some of the gestures used in Spanish-speaking countries.
2. Make one of the gestures on the page and have your partner say its meaning aloud. Take turns.

¡En absoluto!

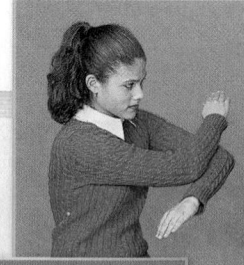

¡En absoluto!
To show "No way!" start with your forearms crossed. Uncross your arms quickly and straighten them completely.

¡Qué loco!
To show that someone is being silly, place your finger against your temple and rotate your wrist back and forth.

¡Mucha gente!
To show that a place is crowded with people, bunch the fingers of both your hands together and then straighten your fingers. Repeat.

¡Ojo!
To show "Watch out!" use your finger to point to your eye. Tug lightly on the skin below your eye.

❖ Proyecto ② Los refranes

Illustrate one of these **refranes** and explain what it means.
1. El que busca, encuentra.
2. Quien va a Sevilla pierde su silla.
3. Donde una puerta se cierra, otra se abre.

Materials for illustrating los refranes
Colored pens or pencils
Paper

Instructions
On a piece of paper, draw the **refrán** that you selected.

❖ En tu comunidad

It is important to understand the meanings of gestures in different cultures. Why would this be especially useful in the business world?

En resumen
Vocabulario y gramática

ANiMaTeDGRaMMaR
Interactive Flashcards
my.hrw.com

Vocabulario

Talk About Staying Healthy

enfermo(a)	*sick*	levantar pesas	*to lift weights*
fuerte	*strong*	la salud	*health*
herido(a)	*hurt*	sano(a)	*healthy*

Parts of the Body

la boca	*mouth*	la nariz	*nose*
el brazo	*arm*	(*pl.* las narices)	
la cabeza	*head*	el ojo	*eye*
el corazón (*pl.* los corazones)	*heart*	la oreja	*ear*
		el pie	*foot*
el cuerpo	*body*	la piel	*skin*
el estómago	*stomach*	la pierna	*leg*
la mano	*hand*	la rodilla	*knee*
		el tobillo	*ankle*

Outdoor Activities

el bloqueador de sol	*sunscreen*	hacer esquí acuático	*to water-ski*
bucear	*to scuba-dive*	el mar	*sea*
caminar	*to walk*	la playa	*beach*
		tomar el sol	*to sunbathe*

Make Excuses

doler (ue)	*to hurt, to ache*
Lo siento.	*I'm sorry.*

Other Words and Phrases

anoche	*last night*
ayer	*yesterday*
comenzar (ie)	*to begin*
terminar	*to end*
¿Qué hiciste (tú)?	*What did you do?*
¿Qué hicieron ustedes?	*What did you do?*

Gramática

Nota gramatical: The verb **doler** p. 330

Preterite of Regular -ar Verbs

To form the **preterite** of a regular **-ar** verb, add the appropriate preterite ending to the verb's stem.

nadar to swim	
nad**é**	nad**amos**
nad**aste**	nad**asteis**
nad**ó**	nad**aron**

Preterite of -car, -gar, -zar Verbs

Regular verbs that end in **-car, -gar,** or **-zar** have a spelling change in the **yo** form of the preterite.

buscar	c	*becomes*	qu	(yo)	**busqué**
jugar	g	*becomes*	gu	(yo)	**jugué**
almorzar	z	*becomes*	c	(yo)	**almorcé**

Repaso de la lección

¡LLEGADA!

@HOMETUTOR
my.hrw.com

¡AvanzaRap!
DVD
Sing and Learn

Now you can
- talk about parts of the body
- make excuses
- say what you did
- talk about staying healthy

Using
- the verb **doler**
- preterite of regular **-ar** verbs
- preterite of **-car, -gar, -zar** verbs

To review
- preterite of regular **-ar** verbs p. 331
- preterite of **-car, -gar, -zar** verbs p. 336

AUDIO

1 | Listen and understand

Elisa describe un día en la playa. Escucha y escribe si ella hizo o no las siguientes actividades. *(Listen to Elisa's description. Then write whether or not she did the following activities.)*

modelo: usar bloqueador de sol
Elisa usó bloqueador de sol.

1. tomar el sol
2. bucear
3. caminar
4. almorzar

5. jugar al voleibol
6. descansar
7. tocar la guitarra
8. cantar

To review
- the verb **doler** p. 330

2 | Talk about parts of the body

Estas personas van a la enfermería de la escuela. Explica qué les duele.
(Explain why these people are going to the school nurse.)

modelo: Andrés
A Andrés le duele la cabeza.

 1. Esteban

 4. usted

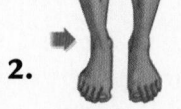 2. Amalia y Patricio

 5. nosotros

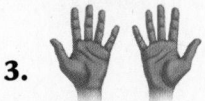 3. yo

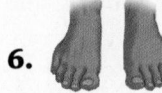 6. tú

To review
- preterite of regular **-ar** verbs p. 331

3 | Talk about staying healthy

Todas las personas en la familia de Guillermo son sanas. ¿Qué hicieron ayer? Completa el párrafo con la forma correcta del verbo apropiado. *(Complete the paragraph with the correct form of the appropriate verb.)*

preparar	patinar	levantar
bucear	montar	nadar

A mi familia y a mí nos gusta ser sanos. Ayer mi hermano Marcos y yo __1.__ pesas antes de jugar al fútbol. Mi papá __2.__ en la piscina, y mi mamá y mi tía __3.__ en el mar. Mi hermana Carlota __4.__ una ensalada para todos nosotros. Después del almuerzo, yo __5.__ en bicicleta y mis hermanos __6.__ en línea en el parque.

To review
- preterite of **-car, -gar, -zar** verbs p. 336

4 | Say what you did

Lee lo que hizo Carolina ayer y escribe si también lo hiciste tú. *(Read what Carolina did yesterday and write whether or not you did the same thing.)*

modelo: Carolina sacó la basura.
Yo también saqué la basura. (Yo no saqué la basura.)

1. Llegó tarde a la escuela.
2. Tocó la guitarra.
3. Comenzó a leer un libro.
4. Practicó deportes.
5. Jugó al voleibol.
6. Almorzó a las doce y media.
7. Pagó la cuenta en un restaurante.
8. Empezó la tarea.

To review
- Beaches p. 299
- Comparación cultural pp. 332, 338
- Lectura cultural pp. 342–343

5 | Dominican Republic and Venezuela

Comparación cultural

Answer these culture questions.

1. What are beaches in the Dominican Republic known for?
2. What are some common themes of Amaya Salazar's artwork?
3. What can you see and do at Santo Domingo's **Festival del Merengue**?
4. Where are Félix Sánchez and Daniela Larreal from and what sports do they play? What competitions have they participated in?

Get Help Online my.hrw.com

República
Dominicana

Honduras

Venezuela

AUDIO

Deportes
favoritos

Lectura y escritura

1 **Leer** Choices of favorite sports vary around the world. Read what Felipe, Gloria, and Agustín say about their favorite sports.

2 **Escribir** Using the three descriptions as models, write a short paragraph about your favorite sport.

STRATEGY **Escribir**

Use a sports chart
To write about your favorite sport, complete a chart like the one shown.

Categoría	Detalles
nombre del deporte	
lugar	
participantes	
equipo necesario	
ropa apropiada	

Step 1 Complete the chart with information about your sport. Include details about where it is played, who participates, what equipment is needed, and what clothes should be worn.

Step 2 Write your paragraph. Make sure to include all the information from your chart. Check your writing by yourself or with help from a friend. Make final corrections.

Compara con tu mundo

Use the paragraph you wrote to compare your favorite sport to a sport described by *one* of the three students. How are they similar? How are they different?

Cuaderno *pp. 292–294*   Cuaderno para hispanohablantes *pp. 292–294*

CULTURA Interactiva
my.hrw.com
See these pages come alive!

República Dominicana

Felipe

¡Hola! Me llamo Felipe y vivo en Punta Cana, cerca del mar. Ayer pasé el día en la playa con mis amigos. Después de nadar un rato, jugamos un partido de voleibol con ocho jugadores. Mi equipo comprende las reglas pero ayer no ganó el partido. El voleibol es mi deporte favorito porque puedo jugar con mis amigos y no es peligroso.

Honduras

Gloria

¿Qué tal? Me llamo Gloria y vivo en La Ceiba, el lugar perfecto para practicar deportes acuáticos. Mi deporte favorito es el rafting. Uno de los mejores ríos para practicar rafting en Honduras es el río Cangreja. La semana pasada, mis hermanos y yo alquilamos una balsa[1] para navegar el río. Es una actividad muy divertida.

———
[1] raft

Venezuela

Agustín

¡Hola! Me llamo Agustín. Soy aficionado de los deportes. Me gusta mucho el béisbol, pero me gusta más el básquetbol porque soy alto y tengo las piernas y los brazos largos[2]. También me gusta correr y saltar[3]. Mis amigos y yo jugamos casi todos los días en una cancha cerca de mi casa en Caracas.

———
[2] long   [3] to jump

Repaso inclusivo
♻ Options for Review

¡AvanzaRap!
DVD
Sing and Learn

Digital
performance space

1 | Listen, understand, and compare

Escuchar

Listen to a sports broadcast from the Dominican Republic. Then answer the following questions.

1. ¿Qué tiempo hace en el campo?
2. ¿A qué juega Mariano Sandoval?
3. ¿De dónde es Sandoval?
4. ¿Cómo juega él?
5. ¿Por qué dice Sandoval que es un buen jugador?

Have you ever excelled at something? Who influenced you and how?

2 | Be a sports commentator

Hablar

You have been asked to present a student's view on sports for a Spanish-language channel on television. Prepare a commentary on your favorite sport. Include when and where it is played, why it is important to you, and information on teams and/or athletes. You may want to videotape your commentary or present it live to the class.

3 | Talk with the school nurse

Hablar

Role-play a conversation with the school nurse. You are injured and you decide to go to the nurse's office. Tell your partner what hurts and name three activities that you did recently. He or she will make a connection between the activities and your injuries and make some recommendations for getting better. In your conversation, use some of the gestures you have learned. Your conversation should be at least four minutes long.

4 | Write a blog entry

Escribir

Write a blog entry about sports and activities people can do each season of the year and where they can go to do them. Ask readers questions about their favorite sports, and how they practice if the weather is bad. Remember to use appropriate style and register for a blog, especially when addressing your readers. (To find examples online, use the keywords "blog deportivo" or "blog de bienestar.")

5 | Agree on what to watch

Hablar

You and a partner have to decide what to watch on television. Choose a sporting event and compare it to the sporting event that your partner chose. Try to convince your partner to watch what you want to watch. Your conversation should be at least four minutes long.

6 | Plan a class trip

Hablar
Escribir

Work in a group of five to plan a class trip to Punta Cana, Dominican Republic. Each person will text a list of activities to do in Punta Cana. To pick the top five, list all the activities and allow each participant to choose one. Then, text or e-mail to decide how long the trip will be and when people will participate in the various activities.

7 | Compare classes

Leer
Escribir

Silvia is in her second year of high school. Read her report cards from last year and this year. Write a paragraph about what she studied and did during her first year and the classes she has and activities she does now. Then compare her grades and give possible reasons for why her grades are different from one year to the next. Your paragraph should have at least six sentences.

Escuela Secundaria
de Santo Domingo

Silvia Ibáñez
Primer año

Clase	Nota final
Matemáticas – Álgebra I	A
Arte	B
Inglés I	B
Ciencias Naturales	C
Literatura	A
Música	B

Actividades extracurriculares:
Equipo de natación
Equipo de voleibol

Escuela Secundaria
de Santo Domingo

Silvia Ibáñez
Segundo año

Clase	Nota final
Ciencias – Biología	B
Historia	A
Música	A
Matemáticas – Geometría	A
Literatura	B
Inglés II	A

Actividades extracurriculares:
Banda musical (trompeta)
Equipo de voleibol

Argentina

¡Una semana fenomenal!

Lección 1

Tema: **En el cibercafé**

Lección 2

Tema: **Un día en el parque de diversiones**

«¡Hola!

Somos Florencia y Mariano.
Vivimos en Argentina.»

Bolivia

Océano
Pacífico

Paraguay

Argentina

Rosario Uruguay

Buenos Aires

Chile

Mar del Plata

Océano
Atlántico

Ushuaia

Población: 43.431.886

Área: 1.068.302 millas cuadradas,
el país hispanohablante más grande
del mundo

Capital: Buenos Aires

Moneda: el peso argentino

Idioma: español

Comida típica: asado, matambre,
dulce de leche

Gente famosa: Norma Aleandro (actriz),
Jorge Luis Borges (escritor), César Milstein
(biólogo), Mercedes Sosa (cantante)

El Obelisco en la Plaza de la República, Buenos Aires

◀ **Modernidad y tradición** Buenos Aires is often called "Paris of the Americas," in part due to its European-style architecture mixed with modern elements, such as **El Obelisco** (Obelisk) in the Plaza de la República. At 400 feet across, the Avenida 9 de Julio leading up to the plaza is considered the widest avenue in the world. *What landmarks does your community have?*

La identidad nacional y el gaucho **Los gauchos** are considered cultural icons in Argentina. They lead an independent and simple life, raising cattle on the plains (**las pampas**). *How do **gauchos** compare to the cowboys of the western United States?* ▶

Gauchos y sus caballos en un bosque petrificado cerca de Sarmiento, Argentina

El Barrio de San Telmo, Buenos Aires

◀ **Un baile muy popular** On Sundays in Barrio de San Telmo, you can see **tango** dancers and hear the accordion-like instrument **el bandoneón.** Most agree that the now-famous **tango** originated in working-class neighborhoods of Buenos Aires at the end of the 19th century. *What are some popular dances in the U.S.?*

LECCIÓN
1

Tema:

En el cibercafé

¡AVANZA!

In this lesson you will learn to
- talk about technology
- talk about a series of events
- say what you did
- talk about indefinite or negative situations

using
- preterite of regular **-er** and **-ir** verbs
- affirmative and negative words

♻ *¿Recuerdas?*
- affirmative **tú** commands
- telling time
- foods and beverages
- preterite of regular **-ar** verbs

Comparación cultural

In this lesson you will learn about
- the use of **lunfardo** in Argentina
- the city of Mar del Plata
- protecting your computer

Compara con tu mundo
These teens are drinking a tea-like beverage called **mate.** Drinking **mate** involves a special cup, often made out of a dried, decorated gourd, with a metal or wood straw, called a **bombilla.** *Does your region have a special beverage or food? What is it?*

¿Qué ves?
Mira la foto
¿Son amigos estas personas?

¿Tienen sed o tienen hambre?

¿Qué hace la chica de la blusa roja?

MODES OF COMMUNICATION

INTERPRETIVE	INTERPERSONAL	PRESENTATIONAL
Listen to a radio review about a place to go after school. Read a questionnaire about computer viruses.	Discuss how to do various things on the computer. Interview a classmate about an event that happened at school.	Explain how you use a computer and technology. Write and conduct a survey and present the results.

La Casa Rosada
Buenos Aires, Argentina

❊ Presentación de VOCABULARIO

VIDEO DVD

AUDIO

A ¡Hola! Me llamo Florencia. **Anteayer** pasé un rato con mis amigos Mariano y Luciana. **Tomamos fotos** delante de la Casa Rosada.

tomar fotos

la semana pasada

abril

ayer hoy

anteayer

B Hoy, Mariano y yo estamos en la biblioteca. Aquí **navegamos por Internet,** usamos **el mensajero instantáneo** y **mandamos** correos electrónicos. Quiero mandar las fotos que tomé anteayer.

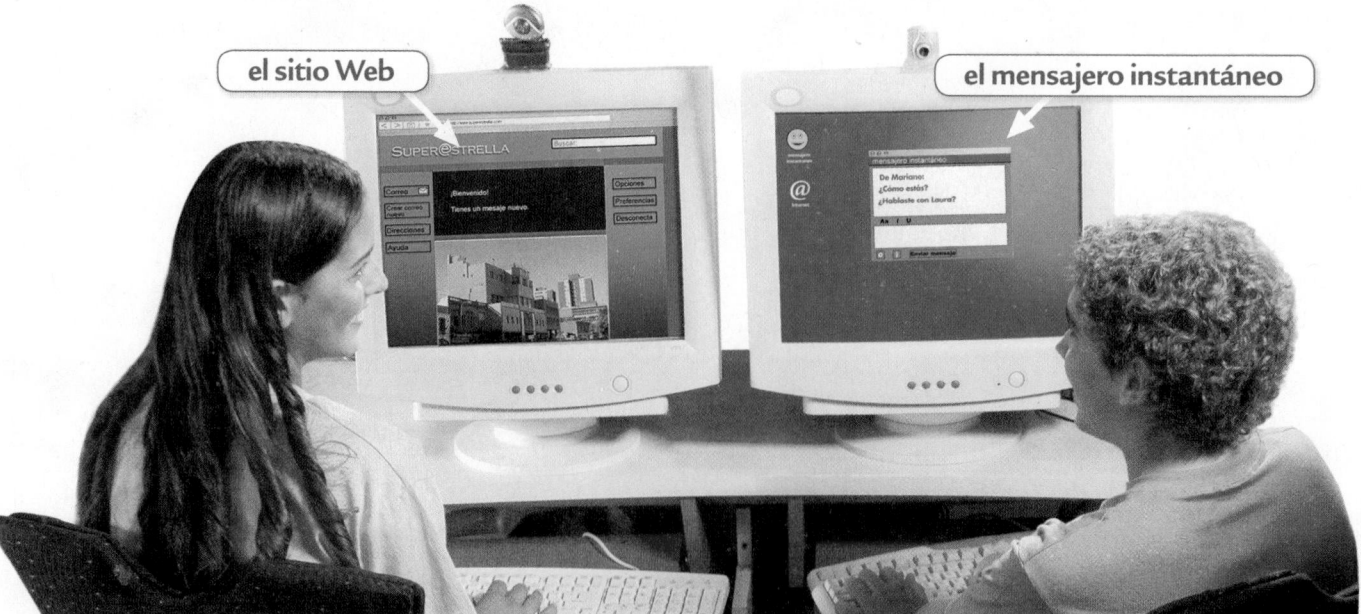

el sitio Web

el mensajero instantáneo

C Es fácil mandarlas y no cuesta **nada.** Primero **conecto a Internet.** Cuando **estoy en línea,** escribo un correo electrónico con las fotos. **Por fin,** pongo **la dirección electrónica** de mi amiga y **hago clic en el icono** para mandarlas.

la pantalla

la dirección electrónica

la cámara digital

el teclado

hacer clic en

el ratón

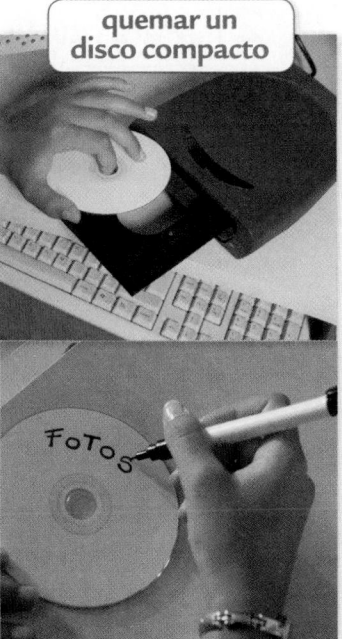

quemar un disco compacto

FOTOS

Más vocabulario

el año pasado *last year*
entonces *then, so*
luego *later, then*
más tarde *later on*

Expansión de vocabulario p. R8

la cámara digital

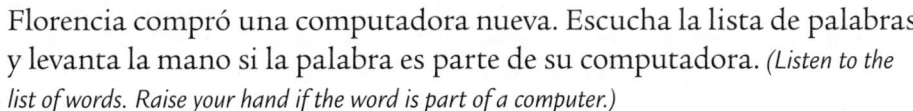

¡A responder!   Escuchar

Florencia compró una computadora nueva. Escucha la lista de palabras y levanta la mano si la palabra es parte de su computadora. *(Listen to the list of words. Raise your hand if the word is part of a computer.)*

✳ Práctica de VOCABULARIO

1 | El mundo digital

Leer | Empareja las frases para describir computadoras. *(Match the phrases.)*

1. Florencia toma fotos
2. Conectamos a Internet
3. Hago clic
4. Mariano navega
5. Uso el ratón
6. Voy a quemar

a. por Internet en la biblioteca.
b. con su cámara digital.
c. un disco compacto.
d. para estar en línea.
e. en el icono para abrir un sitio Web.
f. para hacer clic en los iconos.

> **Expansión**
> Draw a computer and label as many parts as you can.

2 | ¿Para qué usas...?

Hablar
Escribir | Describe para qué usas cada cosa que ves en las fotos. *(Tell how you use the items pictured below.)*

escribir en la computadora	hacer clic
tomar fotos	mirar fotos
buscar una película	hablar con amigos
mandar correos electrónicos	

Cinelux
Con lluvia o con sol
9:00 11:00 4:00
El pueblo fantasma
1:00 3:00 7:00

modelo: Uso **el sitio Web** para **buscar una película.**

1.

2.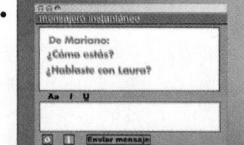

3.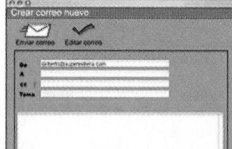

4.

5.

6.

Más práctica   Cuaderno *pp. 295–297*   Cuaderno para hispanohablantes *pp. 295–298*

Get Help Online
my.hrw.com

PARA Y PIENSA

Did you get it?
1. Name three parts of a computer.
2. Name three things you can do on the Internet.

VOCABULARIO en contexto

¡AVANZA!

Goal: Pay attention to the words Florencia uses to put events in order. Then practice these words to talk about a series of events. *Actividades 3–5*

♻ *¿Recuerdas?* Affirmative **tú** commands p. 282

Telehistoria escena 1

@**HOMETUTOR** View, Read
my.hrw.com and Record

STRATEGIES

Cuando lees
List related words This conversation includes several expressions for time-sequencing, such as **luego.** While reading, list them and add any others you know.

Cuando escuchas
Listen for sequences Listen for places Alicia's T-shirt has been. Write the names of cities, states, and countries, using arrows for sequencing.

VIDEO
DVD

AUDIO

Florencia: ¡Mariano! Mira, tengo un correo electrónico de Alicia.

Mariano: ¿Qué dice, Florencia? No puedo ver la pantalla.

Florencia: Alicia quiere el autógrafo de Trini Salgado en su camiseta.

Mariano: ¡Qué bárbaro tener el autógrafo de una jugadora de fútbol famosa como Trini Salgado!

Florencia: Alicia mandó la camiseta a Sandra, una amiga que vive en Texas. Después, Sandra la mandó a un amigo de Puebla, en México, pero tampoco la encontró.

Mariano: ¿Y entonces?

Florencia: Luego, su amigo de México mandó la camiseta a Puerto Rico. Más tarde, sus amigos mandaron la camiseta a España, y entonces a Ecuador y a la República Dominicana. Y por fin, anteayer la mandaron aquí a Buenos Aires. ¡Porque Trini está aquí!

Continuará... p. 364

También se dice

Argentina Mariano uses the phrase **¡Qué bárbaro!** to say *Cool!* In other Spanish-speaking countries you might hear:
• **Perú, Chile, Ecuador** **¡Qué bacán!**
• **México** **¡Qué padre!**
• **España** **¡Qué guay!**
• **muchos países** **¡Qué chévere!**

3 | *Comprensión del episodio* ¿Adónde la mandaron?

Escuchar
Leer

Usa las palabras de la lista para indicar el orden y los lugares adonde mandaron la camiseta de Alicia. *(Use the words in the list to write the order of the places where they sent Alicia's T-shirt.)*

entonces	más tarde
luego	por fin

modelo: Primero, Alicia mandó la camiseta de Miami a Texas. Luego...

4 | ¿En qué orden?

Escuchar

Escucha la descripción de cómo Florencia tomó fotos y se las mandó a sus amigas. Luego indica el orden correcto de los dibujos. *(Listen to the description and put the drawings in order.)*

a.

b.

c.

d.

e.

f.

> **Expansión**
> Write five sentences to tell how you use the computer at home or at school.

5 | ¿Cómo lo hago?   *¿Recuerdas?* Affirmative **tú** commands p. 282

Hablar

Pregúntale a otro(a) estudiante cómo hacer varias cosas en la computadora.
(Ask a partner how to do these things.)

A ¿Cómo uso una cámara digital?

B Toma fotos. Luego ponlas en la computadora y míralas en la pantalla.

> navegar por Internet
> usar una cámara digital
> mandar fotos
> usar el mensajero instantáneo
> mandar un correo electrónico
> ¿?

Get Help Online
my.hrw.com

PARA Y PIENSA

Did you get it? Put the following sentences in order.
    a. Más tarde, Trini va a Puerto Rico y a España.
    b. Luego, Trini está en Puebla, México.
    c. Por fin, Trini está en Buenos Aires.
    d. Primero, Trini llega a San Antonio.

Unidad 7 Argentina
360 trescientos sesenta

Presentación de GRAMÁTICA

¡AVANZA! **Goal:** Learn about the preterite forms of **-er** and **-ir** verbs. Then practice using these verbs to say what you and others did. *Actividades 6–9*

♻ *¿Recuerdas?* Telling time p. 90, foods and beverages pp. 33, 140, 218

English Grammar Connection: Remember that the **preterite** is a tense used to express an action completed at a definite time in the past (see p. 331). In English, regular verbs in the past tense end in *-ed*.

Preterite of Regular -er and -ir Verbs

Regular **-er** and **-ir** verbs follow a pattern similar to regular **-ar** verbs in the **preterite.** How do you form the **preterite** of regular **-er** and **-ir** verbs?

Here's how:

In the preterite, **-er** and **-ir** verb endings are identical.

vender *to sell*	
vend**í**	vend**imos**
vend**iste**	vend**isteis**
vend**ió**	vend**ieron**

escribir *to write*	
escrib**í**	escrib**imos**
escrib**iste**	escrib**isteis**
escrib**ió**	escrib**ieron**

The **yo** forms and the **usted/él/ella** forms take accents.

Vendí la computadora.
*I **sold** the computer.*

Tomás **escrib**ió un correo electrónico.
*Tomás **wrote** an e-mail.*

The **nosotros(as)** form of regular **-ir** verbs is the same in both the present and the preterite. Use context clues to determine the tense of the verb.

Salimos a las ocho **anoche.**
*We **left** at eight o'clock **last night.***

The word **anoche** tells you that **salimos** is in the preterite tense.

Más práctica
Cuaderno *pp. 298–300*
Cuaderno para hispanohablantes *pp. 299–301*

@HOMETUTOR my.hrw.com
Leveled Practice
🌐 Conjuguemos.com

Práctica de GRAMÁTICA

6 | ¿Cuándo volvieron? ♻️ *¿Recuerdas?* Telling time p. 90

**Hablar
Escribir**

Mariano y sus amigos salieron ayer. Indica cuándo volvieron, según la hora a la que salieron y cuántas horas pasaron fuera de casa. *(Tell when these people came home, according to the time they left and how long they were out.)*

> **modelo:** Mariano / 4:00 (dos horas)
> Mariano salió a las cuatro y volvió a las seis.

1. Mariano y yo / 8:30 (siete horas)
2. usted / 9:20 (dos horas)
3. yo / 6:40 (una hora)
4. Florencia y Ana / 10:05 (cuatro horas)
5. tú / 1:15 (tres horas)
6. Florencia / 2:45 (seis horas)

> **Expansión**
> Tell what time you went out and came home yesterday and the day before.

7 | Mariano y su familia

**Leer
Escribir**

Mariano le escribió un correo electrónico a Luciana. Complétalo con la forma correcta del pretérito del verbo apropiado. *(Complete Mariano's e-mail.)*

```
Yo te ___1.___ (escribir / correr) un correo electrónico
ayer y mandé unas fotos. ¿Tú las ___2.___ (vivir / recibir)?
Mi familia y yo ___3.___ (perder / salir) a un restaurante.
Mis padres ___4.___ (comer / deber) churrasco, el bistec
de Argentina. De postre mi hermana y yo ___5.___ (abrir /
compartir) un pastel y mi padre ___6.___ (subir / beber)
un café. Luego nosotros ___7.___ (volver / ver) a casa.
```

Comparación cultural

El famoso Carlos Gardel

El lunfardo

How do slang words develop? Lunfardo is a variety of slang that originated among the immigrant populations of Buenos Aires, **Argentina,** during the early 20th century. Many words were influenced by other languages, especially Italian, while others were created by reversing the syllables of Spanish terms. For example, *amigos* became *gomías* and *pizza* became *zapi*. *Lunfardo* appeared in many tango lyrics, such as those popularized by Carlos Gardel. His music helped introduce *lunfardo* to the general public. Many people in Argentina still use some of these words in their informal speech, often in a playful or humorous manner.

Compara con tu mundo *What slang terms do you know that mean "Great!"?*

8 La semana pasada

Hablar

Habla con otro(a) estudiante sobre las actividades que hizo la semana pasada. *(Talk with a partner about activities he or she did last week.)*

salir	recibir	escribir
barrer	comer	correr
beber		

A ¿Saliste con tus amigos la semana pasada?

B Sí, salí con mis amigos al cine. (No, no salí con mis amigos.)

1.
2.
3.
4.
5.
6.

9 Una encuesta

 ¿Recuerdas? Foods and beverages pp. 33, 140, 218

Hablar Escribir

Haz una encuesta sobre qué comieron y bebieron los estudiantes de tu clase ayer. Presenta los resultados a la clase. *(Take a survey of what your classmates ate and drank yesterday. Report your findings to the class.)*

AUDIO

Pronunciación   La combinación qu

You already know that **c** before **a, o, u,** and consonants makes the sound of the English *k*. To make this sound before **e** and **i** in Spanish, use **qu.**

Listen and repeat.

que	→	queso	pequeño	raqueta	quemar
qui	→	tranquilo	quince	quiero	equipo

¿Quién tiene que hacer los quehaceres? ¿Quieres ir al parque?

Más práctica   Cuaderno *pp. 298–300*   Cuaderno para hispanohablantes *pp. 299–301*

 **Get Help Online**
my.hrw.com

PARA Y PIENSA

Did you get it? Fill in the preterite form of the verb in parentheses.
1. Anteayer yo _____ la cena con mi amiga Teresa. (comer)
2. ¿ _____ tú muchos regalos para tu cumpleaños? (recibir)

Lección 1
trescientos sesenta y tres   **363**

❋GRAMÁTICA en contexto

¡AVANZA! **Goal:** Listen to Florencia and Mariano talk about what happened the day before. Then use the preterite of **-er** and **-ir** verbs to describe what you did recently. *Actividades 10–11*

Telehistoria escena 2

@**HOMETUTOR** View, Read
my.hrw.com and Record

STRATEGIES

Cuando lees
Locate and practice key phrases
Read the scene, finding phrases about the Internet and writing or receiving e-mails. Repeat each one (aloud or to yourself) until you know it and can use it in conversation.

Cuando escuchas
Use visual clues while listening
While listening to the video, search for visual clues that tell you where Trini is going to be. How do the characters' movements keep them from finding out?

VIDEO DVD

AUDIO

Mariano: Florencia, ¿ahora qué va a pasar con la camiseta de Alicia?

Florencia: Anoche cuando volví a casa, recibí otro correo electrónico de Alicia.

Florencia takes a printout of the e-mail from her bag.

Florencia: Aquí está. Compartimos muchas ideas anoche. Escribió que debemos buscar a Trini en el estadio.

Mariano: Pero, ¿cuándo?

Florencia: No sé. No recibí mucha información. Tenemos que navegar por Internet para buscar la fecha y la hora. ¿Salimos para el cibercafé?

As they leave, Florencia leaves her camera on the table in the restaurant.

Continuará... p. 369

10 | Comprensión del episodio   ¿Qué necesitan saber?

**Escuchar
Leer**

Contesta las preguntas. *(Answer the questions.)*

1. ¿Qué recibió Florencia anoche?

2. ¿Quiénes compartieron ideas?

3. ¿Quién escribió que deben buscar a Trini en el estadio?

4. ¿Cómo van a buscar información Florencia y Mariano sobre la fecha y la hora?

5. ¿Adónde van ellos después?

11 | ¿Pasaste una semana fenomenal?

**Leer
Escribir**

Tu amigo(a) te manda este cuestionario. Complétalo y mándale los resultados. *(Take this quiz and send the results to your friend.)*

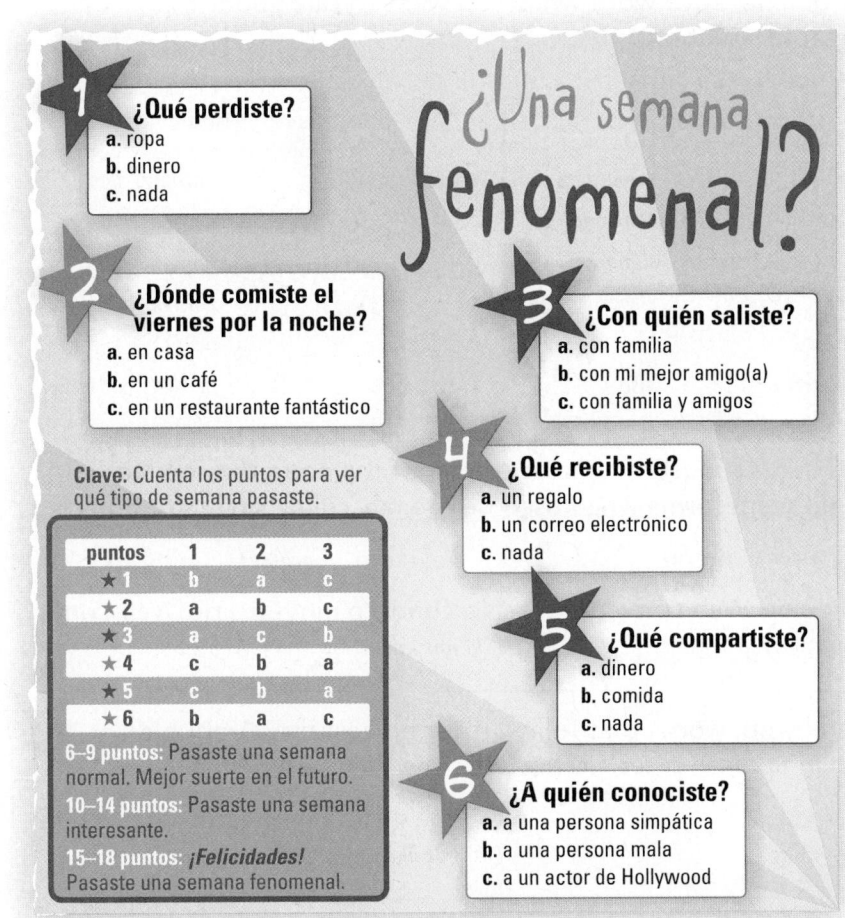

¿Una semana fenomenal?

1 ¿Qué perdiste?
a. ropa
b. dinero
c. nada

2 ¿Dónde comiste el viernes por la noche?
a. en casa
b. en un café
c. en un restaurante fantástico

3 ¿Con quién saliste?
a. con familia
b. con mi mejor amigo(a)
c. con familia y amigos

4 ¿Qué recibiste?
a. un regalo
b. un correo electrónico
c. nada

5 ¿Qué compartiste?
a. dinero
b. comida
c. nada

6 ¿A quién conociste?
a. a una persona simpática
b. a una persona mala
c. a un actor de Hollywood

Clave: Cuenta los puntos para ver qué tipo de semana pasaste.

puntos	1	2	3
★1	b	a	c
★2	a	b	c
★3	a	c	b
★4	c	b	a
★5	c	b	a
★6	b	a	c

6–9 puntos: Pasaste una semana normal. Mejor suerte en el futuro.
10–14 puntos: Pasaste una semana interesante.
15–18 puntos: *¡Felicidades!* Pasaste una semana fenomenal.

Expansión
Compare and contrast your answers with your friend's.

Get Help Online
my.hrw.com

PARA Y PIENSA

Did you get it? Complete each sentence with the preterite form of the appropriate verb: **salir, compartir,** or **recibir.**

1. Florencia _____ un correo electrónico de Alicia.

2. Alicia y Florencia _____ muchas ideas.

3. Florencia y Mariano _____ para el cibercafé.

✦ Presentación de GRAMÁTICA

¡AVANZA! **Goal:** Learn how to use affirmative and negative words. Then practice them to talk about indefinite or negative situations. **Actividades 12–15**

♻ **¿Recuerdas?** Preterite of regular -ar verbs p. 331

English Grammar Connection: A **double negative** is the use of two **negative words** to express a negative idea. Double negatives are considered incorrect in English. In Spanish, they are often required.

There's **nobody** at the door.   **No** hay **nadie** en la puerta.

Affirmative and Negative Words

ANIMATEDGRAMMAR
my.hrw.com

Use an **affirmative** or a **negative** word when you want to talk about an indefinite or negative situation.

Here's how:

Affirmative Words		Negative Words	
algo	something	nada	nothing
alguien	someone	nadie	no one, nobody
algún/alguno(a)	some, any	ningún/ninguno(a)	none, not any
o... o	either . . . or	ni... ni	neither . . . nor
siempre	always	nunca	never
también	also	tampoco	neither, not either

Alguno(a) and **ninguno(a)** must match the gender of the noun they replace or modify. They have different forms when used before masculine singular nouns.

alguno *becomes* **algún**   **ninguno** *becomes* **ningún**

¿Conoces **algún** sitio Web cómico?   No conozco **ningún** sitio Web cómico.
*Do you know **any** funny Web sites?*   *I do **not** know **any** funny Web sites.*

If a verb is preceded by **no,** words that follow must be negative. A double negative is required in Spanish when **no** precedes the verb.

No queremos **nada.**   **No** me gusta **ninguna** cámara digital.
*We do **not** want **anything.***   *I do **not** like **any** digital cameras.*

However, if the negative word comes before the verb, there is no need to use **no.**

Mi padre **nunca** usa la computadora.   **Nadie** navega por Internet ahora.
*My father **never** uses the computer.*   ***No one** is surfing the Web now.*

Más práctica
Cuaderno *pp. 301–303*
Cuaderno para hispanohablantes *pp. 302–305*

@**HOMETUTOR** my.hrw.com
Leveled Practice

❋ Práctica de GRAMÁTICA

12 | ¡Qué negativa!

Hablar
Escribir

Florencia no quiere hacer nada hoy. Completa la conversación con las formas correctas de palabras afirmativas y negativas. *(Complete the conversation with affirmative and negative words.)*

Mariano

Florencia

¿Quieres ver **1.** película en el cine Rex?

¿Quieres comprar **3.** en la tienda?

¿Quieres pasar un rato con **5.** ?

¿Quieres practicar **7.** deporte?

No, no quiero ver **2.** película en el cine Rex.

No, no quiero comprar **4.** en la tienda.

No, no quiero pasar un rato con **6.** .

No, no quiero practicar **8.** deporte.

> **Expansión**
> Give your own answers for Mariano's questions.

Nota gramatical

Ningunos(as) is used only with nouns that are not typically singular, such as **jeans.**

No compro ningunos jeans.   *I'm **not** buying **any jeans.***

13 | El domingo pasado

Hablar

Pregúntale a otro(a) estudiante si hizo estas cosas el domingo pasado. Te va a decir que no las hizo. *(Ask a partner whether he or she did these things last Sunday. He or she will say no.)*

1. beber algunos refrescos
2. usar el mensajero instantáneo con alguien
3. recibir algo especial de un amigo
4. tomar algunas fotos con una cámara digital
5. salir con alguien
6. escribir algún correo electrónico
7. vender algo
8. quemar algún disco compacto

> **A** ¿Comiste pizza y papas fritas?

> **B** No, no comí ni pizza ni papas fritas.

14 ¿Y tú? ¿*Recuerdas?* Preterite of regular **-ar** verbs p. 331

Hablar
Escribir

Contesta las preguntas sobre lo que hiciste. Explica tus respuestas si es posible. (*Answer the questions about what you did. Explain your answers whenever possible.*)

modelo: ¿Aprendiste algo en la clase de español la semana pasada?
Sí, aprendí algo la semana pasada. Aprendí el vocabulario nuevo.
(No, no aprendí nada.)

1. ¿Estudiaste con alguien anteayer?

2. ¿Comiste algunas galletas anoche?

3. ¿Perdiste algo el año pasado?

4. ¿Compraste algo la semana pasada?

5. ¿Ayudaste a alguien el sábado pasado?

6. ¿Practicaste algún deporte ayer?

7. ¿Escribiste algo anoche?

8. ¿Compartiste algo con alguien ayer?

Expansión
Ask a partner these questions and write down the answers.

15 ¿Qué hay en la playa?

Hablar

Comparación cultural

Las playas de Mar del Plata

What features and attractions are most popular for tourists? Mar del Plata is a city with miles of beaches along the Atlantic Ocean. It is a popular destination for Buenos Aires residents and other tourists during the summer, especially between December and February. Visitors can participate in a variety of activities such as sunbathing, surfing, scuba diving, and fishing.

Las playas de Mar del Plata

Compara con tu mundo *During the summer months, what are popular destinations in your area? What are common activities in these places?*

Pregúntale a otro(a) estudiante sobre la foto. Usa palabras afirmativas y negativas. (*Ask your partner about the photo. Use affirmative and negative words.*)

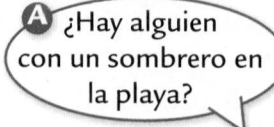

A ¿Hay alguien con un sombrero en la playa?

B No, no hay nadie con un sombrero. ¿Hay algo azul?

Más práctica   Cuaderno *pp. 301–303*   Cuaderno para hispanohablantes *pp. 302–305*

 **Get Help Online**
my.hrw.com

PARA Y PIENSA

Did you get it? Write the opposite of these sentences.
1. Siempre recibo algunos correos electrónicos.
2. Nadie escribe nada con el mensajero instantáneo.
3. A Beatriz le gusta navegar por Internet y estar en línea.

❖ Todo junto

Goal: *Show what you know* Notice the affirmative and negative words used to talk about Trini in Buenos Aires. Then use these words and the preterite of **-er** and **-ir** verbs to talk about past actions. *Actividades 16–20*

Telehistoria completa

 @**HOMETUTOR** **View, Read and Record** my.hrw.com

STRATEGIES

 **Cuando lees**
Notice the information exchange
While reading, notice the information exchange. What does the waiter tell Mariano and Florencia? How does he help them solve their problem?

Cuando escuchas
Practice what you hear Listen to how the speakers emphasize negative expressions (**no, nada, nadie, ni... ni**). After listening, say these sentences with proper emphasis. Remember this for future communication.

 **Escena 1** *Resumen*
Florencia recibe un correo electrónico de Alicia porque Trini Salgado va a estar en Buenos Aires. Sus amigos mandan la camiseta a Argentina.

 **Escena 2** *Resumen*
Alicia escribe que Trini va a estar en el estadio. Pero Florencia y Mariano tienen que navegar por Internet para buscar más información.

 VIDEO DVD

AUDIO

Escena 3

Florencia: ¡Señor, por favor! ¿Tiene usted mi cámara?

Camarero: Sí, sí, tranquila. Aquí está. ¿Qué pasa? ¿Necesitan algo?

Mariano: No, nada. Gracias. Queremos ir al estadio para ver a Trini Salgado, pero no sabemos ni la fecha ni la hora. Nadie sabe cuándo va a llegar ella.

Florencia: Usted tampoco sabe, ¿no?

Camarero: No sé nada del estadio, pero sé que Trini Salgado va a estar en el Parque de la Costa en El Tigre, el sábado.

Florencia: ¿Sí? ¿Cómo lo sabe?

Camarero: Mira, allí dice. *(He points to a poster in the restaurant's window.)*

Mariano: ¡Florencia! Nadie encontró a Trini... ni en Estados Unidos... ni en Puerto Rico... tampoco en España. Pero ahora, tú vas a tener el autógrafo.

16 | Comprensión de los episodios ¿Estás seguro(a)?

Escuchar
Leer

Indica si estas oraciones son ciertas o falsas. Corrige las oraciones falsas con palabras afirmativas o negativas. *(Tell if these sentences are true or false. Correct the false sentences, using affirmative or negative words.)*

1. Florencia recibió algo de Alicia.
2. No van a buscar a nadie en el estadio.
3. El camarero no tiene nada de Florencia.
4. El camarero sabe algo de Trini en el estadio.
5. Nadie encontró a Trini en Estados Unidos.
6. También la encontraron en España.

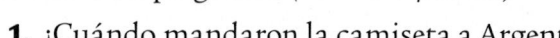

17 | Comprensión de los episodios ¿Lo sabes?

Escuchar
Leer

Contesta las preguntas. *(Answer the questions.)*

1. ¿Cuándo mandaron la camiseta a Argentina? ¿Por qué?
2. ¿Qué recibió Florencia cuando volvió a casa?
3. ¿Con quién compartió ideas Florencia?
4. ¿Qué perdió Florencia?
5. ¿Alguien sabe cuándo Trini va a llegar al estadio?
6. ¿Qué no saben Florencia y Mariano?

18 | Los reporteros

Hablar

> **STRATEGY Hablar**
> **Choose an interesting topic** Decide with your partner whether to talk about something interesting that actually occurred or something amazing that you can pretend happened. That way, whatever you choose to talk about in your interview will be of interest to listeners.

Eres reportero(a). Entrevista a otro(a) estudiante sobre algo que pasó en la escuela. *(Interview a partner about something that happened at school.)*

A Estamos aquí en la cafetería. Alguien habló con el director de la escuela y ya no sirven refrescos. ¿Qué piensas, Víctor?

B ¡No me gusta! No hay nada bueno para beber. Ayer bebí leche...

Expansión
Turn your interview into an article.

19 | Integración

Leer
Escuchar
Hablar

Lee la página Web y escucha el programa de radio. Explica a qué lugar prefieres ir después de las clases y por qué. *(Read the Web page and listen to the radio program. Then tell where you prefer to go after school and why.)*

Fuente 1 Página Web

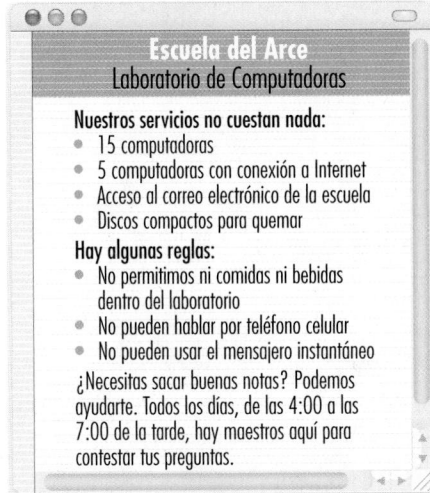

Escuela del Arce
Laboratorio de Computadoras

Nuestros servicios no cuestan nada:
* 15 computadoras
* 5 computadoras con conexión a Internet
* Acceso al correo electrónico de la escuela
* Discos compactos para quemar

Hay algunas reglas:
* No permitimos ni comidas ni bebidas dentro del laboratorio
* No pueden hablar por teléfono celular
* No pueden usar el mensajero instantáneo

¿Necesitas sacar buenas notas? Podemos ayudarte. Todos los días, de las 4:00 a las 7:00 de la tarde, hay maestros aquí para contestar tus preguntas.

Fuente 2 Programa de radio

Listen and take notes
* ¿Qué lugar buscó Raquel?
* ¿Qué hay allí?
* ¿Qué pasó allí?

modelo: Después de las clases prefiero ir al... porque...

---

20 | Teclados y ratones

Escribir

Escribe un artículo para una revista sobre computadoras. Di cómo usaste la tecnología ayer y cómo usas la computadora en tu vida diaria. *(Write an article for a computer magazine about your computer use.)*

modelo: Me gusta usar la computadora. Ayer navegué por Internet, pero no escribí ningún correo electrónico. Siempre uso el mensajero instantáneo para...

Writing Criteria	Excellent	Good	Needs Work
Content	Your article includes a lot of information.	Your article includes some information.	Your article includes little information.
Communication	Most of your article is organized and easy to follow.	Parts of your article are organized and easy to follow.	Your article is disorganized and hard to follow.
Accuracy	Your article has few mistakes in grammar and vocabulary.	Your article has some mistakes in grammar and vocabulary.	Your article has many mistakes in grammar and vocabulary.

Expansión
Compare your article with a classmate's.

Más práctica   Cuaderno *pp. 304–305*   Cuaderno para hispanohablantes *pp. 306–307*

Get Help Online
my.hrw.com

PARA Y PIENSA

Did you get it? Answer the following questions negatively.
1. ¿Perdió algo Mariano?
2. ¿Recibió Florencia la fecha o la hora?
3. ¿Escribió Mariano algún correo electrónico?

Lectura

¡AVANZA! **Goal:** Take this virus-protection questionnaire. Then talk about computer viruses and how you protect your computer.

AUDIO

Un cuestionario sobre las computadoras

Cuestionario: Protección para tu PC

✕ www.antivirus.ar

Cuestionario: Protección para tu PC

¿Qué pasa cuando un virus infecta tu computadora? El virus funciona como un borrador. Puede destruir tus archivos[1]. Puede afectar tu acceso a Internet y el sistema del correo electrónico. Otras personas pueden ver tus datos[2] personales. ¿Conoces las medidas[3] básicas que debes tomar como protección contra[4] los virus? Toma este cuestionario para saber.

1. **¿Cuál de los siguientes *no* es un método típico de propagación de los virus?**

   A. programas que se descargan[5] de Internet
   B. archivos adjuntos[6] a correos electrónicos
   C. la provisión de datos personales en un sitio Web no seguro[7]
   D. software pirata

---

[1] files   [2] information   [3] measures   [4] against
[5] are downloaded   [6] attached   [7] secure, safe

STRATEGY Leer
Use a cause-and-effect chart
Make a cause-and-effect chart for computer viruses. This will help you understand the text.

```
  software pirata
        |
        v
    un virus
        |
        v
  perder archivos
       /    \
      v      v
  [    ]   [    ]
```

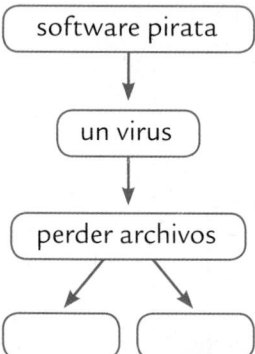

Cuestionario: Protección para tu PC

   www.antivirus.ar

Cuestionario: Protección para tu PC

Centro de Protección

Introd ucción
Protege tu equipo
Recursos

2. Cierto o falso: Después de instalar software antivirus, la computadora está completamente protegida[8].
  A. cierto
  B. falso

3. ¿Qué es un firewall de Internet?
  A. una contraseña[9] segura
  B. un artículo de asbesto que protege la computadora de las llamas[10]
  C. un candado[11] que puedes poner en la computadora para impedir acceso no autorizado
  D. software o hardware que ayuda a proteger la computadora contra ataques como los virus

HAZ CLIC

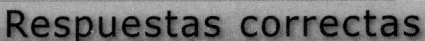

Respuestas correctas

1. C: la provisión de datos personales en un sitio Web no seguro
2. B: falso
3. D: software o hardware que ayuda a proteger la computadora contra ataques como los virus

[8] protected   [9] password   [10] flames   [11] padlock

PARA Y PIENSA

¿Comprendiste?
1. ¿Por qué son peligrosos los virus?
2. ¿Cuáles son los métodos típicos de propagación de los virus?
3. ¿Cómo se llama el software o hardware que ayuda a proteger la computadora contra ataques como los virus?

¿Y tú?
¿Qué medidas antivirus tomas cuando usas la computadora?

Lección 1
trescientos setenta y tres   **373**

Conexiones   *El lenguaje*

Los juegos de lenguaje

Jeringozo is a language game played by children in Argentina. To say a word in **jeringozo,** divide the word into syllables. After each one, add a syllable consisting of **p** and the vowel sound of the original syllable. For example:

tarde

tar + *pa* | de + *pe* = tar*pa*de*pe*
(Pronounced tárpa-dépe)

mesa

me + *pe* | sa + *pa* = me*pe*sa*pa*
(Pronounced mépe-sápa)

If a syllable has more than one vowel, the stressed vowel is used:
bueno = **bue*pe*nopo** *(buépe-nópo)*. Accents are omitted when writing in **jeringozo.** Try saying and writing the following words in **jeringozo:**

Argentina   semana   durante   favorito

Now that you have mastered it, try saying **República Dominicana**!

El juego de jeringozo

¡Hopolapa, apamipigapa!

¡Buepenospo dipiaspa!

Proyecto 1 *Las ciencias sociales*

Can you think of a game children play in English that is similar to **jeringozo**? Describe the game. How do you think these language games are invented? What purpose do they serve?

Proyecto 2 *La geografía*

Children in Chile play a variation of **jeringozo.** Look at the map of South America on page xlii. Examine the location and geographical features of Argentina and Chile. Write a paragraph about how you think geography affects the cultures of these two countries. Why would they have cultural similarities? Why might they also have cultural differences?

Proyecto 3 *Las ciencias*

The word *Argentina* comes from *argentum,* the Latin word for silver. It has this name because Spanish explorers hoped to find silver there. Research and write about this valuable metal. What characteristics does it have that make it desirable?

Espuelas de plata (Silver spurs)

En resumen
Vocabulario y gramática

ANiMaTeDGRaMMaR
Interactive Flashcards
my.hrw.com

Vocabulario

Talk About Technology

la cámara digital	digital camera	navegar por Internet	to surf the Internet
conectar a Internet	to connect to the Internet	la pantalla	screen
la dirección (pl. las direcciones) electrónica	e-mail address	quemar un disco compacto	to burn a CD
estar en línea	to be online	el ratón (pl. los ratones)	mouse
hacer clic en	to click on	el sitio Web	Web site
el icono	icon	el teclado	keyboard
mandar	to send	tomar fotos	to take photos
el mensajero instantáneo	instant messaging		

Talk About Events

anteayer	the day before yesterday
el año pasado	last year
entonces	then, so
luego	later, then
más tarde	later on
por fin	finally
la semana pasada	last week

Talk About Negative or Indefinite Situations

algo	something	ni... ni	neither . . . nor
alguien	someone	ningún / ninguno(a)	none, not any
algún / alguno(a)	some, any	o... o	either . . . or
nada	nothing	tampoco	neither, not either
nadie	no one, nobody		

Gramática

Nota gramatical: ningunos(as) *p. 367*

Preterite of Regular -er and -ir Verbs

In the preterite, **-er** and **-ir** verb endings are identical.

vender	*to sell*
vendí	vendimos
vendiste	vendisteis
vendió	vendieron

escribir	*to write*
escribí	escribimos
escribiste	escribisteis
escribió	escribieron

Affirmative and Negative Words

Affirmative Words		Negative Words	
algo	something	nada	nothing
alguien	someone	nadie	no one, nobody
algún/alguno(a)	some, any	ningún/ninguno(a)	none, not any
o... o	either . . . or	ni... ni	neither . . . nor
siempre	always	nunca	never
también	also	tampoco	neither, not either

Alguno(a) and **ninguno(a)** must match the gender of the noun they replace or modify. They have different forms when used before masculine singular nouns.

Repaso de la lección

¡LLEGADA!

Now you can
- talk about technology
- talk about a series of events
- say what you did
- talk about indefinite or negative situations

Using
- preterite of regular **-er** and **-ir** verbs
- affirmative and negative words

To review
- preterite of regular **-er** and **-ir** verbs p. 361
- affirmative and negative words p. 366

1 Listen and understand

AUDIO

Diana habla con Ramiro sobre su computadora. Escucha y escribe si las oraciones son ciertas o falsas. *(Listen and write whether the statements are true or false.)*

1. Diana piensa que hay algún problema con su computadora.
2. Diana recibió correos electrónicos ayer.
3. A Diana y a sus amigos les gusta usar Internet.
4. Ramiro no encontró ningún problema con la computadora.
5. Diana recibió fotos de sus amigos ayer.
6. Diana no quemó ningún disco compacto anteayer.

To review
- preterite of regular **-er** and **-ir** verbs p. 361

2 Talk about a series of events

Completa el correo electrónico con la forma correcta del pretérito del verbo apropiado. *(Complete the e-mail with the correct preterite form of the appropriate verb.)*

abrir	recibir
comer	salir
compartir	subir
envolver	volver

Hola, Inés. ¿Qué tal? La semana pasada celebré mi cumpleaños. Primero mi familia y yo __1.__ a comer en un restaurante. De primer plato mi hermana __2.__ pescado. Nunca como mucha carne, entonces yo __3.__ un bistec grande con mi padre. Más tarde nosotros __4.__ a casa y cuando yo __5.__ las escaleras, vi una sorpresa: ¡unos regalos! Entonces yo los __6.__ : un videojuego de mi hermana y una cámara de mi madre. Después mi padre me explicó que él no __7.__ su regalo con papel. ¡De mi padre, yo __8.__ un perro! ¡Qué bárbaro!

To review
- preterite of regular **-er** and **-ir** verbs p. 361

3 | Say what you did

Escribe lo que hicieron estas personas la semana pasada. Luego escribe si tú lo hiciste o no. *(Write what people did last week. Then write whether or not you did that activity.)*

> **modelo:** el señor Cruz / a casa tarde.
> El señor Cruz volvió a casa tarde.
> Yo no volví a casa tarde.
> *(Yo también volví a casa tarde.)*

barrer	recibir
beber	correr
aprender	escribir
volver	perder
comer	

1. tú / un correo electrónico
2. mis amigos y yo / una pizza
3. Marta / refrescos
4. el jugador / el partido
5. Paca y Teresa / al parque
6. usted / el suelo
7. Isabel / regalos
8. mis hermanos / español

To review
- affirmative and negative words p. 366

4 | Talk about indefinite or negative situations

Juan y Juana son hermanos muy diferentes. Lee lo que dice Juan y escribe lo que responde Juana. Usa palabras afirmativas y negativas. *(Use affirmative or negative words to give Juana's opposite responses to her brother Juan's statements.)*

> **modelo:** Conozco algunos sitios Web muy interesantes.
> No conozco ningún sitio Web muy interesante.

1. Siempre recibo correos electrónicos de mis amigos.
2. No mandé nada por Internet anteayer.
3. No hay ningún problema con mi computadora.
4. Los sábados quemo un disco compacto o navego por Internet.
5. Ayer tomé fotos de alguien.
6. Nunca uso cámaras digitales.

To review
- **gauchos** p. 353
- Comparación cultural pp. 354, 362, 368

5 | Argentina

Comparación cultural

Answer these culture questions.

1. What do **gauchos** do?
2. What is **mate** and how is it served?
3. What is **lunfardo**? Give an example of a **lunfardo** word.
4. When and why do many people go to Mar del Plata, Argentina?

Más práctica Cuaderno *pp. 306–317* Cuaderno para hispanohablantes *pp. 308–317*

Get Help Online
my.hrw.com

Argentina

Tema:

Un día en el parque de diversiones

¡AVANZA!

In this lesson you will learn to
- talk on the phone
- say where you went, how it was, and what you did
- extend invitations

using
- **¡Qué** + adjective!
- preterite of **ir, ser,** and **hacer**
- pronouns after prepositions

♻ ¿Recuerdas?
- noun-adjective agreement
- places around town
- stem-changing verbs: **e → i**

ENTRADA

Comparación cultural

In this lesson you will learn about
- family names
- artist Benito Quinquela Martín and Argentinean cuisine
- places to visit in Argentina, Bolivia, and Nicaragua

Compara con tu mundo
El Parque de la Costa is near Buenos Aires. With over 50 rides, it is the largest amusement park in South America. *Have you visited an amusement park? What rides do you like? If you haven't, would you like to go?*

¿Qué ves?

Mira la foto

¿Están delante del cine los amigos?

¿Tiene Mariano una mochila o una chaqueta?

¿Qué tiene Florencia en las manos?

MODES OF COMMUNICATION

INTERPRETIVE	INTERPERSONAL	PRESENTATIONAL
Read and listen to two invitations and respond to both.

Understand a phone conversation. | Conduct several phone conversations.

Respond to an e-mail giving advice. | Write a social media post about a trip you took.

Describe a place you visited and compare it to trips students in Spanish-speaking countries took. |

El Parque de la Costa
El Tigre, Argentina

Presentación de VOCABULARIO

¡AVANZA! **Goal:** Learn about Mariano's trip to the amusement park with his friends. Then practice what you have learned to talk on the phone about where you like to go with your friends. *Actividades 1–2*

VIDEO DVD

AUDIO

A Voy a **llamar** a Florencia para invitarla a hacer algo este **fin de semana.**

llamar

el teléfono celular

Mariano

Florencia

B

Mariano: ¿**Aló?** ¿**Puedo hablar con** Florencia?

Florencia: Hola, Mariano. Soy yo, Florencia.

Mariano: Hola, Florencia. ¿**Quieres acompañarme al zoológico?** **Te invito.**

Florencia: Lo siento. No me gusta mucho ir al zoológico.

Mariano: ¿**Te gustaría** ir a **la feria** del libro el sábado?

Florencia: ¡**Qué lástima!** El sábado no puedo, pero **me gustaría** hacer algo el domingo.

Mariano: Voy a ir al **parque de diversiones con** Luciana. ¿Quieres ir?

Florencia: ¡**Claro que sí!** Hasta el domingo.

ZOO DE BUENOS
18 HECTAREAS DE PARQUE · 350 ESPECIES

el zoológico

la feria

el acuario

el museo

C Hola, Florencia.
Hola, Luciana.
Vamos a comprar
los boletos. Primero
quiero **subir a la
vuelta al mundo.**

el parque de diversiones

la vuelta al mundo

el boleto

D No voy a subir a **la montaña rusa** porque **tengo miedo.**
Luciana y yo preferimos **los autitos chocadores.**
Son más divertidos.

la montaña rusa

¡Qué miedo!

los autitos chocadores

¡Qué divertido!

Más vocabulario

dejar un mensaje *to leave a message*

la llamada *phone call*

¿Está...? *Is . . . there?*

No, no está. *No, he's/she's not here.*

Sí, me encantaría. *Yes, I would love to.*

Un momento. *One moment.*

Expansión de vocabulario p. R8

@**HOMETUTOR**
my.hrw.com

**Interactive
Flashcards**

¡A responder!   Escuchar

Mariano invita a Luciana al museo. Escucha sus respuestas y señala con
el pulgar hacia arriba si ella acepta la invitación o con el pulgar hacia
abajo si no la acepta. *(Listen to Luciana's responses to Mariano's invitation. Make a
thumbs-up sign if she accepts or a thumbs-down sign if she declines.)*

Práctica de VOCABULARIO

1 | Conversaciones por teléfono

Leer | Completa las conversaciones. *(Complete these phone conversations.)*

1. ¿Quieres acompañarme a la feria?
  a. ¿Aló?
  b. ¡Claro que sí!
  c. Tienes una llamada.

2. ¿Puedo hablar con Julieta?
  a. No, no está.
  b. Sí, me encantaría.
  c. ¡Qué lástima!

3. ¿Está Manuel?
  a. ¿Puedo hablar con él?
  b. Te invito.
  c. Un momento.

4. ¿Aló?
  a. Un momento.
  b. ¿Puedo hablar con Rafael?
  c. ¿Puedo dejar un mensaje?

5. No, no está.
  a. ¡Claro que sí!
  b. Me gustaría dejar un mensaje.
  c. ¿Te gustaría ir a la feria?

6. ¿Te gustaría ir al museo?
  a. ¡Qué miedo!
  b. Lo siento, pero no puedo.
  c. ¿Quieres dejar un mensaje?

> **Expansión**
> Write the next part of each conversation.

2 | Los boletos

Hablar Escribir | Mariano tiene boletos para las atracciones del parque de diversiones y otros lugares. Mira el boleto e identifica para qué es. *(Identify what each ticket is for.)*

modelo: El boleto es para **la feria** del libro.

1.
2.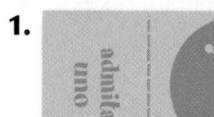
3.

4.
5.
6.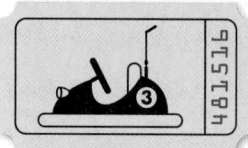

Más práctica   Cuaderno *pp. 318–320*   Cuaderno para hispanohablantes *pp. 318–321*

Get Help Online
my.hrw.com

PARA Y PIENSA

Did you get it?
1. Name two amusement park rides.
2. Name four places that might require you to buy tickets.

VOCABULARIO en contexto

¡AVANZA!

Goal: Listen to Florencia and Mariano talk about the things they see at an amusement park. Then use **Qué** + adjective to describe the different activities you do. *Actividades 3–4*

 ¿Recuerdas? Noun-adjective agreement p. 66

Telehistoria escena 1

@HOMETUTOR View, Read
my.hrw.com and Record

STRATEGIES

VIDEO DVD

AUDIO

Cuando lees
Map the scene Draw a map of the park, using arrows and the initials **M, L,** and **F** for the characters' changing locations. Then use location expressions, such as **cerca de...,** to write sentences describing where they are.

Cuando escuchas
Link words and visual images
Match the location expressions you hear with visual images. For example, when you hear **la montaña rusa,** visualize the roller coaster.

Luciana   Mariano

Florencia

Florencia: *(muttering to herself)* ¿Dónde está Mariano? Tengo que llamarlo a su teléfono celular.

Mariano is also at the amusement park, with his friend Luciana.

Mariano: *(answering phone)* Hola, Florencia. Sí, Luciana y yo estamos en el Parque de la Costa. Compramos nuestros boletos.

Florencia: Yo también. ¿Pueden ver la montaña rusa?

Mariano: Sí, pero estamos más cerca de la vuelta al mundo.

Florencia: Ahora veo la vuelta al mundo. Ustedes deben estar cerca.

Mariano: Sí, sí. Veo la montaña rusa, pero no te veo.

Florencia and Mariano both walk backward, looking for each other.

Luciana: ¿Por qué no encontramos a Florencia delante de los autitos chocadores?

As she says this, Mariano and Florencia suddenly bump into each other.

Continuará... p. 388

También se dice

Argentina To say that he and Luciana are near the Ferris wheel, Mariano uses the words **la vuelta al mundo.** In other Spanish-speaking countries you might hear:
• **España** **la noria**
• **México** **la rueda de la fortuna**
• **Puerto Rico** **la estrella**
• **Perú, Colombia y otros países** **la rueda de Chicago**

3 | Comprensión del episodio   ¿Dónde están?

Escuchar
Leer

Empareja las frases para describir el episodio. *(Match the following sentence starters with logical endings according to the episode.)*

1. Florencia y Mariano hablan por

2. Florencia, Luciana y Mariano están

3. Luciana y Mariano compran

4. Todos pueden ver

5. Mariano y Luciana están

a. la montaña rusa.

b. sus boletos.

c. cerca de la vuelta al mundo.

d. teléfono celular.

e. en el parque de diversiones.

> **Expansión**
> Predict what will happen in the next episode of the Telehistoria.

Nota gramatical   ♻ *¿Recuerdas?* Noun-adjective agreement p. 66

To express *How* + **adjective,** use **Qué** + **adjective** in the masculine singular form.

¡**Qué divertido**!
How fun!

¡**Qué aburrido**!
How boring!

Use the feminine form only when a feminine noun is being described.

4 | Invitaciones

Hablar

Estás en Argentina con un(a) amigo(a). Invita a otro(a) estudiante a varios lugares y atracciones. Él o ella va a dar su opinión y aceptar o no tu invitación. *(Invite a classmate to various places and attractions. He or she will give an opinion and accept or decline your invitation.)*

A ¿Te gustaría subir a la montaña rusa?

B ¡Qué peligroso! No, no me gustaría.

Diversiones en **Argentina**

¿Te gustaría conocer Argentina? Visita las atracciones de este país interesante y divertido.

Get Help Online
my.hrw.com

PARA Y PIENSA

Did you get it? Describe the following, using **Qué** + an adjective.

1. Ir al parque es divertido.

2. La pantalla es pequeña.

3. El museo es interesante.

4. Las fotos son grandes.

Presentación de GRAMÁTICA

Goal: Learn about the irregular preterite forms of **ir, ser,** and **hacer.** Then practice these forms to say where you went and what you did, and tell how it was. *Actividades 5–8*

English Grammar Connection: Irregular verbs do not follow the pattern of regular verbs. In English, irregular verbs in the past tense do not end in *-ed.*

She **went** to the aquarium.   Ella **fue** al acuario.

⬆ **irregular verb**   ⬆ **irregular verb**

Preterite of ir, ser, and hacer

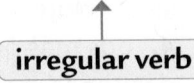
ANIMATEDGRAMMAR
my.hrw.com

Ir, ser, and **hacer** are irregular in the preterite tense. How do you form the preterite of these verbs?

Here's how: The preterite forms of **ir** and **ser** are exactly the same.

ir *to go* / ser *to be*	
fui	fuimos
fuiste	fuisteis
fue	fueron

Use context clues to determine which verb is being used.

Fuimos a la feria.   ¡**Fue** un día divertido!
***We went** to the fair.*   ***It was** a fun day!*

Like **ir** and **ser,** the preterite forms of **hacer** have no accents.

hacer *to do, to make*	
hice	hicimos
hiciste	hicisteis
hizo	hicieron

*Notice that the **c** becomes **z** before **o.**

¿Qué **hiciste** ayer?   Él **hizo** la tarea.
*What **did you do** yesterday?*   *He **did** homework.*

Más práctica
Cuaderno *pp. 321–323*
Cuaderno para hispanohablantes *pp. 322–324*

@**HOMETUTOR** my.hrw.com
Leveled Practice
🌐 Conjuguemos.com

Práctica de GRAMÁTICA

5 | Muchísimas llamadas

Leer Escribir

El sábado y el domingo Florencia, Mariano y Luciana hicieron 40 llamadas por teléfono. Completa la descripción de Mariano con la forma apropiada del pretérito de **hacer**. Luego contesta las preguntas 7 y 8. *(Complete Mariano's description with the correct preterite form of **hacer**. Then answer questions 7 and 8.)*

El fin de semana pasado, mis amigas y yo **1.** 40 llamadas por teléfono. ¡Qué bárbaro! Luciana **2.** cinco llamadas el sábado. Luciana y Florencia **3.** el mismo (*same*) número de llamadas el domingo. Yo **4.** dos más que ellas el domingo. Una persona en el grupo **5.** ocho llamadas cada (*each*) día. Florencia **6.** dos más que Luciana el sábado. ¿Cuántas llamadas **7.** cada persona? ¿Cuántas llamadas **8.** tú el fin de semana pasado?

6 | ¿Cómo fue el día?

Hablar Escribir

Muchas personas salieron ayer. Explica adónde fueron y si fue divertido o aburrido. *(Tell where these people went and if it was fun or boring.)*

modelo: nosotros / parque de diversiones / 🙂
Fuimos al parque de diversiones. Fue divertido.

1. yo / museo / 🙂
2. ustedes / acuario / 🙁
3. mis amigos y yo / cine / 🙁
4. Florencia / centro / 🙂
5. tú / zoológico / 🙂
6. mis padres / feria / 🙁

Expansión
Interview your classmates to find out where they went yesterday and how it was.

Comparación cultural

El puerto de La Boca

How do paintings reflect a city's character? People from Buenos Aires, **Argentina,** are called *porteños*, meaning "people of the port." This reflects the essential role of the port in the nation's development. La Boca, the city's first port, is a famous neighborhood of Buenos Aires known for its brightly colored buildings. The artist Benito Quinquela Martín grew up in La Boca in the early 20th century, during the height of the port's development. His paintings capture the neighborhood's color and port activities.

Compara con tu mundo *What are some port cities in the United States?*

Día de Trabajo (1948), Benito Quinquela Martín

7 Fueron a diferentes lugares

Escuchar
Escribir

Escucha las descripciones y contesta las preguntas. *(Listen and answer the questions.)*

1.

a. ¿Quiénes fueron?
b. ¿Qué hicieron?
c. ¿Cómo fue?

2.

a. ¿Quiénes fueron?
b. ¿Qué hicieron?
c. ¿Cómo fue?

3.

a. ¿Quiénes fueron?
b. ¿Qué hicieron?
c. ¿Cómo fue?

8 ¡Qué divertido!

Hablar

Habla con otro(a) estudiante sobre adónde fuiste y qué hiciste el fin de semana pasado. *(Talk with a partner about where you went and what you did last weekend.)*

A ¿Fuiste al centro?

¿Qué hicieron ustedes allí?

B Sí, fui al centro con mi familia.

Fuimos al cine y...

Estudiante Ⓐ

1. el parque de diversiones
2. el centro
3. el museo
4. la playa
5. el zoológico
6. el estadio
7. el restaurante
8. ¿?

Estudiante Ⓑ

ir de compras
mirar...
hacer esquí acuático
subir a...
pasar un rato
comer
pasear
¿?

Expansión
Write a summary of where you went and what you did last weekend.

Más práctica   Cuaderno *pp. 321–323*   Cuaderno para hispanohablantes *pp. 322–324*

Get Help Online
my.hrw.com

PARA Y PIENSA

Did you get it?   Complete the following sentences with the correct preterite form of **hacer** and **ir** or **ser**. Then tell whether you used **ir** or **ser**.
1. Nosotros _____ la tarea; _____ muy fácil.
2. Yo _____ a la playa. _____ esquí acuático.
3. ¿ _____ ellos al parque? ¿Y qué _____ allí?

GRAMÁTICA en contexto

¡AVANZA! **Goal:** Notice how Mariano, Florencia, and Luciana use the preterite tense to talk about what they and others did. Then use **ir, ser,** and **hacer** in the preterite to ask about what others did. *Actividades 9–10*

♻ *¿Recuerdas?* Places around town p. 219

Telehistoria escena 2

@**HOMETUTOR** View, Read
my.hrw.com and Record

STRATEGIES

Cuando lees
Identify verb forms in context
Identify preterite-tense forms of **ir** in this scene. For each, find out where the character(s) went and why.

Cuando escuchas
Sort out the speakers In this scene, characters use **dice que...** to report what another person says. Listen for who reports what was said. What information do they report?

VIDEO
DVD

AUDIO

Luciana: ¡Ay! Che, Mariano, ¿adónde fuiste?

Mariano: Yo fui a ver dónde podemos encontrar a Trini. Sé dónde está.

Luciana: ¿Cómo lo sabes?

Mariano: Fue el señor de la ventanilla. Él dice que Trini fue a la vuelta al mundo.

Florencia: Mariano, ¡qué bárbaro! ¡Vamos!

They start to walk. Florencia stops to speak to someone, then catches up.

Florencia: El señor dice que Trini y sus amigos fueron a comer.

Mariano: ¿Trini fue a comer? ¡Ay, no! ¿Qué podemos hacer? Tenemos que ir a buscarla.

They reach the food court but don't see Trini.

Luciana: Fuimos a la vuelta al mundo, fuimos al restaurante. ¿Dónde está Trini? Nunca la vamos a encontrar.

Continuará... p. 393

También se dice

Argentina Luciana uses the word **che** to greet Mariano in a friendly way. In other Spanish-speaking countries you might hear:
• **México** **cuate**
• **España** **tío(a), colega**
• **Colombia** **llave**
• **Puerto Rico, Venezuela y otros países** **pana**

9 *Comprensión del episodio* Fueron a buscarla

Escuchar
Leer

Contesta las preguntas. *(Answer the questions.)*

1. ¿Quién habló con el señor de la ventanilla?

2. ¿Quién fue a la vuelta al mundo?

3. ¿Quién habló con otro señor en el parque?

4. ¿Qué dice el señor?

5. ¿Por qué fueron al restaurante los chicos?

6. ¿Quién dice que nunca van a encontrar a Trini?

10 ¡A jugar! Adivina   *¿Recuerdas?* Places around town p. 219

Hablar

Trabaja con otros estudiantes. Sin decir adónde fuiste, explícales que hiciste. Ellos tienen que adivinar el lugar. *(Give clues about what you did so your partners can guess where you went.)*

un partido de...   el parque de
el cine   diversiones
el centro comercial   un concierto
la playa   ¿ ?
el museo

A Compré bloqueador de sol y nadé en el mar.

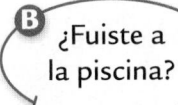 **B** ¿Fuiste a la piscina?

 **C** ¿Fuiste a la playa?

Expansión
For each place, tell how you got there and how it was.

AUDIO

Pronunciación   Las letras LL y Y

The letter combination **ll** in Spanish sounds like the English *y* in *yet*. The **y** has the same sound unless it stands alone or is at the end of a word, in which case the **y** is pronounced like the *ee* in the English word *see*.

Listen and repeat.

llamar	tobi**ll**o	rodi**ll**a	e**ll**a	ga**ll**eta
yo	a**y**er	pla**y**a	ma**y**o	desa**y**uno
y	ha**y**	mu**y**	ho**y**	

Yo me **ll**amo Marco **y** e**ll**a es **Y**olanda.

Hoy vo**y** a la pla**y**a de Marbe**ll**a. Es mu**y** bonita.

 **Get Help Online**
my.hrw.com

PARA
Y
PIENSA

Did you get it?   Ask Mariano the questions to which he would provide these statements as answers. Use **ir, ser,** and **hacer.**

1. Florencia, Luciana y yo fuimos al restaurante.

2. Yo hablé con el señor de la ventanilla.

3. El día fue divertido.

Lección 2
trescientos ochenta y nueve **389**

Presentación de GRAMÁTICA

¡AVANZA! **Goal:** Learn what pronouns are used after prepositions. Then practice them to give and accept or decline invitations. *Actividades 11–14*

♻ *¿Recuerdas?* Stem-changing verbs: **e → i** p. 228

English Grammar Connection: Prepositions (such as *at, for, in, on,* and *with* in English) link a noun or a **pronoun** with another word in a sentence. In both English and Spanish, some of the pronouns that follow these prepositions are different from the subject pronouns.

I have a ticket. The ticket is **for me.**   **Yo** tengo un boleto. El boleto es **para mí.**

Pronouns After Prepositions

ANIMATEDGRAMMAR
my.hrw.com

Use **pronouns** after **prepositions** like **a, con, de,** and **para.**

Here's how: Pronouns that follow prepositions are the same as the subject pronouns in all forms except **mí** (**yo**) and **ti** (**tú**).

Pronouns After Prepositions	
mí	nosotros(as)
ti	vosotros(as)
usted, él, ella	ustedes, ellos(as)

La montaña rusa está **detrás de mí.**
*The roller coaster is **behind me.***

El teléfono celular está **cerca de ti.**
*The cellular phone is **near you.***

When you use **mí** and **ti** after the preposition **con,** they combine with **con** to form the words **conmigo** and **contigo.**

¿Vas al museo **conmigo?**
*Are you going to the museum **with me?***

Sí, voy **contigo.**
*Yes, I'm going **with you.***

♻ *¿Recuerdas?* You use these pronouns with verbs like **gustar** to emphasize or clarify which person you are talking about (see p. 42).

A **él** le **gusta** ir al zoológico.   *He likes to go to the zoo.*

A **ella** le **gusta** ir al zoológico.   *She likes to go to the zoo.*

A **usted** le **gusta** ir al zoológico.   *You like to go to the zoo.*

Más práctica
Cuaderno *pp. 324–326*
Cuaderno para hispanohablantes *pp. 325–328*

@HOMETUTOR my.hrw.com
Leveled Practice

Práctica de GRAMÁTICA

11 | Invitaciones para ella

Escribir

Hoy hace sol y Luciana prefiere hacer algo al aire libre. Sus amigos la invitan a varios lugares. Escribe sus respuestas, usando pronombres. *(Luciana wants to do something outdoors. Write her responses to these invitations, using pronouns.)*

> **modelo:** ¿Quieres ir al cine con nosotros?
> No, no quiero ir al cine con ustedes.

1. ¿Te gustaría ir a la playa conmigo?
2. ¿Quieres comprar ropa para ti en el centro comercial?
3. ¿Quieres tomar fotos de nosotros en el parque?
4. ¿Te gustaría ir al Café Internet con Mariano y Florencia?
5. ¿Puedes preparar la comida para mí y para mi hermano?
6. ¿Puedo ir al zoológico contigo?

12 | Te invito

Hablar

Llama a otro(a) estudiante por teléfono para hacerle invitaciones a estos lugares. Él o ella va a decir que va con otra(s) persona(s). *(Make phone calls to invite a classmate to go to these places. Your partner will say that he or she is going with someone else.)*

modelo: mis tíos

A ¿Aló? ¿Puedo hablar con Ana?

B Hola, Laura. Soy yo. ¿Cómo estás?

Bien. ¿Te gustaría ir al museo conmigo?

Lo siento, pero no puedo ir contigo. Voy a ir con mis tíos.

1. él

2. ellas

3. mi hermano

4. ellos

5. mis padres

6. ella

> **Expansión**
> Invite your partner to three more places.

13 | ¿Y tú?

Hablar
Escribir

Contesta las preguntas. Usa pronombres en tus respuestas. *(Answer the questions, using pronouns.)*

1. ¿Te gustaría subir a una montaña rusa con tus amigos?

2. ¿Tienes miedo cuando no hay nadie contigo?

3. ¿Qué hay delante de ti ahora?

4. ¿A qué museo te gustaría ir con los estudiantes de tu clase?

5. ¿Qué te gusta hacer con tus amigos durante el fin de semana?

6. ¿Cómo contestas el teléfono cuando hay una llamada para ti?

> **Expansión**
> Write five original questions using prepositions for your classmates to answer.

14 | En un restaurante argentino   **¿Recuerdas?** Stem-changing verbs: e → i p. 228

Escribir

Comparación cultural

La comida argentina

What factors influence a country's cuisine? In the late 18th century, many *estancias,* or ranches, were developed on the sprawling grasslands, or *pampas,* of **Argentina.** More beef is eaten per person in Argentina than in any other country. Some people may have *bife,* or steak, twice a day. A traditional weekend activity of many Argentines is an *asado,* or outdoor barbecue with family and friends. Steakhouses, known as *parrillas,* are also common. Argentinean cuisine is not limited to meat, however. Because of Argentina's many Italian immigrants, dishes such as pizza and pasta are also popular.

Un gaucho prepara bife en una estancia

Restaurante Mirasol	
Parrilla	
Bife de chorizo	$11,00
Bife de lomo	$12,00
Pastas	
Ravioles de ricota	$9,00
Canelones	$9,00
Pizzas	
Cuatro quesos	
Vegetariana *(espinaca y tomates)*	
mediana: $11,50	grande: $15,00

Compara con tu mundo *What has influenced the common foods available in your area?*

Escribe sobre una visita a este restaurante. Di quiénes van contigo y describe qué piden y por qué. *(Write about a trip to this restaurant. Tell who goes with you, what they order, and why.)*

modelo: Mis padres y mi hermano van conmigo al Restaurante Mirasol.
Mi padre pide el bife de chorizo porque a él le gusta la carne...

Más práctica Cuaderno *pp. 324–326* Cuaderno para hispanohablantes *pp. 325–328*

PARA Y PIENSA

Get Help Online
my.hrw.com

Did you get it? Complete the sentences with the correct pronoun according to the hint in parentheses.

1. ¿Te gustaría ir con _____ ? (Simón y yo)

2. El boleto es para _____ . (tú)

3. Quiero ir con _____ . (mis amigos)

✾ Todo junto

¡AVANZA!

Goal: *Show what you know* Pay attention to the different characters and their roles in this scene. Then practice using the preterite forms of **ir, ser,** and **hacer** and prepositions after pronouns to tell a friend what activities you did. *Actividades 15–19*

Telehistoria completa

@**HOMETUTOR** View, Read and Record
my.hrw.com

STRATEGIES

Cuando lees
Recall and reason As you read, recall the previous scenes to understand how hard the teenagers have tried to find Trini Salgado. Analyze why another woman shows up at the information booth.

Cuando escuchas
Identify appropriate expressions and register Pay attention to the language Florencia uses to assign tasks. How does it compare to the language the announcer uses to call Trini Salgado? What differences can you identify?

Escena 1 *Resumen*
Florencia va al parque de diversiones para buscar a Trini Salgado, pero primero necesita encontrar a Mariano y a su amiga, Luciana.

Escena 2 *Resumen*
Los amigos van a la vuelta al mundo y al restaurante para buscar a Trini Salgado, pero no la encuentran.

VIDEO
DVD

AUDIO

Escena 3

Luciana: *(eyeing a food stand)* Empanadas, ¡qué ricas! Voy a comprar unas.

Florencia: Gracias, Luciana. ¿Por qué no compras un refresco para mí, y unas empanadas para nosotros dos? Y Mariano, ¿te gustaría venir conmigo a buscar a Trini a los autitos chocadores?

Luciana speaks with a manager, who makes an announcement over the loudspeaker.

(crackling) «Atención, por favor, señorita Trini Salgado, por favor, la esperan en la puerta, señorita Trini Salgado».

Florencia y Mariano: ¡Vamos!

A woman, not the famous soccer player, arrives at the booth.

Mujer: Señor, ¡yo soy Trini Salgado!

Florencia: ¿Trini Salgado? ¿La jugadora de fútbol?

Mujer: *(confused)* ¿La jugadora de fútbol?

15 | Comprensión de los episodios   ¡No es cierto!

Escuchar
Leer

Corrige los errores en estas oraciones. *(Correct the errors.)*

1. Luciana y Mariano compraron boletos para el zoológico.
2. Luciana y Mariano hablaron por teléfono.
3. Florencia habló con el señor de la ventanilla.
4. Luciana fue a comprar hamburguesas y un café.
5. Florencia invitó a Mariano a acompañarla a la montaña rusa para buscar a Trini.
6. Los amigos encontraron a Trini Salgado, la jugadora de fútbol.

16 | Comprensión de los episodios   ¿Qué pasó?

Escuchar
Leer

Explica lo que pasó en los episodios. Menciona como mínimo dos cosas para cada foto. *(Tell what happened in the episodes. Mention at least two things for each.)*

1.    **2.**    **3.**

17 | Unas llamadas telefónicas

Digital **performance space**

Hablar

STRATEGY Hablar

Use appropriate expressions When you make a phone call, you need to use appropriate expressions and register depending on the conversation. When you talk to a friend, you can be very informal, but remember that with other people you may have to be a little more formal. Below you will find some ideas to use during a phone conversation. Use as many as possible and make them understandable to your partner.

Trabaja con otro(a) estudiante. Haz varias llamadas por teléfono, usando las ideas de la lista. Presenta la mejor conversación a la clase. *(Have phone conversations with a partner, using the ideas on the list. Share your best conversation with the class.)*

Para organizarte:
- Invita a la persona al parque de diversiones o a otro lugar.
- Habla sobre adónde fuiste y qué hiciste durante la semana pasada.
- ¿ ?

A ¿Aló?

B Buenas tardes. ¿Puedo hablar con Andrew, por favor?

Expansión
Leave a phone message for your teacher asking to meet to discuss your grades.

18 | Integración

Digital **performance**)) **space**

Leer
Escuchar
Hablar

Lee la nota y escucha el mensaje telefónico. Decide qué invitación quieres aceptar, y deja un mensaje para Álvaro y después para Carlos para decirles si vas a ir o no. *(Decide which invitation you want to accept and then respond to both invitations.)*

Fuente 1 Nota

> 3 P.M.
>
> Llamó Álvaro. Ayer fue a la ventanilla del zoológico y compró dos boletos. Tienen una exhibición con elefantes y gorilas de África. Quiere saber si te gustaría ir con él mañana, a la una y media de la tarde. Álvaro te invita; no necesitas dinero. Llámalo a su casa, y si no está allí, deja un mensaje en su teléfono celular.

Fuente 2 Mensaje telefónico

Listen and take notes
- ¿Qué hizo Carlos anteayer?
- ¿Qué quiere hacer mañana?
- ¿Cuál es el problema?

modelo: Hola,... Me gustaría...
(Hola,... Lo siento...)

19 | Un post para tus amigos

Digital **performance**)) **space**

Escribir

Escribe un post para tus amigos en las redes sociales.
Habla sobre adónde fuiste la semana pasada y qué hiciste. Incluye una invitación para volver con tus amigos al mismo lugar. *(Write a social media post for your friends. Talk about where you went and what you did last week. Include an invitation to go back together to the same place.)*

modelo: ¿Sabes qué? La semana pasada fui a la feria con mis amigos. Compré helados para ellos y...

Writing Criteria	Excellent	Good	Needs Work
Content	Your post contains a detailed invitation.	Your post contains a brief invitation.	Your post doesn't include an invitation.
Communication	Most of your post is organized and easy to follow.	Parts of your post are organized and easy to follow.	Your post is disorganized and hard to follow.
Accuracy	Your post has few mistakes in grammar and vocabulary.	Your post has some mistakes in grammar and vocabulary.	Your post has many mistakes in grammar and vocabulary.

Expansión
Write your friends' responses to your invitation.

Más práctica   Cuaderno *pp. 327–328*   Cuaderno para hispanohablantes *pp. 329–330*

PARA Y PIENSA

Get Help Online
my.hrw.com

Did you get it? Create sentences using the preterite form of each verb and the correct pronoun after each preposition.
1. Florencia / hacer / una cena para (Mariano)
2. Las empanadas / ser / para (Florencia y Mariano)
3. Mariano / ir / con (Florencia) a los autitos chocadores

Lectura cultural

¡AVANZA! **Goal:** Read about non-traditional museums in Argentina and Bolivia. Then compare the two museums and talk about museums that you have visited.

Comparación cultural

AUDIO

Museos excepcionales

STRATEGY Leer

Compare museums Make a table to compare the two museums by name (**nombre**), location (**ubicación**), focus (**enfoque**), and exhibits (**exhibiciones**).

	1.	2.
nombre		
ubicación		
enfoque		
exhibiciones		

¿Qué imaginas cuando piensas en un museo? Muchas personas imaginan cuartos formales con obras [1] de arte. Hay museos en Latinoamérica que celebran su cultura y también dan una experiencia diferente, sin [2] tantas restricciones como un museo tradicional.

El Museo al Aire Libre [3] no tiene ni puertas ni paredes [4], pero es uno de los museos más populares de Buenos Aires. Está en el corazón de La Boca, una sección de Buenos Aires cerca del mar, en una calle pequeña que se llama el Caminito. Allí viven muchos artistas argentinos en sus famosas casas multicolores.

---

[1] works   [2] without   [3] Open-air   [4] walls

Argentina

El Museo al Aire Libre en Buenos Aires, Argentina

El Museo de Instrumentos Musicales en La Paz, Bolivia

Bolivia

El Caminito sirve como un marco[5] natural para diversas obras de arte: pinturas[6], esculturas y murales. Es posible caminar por la calle, ver obras de arte, comer en cafés, escuchar música y mirar a personas que bailan el tango.

La cultura boliviana, especialmente la música, tiene dos orígenes: indígena[7] y español. En el centro de La Paz, Bolivia, la calle Jaén tiene varios museos de arte donde puedes ver obras indígenas. El Museo de Instrumentos Musicales es un poco diferente de los otros. En este museo interactivo, ¡puedes tocar algunos de los instrumentos! Allí hay exhibiciones de instrumentos precolombinos, instrumentos de viento y tambores[8]. Puedes tocar instrumentos como el charango, una guitarra pequeña de influencia española.

---

[5] frame   [6] paintings   [7] indigenous   [8] drums

PARA Y PIENSA

¿Comprendiste?

1. ¿Dónde está el Museo al Aire Libre? ¿Y el Museo de Instrumentos Musicales?
2. ¿Qué hay en los dos museos?
3. ¿Por qué no es tradicional el museo de Buenos Aires? ¿Y el museo de La Paz?

¿Y tú?

¿Alguna vez fuiste a un museo? ¿Con quién? ¿Te gustaría visitar el Museo al Aire Libre o el Museo de Instrumentos Musicales? ¿Por qué?

Proyectos culturales

Comparación cultural

Nombres y apellidos

How do last names show family ties across generations? In English-speaking countries, people traditionally inherit one last name, from their father. In Spanish-speaking countries, many people inherit two last names (**apellidos**); the first is the father's, the second is the mother's. Look at the chart to see how this works. Which names represent the father and which ones represent the mother?

Alejandro García Montoya
Guadalupe Saavedra Alderete
Lorenzo Robledo Trujillo
Esperanza Landa Córdoba
Gregorio García Saavedra
Margarita Robledo Landa
Marisol Antonia García Robledo

Proyecto 1 *Family tree*

Make a family tree of your family or a family you know.

Instructions for family tree
Draw a family tree chart like the one above to show how the family names of you, your parents, and grandparents would change using the Spanish tradition of two last names.

Proyecto 2 *Photo album*

Make a photo album of your immediate family or one you know. Use two last names to label the people in your photos.

Materials for photo album
Photos or copies of photos
Construction paper
Glue or tape
Cardboard and cord or ribbon

Instructions

1. Make a page for each person you want to include in your album, using construction paper. Label the page with his or her name or write a caption below each photo. Use the two last names. You may include the date of birth or words that describe the person's interests and personality.
2. Make a cover for your family album. Punch holes in the cover and pages. Bind them together with cord or ribbon.

En tu comunidad

If you know any native speakers of Spanish, ask them about their own last names. Do they have two surnames? If so, do they ordinarily use both of them?

En resumen
Vocabulario y gramática

Vocabulario

At the Amusement Park

los autitos chocadores	*bumper cars*	¡Qué divertido!	*How fun!*
el boleto	*ticket*	¡Qué miedo!	*How scary!*
la montaña rusa	*roller coaster*	tener miedo	*to be afraid*
subir a	*to ride*	la vuelta al mundo	*Ferris wheel*

Places of Interest

el acuario	*aquarium*
la feria	*fair*
el museo	*museum*
el parque de diversiones	*amusement park*
el zoológico	*zoo*

Make a Phone Call

dejar un mensaje	*to leave a message*
la llamada	*phone call*
llamar	*to call (by phone)*
el teléfono celular	*cellular phone*

Extend Invitations

¿Quieres acompañarme a...?	*Would you like to come with me to . . . ?*
¿Te gustaría...?	*Would you like . . . ?*
Te invito.	*I'll treat you. / I invite you.*

Other Words and Phrases

con	*with*
el fin de semana	*weekend*

Talk on the Phone

¿Aló?	*Hello?*
¿Está...?	*Is . . . there?*
No, no está.	*No, he's / she's not.*
¿Puedo hablar con...?	*May I speak with . . . ?*
Un momento.	*One moment.*

Accept

¡Claro que sí!	*Of course!*
Me gustaría...	*I would like . . .*
Sí, me encantaría.	*Yes, I would love to.*

Decline

¡Qué lástima!	*What a shame!*

Gramática

Nota gramatical: ¡Qué + adjective! *p.384*

Preterite of ir, ser, and hacer

Ir, ser, and **hacer** are irregular in the preterite tense. The preterite forms of **ir** and **ser** are exactly the same.

ir *to go* / **ser** *to be*	
fui	fuimos
fuiste	fuisteis
fue	fueron

hacer *to do, to make*	
hice	hicimos
hiciste	hicisteis
hizo	hicieron

Pronouns After Prepositions

Pronouns that follow prepositions are the same as the subject pronouns except **mí (yo)** and **ti (tú)**.

Pronouns After Prepositions	
mí	nosotros(as)
ti	vosotros(as)
usted, él, ella	ustedes, ellos(as)

The preposition **con** combines with **mí** and **ti** to form the words **conmigo** and **contigo**.

¡AvanzaRap!
DVD
Sing and Learn

@**HOMETUTOR**
my.hrw.com

¡LLEGADA!

Now you can
- talk on the phone
- say where you went, how it was, and what you did
- extend invitations

Using
- ¡**Qué** + adjective!
- preterite of **ir, ser,** and **hacer**
- pronouns after prepositions

To review
- ¡**Qué** + adjective! p. 384
- pronouns after prepositions p. 390

1 Listen and understand

AUDIO

Escucha las conversaciones. En una hoja de papel, escribe **sí** si el (la) invitado(a) acepta la invitación, o **no** si no la acepta. *(Listen to the conversations. On a separate sheet of paper, write **sí** or **no** to tell whether or not each invitation is accepted.)*

To review
- ¡**Qué** + adjective! p. 384

2 Extend invitations

Jaime invita a Laura a salir con él. Escribe sus invitaciones y las respuestas de Laura. *(Write Jaime's invitations to Laura. Then write her responses.)*

modelo: no / horrible
Jaime: ¿Quieres acompañarme a la feria?
Laura: No. ¡Qué horrible!

1. sí / interesante

2. sí / bonito

3. no / aburrido

4. sí / divertido

5. no / peligroso

6. sí / bueno

To review
• pronouns after prepositions p. 390

3 | Talk on the phone

Completa esta conversación. Usa **con** o **para** y el pronombre correcto.
*(Complete the conversation with **con** or **para** and the correct pronoun.)*

—¿Bueno?

—¿Está Manuel?

—Sí, soy yo.

—Manuel, soy Guillermo. ¿Te gustaría ir al acuario **1.** ? Te invito.
 Ya tengo un boleto **2.** , y si quieres acompañarme, puedo comprar
 un boleto **3.** .

—Lo siento, Guillermo, pero no puedo ir **4.** . Carlos y Beatriz quieren ir
 al museo y voy **5.** . ¿Por qué no vienes **6.** ? Vamos a salir a las diez.

—Mi hermano también quiere ir. Voy a hablar **7.** para ver
 si puede.

—Está bien. Hasta luego.

To review
• preterite of **ir, ser,** and **hacer** p. 385

4 | Say where you went, how it was, and what you did

Luisa habla con Gregorio. Lee las respuestas de Gregorio y escribe las
preguntas de Luisa. Usa los verbos **ir, ser** y **hacer.** *(Write Luisa's questions based on
Gregorio's answers. Use **ir, ser,** and **hacer.**)*

modelo: Hice muchas cosas el sábado. (¿Qué?)
 ¿Qué hiciste el sábado?

1. El viernes fui al cine. (¿Adónde?)
2. La película fue muy interesante. (¿Cómo?)
3. Lucas fue conmigo. (¿Quién?)
4. Hicimos algo muy divertido después. (¿Qué?)
5. Fuimos al nuevo café. (¿Adónde?)
6. La comida fue buena. (¿Cómo?)

To review
• Comparación cultural pp. 378, 386, 392
• Lectura cultural pp. 396–397

5 | Argentina and Bolivia

Comparación cultural

Answer these culture questions.

1. Where is El Parque de la Costa and what can you do there?
2. To whom does the term **porteños** refer and why?
3. What foods are popular in Argentina and why? What is an **asado**?
4. Describe what you can find on **el Caminito** in Buenos Aires and
 calle Jaén in La Paz.

Más práctica Cuaderno *pp. 329–340* Cuaderno para hispanohablantes *pp. 331–340*

Get Help Online
my.hrw.com

Nicaragua

Bolivia

Argentina

AUDIO

¿Conoces un lugar divertido?

Lectura y escritura

1 **Leer** People like to go to different places to have fun. Read about the places that Luis, Liliana, and Eva visited.

2 **Escribir** Using the three descriptions as models, write a short paragraph about a place you recently visited.

> **STRATEGY Escribir**
>
> **Make an activity timeline** Make a timeline of your activities. What did you do first, second, third, and so on? Use the timeline to guide your writing.
>
>
>
> Primero   Segundo   Tercero

Step 1 Complete the timeline, showing what you did first, second, third, and so on.

Step 2 Write your paragraph, including all the activities on your timeline. Check your writing by yourself or with help from a friend. Make final corrections.

Compara con tu mundo

Use the paragraph you wrote to compare your visit to a visit described by *one* of the three students. Are the activities similar? In what ways are they different?

Cuaderno *pp. 341–343*   Cuaderno para hispanohablantes *pp. 341–343*

Bolivia — Luis

¿Qué tal? Soy Luis y vivo en La Paz, en las montañas de los Andes. Anteayer mis amigos y yo hicimos algo divertido. Primero fuimos al Paseo el Prado, una calle divertida. Allí caminamos y miramos los restaurantes y las tiendas. Por fin llegamos a la Plaza del Estudiante. Encontramos a otros amigos allí. Hizo buen tiempo, entonces hablamos y paseamos en la plaza. ¡Qué bonito!

Argentina — Liliana

¡Hola! Me llamo Liliana y soy de Buenos Aires. Ayer mi hermana y yo fuimos a un parque de diversiones cerca de mi casa. Primero nosotras subimos a la montaña rusa, pero a mí no me gustó. ¡Qué miedo! Me gustaron más los autitos chocadores. Más tarde comimos unas hamburguesas. Luego miramos un espectáculo de láser[1]. Volvimos a casa en la noche, cuando cerró el parque. ¡Qué bárbaro!

[1] **espectáculo...** laser show

Nicaragua — Eva

Me llamo Eva y soy de Managua. El jueves pasado mis padres y yo fuimos a Masaya, el centro folklórico de Nicaragua. Todos los jueves, en el Mercado Nacional de Artesanías[2] celebran las Verbenas de Masaya: un festival folklórico de danza y música. Los artistas llevan trajes[3] de muchos colores. ¡Tomé unas fotos fabulosas! Después compramos artesanías y comimos comidas típicas de Nicaragua. ¡Fue muy divertido!

[2] **Mercado...** National Handicraft Market   [3] costumes

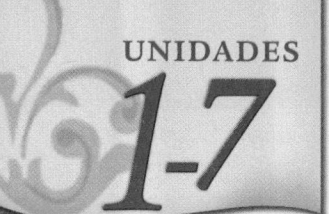
Repaso inclusivo
♻ Options for Review

¡AvanzaRap!
DVD
Sing and Learn

Digital
performance space

1 | Listen, understand, and compare

Escuchar

Listen to the phone conversation. Then answer the following questions.

1. ¿Quién llama a Jaime?
2. ¿Quién contesta el teléfono en la casa de Jaime?
3. ¿Adónde fue Jaime?
4. ¿Quiere dejar un mensaje Teresa?
5. ¿Qué quiere hacer Teresa hoy? ¿Con quién?
6. ¿Cuál es el número del teléfono celular de Jaime?

Who do you like to do things with on the weekends? Where do you go?

2 | Present a trip

Hablar

Prepare a presentation about the last trip or outing that you took. Make a poster out of your own photos or magazine clippings and give your poster a title. Use it as a visual cue while you talk about where you went and with whom, when and how you got there, and what you did. Your presentation should be at least three minutes long.

3 | Talk with a fellow passenger

Hablar

You are on a plane returning home after a long weekend trip. You strike up a conversation with the teen sitting next to you. Find out as much as you can about him or her: name, age, where he or she is from, where he or she is going, and what he or she is going to do there. Your partner will also ask where you went and what you did there. Your conversation should be at least three minutes long.

4 | Write a computer guide

Escribir

While working at your summer job in a cybercafé, you are asked to create a guide for Spanish-speaking customers. Include the café's name, location, hours, and prices. Explain what kinds of computers the café has and what customers are able to do there, and give step-by-step instructions for those who are unfamiliar with Internet activities. Your guide should have illustrations and at least eight sentences.

5 | Tell what is true or false

Hablar

Work in a group of three. Take turns making statements about things you or someone you know did or about your life now. Most of the statements should be true but some should be made-up. The other members of your group will say whether they think each statement is true or false. The winner is the person who guessed correctly the most.

6 | Create a TV ad

Hablar

Work with a partner. Use the Internet to research an amusement park in a Spanish-speaking country. Then write the script for a TV ad for the park, mentioning the name, days and hours of operation, prices, and rides, including any special facts or features. Also tell people how they can get there from the nearest city. Record the ad or present it to the class.

7 | Give advice to another teen

Leer Escribir

You run an advice column on the Web for other teens. Read this e-mail that a student sent to you and write a response, telling him what to do. Use affirmative **tú** commands, **deber,** and **tener que** in your response. Your e-mail should include at least six pieces of advice.

> Hola. Soy estudiante del primer año de español. Tengo un problema y necesito tu ayuda. Me gusta aprender el español, pero muchas veces saco malas notas en los exámenes. La clase es interesante y escucho a la maestra, pero no entiendo nada. ¿Qué debo hacer?
>
> Muchas gracias.
>
> Estudiante nervioso

Costa Rica

❧❧

Una rutina diferente

Océano
Atlántico

Lección 1

Tema: **Pensando en las vacaciones**

Lección 2

Tema: **¡Vamos de vacaciones!**

República
Dominicana

Cuba   Puerto
Rico

Golfo de México

México

Honduras   *Mar Caribe*

Nicaragua

Guatemala
El Salvador

Panamá

«¡Hola!

Somos Jorge y Susana.
Vivimos en San José, Costa Rica.»

Costa Rica

*Océano
Pacífico*

Venezuela

Colombia

Ecuador

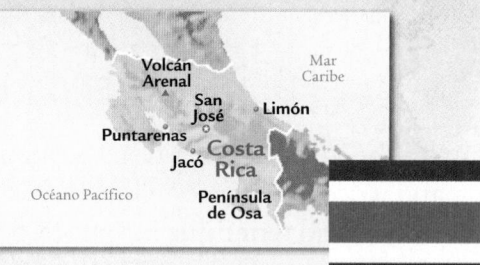

Volcán
Arenal   *Mar
Caribe*
San
José   •Limón
Puntarenas ○
Jacó   ○ Costa
Rica
Océano Pacífico   Península
de Osa

Población: 4.814.144

Área: 19.730 millas cuadradas

Capital: San José

Moneda: el colón (por Cristóbal Colón)

Idioma: español

Comida típica: gallo pinto, casado, sopa negra

Gente famosa: Óscar Arias Sánchez (político),
José Figueres Ferrer (político), Claudia Poll
(atleta), Francisco Zúñiga (artista)

Casado

La naturaleza: un lugar para relajarse
The active Arenal Volcano provides immense heat to the waters nearby, which creates the Tabacón hot springs. Costa Ricans and other tourists come here to relax and enjoy the health benefits of the springs' mineral water pools. *Where can people go to relax and experience nature in your area?* ▶

Las aguas termales de Tabacón y el Volcán Arenal

◀ **Los deportes acuáticos** Costa Rica's Pacific coast has dozens of beaches where tourists come to sunbathe and swim. More daring water sports, especially surfing, are also very popular. Costa Rica recently hosted the World Surf Kayak Championship. *Where can people practice water sports where you live?*

Un competidor de surf kayac en Puntarenas

Las artesanías de madera The town of Sarchí holds an annual festival for their **carretas,** or wooden oxcarts. The carts were used to transport coffee in Costa Rica in the 1800s, before the construction of the railroad. Today's **carretas** are elaborately painted by hand, often have musical wheels, and can be found in all sizes, even as miniature souvenirs. *What typical handicrafts are made in the United States?* ▶

Las carretas, artesanías típicas de Sarchí

Costa Rica

Lección 1

Tema:

Pensando en las vacaciones

∙∙∙ ∙∙∙

¡AVANZA! **In this lesson you will learn to**
- talk about a typical day
- talk about what you are doing
- talk about your daily routine while on vacation

using
- reflexive verbs
- present progressive

♻ **¿Recuerdas?**
- preterite of **hacer,** chores, houses
- direct object pronouns
- parts of the body, telling time

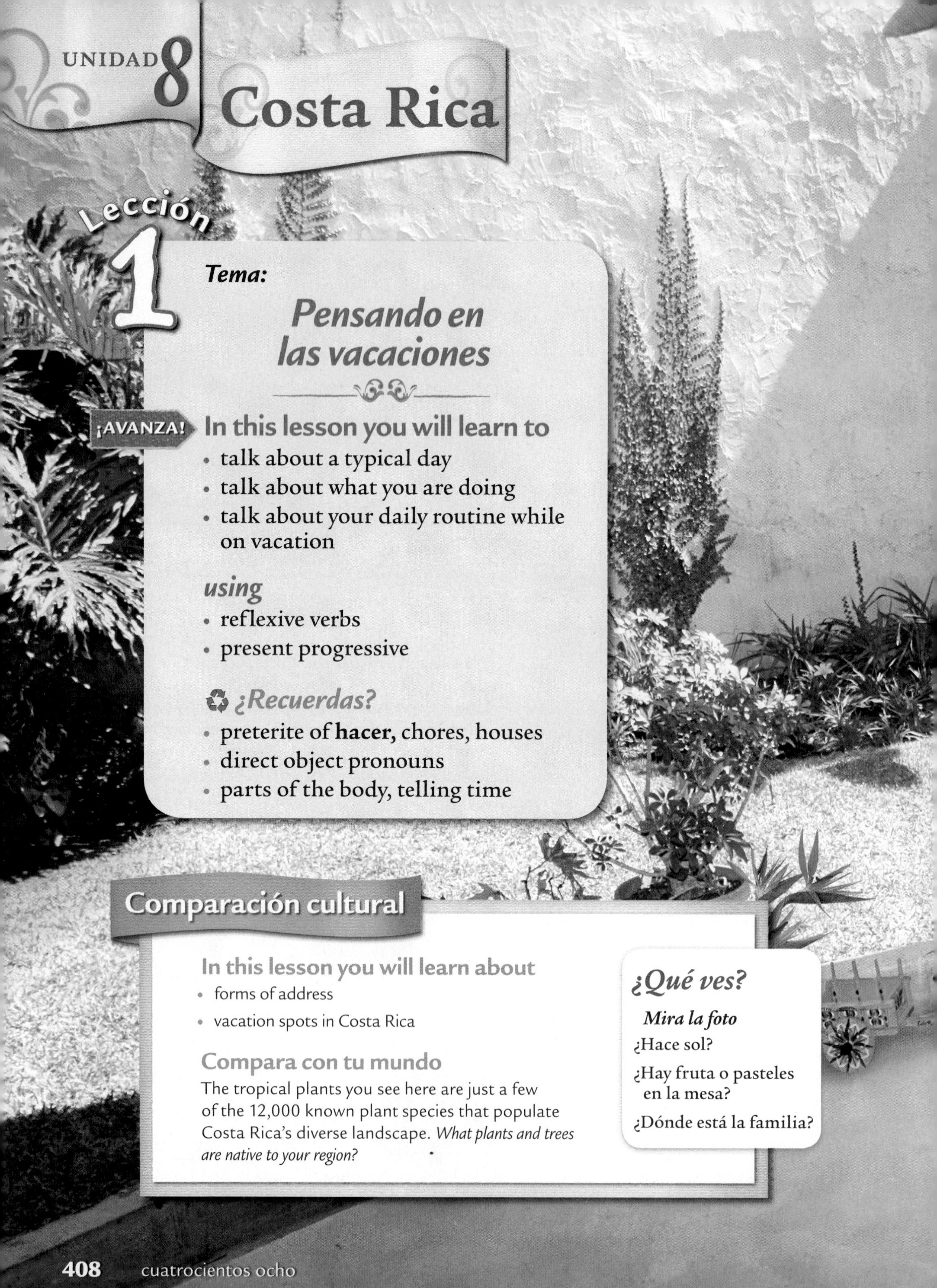

Comparación cultural

In this lesson you will learn about
- forms of address
- vacation spots in Costa Rica

Compara con tu mundo
The tropical plants you see here are just a few of the 12,000 known plant species that populate Costa Rica's diverse landscape. *What plants and trees are native to your region?*

¿Qué ves?
Mira la foto
¿Hace sol?
¿Hay fruta o pasteles en la mesa?
¿Dónde está la familia?

MODES OF COMMUNICATION

INTERPRETIVE	INTERPERSONAL	PRESENTATIONAL
Read a description of someone's trip and identify places and events. Listen to people talking about their daily routines and identify details.	Describe your daily routine to others. Discuss how your routine changes when you are on vacation.	Describe someone else's weekend routine. Write a blog entry about a trip you are taking.

Una familia habla de las vacaciones
San José, Costa Rica

✤ Presentación de VOCABULARIO

¡AVANZA!
Goal: Learn about the daily routines of Susana and Jorge and where they would like to go on vacation. Then practice what you have lea rned to talk about your daily routine and trips you've taken. *Actividades 1–2*

♲ *¿Recuerdas?* Preterite of **hacer** p. 385

VIDEO DVD

AUDIO

A ¡Hola! Me llamo Susana. En los días de escuela **me acuesto** muy temprano. **Normalmente** tengo que **despertarme** a las seis. Antes del desayuno voy al baño para **lavarme la cara** y **maquillarme.**

acostarse

dormirse

despertarse

levantarse

lavarse la cara

maquillarse

B **Generalmente** mi hermano Jorge **se levanta** tarde y pasa mucho tiempo en el baño. **Se afeita, se ducha** y usa **el secador de pelo** para **secarse el pelo.** Siempre usa mi **pasta de dientes** para **cepillarse los dientes.** No es fácil vivir con él.

el champú

la toalla

el secador de pelo

afeitarse

el jabón

el peine

el cepillo de dientes

la pasta de dientes

Unidad 8 Costa Rica
410 cuatrocientos diez

C Después de **peinarse** y **vestirse**, Jorge **se pone** una chaqueta para ir a la escuela. Está contento porque mañana vamos **de vacaciones**.

peinarse

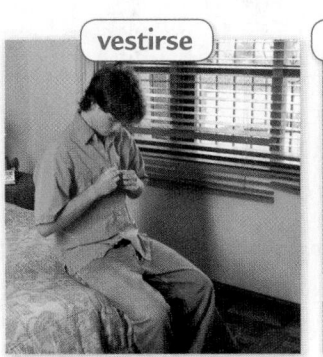
vestirse

ponerse la chaqueta

D Para **las vacaciones**, mi familia y yo vamos a **hacer un viaje**. A mí me gustaría ir a **la ciudad**, pero Jorge quiere ir al **campo**.

la ciudad

el campo

E Mamá prefiere hacer un viaje **en tren** y papá quiere hacer un viaje **en barco**.

en tren

en barco

Más vocabulario

en avión *by plane*
el hotel *hotel*
esperar *to wait (for)*
quedarse en *to stay in*
la rutina *routine*
bañarse *to take a bath*
lavarse *to wash oneself*
secarse *to dry oneself*
Expansión de vocabulario p. R9

@HOMETUTOR my.hrw.com **Interactive Flashcards**

¡A responder!   Escuchar

Escucha la rutina de Jorge. Mientras escuchas, representa las acciones.
(Listen to Jorge's routine and act out the verbs as you hear them.)

Práctica de VOCABULARIO

1 | ¿Qué usas?

Leer | Empareja cada actividad con el objeto correspondiente. *(Match each activity with the item that someone would need to do the activity.)*

1. secarse el cuerpo
2. bañarse
3. lavarse el pelo
4. secarse el pelo
5. peinarse
6. cepillarse los dientes
7. vestirse
8. maquillarse

a. el cepillo de dientes
b. la ropa
c. el champú
d. la toalla
e. el espejo
f. el jabón
g. el peine
h. el secador de pelo

Expansión
Make a list of the items you used while getting ready for school this morning.

2 | Las vacaciones   ♻ ¿*Recuerdas?* Preterite of **hacer** p. 385

Hablar | Pregúntale a otro(a) estudiante si hizo estas cosas durante las vacaciones. *(Ask a partner if he or she did the following things during vacation.)*

modelo: hacer un viaje en

A ¿Hiciste un viaje en coche?

B Sí, hice un viaje en coche el año pasado.

1. hacer un viaje en

2. hacer un viaje en

3. hacer un viaje en

4. hacer un viaje a

5. hacer un viaje a

6. hacer un viaje a

Más práctica   Cuaderno *pp. 344–346*   Cuaderno para hispanohablantes *pp. 344–347*

🌐 Get Help Online
my.hrw.com

PARA Y PIENSA

Did you get it?

1. Name three morning activities and three nighttime activities in your daily routine.

2. Name three ways to travel.

Unidad 8 Costa Rica
412 cuatrocientos doce

 **VOCABULARIO en contexto**

 ¡AVANZA! **Goal:** Identify the words Susana uses to talk about what she would like to do on vacation. Then use the words to talk about being on vacation. *Actividades 3–4*

♻ *¿Recuerdas?* Direct object pronouns p. 204

Telehistoria escena 1

@ **HOMETUTOR** View, Read
my.hrw.com and Record

STRATEGIES

Cuando lees
Group the travel expressions While reading, group the scene's expressions for vacation destinations and modes of transportation. What are some other destinations and modes of transportation?

Cuando escuchas
Understand the interruption
Notice the interruption. Who interrupts whom? What is each person doing at the time? What is the response? How do you think the parents feel when they arrive?

VIDEO
DVD

AUDIO

Papá
Mamá
Jorge
Susana

Susana reads about vacations as she waits for her brother so they can leave for school.

Susana: *(daydreaming)* Voy a hacer un viaje con mi familia. Podemos ir en avión, en barco...

Jorge: *(yelling from the other room)* ¡Susana!

Susana: *(ignoring him)* ¿Voy al campo o a la ciudad? El año pasado mi familia y yo fuimos al campo. Pero yo generalmente prefiero...

Jorge: ¡Susana! ¿Qué haces?

She goes to the kitchen. Jorge is sitting calmly at the table, shaking an empty milk carton.

Jorge: Susana, ¿dónde está la leche?

Susana: ¡Mamá, papá!

Their parents come running into the kitchen.

Mamá: Susana, ¿qué?

Susana: Mi hermano es imposible. ¡Me voy a quedar en un hotel!

Continuará... p. 418

3 | *Comprensión del episodio* Las vacaciones de Susana

Escuchar
Leer

Contesta las preguntas. *(Answer the questions.)*

1. ¿Qué va a hacer Susana?
2. ¿Con quién quiere ir de vacaciones?
3. ¿Cómo pueden hacer el viaje?
4. ¿Adónde pueden ir de vacaciones?
5. ¿Adónde fueron el año pasado?
6. ¿Quién es Jorge?
7. ¿Cómo es Jorge?

4 | En el hotel *¿Recuerdas?* Direct object pronouns p. 204

Hablar

Estás de vacaciones y perdiste la maleta. Dile a otro(a) estudiante las cosas que no tienes. Basado en la tarjeta, él o ella te va a decir si en el hotel las tienen o no. *(Tell your partner the items that you don't have. He or she will tell you if they are available at the hotel.)*

A No tengo el reloj.

B Está bien. En el hotel lo tienen.

¿NECESITA USTED ALGO?
PARA SU SERVICIO TENEMOS:
☼ toallas para la playa
☼ champú   ☼ jabón
☼ secadores de pelo   ☼ relojes
                  ☼ peines
USTED PUEDE LLAMAR A LA EXTENSIÓN 227.

1.
2.
3.
4.

5.
6.
7.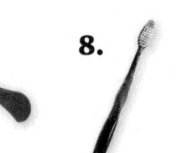
8.

Expansión
Write a list of items you would pack to stay overnight at a friend's house. Compare your list with a partner's.

Get Help Online
my.hrw.com

PARA Y PIENSA

Did you get it? Complete each sentence with the most logical word, based on the Telehistoria: **la ciudad, unas vacaciones,** or **un hotel.**

1. Susana quiere tomar _____ .
2. Susana no quiere ir al campo; prefiere ir a _____ .
3. Susana quiere quedarse en _____ para estar lejos de Jorge.

Unidad 8 Costa Rica

Presentación de GRAMÁTICA

Goal: Learn how to form and use reflexive verbs. Then use these verbs to describe the daily routines of yourself and others. *Actividades 5–8*

♻ *¿Recuerdas?* Parts of the body p. 327

English Grammar Connection: Reflexive verbs and **reflexive pronouns** show that the subject of a sentence both does and receives the action of the verb. The reflexive pronouns in English end in *-self* or *-selves*.

> She **dried herself** with a towel.   Ella **se secó** con una toalla.

Reflexive Verbs

ANIMATED GRAMMAR
my.hrw.com

Use **reflexive pronouns** with **reflexive verbs** when the subject in a sentence is the same as its object.

Here's how:

lavarse *to wash oneself*	
me lavo	**nos** lavamos
te lavas	**os** laváis
se lava	**se** lavan

Many verbs can be used with or without reflexive pronouns. When there is no reflexive pronoun, the person doing the action does not receive the action.

reflexive   *not reflexive*

Anita **se lava.**   Anita **lava** los platos.

*Anita **washes herself.***   *Anita **washes** the dishes.*

Do *not* use possessive adjectives with **reflexive verbs.** Use the **definite article** instead.

> Anita **se lava la** cara.   *Anita **is washing** her face.*

When an infinitive follows a conjugated verb, the **reflexive pronoun** can be placed before the **conjugated verb** or attached to the **infinitive.**

> **Me** voy a **acostar** a las once.   *I'm going **to go to bed** at eleven.*
> *or* Voy a **acostarme** a las once.

Some verbs have different meanings when used reflexively.

> **dormir** *to sleep* → **dormirse** *to fall asleep*
> **poner** *to put* → **ponerse** *to put on (clothes)*

Más práctica
Cuaderno *pp. 347–349*
Cuaderno para hispanohablantes *pp. 348–350*

@HOMETUTOR my.hrw.com
Leveled Practice
🌐 Conjuguemos.com

Práctica de GRAMÁTICA

5 | ¡Se lavan!   ♻ ¿Recuerdas? Parts of the body p. 327

Hablar
Escribir

Explica qué se lavan estas personas. *(Tell what these people wash.)*

1. tú

2. nosotros

3. Jorge

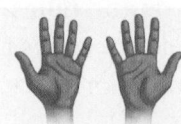

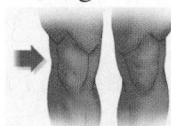

4. yo

5. ustedes

6. los chicos

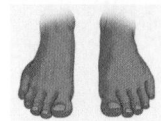

6 | ¿Qué hacen primero?

Hablar
Escribir

Explica el orden lógico en que las siguientes personas hacen estas actividades. *(Explain the logical order in which the following people do these activities.)*

> **modelo:** yo (dormirse / acostarse)
> Primero me acuesto y luego me duermo.

1. mi familia y yo (despertarse / levantarse)
2. tú (vestirse / ducharse)
3. mis amigas (maquillarse / bañarse)
4. usted (secarse / ponerse la ropa)
5. mi padre (afeitarse / secarse la cara)
6. yo (cepillarse los dientes / acostarse)

> **Expansión**
> Compare the order of your regular morning or nighttime activities with those of a partner.

Comparación cultural

Volcán Arenal,
Costa Rica

El paisaje de Costa Rica

How can a country's geography affect daily life? **Costa Rica's** varied landscape includes mountain ranges, active volcanoes, tropical rain forests, rivers, and sandy beaches. Volcán Arenal is one of the ten most active volcanoes in the world, producing glowing red lava and ash columns almost every day. After a major eruption in 1968 which buried several communities, the town of La Fortuna became the area's main village. The volcano heats several hot springs in the area and has become a major tourist attraction.

Compara con tu mundo *How does the landscape of your area compare to Costa Rica? What features are similar or different?*

7 | Lorena y Napoleón

Hablar
Escribir

Describe el día de Lorena y su perro Napoleón. Usa la forma reflexiva si es necesario. *(Describe Lorena and Napoleón's day, using reflexive verbs when needed.)*

modelo: Lorena despierta a Napoleón.

1.

2.

3.

4.

5.

6.

8 | ¿Cuándo lo hacen?

Hablar

Habla con otros(as) estudiantes sobre cuándo haces estas actividades. *(Talk about when you generally do these activities.)*

modelo: afeitarse

> **A** ¿Cuándo se afeitan ustedes generalmente?

> **B** Me afeito la cara cuando voy a una fiesta.

> **C** Nunca me afeito.

cuando...
nunca
antes de...
después de...
a la(s)...
¿ ?

1. cepillarse los dientes
2. mirarse en el espejo
3. ducharse

4. levantarse
5. secarse el pelo
6. maquillarse

7. bañarse
8. acostarse
9. lavarse las manos

Expansión
Report the activities you have in common to the class.

Más práctica Cuaderno *pp. 347–349* Cuaderno para hispanohablantes *pp. 348–350*

 **Get Help Online**
my.hrw.com

PARA Y PIENSA

Did you get it? Create sentences using the following information. Use reflexive pronouns only when necessary.

1. yo / lavar(se) / las manos
2. los chicos / secar(se) / el perro

3. Juana y yo / poner(se) / la mesa
4. mi abuelo / afeitar(se) / la cara

GRAMÁTICA en contexto

¡AVANZA! **Goal:** Focus on the reflexive verbs Susana, Jorge, and their father use to talk about their vacation schedules. Then use these reflexive verbs to talk about different routines. *Actividades 9–10*

Telehistoria escena 2

@HOMETUTOR **View, Read and Record**
my.hrw.com

STRATEGIES

Cuando lees
Compare daily routines While reading, make a note of Jorge's regular daily routine. How do you think his routine will change when he is on vacation?

Cuando escuchas
Listen for persuasion Jorge repeatedly asks his father about going to the beach. Listen to how Jorge tries to persuade him and how his father responds each time. What persuasive techniques would you try?

VIDEO
DVD

AUDIO

Susana and Jorge are at home eating lunch with their father.

Susana: ¿Y mamá? ¿Dónde está?

Papá: En la oficina. Ahora ustedes tienen vacaciones, ¿no? ¿Qué planes tienen?

Jorge: Queremos ir a la playa el sábado. ¿Podemos?

Papá: Sí, pero el primer autobús a Playa Jacó sale a las nueve. Con tu rutina, Jorge, debes acostarte a las diez, para levantarte a las seis de la mañana. Necesitas tiempo para ducharte, lavarte el pelo, secarte el pelo, peinarte, ponerte la ropa...

Jorge: *(with a horrified look)* ¿Despertarme a las seis? Normalmente me levanto temprano y me visto rápidamente para ir a la escuela, pero ¡estoy de vacaciones! Papá, ¿podemos ir a la playa en carro?

Papá: No, tengo que ir a la oficina el sábado.

Jorge: *(mischievously)* ¿Puedo usar yo el carro?

Susana and their father look at Jorge in amazement.

Continuará... p. 423

También se dice

Costa Rica To ask his father about using the car, Jorge says **el carro**. In other Spanish-speaking countries you might hear:
• **España el coche**
• **México la nave**
• **Venezuela, Cuba la máquina**
• **muchos países el auto, el automóvil, el vehículo**

9 *Comprensión del episodio* Planes para el sábado

Escuchar
Leer

Empareja las frases para describir el episodio. *(Match phrases from the columns to create accurate sentences according to the episode.)*

1. La madre está
2. Jorge y Susana quieren ir
3. Normalmente Jorge
4. Jorge quiere despertarse
5. No pueden ir en coche

a. se levanta temprano.
b. en la oficina.
c. más tarde el sábado.
d. porque su padre tiene que trabajar.
e. a la playa.

10 La rutina de Susana

Escuchar
Escribir

Susana habla de lo que hace los sábados. Escucha la descripción y pon las fotos en orden según lo que dice. Luego escribe un párrafo para describir su rutina. *(Listen to Susana's description and put the drawings in order. Then write a paragraph.)*

Expansión
Write about what you did last Saturday.

AUDIO

Pronunciación   Los diptongos

In Spanish, vowels are divided into two categories: strong and weak. **A, e,** and **o** are the strong vowels; **i** and **u** are weak. A weak vowel with another vowel forms one sound, called a diphthong.

ig**ua**lmente   demas**ia**do   af**ei**tarse   c**iu**dad

If there are two consecutive vowels, and one has an accent mark, then each vowel is pronounced separately. The same is true for two strong vowels.

día   país   frío   leí   toalla   zoológico   peor   leer

Get Help Online
my.hrw.com

PARA
Y
PIENSA

Did you get it?   Complete these sentences with the correct form of **acostarse** or **levantarse,** based on the Telehistoria.
1. Jorge debe _____ a las diez si quiere tomar el autobús a las nueve.
2. Cuando está de vacaciones, Jorge no _____ a las seis.

Presentación de GRAMÁTICA

 ¡AVANZA! **Goal:** Learn how to form the present progressive tense of the verbs you know. Then practice this tense to talk about what people are doing right now. *Actividades 11–14*

♻ *¿Recuerdas?* Chores p. 272, houses p. 248

English Grammar Connection: In both English and Spanish, the **present progressive** tense is used to say that an action is in progress at this moment.

Roberto **is skating** in the park.   Roberto **está patinando** en el parque.

Present Progressive

To form the present progressive in Spanish, use the present tense of **estar** + a **present participle.**

Here's how: To form the **present participle** of a verb, drop the ending of the infinitive and add **-ando** or **-iendo.**

-ar verbs	**-er** verbs	**-ir** verbs
camin**ar** ← **ando**	pon**er** ← **iendo**	abr**ir** ← **iendo**
ar ar	*er er*	*ir ir*
caminando	**pon**iendo	**abr**iendo

Estamos poniendo** la mesa.**   *We are setting the table.*

When the stem of an **-er** or **-ir** verb ends in a vowel, change the **-iendo** to **-yendo.**

leer → le**y**endo   traer → tra**y**endo

The **e → i** stem-changing verbs have a vowel change in the stem.

p**e**dir → p**i**diendo   s**e**rvir → s**i**rviendo   v**e**stir → v**i**stiendo

Some other verbs also have a vowel change in the stem.

d**e**cir → d**i**ciendo   v**e**nir → v**i**niendo   d**o**rmir → d**u**rmiendo

Place **pronouns** before the conjugated form of **estar** or attach them to the end of the **present participle.** Add an **accent** when you attach a pronoun.

Me estoy vistiendo. *or* **Estoy vistiéndome.** *I'm getting dressed.*
before⬆   *attached*⬆

Más práctica
Cuaderno *pp. 350–352*
Cuaderno para hispanohablantes *pp. 351–354*

@HOMETUTOR my.hrw.com
Leveled Practice
🌐 Conjuguemos.com

Práctica de GRAMÁTICA

11 | ¿De vacaciones o no?   ♻ ¿Recuerdas? Chores p. 272

¿Recuerdas? Chores p. 272

Hablar
Escribir

Completa las siguientes oraciones y decide si estas personas están de vacaciones o no. *(Complete the sentences and decide who is on vacation.)*

> **modelo:** Jorge _____ la basura. (sacar)
> Jorge **está sacando** la basura. No está de vacaciones.

1. Susana y Jorge _____ el sol en la playa. (tomar)
2. Nosotros _____ el autobús para ir a la escuela. (esperar)
3. Mi amigo _____ un viaje al campo. (hacer)
4. Tú _____ la mesa. (poner)
5. Yo _____ el suelo. (barrer)
6. Ustedes _____ un libro en la playa. (leer)

> **Expansión**
> Write three sentences about what people in your class are doing right now.

12 | ¿Qué están haciendo?

Escribir

Mira las fotos de las vacaciones y escribe lo que están haciendo estas personas. *(Write what these people are doing.)*

levantarse tarde	ponerse bloqueador de sol
hacer un viaje en barco	servir comida
nadar en la piscina	quedarse en un buen hotel
hacer esquí acuático	

> **modelo:** mi madre
> Mi madre se está poniendo bloqueador de sol. (Mi madre está poniéndose bloqueador de sol.)

1. nosotros   **2.** yo   **3.** mis amigos

4. usted   **5.** el camarero   **6.** mi padre

13 ¿Dónde estoy? ♻️ ¿Recuerdas? Houses p. 248

Hablar

Describe qué estás haciendo y otro(a) estudiante va a adivinar dónde estás en la casa. *(Tell what you are doing so that a partner can guess where you are in the house.)*

modelo: cepillarse

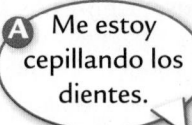

A Me estoy cepillando los dientes.

B Estás en el baño.

Estudiante A

1. cocinar	5. ducharse
2. leer	6. vestirse
3. dormirse	7. jugar...
4. mirar...	8. ¿ ?

Estudiante B

la sala
el baño
el cuarto
la cocina
el jardín
¿ ?

Expansión
Say what items you are using for each activity.

14 Por teléfono

Hablar

Comparación cultural

El uso de usted, tú y vos

How do forms of address differ among countries? Informal and formal address vary in the Spanish-speaking world. In both **Costa Rica** and **Uruguay,** *vos* is used rather than *tú*. In Costa Rica, family members often use *usted;* however, in Uruguay, *usted* is rarely used within a family. In **Ecuador,** some families may use *usted* as a sign of respect, but many families use *tú*.

Una tira cómica de Francisco Munguía

Compara con tu mundo *How does your language change depending on the situation you are in?*

Eres de Costa Rica y hablas por teléfono con tu hermano(a). Usa la forma **usted.** *(Role-play a telephone conversation. Use usted.)*

A Hola, Diego. ¿Qué está haciendo?

B Estoy estudiando. ¿Y usted?

Más práctica Cuaderno *pp. 350–352* Cuaderno para hispanohablantes *pp. 351–354*

🌐 **Get Help Online**
my.hrw.com

PARA Y PIENSA

Did you get it? Complete each sentence with the correct present progressive form of the verb in parentheses.
1. Todos los días a las ocho de la mañana yo _____ . (ducharse)
2. Tú siempre _____ cuando queremos ir a la playa. (dormir)
3. Nosotros _____ para ir a la escuela. (vestirse)

Todo junto

¡AVANZA!

Goal: *Show what you know* Notice how Susana and Jorge use the present progressive in their conversation. Then use this tense and reflexive verbs to talk about your daily routine while on vacation. ***Actividades 15–19***

¿Recuerdas? Telling time p. 90

Telehistoria completa

@HOMETUTOR View, Read and Record
my.hrw.com

STRATEGIES

Cuando lees
Analyze differences in behavior
While reading, discover the differences in behavior between Jorge and Susana. How do they react to being late?

Cuando escuchas
Listen for attempts to control Listen for differences in intonation as Jorge and Susana each try to gain control over the situation. How does each person sound? Why? What is their father's role?

Escena 1 *Resumen*
Susana va a hacer un viaje con su familia, pero su hermano, Jorge, es imposible.

Escena 2 *Resumen*
Jorge y Susana quieren ir a la playa en coche el sábado, pero su padre tiene que ir a la oficina.

Escena 3

VIDEO DVD

AUDIO

Susana and Jorge are finishing breakfast in the kitchen. Their father waits in the car.

Susana: *(impatiently)* Jorge, estás comiendo y comiendo. ¡Por favor! ¿Quieres ir al centro comercial o no? Papá nos está esperando. Tiene que ir a la oficina.

Jorge keeps eating and ignores his sister.

Susana: Jorge, ¿no me escuchas? ¡Nos está llamando papá!

Jorge: Pero estoy comiendo el desayuno...

Susana wraps up his breakfast.

Susana: ¡Vamos, ahora! ¿No me estás escuchando? Papá está esperando. ¡Toma la mochila!

Jorge: Un momento, hay algo... Necesito algo importante. Pero, ¿qué puede ser?

Jorge unknowingly leaves Alicia's T-shirt behind.

15 | Comprensión de los episodios   ¿Cierto o falso?

Escuchar
Leer

Decide si estas oraciones son ciertas o falsas. Corrige las falsas.
(Tell if these sentences are true or false. Correct the false ones.)

1. Susana va a hacer un viaje con sus amigas.

2. Jorge y Susana quieren ir a la playa el sábado.

3. Su padre piensa que Jorge debe levantarse temprano para hacer su rutina.

4. Susana y Jorge pueden ir en coche a la playa porque su padre no tiene que trabajar el sábado.

5. Susana y Jorge necesitan salir porque su padre los está esperando.

6. Jorge sabe qué necesita para ir al centro comercial.

16 | Comprensión de los episodios   ¿Qué está pasando?

Escuchar
Leer

Describe qué está pasando en cada foto, según los episodios. *(Tell what is happening in each picture, according to the episodes.)*

modelo: Susana está pensando en unas vacaciones. No está escuchando a Jorge.

1. **2.** **3.**

17 | ¿Quién está de vacaciones?

 **¿Recuerdas?**
Telling time p. 90

Digital
performance space

Hablar

> **STRATEGY Hablar**
> **Use clock faces to link times and activities** Organize your drawings by including clock faces with your daily routine. Practice narrating your routine using the clocks, then get together with your partner to ask and answer questions.

En una hoja de papel, dibuja tu rutina diaria cuando estás de vacaciones. Otro(a) estudiante va a dibujar su rutina diaria durante un día escolar típico. Haz preguntas sobre los dibujos. *(Draw your daily routine while on vacation. Your partner will draw his or her daily routine during a typical school day. Ask questions about the drawings.)*

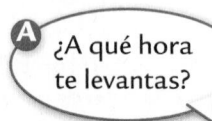

A ¿A qué hora te levantas?

B Me levanto a las seis porque tengo que ir a la escuela.

Expansión
Choose different destinations for your vacations and compare your activities.

18 | Integración

Leer
Escuchar
Hablar

Quieres hablar por Internet antes de las clases con dos amigos de Costa Rica. Lee el correo electrónico y escucha el mensaje telefónico. Decide si pueden hacerlo y explica por qué. *(Decide if the three of you can be online together before school. Explain why or why not.)*

Fuente 1 Correo electrónico

Hola, ¿qué tal? Tenemos que decidir a qué hora vamos a estar en línea mañana. Normalmente me levanto a las siete menos veinte de la mañana. Me lavo la cara y luego me visto. Entonces voy a la sala para ver un programa de televisión a las siete. Termina a las siete y media. A las ocho menos cuarto me pongo los zapatos y la chaqueta y salgo para la escuela. ¿Y tú? ¿Qué haces antes de las clases?
Ignacio

Fuente 2 Mensaje telefónico

Listen and take notes
• ¿A qué hora se levantó hoy Carmen?
• ¿Cuándo está ocupada?
• ¿Cuándo puede estar en línea?

modelo: Ignacio, Carmen y yo podemos estar en línea a las... porque... (No podemos estar en línea porque...)

19 | Un viaje fenomenal

Escribir

Haces un viaje fenomenal. Escribe un blog para describir dónde estás, cómo es tu rutina y qué estás haciendo en el viaje. *(You are on a great trip. Write a blog that describes where you are, what your daily routine is, and what you are doing on your trip.)*

modelo: sábado, 12 de junio 10:00
Estoy en Guanacaste. Acabo de levantarme y estoy comiendo el desayuno y bebiendo jugo al lado de la playa. Voy a...

Writing Criteria	Excellent	Good	Needs Work
Content	Your blog includes a lot of information.	Your blog includes some information.	Your blog includes little information.
Communication	Most of your blog is organized and easy to follow.	Parts of your blog are organized and easy to follow.	Your blog is disorganized and hard to follow.
Accuracy	Your blog has few mistakes in grammar and vocabulary.	Your blog has some mistakes in grammar and vocabulary.	Your blog has many mistakes in grammar and vocabulary.

Más práctica   Cuaderno *pp. 353–354*   Cuaderno para hispanohablantes *pp. 355–356*

Get Help Online
my.hrw.com

PARA Y PIENSA

Did you get it?   Tell what Jorge and Susana are doing before going to the mall, using this information and the present progressive.
1. Jorge / peinarse
2. Susana / maquillarse
3. los hermanos / cepillarse los dientes
4. Jorge / ponerse la chaqueta

Lectura

AUDIO

Additional readings at **my.hrw.com**
SPANISH
InterActive Reader

¡AVANZA! **Goal:** Read the captions from the scrapbook of a student who went on vacation to Costa Rica. Then talk about her vacation and compare it with what you would like to do.

Mi viaje a Costa Rica

El año pasado Sara y su familia hicieron un viaje a Costa Rica. Cuando volvieron a Miami, Sara hizo un álbum con fotos y recuerdos de sus experiencias.

STRATEGY Leer

Use an "L" to link place and event Draw L's like the ones below. On the tall part, write the name of the place. On the low part, write events and activities.

¡Papá nunca tiene miedo! Aquí está en un zip line. Aquí va de árbol en árbol en un cable de metal.

Fuimos todos al bosque nuboso[1] en Monteverde. Es una reserva biológica con muchos tipos de árboles[2] y pájaros[3]. Es un lugar ideal para caminar y tomar fotos.

¿Qué están mirando mi mamá y mis hermanos? No es un pájaro y no es un avión… Es Papá.

Vimos un tucán. Es un pájaro bonito de muchos colores. Es típico de Costa Rica. Allí hay más de 850 especies de pájaros.

---

[1] **bosque…** cloud forest   [2] trees   [3] birds

Un día fuimos a Escazú. Estoy comprando regalos para mis amigos en Miami. También compré una pequeña máscara de barro.⁴

En San José, nos quedamos en un hotel en el centro. El hotel está cerca de la Plaza Central y la Catedral Metropolitana.

Hicimos un viaje en avión de San José a Tambor (en la costa del Pacífico de Costa Rica). Pasamos tres días en Montezuma. Descansamos en la playa, tomamos el sol y buceamos. ¡Fue mi parte favorita de las vacaciones!

⁴ **máscara...** clay mask

PARA Y PIENSA

¿Comprendiste?

1. ¿Adónde fueron Sara y su famila en Monteverde? Si te gusta ver pájaros, ¿es Costa Rica un buen lugar? ¿Por qué?
2. ¿Dónde está el hotel donde se quedaron Sara y su familia?
3. ¿Qué hizo Sara en Escazú?
4. ¿Está Tambor cerca o lejos de San José? ¿Cómo lo sabes?

¿Y tú?

¿Qué te gustaría hacer de vacaciones en Costa Rica?

✳ Conexiones *Las ciencias*

¡Vamos al museo!

In addition to outdoor activities, visitors at **Parque La Sabana** in Costa Rica can enjoy **el Museo de Ciencias Naturales La Salle,** a museum dedicated to nature and science located in the southwest corner of the park. The museum is divided into various sections: **minerales y rocas, paleontología, invertebrados, malacología, artrópodos, insectos, vertebrados, ornitología, mamíferos,** and **esqueletos.** There are more than 55,000 exhibits on permanent display.

Choose five sections of the museum and find their meanings in a dictionary. Then make a list of two or three items you might see on exhibit for each of the five sections.

Museo de Ciencias Naturales La Salle

¡Ve el esqueleto de un mamut enorme en la exhibición de paleontología!
lunes a sábado, 8 a.m.–4 p.m.
domingo, 9 a.m.–5 p.m.
adultos ₡400, niños ₡300

Para más información llama:
Teléfono: 232-4876 **Fax:** 231-1920
o visita nuestro sitio Web

Proyecto **1** *Las matemáticas*

Your Spanish class has taken a trip to Costa Rica. Calculate how much it will cost in **colones** (symbol ₡) for everyone in your class to visit the museum. Then use a current exchange rate to calculate the cost in U.S. dollars. Write out your calculations in Spanish.

Proyecto **2** *El lenguaje*

Many scientific terms in Spanish and English are similar due in part to their common Latin and Greek roots. Research the Latin and Greek roots of the following words:

zoología   paleontología   ornitología

Proyecto **3** *El arte*

Make a list of six to ten animals or insects that may be found in **Parque La Sabana** or **el Museo de Ciencias Naturales La Salle.** If you need more animal names, see page R8. Make a poster containing illustrations of each with captions in Spanish.

Una mariposa

En resumen
Vocabulario y gramática

Vocabulario

Talk About a Daily Routine

acostarse (ue)	to go to bed	lavarse la cara	to wash one's face
afeitarse	to shave oneself	levantarse	to get up
bañarse	to take a bath	maquillarse	to put on makeup
cepillarse los dientes	to brush one's teeth	peinarse	to comb one's hair
despertarse (ie)	to wake up	ponerse (la ropa)	to put on (clothes), to get dressed
dormirse (ue)	to fall asleep	secarse	to dry oneself
ducharse	to take a shower	secarse el pelo	to dry one's hair
lavarse	to wash oneself	vestirse (i)	to get dressed

Talk About Grooming

el cepillo (de dientes)	brush (toothbrush)	el peine	comb
el champú	shampoo	el secador de pelo	hair dryer
el jabón	soap	la toalla	towel
la pasta de dientes	toothpaste		

Talk About a Typical Day

generalmente	generally
normalmente	normally
la rutina	routine

Other Words and Phrases

el campo	the country, countryside
la ciudad	city
esperar	to wait (for)
hacer un viaje	to take a trip
en avión	by plane
en barco	by boat
en tren	by train
el hotel	hotel
quedarse en	to stay in
las vacaciones	vacation
de vacaciones	on vacation

Gramática

Reflexive Verbs

Use **reflexive pronouns** with **reflexive verbs** when the subject in a sentence is the same as its object.

lavarse *to wash oneself*	
me lavo	**nos** lavamos
te lavas	**os** laváis
se lava	**se** lavan

Present Progressive

To form the present progressive in Spanish, use the present tense of **estar** + **present participle.**

-ar verbs	-er verbs	-ir verbs
cami**nar** ~~ar~~ **ando**	po**ner** ~~er~~ **iendo**	ab**rir** ~~ir~~ **iendo**
cami**nando**	po**niendo**	ab**riendo**

Some verbs have a spelling change or a stem change in the present participle.

Repaso de la lección

Now you can
- talk about a typical day
- talk about what you are doing
- talk about your daily routine while on vacation

Using
- reflexive verbs
- present progressive

To review
- reflexive verbs p. 415
- present progressive p. 420

1 | **Listen and understand**

AUDIO

Escucha a Silvia y a sus hermanos mientras se preparan para ir a la escuela. Indica lo que necesitan y explica por qué. *(Listen to Silvia and her brothers and sisters. Tell what they need and why.)*

a.   **b.**    **c.**

d.    **e.**    **f.**

1. Silvia
2. Roberto
3. Anita
4. Juan
5. Tomás
6. Laura

To review
- reflexive verbs p. 415

2 | **Talk about a typical day**

Escribe a qué hora las siguientes personas hacen estas actividades. *(Write when the following people do these activities.)*

modelo: Pancho / acostarse / 10:00 p.m.
         Pancho se acuesta a las diez de la noche.

1. yo / dormirse / 10:50 p.m.
2. nosotros / cepillarse los dientes / 9:15 p.m.
3. Papá / afeitarse / 6:40 a.m.
4. mi hermana / ducharse / 8:20 a.m.
5. Ignacio y Pablo / levantarse / 7:10 a.m.
6. tú / peinarse / 8:45 a.m.

3 | Talk about your daily routine while on vacation

Julia describe sus vacaciones. Completa la carta con la forma correcta del verbo apropiado. *(Complete the letter with the correct form of the appropriate verb.)*

Hola, Beatriz.

¿Qué pasa? Estoy en un hotel bonito en San José. Mi rutina es muy diferente aquí. Mis padres prefieren **1.** (maquillarse / levantarse) temprano para ir de compras. Yo **2.** (ponerse / despertarse) más tarde, a las diez de la mañana. Después mi hermana y yo **3.** (acostarse / vestirse). Luego salimos a conocer la ciudad.

Mis padres **4.** (acostarse / despertarse) a las diez y media de la noche. Mi hermana y yo **5.** (cepillarse / levantarse) los dientes, y después ella siempre **6.** (ducharse / lavarse) el pelo. Yo leo mi libro y **7.** (dormirse / ponerse) a las doce. ¿Y tú? ¿También **8.** (quedarse / ponerse) en un hotel cuando vas de vacaciones?

4 | Talk about what you are doing

Estas personas no pueden salir porque están ocupadas. Escribe lo que están haciendo. *(Write what the following people are doing right now.)*

modelo: Alberto / correr
Alberto está corriendo.

1. mamá y papá / comer
2. Adriana / hablar por teléfono
3. tú / hacer la tarea
4. ustedes / escribir correos electrónicos
5. yo / cocinar
6. nosotros / envolver un regalo

To review
• **carretas**
p. 407
• **Tabacón**
p. 407
• Comparación
cultural pp. 416,
422

5 | Costa Rica, Ecuador, and Uruguay

Comparación cultural

Answer these culture questions.

1. What are **carretas**? Describe them.
2. Where are the Tabacón hot springs and what can you do there?
3. What types of land features are found in Costa Rica?
4. How do family members address each other in Costa Rica, Ecuador, and Uruguay?

Más práctica   Cuaderno *pp. 355–366*   Cuaderno para hispanohablantes *pp. 357–366*

Get Help Online
my.hrw.com

Costa Rica

Lección 2

Tema:
¡Vamos de vacaciones!

¡AVANZA! **In this lesson you will learn to**
- talk about buying souvenirs on vacation
- talk about vacation activities

using
- indirect object pronouns
- demonstrative adjectives

♻ *¿Recuerdas?*
- family, classroom objects
- numbers from 200 to 1,000,000
- **gustar** with an infinitive
- present progressive

Comparación cultural

In this lesson you will learn about
- transportation and marketplaces
- the coffee industry and desserts from Costa Rica and Uruguay
- travel destinations in Costa Rica, Ecuador, and Uruguay

Compara con tu mundo
This shop has several items depicting tropical birds, such as the **quetzal** and the **tucán.** Costa Rica is home to about five percent of the world's plant and animal species, making it an ideal place for ecotourism. *Where do you like to go and what do you like to do during vacation?*

¿Qué ves?
Mira la foto
¿Están enojados Susana y Jorge?
¿De qué color es la tienda?
¿Qué pueden comprar aquí?

MODES OF COMMUNICATION

INTERPRETIVE	INTERPERSONAL	PRESENTATIONAL
Understand a radio ad to make vacation plans.	Bargain when buying and selling various items.	Write an article for a Web site comparing two different trips.
Read about bargaining in markets in Costa Rica and Uruguay to make comparisons.	Reply to your teacher about where you'd like to study abroad and why.	Describe your ideal daily routine.

Una tienda de artesanías y recuerdos
San José, Costa Rica

✤ Presentación de VOCABULARIO

¡AVANZA! **Goal:** Learn about the activities Susana likes to do on vacation. Then practice what you have learned to talk about buying souvenirs. *Actividades 1–2*

VIDEO DVD

AUDIO

A **Estoy comiendo al aire libre** con mi amiga. Es divertido, pero yo **quisiera** hacer un viaje al campo o al mar.

comer al aire libre

B Me gustaría **hacer surfing, hacer surf de vela, acampar** o **montar a caballo.**

hacer una parrillada

hacer surfing

hacer surf de vela

acampar

dar una caminata

montar a caballo

Más vocabulario

el tiempo libre *free time*	**¿Me deja ver...?** *May I see. . .?*
Le dejo... en... *I'll give. . . to you for. . .*	**¡Qué caro(a)!** *How expensive!*
Le puedo ofrecer... *I can offer you. . .*	**¿Qué es esto?** *What is this?*

Expansión de vocabulario p. R9

C Cuando estoy de vacaciones siempre compro **recuerdos** en **el mercado.** Allí puedes **regatear** y las cosas son más **baratas.**

el mercado

D Hay **artesanías** y **joyas** de buena **calidad.** Quiero comprar **un anillo de oro** pero cuesta **demasiado.** Hay **unos aretes de plata** menos **caros.**

las artesanías

la cerámica

el artículo de madera

las joyas

el anillo

el arete

el collar

@HOMETUTOR
my.hrw.com
Interactive
Flashcards

¡A responder!   Escuchar

Escucha la lista de actividades que Susana quisiera hacer durante las vacaciones. Señala la foto correcta para cada actividad que menciona.

(Point to the photo of each activity that Susana mentions.)

✣ Práctica de VOCABULARIO

1 | ¿Qué hay en la tienda?

**Hablar
Escribir**

Indica qué hay en la tienda, según el anuncio.
(Indicate what items the store has, according to the ad.)

> **modelo:** collares de plata
> No hay collares de plata en la tienda.

1. artículos de madera
2. joyas
3. cerámica
4. anillos de oro
5. collares de madera
6. aretes de plata
7. artesanías
8. anillos de plata

2 | Unos aretes de plata

**Leer
Escribir**

Susana quiere comprar algo en el mercado. Completa la conversación.
(Complete the conversation.)

le dejo	me deja ver	caro
demasiado	quisiera	ofrecer

Susana: Buenas tardes. __1.__ comprar un regalo para mi madre.
¿ __2.__ los aretes de plata?

Vendedor: Sí, claro. Son muy bonitos.

Susana: ¿Cuánto cuestan?

Vendedor: __3.__ los aretes en quince mil quinientos colones.

Susana: ¡Quince mil quinientos! ¡Qué __4.__ ! Le puedo __5.__ trece
mil quinientos.

Vendedor: Lo siento. Son de buena calidad. Le dejo los aretes en
catorce mil.

Susana: ¿Catorce mil? Es __6.__ , pero me gustan mucho. Los compro.

> **Expansión**
> Talk with a partner
> about which of these
> items you would like
> to buy for yourself.

Más práctica   Cuaderno *pp. 367–369*   Cuaderno para hispanohablantes *pp. 367–370*

🌐 **Get Help Online**
my.hrw.com

**PARA
Y
PIENSA**

Did you get it?   Ask to see the following items.

1. earrings
2. silver necklace
3. gold ring
4. wooden handicrafts

VOCABULARIO en contexto

¡AVANZA! **Goal:** Pay attention to the words Susana uses to talk about items in a store. Then practice these words to talk about shopping and what you would and would not like to do in your free time. *Actividades 3–4*

Telehistoria escena 1

@HOMETUTOR View, Read
my.hrw.com and Record

STRATEGIES

Cuando lees
Find the hidden reasons Read between the lines to understand hidden reasons. Why does Susana ask her father to buy a blue car?

Cuando escuchas
Identify appropriate register Does the clerk address Susana in a formal or informal way? How can you tell? Identify at least two words that support your answer.

VIDEO DVD

AUDIO

Vendedora

Susana

Susana and Jorge's father drops them off at a store in his red car that looks like a taxi. One of Susana's classmates is standing outside.

Susana: Gracias, Papi. Pero, ¿por qué no compras un carro nuevo? ¿Un carro azul?

Amiga: Eh, Susanita, ¡qué divertido viajar en taxi todos los días!

Embarrassed, Susana smiles, and she and Jorge enter the shop quickly.

Vendedora: ¿Quiere usted ver algo en especial?

Susana: A ver... ¿este anillo de oro?

Vendedora: Claro que sí.

Susana tries on the ring.

Susana: ¿Cuánto cuesta?

Vendedora: Veinte mil colones.

Susana: ¡Qué caro! Tengo diez mil colones, nada más.

Vendedora: Señorita, no estamos en el mercado. Aquí no regateamos.

A little embarrassed, Susana leaves.

Continuará... p. 442

Escuchar
Leer

Contesta las preguntas. *(Answer the questions.)*

1. ¿A Susana le gusta el coche de su papá? ¿Por qué?
2. ¿Con quién va Susana a la tienda?
3. ¿Qué anillo quiere ver Susana?
4. ¿Cuánto cuesta el anillo?
5. ¿Cuánto dinero tiene Susana?
6. ¿Por qué no regatea la vendedora?

4 | **¡Qué divertido!**

Hablar

Pregúntales a otros estudiantes si les gustaría hacer las siguientes actividades en su tiempo libre. *(Ask if your partners would like to do these activities.)*

A ¿Te gustaría acampar en tu tiempo libre?

B Sí, me gustaría acampar.

C No, no me gustaría acampar.

1.

2.

3.

4.

5.

6.

Expansión
Rank these activities in order of preference. Then, exchange your preferences with a classmate and make plans to do two of them together.

 **Get Help Online**
my.hrw.com

PARA Y PIENSA

Did you get it? Create logical sentences by choosing the correct word.
1. Susana está contenta porque el collar es muy (caro / barato).
2. A ella le gustan (la cerámica / los aretes) de madera.
3. Ella puede regatear en (las artesanías / el mercado).

Presentación de GRAMÁTICA

Goal: Learn how to use indirect object pronouns. Then practice using these pronouns to talk about buying things for people. *Actividades 5–8*

♻ *¿Recuerdas?* Family p. 164, numbers from 200 to 1,000,000 p. 165

English Grammar Connection: In both English and Spanish, **indirect objects** are nouns or pronouns that tell *to whom* or *for whom* the action takes place in a sentence.

Aunt Lola sends **us** gifts.

| indirect object pronoun |

Tía Lola **nos** manda regalos.

| indirect object pronoun |

Indirect Object Pronouns

ANiMaTeDGRaMMaR
my.hrw.com

Use **indirect object pronouns** to clarify to whom or for whom an action takes place.

Here's how: **Indirect object pronouns** use the same words as direct object pronouns except for **le** and **les**.

Singular		Plural	
me	*me*	**nos**	*us*
te	*you (familiar)*	**os**	*you (familiar)*
le	*you (formal), him, her*	**les**	*you, them*

The pronouns **le** and **les** can refer to a variety of people. To clarify what they mean, they are often accompanied by **a** + **noun** or **pronoun**.

Le doy las joyas.
*I'm giving the jewelry **to him/her/you**.*

Le doy las joyas a **Juana**.
*I'm giving the jewelry **to Juana**.*

When a conjugated verb is followed by an infinitive, the same rules for placement apply as for direct object pronouns. The **pronoun** can be placed before the **conjugated verb** or attached to the end of the **infinitive.**

Les voy a **comprar** recuerdos a mis amigos.

or Voy a **comprarles** recuerdos a mis amigos.

I'm going to buy souvenirs for my friends.

Más práctica
Cuaderno *pp. 370–372*
Cuaderno para hispanohablantes *pp. 371–373*

@HOMETUTOR my.hrw.com
Leveled Practice

Práctica de GRAMÁTICA

5 | De compras ♻ *¿Recuerdas?* Family p. 164

Leer

Susana le explica a Jorge qué compran sus padres. Escoge el pronombre de objeto indirecto apropiado (**me, te, le, nos, les**). *(Choose the appropriate indirect object pronoun.)*

> **modelo:** Mamá y papá (te / le) compran un sombrero a nuestra tía.
> Mamá y papá **le** compran un sombrero **a nuestra tía.**

1. Mamá y papá (nos / les) compran un DVD a nosotros.
2. (Le / Les) compran aretes a nuestra abuela.
3. A nuestros primos (le / les) compran un disco compacto.
4. (Me / Te) compran un collar de madera a ti.
5. A mí también (me / les) compran un collar, pero es de plata.
6. (Le / Les) compran artículos de cerámica a su amigo.

6 | ¿Qué les compró?

Escribir

Durante las vacaciones, Susana compró recuerdos. Escribe oraciones para indicar a quiénes les compró estas cosas. *(Write sentences to tell for whom Susana bought these souvenirs.)*

> **modelo:** artículo de madera / padre
> **Le** compró un artículo de madera **a su padre.**

1. collar de madera / madre
2. aretes de plata / yo
3. cerámica / nosotros
4. anillo de oro / tú
5. joyas / amigas
6. aretes de oro / abuelas

> **Expansión**
> Tell for whom you have bought gifts recently.

Comparación cultural

Taxis en el Parque Central en San José

El transporte

How is transportation important to a country? In **Costa Rica,** taxis are generally inexpensive and easy to find, especially in larger cities. You can recognize Costa Rican taxis by their color: airport taxis are orange, while all other taxis are red. Traveling by bus is also common. The capital, San José, has extensive bus lines and almost all areas of the country can be reached by bus. Many travelers also use local airlines to reach popular destinations, such as coastal cities and beaches.

Compara con tu mundo *How does transportation in your area compare to that of Costa Rica?*

7 | La vendedora ¿*Recuerdas?* Numbers from 200 to 1,000,000 p. 165

Hablar
Escribir

Ayer una vendedora vendió muchas cosas en el mercado. Indica a quiénes les vendió estos artículos, según lo que pagaron. *(Based on the amount each person paid, indicate to whom the salesclerk sold these items.)*

> **modelo:** Tú pagaste dieciséis mil cuatrocientos colones.
> Ella **te** vendió **un collar de plata.**

1. Jorge pagó quince mil seiscientos colones.

2. Mis amigos y yo pagamos cinco mil novecientos colones.

3. Susana y su madre pagaron dos mil colones.

4. Yo pagué treinta mil ochocientos colones.

5. La maestra de español pagó veinte mil colones.

6. Ustedes pagaron nueve mil trescientos colones.

Ventas, el 6 de junio	
Artículo	Precio
1 aretes de oro	20.000
2 recuerdos de madera	15.600
3 collar de plata	16.400
4 platos de cerámica	5.900
5 libro de Costa Rica	2.000
6 anillo de plata	9.300
7 collares de oro	30.800
8	
9	
10	
11	

8 | ¿Qué les das a otros?

Hablar

Di qué regalos les das a otras personas. *(Tell what gifts you give to whom.)*

modelo:

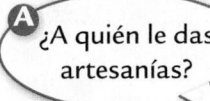
A ¿A quién le das artesanías?

B Le doy artesanías a mi abuela.

1.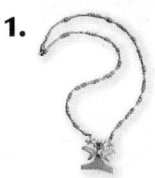

2.

3.

4.

5.

6.

> **Expansión**
> Describe what gifts people gave you last year.

Más práctica   Cuaderno *pp. 370–372*   Cuaderno para hispanohablantes *pp. 371–373*

Get Help Online
my.hrw.com

PARA Y PIENSA

Did you get it?   Give the correct indirect object pronoun.
1. Nosotros _____ damos los recuerdos a nuestros hermanos.
2. A ti _____ quiero comprar un collar de oro.
3. Carlos _____ pide 2.000 colones a nosotros.

❦ GRAMÁTICA en contexto

Goal: Listen to Susana's conversation with the salesclerk. Then use indirect object pronouns to talk about vacation activities and shopping for yourself and others. *Actividades 9–10*

♻ *¿Recuerdas?* **gustar** with an infinitive p. 42

Telehistoria escena 2

@HOMETUTOR   View, Read
my.hrw.com   and Record

VIDEO
DVD

AUDIO

STRATEGIES

Identify keywords and details
Notice at least four expressions normally used in stores. Review the scene, then write these expressions in new sentences.

Identify conversational exchanges
Note how the salesclerk greets Susana and how Susana asks for something. How does Jorge enter the conversation?

Susana and Jorge enter another shop.

Susana: ¡A mí me gustan los collares de madera! *(She looks at a price tag.)* ¡Qué caro!

Vendedor: ¡Buenos días! ¿Los puedo ayudar?

Susana: ¿Me deja ver esa joya? ¿Cuánto cuesta?

Vendedor: Cuesta cincuenta mil colones. Es un poco cara, ¿verdad?

Jorge: A ti te gustan todas las cosas caras.

Vendedor: *(to Susana)* ¿A usted le gustan los aretes de plata?

As Susana looks at the earrings, Jorge turns to see who has just entered the store.

Jorge: Susana...

Susana: *(impatiently)* Y ahora, ¿qué te pasa a ti?

Continuará... p. 447

También se dice

Costa Rica To ask Susana if she likes the earrings, the salesclerk uses **los aretes.** In other Spanish-speaking countries you might hear:
• **Argentina** **los aros**
• **España** **los pendientes, los zarcillos**
• **Puerto Rico** **las pantallas**

9 *Comprensión del episodio* Unas joyas

Escuchar
Leer

Todas estas oraciones son falsas. Corrígelas, según el episodio. *(Correct these false statements.)*

1. A Susana le gustan mucho los aretes de madera.
2. Los collares son muy baratos.
3. Susana quiere ver un recuerdo.
4. El vendedor dice que la joya no es cara.
5. Jorge dice que a Susana le gustan las cosas baratas.

> **Expansión**
> Using the shopping expressions you identified earlier, role-play a conversation between a customer and a salesperson.

10 El viaje ideal *¿Recuerdas?* **gustar** with an infinitive p. 42

Hablar

Habla con un(a) agente de viajes sobre las personas a quienes les gusta hacer estas actividades. Él o ella te va a ofrecer un viaje ideal. *(Tell a travel agent who likes to do these activities. He or she will offer an ideal trip.)*

modelo: hacer un viaje en barco

A A mi hermano le gusta hacer un viaje en barco.

B A él le puedo ofrecer un viaje al mar.

Estudiante Ⓐ
1. hacer surfing
2. montar a caballo
3. ir de compras
4. dar caminatas
5. acampar
6. ¿ ?

Estudiante Ⓑ
la ciudad   el mar
la playa   ¿ ?
el campo

> **Expansión**
> Find out what activities both you and a partner like to do. Agree on an ideal trip to take.

AUDIO

⚙ Pronunciación ⚙ Unir las palabras

Native speakers may seem to speak quickly when they link their words in breath groups. Instead of pronouncing each word separately, they run some words together. This is common in all languages.

Listen and repeat.

¿A qué hora empieza el almuerzo?

Quisiera el anillo de oro y el artículo de madera.

Ella no puede acampar porque está ocupada.

🖥 **Get Help Online**
my.hrw.com

PARA Y PIENSA

Did you get it? Complete each sentence with the correct indirect object pronoun, based on the Telehistoria.

1. A Susana _____ gustan los collares de madera.
2. El vendedor _____ pregunta a Jorge y a Susana si los puede ayudar.
3. Susana quiere saber qué _____ pasa a Jorge.

※Presentación de GRAMÁTICA

Goal: Learn how to point out specific things by using demonstrative adjectives. Then use these words to identify objects. *Actividades 11–14*

♻ *¿Recuerdas?* Present progressive p. 420, classroom objects p. 110

English Grammar Connection: Demonstrative adjectives indicate the location of a person or thing in relation to the speaker. They go before the noun in both English and Spanish.

This necklace is expensive.
demonstrative adjective

Este collar es caro.
demonstrative adjective

Demonstrative Adjectives

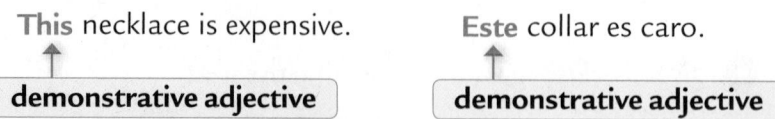
ANIMATED GRAMMAR
my.hrw.com

In Spanish, **demonstrative adjectives** must match the nouns they modify in gender and number.

Here's how:

Masculine

Singular		Plural	
este anillo	*this ring*	**estos** anillos	*these rings*
ese anillo	*that ring*	**esos** anillos	*those rings*
aquel anillo	*that ring (over there)*	**aquellos** anillos	*those rings (over there)*

Feminine

Singular		Plural	
esta camiseta	*this T-shirt*	**estas** camisetas	*these T-shirts*
esa camiseta	*that T-shirt*	**esas** camisetas	*those T-shirts*
aquella camiseta	*that T-shirt (over there)*	**aquellas** camisetas	*those T-shirts (over there)*

No sé si debo comprar **estos** aretes de aquí o **esos** aretes de allí.
*I don't know if I should buy **these** earrings here or **those** earrings there.*

Aquellas cerámicas son muy baratas.
***Those** ceramics **(over there)** are very inexpensive.*

Más práctica
Cuaderno *pp. 373–375*
Cuaderno para hispanohablantes *pp. 374–377*

@**HOMETUTOR** my.hrw.com
Leveled Practice

Práctica de GRAMÁTICA

11 | En el mercado

**Leer
Escribir**

Susana está en el mercado. Escoge el adjetivo demostrativo correcto para completar la conversación. Luego pon las joyas en orden según su proximidad a Susana, empezando con la más cercana. *(Choose the correct demonstrative adjective. Then write a list of the jewelry items in order from the closest to the farthest in relation to Susana.)*

Susana: Me gustan las joyas de plata. ¿Me deja ver __1.__ (aquella / aquel) collar?

Vendedora: Sí, le dejo __2.__ (aquel / aquellos) collar en treinta mil colones.

Susana: Es caro. ¿Y __3.__ (estas / estos) aretes de aquí? ¿Cuánto cuestan?

Vendedora: __4.__ (Esos / Esas) aretes de plata cuestan veinticinco mil colones. Son de buena calidad.

Susana: Me gustan __5.__ (esas / esos) joyas de allí, pero cuestan demasiado.

Vendedora: ¿Le gustaría __6.__ (ese / esa) anillo de plata? Sólo cuesta dieciocho mil colones.

Susana: ¡Está bien! Quisiera comprar __7.__ (esa / ese) anillo.

12 | ¿Qué están haciendo?   *¿Recuerdas?* Present progressive p. 420

**Escuchar
Escribir**

Hay muchas personas en el mercado hoy. Mira el dibujo y escucha las oraciones sobre qué están haciendo. Indica si cada oración es cierta o falsa. *(Listen to the sentences and tell whether they are true or false, according to the drawing.)*

Expansión
Write four true sentences based on the drawing.

13 | Hablando del café

Comparación cultural

El café

Coffee plantation, Costa Rica

How does Costa Rica's climate impact its leading exports? Coffee is one of **Costa Rica's** leading exports. It grows well due to the country's high altitudes, rich soils, and warm temperatures. The coffee harvest takes place between November and January. Workers carefully handpick and sort the berries of the coffee plants, placing only the ripe, red ones in their baskets. The berries are then brought to mills so that the beans can be removed and processed.

Compara con tu mundo *What is an important industry in your area?*

Elena: __1.__ café de Costa Rica me gusta más que __2.__ café que toma Daniel, que es de Indonesia.

Rodrigo: Mi favorito fue __3.__ café que nos sirvió Alejandra la semana pasada.

Alicia: Estoy de acuerdo con Elena. En casa estamos tomando __4.__ cafés que nos compraron mis padres en San José el año pasado, y creo que los de Costa Rica son más sabrosos.

---

14 | ¡A jugar! Veo, veo ♻ *¿Recuerdas?* Classroom objects p. 110

Hablar

Habla con otro(a) estudiante. Describe objetos que ves en la clase. Él o ella va a adivinar qué son, usando adjetivos demostrativos. *(Describe classroom objects for a partner to guess.)*

A Veo una cosa roja.

B ¿Es esta mochila?

No.

¿Es aquella mochila?

Sí.

Expansión
Point out six classroom objects to a partner. He or she will describe them.

Más práctica Cuaderno *pp. 373–375* Cuaderno para hispanohablantes *pp. 374–377*

Get Help Online
my.hrw.com

PARA Y PIENSA

Did you get it? Complete each sentence with the correct demonstrative adjective: **esas, aquellos,** or **este.**

1. _____ aretes son más bonitos que esos aretes.
2. _____ anillo es de oro.
3. La calidad de _____ artesanías es muy buena.

Unidad 8 Costa Rica

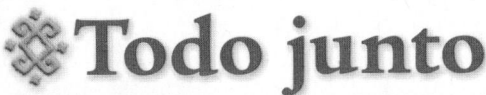

Todo junto

¡AVANZA!

Goal: Show what you know Identify the demonstrative adjectives used to indicate items in a store. Then practice using demonstrative adjectives and indirect object pronouns to bargain and describe vacations.
Actividades 15–19

Telehistoria completa

@HOMETUTOR View, Read and Record
my.hrw.com

STRATEGIES

Find the dramatic turn Read, watch, and/or listen to the scene slowly to discover the dramatic "turn" or change. Why do the teens stop paying attention to the salesclerk? What happens after that?

Identify expressions of courtesy What language does Susana use when she talks to vendors? How is it different from the language she uses with Jorge?

Escena 1 *Resumen*
Jorge y Susana llegan al centro comercial. Susana quiere comprar un anillo, pero es muy caro.

Escena 2 *Resumen*
Susana está hablando con el vendedor en la tienda cuando Jorge ve a alguien.

VIDEO DVD

AUDIO

Escena 3

Vendedor: ¿Y a usted no le gustan aquellos aretes de oro? ¿Ese collar de plata? ¿Estos anillos?

The salesclerk sees that Jorge and Susana have stopped paying attention and leaves.

Jorge: *(excited)* Susana, ¡allí está Trini Salgado, la jugadora de fútbol! Es ella, ¿no? ¿Qué está haciendo?

Susana: Sí, sí, es ella. Está comprando unos aretes.

Jorge: ¡Vamos! Necesito su autógrafo para Alicia. *(He opens his backpack but can't find the T-shirt.)* ¿Dónde está la camiseta de Alicia?

Susana: No sé...

While he looks through his backpack, Trini leaves the store.

15 | Comprensión de los episodios   ¿En qué orden?

Escuchar
Leer

Pon estas oraciones en orden para describir los episodios. *(Put the sentences in order.)*

a. Susana empieza a regatear, pero ella no está en el mercado.

b. Jorge no puede encontrar la camiseta.

c. Jorge le dice a Susana que a ella le gustan las cosas caras.

d. A Susana no le gusta llegar en el coche de su papá.

e. Jorge le dice a Susana que ve a Trini Salgado.

f. Susana le pregunta a Jorge qué le pasa a él.

16 | Comprensión de los episodios   ¿Qué pasó?

Escuchar
Leer

Mira las fotos y describe lo que pasó en los episodios. *(Describe what happened in the episodes.)*

1.

2.

3.

4.

17 | ¡A regatear!

Digital **performance space**

Hablar

STRATEGY Hablar

Be realistic In a real market you would need to be respectful and courteous as you bargain. Review the episodes and pay attention to the expressions and register the characters use. Model your conversation on theirs.

Regatea con otro(a) estudiante. Dibuja los artículos que quieres vender y trata de recibir el mejor precio posible. *(Bargain with your classmates.)*

A Buenas tardes. ¿Me deja ver aquel videojuego?

B Sí. Es de buena calidad. Le dejo este videojuego en treinta dólares...

Expansión
Tell the class what you bought, including the original price and final purchase price. The class will decide if it was a fair deal.

18 | Integración

Leer
Escuchar
Hablar

Lee la guía y escucha el anuncio. Luego di qué te gustaría hacer allí y qué les vas a comprar a tu familia y amigos. *(Read the guide and listen to the ad. Then tell what you would like to do there and what you are going to buy for your family and friends.)*

Fuente 1   Guía turística

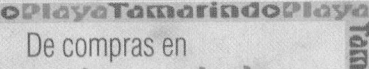

De compras en
Playa Tamarindo

Mercado Costeño En este mercado al aire libre, encuentras ropa, artículos de madera, joyas de madera y café orgánico. Puedes regatear.

Artesanías Iguana Verde Esta tienda tiene artesanías de buena calidad, pero son un poco caras. Venden cerámica, platos de madera y joyas de oro.

Librería Sol Tico Aquí venden libros, discos compactos y mapas decorativos.

Tienda Colibrí En esta tienda hay anillos y aretes de plata, y collares de madera. También venden camisetas y sombreros. Precios baratos.

Fuente 2   Anuncio de radio

Listen and take notes
- ¿Qué actividades hay en la playa?
- ¿Qué puedes hacer si no te gusta el mar?

modelo: En Playa Tamarindo me gustaría...
A... le voy a comprar...

19 | ¡Ya llegan las vacaciones!

Escribir

Escribe una entrada para tu blog comparando dos viajes. Describe a quién le gustaría cada viaje, qué hace la gente durante su tiempo libre, y qué puede comprar y para quién. *(Write an entry in your blog comparing two trips.)*

modelo: Tenemos dos viajes fenomenales. Si a usted le gusta el mar, le podemos ofrecer un viaje a Playa del Coco. Usted puede...

Writing Criteria	Excellent	Good	Needs Work
Content	Your entry includes a lot of information.	Your entry includes some information.	Your entry includes little information.
Communication	Most of your entry is organized and easy to follow.	Parts of your entry are organized and easy to follow.	Your entry is disorganized and hard to follow.
Accuracy	Your entry has few mistakes in grammar and vocabulary.	Your entry has some mistakes in grammar and vocabulary.	Your entry has many mistakes in grammar and vocabulary.

Expansión
Send a text message to a classmate telling which trip you prefer and why. Ask your classmate which trip he or she prefers and why.

Más práctica   Cuaderno *pp. 376–377*   Cuaderno para hispanohablantes *pp. 378–379*

Get Help Online
my.hrw.com

PARA Y PIENSA

Did you get it? Complete each sentence with the correct indirect object pronoun and demonstrative adjective, based on the Telehistoria.
1. Jorge _____ pregunta a Susana si _____ mujer allí es Trini Salgado.
2. El hombre _____ quiere vender a Jorge y a Susana _____ anillos de aquí.

Lectura cultural

Additional readings at my.hrw.com
SPANISH
InterActive Reader

¡AVANZA! **Goal:** Read about markets in Costa Rica and Uruguay. Then compare markets and bargaining in Costa Rica, Uruguay, and the United States.

Comparación cultural

Mercados en Costa Rica y Uruguay

AUDIO

STRATEGY Leer

Diagram comparisons
Use a Venn diagram to compare markets and bargaining in Costa Rica, Uruguay, and the U.S.

Costa Rica

Uruguay   Estados Unidos

En Latinoamérica, muchas ciudades tienen mercados al aire libre, donde puedes ir de compras y encontrar artículos interesantes y de buena calidad. Es muy común regatear en los puestos [1] de estos mercados. Si quieres regatear, hay algunas recomendaciones. Cuando escuchas el primer precio, puedes contestar: «¡Es demasiado!» También es importante ir a varios puestos para encontrar el precio más barato.

_____
[1] stalls

Costa Rica

AL MERCADO

—¿QUÉ LE VENDO, CHOLITA?... ¿QUÉ QUIERE, ENCANTO?
—¡MIRE QUÉ CEBOLLITAS, ESPÍ QUÉ NABOS!

Representación de un mercado, San José, Costa Rica

Mercado de fruta,
Montevideo, Uruguay

Uruguay

El Mercado Central de San José, Costa Rica, se fundó en el año 1880. En los puestos, venden una variedad de cosas, como café, frutas, verduras, pescado, carne, flores[2] y plantas medicinales. También puedes comprar recuerdos. Hay camisetas, joyas y artículos de madera y de cuero[3]. Si tienes hambre, hay restaurantes pequeños que se llaman sodas.

El Mercado del Puerto está cerca del mar en Montevideo, la capital de Uruguay. Se inauguró[4] en 1868. Allí hay artistas locales que venden sus artículos y puedes comprar artesanías en las tiendas. También puedes comer en los restaurantes, donde sirven carne y pescado. La parrillada, un plato con diferentes tipos de carne, es muy popular. Los sábados, muchas personas van a este mercado para almorzar y escuchar música.

---

[2] flowers   [3] leather   [4] opened

PARA
Y
PIENSA

¿Comprendiste?
1. ¿Qué puedes comprar en el Mercado Central? ¿En el Mercado del Puerto?
2. ¿Cuál de los mercados es más viejo?
3. ¿Qué recuerdos hay en el Mercado Central?
4. ¿En qué mercado es popular la parrillada?

¿Y tú?
¿Hay un mercado donde tú vives? Si hay, ¿cómo es? ¿Puedes regatear allí? ¿Dónde puedes regatear en Estados Unidos?

✤ Proyectos culturales

Postres en Costa Rica y Uruguay

How can foods from other Spanish-speaking countries be enjoyed here in the U.S.? Desserts in Spanish-speaking countries may appear to be different from the desserts that you are used to, but if you read the ingredients you'll see that these recipes from **Costa Rica** and **Uruguay** contain foods you could find in your own kitchen or the supermarket. **Plátanos horneados** and **dulce de leche** are prepared in slightly different ways throughout Latin America.

✤ Proyecto **1** *Plátanos horneados*

Costa Rica Plátanos, or plantains, grow in abundance in Latin America and are a dietary staple. This fruit resembles a banana, but it is typically not eaten raw. You know a plantain is ripe when its outer skin has turned from green to black. Ripe plantains are called **maduros.**

Ingredients for plátanos horneados
6 ripe plantains
1 stick of butter
1/2 cup honey
1/4 teaspoon ground cloves

Instructions
Preheat a toaster oven to 300 degrees. Remove the peels of the plantains and cut them in half lengthwise. Place them in a rectangular glass pan and pour the honey over them. Cut the butter into six pieces and place them on top of every other plantain, then sprinkle with the cloves. Cover the pan with aluminum foil and bake for 30 minutes or until the plantains are golden brown.
Optional: Once you remove the plantains from the oven, sprinkle them with cinnamon.

✤ Proyecto **2** *Dulce de leche*

Uruguay Dulce de leche has a sweet, caramel flavor and a texture that resembles fudge. It is often used as a filling for pastries and desserts, but can also be eaten by itself.

Ingredients for dulce de leche
4 cups whole milk
2 cups sugar
1 teaspoon baking soda
1/2 teaspoon vanilla extract

Instructions
Place all the ingredients in a heavy-bottomed saucepan. Bring the liquid to a boil and then reduce to medium heat, stirring frequently until the mixture thickens and turns caramel in color. Cool to room temperature.
Optional: Serve with cookies, bread, or fruit.

En tu comunidad

The work of a professional chef often brings him or her in contact with foods and people from other countries. How would knowing about other languages and cultures help you to be a better chef?

En resumen
Vocabulario y gramática

Vocabulario

Talk About Vacation Activities

acampar	to camp	hacer surf de vela	to windsurf
comer al aire libre	to picnic, to eat outside	hacer surfing	to surf
		montar a caballo	to ride a horse
dar una caminata	to hike	el tiempo libre	free time
hacer una parrillada	to barbecue		

Indicate Position

aquel(aquella)	that (over there)
aquellos(as)	those (over there)
ese(a)	that
esos(as)	those
este(a)	this
estos(as)	these
¿Qué es esto?	What is this?

Talk About Buying Souvenirs

barato(a)	inexpensive
la calidad	quality
caro(a)	expensive
demasiado	too much
el mercado	market
el recuerdo	souvenir

Jewelry and Handicrafts

el anillo	ring
el arete	earring
las artesanías	handicrafts
los artículos	goods
de madera	wood
de oro	gold
de plata	silver
la cerámica	ceramics
el collar	necklace
las joyas	jewelry

Bargaining

Le dejo... en...	I'll give . . . to you for . . .
Le puedo ofrecer...	I can offer you . . .
¿Me deja ver...?	May I see . . . ?
¡Qué caro(a)!	How expensive!
Quisiera...	I would like . . .
regatear	to bargain

Gramática

Indirect Object Pronouns

Indirect object pronouns use the same words as direct object pronouns except for **le** and **les.**

Singular		Plural	
me	me	nos	us
te	you (familiar)	os	you (familiar)
le	you (formal), him, her	les	you, them

Demonstrative Adjectives

In Spanish, **demonstrative adjectives** must match the nouns they modify in gender and number.

Masculine

Singular	Plural
este anillo	estos anillos
ese anillo	esos anillos
aquel anillo	aquellos anillos

Feminine

Singular	Plural
esta camiseta	estas camisetas
esa camiseta	esas camisetas
aquella camiseta	aquellas camisetas

Repaso de la lección

¡LLEGADA!

¡AvanzaRap!
DVD
Sing and Learn

Now you can
- talk about buying souvenirs on vacation
- talk about vacation activities

Using
- indirect object pronouns
- demonstrative adjectives

To review
- indirect object pronouns p. 439
- demonstrative adjectives p. 444

AUDIO

1 Listen and understand

Escucha la conversación entre César y una vendedora. Luego escoge la respuesta correcta. *(Listen and choose the correct word to complete each sentence.)*

1. César busca (un recuerdo / un artículo de madera) para su amiga.
2. La amiga prefiere (las artesanías / las joyas).
3. César piensa que el anillo de (oro / plata) es bonito.
4. El anillo es muy (caro / barato).
5. La amiga de César prefiere las joyas de (oro / plata).
6. La vendedora le deja (los aretes / los anillos) en quince mil.

To review
- indirect object pronouns p. 439

2 Talk about buying souvenirs on vacation

Soledad y su amiga Ana están regateando en un mercado. Completa la conversación con el pronombre de objeto indirecto apropiado.
(Complete the conversation with the appropriate indirect object pronoun.)

Soledad: Buenos días, señor. ¿ **1.** deja ver los collares de oro?

Vendedor: ¡Claro que sí! A usted **2.** dejo el collar más bonito en quince mil colones.

Soledad: ¡Qué caro! Mi amiga también quiere comprar un collar. ¿ **3.** deja ver a nosotras los collares de plata?

Vendedor: Sí, señoritas. A ustedes **4.** dejo dos collares en veinticinco mil colones.

Soledad: Todavía son caros.

Vendedor: Está bien. A usted **5.** dejo los dos collares en veinticuatro mil.

Ana: ¡Gracias, Soledad! ¿Quieres ir al café? **6.** invito.

To review
• demonstrative adjectives p. 444

3 | Talk about vacation activities

Estás de vacaciones y ves a muchas personas en la playa. Indica quiénes están haciendo las siguientes actividades. Usa adjetivos demostrativos. *(Use demonstrative adjectives to indicate who is doing the following activities.)*

modelo: acampar
Estos chicos están acampando.

1. hacer surfing

2. montar a caballo

3. comer al aire libre

4. vender refrescos

5. caminar en la playa

6. hacer surf de vela

7. hacer una parrillada

8. comprar un refresco

To review
• Comparación cultural pp. 432, 440, 446
• Lectura cultural pp. 450–451

4 | Costa Rica and Uruguay

Comparación cultural

Answer these culture questions.

1. Why is Costa Rica a good destination for ecotourism?

2. What are some transportation options in Costa Rica? Describe them.

3. How is coffee harvested in Costa Rica? Why does it grow well there?

4. Where are **el Mercado Central** and **el Mercado del Puerto** located? What foods can you buy at these markets?

Más práctica   Cuaderno *pp. 378–389*   Cuaderno para hispanohablantes *pp. 380–389*

Get Help Online
my.hrw.com

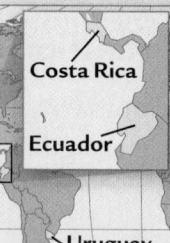

Comparación cultural

Costa Rica

Ecuador

Uruguay

AUDIO

¡De vacaciones!

Lectura y escritura

1 Leer Travel destinations vary around the world. Read and compare where and how Ernesto, Isabel, and Osvaldo are spending their vacations.

2 Escribir Using the three descriptions as models, write a short paragraph about a real or imaginary vacation.

> **STRATEGY Escribir**
> **Use three boxes** Use three boxes to help you describe the vacation.
>
> | Lugar | Actividades | Opinión |
> |---|---|---|

Step 1 Complete the boxes. In the first box write information about the place, in the second box write details about what you usually do there, and in the third box give your opinion about the location.

Step 2 Write your paragraph. Make sure to include all the information from the boxes. Check your writing by yourself or with help from a friend. Make final corrections.

Compara con tu mundo

Use the paragraph you wrote to compare your vacation with a vacation described by *one* of the three students. How are they similar? How are they different?

Cuaderno *pp. 390–392*   Cuaderno para hispanohablantes *pp. 390–392*

my.hrw.com

See these pages come alive!

Uruguay

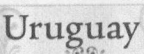

Ernesto

¡Hola! Me llamo Ernesto y vivo en Montevideo. Es febrero, y mis padres y yo estamos de vacaciones en Punta del Este. Generalmente nos quedamos con mi abuela. Su casa está muy cerca de Playa Mansa. Es una playa donde el mar es muy tranquilo. Es ideal para nadar o tomar el sol. Yo prefiero ir a Playa Brava porque tiene más olas[1] y es perfecta para hacer surfing. En las tardes me gusta pasear por el Mercado de los Artesanos. Allí les compro recuerdos a mis amigos.

---
[1] waves

Ecuador

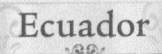

Isabel

¿Qué tal? Me llamo Isabel y soy de Quito. Mi familia y yo estamos pasando unos días de vacaciones en Baños, una ciudad que está en un valle[2], al lado de un volcán. Nos estamos quedando en un hotel que está muy cerca de las cascadas[3] y de las aguas termales[4]. Aquí puedes hacer muchas actividades al aire libre: montar a caballo, dar caminatas por la ruta de las cascadas y montar en bicicleta. ¡Es un lugar fenomenal!

---
[2] valley   [3] waterfalls   [4] hot springs

Costa Rica

Osvaldo

¡Hola! Me llamo Osvaldo y soy de Costa Rica. Estoy pasando las vacaciones de julio en el Parque Nacional Manuel Antonio. El hotel está en un bosque tropical lluvioso[5] pero también tiene una playa en la costa del océano Pacífico. Todas las mañanas, mis padres y yo nos levantamos muy temprano y salimos a dar caminatas en el parque. Allí hay plantas y animales muy exóticos. ¡Me gusta estar en la naturaleza![6]

---
[5] **bosque...** tropical rain forest   [6] nature

cuatrocientos cincuenta y siete   **457**

Repaso inclusivo
♻ Options for Review

Digital
performance space

¡AvanzaRap!
DVD
Sing and Learn

1 | Listen, understand, and compare

Escuchar

Listen to the telephone conversation between Mrs. Daza and her husband. Then answer the following questions.

1. ¿Dónde está la señora Daza y qué está haciendo? ¿Por qué va a llegar tarde?

2. ¿Qué hizo el señor Daza después de trabajar?

3. ¿Qué está haciendo él ahora?

4. ¿Dónde están Luisa y David? ¿Qué están haciendo?

5. ¿Qué va a hacer la familia Daza este sábado? ¿Cuál es el problema?

Does your family eat dinner together? At what time? What do you do as a group on weekends?

2 | Talk about your ideal routine

Hablar

Prepare a presentation about your ideal daily routine. Include what time you get up, the sequence of your morning activities, what your school day is like, and what you do after school. Also include as many details as possible about your perfect day: what you eat, with whom you do different activities, and what the weather is like. Your presentation should be about four minutes long.

3 | Talk about your health

Hablar

You are at the doctor's office for a checkup. You should tell your partner about your general health routine, including when you go to bed, what time you get up, what you eat and drink throughout the day, and what your activities are. Your partner will make recommendations about what you should do differently. Your conversation should be about five minutes long.

4 | Plan a trip

Escribir

You are an intern at a travel agency and have been asked to research possible trips a family of four could make to a Spanish-speaking country. Do research online, then send an e-mail to the family that includes some details about destinations, transportation, costs, and information about regional festivals or cuisine. Ask them questions about their preferences and request they get back to you soon with their answers. Remember to use the appropriate register and style for a work e-mail.

5 | Interview potential roommates

Hablar

Work in a group of four. You are potential roommates at soccer camp. Ask questions to find out about your new roommates' personalities, preferences, and daily routines. Each roommate should give as much detail about himself or herself and then ask questions to others. Each person should speak for at least two minutes.

6 | Mingle at a party

Hablar

In a group of six, role-play a dinner party in which you mingle with other guests. Walk around and introduce yourself to others. Talk about the people that you know in common, what you are studying, what you like to do in your free time, and anything else you find out about the person you are talking to, such as plans for summer vacation. You should spend at least two minutes talking to each person.

7 | Decide where to study

Leer Escribir

This summer you want to study Spanish for a month in Costa Rica. Your Spanish teacher gave you the following information to help you decide which program to choose. Read the descriptions and write a note to your teacher, explaining where you would prefer to study and why. Offer comparisons of the two programs.

Estudia en
¡Costa Rica!

Jacó

En esta ciudad muy pequeña no hay muchas tiendas, pero hay varias playas en el Océano Pacífico. Puedes vivir en una residencia de la escuela, con un(a) compañero(a) de cuarto.

Durante los fines de semana es muy popular hacer surf de vela o esquí acuático. También puedes nadar o tomar el sol en la playa.

Horario
Clases: 7:00–2:30
Almuerzo: 12:00–1:00

Heredia

Heredia es una ciudad pequeña cerca de San José, la capital. Puedes vivir en una casa con una familia con hijos. Las familias con hijos normalmente se acuestan a las diez de la noche. Se levantan a las seis y media para comer el desayuno.

Durante los fines de semana puedes dar caminatas en las áreas verdes y ver muchos animales exóticos. También hay volcanes cerca de la ciudad.

Horario
Clases: 8:00–4:30
Almuerzo: 1:00–3:00

¿?Entre dos

Pair Activities

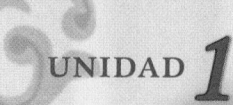

¿Qué les gusta hacer?

Estudiante A

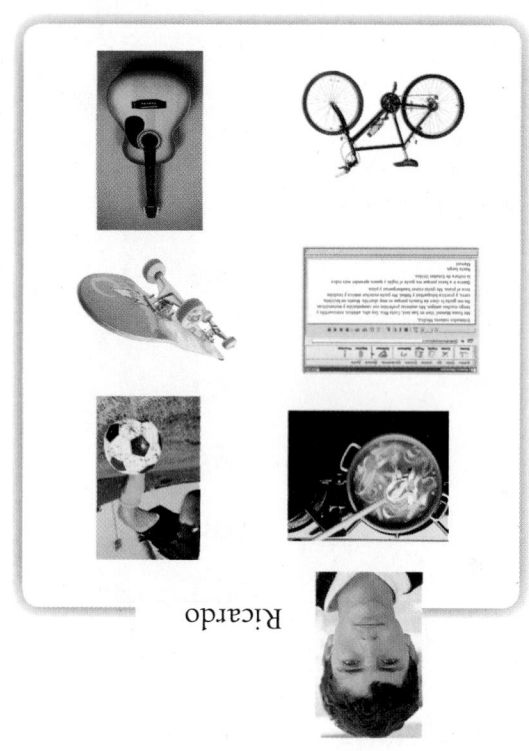

Ricardo

Ricardo and Isabel like to do many things. Look at the pictures on the right to find out what Ricardo likes to do. (Your partner has pictures showing what Isabel likes to do.) Take turns asking each other questions to discover what Ricardo and Isabel like to do.

Estudiante A: A Ricardo le gusta... ¿Y a Isabel?

Estudiante B: A Isabel también le gusta... ¿A Ricardo le gusta...?

What activities do Ricardo and Isabel both like to do?

¿Qué les gusta hacer?

Estudiante B

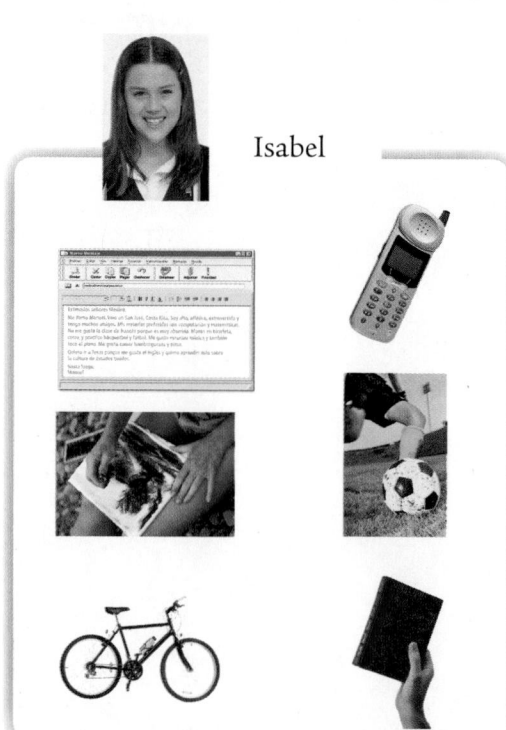

Isabel

Ricardo and Isabel like to do many things. Look at the pictures on the right to find out what Isabel likes to do. (Your partner has pictures showing what Ricardo likes to do.) Take turns asking each other questions to discover what Ricardo and Isabel like to do.

Estudiante A: A Ricardo le gusta... ¿Y a Isabel?

Estudiante B: A Isabel también le gusta... ¿A Ricardo le gusta...?

What activities do Ricardo and Isabel both like to do?

Entre dos · Lección 2

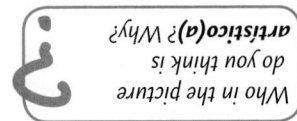

¿ Who in the picture do you think is *artístico(a)*? Why?

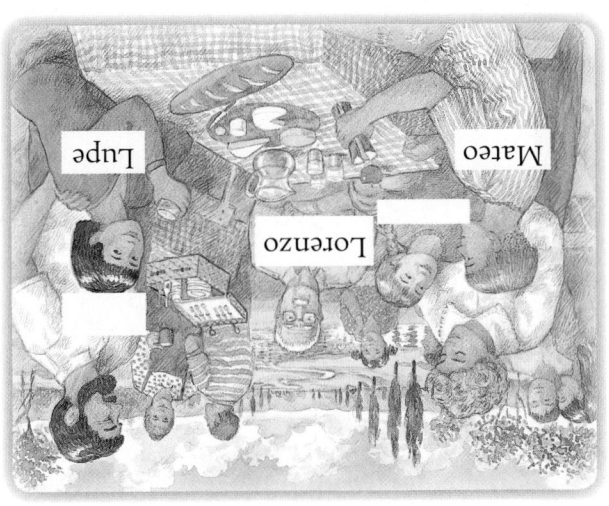

Lupe

Mateo

Lorenzo

Estudiante A

¿Cómo se llaman?

You and your partner want to know the names of the people in the picture. Your picture has the names of three people and your partner's picture has the names of three other people. Take turns asking each other questions and describing people to find out the names of all the people.

Estudiante A: ¿Cómo se llama la chica rubia?

Estudiante B: ¿La chica pequeña y joven?

Estudiante A: Sí.

Estudiante B: Se llama Gabi.
¿Cómo se llama...?

¿Cómo se llaman?

Estudiante B

You and your partner want to know the names of the people in the picture. Your picture has the names of three people and your partner's picture has the names of three other people. Take turns asking each other questions and describing people to find out the names of all the people.

Estudiante A: ¿Cómo se llama la chica rubia?

Estudiante B: ¿La chica pequeña y joven?

Estudiante A: Sí.

Estudiante B: Se llama Gabi.
¿Cómo se llama...?

Marta

Gabi

Tomas

Who in the picture do you think is *artístico(a)*? Why?

Estudiante A

¿What classes do you and your partner have at the same time?

You and your partner want to compare class schedules. Look at your class schedule on the right. Your partner has a different schedule. Ask each other questions to find out what classes you have at various times of the day.

Estudiante A: A las... tengo... ¿Y tú?
Estudiante B: Yo (también) tengo... ¿Qué clase tienes a las...?

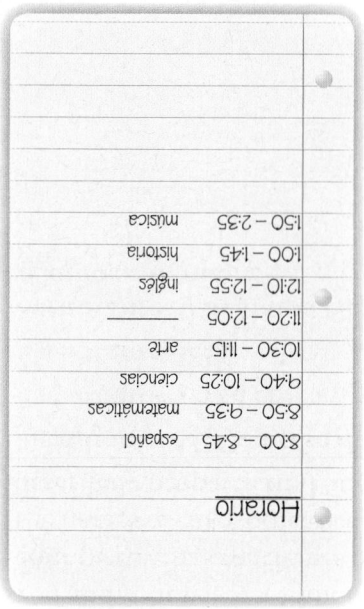

Horario	
8:00 – 8:45	español
8:50 – 9:35	matemáticas
9:40 – 10:25	ciencias
10:30 – 11:15	arte
11:20 – 12:05	——
12:10 – 12:55	inglés
1:00 – 1:45	historia
1:50 – 2:35	música

Horario de clases

Estudiante B

You and your partner want to compare class schedules. Look at your class schedule on the right. Your partner has a different schedule. Ask each other questions to find out what classes you have at various times of the day.

Estudiante A las... tengo... ¿Y tú?
Estudiante B: Yo (también) tengo... ¿Qué clase tienes a las...?

Horario	
8:00 – 8:45	español
8:50 – 9:35	historia
9:40 – 10:25	ciencias
10:30 – 11:15	arte
11:20 – 12:05	inglés
12:10 – 12:55	——
1:00 – 1:45	matemáticas
1:50 – 2:35	música

What classes do you and your partner have at the same time?

Entre dos · Lección 2

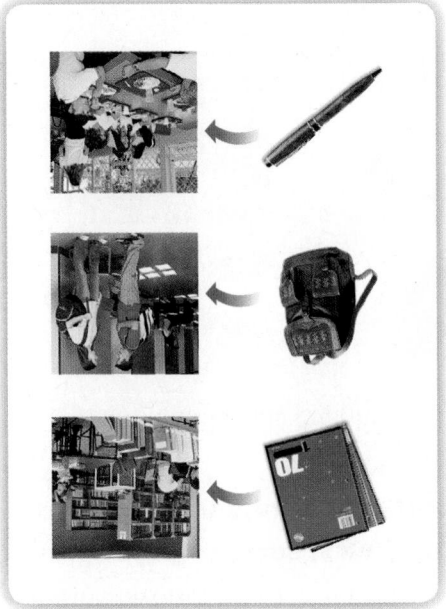

Did you and your partner leave some of the supplies in the same places?

¿Dónde están?

Estudiante A

You and your partner have borrowed some school supplies from friends but have forgotten them at different places in school. Ask your partner where the following friends' supplies are:

> Alejo's and Marta's calculators
>
> Sergio's paper
>
> Julia's pencil

Then, answer your partner's questions based on the images and cues. Take turns doing this activity.

Estudiante A: ¿Dónde está el borrador de la maestra?

Estudiante B: Está en la clase.

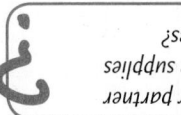

¿Dónde están?

Estudiante B

You and your partner have borrowed some school supplies from friends but have forgotten them at different places in school. Ask your partner where the following friends' supplies are:

> Daniel's backpack
>
> Florencia's and Luis's pens
>
> Félix's notebook

Then, answer your partner's questions based on the images and cues. Take turns doing this activity.

Estudiante A: ¿Dónde está el borrador de la maestra?

Estudiante B: Está en la clase.

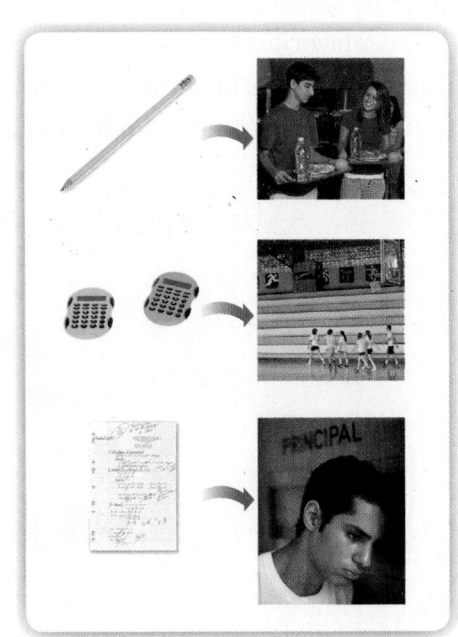

Did you and your partner leave some of the supplies in the same places?

¿Qué le gusta comer?

Estudiante A

You and your partner are discussing what Elena and Mario like and don't like to eat. Look at the pictures below to find out what Elena likes and dislikes. (Your partner has pictures showing what Mario likes and dislikes.) Talk to your partner about Elena's and Mario's favorite foods.

Estudiante A: **A Elena le gusta(n)..., pero no le gusta(n)... ¿Y a Mario?**

Estudiante B: **A Mario no le gusta(n)..., pero le gusta(n)... ¿A Elena le gusta(n)...?**

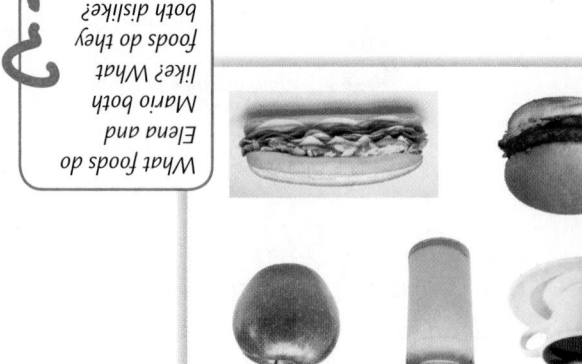

A Elena no le gusta(n)...

A Elena le gusta(n)...

What foods do Elena and Mario both like? What foods do they both dislike?

¿Qué le gusta comer?

Estudiante B

You and your partner are discussing what Elena and Mario like and don't like to eat. Look at the pictures below to find out what Mario likes and dislikes. (Your partner has pictures showing what Elena likes and dislikes.) Talk to your partner about Elena's and Mario's favorite foods.

Estudiante A: **A Elena le gusta(n)..., pero no le gusta(n)... ¿Y a Mario?**

Estudiante B: **A Mario no le gusta(n)..., pero le gusta(n)... ¿A Elena le gusta(n)...?**

A Mario le gusta(n)...   A Mario no le gusta(n)...

What foods do Elena and Mario both like? What foods do they both dislike?

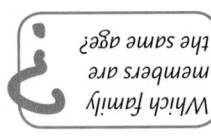

ENTRE DOS UNIDAD 3

Which family members are the same age?

Pedro

53 años   47 años

72 años   69 años

Estudiante A: **¿Cuántos años tiene su...?**

Estudiante B: **Su... tiene...**

You and your partner are looking at Pedro's family tree. You know the age of some of Pedro's family members and your partner knows the age of the other members of Pedro's family. Take turns asking each other how old Pedro's family members are.

Estudiante A

¿Cuántos años tienen?

¿Cuántos años tienen?

Estudiante B

You and your partner are looking at Pedro's family tree. You know the age of some of Pedro's family members and your partner knows the age of the other members of Pedro's family. Take turns asking each other how old Pedro's family members are.

Estudiante A: **¿Cuántos años tiene su...?**

Estudiante B: **Su... tiene...**

47 años   53 años

Pedro   11 años

4 años

Which family members are the same age?

Estudiante A

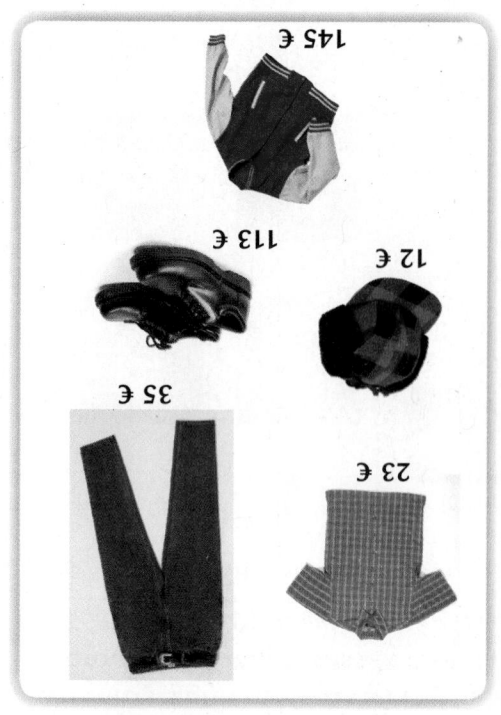

145 €

113 €

12 €

35 €

23 €

¿Cuánto cuesta la ropa de Éster en total? ¿Y de Eduardo?

Estudiante A: **¿Cuánto cuesta(n)...?**

Estudiante B: **Éster quiere comprar...**

Estudiante A: **¿Qué quiere comprar Éster?**

costs. Note the cost of each item.

buying, in what color, and how much each item

asking each other what Éster and Eduardo are

showing what Éster wants to buy.) Take turns

Eduardo wants to buy. (Your partner has pictures

Look at the pictures on the right to find out what

Eduardo and Éster are shopping for clothes.

En la tienda de ropa

En la tienda de ropa

Eduardo and Éster are shopping for clothes. Look at the pictures on the right to find out what Éster wants to buy. (Your partner has pictures showing what Eduardo wants to buy.) Take turns asking each other what Éster and Eduardo are buying, in what color, and how much each item costs. Note the cost of each item.

Estudiante A: **¿Qué quiere comprar Eduardo?**

Estudiante B: **Eduardo quiere comprar...**

Estudiante A: **¿Cuánto cuesta(n)...?**

Estudiante B

49 €

33 €

9 €

89 €

38 €

¿Cuánto cuesta la ropa de Éster en total? ¿Y de Eduardo?

Entre dos · Lección 2

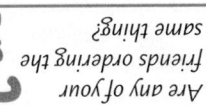

Are any of your friends ordering the same thing?

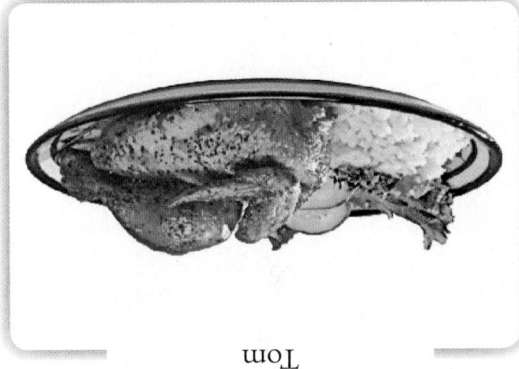

Tom

Julie

Estudiante A: **¿Qué va a pedir Tom?**

Estudiante B: **Tom va a pedir…**

You and your partner are supposed to meet some friends at a restaurant. They are late and they asked you to order for them. Take turns asking each other what your friends are going to order.

Estudiante A

¿Qué van a pedir?

¿Qué van a pedir?

Estudiante B

You and your partner are supposed to meet some friends at a restaurant. They are late and they asked you to order for them. Take turns asking each other what your friends are going to order.

Estudiante A: **¿Qué va a pedir Sara?**

Estudiante B: **Sara va a pedir…**

Sara

Sam

Are any of your friends ordering the same thing?

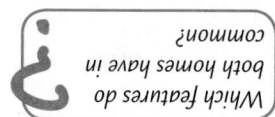

¿
Which features do
both homes have in
common?

Estudiante B: **Sí/No...**

Estudiante A: **¿Tiene comedor?**

Estudiante B: **Sí/No...**

Estudiante A: **¿La casa tiene dos pisos?**

Decide which one you would select and why.

questions about the home you found. Then, ask your partner at least five questions

partner each found a home that would be available. First, answer your partner's

Imagine that you and your family are going to rent a vacation home. You and your

Estudiante A

Un hogar para las vacaciones

Un hogar para las vacaciones

Estudiante B

Imagine that you and your family are going to rent a vacation home. You and
your partner each found a home that would be available. First, ask your partner at
least five questions about the home he or she found. Then, answer your partner's
questions about the home you found. Decide which one you would select and why.

Estudiante A: **¿La casa tiene dos pisos?**

Estudiante B: **Sí/No...**

Estudiante A: **¿Tiene comedor?**

Estudiante B: **Sí/No...**

*Which features do
both homes have in
common?* **?**

Antes de celebrar, hay que limpiar

Estudiante A

Imagine that you and a family member (your partner) want to have a party. You are allowed to have the party as long as you both complete your chores. Take turns asking each other what you are going to do today. First, ask your partner if he or she plans to set the table, wash the dishes, make the bed, cook, and mow the lawn. Then, answer your partner's questions based on the images and clues below.

Estudiante A: **¿Vas a hacer la cama?**

Estudiante B: **Sí/No....**

What are two chores you and your partner still need to do tomorrow?

Antes de celebrar, hay que limpiar

Estudiante B

Imagine that you and a family member (your partner) want to have a party. You are allowed to have the party as long as you both complete your chores. Take turns asking each other what you are going to do today. First, answer your partner's questions based on the images and clues below. Then, ask your partner if he or she plans to sweep, feed the cat, take out the trash, iron, and vacuum.

Estudiante A: **¿Vas a planchar la ropa?**

Estudiante B: **Sí/No...**

X √ √ X √

What are two chores you and your partner still need to do tomorrow?

¿Which sports do Carolina and Enrique have in common?

Estudiante B: **Ella no juega al fútbol americano, pero patina.**

Estudiante A: **Enrique juega al fútbol americano. ¿Y Carolina?**

You and your partner are talking about what sports Enrique and Carolina like to play. Look at Enrique's equipment to see the sports he enjoys. With a partner, talk about what sports Enrique and Carolina do.

Estudiante A

Los deportes

Enrique

Los deportes

You and your partner are talking about what sports Enrique and Carolina like to play. Look at Carolina's equipment to see the sports she enjoys. With a partner, talk about what sports Carolina and Enrique do.

Estudiante A: **Enrique juega al fútbol americano. ¿Y Carolina?**

Estudiante B: **Ella no juega al fútbol americano, pero patina.**

Estudiante B

Carolina

Which sports do Carolina and Enrique have in common?

Entre dos · Lección 2

¡Ay, me duele...!

Estudiante A

You and your partner are doctors. Each of you has information about some patients. Ask each other about patients on your charts. Use the images to tell your partner what the medical problems are. Then, imagine what each patient did to cause that problem.

Estudiante A: **¿Qué le duele a Ana?**

Estudiante B: **Le duele el tobillo. Ayer caminó mucho.**

Sarita

Carlos

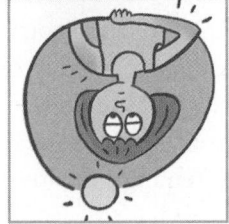

Daniela

	Le duele...	¿Por qué?
Patricia		
Esteban		
Mario		

What would you advise these patients to do to get better?

¡Ay, me duele...!

Estudiante B

You and your partner are doctors. Each of you has information about some patients. Ask each other about patients on your charts. Use the images to tell your partner what the medical problems are. Then, imagine what each patient did to cause that problem.

Estudiante A: **¿Qué le duele a Ana?**

Estudiante B: **Le duele el tobillo. Ayer caminó mucho.**

	Le duele...	¿Por qué?
Daniela		
Carlos		
Sarita		

Patricia

Esteban

Mario

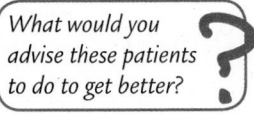

What would you advise these patients to do to get better?

El proyecto

Estudiante A

Roberto

Rita

Luisa y Andrea

You and your partner are in charge of a class project and you want to make sure that all your team members have completed their tasks. Ask your partner who did the tasks listed below. Answer your partner's questions based on the images. Take turns doing this activity.

Use instant messaging
Burn compact discs
Surf the Internet
Buy a new mouse

Estudiante A: **¿Quién habló con el profesor?**
Estudiante B: **... habló con el profesor./ Nadie.**

Which tasks have not yet been completed?

El proyecto

Estudiante B

You and your partner are in charge of a class project and you want to make sure that all your team members have completed their tasks. Ask your partner who did the tasks listed below. Answer your partner's questions based on the images. Take turns doing this activity.

Take photos
Send photos
Look for books in the library
Send e-mails

Estudiante A: **¿Quién habló con el profesor?**
Estudiante B: **... habló con el professor./ Nadie.**

Which tasks have not yet been completed?

Juan y Cristina

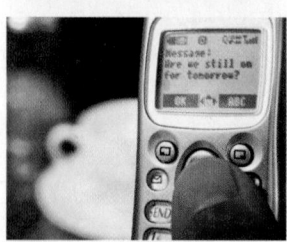

Marcelo

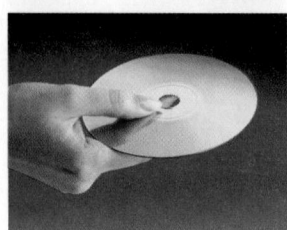

Teresa y yo

Entre dos · Lección 2

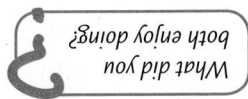

What did you both enjoy doing?

Estudiante B: ... **divertido(a)/aburrido(a). Y tú, ¿qué hiciste?**

Estudiante A: **¿Cómo fue?**

Estudiante B: **Por la mañana, ... y por la tarde...**

Estudiante A: **¿Adónde fuiste el viernes pasado?**

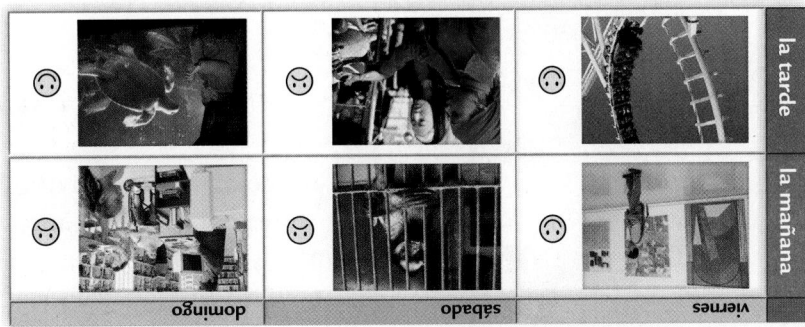

You and your partner are talking about what you did last weekend. Take turns asking and telling each other where you went and whether it was fun or boring.

Estudiante A

El fin de semana pasado

ENTRE DOS UNIT 7

El fin de semana pasado

Estudiante B

You and your partner are talking about what you did last weekend. Take turns asking and telling each other where you went and whether it was fun or boring.

Estudiante A: **¿Adónde fuiste el viernes pasado?**

Estudiante B: **Por la mañana, ... y por la tarde...**

Estudiante A: **¿Cómo fue?**

Estudiante B: **... divertido(a)/aburrido(a). Y tú, ¿qué hiciste?**

What did you both enjoy doing?

¿Who is almost ready to leave?

Diego

Isabel

Sergio

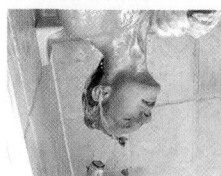

Mateo

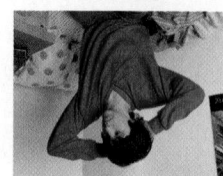

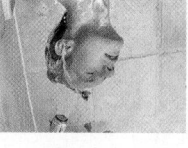

Estudiante A: ¿Qué está haciendo...?
Estudiante B: Está...

doing.
about what the people in the images below are
Elena. Then, answer your partner's questions
Sr. Costas, Cris, la Sra. Vásquez, Rafael, Rita, and
partner what the following people are doing: el
everyone gets to the airport on time. Ask your
and your partner are trying to make sure that
Your class is leaving for a trip to Spain today. You

¡Date prisa!

Sofía

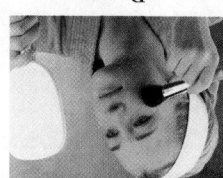

Rosa

Estudiante A

¡Date prisa!

Estudiante B

Your class is leaving today for a trip to Spain. You and your partner are trying to make sure that everyone gets to the airport on time. Answer your partner's questions about what the people in the images are doing. Then, ask your partner what these people are doing: Rosa, Sofía, Mateo, Sergio, Isabel, and Diego.

Estudiante A: **¿Qué está haciendo...?**
Estudiante B: **Está...**

el Sr. Costas

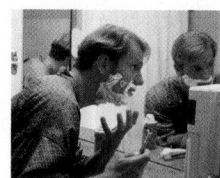

Cris

la Sra. Vásquez

Rita

Rafael

Elena

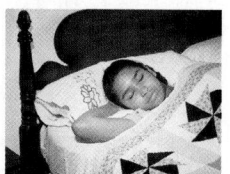

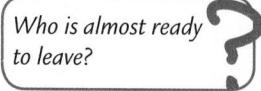
Who is almost ready to leave?

Entre dos · Lección 2

De vacaciones

You and your partner are organizing a summer camp and are trying to decide what activities to include. Ask your partner what the teens on your list would like to do. Answer your partner's questions based on the images. Take turns doing the activity.

Estudiante A: **¿Qué le gustaría hacer a Miguel?**

Estudiante B: **A Miguel le gustaría...**

Miguel	Pablo
Susana	Jorge
María	Carlos

What are the two activities that more than one person would like?

Estudiante A

Raquel

Paloma

Juan

Rosa

Ana

Gabi

De vacaciones

You and your partner are organizing a summer camp and are trying to decide what activities to include. Ask your partner what the teens on your list would like to do. Answer your partner's questions based on the images. Take turns doing the activity.

Estudiante A: **¿Qué le gustaría hacer a Miguel?**

Estudiante B: **A Miguel le gustaría...**

Estudiante B

Miguel

Pablo

Susana

Jorge

Maria

Carlos

Gabi	Ana
Rosa	Juan
Paloma	Raquel

What are the two activities that more than one person would like?

Recursos

Lección 1
¿Qué te gusta hacer?

Talk About Activities

cuidar niños	to baby-sit
pintar	to paint
la reunión	meeting
el club	club
manejar	to drive
trabajar a tiempo parcial	to work part-time
trabajar de voluntario	to volunteer
tocar un instrumento	to play an instrument

Instruments

el piano	piano
el clarinete	clarinet
la flauta	flute
el saxofón	saxophone
el tambor	drum
la trompeta	trumpet
la viola	viola
el violín	violin

Snack Foods and Beverages

la merienda	snack
las papitas	chips
las galletas saladas	crackers
las galletitas	cookies
el chicle	chewing gum
los dulces	candy
la limonada	lemonade

Lección 2
Mis amigos y yo

Describe Yourself and Others

Personality

listo(a)	clever / smart
callado(a)	quiet
extrovertido(a)	outgoing
tímido(a)	shy
sincero(a)	sincere
tonto(a)	silly
travieso(a)	mischievous
paciente	patient
talentoso(a)	talented
creativo(a)	creative
ambicioso(a)	ambitious

Appearance

el pelo oscuro	dark hair
el pelo rizado	curly hair
el pelo lacio	straight hair
calvo(a)	bald
los frenillos	braces

People

el (la) policía	police officer
el actor	actor
la actriz	actress
el (la) compañero(a) de clase	classmate
el (la) bombero(a)	firefighter
el (la) secretario(a)	secretary
el jefe, la jefa	boss

Unidad 2

Expansión de vocabulario

Lección 1
Somos estudiantes

Tell Time and Discuss Daily Schedules

la medianoche	midnight
el mediodía	noon

Describing Classes

School Subjects	
la asignatura	school subject
la educación física	physical education
las ciencias sociales	social studies
la geometría	geometry
la geografía	geography
el álgebra	algebra
la lengua, el idioma	language
la literatura	literature
la biología	biology
la química	chemistry
la banda	band
el coro	choir
la orquesta	orchestra
la hora de estudio	study hall
In School	
la asamblea	assembly
el recreo	recess, break
Classroom Activities	
preguntar	to ask
la respuesta	answer
la prueba	test, quiz

Describe Frequency

cada	each
a veces	sometimes
¿Con qué frecuencia...?	How often. . . ?
rara vez	rarely

Other Words and Phrases

terminar	to finish
esperar	to wait (for)
mientras	while
otra vez	again

Lección 2
En la escuela

Describe Classroom Objects

la carpeta	folder
las tijeras	scissors
la regla	ruler
el diccionario	dictionary
la impresora	printer
la bandera	flag
el globo	globe

Places in School

la sala de clase	classroom
el casillero	locker
el auditorio	auditorium

Say Where Things Are Located

entre	between
fuera (de)	out / outside (of)
(a la) derecha (de)	(to the) right (of)
(a la) izquierda (de)	(to the) left (of)
aquí	here
allí	there
enfrente (de)	across from, facing

Talk About How You Feel

feliz, alegre	happy
preocupado(a)	worried
listo(a)	ready
Estoy de acuerdo.	I agree.

Other Words and Phrases

mismo(a)	same
según	according to
creer	to think, to believe
especialmente	especially
olvidar	to forget
sobre	about
además	besides, further
suficiente, bastante	enough
sin	without

Lección 1
Mi comida favorita

Talk About Foods and Beverages

For Breakfast	
desayunar	to have breakfast
la mantequilla	butter
la miel	honey
el pan tostado	toast
el batido	milkshake, smoothie
For Lunch	
la bolsa	bag
la mantequilla de cacahuate	peanut butter
la jalea	jelly
el atún	tuna
la ensalada	salad
Fruit	
el plátano	banana; plantain
la toronja	grapefruit
la piña	pineapple
el durazno	peach
el limón	lemon
la sandía	watermelon

Lección 2
En mi familia

Talk About Family

el esposo	husband
la esposa	wife
la hermanastra	stepsister
el hermanastro	stepbrother
la media hermana	half-sister
el medio hermano	half-brother
el nieto	grandson
la nieta	granddaughter
el sobrino	nephew
la sobrina	niece
el (la) bebé	baby

Pets

el pájaro	bird
el pez (*pl.* los peces)	fish
el conejo	rabbit
el lagarto	lizard
la rana	frog
el hámster	hamster

Unidad 4 — Expansión de vocabulario

Lección 1
¡Vamos de compras!

Describe Clothing

las botas	boots
el impermeable	raincoat
la falda	skirt
el suéter	sweater
la sudadera (con capucha)	(hooded) sweatshirt
los pantalones deportivos	sweatpants
el abrigo	coat
los zapatos de tenis	tennis shoes, sneakers
el pijama	pajamas
las sandalias	sandals
la gorra	baseball cap
las gafas de sol	sunglasses
los guantes	gloves
la bufanda	scarf
el paraguas	umbrella
la bolsa	bag, purse

Colors

morado(a)	purple
rosado(a)	pink
gris	gray

Discuss Seasons

el norte	north
el sur	south
el este	east
el oeste	west

Lección 2
¿Qué hacemos esta noche?

Describe Places In Town

la iglesia	church
el edificio	building
el centro de videojuegos	arcade
la piscina	pool
la acera	sidewalk
el correo	post office
la librería	bookstore
la zapatería	shoe store
el templo	temple
la tienda de discos	music store

Music

el rap	rap
alternativa	alternative
la música electrónica	electronic music, techno
la canción	song
la letra	lyrics

In a Restaurant

la cuchara	spoon
el cuchillo	knife
el tenedor	fork
el vaso	glass
la servilleta	napkin
el tazón	bowl
la taza	cup

For Dinner

el puerco	pork
el pavo	turkey
los fideos	noodles
la salsa	sauce
la pimienta	pepper
la sal	salt
los mariscos	seafood

Vegetables

la zanahoria	carrot
la lechuga	lettuce
el maíz	corn

Lección 1
Vivimos aquí

Describe A House

el garaje	garage
la pared	wall
el traspatio	back yard
antiguo(a)	old, ancient
la cerca	fence

Describe Household Items

el congelador	freezer
la estufa	stove
el refrigerador	refrigerator
el lavaplatos	dishwasher
el microondas	microwave
la videograbadora	VCR
el teléfono celular	cellular phone
los audífonos	headphones

Lección 2
Una fiesta en casa

Plan a Party

sorprender	to surprise
el aniversario	anniversary
el confeti	confetti
la celebración	celebration
el día festivo	holiday
el ponche	punch
los juegos	games
los premios	prizes

Holidays/Celebrations

el bautizo	baptism
la graduación	graduation
la Navidad	Christmas
la Nochebuena	Christmas Eve
la Pascua Florida	Easter
el Ramadán	Ramadan
Rosh Hashaná	Rosh Hashanah
la Jánuca	Hanukkah
la Nochevieja	New Year's Eve
el día de Año Nuevo	New Year's Day
la confirmación	confirmation
el bar / bat mitzvá	bar / bat mitzvah

Talk About Gifts

la tarjeta de cumpleaños	birthday card
la tarjeta de regalo	gift card
el certificado de regalo	gift certificate

Talk About Chores and Responsibilities

quitar la mesa	to clear the table
el estipendio	allowance

Unidad 6

Expansión de vocabulario

Lección 1
¿Cuál es tu deporte favorito?

Sports

esquiar	to ski
hacer snowboard	to snowboard
el gol	goal
el hockey	hockey
el golf	golf
la gimnasia	gymnastics
el jonrón	homerun
los deportes de pista y campo	track and field
correr a campo traviesa	to run cross country
el (la) porrista	cheerleader
la carrera	race
las artes marciales	martial arts
caerse	to fall
saltar	to jump
hacer trucos	to do tricks

Locations and People

la pista	track
el (la) entrenador(a)	coach
el (la) capitán del equipo	team captain
el árbitro	referee, umpire

Lección 2
La salud

Talking About Staying Healthy

el (la) doctor(a)	doctor
el (la) paciente	patient
el consultorio	doctor's office
tener una cita	to have an appointment
la alergia	allergy
la gripe	flu
el resfriado	cold
estornudar	to sneeze
toser	to cough
la medicina	medicine

Parts of the Body

el dedo	finger
el dedo de pie	toe
el cuello	neck
la espalda	back
la garganta	throat
el hombro	shoulder
el oído	inner ear
la muñeca	wrist

Outdoor activities

las máquinas para hacer ejercicio	exercise machines
remar	to row
hacer aeróbicos	to do aerobics

The Beach

la arena	sand
el traje de baño	bathing suit
el tiburón	shark
el delfín	dolphin
la toalla	towel
las olas	waves
el (la) salvavidas	lifeguard

Lección 1
En el cibercafé

Talk About Technology

el apodo	screen name
la contraseña	password
cortar y pegar	to cut and paste
borrar	to delete
el archivo adjunto	attachment
la sonrisa, la carita feliz (emoticono)	smiley face (emoticon)
escribir a máquina	to type
charlar en línea	to chat
la cadena de e-mail	e-mail chain (forward)
arroba	@ (at)
punto com	.com (dot com)
el enlace	link
el blog	blog
bajar música	to download music
el tocador de mp3 (eme pe tres)	mp3 player
comenzar / terminar la sesión	to log on / to log off

Lección 2
Un día en el parque de diversiones

At the Amusement Park

el carrusel	carousel
el tobogán acuático	water slide
el espectáculo	show

Places of Interest

At the Aquarium

la ballena	whale
el pez (pl. los peces)	fish
la tortuga	turtle
la foca	seal

At the Fair

los juegos mecánicos	rides
el algodón de azúcar	cotton candy
los animales de peluche	stuffed animals

At the Zoo

el león	lion
el tigre	tiger
el oso	bear
el canguro	kangaroo
el pingüino	penguin
el mono	monkey
el hipopótamo	hippopotamus
la jirafa	giraffe
la jaula	cage

Extend Invitations

Decline

¿Quizás otra vez?	Maybe another time?

Make a Phone Call

¿De parte de quién?	Who's calling?
¿Puedo tomar un mensaje?	Can I take a message?
Puedo llamar más tarde.	I can call back later.

Unidad 8

Expansión de vocabulario

Lección 1
Pensando en las vacaciones

Talk About a Daily Routine

el despertador	alarm clock
rizarse el pelo	to curl one's hair
alisarse el pelo	to straighten one's hair
Talk About Grooming	
el desodorante	deodorant
la seda dental	dental floss
el acondicionador	conditioner
la loción	lotion
el gel	hair gel
el lápiz labial	lipstick
el rímel	mascara
la sombra de ojos	eye shadow
el perfume	perfume
la colonia	cologne

Discussing a Vacation

el lago	lake
el río	river
hacer / tener una reservación	to make / have a reservation
el aeropuerto	airport

Lección 2
¡Vamos de vacaciones!

Talk About Vacation Activities

la tienda de campaña	tent
la cabaña	cabin
ver las atracciones	to go sightseeing
pescar	to go fishing
mandar tarjetas postales	to send postcards
el (la) turista	tourist

Talk About Shopping

el dinero en efectivo	cash
la tarjeta de crédito	credit card
probarse la ropa	to try on clothing
el probador	fitting room
el recibo	receipt
la moneda	coin
la talla	(clothing) size
la vitrina	store window
gastar	to spend
la caja	cash register
la billetera	wallet
el cajero automático	automatic teller machine
Jewelry and Handicrafts	
la pulsera	bracelet
la joyería	jewelry store
brillante	shiny
el diamante	diamond
Bargaining	
¿Tiene otros(as)?	Do you have others?

Para y piensa
Self-Check Answers

Lección preliminar

p. 5
1. Buenos días.
2. ¿Cómo estás?
Answers may vary but can include:
3. Adiós, hasta mañana, hasta luego.

p. 9
1. c.
2. a.
3. b.

p. 11
1. See p. 10

p. 15
1. b.
2. a.
3. c.

p. 17
1. seis - dos - cinco - uno - cuatro - dos - cero - nueve
2. tres - siete - cero - ocho - nueve - dos - seis - tres
3. cuatro - uno - ocho - cinco - dos - siete - seis - cero

p. 19
1. lunes
2. mañana

p. 21
1. b.
2. a.
3. c.

p. 24
1. ¿Cómo se dice *please*?
2. ¿Comprendes?

Unidad 1 Estados Unidos

Lección 1

p. 34 Práctica de vocabulario
1. escuchar música
2. hacer la tarea

p. 36 Vocabulario en contexto
1. jugar
2. música
3. comer

p. 39 Práctica de gramática
1. Cristóbal y yo somos de Honduras.
2. Tomás es de la República Dominicana.
3. Yo soy de México.

p. 41 Gramática en contexto
1. El Sr. Costas es de la Florida.
2. Alicia es de Miami.
3. Teresa y Miguel son de Honduras y Cuba.

p. 44 Práctica de gramática
1. Le gusta
2. Te gusta
3. Nos gusta

p. 47 Todo junto
1. Teresa es de Honduras. Le gusta tocar la guitarra.
2. Alicia es de Miami. Le gusta comer.
3. Miguel es de Cuba. Le gusta mirar la televisión.

Lección 2

p. 58 Práctica de vocabulario
1. Juan es bajo.
2. David es artístico.
3. Carlos es serio.

p. 60 Vocabulario en contexto
1. perezoso
2. atlético
3. estudioso

p. 63 Práctica de gramática
1. la televisión
2. unas frutas
3. el libro
4. unos hombres

p. 65 Gramática en contexto
1. Ricardo es un amigo de Alberto.
2. Marta y Carla son unas chicas de una clase de español.
3. Ana es una chica muy inteligente.

p. 68 Práctica de gramática
1. una estudiante desorganizada
2. unos chicos simpáticos
3. unas mujeres trabajadoras
4. un hombre grande

p. 71 Todo junto
1. Alberto es un chico simpático.
2. Ricardo es un estudiante trabajador.
3. Sandra es una persona organizada.

Unidad 2 México

Lección 1

p. 88 Práctica de vocabulario
1. Me gusta dibujar en la clase de arte.
2. Hay veintitrés chicos en la clase de matemáticas.

p. 90 Vocabulario en contexto
1. a las diez y cuarto (a las diez y quince)
2. las ocho y veinte
3. a las siete

p. 93 Práctica de gramática
1. Juan nunca tiene que preparar la comida.
2. Tenemos la clase de inglés todos los días.
3. Siempre tengo que usar la computadora.

p. 95 Gramática en contexto
1. tienen
2. tiene que
3. tienen

p. 98 Práctica de gramática
1. usamos
2. preparo
3. dibujan
4. Necesitas

p. 101 Todo junto
1. toma
2. practicar
3. estudian

Lección 2

p. 112 Práctica de vocabulario
Answers may vary but can include:
1. el baño, el gimnasio, la cafetería, la biblioteca, etc.
2. el mapa, el escritorio, la silla, el reloj, etc.

p. 114 Vocabulario en contexto
1. la biblioteca
2. el gimnasio
3. la biblioteca

p. 117 Práctica de gramática
1. Estoy cerca de las ventanas.
2. Pablo, ¿estás nervioso?

p. 119 Gramática en contexto
Answers may vary but can include:
1. Pablo y Claudia están en la biblioteca.
2. Pablo está nervioso.
3. Pablo tiene que estar en el gimnasio a las cinco.

p. 122 Práctica de gramática
1. Teresa va a la cafetería.
2. Los estudiantes van a la oficina del director.
3. Nosotros vamos al gimnasio.
4. Yo voy a la clase de matemáticas.

p. 125 Todo junto
1. está; va a
2. están; van a
3. está; va a

Unidad 3 Puerto Rico

Lección 1

p. 142 Práctica de vocabulario
Answers may vary but can include:
1. los huevos, el cereal, el yogur, la fruta
2. el sándwich, la sopa, la hamburguesa

p. 144 Vocabulario en contexto
1. Quiénes
2. Cuándo
3. Por qué

p. 147 Práctica de gramática
1. Me gustan los huevos para el desayuno.
2. A José le gusta la pizza con jamón.
3. ¿Por qué no te gusta la fruta?

p. 149 Gramática en contexto
1. gusta
2. gusta
3. gustan

p. 152 Práctica de gramática
1. hacen; comen   3. hace; bebe
2. haces; leo

p. 155 Todo junto
1. gusta; come
2. gustan; comparten

Lección 2

p. 166 Práctica de vocabulario
1. hijo   3. hermanas
2. padres

p. 168 Vocabulario en contexto
1. Marisol tiene catorce años.
2. El gato de la familia Vélez tiene ocho años.
3. Los padres de Marisol tienen cincuenta y dos años.

p. 171 Práctica de gramática
1. mi; el seis de septiembre
2. nuestro; el veinticinco de enero.
3. su; el diecisiete de abril.

p. 173 Gramática en contexto
1. El cumpleaños de Camila es el doce de junio.
2. El cumpleaños de Éster es el primero de octubre.
3. El cumpleaños de Tito es el veintiocho de marzo.
4. El cumpleaños de Celia es el diecisiete de enero.

p. 176 Práctica de gramática
1. Mi hermano es más alto que mi padre.
2. Me gustan las manzanas tanto como las bananas.
3. La clase de matemáticas es mejor que la clase de arte.

p. 179 Todo junto
1. Sus perros son tan grandes como Marisol.
2. Su primo es menor que él.
3. Sus perros son más perezosos que los gatos.

Unidad 4 España

Lección 1

p. 196 Práctica de vocabulario
1. ¿Cuánto cuestan los calcetines blancos?
2. ¿Cuánto cuesta el vestido azul?
3. ¿Cuánto cuesta la chaqueta anaranjada?
4. ¿Cuánto cuestan los pantalones cortos rojos?

p. 198 Vocabulario en contexto
1. tiene frío
2. tiene calor
3. tiene frío

p. 201 Práctica de gramática
1. pienso
2. empieza
3. cierra

p. 203 Gramática en contexto
1. entiende
2. prefiere
3. quiere

p. 206 Práctica de gramática
1. los
2. La
3. Las

p. 209 Todo junto
1. Sí, Enrique la necesita.
2. Sí, Enrique lo prefiere.
3. Sí, Enrique la quiere comprar. (Sí, Enrique quiere comprarla.)

Lección 2

p. 220 Práctica de vocabulario
Answers may vary but can include:
1. El menú, el (la) camarero(a), la cuenta, los platos principales, etc.
2. El teatro, el parque, el cine, etc.

p. 222 Vocabulario en contexto
1. en autobús
2. a pie
3. en coche

p. 225 Práctica de gramática
1. cuesta
2. almorzamos
3. duermo
4. pueden

p. 227 Gramática en contexto
1. puede
2. encuentra
3. vuelve

p. 230 Práctica de gramática
1. sirven
2. sirve
3. pedimos

p. 233 Todo junto
1. almuerzan
2. pide
3. puede

Unidad 5 Ecuador

Lección 1

p. 250 Práctica de vocabulario
Answers may vary but can include:
1. el sillón, el sofá, el televisor, la alfombra
2. la cama, el armario, la lámpara, la cómoda

p. 252 Vocabulario en contexto
Answers may vary but can include:
1. el disco compacto, el tocadiscos compactos, el radio
2. la lámpara, el sillón
3. el sofá, el televisor

p. 255 Práctica de gramática
1. estamos
2. estoy
3. es
4. son

p. 257 Gramática en contexto
1. es
2. están
3. está

p. 260 Práctica de gramática
1. Estoy en el sexto piso.
2. Estoy en el noveno piso.
3. Estoy en el segundo piso.
4. Estoy en el tercer piso.

p. 263 Todo junto
1. es; está
2. séptimo

Lección 2

p. 274 Práctica de vocabulario
Answers may vary but can include:
Cocinar, poner la mesa, decorar, limpiar la cocina

p. 276 Vocabulario en contexto
1. la basura
2. el césped
3. la aspiradora

p. 279 Práctica de gramática
1. pongo
2. dice
3. traigo

p. 281 Gramática en contexto
1. dice; viene
2. trae

p. 284 Práctica de gramática
1. Decora la sala. Acabo de decorarla. (La acabo de decorar.)
2. Haz los quehaceres. Acabo de hacerlos. (Los acabo de hacer.)
3. Corta el césped. Acabo de cortarlo. (Lo acabo de cortar.)

p. 287 Todo junto
Answers may vary but can include:
Pasa la aspiradora. Lava los platos. Limpia la cocina.

Unidad 6 República Dominicana

Lección 1

p. 304 Práctica de vocabulario
1. una cancha, una bola
2. un campo, un bate, un guante, un casco, una pelota
3. una cancha, una pelota, una raqueta

p. 306 Vocabulario en contexto
1. la ganadora
2. la natación
3. un casco

p. 309 Práctica de gramática
1. Ana y yo jugamos al béisbol.
2. Ustedes juegan al básquetbol.
3. El hermano de Rosa juega al voleibol.
4. Yo juego al tenis.

p. 311 Gramática en contexto
1. juega
2. juegan
3. jugar

p. 314 Práctica de gramática
1. Saben
2. conozco a
3. sabemos

p. 317 Todo junto
sabe; conocen; saben

Lección 2

p. 328 Práctica de vocabulario
Answers may vary but can include:
1. la boca, la nariz, los ojos, las orejas
2. el tobillo, el pie, la rodilla

p. 330 Vocabulario en contexto
1. le duele
2. le duelen

p. 333 Práctica de gramática
1. buceamos
2. tomaste
3. levantaron

p. 335 Gramática en contexto
1. Isabel y Mario llevaron cascos.
2. Mario no montó en bicicleta muy bien.
3. El señor de las frutas caminó delante de Mario.

p. 338 Práctica de gramática
1. llegué
2. jugaron
3. comenzó
4. practiqué

p. 341 Todo junto
1. comenzó
2. encontraron

Unidad 7 Argentina

Lección 1

p. 358 Práctica de vocabulario
Answers may vary but can include:
1. la pantalla, el ratón, el teclado
2. usar el mensajero instantáneo, navegar por Internet, mandar fotos, buscar un sitio Web

p. 360 Vocabulario en contexto
1. Primero, Trini llega a San Antonio.
2. Luego, Trini está en Puebla, México.
3. Más tarde, Trini va a Puerto Rico y a España.
4. Por fin, Trini está en Buenos Aires.

p. 363 Práctica de gramática
1. comí
2. Recibiste

p. 365 Gramática en contexto
1. recibió
2. compartieron
3. salieron

p. 368 Práctica de gramática
1. Nunca recibo ningún correo electrónico.
2. Alguien escribe algo con el mensajero instantáneo.
3. A Beatriz no le gusta ni navegar por Internet ni estar en línea.

p. 371 Todo junto
1. No, Mariano no perdió nada.
2. No, Florencia no recibió ni la fecha ni la hora.
3. No, Mariano no le escribió ningún correo electrónico a Alicia.

Lección 2

p. 382 Práctica de vocabulario
Answers may vary but can include:
1. la vuelta al mundo, la montaña rusa, los autitos chocadores
2. el zoológico, el museo, el acuario, el parque de diversiones

p. 384 Vocabulario en contexto
1. ¡Qué divertido!
2. ¡Qué pequeña!
3. ¡Qué interesante!
4. ¡Qué grandes!

p. 387 Práctica de gramática
1. hicimos; fue (ser)
2. fui (ir); Hice
3. Fueron (ir); hicieron

p. 389 Gramática en contexto
1. ¿Adónde fueron Florencia, Luciana y tú?
2. ¿Qué hiciste?
3. ¿Cómo fue el día?

p. 392 Práctica de gramática
1. nosotros
2. ti
3. ellos

p. 395 Todo junto
1. Florencia hizo una cena para él.
2. Las empanadas fueron para ellos.
3. Mariano fue con ella a los autitos chocadores.

Unidad 8 Costa Rica

Lección 1

p. 412 Práctica de vocabulario
Answers may vary but can include:
1. levantarse, lavarse la cara, maquillarse, lavarse el pelo, secarse el pelo, ducharse, afeitarse, cepillarse los dientes, vestirse
2. en barco, en tren, en avión

p. 414 Vocabulario en contexto
1. unas vacaciones
2. la ciudad
3. un hotel

p. 417 Práctica de gramática
1. Yo me lavo las manos.
2. Los chicos secan al perro.
3. Juana y yo ponemos la mesa.
4. Mi abuelo se afeita la cara.

p. 419 Gramática en contexto
1. acostarse
2. se levanta

p. 422 Práctica de gramática
1. me estoy duchando (estoy duchándome)
2. estás durmiendo
3. nos estamos vistiendo (estamos vistiéndonos)

p. 425 Todo junto
1. Jorge se está peinando. (Jorge está peinándose.)
2. Susana se está maquillando. (Susana está maquillándose.)
3. Los hermanos se están cepillando los dientes. (Los hermanos están cepillándose los dientes.)
4. Jorge se está poniendo la chaqueta. (Jorge está poniéndose la chaqueta.)

Lección 2

p. 436 Práctica de vocabulario
1. ¿Me deja ver los aretes?
2. ¿Me deja ver el collar de plata?
3. ¿Me deja ver el anillo de oro?
4. ¿Me deja ver las artesanías de madera?

p. 438 Vocabulario en contexto
1. barato
2. los aretes
3. el mercado

p. 441 Práctica de gramática
1. les
2. te
3. nos

p. 443 Gramática en contexto
1. le
2. les
3. le

p. 446 Práctica de gramática
1. Aquellos
2. Este
3. esas

p. 449 Todo junto
1. le; esa
2. les; estos

Resumen de gramática

Nouns, Articles, and Pronouns

Nouns

Nouns identify people, animals, places, and things. All Spanish nouns, even if they refer to objects, are either **masculine** or **feminine.** They are also either **singular** or **plural.**

Nouns ending in **-o** are usually masculine; nouns ending in **-a** are usually feminine.

To form the **plural** of a noun, add **-s** if the noun ends in a vowel; add **-es** if it ends in a consonant.

Singular Nouns		Plural Nouns	
Masculine	**Feminine**	**Masculine**	**Feminine**
abuelo	abuela	abuelos	abuelas
chico	chica	chicos	chicas
hombre	mujer	hombres	mujeres
papel	pluma	papeles	plumas
zapato	blusa	zapatos	blusas

Articles

Articles identify the class of a noun: masculine or feminine, singular or plural. **Definite articles** are the equivalent of the English word *the.* **Indefinite articles** are the equivalent of *a, an,* or *some.*

Definite Articles	Masculine	Feminine		Indefinite Articles	Masculine	Feminine
Singular	el chico	la chica		**Singular**	un chico	una chica
Plural	los chicos	las chicas		**Plural**	unos chicos	unas chicas

Pronouns

Pronouns take the place of nouns. The pronoun used is determined by its function or purpose in a sentence.

Subject Pronouns	
yo	nosotros(as)
tú	vosotros(as)
usted	ustedes
él, ella	ellos(as)

Direct Object Pronouns	
me	nos
te	os
lo, la	los, las

Indirect Object Pronouns	
me	nos
te	os
le	les

Pronouns After Prepositions	
mí	nosotros(as)
ti	vosotros(as)
usted	ustedes
él, ella	ellos(as)

Reflexive Pronouns	
me	nos
te	os
se	se

Adjectives

Adjectives describe nouns. In Spanish, adjectives match the **gender** and **number** of the nouns they describe. To make an adjective plural, add **-s** if it ends in a vowel; add **-es** if it ends in a consonant. The adjective usually comes after the noun in Spanish.

Adjectives	Masculine	Feminine
Singular	el chico alto	la chica alta
	el chico inteligente	la chica inteligente
	el chico joven	la chica joven
	el chico trabajador	la chica trabajadora
Plural	los chicos altos	las chicas altas
	los chicos inteligentes	las chicas inteligentes
	los chicos jóvenes	las chicas jóvenes
	los chicos trabajadores	las chicas trabajadoras

Adjectives (continued)

Sometimes adjectives are shortened when they are placed in front of a masculine singular noun.

Shortened Forms

alguno	**algún** chico
bueno	**buen** chico
malo	**mal** chico
ninguno	**ningún** chico
primero	**primer** chico
tercero	**tercer** chico

Possessive adjectives indicate who owns something or describe a relationship between people or things. They agree in number with the nouns they describe. **Nuestro(a)** and **vuestro(a)** must also agree in gender with the nouns they describe.

Possessive Adjectives

	Masculine		Feminine	
Singular	**mi** amigo	**nuestro** amigo	**mi** amiga	**nuestra** amiga
	tu amigo	**vuestro** amigo	**tu** amiga	**vuestra** amiga
	su amigo	**su** amigo	**su** amiga	**su** amiga
Plural	**mis** amigos	**nuestros** amigos	**mis** amigas	**nuestras** amigas
	tus amigos	**vuestros** amigos	**tus** amigas	**vuestras** amigas
	sus amigos	**sus** amigos	**sus** amigas	**sus** amigas

Demonstrative adjectives describe the location of a person or a thing in relation to the speaker. Their English equivalents are *this, that, these,* and *those*.

Demonstrative Adjectives

	Masculine	Feminine
Singular	**este** chico	**esta** chica
	ese chico	**esa** chica
	aquel chico	**aquella** chica
Plural	**estos** chicos	**estas** chicas
	esos chicos	**esas** chicas
	aquellos chicos	**aquellas** chicas

Comparatives

Comparatives are used to compare two people or things.

Comparatives		
más (+)	**menos (−)**	**tan, tanto (=)**
más serio **que...**	**menos** serio **que...**	**tan** serio **como...**
Me gusta leer **más que** pasear.	Me gusta pasear **menos que** leer.	Me gusta hablar **tanto como** escuchar.

There are a few irregular comparative words. When talking about the age of people, use **mayor** and **menor.** When talking about qualities, use **mejor** and **peor.**

Age	Quality
mayor	mejor
menor	peor

Affirmative and Negative Words

Affirmative or **negative** words are used to talk about indefinite or negative situations.

Affirmative Words	Negative Words
algo	nada
alguien	nadie
algún/alguno(a)	ningún/ninguno(a)
o... o	ni... ni
siempre	nunca
también	tampoco

Verbs: Present Tense

Regular Verbs

Regular verbs ending in **-ar, -er,** or **-ir** always have regular endings in the present tense.

-ar Verbs		-er Verbs		-ir Verbs	
habl**o**	habl**amos**	vend**o**	vend**emos**	compart**o**	compart**imos**
habl**as**	habl**áis**	vend**es**	vend**éis**	compart**es**	compart**ís**
habl**a**	habl**an**	vend**e**	vend**en**	compart**e**	compart**en**

Verbs with Irregular yo Forms

Some verbs have regular forms in the present tense except for the **yo** form.

conocer		dar		hacer	
cono**zco**	conocemos	d**oy**	damos	ha**go**	hacemos
conoces	conocéis	das	dais	haces	hacéis
conoce	conocen	da	dan	hace	hacen

poner		saber		salir	
pon**go**	ponemos	s**é**	sabemos	sal**go**	salimos
pones	ponéis	sabes	sabéis	sales	salís
pone	ponen	sabe	saben	sale	salen

traer		ver	
tra**igo**	traemos	v**eo**	vemos
traes	traéis	ves	veis
trae	traen	ve	ven

Resumen de gramática

Verbs: Present Tense (continued)

Stem-Changing Verbs

e → ie

quiero	queremos
quieres	queréis
quiere	quieren

Other **e → ie** stem-changing verbs are **cerrar, comenzar, despertarse, empezar, entender, pensar, perder,** and **preferir.**

o → ue

puedo	podemos
puedes	podéis
puede	pueden

Other **o → ue** stem-changing verbs are **acostarse, almorzar, costar, doler, dormir, encontrar, envolver,** and **volver.**

e → i

sirvo	servimos
sirves	servís
sirve	sirven

Other **e → i** stem-changing verbs are **pedir** and **vestirse.**

u → ue

juego	jugamos
juegas	jugáis
juega	juegan

Jugar is the only verb with a **u → ue** stem change.

Irregular Verbs

The following verbs are irregular in the present tense.

decir

digo	decimos
dices	decís
dice	dicen

estar

estoy	estamos
estás	estáis
está	están

ir

voy	vamos
vas	vais
va	van

ser

soy	somos
eres	sois
es	son

tener

tengo	tenemos
tienes	tenéis
tiene	tienen

venir

vengo	venimos
vienes	venís
viene	vienen

Verbs: Present Participles

Present participles are used with a form of **estar** to say that an action is in progress at this moment.

Regular Participles

-ar Verbs	-er Verbs	-ir Verbs
camin**ando**	hac**iendo**	abr**iendo**
habl**ando**	pon**iendo**	compart**iendo**
jug**ando**	vend**iendo**	sal**iendo**

Stem Changes

decir	**di**ciendo
dormir	**du**rmiendo
pedir	**pi**diendo
servir	**si**rviendo
venir	**vi**niendo
vestir	**vi**stiendo

y Spelling Change

leer	le**y**endo
traer	tra**y**endo

Verbs: Affirmative tú Commands

Affirmative tú commands are used to tell a friend or family member to do something. Regular affirmative **tú** commands are the same as the **él/ella forms** in the present tense.

Regular Affirmative tú Commands

-ar Verbs	-er Verbs	-ir Verbs
lava	barre	abre
cierra	entiende	duerme
almuerza	vuelve	pide

Irregular Affirmative tú Commands

Infinitive	Affirmative tú Command
decir	**di**
hacer	**haz**
ir	**ve**
poner	**pon**
salir	**sal**
ser	**sé**
tener	**ten**
venir	**ven**

Verbs: Preterite Tense

Regular Verbs

Regular preterite verbs ending in **-ar, -er,** or **-ir** have regular endings.

-ar Verbs

nadé	nadamos
nadaste	nadasteis
nadó	nadaron

-er Verbs

vendí	vendimos
vendiste	vendisteis
vendió	vendieron

-ir Verbs

escribí	escribimos
escribiste	escribisteis
escribió	escribieron

Verbs with Spelling Changes

-car Verbs

busqué	buscamos
buscaste	buscasteis
buscó	buscaron

-gar Verbs

jugué	jugamos
jugaste	jugasteis
jugó	jugaron

-zar Verbs

almorcé	almorzamos
almorzaste	almorzasteis
almorzó	almorzaron

Note: The verb **leer** also has a spelling change in the preterite. You will learn about this in Level 2.

Irregular Verbs

hacer

hice	hicimos
hiciste	hicisteis
hizo	hicieron

ir

fui	fuimos
fuiste	fuisteis
fue	fueron

ser

fui	fuimos
fuiste	fuisteis
fue	fueron

Note: The verbs **dormir, pedir, preferir,** and **servir** have a stem change in the preterite tense. The verbs **dar, decir, estar, poner, querer, saber, tener,** and **traer** are irregular in the preterite tense. You will learn about the preterite of these verbs in Level 2.

Glosario español-inglés

This Spanish-English glossary contains all the active vocabulary words that appear in the text as well as passive vocabulary lists.

a to, at
  A la(s)... At... o'clock. **2.1**
  a pie on foot **4.2**
  ¿A qué hora es/son...? At what time is/are...? **2.1**
abril April **3.2**
abrir to open **5.2**
la abuela grandmother **3.2**
el abuelo grandfather **3.2**
los abuelos grandparents **3.2**
aburrido(a) boring **2.2**
acabar de... to have just... **5.2**
acampar to camp **8.2**
acompañar to go *or* come with
  ¿Quieres acompañarme a...? Would you like to come with me to...? **7.2**
acostarse (ue) to go to bed **8.1**
la actividad activity **1.1**
el acuario aquarium **7.2**
Adiós. Goodbye. **LP**
adivinar to guess
adjunto(a) attached
adónde (to) where **2.2**
  ¿Adónde vas? Where are you going? **2.2**
afeitarse to shave oneself **8.1**
el (la) aficionado(a) fan, sports fan **6.1**
agosto August **3.2**
el agua (*fem.*) water **1.1**
  las aguas termales hot springs
ahora now **3.1**
el aire air
  al aire libre outside; open-air **8.2**
al to the **2.2**
  al aire libre outside; open-air **8.2**
  al lado (de) next to **2.2**
alegre happy; upbeat
la alfombra rug **5.1**

algo something **7.1**
alguien someone **7.1**
alguno(a) some, any **7.1**
allí there **4.2**
el almacén (*pl.* los almacenes) department store
almorzar (ue) to eat lunch **4.2**
el almuerzo lunch **3.1**
¿Aló? Hello? (on telephone) **7.2**
alquilar to rent **1.1**
  alquilar un DVD to rent a DVD **1.1**
alto(a) tall **1.2**
amarillo(a) yellow **4.1**
el (la) amigo(a) friend **1.2**
anaranjado(a) orange (color) **4.1**
andar en patineta to skateboard **1.1**
el anillo ring **8.2**
el ánimo spirit
anoche last night **6.2**
anteayer the day before yesterday **7.1**
antes (de) before **1.1**
la antorcha torch
el anuncio advertisement; announcement
el año year **3.2**
  el Año Nuevo New Year
  el año pasado last year **7.1**
  ¿Cuántos años tienes? How old are you? **3.2**
  tener... años to be... years old **3.2**
el apartamento apartment **5.1**
aprender to learn **1.1**
  aprender el español to learn Spanish **1.1**
los apuntes notes **2.1**
  tomar apuntes to take notes **2.1**
aquel (aquella) that (over there) **8.2**
aquellos(as) those (over there) **8.2**
aquí here **4.2**
el árbol tree

  el árbol de Navidad Christmas tree
el archivo file
el arete earring **8.2**
el armario closet; armoire **5.1**
el arrecife de coral coral reef
el arroz rice **4.2**
el arte art **2.1**
  las artes marciales martial arts
las artesanías handicrafts **8.2**
el artículo article
los artículos goods **8.2**
  los artículos deportivos sporting goods
artístico(a) artistic **1.2**
la aspiradora vacuum cleaner **5.2**
el (la) atleta athlete **6.1**
atlético(a) athletic **1.2**
los autitos chocadores bumper cars **7.2**
el autobús (*pl.* los autobuses) bus **4.2**
  en autobús by bus **4.2**
avanzar to advance, to move ahead
  ¡Avanza! Advance!, Move ahead!
  avancemos let's advance, let's move ahead
el avión (*pl.* los aviones) airplane **8.1**
  en avión by plane **8.1**
ayer yesterday **6.2**
el aymara indigenous language of Bolivia and Peru
ayudar to help **5.2**
azul blue **4.1**

bailar to dance **5.2**
el (la) bailarín(ina) (*pl.* los bailarines) dancer
el baile dance
bajar to descend **5.1**
bajo(a) short (height) **1.2**

RECURSOS
R24 Glosario español-inglés

la balsa raft

la banana banana **3.1**

la banda musical band

la bandera flag

bañarse to take a bath **8.1**

el baño bathroom **2.2**

barato(a) inexpensive **8.2**

el barco boat **8.1**

    en barco by boat **8.1**

barrer to sweep **5.2**

    barrer el suelo to sweep the floor **5.2**

el básquetbol basketball (the sport) **6.1**

la basura trash, garbage **5.2**

la batalla battle

el bate (baseball) bat **6.1**

beber to drink **1.1**

la bebida beverage, drink **3.1**

el béisbol baseball (the sport) **6.1**

la biblioteca library **2.2**

la bicicleta bicycle **1.1**

bien well, fine **LP**

    Bien. ¿Y tú/usted? Fine. And you? (familiar/formal) **LP**

    Muy bien. ¿Y tú/usted? Very well. And you? (familiar/formal) **LP**

el bistec beef **4.2**

blanco(a) white **4.1**

el bloqueador de sol sunscreen **6.2**

la blusa blouse **4.1**

la boca mouth **6.2**

el boleto ticket **7.2**

bonito(a) pretty **1.2**

el borrador eraser **2.2**

el bosque forest

    el bosque nuboso cloud forest

    el bosque tropical lluvioso tropical rain forest

el bote boat

el brazo arm **6.2**

el brindis celebratory toast

el brócoli broccoli **4.2**

bucear to scuba-dive **6.2**

bueno(a) good **1.2**

    Buenos días. Good morning. **LP**

    Buenas noches. Good evening; Good night. **LP**

    Buenas tardes. Good afternoon. **LP**

buscar to look for **5.2**

C

el caballo horse

    montar a caballo to ride horses **8.2**

la cabeza head **6.2**

cada each; every

el café coffee; café **3.1**, **4.2**

la cafetería cafeteria **2.2**

la calavera skull

el calcetín (*pl.* **los calcetines**) sock **4.1**

la calculadora calculator **2.2**

la calidad quality **8.2**

caliente hot

la calle street **4.2**

el calor heat

    Hace calor. It is hot. **LP**

    tener calor to be hot (person) **4.1**

la cama bed **5.1**

    hacer la cama to make the bed **5.2**

la cámara camera **7.1**

    la cámara digital digital camera **7.1**

el (la) camarero(a) (food) server **4.2**

el cambio change

caminar to walk **6.2**

la caminata hike **8.2**

    dar una caminata to hike **8.2**

la camisa shirt **4.1**

la camiseta T-shirt **4.1**

el campeón (*pl.* **los campeones**), **la campeona** champion **6.1**

el campo field (sports) **6.1**; the country, countryside **8.1**

la cancha court (sports) **6.1**

cansado(a) tired **2.2**

cantar to sing **5.2**

carnaval carnival

la carne meat **4.2**

caro(a) expensive **8.2**

    ¡Qué caro(a)! How expensive! **8.2**

la carrera (sports) race

la carreta horse-drawn carriage

el carro car

la casa house **5.1**

la cascada waterfall

el cascarón (*pl.* **los cascarones**) confetti-filled egg

el casco helmet **6.1**

la caseta small house or tent

casi almost **2.1**

castaño(a) brown (hair) **1.2**

catorce fourteen **2.1**

celebrar to celebrate **5.2**

el cementerio cemetery

la cena dinner **3.1**

el centro center, downtown **4.2**

    el centro comercial shopping center, mall **4.1**

cepillar to brush **8.1**

    cepillarse los dientes to brush one's teeth **8.1**

el cepillo brush **8.1**

    el cepillo de dientes toothbrush **8.1**

la cerámica ceramics **8.2**

cerca (de) near (to) **2.2**

el cereal cereal **3.1**

cero zero **LP**

cerrar (ie) to close **4.1**

el césped grass, lawn **5.2**

el champú shampoo **8.1**

la chaqueta jacket **4.1**

la chica girl **1.2**

el chico boy **1.2**

cien one hundred **2.1**

las ciencias science **2.1**

ciento(a) one hundred **3.2**

cierto(a) true

cinco five **LP**

cincuenta fifty **2.1**

el cine movie theater; the movies **4.2**

la ciudad city **8.1**

¡Claro que sí! Of course! **7.2**

la clase class, classroom **LP**; kind, type

el coche car **4.2**

    en coche by car **4.2**

la cocina kitchen **5.1**

cocinar to cook **5.2**

el colegio high school

el collar necklace **8.2**

el color color

    ¿De qué color es/son...? What color is/are...?

el comedor dining room **5.1**

comenzar (ie) to begin **6.2**

comer to eat **1.1**

    comer al aire libre to picnic, to eat outside **8.2**

cómico(a) funny **1.2**

la comida meal; food **1.1**, **3.1**

como as, like

¿Cómo...? How...? **3.1**

    ¿Cómo eres? What are you like? **1.2**

    ¿Cómo estás? How are you? (familiar) **LP**

¿Cómo está usted? How are you? (formal) **LP**

¿Cómo se llama? What's his/her/your (formal) name? **LP**

¿Cómo te llamas? What's your name? (familiar) **LP**

la cómoda dresser **5.1**

comparar to compare

compartir to share **3.1**

comprar to buy **1.1**

comprender to understand **6.1**

¿Comprendiste? Did you understand?

la computación computer studies

la computadora computer **2.1**

común common

con with **7.2**

el concierto concert **4.2**

conectar to connect **7.1**

conectar a Internet to connect to the Internet **7.1**

conmigo with me **7.2**

conocer (conozco) to know, to be familiar with; to meet **6.1**

contento(a) happy **2.2**

contestar to answer **2.1**

contigo with you **7.2**

contra against

la contraseña password

el corazón (pl. los corazones) heart **6.2**

corregir to correct·

el correo electrónico e-mail **1.1**

correr to run **1.1**

cortar to cut **5.2**

cortar el césped to cut the grass **5.2**

la cortina curtain **5.1**

la cosa thing **5.1**

costar (ue) to cost **4.2**

¿Cuánto cuesta(n)? How much does it (do they) cost? **4.1**

Cuesta(n)... It (They) cost... **4.1**

la Cremà burning of papier-mâché figures during Las Fallas

el cuaderno notebook **2.2**

el cuadro painting

¿Cuál(es)? Which?; What? **3.1**

¿Cuál es la fecha? What is the date? **3.2**

¿Cuál es tu/su número de teléfono? What is your phone number? (familiar/formal) **LP**

cuando when **2.2**

¿Cuándo? When? **2.2**

cuánto(a) how much **3.2**

¿Cuánto cuesta(n)? How much does it (do they) cost? **4.1**

cuántos(as) how many **3.2**

¿Cuántos(as)...? How many...? **2.1**

¿Cuántos años tienes? How old are you? **3.2**

cuarenta forty **2.1**

cuarto quarter **2.1**

... y cuarto quarter past... (the hour) **2.1**

el cuarto room; bedroom **5.1**

cuarto(a) fourth **5.1**

cuatro four **LP**

cuatrocientos(as) four hundred **3.2**

la cuenta bill (in a restaurant) **4.2**

el cuero leather

el cuerpo body **6.2**

el cumpleaños birthday **3.2**

¡Feliz cumpleaños! Happy birthday! **3.2**

D

dar (doy) to give **5.2**

dar una caminata to hike **8.2**

dar una fiesta to give a party **5.2**

darle de comer al perro to feed the dog **5.2**

los datos information

de of, from **1.1**

de madera wood (made of wood) **8.2**

de la mañana in the morning (with a time) **2.1**

De nada. You're welcome. **LP**

de la noche at night (with a time) **2.1**

de oro gold (made of gold) **8.2**

de plata silver (made of silver) **8.2**

¿De qué color es/son...? What color is/are...?

de la tarde in the afternoon (with a time) **2.1**

de vacaciones on vacation **8.1**

de vez en cuando once in a while **2.1**

debajo (de) underneath, under **2.2**

deber should, ought to **5.2**

décimo(a) tenth **5.1**

decir to say **5.2**

también se dice... you can also say...

la decoración (pl. las decoraciones) decoration **5.2**

decorar to decorate **5.2**

dejar to leave

dejar un mensaje to leave a message **7.2**

Le dejo... en... I'll give... to you for... (a price) **8.2**

¿Me deja ver...? May I see...? **8.2**

del (de la) of or from the **2.2**

delante (de) in front (of) **2.2**

demasiado too much **8.2**

dentro (de) inside (of) **2.2**

los deportes sports **1.1**

deprimido(a) depressed **2.2**

derecho(a) right

el desayuno breakfast **3.1**

descansar to rest **1.1**

descargar to download

desde from

desear to wish, to want

el desfile parade

desorganizado(a) disorganized **1.2**

despertarse (ie) to wake up **8.1**

después (de) afterward; after **1.1**

destruir to destroy

detrás (de) behind **2.2**

el día day **LP**

Buenos días. Good morning. **LP**

¿Qué día es hoy? What day is today? **LP**

todos los días every day **2.1**

dibujar to draw **1.1**

el dibujo drawing

diciembre December **3.2**

diecinueve nineteen **2.1**

dieciocho eighteen **2.1**

dieciséis sixteen **2.1**

diecisiete seventeen **2.1**

diez ten **LP**

diferente different

difícil difficult **2.1**

el difunto deceased

el dinero money **4.1**

la dirección (pl. las direcciones) address **7.1**

la dirección electrónica e-mail address **7.1**

el (la) director(a) principal **2.2**

el disco compacto compact disc **5.1**

   quemar un disco compacto to burn a CD **7.1**

el disfraz (*pl.* **los disfraces**) costume

divertido(a) fun **2.2**

   ¡Qué divertido! How fun! **7.2**

doce twelve **2.1**

el (la) doctor(a) doctor

el dólar dollar **4.1**

doler (ue) to hurt, to ache **6.2**

domingo Sunday **LP**

donde where

   ¿De dónde eres? Where are you from? (familiar) **LP**

   ¿De dónde es? Where is he/she from? **LP**

   ¿De dónde es usted? Where are you from? (formal) **LP**

   ¿Dónde? Where? **2.2**

dormir (ue) to sleep **4.2**

dormirse (ue) to fall asleep **8.1**

dos two **LP**

doscientos(as) two hundred **3.2**

ducharse to take a shower **8.1**

durante during **4.1**

el DVD DVD **1.1**

el ecoturismo ecotourism

el ejercicio exercise

el ejército army

él he **1.1**; him **7.2**

ella she **1.1**; her **7.2**

ellos(as) they **1.1**; them **7.2**

emocionado(a) excited **2.2**

emparejar to match

empezar (ie) to begin **4.1**

en in **2.1**; on

   en autobús by bus **4.2**

   en avión by plane **8.1**

   en barco by boat **8.1**

   en coche by car **4.2**

   en línea online **7.1**

   en tren by train **8.1**

Encantado(a). Delighted; Pleased to meet you. **LP**

encima (de) on top (of) **2.2**

encontrar (ue) to find **4.2**

la encuesta survey

enero January **3.2**

enfermo(a) sick **6.2**

enojado(a) angry **2.2**

la ensalada salad **4.2**

enseñar to teach **2.1**

entender (ie) to understand **4.1**

entonces then, so **7.1**

la entrada ticket **4.2**

entrar to enter

la entrevista interview

entrevistar to interview

envolver (ue) to wrap **5.2**

el equipo team **6.1**

la escalera stairs **5.1**

la escena scene

escribir to write **1.1**

   escribir correos electrónicos to write e-mails **1.1**

el escritorio desk **2.2**

la escritura writing

escuchar to listen (to) **1.1**

   escuchar música to listen to music **1.1**

la escuela school **1.1**

   la escuela secundaria high school

ese(a) that **8.2**

esos(as) those **8.2**

el español Spanish **2.1**

especial special

el espejo mirror **5.1**

esperar to wait (for) **8.1**

el esqueleto skeleton

la estación (*pl.* **las estaciones**) season **4.1**

el estadio stadium **6.1**

la estancia ranch

estar to be **2.2**

   ¿Está...? Is... there? **7.2**

   ¿Está bien? OK?

   estar en línea to be online **7.1**

   No, no está. No, he's/she's not here. **7.2**

este(a) this **8.2**

el estómago stomach **6.2**

estos(as) these **8.2**

el (la) estudiante student **1.2**

estudiar to study **1.1**

estudioso(a) studious **1.2**

el euro euro **4.1**

el examen (*pl.* **los exámenes**) test, exam **2.1**

fácil easy **2.1**

falso(a) false

las fallas displays of large papier-mâché figures

el (la) fallero(a) celebrant of *Las Fallas*

la familia family **3.2**

favorito(a) favorite **6.1**

febrero February **3.2**

la fecha date **3.2**

   ¿Cuál es la fecha? What is the date? **3.2**

   la fecha de nacimiento birth date **3.2**

feliz happy

   ¡Feliz cumpleaños! Happy birthday! **3.2**

feo(a) ugly **4.1**

la feria fair **7.2**

la fiesta party; holiday

   la fiesta de sorpresa surprise party **5.2**

   la fiesta nacional national holiday

   la fiesta patria patriotic holiday

el fin end

   el fin de semana weekend **7.2**

   por fin finally **7.1**

la flor flower

la foto photo, picture **7.1**

   tomar fotos to take photos **7.1**

el (la) francés(esa) (*pl.* **los franceses**) French

los frijoles beans **4.2**

el frío cold

   Hace frío. It is cold. **LP**

   tener frío to be cold **4.1**

la fruta fruit **1.1**

los fuegos artificiales fireworks

la fuente source; fountain

fuerte strong **6.2**

el fútbol soccer (the sport) **1.1**

el fútbol americano football (the sport) **6.1**

la galleta cookie **1.1**

ganador(a) winning

el (la) ganador(a) winner **6.1**

ganar to win **6.1**

el (la) gato(a) cat **3.2**

generalmente generally **8.1**

el gimnasio gymnasium **2.2**

el globo balloon **5.2**

el gorro winter hat **4.1**

Gracias. Thank you. **LP**

   Muchas gracias. Thank you very much. **LP**

la gramática grammar
grande big, large; great **1.2**
el grito shout
el guante glove **6.1**
guapo(a) good-looking **1.2**
la guitarra guitar **1.1**
gustar
    Me gusta... I like... **1.1**
    Me gustaría... I would like... **7.2**
    No me gusta... I don't like... **1.1**
    ¿Qué te gusta hacer? What do you like to do? **1.1**
    ¿Te gusta...? Do you like...? **1.1**
    ¿Te gustaría...? Would you like...? **7.2**
el gusto pleasure
    El gusto es mío. The pleasure is mine. **LP**
    Mucho gusto. Nice to meet you. **LP**

hablar to talk, to speak **1.1**
    hablar por teléfono to talk on the phone **1.1**
    ¿Puedo hablar con...? May I speak with...? **7.2**
hacer (hago) to make, to do **3.1**
    Hace calor. It is hot. **LP**
    Hace frío. It is cold. **LP**
    Hace sol. It is sunny. **LP**
    Hace viento. It is windy. **LP**
    hacer la cama to make the bed **5.2**
    hacer clic en to click on **7.1**
    hacer esquí acuático to water-ski **6.2**
    hacer una parrillada to barbecue **8.2**
    hacer surf de vela to windsurf **8.2**
    hacer surfing to surf **8.2**
    hacer la tarea to do homework **1.1**
    hacer un viaje to take a trip **8.1**
    ¿Qué hicieron ustedes? What did you do? (pl., formal) **6.2**
    ¿Qué hiciste tú? What did you do? (sing., familiar) **6.2**
    ¿Qué tiempo hace? What is the weather like? **LP**
    hacerse to become
    el hambre hunger

tener hambre to be hungry **3.1**
la hamburguesa hamburger **3.1**
hasta until
    Hasta luego. See you later. **LP**
    Hasta mañana. See you tomorrow. **LP**
hay... there is/are... **2.1**
    hay que... one has to..., one must... **5.2**
el helado ice cream **1.1**
herido(a) hurt **6.2**
la hermana sister **3.2**
el hermano brother **3.2**
los hermanos brothers, brother(s) and sister(s) **3.2**
la hija daughter **3.2**
el hijo son **3.2**
los hijos children, son(s) and daughter(s) **3.2**
la hispanidad cultural community of Spanish speakers
la historia history **2.1**
Hola. Hello; Hi. **LP**
el hombre man **1.2**
la hora hour; time **2.1**
    ¿A qué hora es/son...? At what time is/are...? **2.1**
    ¿Qué hora es? What time is it? **2.1**
el horario schedule **2.1**
horrible horrible **3.1**
el hotel hotel **8.1**
hoy today **LP**
    ¿Qué día es hoy? What day is today? **LP**
    Hoy es... Today is... **LP**
el huevo egg **3.1**

el icono icon **7.1**
ideal ideal **5.1**
el idioma language
Igualmente. Same here; Likewise. **LP**
importante important **3.1**
    Es importante. It's important. **3.1**
los incas Incas, an indigenous South American people
la independencia independence
la información information
el inglés English **2.1**
inteligente intelligent **1.2**

interesante interesting **2.2**
Internet Internet **7.1**
    conectar a Internet to connect to the Internet **7.1**
    navegar por Internet to surf the Web **7.1**
el invierno winter **4.1**
los invitados guests **5.2**
invitar to invite **5.2**
    invitar a to invite (someone) **5.2**
    Te invito. I invite you; I'll treat you. **7.2**
ir to go **2.2**
    ir a... to be going to... **4.2**
    ir de compras to go shopping **4.1**
    Vamos a... Let's... **4.2**
izquierdo(a) left

el jabón (*pl.* **los jabones**) soap **8.1**
el jamón (*pl.* **los jamones**) ham **3.1**
el jardín (*pl.* **los jardines**) garden **5.1**
los jeans jeans **4.1**
joven (*pl.* **jóvenes**) young **1.2**
las joyas jewelry **8.2**
jueves Thursday **LP**
el (la) jugador(a) player **6.1**
jugar (ue) to play (sports or games) **1.1**
    jugar al fútbol to play soccer **1.1**
el jugo juice **1.1**
    el jugo de naranja orange juice **3.1**
julio July **3.2**
junio June **3.2**

el lado side
    al lado (de) next to **2.2**
el lago lake
la lámpara lamp **5.1**
el lápiz (*pl.* **los lápices**) pencil **2.2**
largo(a) long
lavar to wash **5.2**
    lavarse to wash oneself **8.1**

lavarse la cara to wash one's face **8.1**
lavar los platos to wash the dishes **5.2**
la lección (*pl.* **las lecciones**) lesson
la leche milk **3.1**
el lector DVD DVD player **5.1**
la lectura reading
leer to read **1.1**
leer un libro to read a book **1.1**
lejos (de) far (from) **2.2**
las lentejas lentils
levantar to lift **6.2**; to raise
levantar pesas to lift weights **6.2**
levantarse to get up **8.1**
el libertador liberator
el libro book **1.1**
limpiar to clean **5.2**
limpiar la cocina to clean the kitchen **5.2**
limpio(a) clean **5.2**
la llamada phone call **7.2**
llamar to call (by phone) **7.2**
llamarse to be called
¿Cómo se llama? What's his/her/your (formal) name? **LP**
¿Cómo te llamas? What's your name? (familiar) **LP**
Me llamo... My name is... **LP**
Se llama... His/Her name is... **LP**
la llegada arrival
llegar to arrive **2.1**
llevar to wear **4.1**
llover (ue) to rain **LP**
Llueve. It is raining. **LP**
Lo siento. I'm sorry. **6.2**
luego later, then **7.1**
Hasta luego. See you later. **LP**
el lugar place **4.2**
lunes Monday **LP**

la madera wood **8.2**
de madera wood (made of wood) **8.2**
la madrastra stepmother **3.2**
la madre mother **3.2**
el (la) maestro(a) teacher **LP**
malo(a) bad **1.2**
Mal. ¿Y tú/usted? Bad. And you? (familiar/formal) **LP**

mandar to send **7.1**
la mano hand **6.2**
la manzana apple **3.1**
mañana tomorrow **LP**
Hasta mañana. See you tomorrow. **LP**
Mañana es... Tomorrow is... **LP**
la mañana morning **2.1**
de la mañana in the morning (with a time) **2.1**
el mapa map **2.2**
maquillarse to put on makeup **8.1**
el mar sea **6.2**
marrón (*pl.* **marrones**) brown **4.1**
martes Tuesday **LP**
marzo March **3.2**
la mascletà firecracker explosions during *Las Fallas*
más more **1.1**
Más o menos. ¿Y tú/usted? So-so. And you? (familiar/formal) **LP**
más que... more than... **3.2**
más... que more... than **3.2**
más tarde later (on) **7.1**
la máscara mask
las matemáticas math **2.1**
mayo May **3.2**
mayor older **3.2**
la medianoche midnight
medio(a) half
...y media half past... (the hour) **2.1**
mejor better **3.2**
menor younger **3.2**
menos less
...menos (diez) (ten) to/before... (the hour) **2.1**
menos que... less than... **3.2**
menos... que less... than **3.2**
el mensaje message **7.2**
dejar un mensaje to leave a message **7.2**
el mensaje instantáneo instant message
el mensajero instantáneo instant messaging **7.1**
el menú menu **4.2**
el mercado market **8.2**
el mercado al aire libre open-air market
el mes month **3.2**
la mesa table **4.2**
poner la mesa to set the table **5.2**
el metro meter
mí me **7.2**

mi my **3.2**
el miedo fear
¡Qué miedo! How scary! **7.2**
tener miedo to be afraid **7.2**
miércoles Wednesday **LP**
mil thousand, one thousand **3.2**
un millón (de) million, one million **3.2**
el minuto minute **2.1**
mirar to watch **1.1**; to look at
mirar la televisión to watch television **1.1**
mismo(a) same
la mochila backpack **2.2**
el momento moment
Un momento. One moment. **7.2**
la montaña rusa roller coaster **7.2**
montar to ride **1.1**
montar a caballo to ride a horse **8.2**
montar en bicicleta to ride a bike **1.1**
mucho a lot **2.1**
Mucho gusto. Nice to meet you. **LP**
muchos(as) many **2.1**
muchas veces often, many times **2.1**
los muebles furniture **5.1**
la mujer woman **1.2**
el mundo world
el museo museum **7.2**
la música music **1.1**
la música folklórica folk music
la música rock rock music **4.2**
el (la) músico(a) musician
muy very **1.2**
Muy bien. ¿Y tú/usted? Very well. And you? (familiar/formal) **LP**

nacer to be born
nada nothing **7.1**
De nada. You're welcome. **LP**
nadar to swim **6.1**
nadie no one, nobody **7.1**
la naranja orange (fruit) **3.1**
la nariz (*pl.* **las narices**) nose **6.2**
la natación swimming **6.1**
la naturaleza nature
navegar por Internet to surf the Web **7.1**
la Navidad Christmas

necesitar to need **2.1**
negro(a) black **4.1**
nervioso(a) nervous **2.2**
nevar (ie) to snow **LP**
   Nieva. It is snowing. **LP**
ni... ni neither... nor **7.1**
la nieve snow
ninguno(a) none, not any **7.1**
el ninot (*pl.* **los ninots**) large
   papier-mâché figure
no no **LP**
la noche night **2.1**; evening **LP**
   Buenas noches. Good evening;
      Good night. **LP**
   de la noche at night (with a
      time) **2.1**
la Nochebuena Christmas Eve
la Nochevieja New Year's Eve
el nombre name
normalmente normally **8.1**
nosotros(as) we **1.1**; us **7.2**
la nota grade (on a test) **2.1**
   sacar una buena/mala nota to
      get a good/bad grade **2.1**
novecientos(as) nine hundred **3.2**
noveno(a) ninth **5.1**
noventa ninety **2.1**
noviembre November **3.2**
nuestro(a) our **3.2**
nueve nine **LP**
nuevo(a) new **4.1**
el número number **LP**
   el número de teléfono phone
      number **LP**
nunca never **2.1**
nutritivo(a) nutritious **3.1**

o or **1.1**
   o... o either... or **7.1**
la obra work (of art)
ocho eight **LP**
ochocientos(as) eight hundred **3.2**
octavo(a) eighth **5.1**
octubre October **3.2**
ocupado(a) busy **2.2**
la oficina office **2.2**
   la oficina del (de la)
     director(a) principal's office **2.2**
ofrecer (ofrezco) to offer
   Le puedo ofrecer... I can offer
     you... (a price) **8.2**
el ojo eye **6.2**

once eleven **2.1**
la oración (*pl.* **las oraciones**)
   sentence
la oreja ear **6.2**
organizado(a) organized **1.2**
el oro gold
   de oro gold (made of gold) **8.2**
el otoño autumn, fall **4.1**
otro(a) other **3.1**

el padrastro stepfather **3.2**
el padre father **3.2**
los padres parents **3.2**
pagar to pay **4.1**
la página page
el país country, nation **LP**
el pájaro bird
el pan bread **3.1**
   el pan de muertos special bread
     made for *Día de los Muertos*
la pantalla screen **7.1**
los pantalones pants **4.1**
   los pantalones cortos
     shorts **4.1**
la papa potato **1.1**
   las papas fritas French fries **1.1**
el papel paper **2.2**
   el papel de regalo wrapping
     paper **5.2**
   el papel picado paper cutouts
para for; in order to **3.1**
parar to stop
   Para y piensa. Stop and think.
la pared wall
la pareja pair
el párrafo paragraph
la parrillada barbecue **8.2**
   hacer una parrillada to
     barbecue **8.2**
el parque park **4.2**
   el parque de diversiones
     amusement park **7.2**
la parte part
el partido game (in sports) **6.1**
el pasado the past
pasado(a) past **7.1**
   el año pasado last year **7.1**
   la semana pasada last week **7.1**
pasar to happen
   pasar la aspiradora to
     vacuum **5.2**
   pasar un rato con los amigos to

spend time with friends **1.1**
¿Qué pasa? What's
   happening? **LP**
¿Qué te pasa (a ti)? What's the
   matter (with you)?
pasear to go for a walk **1.1**
el paseo walk, stroll; ride
el pasillo hall **2.2**
la pasta de dientes toothpaste **8.1**
el pastel cake **4.2**
la patata potato **4.2**
patinar to skate **6.1**
   patinar en línea to in-line
     skate **6.1**
los patines en línea in-line
   skates **6.1**
el patio patio **5.1**
pedir (i) to order, to ask for **4.2**
peinarse to comb one's hair **8.1**
el peine comb **8.1**
la película movie **4.2**
peligroso(a) dangerous **6.1**
pelirrojo(a) red-haired **1.2**
el pelo hair **1.2**
   el pelo castaño/rubio brown/
     blond hair **1.2**
la pelota ball **6.1**
pensar (ie) to think; to plan **4.1**
peor worse **3.2**
pequeño(a) little, small **1.2**
perder (ie) to lose **6.1**
Perdón. Excuse me. **LP**
perezoso(a) lazy **1.2**
el periódico newspaper
   el periódico escolar student
     newspaper
pero but **1.1**
el (la) perro(a) dog **3.2**
la persona person **1.2**
el pescado fish (as food) **4.2**
el pie foot **6.2**
   a pie on foot **4.2**
la piel skin **6.2**
la pierna leg **6.2**
la pintura painting
la piscina swimming pool **6.1**
el piso floor (of a building) **5.1**
   primer piso second floor (first
     floor above ground floor) **5.1**
la pista track; clue
el pizarrón (*pl.* **los pizarrones**)
   chalkboard, board **2.2**
la pizza pizza **1.1**
planchar to iron **5.2**
la planta plant
la planta baja first floor, ground

floor **5.1**
la plata silver
  de plata silver (made of silver) **8.2**
el plato plate; dish; course
  el plato principal main course **4.2**
la playa beach **6.2**
la pluma pen **2.2**
un poco a little **1.2**
pocos(as) few
poder (ue) to be able, can **4.2**
  Le puedo ofrecer... I can offer you... **8.2**
  ¿Puedo hablar con...? May I speak with...? **7.2**
el pollo chicken **4.2**
poner (pongo) to put, to place **5.2**
  poner la mesa to set the table **5.2**
ponerse (me pongo) to put on **8.1**
  ponerse la ropa to put one's clothes on, to get dressed **8.1**
por for, per
  Por favor. Please. **LP**
  por fin finally **7.1**
  ¿Por qué? Why? **3.1**
porque because **1.2**
el postre dessert **4.2**
  de postre for dessert **4.2**
practicar to practice **1.1**
  practicar deportes to play or practice sports **1.1**
el precio price **4.1**
preferir (ie) to prefer **4.1**
la pregunta question
el premio award
preparar to prepare **1.1**
  preparar la comida to prepare food, to make a meal **1.1**
presentar to introduce **LP**
  Te/Le presento a... Let me introduce you to... (familiar/ formal) **LP**
la primavera spring **4.1**
primero(a) first **5.1**
  el primero de... the first of... (date) **3.2**
el (la) primo(a) cousin **3.2**
los primos cousins **3.2**
el problema problem **2.2**
la procesión (pl. las procesiones) procession
proclamar to declare
la propina tip (in a restaurant) **4.2**

proteger (protejo) to protect
el pueblo town
la puerta door **2.2**

¿Qué? What? **3.1**
  ¿De qué color es/son...? What color is/are...?
  ¡Qué bárbaro! How cool!
  ¡Qué caro(a)! How expensive! **8.2**
  ¡Qué divertido! How fun! **7.2**
  ¡Qué lástima! What a shame! **7.2**
  ¡Qué miedo! How scary! **7.2**
  ¿Qué día es hoy? What day is today? **LP**
  ¿Qué es esto? What is this? **8.2**
  ¿Qué hicieron ustedes? What did you do? (pl., formal) **6.2**
  ¿Qué hiciste tú? What did you do? (sing., familiar) **6.2**
  ¿Qué hora es? What time is it? **2.1**
  ¿Qué pasa? What's happening? **LP**
  ¿Qué tal? How's it going? **LP**
  ¿Qué te gusta hacer? What do you like to do? **1.1**
  ¿Qué tiempo hace? What is the weather like? **LP**
el quechua indigenous language from South America
quedarse en to stay in **8.1**
los quehaceres chores **5.2**
quemar to burn
  quemar un disco compacto to burn a CD **7.1**
querer (ie) to want **4.1**
  ¿Quieres acompañarme a...? Would you like to come with me to...? **7.2**
  Quisiera... I would like... **8.2**
el queso cheese **3.1**
  el queso crema cream cheese
¿Quién(es)? Who? **3.1**
  ¿Quién es? Who is he/she/it? **LP**
quince fifteen **2.1**
quinientos(as) five hundred **3.2**
quinto(a) fifth **5.1**

el radio radio **5.1**
rápido(a) fast
la raqueta racket (in sports) **6.1**
un rato a while, a short time
el ratón (pl. los ratones) mouse **7.1**
la raza (human) race
la razón (pl. las razones) reason
  tener razón to be right **4.1**
recibir to receive **5.2**
la reconstrucción (pl. las reconstrucciones) reenactment
recordar (ue) to remember
  ¿Recuerdas? Do you remember?
el recorrido run, journey
el recreo recess
el recuerdo souvenir **8.2**
el refresco soft drink **1.1**
regalar to give (a gift)
el regalo present, gift **5.2**
regatear to bargain **8.2**
la regla rule
regular OK **LP**
  Regular. ¿Y tú/usted? OK. And you? (familiar/formal) **LP**
el reloj watch; clock **2.2**
el repaso review
responder to reply
la respuesta answer
el restaurante restaurant **4.2**
el resultado result
el resumen summary
  en resumen in summary
los Reyes Magos Three Kings
rico(a) tasty, delicious; rich **3.1**
la rodilla knee **6.2**
rojo(a) red **4.1**
la ropa clothing **4.1**
la rosca de reyes sweet bread eaten on January 6
rubio(a) blond **1.2**
la rutina routine **8.1**

sábado Saturday **LP**
saber (sé) to know (a fact, how to do something) **6.1**
sacar to take out
  sacar la basura to take out the trash **5.2**
  sacar una buena/mala nota to get a good/bad grade **2.1**
la sala living room **5.1**
salir (salgo) to leave, to go out **5.2**

la salud health **6.2**

¡Saludos! Greetings!

   Saludos desde... Greetings from...

el sándwich sandwich **3.1**

   el sándwich de jamón y queso ham and cheese sandwich **3.1**

sano(a) healthy **6.2**

el santo saint

el secador de pelo to hair dryer **8.1**

secar to dry

   secarse to dry oneself **8.1**

   secarse el pelo to dry one's hair **8.1**

el secreto secret **5.2**

la sed thirst

   tener sed to be thirsty **3.1**

según according to

segundo(a) second **5.1**

seguro(a) secure, safe

seis six **LP**

seiscientos(as) six hundred **3.2**

la semana week **LP**

   el fin de semana weekend **7.2**

   la semana pasada last week **7.1**

   Semana Santa Holy Week

Señor (Sr.) Mr. **LP**

Señora (Sra.) Mrs. **LP**

Señorita (Srta.) Miss **LP**

sentir to feel

   Lo siento. I'm sorry. **6.2**

septiembre September **3.2**

séptimo(a) seventh **5.1**

ser to be **1.1**

   Es de... He/She is from... **LP**

   Es el... de... It's the... of... (day and month) **3.2**

   Es la.../Son las... It is... o'clock. **2.1**

   Soy de... I'm from... **LP**

serio(a) serious **1.2**

servir (i) to serve **4.2**

sesenta sixty **2.1**

setecientos(as) seven hundred **3.2**

setenta seventy **2.1**

sexto(a) sixth **5.1**

si if **5.2**

sí yes **LP**

   ¡Claro que sí! Of course! **7.2**

   Sí, me encantaría. Yes, I would love to. **7.2**

siempre always **2.1**

siete seven **LP**

siguiente following

la silla chair **2.2**

el sillón (*pl.* **los sillones**) armchair **5.1**

simpático(a) nice, friendly **1.2**

sin without

el sitio Web Web site **7.1**

sobre about; on

el sofá sofa, couch **5.1**

el sol sun **LP**

   el bloqueador de sol sunscreen **6.2**

   Hace sol. It is sunny. **LP**

   tomar el sol to sunbathe **6.2**

el sombrero hat **4.1**

la sopa soup **3.1**

la sorpresa surprise **5.2**

su his, her, its, their, your (formal) **3.2**

subir to go up **5.1**

   subir a la vuelta al mundo/la montaña rusa to ride the Ferris wheel/roller coaster **7.2**

sucio(a) dirty **5.2**

el suelo floor (of a room) **5.1**

la suerte luck

   tener suerte to be lucky **4.1**

el supermercado supermarket

T

tal vez perhaps, maybe **4.2**

también also, too **1.1**

   también se dice... you can also say...

tampoco neither, not either **7.1**

tan... como as... as **3.2**

tanto como... as much as... **3.2**

tanto(a) so much

tantos(as) so many

tarde late **2.1**

la tarde afternoon **2.1**

   Buenas tardes. Good afternoon. **LP**

   de la tarde in the afternoon (with a time) **2.1**

   más tarde later (on) **7.1**

la tarea homework **1.1**

la tarjeta postal postcard

el teatro theater **4.2**

el teclado keyboard **7.1**

el teléfono telephone **7.2**

   ¿Cuál es tu/su número de teléfono? What is your phone number? (familiar/formal) **LP**

   Mi número de teléfono es... My phone number is... **LP**

   el teléfono celular cellular telephone **7.2**

la televisión television **1.1**

el televisor television set **5.1**

el tema theme

temprano early **2.1**

tener to have **2.1**

   ¿Cuántos años tienes? How old are you? **3.2**

   tener... años to be... years old **3.2**

   tener calor to be hot **4.1**

   tener frío to be cold **4.1**

   tener ganas de... to feel like... **3.1**

   tener hambre to be hungry **3.1**

   tener miedo to be afraid **7.2**

   tener que... to have to... **2.1**

   tener razón to be right **4.1**

   tener sed to be thirsty **3.1**

   tener suerte to be lucky **4.1**

el tenis tennis **6.1**

tercero(a) third **5.1**

terminar to end **6.2**

ti you (sing., familiar) **7.2**

la tía aunt **3.2**

el tiempo weather **LP**; time **8.2**

   el tiempo libre free time **8.2**

   ¿Qué tiempo hace? What is the weather like? **LP**

la tienda store **4.1**

el tío uncle **3.2**

los tíos uncles, uncle(s) and aunt(s) **3.2**

típico(a) typical

el tipo type

la tiza chalk **2.2**

la toalla towel **8.1**

el tobillo ankle **6.2**

el tocadiscos compactos CD player **5.1**

tocar to play (an instrument) **1.1**

   tocar la guitarra to play the guitar **1.1**

todavía still; yet **5.2**

todo junto all together

todos(as) all **1.2**

   todos los días every day **2.1**

tomar to take **4.2**

   tomar apuntes to take notes **2.1**

tomar fotos to take photos **7.1**
tomar el sol to sunbathe **6.2**
el tomate tomato **4.2**
trabajador(a) hard-working **1.2**
trabajar to work **1.1**
traer (traigo) to bring **5.2**
el traje costume
tranquilo(a) calm **2.2**
trece thirteen **2.1**
treinta thirty **2.1**
treinta y uno thirty-one **2.1**
el tren train **8.1**
　　en tren by train **8.1**
tres three **LP**
trescientos(as) three hundred **3.2**
triste sad **2.2**
tu your (sing., familiar) **3.2**
tú you (sing., familiar) **1.1**
el turismo tourism
el turrón (*pl.* los turrones) almond nougat candy

último(a) last
la unidad unit
uno one **LP**
usar to use **2.1**
　　usar la computadora to use the computer **2.1**
usted you (sing., formal) **1.1, 7.2**
ustedes you (pl.) **1.1**
la uva grape **3.1**
　　las doce uvas twelve grapes (eaten on New Year's Eve)

las vacaciones vacation **8.1**
　　de vacaciones on vacation **8.1**
¡Vale! OK!
el valle valley
varios(as) various
veinte twenty **2.1**
veintiuno twenty-one **2.1**
el (la) vendedor(a) salesclerk
vender to sell **3.1**
venir to come **5.2**
la ventana window **2.2**
la ventanilla ticket window **4.2**
ver (veo) to see **4.2**
　　¿Me deja ver...? May I see...? **8.2**
el verano summer **4.1**
la verdad truth
　　¿Verdad? Really?; Right? **LP**
verde green **4.1**
las verduras vegetables **4.2**
el vestido dress **4.1**
vestirse (i) to get dressed **8.1**
la vez (*pl.* las veces) time
　　a veces sometimes
　　de vez en cuando once in a while **2.1**
　　muchas veces often, many times **2.1**
　　tal vez maybe **4.2**
el viaje trip, journey
　　hacer un viaje to take a trip **8.1**
la vida life
el videojuego video game **5.1**
viejo(a) old **1.2**
el viento wind
　　Hace viento. It is windy. **LP**

viernes Friday **LP**
el villancico seasonal children's song
visitar to visit
vivir to live **3.2**
el vocabulario vocabulary
el voleibol volleyball (the sport) **6.1**
volver (ue) to return, to come back **4.2**
vosotros(as) you (pl. familiar) **1.1, 7.2**
la vuelta al mundo Ferris wheel **7.2**
vuestro(a) your (pl., familiar) **3.2**

y and
　　...y (diez) (ten) past... (the hour) **2.1**
　　...y cuarto quarter past... (the hour) **2.1**
　　...y media half past... (the hour) **2.1**
¿Y tú? And you? (familiar) **LP**
¿Y usted? And you? (formal) **LP**
ya already **3.2**
yo I **1.1**
el yogur yogurt **3.1**

el zapato shoe **4.1**
el zoológico zoo **7.2**

Glosario inglés-español

This Spanish-English glossary contains all the active vocabulary words that appear in the text as well as passive vocabulary lists.

about sobre
to accompany acompañar **7.2**
according to según
to ache doler (ue) **6.2**
activity la actividad **1.1**
address la dirección (*pl.* las direcciones) **7.1**
   e-mail address la dirección electrónica **7.1**
to advance avanzar
advertisement el anuncio
afraid: to be afraid tener miedo **7.2**
after después (de) **1.1**
afternoon la tarde **2.1**
   Good afternoon. Buenas tardes. **LP**
   in the afternoon de la tarde **2.1**
afterward después **1.1**
against contra
air el aire
airplane el avión (*pl.* los aviones) **8.1**
   by plane en avión **8.1**
all todos(as) **1.2**
all together todo junto
almost casi **2.1**
already ya **3.2**
also también **1.1**
always siempre **2.1**
and y
angry enojado(a) **2.2**
ankle el tobillo **6.2**
announcement el anuncio
answer la respuesta
to answer contestar **2.1**
any alguno(a) **7.1**
   not any ninguno(a) **7.1**
apartment el apartamento **5.1**
apple la manzana **3.1**
April abril **3.2**
aquarium el acuario **7.2**

arm el brazo **6.2**
armchair el sillón (*pl.* los sillones) **5.1**
armoire el armario **5.1**
arrival la llegada
to arrive llegar **2.1**
art el arte **2.1**
   martial arts las artes marciales
article el artículo
artistic artístico(a) **1.2**
as como
   as... as tan... como **3.2**
   as much as... tanto como... **3.2**
to ask for pedir (i) **4.2**
at a
   at night de la noche **2.1**
   At... o'clock. A la(s)... **2.1**
   At what time is/are...? ¿A qué hora es/son...? **2.1**
athlete el (la) atleta **6.1**
athletic atlético(a) **1.2**
attached adjunto(a)
August agosto **3.2**
aunt la tía **3.2**
autumn el otoño **4.1**
award el premio

backpack la mochila **2.2**
bad malo(a) **1.2**
   Bad. And you? (familiar/formal) Mal. ¿Y tú/usted? **LP**
ball la pelota **6.1**
balloon el globo **5.2**
banana la banana **3.1**
barbecue la parrillada **8.2**
to barbecue hacer una parrillada **8.2**
to bargain regatear **8.2**
baseball el béisbol **6.1**
   (baseball) bat el bate **6.1**
basketball el básquetbol **6.1**
bathroom el baño **2.2**

to be ser **1.1**; estar **2.2**
   to be able poder (ue) **4.2**
   to be afraid tener miedo **7.2**
   to be called llamarse
   to be cold tener frío **4.1**
   to be familiar with conocer (conozco) **6.1**
   to be hot tener calor **4.1**
   to be hungry tener hambre **3.1**
   to be lucky tener suerte **4.1**
   to be online estar en línea **7.1**
   to be right tener razón **4.1**
   to be thirsty tener sed **3.1**
   to be... years old tener... años **3.2**
beach la playa **6.2**
beans los frijoles **4.2**
because porque **1.2**
to become hacerse
bed la cama **5.1**
   to go to bed acostarse (ue) **8.1**
   to make the bed hacer la cama **5.2**
bedroom el cuarto **5.1**
beef el bistec **4.2**
before antes (de) **1.1**; menos (with a time) **2.1**
to begin empezar (ie) **4.1**, comenzar (ie) **6.2**
behind detrás (de) **2.2**
better mejor **3.2**
beverage la bebida **3.1**
bicycle la bicicleta **1.1**
big grande **1.2**
bill (in a restaurant) la cuenta **4.2**
bird el pájaro
birth date la fecha de nacimiento **3.2**
birthday el cumpleaños **3.2**
   Happy birthday! ¡Feliz cumpleaños! **3.2**
black negro(a) **4.1**
blond rubio(a) **1.2**
blouse la blusa **4.1**
blue azul **4.1**

board el pizarrón (*pl.* los pizarrones) **2.2**

boat el barco **8.1**, el bote
  by boat en barco **8.1**

body el cuerpo **6.2**

book el libro **1.1**

boring aburrido(a) **2.2**

boy el chico **1.2**

bread el pan **3.1**

breakfast el desayuno **3.1**

to bring traer (traigo) **5.2**

broccoli el brócoli **4.2**

brother el hermano **3.2**

brown marrón (*pl.* marrones) **4.1**
  brown hair el pelo castaño **1.2**

brush el cepillo **8.1**

to brush cepillar
  to brush one's teeth cepillarse los dientes **8.1**

bumper cars los autitos chocadores **7.2**

burn: to burn a CD quemar un disco compacto **7.1**

bus el autobús (*pl.* los autobuses) **4.2**
  by bus en autobús **4.2**

busy ocupado(a) **2.2**

but pero **1.1**

to buy comprar **1.1**

café el café **4.2**

cafeteria la cafetería **2.2**

cake el pastel **4.2**

calculator la calculadora **2.2**

call la llamada **7.2**

to call llamar **7.2**

calm tranquilo(a) **2.2**

camera la cámara **7.1**
  digital camera la cámara digital **7.1**

to camp acampar **8.2**

can (to be able) poder (ue) **4.2**
  I can offer you... Le puedo ofrecer... **8.2**

car el coche **4.2**; el carro
  by car en coche **4.2**

cat el (la) gato(a) **3.2**

CD player el tocadiscos compactos **5.1**

to celebrate celebrar **5.2**

cellular phone el teléfono celular **7.2**

center el centro **4.2**

ceramics la cerámica **8.2**

cereal el cereal **3.1**

chair la silla **2.2**

chalk la tiza **2.2**

chalkboard el pizarrón (*pl.* los pizarrones) **2.2**

champion el campeón (*pl.* los campeones), la campeona **6.1**

change el cambio

cheese el queso **3.1**
  cream cheese el queso crema

chicken el pollo **4.2**

children los hijos **3.2**

chores los quehaceres **5.2**

Christmas la Navidad
  Christmas tree el árbol de Navidad

city la ciudad **8.1**

class la clase **LP**

classroom la clase **LP**

clean limpio(a) **5.2**

to clean limpiar **5.2**

to click on hacer clic en **7.1**

clock el reloj **2.2**

to close cerrar (ie) **4.1**

closet el armario **5.1**

clothing la ropa **4.1**

clue la pista

coffee el café **3.1**

cold el frío **4.1**
  It is cold. Hace frío. **LP**
  to be cold tener frío **4.1**

color el color
  What color is/are...? ¿De qué color es/son...?

comb el peine **8.1**
  to comb one's hair peinarse **8.1**

to come venir **5.2**
  to come back volver (ue) **4.2**
  to come with acompañar **7.2**

common común

compact disc el disco compacto **5.1**

to compare comparar

computer la computadora **2.1**
  computer studies la computación

concert el concierto **4.2**

to connect conectar **7.1**
  to connect to the Internet conectar a Internet **7.1**

to cook cocinar **5.2**

cookie la galleta **1.1**

coral reef el arrecife de coral

to correct corregir

to cost costar (ue) **4.2**
  How much does it (do they) cost? ¿Cuánto cuesta(n)? **4.1**
  It (They) cost... Cuesta(n)... **4.1**

costume el disfraz (*pl.* los disfraces),

el traje

couch el sofá **5.1**

country el campo **8.1**; el país **LP**

course el plato
  main course el plato principal **4.2**

court la cancha **6.1**

cousin el (la) primo(a) **3.2**

curtain la cortina **5.1**

to cut cortar **5.2**
  to cut the grass cortar el césped **5.2**

dance el baile

to dance bailar **5.2**

dangerous peligroso(a) **6.1**

date la fecha **3.2**
  birth date la fecha de nacimiento **3.2**
  What is the date? ¿Cuál es la fecha? **3.2**

daughter la hija **3.2**

day el día **LP**
  the day before yesterday anteayer **7.1**
  every day todos los días **2.1**
  What day is today? ¿Qué día es hoy? **LP**

December diciembre **3.2**

to decorate decorar **5.2**

decoration la decoración (*pl.* las decoraciones) **5.2**

delicious rico(a) **3.1**

Delighted. Encantado(a). **LP**

department store el almacén (*pl.* los almacenes)

depressed deprimido(a) **2.2**

to descend bajar **5.1**

desk el escritorio **2.2**

dessert el postre **4.2**
  for dessert de postre **4.2**

to destroy destruir

different diferente

difficult difícil **2.1**

dining room el comedor **5.1**

dinner la cena **3.1**

dirty sucio(a) **5.2**

dish el plato
  main dish el plato principal **4.2**

disorganized desorganizado(a) **1.2**

to do hacer (hago) **3.1**

doctor el (la) doctor(a)

dog el (la) perro(a) **3.2**

dollar el dólar **4.1**

door la puerta **2.2**
to download descargar
downtown el centro **4.2**
to draw dibujar **1.1**
drawing el dibujo
dress el vestido **4.1**
dresser la cómoda **5.1**
drink la bebida **3.1**
to drink beber **1.1**
to dry secar
    to dry one's hair secarse el
      pelo **8.1**
    to dry oneself secarse **8.1**
during durante **4.1**
DVD el DVD **1.1**
    DVD player el lector DVD **5.1**

each cada
ear la oreja **6.2**
early temprano **2.1**
earring el arete **8.2**
easy fácil **2.1**
to eat comer **1.1**
    to eat lunch almorzar (ue) **4.2**
    to eat outside comer al aire
      libre **8.2**
ecotourism el ecoturismo
egg el huevo **3.1**
eight ocho **LP**
eight hundred ochocientos(as) **3.2**
eighteen dieciocho **2.1**
eighth octavo(a) **5.1**
either
    either... or o... o **7.1**
    not either tampoco **7.1**
eleven once **2.1**
e-mail el correo electrónico **1.1**
    e-mail address la dirección (*pl.*
    las direcciones) electrónica **7.1**
to end terminar **6.2**
English el inglés **2.1**
to enter entrar
eraser el borrador **2.2**
euro el euro **4.1**
evening la noche **LP**
    Good evening. Buenas
      noches. **LP**
every cada
    every day todos los días **2.1**
exam el examen (*pl.* los
    exámenes) **2.1**

excited emocionado(a) **2.2**
Excuse me. Perdón. **LP**
exercise el ejercicio
expensive caro(a) **8.2**
    How expensive! ¡Qué
      caro(a)! **8.2**
eye el ojo **6.2**

fair la feria **7.2**
fall el otoño **4.1**
to fall asleep dormirse (ue) **8.1**
false falso(a)
family la familia **3.2**
fan el (la) aficionado(a) **6.1**
far (from) lejos (de) **2.2**
fast rápido(a)
father el padre **3.2**
favorite favorito(a) **6.1**
fear el miedo **7.2**
February febrero **3.2**
to feed darle(s) de comer **5.2**
    to feed the dog darle de comer
      al perro
to feel sentir (ie)
    to feel like... tener ganas
      de... **3.1**
Ferris wheel la vuelta al
    mundo **7.2**
few pocos(as)
field el campo **6.1**
fifteen quince **2.1**
fifth quinto(a) **5.1**
fifty cincuenta **2.1**
file el archivo
finally por fin **7.1**
to find encontrar (ue) **4.2**
fine bien **LP**
    Fine. And you? (familiar/
    formal) Bien. ¿Y tú/usted? **LP**
fireworks los fuegos artificiales
first primero(a) **5.1**
    the first of... el primero de... **3.2**
fish el pescado **4.2**
five cinco **LP**
five hundred quinientos(as) **3.2**
flag la bandera
floor el piso; el suelo **5.1**
    first *or* ground floor la planta
      baja **5.1**
    second floor (first above
    ground) el primer piso **5.1**

flower la flor
following siguiente
food la comida **1.1, 3.1**
food server el (la) camarero(a) **4.2**
foot el pie **6.2**
    on foot a pie **4.2**
football el fútbol americano **6.1**
for para **3.1**; por
forest el bosque
    cloud forest el bosque nuboso
    tropical rain forest el bosque
      tropical lluvioso
forty cuarenta **2.1**
fountain la fuente
four cuatro **LP**
four
    hundred cuatrocientos(as) **3.2**
fourteen catorce **2.1**
fourth cuarto(a) **5.1**
free time el tiempo libre **8.2**
French fries las papas fritas **1.1**
Friday viernes **LP**
friend el (la) amigo(a) **1.2**
    to spend time with friends
      pasar un rato con los amigos **1.1**
from de **1.1**; desde
front: in front (of) delante
    (de) **2.2**
fruit la fruta **1.1**
fun divertido(a) **2.2**
    How fun! ¡Qué divertido! **7.2**
funny cómico(a) **1.2**
furniture los muebles **5.1**

game el partido **6.1**
garbage la basura **5.2**
garden el jardín (*pl.* los
    jardines) **5.1**
generally generalmente **8.1**
to get
    to get dressed vestirse (i) **8.1**
    to get up levantarse **8.1**
gift el regalo **5.2**
girl la chica **1.2**
to give dar (doy) **5.2**; regalar
glove el guante **6.1**
to go ir **2.2**
    to be going to... ir a... **4.2**
    to go for a walk pasear **1.1**
    to go out salir (salgo) **5.2**
    to go shopping ir de

compras **4.1**
to go to bed acostarse (ue) **8.1**
to go up subir **5.1**
to go with acompañar **7.2**
gold el oro
(made of) gold de oro **8.2**
good bueno(a) **1.2**
Good afternoon. Buenas tardes. **LP**
Good evening. Buenas noches. **LP**
Good morning. Buenos días. **LP**
Good night. Buenas noches. **LP**
Goodbye. Adiós. **LP**
good-looking guapo(a) **1.2**
goods los artículos **8.2**
sporting goods los artículos deportivos
grade la nota **2.1**
to get a good/bad grade sacar una buena/mala nota **2.1**
grammar la grámatica
grandfather el abuelo **3.2**
grandmother la abuela **3.2**
grandparents los abuelos **3.2**
grape la uva **3.1**
grass el césped **5.2**
to cut the grass cortar el césped **5.2**
green verde **4.1**
Greetings! ¡Saludos!
Greetings from... Saludos desde...
to guess adivinar
guests los invitados **5.2**
guitar la guitarra **1.1**
gymnasium el gimnasio **2.2**

hair el pelo **1.2**
blond hair pelo rubio **1.2**
brown hair pelo castaño **1.2**
hair dryer el secador de pelo **8.1**
half medio(a)
half past... ... y media **2.1**
hall el pasillo **2.2**
ham el jamón (*pl.* los jamones) **3.1**
hamburger la hamburguesa **3.1**
hand la mano **6.2**
handicrafts las artesanías **8.2**
to happen pasar

What's happening? ¿Qué pasa? **LP**
happy contento(a) **2.2**; feliz **3.2**; alegre
Happy birthday! ¡Feliz cumpleaños! **3.2**
hard-working trabajador(a) **1.2**
hat el sombrero **4.1**
winter hat el gorro **4.1**
to have tener **2.1**
one has to... hay que... **5.2**
to have just... acabar de... **5.2**
to have to... tener que... **2.1**
he él **1.1**
head la cabeza **6.2**
health la salud **6.2**
healthy sano(a) **6.2**
heart el corazón (*pl.* los corazones) **6.2**
heat el calor
Hello. Hola. **LP**
Hello? ¿Aló? **7.2**
helmet el casco **6.1**
to help ayudar **5.2**
her su **3.2**; ella **7.2**
here aquí **4.2**
Hi. Hola. **LP**
high school el colegio, la escuela secundaria
hike la caminata **8.2**
to hike dar una caminata **8.2**
him él **7.2**
his su **3.2**
history la historia **2.1**
homework la tarea **1.1**
to do homework hacer la tarea **1.1**
horrible horrible **3.1**
horse el caballo **8.2**
to ride a horse montar a caballo **8.2**
hot caliente
It is hot. Hace calor. **LP**
to be hot tener calor **4.1**
hotel el hotel **8.1**
hour la hora **2.1**
house la casa **5.1**
How...? ¿Cómo...? **3.1**
How are you? ¿Cómo estás? (familiar); ¿Cómo está usted? (formal) **LP**
How cool! ¡Qué bárbaro!
How expensive! ¡Qué caro(a)! **8.2**
How fun! ¡Qué divertido! **7.2**
How many...? ¿Cuántos(as)...? **2.1**

How old are you? ¿Cuántos años tienes? **3.2**
How scary! ¡Qué miedo! **7.2**
How's it going? ¿Qué tal? **LP**
how many cuántos(as) **3.2**
how much cuánto(a) **3.2**
How much does it (do they) cost? ¿Cuánto cuesta(n)? **4.1**
hungry: to be hungry tener hambre **3.1**
hurt herido(a) **6.2**
to hurt doler (ue) **6.2**

I yo **1.1**
I'm sorry. Lo siento. **6.2**
ice cream el helado **1.1**
icon el icono **7.1**
ideal ideal **5.1**
if si **5.2**
important importante **3.1**
It's imporant. Es importante. **3.1**
in en **2.1**
in front (of) delante (de) **2.2**
in order to para **3.1**
in the afternoon de la tarde **2.1**
in the morning de la mañana **2.1**
inexpensive barato(a) **8.2**
information la información; los datos
in-line skates los patines en línea **6.1**
to in-line skate patinar en línea **6.1**
inside (of) dentro (de) **2.2**
instant message el mensaje instantáneo
instant messaging el mensajero instantáneo **7.1**
intelligent inteligente **1.2**
interesting interesante **2.2**
Internet Internet **7.1**
to connect to the Internet conectar a Internet **7.1**
interview la entrevista
to interview entrevistar
to introduce presentar **LP**
Let me introduce you to... Te/Le presento a... (familiar/formal) **LP**
to invite invitar **5.2**
I invite you. Te invito. **7.2**
to iron planchar **5.2**
its su **3.2**

jacket la chaqueta **4.1**
January enero **3.2**
jeans los jeans **4.1**
jewelry las joyas **8.2**
juice el jugo **1.1**
    orange juice el jugo de
    naranja **3.1**
July julio **3.2**
June junio **3.2**

keyboard el teclado **7.1**
kind la clase
kitchen la cocina **5.1**
knee la rodilla **6.2**
to know
    (a fact; how to do
    something) saber (sé) **6.1**
    (a person) conocer
    (conozco) **6.1**

lake el lago
lamp la lámpara **5.1**
language el idioma, el lenguaje
large grande **1.2**
last último(a)
    last night anoche **6.2**
    last week la semana pasada **7.1**
    last year el año pasado **7.1**
late tarde **2.1**
later luego **7.1**
    later (on) más tarde **7.1**
    See you later. Hasta luego. **LP**
lawn el césped **5.2**
lazy perezoso(a) **1.2**
to learn aprender **1.1**
    to learn Spanish aprender el
    español **1.1**
leather el cuero
to leave salir (salgo) **5.2**; dejar **7.2**
left izquierdo(a)
leg la pierna **6.2**
less menos
    less than... menos que... **3.2**
    less... than menos... que **3.2**
lesson la lección
Let's... Vamos a... **4.2**

library la biblioteca **2.2**
life la vida
to lift levantar **6.2**
    to lift weights levantar
    pesas **6.2**
like como
to like
    Do you like...? ¿Te gusta...? **1.1**
    I don't like... No me gusta... **1.1**
    I like... Me gusta... **1.1**
    I would like... Me gustaría... **7.2**;
    Quisiera... **8.2**
    What do you like to do? ¿Qué
    te gusta hacer? **1.1**
    Would you like...? ¿Te
    gustaría...? **7.2**
Likewise. Igualmente. **LP**
to listen (to) escuchar **1.1**
    to listen to music escuchar
    música **1.1**
little pequeño(a) **1.2**
    a little un poco **1.2**
to live vivir **3.2**
living room la sala **5.1**
long largo(a)
to look (at) mirar
    to look for buscar **5.2**
to lose perder (ie) **6.1**
a lot mucho **2.1**
luck la suerte
    to be lucky tener suerte **4.1**
lunch el almuerzo **3.1**
    to eat lunch almorzar (ue) **4.2**

to make hacer (hago) **3.1**
    to make the bed hacer la
    cama **5.2**
mall el centro comercial **4.1**
man el hombre **1.2**
many muchos(as) **2.1**
    many times muchas veces **2.1**
map el mapa **2.2**
March marzo **3.2**
market el mercado **8.2**
    open-air market el mercado al
    aire libre
to match emparejar
math las matemáticas **2.1**
May mayo **3.2**
maybe tal vez **4.2**
me mí **7.2**
meal la comida **1.1, 3.1**
meat la carne **4.2**

to meet conocer (conozco) **6.1**
    Nice to meet you. Mucho
    gusto. **LP**
menu el menú **4.2**
message el mensaje **7.2**
    instant message el mensaje
    instantáneo **7.1**
    to leave a message dejar un
    mensaje **7.2**
meter el metro
milk la leche **3.1**
million un millón (de) **3.2**
minute el minuto **2.1**
mirror el espejo **5.1**
Miss Señorita (Srta.) **LP**
moment el momento **7.2**
    One moment. Un
    momento. **7.2**
Monday lunes **LP**
money el dinero **4.1**
month el mes **3.2**
more más **1.1**
    more than... más que... **3.2**
    more... than más... que **3.2**
morning la mañana **2.1**
    Good morning. Buenos
    días. **LP**
    in the morning de la
    mañana **2.1**
mother la madre **3.2**
mouse el ratón (*pl.* los ratones) **7.1**
mouth la boca **6.2**
movie la película **4.2**
movie theater el cine **4.2**
the movies el cine **4.2**
Mr. Señor (Sr.) **LP**
Mrs. Señora (Sra.) **LP**
museum el museo **7.2**
music la música **1.1**
    folk music la música folklórica
    rock music la música rock **4.2**
must: one must... hay que... **5.2**
my mi **3.2**

name el nombre
    His/Her name is... Se
    llama... **LP**
    My name is... Me llamo... **LP**
    What's his/her/your (formal)
    name? ¿Cómo se llama? **LP**
    What's your (familiar)
    name? ¿Cómo te llamas? **LP**
nature la naturaleza

near (to) cerca (de) **2.2**
necklace el collar **8.2**
to need necesitar **2.1**
neither tampoco **7.1**
   neither... nor ni... ni **7.1**
nervous nervioso(a) **2.2**
never nunca **2.1**
new nuevo(a) **4.1**
   New Year el Año Nuevo
newspaper el periódico
   student newspaper el periódico
   escolar
next to al lado (de) **2.2**
nice simpático(a) **1.2**
   Nice to meet you. Mucho
   gusto. **LP**
night la noche **2.1**
   at night de la noche **2.1**
   Good night. Buenas noches. **LP**
   last night anoche **6.2**
nine nueve **LP**
nine hundred novecientos(as) **3.2**
nineteen diecinueve **2.1**
ninety noventa **2.1**
ninth noveno(a) **5.1**
no no **LP**
nobody nadie **7.1**
no one nadie **7.1**
none ninguno(a) **7.1**
normally normalmente **8.1**
nose la nariz (*pl.* las narices) **6.2**
notebook el cuaderno **2.2**
notes los apuntes **2.1**
   to take notes tomar apuntes **2.1**
nothing nada **7.1**
November noviembre **3.2**
now ahora **3.1**
number el número **LP**
   phone number el número de
   teléfono **LP**
nutritious nutritivo(a) **3.1**

o'clock: It is... o'clock. Es la.../Son
   las... **2.1**
October octubre **3.2**
of de **1.1**
   Of course! ¡Claro que sí! **7.2**
to offer ofrecer **8.2**
office la oficina **2.2**
   principal's office la oficina del
   (de la) director(a) **2.2**
often muchas veces **2.1**

OK
   OK! ¡Vale!
   OK? ¿Está bien?
   OK. And you? Regular. ¿Y tú/
   usted? (familiar/formal) **LP**
old viejo(a) **1.2**
   How old are you? ¿Cuántos
   años tienes? **3.2**
   to be... years old tener...
   años **3.2**
older mayor **3.2**
on en; sobre
   on foot a pie **4.2**
   on top (of) encima (de) **2.2**
   on vacation de vacaciones **8.1**
once: once in a while de vez en
   cuando **2.1**
one uno **LP**
one hundred cien **2.1**
one thousand mil **3.2**
online en línea **7.1**
to open abrir **5.2**
open-air al aire libre **8.2**
or o **1.1**
orange (color) anaranjado(a) **4.1**
orange (fruit) la naranja **3.1**
to order pedir (i) **4.2**
organized organizado(a) **1.2**
other otro(a) **3.1**
ought to deber **5.2**
our nuestro(a) **3.2**
outside al aire libre **8.2**

page la página
painting el cuadro, la pintura
pair la pareja
pants los pantalones **4.1**
paper el papel **2.2**
   wrapping paper el papel de
   regalo **5.2**
parade el desfile
paragraph el párrafo
parents los padres **3.2**
park el parque **4.2**
   amusement park el parque de
   diversiones **7.2**
part la parte
party la fiesta
   surprise party la fiesta de
   sorpresa **5.2**
password la contraseña
past pasado(a) **7.1**

half past... ...y media **2.1**
   quarter past... ...y cuarto **2.1**
the past el pasado
patio el patio **5.1**
to pay pagar **4.1**
pen la pluma **2.2**
pencil el lápiz (*pl.* los lápices) **2.2**
perhaps tal vez **4.2**
person la persona **1.2**
phone el teléfono **LP**
   phone call la llamada **7.2**
   **What is your phone
   number?** ¿Cuál es tu/su número
   de teléfono? (familiar/formal) **LP**
   My phone number is... Mi
   número de teléfono es... **LP**
photo la foto **7.1**
   to take photos tomar fotos **7.1**
to picnic comer al aire libre **8.2**
picture la foto **7.1**
pizza la pizza **1.1**
place el lugar **4.2**
to place poner (pongo) **5.2**
to plan pensar (ie) **4.1**
plant la planta
plate el plato
to play
   (an instrument) tocar **1.1**
   (games) jugar (ue) **1.1**
   (sports) jugar (ue), practicar **1.1**
player el (la) jugador(a) **6.1**
Please. Por favor. **LP**
   **Pleased to meet
   you.** Encantado(a). **LP**
pleasure el gusto **LP**
   The pleasure is mine. El gusto es
   mío. **LP**
post card la tarjeta postal
potato la papa **1.1**; la patata **4.2**
to practice practicar **1.1**
to prefer preferir (ie) **4.1**
to prepare preparar **1.1**
   to prepare food/a meal preparar
   la comida **1.1**
present el regalo **5.2**
pretty bonito(a) **1.2**
price el precio **4.1**
principal el (la) director(a) **2.2**
problem el problema **2.2**
to protect proteger (protejo)
to put poner (pongo) **5.2**
   to put on (clothes) ponerse
   (me pongo) (la ropa) **8.1**
   to put on makeup
   maquillarse **8.1**

Q

quality la calidad **8.2**
quarter (to) (menos) cuarto **2.1**
quarter past ... y cuarto **2.1**
question la pregunta

R

race la carrera
racket la raqueta **6.1**
radio el radio **5.1**
raft la balsa
to rain llover (ue) **LP**
   It is raining. Llueve. **LP**
to raise levantar
ranch la estancia
to read leer **1.1**
   to read a book leer un libro **1.1**
reading la lectura
Really? ¿Verdad?
to receive recibir **5.2**
recess el recreo
red rojo(a) **4.1**
red-haired pelirrojo(a) **1.2**
to remember recordar (ue)
to rent alquilar **1.1**
   to rent a DVD alquilar un DVD **1.1**
to reply responder
to rest descansar **1.1**
restaurant el restaurante **4.2**
result el resultado
to return volver (ue) **4.2**
review el repaso
rice el arroz **4.2**
rich rico(a)
to ride montar **1.1**; subir a **7.2**
   to ride a bike montar en bicicleta **1.1**
   to ride a horse montar a caballo **8.2**
   to ride the Ferris wheel/roller coaster subir a la vuelta al mundo/la montaña rusa **7.2**
right derecho(a)
   Right? ¿Verdad? **LP**
   to be right tener razón **4.1**
ring el anillo **8.2**
roller coaster la montaña rusa **7.2**
room el cuarto **5.1**
routine la rutina **8.1**

rug la alfombra **5.1**
rule la regla **6.1**
to run correr **1.1**

S

sad triste **2.2**
safe seguro(a)
salad la ensalada **4.2**
salesclerk el (la) vendedor(a)
same mismo(a)
   Same here. Igualmente. **LP**
sandwich el sándwich **3.1**
   ham and cheese sandwich el sándwich de jamón y queso **3.1**
Saturday sábado **LP**
to say decir **5.2**
scary: How scary! ¡Qué miedo! **7.2**
scene la escena
schedule el horario **2.1**
school la escuela **1.1**
   high school el colegio, la escuela secundaria
science las ciencias **2.1**
screen la pantalla **7.1**
to scuba-dive bucear **6.2**
sea el mar **6.2**
season la estación (*pl.* las estaciones) **4.1**
second segundo(a) **5.1**
secret el secreto **5.2**
secure seguro(a)
to see ver (veo) **4.2**
   May I see...? ¿Me deja ver...? **8.2**
   See you later. Hasta luego. **LP**
   See you tomorrow. Hasta mañana. **LP**
to sell vender **3.1**
to send mandar **7.1**
sentence la oración (*pl.* las oraciones)
September septiembre **3.2**
serious serio(a) **1.2**
to serve servir (i) **4.2**
set: to set the table poner (pongo) la mesa **5.2**
seven siete **LP**
seven hundred setecientos(as) **3.2**
seventeen diecisiete **2.1**
seventh séptimo(a) **5.1**
seventy setenta **2.1**
shame: What a shame! ¡Qué lástima! **7.2**
shampoo el champú **8.1**

to share compartir **3.1**
to shave oneself afeitarse **8.1**
she ella **1.1**
shirt la camisa **4.1**
shoe el zapato **4.1**
shop: to go shopping ir de compras **4.1**
shopping center el centro comercial **4.1**
short (height) bajo(a) **1.2**
shorts los pantalones cortos **4.1**
should deber **5.2**
shower: to take a shower ducharse **8.1**
sick enfermo(a) **6.2**
silver la plata
   (made of) silver de plata **8.2**
to sing cantar **5.2**
sister la hermana **3.2**
six seis **LP**
six hundred seiscientos(as) **3.2**
sixteen dieciséis **2.1**
sixth sexto(a) **5.1**
sixty sesenta **2.1**
to skate patinar **6.1**
   to in-line skate patinar en línea **6.1**
to skateboard andar en patineta **1.1**
skin la piel **6.2**
to sleep dormir (ue) **4.2**
small pequeño(a) **1.2**
snow la nieve
to snow nevar (ie) **LP**
   It is snowing. Nieva. **LP**
so entonces **7.1**
   so many tantos(as)
   so much tanto(a)
soap el jabón (*pl.* los jabones) **8.1**
soccer el fútbol **1.1**
sock el calcetín (*pl.* los calcetines) **4.1**
sofa el sofá **5.1**
soft drink el refresco **1.1**
some alguno(a) **7.1**
someone alguien **7.1**
something algo **7.1**
sometimes a veces
son el hijo **3.2**
sorry: I'm sorry. Lo siento. **6.2**
So-so. And you? Más o menos. ¿Y tú/usted? (familiar/formal) **LP**
soup la sopa **3.1**
source la fuente
souvenir el recuerdo **8.2**

Spanish el español **2.1**
to speak hablar **1.1**
   May I speak with...? ¿Puedo hablar con...? **7.2**
special especial
to spend: to spend time with friends pasar un rato con los amigos **1.1**
spirit el ánimo
sports los deportes **1.1**
spring la primavera **4.1**
stadium el estadio **6.1**
stairs la escalera **5.1**
to stay in quedarse en **8.1**
stepfather el padrastro **3.2**
stepmother la madrastra **3.2**
still todavía **5.2**
stomach el estómago **6.2**
to stop parar
store la tienda **4.1**
street la calle **4.2**
strong fuerte **6.2**
student el (la) estudiante **1.2**
studious estudioso(a) **1.2**
to study estudiar **1.1**
summary el resumen
   in summary en resumen
summer el verano **4.1**
sun el sol **LP**
   It is sunny. Hace sol. **LP**
to sunbathe tomar el sol **6.2**
Sunday domingo **LP**
sunscreen el bloqueador de sol **6.2**
supermarket el supermercado
to surf hacer surfing **8.2**
   to surf the Web navegar por Internet **7.1**
surprise la sorpresa **5.2**
survey la encuesta
to sweep barrer **5.2**
   to sweep the floor barrer el suelo **5.2**
to swim nadar **6.1**
swimming la natación **6.1**
swimming pool la piscina **6.1**

table la mesa **4.2**
   to set the table poner la mesa **5.2**
to take tomar **4.2**
   to take a bath bañarse **8.1**
   to take a shower ducharse **8.1**

to take a trip hacer un viaje **8.1**
   to take notes tomar apuntes **2.1**
   to take out the trash sacar la basura **5.2**
   to take photos tomar fotos **7.1**
to talk hablar **1.1**
   to talk on the phone hablar por teléfono **1.1**
tall alto(a) **1.2**
tasty rico(a) **3.1**
to teach enseñar **2.1**
teacher el (la) maestro(a) **LP**
team el equipo **6.1**
telephone el teléfono **7.2**
   cellular telephone el teléfono celular **7.2**
   My phone number is... Mi número de teléfono es... **LP**
   What is your phone number? (familiar/formal) ¿Cuál es tu/su número de teléfono? **LP**
television la televisión **1.1**
television set el televisor **5.1**
ten diez **LP**
tennis el tenis **6.1**
tenth décimo(a) **5.1**
test el examen (*pl.* los exámenes) **2.1**
Thank you. Gracias. **LP**
   Thank you very much. Muchas gracias. **LP**
that ese(a) **8.2**
   that (over there) aquel (aquella) **8.2**
theater el teatro **4.2**
their su **3.2**
them ellos(as) **7.2**
theme el tema
then luego; entonces **7.1**
there allí **4.2**
   there is/are... hay... **2.1**
these estos(as) **8.2**
they ellos(as) **1.1**
thing la cosa **5.1**
to think pensar (ie) **4.1**
third tercero(a) **5.1**
thirst la sed
   to be thirsty tener sed **3.1**
thirteen trece **2.1**
thirty treinta **2.1**
thirty-one treinta y uno **2.1**
this este(a) **8.2**
those esos(as) **8.2**
   those (over there) aquellos(as) **8.2**

thousand mil **3.2**
three tres **LP**
three hundred trescientos(as) **3.2**
Thursday jueves **LP**
ticket la entrada **4.2**; el boleto **7.2**
time la hora **2.1**; la vez; el tiempo **8.2**
   At what time is/are...? ¿A qué hora es/son...? **2.1**
   free time el tiempo libre **8.2**
   What time is it? ¿Qué hora es? **2.1**
tip la propina **4.2**
tired cansado(a) **2.2**
to menos (with a time) **2.1**; a
today hoy **LP**
   Today is... Hoy es... **LP**
   What day is today? ¿Qué día es hoy? **LP**
tomato el tomate **4.2**
tomorrow mañana **LP**
   See you tomorrow. Hasta mañana. **LP**
   Tomorrow is... Mañana es... **LP**
too también **1.1**
too much demasiado **8.2**
toothbrush el cepillo de dientes **8.1**
toothpaste la pasta de dientes **8.1**
tourism el turismo
towel la toalla **8.1**
town el pueblo
track la pista
train el tren **8.1**
   by train en tren **8.1**
trash la basura **5.2**
tree el árbol
trip el viaje **8.1**
true cierto(a)
truth la verdad
T-shirt la camiseta **4.1**
Tuesday martes **LP**
twelve doce **2.1**
twenty veinte **2.1**
twenty-one veintiuno **2.1**
two dos **LP**
two hundred doscientos(as) **3.2**
type el tipo; la clase
typical típico(a)

ugly feo(a) **4.1**
uncle el tío **3.2**
under debajo (de) **2.2**
underneath debajo (de) **2.2**

GLOSARIO inglés-español

to understand entender (ie) **4.1**; comprender **6.1**
  Did you understand? ¿Comprendiste?
unit la unidad
until hasta
us nosotros(as) **7.2**
to use usar **2.1**
  to use the computer usar la computadora **2.1**

vacation las vacaciones **8.1**
  on vacation de vacaciones **8.1**
to vacuum pasar la aspiradora **5.2**
vacuum cleaner la aspiradora **5.2**
valley el valle
various varios(as)
vegetables las verduras **4.2**
very muy **1.2**
  Very well. And you? Muy bien. ¿Y tú/usted? (familiar/ formal) **LP**
video game el videojuego **5.1**
to visit visitar
vocabulary vocabulario
volleyball el voleibol **6.1**

to wait (for) esperar **8.1**
waiter el camarero **4.2**
waitress la camarera **4.2**
to wake up despertarse (ie) **8.1**
to walk caminar **6.2**
  to go for a walk pasear **1.1**
wall la pared
to want querer (ie) **4.1**; desear
to wash lavar **5.2**
  to wash one's face lavarse la cara **8.1**
  to wash oneself lavarse **8.1**
watch el reloj **2.2**
to watch mirar **1.1**
  to watch television mirar la televisión **1.1**
water el agua (fem.) **1.1**
waterfall la cascada
to water-ski hacer esquí acuático **6.2**

we nosotros(as) **1.1**
to wear llevar **4.1**
weather el tiempo **LP**
  What is the weather like? ¿Qué tiempo hace? **LP**
Web site el sitio Web **7.1**
Wednesday miércoles **LP**
week la semana **LP**
  last week la semana pasada **7.1**
weekend el fin de semana **7.2**
welcome: You're welcome. De nada. **LP**
well bien **LP**
  Very well. And you? Muy bien. ¿Y tú/usted? (familiar/ formal) **LP**
what qué
  What? ¿Qué?; ¿Cuál? **3.1**
  What a shame! ¡Qué lástima! **7.2**
  What are you like? ¿Cómo eres? **1.2**
  What color is/are...? ¿De qué color es/son...?
  What day is today? ¿Qué día es hoy? **LP**
  What did you do? (pl., formal) ¿Qué hicieron ustedes? **6.2**
  What did you do? (sing., familiar) ¿Qué hiciste tú? **6.2**
  What do you like to do? ¿Qué te gusta hacer? **1.1**
  What is the date? ¿Cuál es la fecha? **3.2**
  What is the weather like? ¿Qué tiempo hace? **LP**
  What is this? ¿Qué es esto? **8.2**
  What is your phone number? (familiar/formal) ¿Cuál es tu/su número de teléfono? **LP**
  What time is it? ¿Qué hora es? **2.1**
  What's happening? ¿Qué pasa? **LP**
  What's his/her/your (formal) name? ¿Cómo se llama? **LP**
  What's your (familiar) name? ¿Cómo te llamas? **LP**
when cuando **2.2**
  When? ¿Cuándo? **2.2**
where donde
  Where? ¿Dónde? **2.2**
  (To) Where? ¿Adónde? **2.2**
  Where are you from?

¿De dónde eres (familiar)/es usted (formal)? **LP**
  Where are you going? ¿Adónde vas? **2.2**
  Where is he/she from? ¿De dónde es? **LP**
Which? ¿Cuál(es)? **3.1**
a while un rato
  once in a while de vez en cuando **2.1**
white blanco(a) **4.1**
Who? ¿Quién(es)? **3.1**
  Who is he/she/it? ¿Quién es? **LP**
Why? ¿Por qué? **3.1**
to win ganar **6.1**
wind el viento
  It is windy. Hace viento. **LP**
window la ventana **2.2**
  ticket window la ventanilla **4.2**
to windsurf hacer surf de vela **8.2**
winner el (la) ganador(a) **6.1**
winning ganador(a)
winter el invierno **4.1**
to wish desear
with con **7.2**
  with me conmigo **7.2**
  with you contigo **7.2**
without sin
woman la mujer **1.2**
wood la madera **8**
  made of wood de madera **8.2**
work (of art) la obra
to work trabajar **1.1**
world el mundo
worse peor **3.2**
to wrap envolver (ue) **5.2**
wrapping paper el papel de regalo **5.2**
to write escribir **1.1**
  to write e-mails escribir correos electrónicos **1.1**
writing la escritura

year el año **3.2**
  last year el año pasado **7.1**
  New Year el Año Nuevo
  to be... years old tener... años **3.2**
yellow amarillo(a) **4.1**
yes sí **LP**

Yes, I would love to. Sí, me encantaría. **7.2**

yesterday ayer **6.2**
   the day before yesterday anteayer **7.1**

yet todavía **5.2**

yogurt el yogur **3.1**

you
   (sing., familiar) tú **1.1**; ti **7.2**
   (sing., formal) usted **1.1, 7.2**
   (pl., familiar) vosotros(as) **1.1,**
   (pl.) ustedes **1.1**

young joven (*pl.* jóvenes) **1.2**

younger menor **3.2**

your
   (sing., familiar) tu **3.2**
   (pl., familiar) vuestro(a) **3.2**
   (formal) su **3.2**

zero cero **LP**

zoo el zoológico **7.2**

✤Índice

Índice

L

La Boca (Buenos Aires), 386

Landscape near El Escorial (Zuloaga y Zabaleta), 236

language
- gestures, 344
- **jeringozo,** 374
- language games, 374
- **lunfardo,** 362
- proverbs, 344
- Quechua, 266
- *See also* Spanish; vocabulary

Lavandera (Tufiño), 176

lavar, affirmative **tú** command, 282, 291

lavarse, present tense, 415, 429

legua, 50

leisure. *See* recreation

le(s), 439, 453

likes, expressing, 32, 33, 42, 45, 51, 63, 145, 148, 159

Lira, Pedro, 236

listening strategies
- attempts to control, 423
- attitude changes, 153
- body language, 280
- cognates, 45, 99, 275
- commands, 285
- comparing characters' approaches, 393
- contrasts, 231
- drawing a map, 251
- emotions, 113
- enter the scene, 221
- feelings, 118
- finding the real feelings, 256
- guesses, 40
- humor, 59
- identifying causes, 226
- intensity, 207
- implied meaning, 339
- intonation, 35, 117
- linking words and visual images, 383
- listen for goals, 315
- listening for action, 329
- listening for incomplete sentences, 334
- listening for sequences, 359
- listening for wishes, 197
- listening to problems and
  - imagining solutions, 447
- mental pictures, 148
- motive, 94, 143
- non-responses, listening for, 305
- parts of a scene, 69
- persuasion, 418
- practicing what you hear, 369
- problems expressed, 123
- questions, 89
- reactions, 261
- remember, listen, and predict, 167, 177
- sort out the speakers, 388
- stereotypes, disregarding, 202
- stressed words, 310
- teasing, 437
- tracking people and actions, 172
- "turn-taking" tactics, 442
- understanding the interruption, 413
- unstated wishes, 64
- visual clues while listening, 364

llave, 388

location, expressing, 115, 123, 129, 253, 267, 444

Lomas Garza, Carmen, 68

López, Raúl, 60

lunfardo, 362

M

Madrid (Spain), 234

maduros, 452

making excuses, 345

mamama, 167

maps
- Argentina, 352
- Costa Rica, 406
- de Soto expedition, 50
- Dominican Republic, 298
- Ecuador, 244
- hurricane route, 158
- Mexico, 82
- Puerto Rico, 136
- Spain, 190
- Spanish-speaking world, 12, 13
- United States, 28
- Zempoala (Mexico), 104

máquina, 418

Mar del Plata (Argentina), 368

masculine. *See* gender

masculine adjectives, 61

masculine nouns, 61
- form of numbers before, 88

mate, 354

Maya ruins, 83

meals
- restaurants, 218, 219, 237
- **sobremesa,** 162-163
- vocabulary, 140-142, 159
- *See also* food

Medina, Juan, 314

Las meninas, (Velázquez), 230

menu, ordering from, 218, 219, 237

mercados, 450-451

merengue, 338

Mexico, 82-83
- art of, 97, 122, 128
- celebrations of, C4–C5, C6–C7, C8–C9, C10–C11, C14–C15, C18–C19, C20–C21
- cooking and foods of, 60, 74, 82
- famous persons from, 82
- indigenous cultures, 116, 122
- location on map, 12, 13, 82
- map of, 82
- Mexican-American culture, 68
- murals, 83, 97
- scenes of, 83, 85, 109, 126, 127
- school uniforms, 84, 92
- **Serie del Caribe,** 308
- statistics, 82
- student life, 84, 85, 92, 108, 109
- televised secondary school, 104
- Tex-Mex food, 60
- traditional foods of, 60
- **Universidad Nacional Autónoma de México** (UNAM), 83
- vocabulary variations by country, 64, 94, 110, 118, 197, 221, 251, 305, 359, 383, 388, 418
- yarn painting, 128
- Zempoala (town), 104

mí, 390

Miami
- beach, 31
- Cuban-American art, 44
- Little Havana (**Calle Ocho**), 29
- **Los Premios Juventud,** 41
- recreation, 35, 73
- scenes of, 29, 31, 73

Índice

micro, 221
Mitad del Mundo monument (Ecuador), 260
molas, 290
money
  of Argentina, 352
  of Costa Rica, 406
  of Dominican Republic, 298
  of Ecuador, 244
  of Mexico, 82
  of Puerto Rico, 136
  of Spain, 190
  of Venezuela, C24
montar en bicicleta, 35
Montevideo (Uruguay), 451
months, 165
Moors, 212
Muchacho con cachucha (Colson), 314
murals, 9, 83, 97
Museo al Aire Libre (Buenos Aires), 396-397
Museo de Ciencias Naturales La Salle (Costa Rica), 428
Museo de Instrumentos Musicales (Bolivia), 397
museums
  in Argentina, 396-397
  in Bolivia, 397
  in Costa Rica, 428
Music (Cortada), 44
music
  Andean, 182
  in celebrations, C2, C3, C20
  Cuban-American, 44
  Festival del Merengue, 338
  instruments of Puerto Rico and Peru, 182
  merengue, 338
  Los Premios Juventud, 41
  of Puerto Rico, 181
  sevillanas, 191
  of Spain, 191, 212
  Tex-Mex music, 50
musical instruments
  of Argentina, 353
  in celebrations, C2
  Museo de Instrumentos Musicales (Bolivia), 397
  of Puerto Rico and Peru, 182
musical stars, **Los Premios Juventud,** 41

N

ñ (letter), 65
nadar, preterite tense, 331, 345
names, 4, 398
National Museum of Anthropology (Mexico City), 116
native cultures, C6, C7, C8, C9, C22, C23, 116, 122, 225, 266, 284
nave, 418
Las Navidades, C10–C11
negative words, 366-367, 375
New York City, 1, 9
Nicaragua
  celebrations of, C4-C5
  location on map, 12, 13
Niña campesina sonriente (Sayán Polo), 176
ninguno(a), 366, 367, 375
Nochebuena (Toaquiza), 255
noria, 383
nouns
  defined, 66
  definite articles for, 61, 75
  gender, 61
  gustar +, 145, 159
  indefinite articles for, 61, 75
  noun-adjective agreement, 66, 75, 384
  possession, expressing, 164
  singular/plural, 61
number
  agreement of demonstrative adjectives, 444, 453
  agreement of possessive adjectives, 169, 172
  noun-adjective agreement, 66, 75, 384
  ordinal number agreement, 258, 267
numbers
  from 1 to 10, 16
  from 11 to 100, 87
  from 200 to 1,000,000, 165
  before masculine and feminine nouns, 88
  date of birth, 171, 173
  expressing age, 168
  ordinal numbers, 258-259, 267
  telephone numbers, 16, 25

O

o→ue stem-changing verbs, present tense, 223, 237
El Obelisco (Buenos Aires), 353
olives, 212
opposites, 58
órale, 197
ordinal numbers, 258-259, 267
origin, expressing, 14, 25, 37, 38, 253
Ortiz, David, 308
Otavalo (Ecuador), 245, 284, 290

P

pampas, 353
pana, 388
Panama
  celebrations of, C10–C11
  dance in, 289
  location on map, 12, 13
  scenes of, 289
  textiles, 290
pantallas, 442
papas fritas, 64
papitas, 64
Paraguay
  celebrations of, C14–C15
  indigenous cultures, 116
  location on map, 12, 13
Parque de la Costa (Argentina), 378, 379
Parque del Retiro (Spain), 234
Parque La Sabana (Costa Rica), 428
parrilla, 392
Partido Independista Puertorriqueño, 170
Partido Nuevo Progresista, 170
Partido Popular Democrático, 170
parts of the body, 327
party planning, vocabulary, 272, 291
Paseo del Río (San Antonio), 54, 55, 72
pastel, 280
patatas fritas, 64
pedir, 228
pendientes, 442
pensar, 199
perder, 199
Pérez, Oliver, 308

Q

Índice

Créditos

Acknowledgments

"Invierno tardío" from *Obra poética completa 1967 - 2010* by Antonio Colinas. Text copyright © 2011 by Antonio Colinas. Reprinted by permission of Ediciones Siruela.